NEW TESTAMENT INTERPRETATION

NEW TESTAMENT INTERPRETATION

Essays on Principles and Methods

edited by

I. Howard Marshall

Senior Lecturer in New Testament Exegesis
University of Aberdeen

EXETER
THE PATERNOSTER PRESS

ISBN:
Casebound: 0 85364 196 X
Study Edition: 0 85364 204 4

AUSTRALIA:
Emu Book Agencies Pty., Ltd.,
63, Berry St., Granville, 2142, N.S.W.

SOUTH AFRICA:
Oxford University Press,
P.O. Box 1141, Cape Town

Typeset by Input Typesetting Ltd
and Printed in Great Britain for The Paternoster Press,
Paternoster House, 3 Mount Radford Crescent, Exeter, Devon
by Butler and Tanner Ltd Frome

CONTENTS

EDITOR'S FOREWORD

Although the interpretation of the New Testament has been the subject of much discussion in recent years, it is hard to find any books which sum up the results of this discussion and offer a comprehensive and practical guide to the task of interpretation. It was with this lack in mind that the New Testament Study Group of the Tyndale Fellowship for Biblical Research took up the theme at its meeting in July 1973. The papers which were presented then have been revised and are now offered to a wider public in the hope that they may be found of value as an attempt to cover this important area of study.

The field of New Testament interpretation is an enormous one, and it perhaps deserves several volumes rather than one. We cannot, therefore, claim to have done justice to the subject, whether as a whole or in detail, but we hope that this collection of essays may be sufficiently comprehensive and succinct to offer a basic guide to students and to all who are concerned to interpret the New Testament in the modern world.

Four main areas have claimed our attention. First, there is the question of the presuppositions with which one approaches the subject. We have tried to submit both our own presuppositions and those of scholars from other schools of thought to careful scrutiny. Second, we have looked at the various types of critical study which contribute to the exegesis of the text of the New Testament. Third, we have attempted to deal with the actual methods of exegesis itself. Finally, we have been very conscious that New Testament interpretation is not concerned solely to lay bare the meaning of the text for its original readers but reaches its goal only when it examines the meaning of the text for today and allows the text to affect our own attitudes and understanding. Indeed, it is impossible to achieve either of these two theoretically separable aims in isolation from the other. Hence the book ends on a practical note, and, if it is biased in the direction of expository preaching, this is because of the needs of our intended audience, many of whom will be engaged in the ministry of the Word, and it reflects our conviction that exposition presupposes careful exegesis.

The subject of biblical interpretation is one that can sharply divide students of different schools of thought. We have written as conservative evangelicals who combine a high regard for the authority of Holy Scripture with the belief that we are called to study it with the full use of our minds. It is inevitable that not all will agree with everything that we say, and it should be emphasised that the statements in this book carry no sort of *imprimatur*. Although the contributors share the same general outlook, each is responsible only for his own share in the volume, and the reader may detect points at which some of us disagree with one another. This plurality of opinions is not surprising, and is not necessarily a bad thing. We are writing on a theme which has received comparatively little study in the past, and conservative evangelicals in particular have been slow to work out the implications of their view of Scripture for the task of interpretation and vice-versa. In some ways, therefore, this volume is no more than a first and very tentative attempt to grapple with some of the problems. Hypothesis and conjecture are inevitable at this stage; nevertheless, we have thought it right to publish our views, in the hope that our book may stimulate discussion and lead to a fuller appreciation of truth.

As a result of the economic crisis which has affected many publishers in this country this book has been a long time in production. We regret that it has not been possible to bring our essays fully up to date and to take the most recent discussions of our subject into account. For example, it has not been possible to devote any space to structuralism, a topic which has moved to the forefront of discussion since this book was originally planned.

As editor, I should like to express my thanks to all the essayists whose work has appeared in this book. I should also like to express the appreciation of all the contributors to Norman Hillyer, who compiled the indexes, to the staff at Tyndale House, Cambridge, to the Paternoster Press, and to all the others who have helped towards the publication of this book.

I. HOWARD MARSHALL

ABBREVIATIONS

AG	W. F. Arndt and F. W. Gingrich, *A Greek-English Lexicon of the New Testament and Other Early Christian Literature* (Cambridge 1957)
ATR	*Anglican Theological Review*
BJRL	*Bulletin of the John Rylands Library*
BZ	*Biblische Zeitschrift*
BZNW	*Beiheft zur Zeitschrift für die neutestamentliche Wissenschaft*
CBQ	*Catholic Biblical Quarterly*
EQ	*The Evangelical Quarterly*
ETL	*Ephemerides Theologicae Lovanienses*
Exp.T	*The Expository Times*
JBL	*Journal of Biblical Literature*
JTh.Ch.	*Journal for Theology and the Church*
JTS	*Journal of Theological Studies*
MM	J. H. Moulton and G. Milligan, *The Vocabulary of the Greek New Testament Illustrated from the Papyri and other Non-Literary Sources* (London 1914–29)
NIDNTT	C. Brown (ed.), *The New International Dictionary of New Testament Theology* (Exeter 1975–78)
Nov.T	*Novum Testamentum*
NTS	*New Testament Studies*
Rev.Bén.	*Revue Bénedictine*
RGG	*Die Religion in Geschichte und Gegenwart* (Tübingen 1957–65[3])
SB	H. L. Strack and P. Billerbeck, *Kommentar zum Neuen Testament aus Talmud und Midrasch* (München 1956[3])
SJT	*Scottish Journal of Theology*
TDNT	G. Kittel and G. Friedrich, *Theological Dictionary of the New Testament* (E.T. Grand Rapids 1964–74)
Th.Z	*Theologische Zeitschrift*
TLZ	*Theologische Literaturzeitung*
TSFB	*Theological Students' Fellowship Bulletin*
TU	*Texte und Untersuchungen*
Tyn.B	*Tyndale Bulletin*
VC	*Vigiliae Christianae*
ZNW	*Zeitschrift für die neutestamentliche Wissenschaft*
ZRGG	*Zeitschrift für Religions- und Geistesgeschichte*
ZTK	*Zeitschrift für Theologie und Kirche*

CHAPTER I

INTRODUCTION

I. H. Marshall

The aim of this symposium is to establish the principles and methods involved in understanding the New Testament. The problem of interpreting a passage from the Bible is one to which we would all like to find the key, some simple and easy formula that will enable us to approach any text of Scripture and quickly establish its meaning. Alas, there is no such simple answer, but it is possible to indicate some general principles and types of approach which will enable us to wrestle with the text and come to an understanding of it.

The problem of course is not one confined to study of the New Testament or indeed of the Bible as a whole. It is part of the general problem of hermeneutics, i.e. the attempt to understand anything that somebody else has said or written. It follows that much of what will be said in this volume would also apply to any other material that requires interpretation, especially to similar texts from the ancient world. The New Testament, however, poses distinctive problems because of its own individual literary characteristics and also because Christians regard it as the Word of God. Our discussion, therefore, will concentrate on the problems of hermeneutics as they apply to the New Testament in particular.

I. *Some Hermeneutical Questions*

In order to appreciate the nature of these problems it may be useful for us at the outset to examine a passage from the New Testament. For this purpose let us look at John 4:1–45, a passage which has the merits of illustrating a variety of points and also of being a fairly familiar story. How does one begin to understand it?

The starting point is no doubt to establish the correct wording of the passage. Different editions of the Greek New Testament vary in their wording according to their editors' estimate of the relative reliability of the early manuscripts. We shall, however, forbear to deal in this volume with *textual criticism* in any detail, since the matter is a technical one and there already exist excellent manuals on the subject.[1] So far as the present passage is concerned, it may be assumed that the average modern edition of the Greek New Testament gives the text with sufficient accuracy.

A second stage consists in understanding the vocabulary, grammar and syntax of the passage in order to give a good *translation* of it into English. It is to be feared that many of us start from the English text, and, to be sure, one does not need to know Greek in order to understand the New Testament; at least, the individual may not need to do so, provided that in his language group there are others who do possess and share this knowledge with the rest of the community. Translation is of great importance, and there is a case that it is the goal of interpretation rather than a preliminary stage on the journey, since the precise character of a translation is moulded by our total understanding of the passage in the light of the factors that have still to be considered.[2] Its importance may be quickly illustrated by two points.

First, the central figure in the story is a *γυνή*, regularly translated as "woman" – "the woman of Samaria". What visual image does that word convey to you? To me it is a word that suggests somebody approaching middle-age or even old-age, and it has a faintly derogatory air; one has only to think of the subtle difference in tone between church intimations about "the *Women's* Meeting" or "the *Ladies*' Guild" and the way in which one type of *women's* meeting has to be called "the *Young Wives*' Group" in order to attract members! Suppose that we translated by "lady" (a perfectly correct equivalent of *γυνή*) or even by "girl"? "Woman" tends to put her on the shelf, but the story implies that she was possibly youthful and attractive.

Second, the word "living", used of the water offered to her by Jesus, poses a problem. In Greek it could be used to mean "running", as opposed to stagnant, water. This ambiguity between "running" and "living" may be significant in the story. How does one get it over in English? And does the fact of this ambiguity mean that other words also in John may be used with a double sense?

Translation, therefore, is important both for the meaning and for the "feel" of the incident.

A third stage in understanding is concerned with *background*. It may be useful to know something about the geography of the scene, the historical state of Jewish-Samaritan relationships and matters of this kind. A knowledge of the character of the author of the Gospel and his intended audience will help us to appreciate the point of the story. Much of this can be found fairly simply from reference books.

But where did the author get the story from? The Gospel of John is based on information gathered from various *sources* by the author. Can we distinguish between such information in its earliest form and the way in which the author has used it? Where did he get this particular story? Some parts of it deal with a private conversation between Jesus and the woman: which of them passed it on? Or has John written the story up in the manner he thought appropriate? These are tricky questions, and the experts differ in their answers.[3] But, however difficult the problem may be, it is surely relevant for our understanding of the story to know whether it is a historical report about an actual conversation, or a narrative developed by the evangelist to bring out points which he thought to be significant for his readers, or a mixture of these two.

This point brings us to our next question: what is the *form* and *function* of this narrative in the Gospel? Our immediate inclination is perhaps to see it simply as a historical episode. Let me say that I personally find no difficulty in accepting it as substantially the story of something that actually happened: Jesus met a woman by a well and held a conversation with her in which he led her to realise that he was the Messiah, and as a result of her conversion and Jesus' contact with other people from Sychar they too came to believe in him. To say this is to make a decision about the *form* of the story. But this is an insufficient answer. We have still to ask, Why is this story in the Gospel, and what is its function at this particular point? It is the question of *context*.

According to John's own statement of purpose in 20: 30f., a story like this is included so that the readers of the Gospel may themselves come to faith in Jesus. It is, therefore, not simply an interesting story, but it has a lesson to teach, namely that, just as the Samaritans came to faith, so the reader also ought to believe in Jesus, the Saviour of the world.

Granted this point, however, what is the precise function of this story at this point in the narrative? It is true that John provides chronological links with what precedes and what follows the story, but this does not completely solve the problem. John has presented only a few of the stories that he knew about Jesus (Jn. 20:30); why did he include *this* one? And did he put it here simply because of chronology?

One commentator at least has seen in our story a kind of foil to the preceding story of Nicodemus. Here is an example of belief to be placed over against Nicodemus' difficulty in accepting the idea of rebirth, so that each story may throw light on the other.[4] Or again the story may be part of a series in which the gospel message is seen to be not merely for Jews but also for Samaritans and ultimately for the whole world.[5] Or again there may be a contrast between the old ways of Jews and Samaritans – symbolised by water in jars or wells – and the new life offered by Jesus and symbolised by wine and living water.[6] Some or all of these suggestions may be true, and they add precision and fullness to our understanding of the story.

More than one writer has detected a kind of dramatic *form* in the way the story is told. The story is said to be presented like a play on a forestage and a backstage, with the centre of interest shifting to and fro, from the well to the town, from the woman to the disciples and to the townsfolk. A similar kind of structure is to be found elsewhere, e.g. in John 9, and this raises the question whether we have discovered a technique of presentation used by John, the appreciation of which may help us to understand the structure of the story.[7]

Then there is the question of double meaning, already hinted at earlier. At the beginning of the story there is a time note, that Jesus was at the well at the sixth hour. Details of time and place are common enough in John, and may be claimed as evidence for eye-witness testimony. But it has also been observed that in John 19:14 the same time note occurs to indicate the moment when Jesus was condemned and delivered to his executioners: is the reader meant to link these two events theologically and let them mutually interpret each other? [8]

Again, Jesus reproached the woman for having had five husbands. Such immorality is perfectly credible, even in the pre-film and pop-star era, and is an entirely valid reason for needing to hear the gospel. But it has been suggested that the reference is an allegorical one to the five false gods of the Samaritans mentioned in 2 Kings 17:30f., and this would tie in with the condemnation of Samaritan piety in John 4:22. [9]

If these suggestions of allegory are present, two questions arise. How does one recognise that allegory is present? And does the presence of this amount of allegory justify us in searching for more of it in less likely places in the story? [10] A related problem is that of *symbolism*. Water is undoubtedly used here by Jesus as a religious symbol, and therefore we require to ask what ideas would be conjured up for John's readers by the religious use of the term "water".[11] It is equally important to ask how these ideas can be made relevant and understandable to a modern reader who may not appreciate the symbolism.

With the mention of the modern reader we pass, finally, to a further question regarding the interpretation of the story which may take us beyond the original intention of John. It may be illustrated by mentioning two types of exposition. One or two writers have seen in this story an example of *how Jesus dealt pastorally* with the woman in leading her to conversion. They have then suggested that the story provides an example for his followers to employ in their own activity of personal evangelism. [12] This is surely a valid interpretation of the story, but is it one intended by John himself? Two answers seem to be possible here. John might say to us, "I hadn't consciously thought of the story like that, but now that you suggest it to me, I would agree that you could also understand it in that way. My primary purpose was of course to help the unbeliever who can see himself in the picture of the woman, but naturally it could have the secondary purpose of helping the Christian evangelist to model himself on Jesus." A passage, therefore, may have a further interpretation or application, which was not present to the author, but is legitimate because it can be held to fit in with his intentions. Or John might say that he did intend this secondary, pastoral purpose of the story. If so, the question arises as to how far he has been influenced, consciously or unconsciously, by the needs of the church for advice on this pastoral problem and hence how far the historical narrative has been presented or even adapted in order to draw out these lessons. [13]

Another school of thought interprets the story in an *existential* manner. It is an expression of the way in which a person comes to self-awareness regarding his being and enters into "authentic existence". Thus R. Bultmann heads verses 16–19 "The Revelation as the Disclosure of Man's Being". The ideas of a gift of salvation and of faith in the traditional sense disappear, and are replaced in effect by categories drawn from existentialist philosophy. [14]

Whether this is a legitimate interpretation of John or is rather "read into the text" [15] is a matter for discussion.

II *Possible Methods of Interpretation*

It is time to draw the lines together. A sufficiently bewildering set of exegetical possibilities has now been produced to raise some doubts regarding the good Reformed doctrine of the perspicuity of Holy Scripture. The purpose of this introduction, however, is certainly not to lead the reader to doubt and despair, but rather to raise the questions that must be faced by defenders of this doctrine, so that in the end their acceptance of it may rest on a more solid basis than mere formal assent. Our aim has been to try to indicate the nature of some of the problems which will be developed at greater length later in this book. We may, however, make some tentative suggestions that should be borne in mind as the reader proceeds further.

First, in interpreting a passage a number of different lines of investigation must be followed. Textual and linguistic study, research into background, study of sources, form and context – all these have their vital part to play in exegesis.

Second, we have in effect uncovered three main levels of understanding. There is the "historical" level in which we treat the story as plain history with its own implicit meaning. There is the "Johannine" level in which we explore the uses that John may consciously have made of the story to bring out what he regarded as its full meaning and in order that the story may contribute to the total impact made by the Gospel.[16] And there is the "interpreter's" level in which we may gain impressions from the story which were not consciously in the author's mind, but may nevertheless be valid insights into his message. Moreover, at any of these levels a given passage may have a number of different interpretations, or rather its interpretation may have different facets. There may be a "straight" meaning and a less direct one, organically related to it.

Third, our aim is to discover what the text meant in the mind of its original author for his intended audience. Exegesis seeks for an interpretation of a passage which will account satisfactorily for all the features of that passage, both on its own and in its context. This context includes both the historical environment of the New Testament and also the literary environment of the work in which it occurs – in the example above, the Johannine literature. This may produce an appearance of circularity, since the context itself needs to be interpreted, and the meaning of John's Gospel as a whole depends upon the meaning of the various individual passages, including ch. 4 itself. The circle, however, need not be a vicious one, and a better analogy is provided by dialogue; the whole and the parts question each other, so to speak, and hence knowledge of both is gradually built up.

Fourth, how far can we go beyond the meaning intended for the original readers and reach a meaning for ourselves? As indicated earlier, I would be prepared to accept a "pastoral" interpretation of John 4, even if this was not in the author's mind, but I would be inclined to doubt the particular existentialist interpretation given by Bultmann – or at least I shrewdly suspect that John himself would say "No" to it if he was confronted by it. But is John's verdict (or my guess regarding it) the criterion? It could, for example, be argued that the significance of a story may lie in the unconscious motifs which come to expression in it, especially in the symbolism employed. Thus, to take an extreme example, the significance of a schizophrenic drawing lies not so much in the "objective" interpretation of it which the artist might give, but rather in the "subjective" reflection of the pathological state of his mind to which he unconsciously testified. It could be that in Scripture too there was a meaning different from that intended by the author. Though John himself might deny the existentialist interpretation of his Gospel, it could be argued that unconsciously he has been laid hold of by the existential plight of man and has been led to express it in the religious categories which made sense to him and which he felt to be objectively true, but which are merely one way of expressing an essentially human situation nowadays described more aptly in the language of Heidegger.

A more traditional Christian might prefer to argue for a *sensus plenior* in Scripture. Divine inspiration may have given to a passage a deeper meaning of which the author himself was unconscious. John himself tells us that certain texts in the book of Isaiah were written because the prophet saw the glory of Jesus and spoke of him (Jn. 12:41). We can, I think, be certain that a pre-Christian commentator on Isaiah would not have perceived this interpretation of such passages, nor is it exactly fashionable among modern commentators, and we may feel that the prophet himself saw the glory dimly; but looking back from our Christian vantage point we may truly say "The prophet was speaking about Jesus", and use these passages to throw light on him. Here we reach a point where the category of divine inspiration must be brought into the discussion and a purely human interpretation is inadequate.

How, then, are we to interpret the New Testament for a modern audience? Even if some of the writers did compose their works in the hope that posterity would value them and not simply consign them to the waste papyrus basket, they cannot have known how posterity in its different situation would understand them. The task of exposition is surely to put the audience into the position where it can feel for itself the original impact of the story. It can then pick up the original meaning, together with any fresh elements that may have accrued to it.

It may, however, be argued that regaining the original meaning is impossible, alike for the exegete and the congregation. For exegesis and exposition involve two-way traffic, as the modern student inevitably contributes something of himself to the exposition. This problem of dialogue between a modern reader and an ancient text is a complicated one, but the effects of the process need not necessarily be harmful; the significance of the doctrine of inspiration is surely that the message of the New Testament rings true in every generation. Certain situations, however, may enable us to feel its impact in a more telling manner. I have long had a theoretical knowledge of 1

Thessalonians 3, and could expound it to a congregation. But something happened to that chapter for me on 24th January, 1969. The visiting preacher that day in Christ's College, Aberdeen, was the aged Professor Josef Hromadka of Czechoslovakia, and as he read those verses I saw how he felt himself to be in Paul's situation, normally prevented by Satan from visiting his friends in the west, and longing both to draw comfort from them and to know that they (i.e. you and I) hold fast to their faith.

Perhaps this sort of experience could happen with any secular text – "some chorus ending from Euripides". We as Christians have something more to do. The passages which we interpret must be the means through which God speaks to men and women today. Our belief in the inspiration of the Bible is thus a testimony that New Testament exegesis is not just a problem; it is a real possibility. God can and does speak to men through even the most ignorant of expositors of his Word. At the same time he calls on us to devote ourselves to his Word and to use every resource to make its message the more clear. Sadly the history of the church demonstrates the evils that can arise from false interpretations of the New Testament; our task is to avoid such errors by seeking a true understanding.

It is to that end that this book is written. This chapter has done no more than introduce the reader to some of the areas that require discussion and to arouse problems that the student must tackle. In the ensuing chapters these points will be taken up in greater detail and, it is hoped, some indication given of the answers to them.

NOTES

1. B. M. Metzger, *The Text of the New Testament* (Oxford 1968^2); cf. J. H. Greenlee, *Introduction to New Testament Textual Criticism* (Grand Rapids 1964); J. N. Birdsall, "The New Testament Text", in P. R. Ackroyd and C. F. Evans, *The Cambridge History of the Bible* Vol. I (Cambridge 1970), pp. 308–377.

2. The "circular" nature of interpretation is evident at this point. On the basis of a provisional translation of a passage, one proceeds to interpret the details; this in turn may lead to a revision of the translation. See further p. 15.

3. R. Bultmann (*The Gospel of John* (Oxford 1971), p. 175) attempts to distinguish between a piece of tradition used by John and the additions which John has made. C. K. Barrett (*The Gospel according to St John* (London 1955), p. 191) states that a pre-Johannine nucleus of the story cannot be isolated, while R. Schnackenburg (*The Gospel according to St John* Vol. I (London 1968), p. 420) speaks of the way in which the Evangelist has skilfully constructed his narrative. Commentators are in general agreed that the narrative rests upon tradition, and that the tradition has a historical basis (R. E. Brown, *The Gospel according to John: I–XII* (New York 1966), pp. 175f.).

4. B. F. Westcott, *The Gospel according to St John* (London 1882), p. 67.

5. E.g. J. Marsh, *Saint John* (London 1968), pp. 207f.

6. E.g. A. M. Hunter, *The Gospel according to John* (Cambridge 1965), p. 45.

7. C. H. Dodd, *The Interpretation of the Fourth Gospel* (Cambridge 1954), p. 315.

8. R. H. Lightfoot, *St John's Gospel* (Oxford 1956), p. 122.

9. E. C. Hoskyns and F. N. Davey, *The Fourth Gospel* (London 1947), pp. 242f.

10. It must be admitted that neither of these examples of allegory is particularly convincing. The first is unlikely because the reader does not yet know that the sixth hour is to be the hour of the crucifixion, and when he does reach that point in the story he may not note the coincidence with the hour in ch. 4. As for the second, (a) the woman had six husbands in total, not five; (b) 2 Kings lists seven deities, not five; (c) while the number five does occur in the account of the Samaritans in Josephus (*Ant.* 9:288), it is doubtful whether John is dependent upon him rather than upon the Old Testament itself. We may also doubt whether John does in fact use allegory anywhere (W. F. Howard, *The Fourth Gospel in Recent Criticism and Interpretation* (London 1955[4]), pp. 182f.).
11. R. Bultmann, *op. cit.*, pp. 182–186; R. E. Brown, *op. cit.*, pp. 178–180.
12. W. Temple (*Readings in St John's Gospel* (London 1945), pp. 65–68) considers the narrative as "an example of the Lord's pastoral dealing", but proceeds to apply it to the way in which he deals with "my soul" rather than as an example for the Christian evangelist.
13. Compare the way in which the treatment of the blind man in John 9 is often thought to be based upon the Jewish excommunication of Christians in apostolic times rather than upon actual history in the time of Jesus. See J. L. Martyn, *History and Theology in the Fourth Gospel* (New York 1968).
14. R. Bultmann, op. cit., p. 187.
15. R. Schnackenburg, op. cit., p. 433.
16. One should note that this second level may comprise a number of "mezzanine" levels at which the significance of the tradition for its various bearers should be considered. In the case of the Gospel of John it has been suggested that some of the narrative material comes from a 'Gospel of Signs', in which case it may have had one meaning for the author of this source and another meaning for the author of the final work (R. T. Fortna, *The Gospel of Signs*, Cambridge 1970).

PART ONE

The Background to Interpretation

CHAPTER II

THE HISTORY OF NEW TESTAMENT STUDY

F. F. Bruce

The interpretation of the Old Testament in the New is a subject on which books are still being written and examination candidates still questioned. The interpretation of earlier parts of the Old Testament in its later parts is a subject on which much more work remains to be done; it forms the first chapter in the history of Old Testament interpretation. Similarly the first chapter of a history of New Testament interpretation should be devoted to a study of the interpretation of earlier parts of the New Testament in its later parts.

I. *The Early Church and the Middle Ages*

1. THE APOSTOLIC AGE

There is not the same degree of internal interpretation within the New Testament as is present in the Old, but some examples are readily recognized. Within a single Gospel, for instance, there are interpretations of parables (cf. Mk. 4:3–8 with 14–20, or Mt. 13:24–30 with 37–43), some of which may belong to the tradition while others are supplied by the evangelist. A later Gospel may interpret words in an earlier Gospel which has served as one of its sources, as when "they see the kingdom of God come with power" (Mk. 9:1) is reworded as "they see the Son of Man coming in his kingdom" (Mt. 16:28) or "Truly this man was the son of God" (Mk. 15:39) becomes "Certainly this man was innocent" (Lk. 23:47).

In particular, the Gospel of John presents the story of Jesus in such a way as to bring out the abiding validity of his person, teaching and work. "Eternal life", which in the Synoptic Gospels is an occasional synonym for "the kingdom of God", now supplants it almost entirely, and is shown to consist in the knowledge of the one true God revealed through Jesus (Jn. 17:3). The wording of the charge on which Jesus was executed, "the King of the Jews", which might seem to have little relevance to the public for which the Fourth Evangelist wrote, is interpreted in Jesus' answers to Pilate's interrogation in Jn. 18:33–38a, where it becomes clear that the kingship he claims belongs wholly to the spiritual realm: his sovereignty is acknowledged by "every one who is of the truth".

Even within the Pauline corpus we have evidence of some interpretation of earlier letters in later ones: the church principles of 1 Corinthians, for example, are reapplied in one direction in Ephesians and in another in the Pastoral Epistles. Again, it has been observed more than once that the scenes accompanying the breaking of the seals in the Apocalypse (Rev. 6:1 ff.) are constructed on a framework not unlike the eschatological discourse of Mk. 13:5ff. and parallels.

2. ORTHODOXY AND HERESY IN THE SECOND CENTURY

The earliest of the Apostolic Fathers, Clement of Rome, engages in some New Testament interpretation in his letter to the Corinthian church (*c.* A.D. 96), although the documents which he quotes had not yet been brought together to form part of one collection. His aim is to discourage envy and partisanship and to encourage a spirit of humility and mutual forbearance among the Corinthians, and he very properly quotes in this sense words from the Sermon on the Mount and pre-eminently from 1 Corinthians, where Paul deprecates party-spirit and inculcates a spirit of love in that church in an earlier generation. For the same purpose Clement quotes other New Testament writings, and especially Hebrews, which was plainly well-known to him. For example, he interprets those who "went about in skins of sheep and goats" (Heb. 11:37) as Elijah and Elisha (1 Clem. 17:1), although these men were not in the original author's mind at this point. (This misinterpretation is sufficient evidence that Clement was not the author of Hebrews – a suggestion made by some in Jerome's day and subsequently.)

The *logos* doctrine of the Johannine prologue was naturally treated by those who had been educated in Greek culture in terms of the *logos* of the philosophers. Thus Justin Martyr argued that men like Socrates, who had embraced the *logos* in the form of true reason were, without knowing it, Christians before Christ, since in due course the *logos* became incarnate in Christ.[1] Ptolemy, a member of the Valentinian school of Gnostics, read into the prologue the first "Ogdoad" in the Valentinian system (of which Logos was one) and so made the evangelist teach developed Valentinianism. It was not difficult for Irenaeus to expose the fallacy in this reasoning.[2] But at a more sober level there was much in the Gospel's vocabulary and conceptual range which lent itself to Valentinian speculation, such as the dispelling of darkness by the true light. The Valentinian *Gospel of Truth,* which may be the work of Valentinus himself, bears evident traces of an attempt to understand the Gospel of John on the part of a man whose presuppositions were those of gnostic dualism.

The gnostic schools, as we might expect, found ample material in the parables of Jesus for the presentation of their own teachings. The Naassenes, for example, interpreted the injunction in the parable of the sower, "He who has ears, let him hear" (Mt. 13:9), to mean: "No one has become a hearer of these mysteries save only the gnostics who are perfected".[3] When the kingdom of heaven is compared to a mustard-seed

(Mt. 13:31), they explained this as "the indivisible point existing in the body which is known to none but the spiritual".[4]

The Gospel of John in particular lent itself to allegorical exegesis. This is not surprising because even today many readers of the narratives in this Gospel are left with a feeling that John is saying more than meets the eye – although certainty about any underlying significance is rarely attainable. When the mother of Jesus appears, for example, are we simply to think of Mary (it is noteworthy that John never calls her by her name) or does she symbolize the believing community, or some part of it? A similar question arises with regard to the disciple whom Jesus loved. And what might be intended by the Samaritan woman's five husbands (Jn. 4:18) or by the remarkable catch of 153 fishes (Jn. 21:11)? If commentators are not content to confine themselves to the literal and surface meaning, their symbolic interpretations are likely to reflect their own mode of thinking rather than the evangelist's intention. Origen, for example, interpreted the five husbands of the five senses, by which the human soul is governed before it comes to faith in Christ, although elsewhere he takes them to mean the five books of the law, which the Samaritans acknowledged as canonical.

The Valentinian Gnostic Heracleon, the first commentator on this Gospel, gave the husbands a significance more in keeping with his own outlook: for him they represent various forms of entanglement with the material order, and only when she has been delivered from them will she be united to the *pleroma*.

3. MARCION AND HIS SCHOOL

Marcion (*c.* A.D. 140), with all his one-sided devotion to Paul as the only faithful disciple of Jesus, showed some appreciation of interpretative method in his approach to Paul's epistles. His revisions of the text of these epistles (excluding the Pastorals) and of Luke's Gospel were based on *a priori* dogma, not on anything resembling what we know today as critical method. But he had a firm grasp of the primacy of literal exegesis. Indeed, it was this that made him so resolutely jettison the Old Testament as irrelevant to the gospel; had he been willing to allegorize it, as many of his orthodox and gnostic contemporaries did, he could have made it convey the same teaching as Paul's epistles – or anything else he chose. Apart from his arbitrary handling of the text, his understanding of the epistles appears to have paid due regard to their historical and geographical setting. This may be inferred from the Marcionite prologues to the epistles (preserved in Latin in many Vulgate manuscripts), which are probably the work of his followers rather than his own and show only occasional signs of distinctive Marcionite doctrine. They make best sense if they are read consecutively according to the order in which the ten epistles were arranged in Marcion's canon, beginning with Galatians.[5]

> The Galatians are Greeks. They first received the word of truth from the apostle, but after his departure they were tempted by false apostles to turn to the law

> and circumcision. The apostle recalls them to belief in the truth, writing to them from Ephesus.

Most of this prologue is based on the contents of the epistle, but the first and last statements are either intelligent guesses or based on tradition. The statement that the Galatians were Greeks may imply that they were not Celts ("North Galatians"); the statement that it was written from Ephesus assigns it to the same period as the Corinthian correspondence.

Romans (surprisingly) is said to have been written from Athens. The Marcionite prologue to this letter distorts its argument, perhaps on the assumption that a church founded by someone other than Paul could not have been taught the true gospel. The Romans, it is said,

> had been visited previously by false apostles and introduced to the law and the prophets under the name of Christ. The apostle recalls them to the true faith of the gospel . . .

In fact, nothing in the letter to the Romans suggests that its recipients had been wrongly taught or had anything to unlearn.

The Epistle to the Ephesians was entitled "To the Laodiceans" in Marcion's canon (an inference, probably, from the language of Col. 4:16).

> The Laodiceans are Asians. Having received the word of truth they persevered in the faith. The apostle commends them, writing to them from prison in Rome.

The letters to the Philippians and Philemon are also said to have been written "from prison in Rome". All the more surprising, then, is it to find a different provenance assigned to the letter to the Colossians:

> The Colossians, like the Laodiceans, are also Asians. They also had been visited previously by false apostles. The apostle did not come to them in person, but sets them right again by means of his epistle; for they had heard the word from Archippus, who received his ministry for them. Therefore the apostle, in bonds, writes to them from Ephesus.

The reference to Archippus is an inference from Col. 4:17. As for the statement that the letter was sent from Ephesus, this is based on nothing in the text and may reflect a tradition that one of Paul's imprisonments had been endured in that city.

For the most part, the Marcionite prologues to the epistles show more objectivity and insight than do the anti-Marcionite prologues to the Gospels, which are valuable chiefly for the material which they preserve from earlier tradition, especially the writings of Papias.

4. IRENAEUS AND ORIGEN

Irenaeus, who left his home in the province of Asia to become bishop of Lyons in the Rhone valley shortly after A.D. 177, was not an interpreter of the New Testament books as such but an expositor and defender of Christian doctrine against heretics. Since, however, he recognized that Christian doctrine, preserved in special purity in the churches of apostolic foundation, was based on Scripture, he was inevitably involved in the exposition of Scripture, and indeed has been described by R. M. Grant as "the father of authoritative exegesis in the Church".[6] If I may quote what I have said elsewhere:

> The apostolic tradition is for him the proper and natural interpretation of Scripture: the faith which he summarizes and expounds is what Scripture teaches. He is convinced of the perspicuity of Scripture; any honest student of Scripture must agree that this is its meaning. Heretics may appeal to Scripture, but if they construct from Scripture something different from the apostolic tradition as preserved in the church their appeal is invalid.[7]

The argument that heretics and others who are outside the true church are incompetent to interpret Scripture since they repudiate the key that unlocks its meaning is elaborated by Tertullian. In his *Prescription against Heretics* he invokes a principle of Roman law to debar them from the right of appealing to Scripture.

While several Christian writers of the second and third centuries engaged incidentally in New Testament exegesis, the first to compile scholarly commentaries was Origen of Alexandria and Caesarea (185–254). "He brought the touch of a master to what had hitherto been nothing much more than the exercise of amateurs."[8] His linguistic and textual equipment was unrivalled; his mastery of the whole realm of contemporary learning was unsurpassed. Yet, even when he brought the whole weight of his scholarly apparatus to bear on the interpretation of the biblical text, he too often failed to appreciate the authors' intention because of the strength of his Platonic presuppositions, so alien to their outlook. In every generation exegetes have their presuppositions, but if they know their business they will beware of thinking that the biblical authors shared those presuppositions. Origen all too often makes the biblical authors teach Platonism instead of what they were really concerned to teach. In particular, his Platonism seems to have made him incapable of sympathizing with the biblical writers' sense of history.

Even when he comes to critical questions like discrepancies between the Gospels, he tends to surmount them by allegorization. For example, John places the cleansing of the temple at an early stage in Jesus' ministry; Matthew and the other Synoptists place it towards the end. The question belongs to the realm of historical criticism, and Origen recognizes that if it is treated on that level it cannot be resolved by harmonistic methods. In any case, he says, the story as it stands contains a number of improbabilities. But if the temple is the soul skilled in reason, to which Jesus ascends from Capernaum, a region of less dignity, so as to purify it from irrational tendencies which still adhere to it, then the improbabilities of the literal accounts disappear and the discrepancies between them become irrelevant.

Similarly, when he deals with Jesus' entry into Jerusalem, he interprets Jesus as the word of God entering the soul (which is called Jerusalem). The ass which the disciples loose is the Old Testament properly interpreted; the colt, which in Matthew's account is distinguished from the parent animal, is the New Testament. The statement that no one had ever sat on it is a reference to those who never submitted to the divine message before the coming of Jesus. This treatment of the record is what we nowadays call demythologization, for Origen regards the literal sense as not only inadequate but as downright unacceptable. He criticizes Heracleon for interpreting the temple-cleansing in a gnostic sense, but Heracleon and he were not so far apart in their approach. Each read his philosophic presuppositions into the text, although Origen's allegorization was more under the control of the catholic rule of faith. Origen, however, did not consistently maintain his allegorical method; after insisting near the beginning of his commentary on John that the temple-cleansing could not be understood otherwise than allegorically, he refers to it later as an exhibition of Jesus' supernatural power. But even when he came to pay more respect to the historical interpretation, he regarded it as less important than the allegorical.

5. THE SCHOOL OF ANTIOCH

The biblical interpretation which characterized the church of Antioch was much more restrained in its practice of allegorization than that current in Alexandria. The great Antiochene exegetes belong to a later period than Clement and Origen: the two greatest figures among them are Theodore of Mopsuestia (350–428) and John of the golden mouth (Chrysostom) (347–407), for the last ten years of his life patriarch of Constantinople.

Theodore, whom later generations venerated as "The Interpreter" *par excellence,* distinguished between the pure exegete and the preacher: the exegete's task was to elucidate obscurities, while the preacher's was to communicate the plain teaching of the gospel. If this distinction be maintained, Theodore was a pure exegete while Chrysostom was an expository preacher – but always a preacher.

The Alexandrians understood biblical inspiration in the Platonic sense of utterance in a state of ecstatic possession. It was fitting therefore that words so imparted should be interpreted mystically if their inner significance was to be laid bare. Theodore and the Antiochenes thought of inspiration rather as a divinely-given quickening of the writers' awareness and understanding, in which their individuality was unimpaired and their intellectual activity remained under their conscious control. It was important therefore in interpreting them to have regard to their particular usage, aims and methods. The literal sense was primary, and it was from it that moral lessons should be drawn; the typological and allegorical senses, while not excluded, were secondary.

The contrast between Theodore and Origen appears most strikingly in their Old Testament interpretation, but it is seen also in their treatment of the New Testament. Theodore treats the Gospel narratives factually: he pays attention to the particles of transition and to the minutiae of grammar and punctuation. He shows some skill in assessing the value of dubious readings and in bringing out the point of a discourse or parable. His consciousness of chronological development in theology as well as in history is illustrated by his recognition that Nathanael's use of the title "Son of God" in John 1:49 cannot have the full force that the title received after Jesus' resurrection. But he has the defects of his qualities: if he does not follow Origen into an excess of spiritualization, he lacks his depth of insight. His main strength is found in his exposition of the letters of Paul. Occasionally his exegesis is controlled by theological presuppositions, but that is true of exegetes in other ages. It would be absurd to see in his work an anticipation of the critical method of the nineteenth century, or even of the grammatico-historical method of the sixteenth; but he had, for his time, an uncommon appreciation of the principles of exegesis and the power of applying them to the effective eliciting of an author's meaning.

Chrysostom's homilies on the New Testament cover Matthew, John, Acts and all the Pauline letters. His biblical interpretation appears in these homilies, and is naturally expressed with a wordiness that is in marked contrast to Theodore's spare style: his homilies on the Pauline letters, for example, are nearly ten times as long as Theodore's exposition of the same documents. But they are firmly based on the Antiochene principles of exegesis so outstandingly exemplified in Theodore's work. He does not eschew allegory completely, but holds that when allegorical interpretation is in order the context itself indicates that this is so, and indicates what form the allegorical interpretation should take.

The Antiochene principles of exegesis were introduced to the west by Junilius Africanus (*c.* 542): he translated into Latin an introduction to biblical study by Paul of Nisibis, which reflects Theodore's methods. But the exegetical principles which became dominant in the mediaeval west owed more to Alexandria than to Antioch.

6. THE LATIN FATHERS

Several of the Latin Fathers of the fourth and fifth centuries wrote notable commentaries on the Pauline epistles: Marius Victorinus (*c.* 300–370) on Galatians, Philippians and Ephesians; Jerome (347–420) on Philemon, Galatians, Ephesians and Titus; Augustine (354–430) on Romans and Galatians; "Ambrosiaster" and Pelagius on all thirteen. Victorinus endeavoured to present the literal sense, but found it difficult to exclude his Neoplatonic philosophy. Jerome's commentaries are marked by his great erudition and acquaintance with classical literature and with previous exegetical work, especially Origen's. He has left us also a commentary on Matthew and a revision of the commentary on Revelation by Victorinus of Pettau (d. 303), from which he removed the original chiliastic interpretations. "Ambrosiaster" draws many illustrations from government and law, and shows a rare interest in the principles underlying legal institutions, for example in his remarks on the institution of slavery in his comment on Col. 4:1. Pelagius has a firm grasp of the principle of justification by grace through faith – which is not easy to reconcile with popular ideas of his teaching – and insists repeatedly on the influence of example on conduct.[9]

In addition to Augustine's Pauline commentaries he has left us works on the Gospels, notably 124 homilies on the Gospel of John, and ten homilies on John's first epistle. There is also a wealth of practical exposition in his *Sermons*. In a number of places he gives free rein to the allegorical method. The stock example is his interpretation of the parable of the Good Samaritan (Lk. 10:30–37) where the man who goes down the Jericho road is Adam (mankind), assaulted by the devil and his angels, uncared for by the Old Testament priesthood and ministry, rescued by Christ and brought by him to the church, which exists for the refreshment of travellers on their way to the heavenly country.[10]

Augustine finds authority for the allegorical (spiritual) method in the words of 2 Cor. 3:6, "the letter kills, but the Spirit gives life." To rest content with the pedestrian level of the literal sense is a mark of soul slavery, when the treasures of the spiritual sense are there to be grasped. When the literal sense cannot be understood in reference to purity of life or soundness of doctrine, it should be concluded that the true sense is spiritual. Above all, that interpretation is to be preferred which promotes the supremacy of love. No one can claim to understand the scriptures properly unless he sees that in every part they teach love to God and love to one's neighbour.[11]

In proposing this last hermeneutical principle for the whole Bible, Augustine follows the precedent of Jesus, for whom the twofold commandment of love summed up the law and the prophets.

7. THE MIDDLE AGES

The quality of Augustine's character and intellect ensured that his example dominated the following centuries in western Christendom. In the standard "fourfold" sense of Scripture, the three non-literal senses were varieties of the spiritual sense. Thus a reference to water in Scripture might have the literal sense of water, but in the moral sense it could denote purity of life; in the allegorical sense, the doctrine of baptism; in the anagogical sense, the water of life in the heavenly Jerusalem. Thus the old jingle summed it up:

Littera gesta docet, quid credas allegoria,
Moralis quid agas, quo tendas anagogia.

("The literal sense teaches what actually happened, the allegorical what you are to believe, the moral how you are to behave, the anagogical where you are going.")

On matters of criticism the judgments of Jerome were remembered and repeated by those biblical scholars in the early Middle Ages who were interested in such subjects. Here we should make special mention of the gifted exegetical school at the Abbey of St. Victor, Paris – Hugh (d. 1141) and his disciples, especially Andrew. But where the interpretation of the New Testament was concerned the primacy of the spiritual sense was generally taken for granted. The one control which kept the quest for the spiritual sense within bounds was the insistence that all interpretation must conform with "the analogy of the faith" – this apostolic expression (Rom. 12:6) being understood of "the faith" in its objective sense, as the body of accepted church doctrine. The unanimity of all scripture was axiomatic, and it was inconceivable that there could be any discrepancy between the interpretation of scripture and the catholic faith.

The *Glossa Ordinaria,* the great mediaeval compilation of biblical annotation, took shape from the eleventh to the fifteenth century. In it each book of the Bible is introduced by the prologue or prologues of Jerome with other prefatory material, while the annotations themselves are written in the margins and between the lines.

For the Pauline epistles, as for the Psalter, a specially elaborate *glossa,* the *Magna Glosatura,* was constructed on the basis of Anselm's *glossa* on these books by his pupil Gilbert de la Porrée and by Peter Lombard.

While biblical exegesis was pursued unremittingly throughout the Middle Ages, the high standard of work which characterized the earlier Middle Ages was not maintained in the subsequent period. The *Glossa Ordinaria* and *Magna Glosatura* became in time the norm for all biblical exposition; lectures on the Bible took the form, as Dr. Beryl Smalley has put it, of "glossing the *Gloss*".[12] This dependence on the work of earlier annotators, masters though they were in their day, inhibited fresh biblical study as thoroughly as rabbinical methods did at an earlier date.

When John Wycliffe and his helpers undertook to make the Bible available to Englishmen in their own language, it was from a conviction that every man was God's "tenant-in-chief", immediately responsible to God and immediately responsible to obey his law. And by God's law Wycliffe meant not canon law but the Bible. It followed, then, that every man must have access to the Bible if he was to know what to obey. Earlier Bible translations in English had concentrated on those parts which were relevant to the liturgy and to the devotional life; but Wycliffe's doctrine of "dominion by grace" led to the conclusion that the whole Bible was applicable to the whole of life and should therefore be available in the vernacular.[13] While this approach to the Bible marked a departure from the dominant line, it was still inevitably mediaeval in conception. There was little appreciation of historical development within the biblical record, and no idea that the Bible's guidance could be ambiguous, in regard either to human relationships or to church order and organization.

II. *Renaissance, Reformation and Counter-Reformation*

1. COLET

John Colet (*c.* 1467–1519), later Dean of St. Paul's, broke with the exegetical methods of mediaeval scholasticism when he returned from the Continent to Oxford in 1496 and lectured on the Pauline epistles, expounding the text in terms of its plain meaning as seen in its historical context. When Desiderius Erasmus (*c.* 1467–1536) came to Oxford in 1498, he was profoundly influenced by Colet, to whom he owed in large measure his insight into the proper methods of biblical interpretation.

2. ERASMUS

Erasmus's contribution to the understanding of the New Testament is seen not only in his successive editions of the Greek New Testament (1516, 1519, 1522, 1527 and 1535) with his accompanying new translation into Latin and notes explaining a number of his Latin renderings, but also in his publication (1505) of Lorenzo Valla's philological annotations on the Latin New Testament and in his own paraphrases of the New Testament Epistles and Gospels (1517 ff.). These paraphrases, though written in Latin, were designed for the common people, and this design was furthered by their being translated into several European languages. The English translation was sponsored and partly undertaken by members of the royal family in the reign of Edward VI. The paraphrases are popular, practical and edifying. The historical and contextually established meaning was primary, but any further form of interpretation that enabled the reader to derive some helpful lesson from the text was pressed into service. Erasmus's exposition of the Lord's Prayer was translated into English by Margaret, daughter of Sir Thomas More.

3. LUTHER

No exegete of the sixteenth century exercised a greater or more far-reaching influence on the course of biblical interpretation than Martin Luther (1483–1546). His place in the history of interpretation cannot be dissociated from his appeal from the authority of church, councils and papacy to the authority of *sola scriptura*. Time and again his attitude comes to clear and concise expression. At the Leipzig disputation (1519) he affirmed:

> No believing Christian can be forced to recognize any authority beyond the sacred scripture, which is exclusively invested with divine right.[14]

At the Diet of Worms (1521) he replied to Johann von Eck's demand that he recant his alleged errors:

> Unless I am convinced by the testimonies of the sacred scriptures or manifest reason . . ., I am bound by the scriptures which I have adduced. My conscience has been taken captive by the Word of God, and I neither can nor will recant, since it is neither safe nor right to act against conscience.[15]

Four years later, in *De Servo Arbitrio* (1525), he replies to Erasmus's *De Libero Arbitrio* (1523) and takes issue with Erasmus's willingness to appeal to catholic dogma where his case could not be established by *sola scriptura,* even when the logic underlying the dogma was obscure or faulty:

> What do you mean, Erasmus? Is it not enough to have submitted your judgment to Scripture? Do you submit it to the Church as well? – why, what can the Church settle that Scripture did not settle first? . . . What is this new-fangled religion of yours, this novel sort of humility, that, by your own example, you would take from us power to judge men's decisions and make us defer uncritically to human authority? Where does God's written Word tell us to do that? . . . Woe to the Christian who doubts the truth of what is commanded him and does not follow it! – for how can he believe what he does not follow?[16]

The Christian must "follow" and understand what the church requires of him, and decide whether it is a valid requirement or not, before he can intelligently submit to it. And the basis of his understanding and his decision must be the Bible.

This implies that Scripture is intelligible and consistent. If men have difficulty in understanding it, that is not because of its inherent obscurity but because of their "ignorance of words and grammar". But if Scripture is as authoritative and perspicuous as this, there must be a clear understanding of the principles of its interpretation. Chief among these principles was an insistence on the plain and literal meaning:

> We must keep to the simple, pure and natural sense of the words, as demanded by grammar and the use of language created by God among men.[17]

Interpretation according to the interpreter's whim or preference is impermissible, and this is too often what allegorical interpretation amounts to. The allegorical method can make the text mean whatever the allegorizer wants it to mean. Only where the wording of a passage points unmistakably to a figurative or metaphorical interpretation is such an interpretation to be adopted.

Moreover, the Scriptures must be read in their original languages if their meaning is to be adequately discovered, and therefore painstaking study of these languages is indispensable. Only so can that "ignorance of words and grammar" be overcome which stands in the way of men's understanding of the biblical message.

But is there one basic biblical message? There is; Luther owed all that he was to his discovery of that message. The message was the gospel of justification by faith. There are some parts of the Bible which convey that message more clearly than others, and it is in the light of those parts that the others are to be read. As for certain biblical writings which seemed to contradict justification by faith, this was sufficient to put their canonicity in question.

> In short, St. John's Gospel and his first Epistle; St. Paul's Epistles, especially those to the Romans, Galatians and Ephesians; and St. Peter's first Epistle – these are the books which show you Christ and teach everything which is necessary and blessed for you to know, even if you never see or hear any other book or teaching. Therefore in comparison with them St. James's Epistle is a right strawy epistle, for it has no evangelical quality about it.[18]

It was not the authors who mattered in the last analysis; it was the content of their writings.

> That which does not teach Christ is not apostolic, even though Peter and Paul be the teachers. On the other hand, that which does teach Christ is apostolic, even though Judas, Annas, Pilate or Herod should propound it.[19]

This expresses, in extreme language, Paul's own sentiments: "Even if we, or an angel from heaven, should preach to you a gospel contrary to that which we preached to you, let him be accursed" (Gal. 1:8); on the other hand, even if some "preach Christ from envy and rivalry", what matter? "Only that in every way, whether in pretence or in truth, Christ is proclaimed; and in that I rejoice" (Phil. 1:15–18).

But with the elimination of those elements whose title to a place in the canon was ruled out by their "unevangelical" content, what remained was self-evidently unanimous.

> The New Testament is one book, in which are written the gospel and the promise of God, together with the history of those who believed and those who did not. Thus every man may be sure that there is only one gospel, only one book in the New Testament, only one faith, and only one promise-giving God.[20]

4. CALVIN

Where Luther is bold, sweeping and prophetic, John Calvin (1509–64) is more scholarly, logical and painstaking. Luther was a preacher; Calvin was a lecturer. His commentaries cover nearly the whole Bible; in the New Testament the absence of a commentary on Revelation is conspicuous (the absence of commentaries on 2 and 3 John might more easily escape notice). Like Luther, he reads and expounds Scripture so as to find Christ there. He served his apprenticeship as a commentator in the commentary on Seneca's *De Clementia* which he wrote at the age of twenty-three, and something of the humanist remained in him alongside the Reformed theologian. He brought to his exegetical task a rare wealth of classical and patristic knowledge. Historical problems and textual discrepancies which crop up in the course of his exegesis he takes in his stride. On questions of introduction he can strike out on an independent course, as when he dates Galatians before the Council of Jerusalem of Acts 15 – although one may wonder how the ethnic Galatians (as he takes the recipients of the letter to be) were evangelized at such an early date![21]

He repudiated the time-honoured allegorical method as wholeheartedly as Luther did: not only did it enable the interpreter to extract whatever sense he wished from the text but it effectively obscured the true sense – the sense intended by the Spirit. He was not disposed to maintain time-honoured interpretations which found proof-texts for Christian doctrine in the most unlikely places, if he thought that they were excluded by the plain sense and context. Thus he was fiercely attacked for denying that the plural form for God, *'elohim,* in Gen. 1:1 and elsewhere pointed to the persons of the Trinity.[22]

At the same time, he was a thoroughly theological expositor. To him Scripture, with all the diversity of its human authorship, was the product of the Spirit. It authenticated itself as such by the inward witness of the Spirit in the reader or hearer, and the purpose of its exposition was to make plain what the Spirit was saying not only to the churches of the first century but to those of the sixteenth. Calvin's exegesis was applied exegesis: those religious groups which attract disapproval in the Gospels and Epistles have their sixteenth-century counterparts in the Church of Rome and the Anabaptist communities.

Before he turned to exegesis, Calvin, at the age of twenty-six, published his *Institutio,* an introduction to Christian doctrine which was to receive unsurpassed recognition as a summary of Reformed theology. In Calvin's intention the whole of the *Institutio* is biblically based; Scripture is quoted copiously from start to finish in support of its successive propositions and arguments. But while many Calvinists since Calvin's day have felt it proper to expound Scripture in the light of the *Institutio,* he himself exercised much greater freedom. If in the course of his exposition he says something which is difficult to square with statements in the *Institutio,* he says it because he believes that that is what the relevant scripture means in its context. If he says on Luke 2:17f. that the shepherds' blazing abroad the news of what they had heard from the angels and seen at Bethlehem had the purpose not so much of bringing the people salvation as of rendering their ignorance inexcusable, there are many other places where he shows himself not unduly bound by his statements on predestination in the *Institutio.* In fact on this particular subject his commentaries show a flexibility which is at times disconcerting to those of his followers who would prefer a line more uniformly consistent with the *Institutio.* Not only does he reckon the elect to outnumber the reprobate – "since admittedly Christ is much more powerful to save than Adam was to ruin" (on Rom. 5:15) – but he affirms in the same context: "Paul makes grace common to all men, not because in fact it extends to all, but because it is offered to all; for although Christ suffered for the sins of the world, and is offered by the goodness of God without distinction to all men, yet not all receive him" (on Rom. 5:18). If such comments are not easily reconciled with inferences which many readers have drawn from the *Institutio,* what matter? Calvin knew that an exegete's business is to bring out the meaning of his text, and that is what he does here. Similarly on the words of institution spoken over the cup in Matt. 26:28 and Mark 14:24 ("my blood . . . which is shed for many") he says: "By the word *many* he means not a part of the world only, but the whole human race." And if, in the parallel passage in Luke 22:20, "for many" is replaced by "for you", this reminds believers to appropriate to themselves personally what has been provided for all: "let us not only remember in general that the world has been redeemed by the blood of Christ, but let each one consider for himself that his own sins have been expiated thereby." Such samples indicate that Calvin the exegete sat quite loose to certain ideas which have come traditionally to be regarded as characteristically "Calvinistic".

In fact, the more objectively grammatico-historical biblical exegesis is, the more widely is it acceptable, whereas exegesis which is controlled by theological *parti-pris* will be appreciated only where that theological outlook is found congenial. How successfully Calvin, in the setting of his day, approached the exegetical ideal is illustrated by the assessment of Jacobus Arminius (1560–1609):

> After the reading of Scripture, which I strenuously inculcate, and more than any other . . . I recommend that the *Commentaries* of Calvin be read . . . For I affirm that in the interpretation of the Scriptures Calvin is incomparable, and that his *Commentaries* are more to be valued than anything that is handed down to us in the writings of the Fathers – so much so that I concede to him a certain spirit of prophecy in which he stands distinguished above others, above most, indeed, above all.[23]

5. A POLEMICAL SITUATION

The wind of change blew much of the time-honoured scholastic methods out of exegetical practice in the Church of Rome as well as among the Reformers. It was a congenial exercise on either side to interpret Scripture in such a way as to score points against the other. The marginalia in the Geneva Bible (1560) and the Rheims New Testament (1582) provide ample illustration of this, not least in the Apocalypse. Perhaps one reason why Calvin published no commentary on this book was that his exegetical conscience could not accommodate itself to the polemical interpretation which was current in his environment. Not that Calvin shrank from polemics, but the principles which prevented him from seeing the Papacy in the "little horn" of Dan. 7:8 (which he interpreted of Julius Caesar and his successors) might perhaps have prevented him from following the fashion of discerning it in some of the sinister figures of the Apocalypse.

Theodorus Bibliander (1504–64), "the father of biblical exegesis in Switzerland",[24] went some way on the Reformed side towards repairing Calvin's omission. In his commentary on the Apocalypse (1549) he maintained the identification of Antichrist with the Papacy (as Calvin did in his exposition of 2 Thess. 2:1–12), but (rather inconsistently, if happily) interpreted the beast of Rev. 13:1 ff. as the Roman Empire and its wound as Nero's death – a wound which was healed with the accession of Vespasian.

With his contemporary Heinrich Bullinger (1504–75), Bibliander returned in some measure to the precedent set by Irenaeus and Victorinus of Pettau, and (whether under the stimulus of their example or not) a similar return is seen in exegesis coming from the Roman camp about the same time. Those fathers lived much closer to the age and situation of the Apocalypse than the Reformers and Counter-Reformers did, and showed how sixteenth-century expositors might extricate themselves from the morass of contemporary polemics and come nearer to discovering what John and the other New Testament writers wished their readers to understand.

III. *The Post-Reformation Period*

1. FLACIUS AND CAMERARIUS

It is commonly believed that the followers of the Reformers shrank from the exegetical freedom which Luther and Calvin enjoyed, sterotyped their insights and conducted biblical exposition along well-defined theological party lines, establishing a new Protestant scholasticism. However much this may have been true of the rank and file, the post-Reformation period produced a succession of independent thinkers.

Matthias Flacius Illyricus (1520–75) published in 1567 his *Clavis Scripturae Sacrae;* it included a discussion of the principles of biblical interpretation which, in the words of W. G. Kümmel, "represents the real beginning of scholarly hermeneutics".[25] Following Luther, he admits only one sense of scripture, the grammatical sense, which normally implies a literal interpretation; only where the literal interpretation is impossible is a symbolical interpretation to be adopted as that which the author intended. He insisted on understanding the text in the sense which it was designed to convey to its original readers; without this insistence, there is no way forward in biblical exegesis.

Joachim Camerarius (1500–74) applied to New Testament interpretation the principles which he had mastered as a classical student. He confined himself to philological exegesis, even in the Apocalypse; he despaired of solving that book's symbolical problems: with regard to them he said (quoting Cicero), "Call the good guesser the best seer".

2. CATHOLIC EXEGESIS

Others, however, made some progress with the symbolism of the Apocalypse by combining the historical with the philological approach. On this basis Johannes Hentenius, who in 1547 wrote a preface for a Latin translation of Arethas's commentary on that book,[26] dated it before A.D. 70, as also did his fellow-Catholic Alfonso Salmeron in his *In Iohannis Apocalypsin Praeludia* (1614). Two Jesuit scholars who made contributions of major importance to its elucidation were Francisco de Ribera (1537–91) and Luis de Alcazar (1554–1613). The former, in his *In sacram beati Ioannis Apostoli et Evangelistae Apocalypsin Commentarii* (1593), interpreted the earlier chapters of John's own day and the later ones of the last three and a half years immediately preceding the parousia. The latter, in his *Vestigatio Arcani Sensus in Apocalypsi* (1614), maintained that the whole book had been fulfilled: what was yet future in John's day was accomplished in the downfall of Roman paganism and the consequent triumph of the church. Even so, neither Ribera nor Alcazar was able completely to break with the church-historical method of apocalyptic interpretation.

3. GROTIUS

Such a break appears in the work of the Dutch jurist Hugo Grotius (1583–1645), who also broke with the Reformed tradition of identifying the Papacy with Antichrist. Grotius's *Annotationes in Novum Testamentum* (1641ff.) carried on the philological and historical method of Flacius Illyricus and Camerarius, and did so more rigorously and in greater detail. So objective was his treatment of the text, in fact, that he was charged with rationalism. He saw that the individual books of the New Testament could best be understood in their respective historical contexts, even if he was not always successful in his attempts to identify those contexts. Thus he saw in 2 Thess. 2:1–12 a reference to the Emperor Gaius's attempt to have his statue set up in the Jerusalem temple, and accordingly dated the epistle *c.* A.D. 40, making it the earliest of the Pauline writings. He inferred from 2

Pet. 3:3f. that that epistle was written after A.D. 70 and therefore not by Peter the apostle; he treated the name "Peter" in the initial salutation as a later addition to the text and conjectured that the author was Simeon, bishop of Jerusalem, who was traditionally martyred under Trajan.

4. BACKGROUND STUDIES

In England John Lightfoot (1602–75) realized the importance of Jewish studies for New Testament interpretation and in his *Horae Hebraicae et Talmudicae* (1658–78) he collected a mass of material from the rabbinical writings illustrating the Gospels, Acts, Romans and 1 Corinthians. Two volumes bearing a similar title (*Horae Ebraicae et Talmudicae in universum Novum Testamentum*) were published in 1733 and 1742 by the German scholar Christian Schöttgen (1687–1751). Johann Jakob Wettstein (1693–1754) published at Amsterdam in 1751–52 a two-volume edition of the Greek New Testament which was noteworthy not only for its departures from the *Textus Receptus* but even more so for its copious apparatus of illustrative material from classical and patristic literature. Another quarry of background material was opened in 1750, when a pioneer comparison of the writings of Philo and the Epistle to the Hebrews was published by Johann Benedikt Carpzov (1720–1803) in his *Sacrae exercitationes in epistulam ad Hebraeos ex Philone Alexandrino.*

5. TEXTUAL STUDIES

The reference to Wettstein's departures from the *Textus Receptus* (which exposed him to charges of heresy) reminds us how pioneer studies in the New Testament text made their contribution to its interpretation. The (English) Geneva version of 1560 was ahead of its time in drawing attention to textual variants; nearly a century later Brian Walton's *Biblia Sacra Polyglotta* (1655–57) incurred the displeasure of John Owen (*Considerations on the Prolegomena and Appendix to the Late Polyglotta,* 1659) for "that bulky collection of various readings which the appendix tenders to the view of every one that doth but cast an eye upon it".[27]

But the collection and publication of "various readings" proceeded apace, well in advance of the discovery of a scientific method of classifying and assessing them. John Mill (1645–1707) published two weeks before his death a reprint of Stephanus's third edition of the Greek text (1550) with an apparatus of about 30,000 variants. Their large number disturbed the faith of young Johann Albrecht Bengel (1687–1752), who accordingly devoted himself to a thorough study of the situation and showed the way to classifying the witnesses to the text and weighing the evidence of the readings. It was he who laid down the rule that in the assessing of variants "the difficult reading is to be preferred to the easy one" (*proclivi scriptioni praestat ardua*). His edition of the Greek Testament (1734) was followed in 1742 by his *Gnomon Novi Testamenti,* comprising concise exegetical notes based especially on context and grammar, regardless of dogmatic tradition (orthodox Lutheran and pietist though he was).

6. SEMLER AND MICHAELIS

A new approach to New Testament interpretation was marked by the *Abhandlung vom freien Gebrauch des Kanons* (1771–75) of Johann Salomo Semler (1725–91), which approached the New Testament canon on a historical basis, and the *Einleitung in die göttlichen Schriften des Neuen Bundes* (first edition, 1750) of Johann David Michaelis (1717–91), the fourth edition of which (1788) carried forward Semler's work by stressing the importance of the historical, as distinct from the theological, approach to the individual documents of the New Testament. Both these men were indebted in some measure to Richard Simon's *Histoire Critique du texte du Nouveau Testament* (1689) and other works, but while Simon was motivated in part by a desire to weaken the force of the Reformers' appeal to the perspicuous authority of Scripture, Semler and Michaelis were subject to no such influences and deserve together to be acknowledged as pioneers in the historico-critical study of the New Testament.

7. THE ENLIGHTENMENT

If the eighteenth-century Enlightenment (*Aufklärung*) did not make a direct contribution to the scientific exegesis of the New Testament, it did, like the English deism which preceded it,[28] create an atmosphere in which people were prepared to consider the matter in a spirit independent of traditional or dogmatic positions. Gotthold Ephraim Lessing (1729–81) not only published the "Wolfenbüttel Fragments" of Hermann Samuel Reimarus (1694–1768) anonymously (1774–78), after their author's death – a work to which Semler made a critical rejoinder – but propounded a new theory regarding the origin of the Gospels. He envisaged a primitive Aramaic Gospel of the Nazarenes which was used by Mark and the other canonical evangelists. This thesis was given a more critical exposition in 1794 by Michaelis's pupil Johann Gottfried Eichhorn (1752–1827) in his study *Über die drey ersten Evangelien*. Another aspect of Lessing's theory was developed by Johann Gottfried Herder (1744–1803), who drew a sharp distinction between the portrait of Jesus in the Gospel of John and that in the other three Gospels and maintained the mutual independence even of the three Synoptic Gospels (*Christliche Schriften* ii, 1796; iii, 1797).

More generally, Lessing's hypothesis of the "ugly ditch" which prevented a transition from "the accidental facts of history" to "the necessary truths of religion" had far-reaching implications for the understanding of the New Testament.

8. GRIESBACH

Semler's pupil Johann Jakob Griesbach (1745–1812) may be said to mark the transition from the "post-Reformation" to the "modern" age of New Testament study. In 1774–75 he published a critical edition of the Greek Testament in his own recension, together with an extensive apparatus. He developed Bengel's method of classifying the witnesses to the text and distinguished three main text-types – the Alexandrian, the Western and the Constantinopolitan – recognizing the third as secondary in time and inferior in value to the other two. In this he set a pattern for New Testament textual criticism which has endured to our own day.

Apart from his textual contributions, he advanced beyond the historical criticism of his immediate predecessors by applying himself to the problems of literary criticism, in that area of New Testament where these problems are most obvious – the Gospels and their interrelationship. This question had been tackled from patristic times: Augustine's *De consensu evangelistarum* had provided a precedent for students throughout many centuries. Gospel harmonies had been drawn up from Tatian's *Diatessaron* (*c.* A.D. 170) onwards: Calvin, instead of writing separate commentaries on the Synoptic Gospels, expounded a harmony of the three. It is to Griesbach, apparently, that we owe the expression "Synoptic Gospels" to designate Matthew, Mark and Luke. In his *Synopsis Evangeliorum* (1776) he argued, against the traditional view that Mark was dependent on Matthew, and Luke on Matthew and Mark, that Mark was dependent mainly on Matthew and partly on Luke – that Mark, in fact, was an unoriginal and poorly informed writer. This was indeed a cul-de-sac in literary criticism, worth mentioning only because Griesbach did at least turn his back on tradition and investigate the literary problem *de novo* – none the less a cul-de-sac for recent attempts to open it up by W. R. Farmer, *The Synoptic Problem* (1970), and J. B. Orchard, *Why Three Synoptic Gospels?* (1975). But Eichhorn was able some years later to point to a more promising way forward by developing Lessing's idea, not the more scholarly Griesbach's.

IV. *The Nineteenth Century*

1. DE WETTE AND LACHMANN

The new approach to biblical criticism and interpretation at the end of the eighteenth and beginning of the nineteenth century is paralleled in other fields of study, especially in classical history and literature. In literary criticism Friedrich August Wolf (1759–1824) achieved a break-through in his *Prolegomena* to Homer (1795); in historical criticism Barthold Georg Niebuhr (1776–1831) opened a new era in the study of Roman history, especially the early period, in his *Römische Geschichte* (1811–32). In Old Testament study progress was made by Alexander Geddes (1737–1802), whose "fragmentary hypothesis" of the composition of the Pentateuch was elaborated by Johann Severin Vater (1771–1826); and by Wilhelm Martin Leberecht de Wette (1780–1849), who traced the progress of the composition of the Pentateuch by the evidence of the historical and prophetical books, and in particular drew attention to the crucial significance of the law of the single sanctuary in Deut. 12:5ff. De Wette made contributions to New Testament scholarship also – in his *Kurzgefasstes exegetisches Handbuch zum Neuen Testament* (1836–48) and his *Lehrbuch der historisch-kritischen Einleitung in die kanonischen Bücher des Neuen Testaments* (1830).

He distinguished three theological strands in the New Testament: the Jewish-Christian (in the Synoptic Gospels, most of Acts, the letters of James, Peter and Jude, and the Apocalypse), the Alexandrian (in Hebrews and the Johannine Gospel and letters) and the Pauline. These represent three separate lines along which the message of Jesus was interpreted and developed.

The work of Karl Lachmann (1793–1851) was wide-ranging: he made contributions of outstanding value to the study of classical and German philology as well as to that of the New Testament. His critical edition of the Greek Testament (first edition, 1831; second edition, 1842–50) aimed at reproducing the fourth-century text and was based exclusively on the evidence of the earliest manuscripts and versions then available. This work stands at the head of the succession of four great critical editions of the nineteenth century, the other three being those of G. F. C. von Tischendorf (first edition, 1841; eighth edition, 1872), S. P. Tregelles (1857–72) and Westcott and Hort (1881). In literary criticism Lachmann is famous for his pioneer essay "De ordine narrationum in evangeliis synopticis" in *Theologische Studien und Kritiken* 8 (1835), 570ff., which paved the way for the general acceptance of Mark's priority over the two other Synoptic Gospels and their dependence on Mark. Lachmann's New Testament investigations had been stimulated by Friedrich Daniel Ernst Schleiermacher (1768–1834) who himself made an influential contribution to Gospel criticism in his essay "Über die Zeugnisse des Papias von unsern beiden ersten Evangelien" in *Theologische Studien und Kritiken* 5 (1832), 735ff. Here he argued that the logia which, according to Papias, Matthew compiled in the "Hebrew" speech should be understood not of our first Gospel but of a collection of the sayings of Jesus.

2. SCHLEIERMACHER AND "LIVES OF JESUS"

Whereas many of the scholars of this period here mentioned were interested primarily, if not exclusively, in the historico-critical approach, Schleiermacher, as a philosopher and theologian, manifested a hermeneutical concern: granted that the historico-critical approach disclosed the intention of the biblical writers in the context of their day, what does their message mean to readers and hearers in the different context of today? The "lower criticism", by which the authentic text was more accurately established, and the "higher criticism", by which the endeavour was made to ascertain the truth about the structure, date and authorship of the biblical documents, were making contributions of high value to the study of Scripture, but could those contributions enrich the present understanding and application of the message of Scripture?

Schleiermacher's attempt to provide a positive answer to this question was unsuccessful because, for all his religious sensitivity, he could not free himself from a basic rationalism. In terms of his psychological appraisal of the gospel narrative, for example, he interpreted the resurrection of Jesus as his resuscitation after *apparent* death, and the supernatural features in the accounts of his appearances to the disciples as due to presuppositions on the part of the latter.

This basic rationalism in Schleiermacher's approach finds expression in his *Leben Jesu,* which was published posthumously in 1864 on the basis of lecture notes taken down by a student. But the rationalizing approach appears most fully developed in H. E. G. Paulus, *Das Leben Jesu als Grundlage einer reinen Geschichte des Urchristentums* (1828). Paulus, says Albert Schweitzer, "had an unconquerable distrust of anything that went outside the boundaries of logical thought";[29] he accepted the gospel story as a whole (setting it in the framework of John's narrative) but rationalized its details so as largely to evacuate them of theological significance and to reduce them to a pedestrian level. The miracles of raising the dead, like the resurrection of Jesus himself, were interpreted in terms of the reanimation of people who were only apparently dead; the superficial piercing of Jesus' side inadvertently performed the beneficial service of a phlebotomy.

To this kind of interpretation the death-blow was administered by *Das Leben Jesu kritisch untersucht,* by David Friedrich Strauss. Volume I of the first edition appeared in May 1835; Volume II followed a few months later. A second, unchanged, edition was published before the end of 1836. The volume of criticism which the work called forth led Strauss to make some concessions to orthodoxy in the third edition (1838), but these were revoked in the fourth edition (1840) – the edition which was translated into English by George Eliot: *The Life of Jesus Critically Examined* (1846). Strauss found it impossible to believe in a transcendent God intervening in the life of the world, and hence found it impossible to accept the gospel witness to Christ. What he provided was a carefully constructed replacement for the gospel story, based on a thorough-going typology of miracle and myth. The rationalistic interpretation of the narrative was thus displaced by a mythological interpretation.

It is perhaps inevitable that attempts to re-tell and interpret the life of Christ should reflect the author's personal philosophy or the climate of opinion which he has absorbed. The romanticism of Ernest Renan's *Vie de Jésus* (1863) and the orthodox reasonableness of F. W. Farrar's *Life of Christ* (1874) are among many similarly-named works which illustrate this. And if today we can look back and add our Amen to George Tyrrell's description of Adolf Harnack's Christ as "the reflection of a Liberal Protestant face, seen at the bottom of a deep well",[30] many of us may be too much involved in our contemporary way of thought to appreciate the equal anachronism of interpreting the gospel in the categories of twentieth-century existentialism. "Indeed", in T. W. Manson's words, "it may be said of all theological schools of thought: By their Lives of Jesus ye shall know them."[31]

3. THE MEYER COMMENTARY

One of the great exegetical achievements of the nineteenth century was the inauguration of the *Kritisch-exegetischer Kommentar über das Neue Testament* by Heinrich August Wilhelm Meyer (1800–73). The first two volumes of this work, comprising text and translation, appeared in 1829; the first volume of the commentary proper (on the Synoptic Gospels) followed in 1832. The Gospels, Acts and major Pauline epistles were handled by Meyer himself; the commentaries on the remaining books were entrusted to three other scholars, among whom F. Düsterdieck, author of the commentary on Revelation, is best known. The series was translated into English and published by T. and T. Clark (1873–95). The commentary was revised in successive editions during Meyer's lifetime, and has been kept up to date to the present day, as new commentators have replaced earlier ones. Among contemporary contributions to the series are those by R. Bultmann on the Gospel and Epistles of John, E. Haenchen on Acts, H. Conzelmann on 1 Corinthians and E. Lohse on Colossians and Philemon, all of which have been translated into English. Meyer was described by Philip Schaff as "the ablest grammatical exegete of the age";[32] he deliberately restricted his commentary to the grammatico-historical plane, regarding theological and hermeneutical problems as out of bounds to the pure exegete. More recent contributors to the series have not felt bound by the founder's limitations.

4. EXEGESIS AT PRINCETON

There was in the middle years of the nineteenth century a resurgence of grammatico-historical exegesis in the Reformed tradition at Princeton Theological Seminary, New Jersey. The outstanding exegete on the faculty was Charles Hodge (1797–1878), who published excellent commentaries on four Pauline epistles – on *Romans* (1835), the best of the four, and to this day one of the most masterly expositions of that epistle, and on *Ephesians* (1856), *1 Corinthians* (1857) and *2 Corinthians* (1859). These works served as prolegomena to his great *Systematic Theology* (1871–73); such an exegetical preparation was (in the words of his son, A. A. Hodge) "more certain to result in a system in all its elements and proportions inspired and controlled by the word of God".[33] His colleague Joseph Addison Alexander (1809–60) was better known for his Old Testament exegesis, but he made two helpful contributions to New Testament study in his commentaries on

Acts (1856) and *Mark* (1858). In the latter he showed his freedom from tradition by his treatment of Mark as an independent author, and not as a mere abbreviator of Matthew.

5. THE TÜBINGEN SCHOOL

A major event in the history of New Testament interpretation was the publication in 1831 in the *Tübinger Zeitschrift für Theologie* of a long essay on the Christ party in the Corinthian church, by Ferdinand Christian Baur.[34] The study of Paul's correspondence convinced Baur that apostolic Christianity, far from being a unity, was marked by a deep cleavage between the church of Jerusalem and the Pauline mission. Whereas the church of Jerusalem, led by Peter and other original associates of Jesus, maintained a judaizing version of Christianity, Paul insisted that the gospel involved the abolition of Jewish legalism and particularism. In addition, the genuineness of Paul's apostleship was questioned by the partisans of Jerusalem, and attempts were made to undermine his authority in the eyes of his converts. There is evidence enough of the sharpness of the conflict between the two sides in the Galatian and Corinthian letters of Paul especially. So thoroughly did this conflict dominate the apostolic age that those New Testament documents which do not reflect it, but present instead a picture of harmony between Peter and Paul, between the Jerusalem church and the Gentile mission, betray by that very fact their post-apostolic perspective. Baur indeed, as he followed what appeared to him to be the logic of the situation, came to ascribe a second-century date not only to Acts, from which the conflict has disappeared, but to the Gospels also. If the Gospels were second-century documents, their value as historical sources for the life and teaching of Jesus was slender indeed, but if the evidence pointed to this conclusion, the conclusion had to be accepted. In the years which followed the publication of his 1831 essay Baur was increasingly influenced by Hegel's philosophy, which saw the historical process developing in a dialectical pattern of thesis, antithesis and synthesis. This pattern seemed to Baur to be exemplified by the course of early Christian history: the first-century thesis and antithesis of Jerusalem rigorism and Pauline proclamation of freedom from law being followed by the second-century synthesis in which these two were reconciled by compromise. But it must be borne in mind that the initial impetus to Baur's interpretation of early Christian history came from his New Testament exegesis, not from Hegelianism. (Nor should it be overlooked that the historical process frequently does exhibit the features of Hegel's dialectic, although it is never permissible to impose that dialectic on a historical sequence which does not correspond to it without distortion.) It is illicit, then, to dismiss Baur's reconstruction of the New Testament record (or, for that matter, Wellhausen's reconstruction of the Old Testament record) [35] on the plea of Hegelian influence. Baur, in fact, drew attention to a crucial factor of apostolic history which had received insufficient attention from his predecessors, and he did so to such good effect as to leave a permanent mark on the subsequent course of New Testament interpretation.

Like other pioneers, however, he stated the problems more convincingly than he proposed solutions to them. His second-century dating of the Gospels, for example, could not be maintained: the establishment of their first-century dating as against Baur's arguments was one of the achievements of the Cambridge school. "It might not be too inaccurate", says C. K. Barrett, "to say that Baur asked the right questions, and that Lightfoot set them in the right historical perspective".[36] Even the latest of the four Gospels cannot be dated after the beginning of the second century. But to say that is to say that the synthesis which Baur dated in the second century was already accomplished, or on the way to accomplishment, in the first: it was taking shape simultaneously with the thesis and antithesis. The task of the New Testament interpreter proved to be more complicated than Baur imagined – not only in the problems of the chronological development of the controversies but in their complexity and diversity. Paul had to contend with more than one kind of judaizing activity in his churches, and he had to contend at the same time with more than one variety of incipient Gnosticism. Not only so: at least one of these varieties of incipient Gnosticism was marked by prominent judaizing features. And these were only some of the human tensions within the primitive Christian church. In Baur's day it was a sufficiently radical advance to recognize that such tensions existed at all; since his recognition that this was so, a good part of New Testament interpretation has had to do with the interplay of these tensions and subsequent *détentes*.

6. "ESSAYS AND REVIEWS"

A great and (to many people) disturbing impression was made in England by Benjamin Jowett's essay of 104 pages "On the Interpretation of Scripture" contributed to the symposium *Essays and Reviews* (1860). Much of the essay is devoted to a plea for the use of those principles of interpretation in Bible study which are applicable to the study of other literature, and for the discontinuance of artificial methods which would not be countenanced in the study of (say) the Greek classics. Although certain aspects of his own argument are as dated as some which he criticized in others, we today should take for granted his protest against forcing Scripture to conform to post-biblical formulations of orthodox doctrine, even when these were adopted by the church as a whole – not to speak of forcing it to conform to sectarian traditions and preferences. At least, *most* of us today would take it for granted – but what is to be said when the quite correct rendering "priestly service" in Rom. 15:16, NEB, is denounced by a Protestant critic because (in his eyes) it may seem to support Roman sacerdotalism? As long as Paul is interpreted as saying not what his words plainly mean but what the interpreter would like them to mean, so long is Jowett's protest necessary. In reference to burning controversies of his day he says:

> Consider, for example, the extraordinary and unreasonable importance attached to single words, sometimes of doubtful meaning, in reference to any of the following subjects:– 1, Divorce; 2, Marriage with a Wife's Sister; 3, Inspiration; 4, the Personality of the Holy Spirit; 5, Infant Baptism; 6, Episcopacy; 7, Divine Right of Kings; 8, Original Sin. . . . It is with Scripture as with oratory, its effect partly depends on the preparation in the mind or in circumstances for the reception of it. There is no use of Scripture, no quotation or misquotation of a word which is not a power in the world, when it embodies the spirit of a great movement or is echoed by the voice of a large party.[37]

Some of the issues listed by Jowett have fallen by the wayside and others have taken their place, but the temptation to decide in advance what Scripture must mean, and compel its words to yield that meaning, has not disappeared entirely. Yet there would be general assent to Jowett's dictum: "Doubt comes in at the window, when Inquiry is denied at the door."[38] There would, indeed, be general recognition of the fact that to approach the New Testament in a spirit of inquiry is not to take an unwarranted liberty with a sacred book, since the New Testament itself invites a spirit of inquiry. "*Interpret the Scripture like any other book,*" urged Jowett; the many respects in which Scripture is *unlike* any other book "will appear in the results of such an interpretation."[39]

Jowett's scholarship was broad rather than exact, and the sentence which has just been quoted, while appearing to some as a glimpse of the obvious, had disturbing implications for others – and not only for obscurantists. Brooke Foss Westcott, for example, could not approve of Jowett's ideas of what was involved in interpreting either Scripture or any other work of comparable seriousness: the minute attention to individual words (not least to particles) which for Westcott was essential to the practice of scholarly exegesis was dismissed by Jowett as a wasting of time on what might be little more than "an excrescence of style".[40]

7. THE CAMBRIDGE SCHOOL

Westcott (1825–1901) was one of the three leaders of the Cambridge school, to which reference has already been made. The other two were Fenton John Anthony Hort (1828–92) and Joseph Barber Lightfoot (1828–89). Westcott and Hort are best known for their critical edition of the Greek New Testament (1881), but all three made pioneer contributions of distinction to the study of the history and literature of the apostolic age and the early church. We have mentioned their establishment of the first-century dating of the Gospels: this was done pre-eminently by Westcott in his *Introduction to the Study of the Gospels* (1851) and more especially his *General Survey of the History of the Canon of the New Testament* (1855), and by Lightfoot in his *Essays on the Work entitled "Supernatural Religion"* (published serially, 1874–77; one-volume edition, 1889). The last-named work not only exposed the incompetence of a writer who had impugned Westcott's integrity in his work on the canon but carried the positive argument substantially forward. Paradoxical as it may seem to say so, Lightfoot's chief contribution to the chronology of the New Testament literature was his encyclopaedic work on *The Apostolic Fathers* (1869–85), in which he validated the traditional dating of the genuine works of Clement of Rome, Ignatius of Antioch and Polycarp of Smyrna in the closing years of the first Christian century and earlier years of the second.

In 1860 the three scholars planned to write a series of commentaries covering the whole New Testament: Lightfoot was to deal with the Pauline Epistles, Hort with the Synoptic Gospels and the Epistles of James, Peter and Jude, and Westcott with the Johannine literature and Hebrews. Lightfoot completed magisterial commentaries on *Galatians* (1865), *Philippians* (1868) and *Colossians and Philemon* (1875); a volume of his *Notes* on some of the other Pauline Epistles was published posthumously (1895). Hort left only fragments of his assignment: uncompleted commentaries on *1 Peter* (1898), *The Apocalypse* (1908), and *James* (1909) were published after his death. Westcott's great commentary on *The Gospel of John* appeared as a volume in the Speaker's Commentary series in 1880 (based on AV); a posthumous adaptation of the commentary to the Greek text appeared in 1908. His commentary on *The Epistles of John* appeared in 1883, that on *Hebrews* in 1889, while an incomplete work on *Ephesians* was edited after his death by J. M. Schulhof and published in 1906.

The members of the Cambridge trio were sufficiently different in outlook and temperament to impose limitations on any attempt to make a composite appraisal of their work: yet it can readily be said that all of them were characterized by a wide, deep and exact scholarship which refused to take short cuts or to cut corners. Their linguistic equipment was complete and detailed; for the rest, Lightfoot's strength lay in the historical interpretation of the documents which he handled, while Westcott was gifted with a rare theological insight, which served him particularly well in his exposition of the thought of the Fourth Gospel. The fact that his commentary on John (the 1880 edition) was reissued by a British publisher so recently as 1958 is eloquent. As for Lightfoot, when one compares his dissertation on the Essenes at the end of his commentary on Colossians and Philemon (1875), first with much else that was written about them in the nineteenth century and then with the new knowledge available in this century since the discovery of the Qumran manuscripts in 1947 and the following years, one can but marvel at the acuteness of his reading of the evidence then available; what he wrote can be amplified today, but there is little if anything which needs to be dismissed as obsolete.

Their pioneer work was taken up by two generations of *epigoni* who, if they did not attain to the first three, nevertheless produced commentaries not unworthy to stand alongside theirs: H. B. Swete on *Mark* (1898) and *Revelation* (1906); J. B. Mayor on *James* (1892) and on *Jude and 2 Peter* (1907), J. A. Robinson on *Ephesians* (1904), G. Milligan on *1 and 2 Thessalonians* (1908) and, another generation further on, E. G. Selwyn on *1 Peter* (1946) and V. Taylor on *Mark* (1952). These volumes were published by Macmillan, as companions to those of the Cambridge trio, all of which (apart from Westcott on the Gospel of John) were published by that house.

V. *The Twentieth Century*

1. THOROUGH-GOING ESCHATOLOGY

With the advent of the twentieth century the centre of gravity in New Testament studies was decisively established in the Gospel tradition. William Wrede's *Das Messiasgeheimnis in den Evangelien* (1901) – not to appear in an English dress until 1972[41] – inaugurated the century's work in this field. According to Wrede's thesis, Jesus' injunction to silence when he is acknowledged to be the Messiah (Mark 8:30) or Son of God (Mark 3:12; cf. 1:25, 34) is not historical truth but a device by which the gospel tradition (first given literary form by Mark) attempted to reconcile the church's belief that Jesus was Messiah and Son of God from the beginning with the fact that this belief did not emerge until after the resurrection. Jesus was indeed Messiah and Son of God all along, so runs the explanation, but he kept it dark. Thus, when three of his disciples heard him acclaimed on the mount of transfiguration as the Father's dear Son, "he charged them to tell no one what they had seen, until the Son of man should have risen from the dead" (Mark 9:9). But in Wrede's account the transfiguration, like Peter's confession at Caesarea Philippi (Mark 8:29), was originally related as a resurrection incident and was artificially transposed back into the setting of the Galilaean ministry.

Wrede's work entitles him to be recognized as the father of Gospel redaction criticism – that approach to the Gospels which makes due acknowledgment of the aim and contribution of each evangelist in his own right. In his hands Mark emerges as a theologian with his personal interpretation of the Gospel tradition. For all the defects in the working out of his thesis, he stands out in this regard as a scholar well ahead of his time.

Wrede's study provided Albert Schweitzer with the terminus for his survey of nineteenth-century Lives of Jesus: *Von Reimarus zu Wrede* (1906; E.T. *The Quest of the Historical Jesus,* 1910). This epoch-making work reviewed the Gospel research of more than a hundred years and found all attempts to come to terms with the historical Jesus unsuccessful – the rationalist, mythical and liberal interpretations alike. The material for constructing an adequate Life of Jesus, especially the material for tracing his psychological development, was simply not available. Instead of unconsciously depicting Jesus in categories familiar at the beginning of the twentieth century, Schweitzer concentrated on the note of impending world-crisis in the Gospels and presented Jesus as an apocalyptic visionary, who at the end exposed himself to arrest and execution in order that his death might precipitate the kingdom of God and the end of history which he had announced but which had proved unexpectedly slow in arriving. In this exposition Schweitzer developed along lines of his own the thought of Johannes Weiss, who in a slim volume entitled *Die Predigt Jesu vom Reiche Gottes* (1892) had argued that in Jesus' view the kingdom which he announced could be established by the cataclysmic act of God only when the guilt of the people, which blocked its advent, was removed – a removal to be effected by Jesus' death as "a ransom for many" (Mark 10:45). The choice, as Schweitzer saw it, lay between the thorough-going scepticism implied by Wrede and the thorough-going eschatology to which Weiss had pointed the way – and for Schweitzer it was thorough-going eschatology that pointed the way forward.

Schweitzer's reinterpretation of the story of Jesus necessitated a fresh look at the sequel to that story – in particular at Paul. His *Geschichte der paulinischen Forschung* (1911; E.T. *Paul and his Interpreters,* 1912) was a continuation of *The Quest of the Historical Jesus* and reached as negative a conclusion about Pauline research as its predecessor had reached about Lives of Jesus; it was followed by his own positive account in *Die Mystik des Apostels Paulus* (1930; E.T. *The Mysticism of Paul the Apostle,* 1931). Paul, according to Schweitzer, shared Jesus' eschatological world-view, the only difference between them in this regard arising from the passage of time: "both are looking towards the same mountain range, but whereas Jesus sees it as lying before Him, Paul already stands upon it and its first slopes are already behind him".[42] While the world had not come to an end with the death and resurrection of Jesus, yet (Paul taught) the eschatological blessings secured thereby were enjoyed in anticipation by believers through their present "mystical" union with Christ mediated by the Spirit through the sacraments.

2. REALIZED AND PRESENT ESCHATOLOGY

Rudolf Otto, in his *Reich Gottes und Menschensohn* (1934; E.T. *The Kingdom of God and the Son of Man,* 1938), saw that the kingdom of God announced by Jesus was not entirely future from the perspective of his ministry; in Jesus' teaching it had begun to break in: "from its futurity it already extends its operation into the present".[43] Otto laid stress on some of the parables of Mark 4 (especially the parable of the four soils and the parable of the seed growing secretly) as embodying Jesus' emphasis on the present inbreaking of the kingdom.

This insight was shared, and carried to (and even beyond) its logical conclusion by C. H. Dodd. Indications of the direction in which Dodd's mind was moving on this question were given in papers published in 1927 and 1930,[44] but his *Parables of the Kingdom* (1935) was a full-scale exposition of "realized eschatology"[45] – of the view that the Kingdom of God arrived with the commencement of Jesus' public ministry, any future reference of the kingdom being reduced to vanishing point. The ministry was, in Jesus' eyes, *the* crisis of world history. Since Jesus' inaugural proclamation was (as Dodd understood it) "the kingdom of God has come", it was impermissible "to represent the death of Jesus as in any sense the condition precedent to the coming of the Kingdom of God".[46]

Such an extreme statement of realized eschatology was criticized for destroying "the cruciality of the cross";[47] but Dodd soon modified his position. "The Kingdom of God", he put it in a book published a year later, "is conceived as coming in the events of the life, death and resurrection of Jesus, and to proclaim these facts, in their proper setting, is to preach the Gospel of the Kingdom of God."[48] Later still he spoke of "realized eschatology" as a "not altogether felicitous term"[49] and expressed a preference for Joachim Jeremias's *sich realisierende Eschatologie* (translated by S. H. Hooke as "an eschatology that is in process of realization").[50] (Jeremias acknowledged himself to be indebted for the phrase to Ernst Haenchen.)[51]

This "realized eschatology" perspective was preserved in some New Testament writings – notably in the later Pauline letters and in the Fourth Gospel – but in most the old futurist eschatology of Judaism reasserted itself, especially because of the postponement of a parousia which did not take place as the immediate sequel to the resurrection of Jesus.

The solid contribution of Dodd's "realized eschatology" to New Testament exegesis has been its emphasis on the ministry of Jesus, not apart from but crowned by the saving event of his accomplished passion and triumph, as the climax of salvation-history. More recently Oscar Cullmann has used in this connexion the analogy of the decisive battle of a campaign in relation to the victory celebrations after the campaign is over. The saving act of God in Christ is the decisive battle; the achievement of the hope of glory at the parousia corresponds to the victory celebrations, but it is the decisive battle that is of crucial importance.[52]

To talk of eschatology as having been in any sense "realized" is to use the term (which traditionally means "the doctrine of the last things") in an extended sense, which might perhaps be justified on the ground that Jesus fulfilled the Old Testament prophecies regarding what would take place "in the last (or latter) days" – a phrase which need not mean much more than "hereafter". But an even greater extension of sense is involved in the use of the term by Rudolf Bultmann and his school of existential exegesis: here every present moment is an "eschatological" moment, in the sense that the answers and questions of the past meet one in the present and evoke the reaction of responsible choice which goes to make that new thing, the future. Bultmann's Gifford Lectures, *History and Eschatology* (1957), provide a good statement of this interpretation.

3. HISTORY OF RELIGION SCHOOL

The "history of religion" (*religionsgeschichtlich*) approach to the New Testament, which endeavoured to set the religious presuppositions of primitive Christianity in their contemporary Near Eastern and Graeco-Roman context, promised at one time to provide powerful help towards its interpretation. Among the most influential works of this school were Richard Reitzenstein's *Die hellenistischen Mysterienreligionen* (1910) and, outstandingly, his *Das iranische Erlösungsmysterium* (1921). The Iranian redemption mystery of the latter work concerned the heavenly being Gayōmart, primal man, who falls in battle against the power of evil and from whom, after his death, the human race springs up. When, at the end of time, Saošyant (the "Saviour") comes to raise the dead. Gayōmart will be raised first and exalted to archangelic status. This "mystery" is not given literary expression until the seventh century A.D., and even in its oral form it cannot well antedate the Sassanian era (A.D. 226). It probably influenced Mandaism and later forms of Gnosticism, but it is anachronistic to see its impact in the New Testament or earlier Gnosticism.[53]

In its simplest form the Gnostic myth tells of a heavenly essence which falls from the upper world of light into the lower world of material darkness and is imprisoned in a multitude of earthly bodies. To liberate this pure essence from its imprisonment a saviour comes from the world of light to impart the true knowledge (*gnōsis*); he is both redeemer and revealer. By acceptance of the revealed knowledge the pure essence is released from the bondage of matter and ascends back to its original abode of light. This myth, especially in its Mandaic elaboration, has been urged as the background of the New Testament teaching (particularly, but not exclusively, in the Fourth Gospel)[54] about the Son of Man who came from heaven to earth to liberate men, not from matter but from sin and death, and who by descending into the grave himself set its captives free. Despite the powerful advocacy of Rudolf Bultmann and some members of his school, however, this account of the matter probably reverses the historical order: it may well be that primal man and the redeemer-revealer were first brought together in Gnosticism under the influence of the gospel story. It is certainly difficult to find convincing evidence of the typical Gnostic myth in a pre-Christian form.

But, quite apart from Iranian and Gnostic influences, there was a tendency to classify Christianity – especially the Gentile Christianity which triumphed – among the mystery religions of the Eastern Mediterranean world. This tendency often appeared at a popular level, among people who had been impressed by works like Sir James Frazer's *The Golden Bough* (1890–1915), without being able to draw the correct inferences from that incomparable repository of facts; but we find it also in scholarly expositions. Kirsopp Lake's *The Earlier Epistles of St. Paul* (1911) is a great work which may be read with much profit over sixty years after its first appearance; but his viewpoint on the New Testament sacraments is expressed in his observation that

> much of the controversy between Catholic and Protestant theologians has found its centre in the doctrine of the Eucharist, and the latter have appealed to primitive Christianity to support their views. From their point of view the appeal fails: the Catholic doctrine is much more nearly primitive than the Protestant. But the Catholic advocate in winning his case has proved still more: the type of

> doctrine which he defends is not only primitive, but pre-Christian. Or, to put the matter in the terms of another controversy, Christianity has not borrowed from the Mystery Religions, because it was always, at least in Europe, a Mystery Religion itself.[55]

The concession "at least in Europe" reminds us that, as is plain from 1 Corinthians, Paul's teaching about baptism and the Lord's Supper was readily interpreted by his Greek converts in terms of the traditional mystery cults. But Lake went farther: Paul, in his eyes, went along with his converts' interpretation so far as to use it as the foundation of his arguments.

New perspectives on Paul have redressed this imbalance. In particular, J. G. Machen provided a judicious assessment on the basis of the evidence in *The Origin of Paul's Religion* (1921), and W. D. Davies, in *Paul and Rabbinic Judaism* (1948), showed how deep and pervasive were Paul's affinities with Pharisaic thought and teaching and provided corroboration of the statement in Acts 22:3 that he received his basic training in the school of Gamaliel.

4. ACTS AND INCIPIENT CATHOLICISM

A major enterprise was launched in 1920 with the first volume of an encyclopaedic work entitled *The Beginnings of Christianity*. The editors (F.J. Foakes Jackson and Kirsopp Lake) assumed that the synoptic problem had found its "general solution" and saw their next task as being "to translate these results into the language of the historian; to show how literary complexities and contradictions reveal the growth of thought and the rise of institutions". In particular, it was necessary to trace in detail the process by which first-century Christianity "achieved a synthesis between the Greco-Oriental and the Jewish religions in the Roman Empire".[56] The first step in the accomplishment of this task was a thorough study of Acts, and to this study they devoted Part I of the enterprise, which ran to five volumes (1920–33). But the enterprise never got beyond Part I. From our viewpoint we can see Part I as a monument marking the end of an era of *Actaforschung* – an era to which giants such as Adolf Harnack and W. M. Ramsay had made outstanding contributions[57] – rather than the beginning of a new one.

The new era was marked by the essays of Martin Dibelius (collected in *Aufsätze zur Apostelgeschichte,* 1951; E.T. *Studies in the Acts of the Apostles,* 1956), by Hans Conzelmann's *Die Mitte der Zeit* (1954; E.T. *The Theology of St. Luke,* 1960) and by Ernst Haenchen's Meyer commentary, *Die Apostelgeschichte* (1956; E.T. *The Acts of the Apostles,* 1971). No longer did archaeology or the history of religion occupy a central place in the study of Acts. In Dibelius's hands stylistic criticism was the key to the interpretation of the book, while in Conzelmann's eyes the author's new time-perspective (in which the "age of Jesus", for his first followers the time of the end, was now followed by the "age of the church", of indefinite duration) was a sure sign of post-apostolic "incipient catholicism" (*Frühkatholizismus*).

Incipient catholicism, in fact, becomes a criterion of post-apostolic date and authorship. It involves not only the resolution of earlier tensions in a new and comprehensive unity (in which, for example, Paul and James reach happy agreement on the terms of the inclusion of Gentiles in the church), but the shift of emphasis from the local church to the church universal, the replacement of the charismatic by an institutional ministry, the recession of the hope of glory at an early parousia in favour of dependence on the present means of grace dispensed through the church and its ministry, and the adoption of a codified confession of faith. Among Lutheran theologians on the continent of Europe there is a tendency to regard such incipient catholicism as a sad declension from the apostolic – especially the Pauline – gospel; those documents in which its features are found, such as Acts, Ephesians and the Pastoral Epistles, are felt to be not only post-apostolic in date but sub-apostolic in standard. In fact, Hans Küng could complain with some justice that Ernst Käsemann and others were in effect establishing a reduced canon within the received canon by relegating to an inferior status anything that savoured of "early catholic decadence".[58] When Heinrich Schlier, a distinguished member of the Bultmann school, became convinced that the incipient catholicism which he had pointed out pre-eminently in Ephesians (e.g., in *Christus und die Kirche im Epheserbrief,* 1930) was part and parcel of apostolic Christianity he not only moved over from the Lutheran confession to the Roman obedience but even, without changing his exegesis of Ephesians, found it possible to recognize it as an authentic Pauline epistle (*Der Brief an die Epheser,* 1957, 1965[5]).[59]

5. THE NEW HERMENEUTIC

The "new hermeneutic" represents a modern endeavour to make the message of the New Testament intelligible and relevant to contemporary man. It is closely related to Rudolf Bultmann's constant affirmation that this message is concerned with human existence, and that it is with human existence that contemporary man is essentially concerned.[60] If, then, he approaches the New Testament with the question of human existence uppermost in his mind, he will find the answer in the New Testament – provided all non-essential stumbling-blocks have been removed from the New Testament by application of the demythologizing programme.[61]

It is not a detached and objective approach to the New Testament that is implied here, such as would be suitable for the study of geometry or astronomy. Where human existence is involved, such objectivity is neither desirable nor attainable. Bultmann is indebted to Martin Heidegger not only for his existential emphasis but also for his view of the nature of knowledge and understanding. For Heidegger there is no clearcut line of demarcation between the knowing subject and the known object: subject and object must be mutually engaged if the knowing process is to start at all. Similarly Bultmann insists that there can be no such thing as "presuppositionless" exegesis:[62] the interpreter, whether he realizes it or not, brings his presuppositions to the text; he comes to it with his own questions, and the answers he gets are determined in part by the questions which he puts. This situation underlies the idea of the "hermeneutical circle" in which the interpretative process is seen as flowing from subject to object, or indeed from object to subject, and back again, as the one interacts with the other.[63] The Bible is not like an Ugaritic text which the Semitist is deciphering for the first time. The Semitist does indeed come to the Ugaritic text with a question which interests him: "What is this text, or this writer, trying to say in relation to the Near Eastern situation of the fourteenth century B.C.?" But this is not an existential question like that which the Bible reader is envisaged as bringing to *his* text: "What is this text saying to me in my situation here and now?" Such a question (a question the importance of which was appreciated by Schleiermacher in his day) already involves a large presupposition – that the New Testament text which I am studying is related not only to the circumstances for which it was originally written but to the modern reader in his circumstances today. Both Bultmann and his followers assure the modern reader that the New Testament, in helping him to understand his own existence, in fact transforms his existence and imparts "authenticity" to it, liberating him from his bondage to the past and enabling him to be "open" towards the future.

One can see the analogy between this account of the matter and the New Testament teaching about justification by faith; one can agree that in the experience of many the analogy may amount to identity. But for this to be so the message of authentic existence should be as vitally related to the person and work of Christ as is the New Testament teaching on justification by faith. Moreover, for those who are not familiar with the vocabulary of existentialism, talk about inauthentic and authentic existence is not more intelligible than the Pauline vocabulary of sin and grace, law and liberty, retribution and acceptance, estrangement and reconciliation. In so far, indeed, as Paul's vocabulary is cast in terms of personal relationships, it may well speak to late twentieth-century man in an idiom with which he finds himself more at home than with that of existential exegesis.

The new hermeneutic takes up where Bultmann leaves off, and marks a substantial advance on his position. His disciple Ernst Fuchs has played a notable part in this: for him, the text of Scripture is properly interpreted when the word of God is proclaimed. Then the language of Scripture awakens faith; it ceases to be mere language and becomes a "language occurrence" (*Sprachereignis*).[64] A similar insight is expressed by Gerhard Ebeling when he speaks of a "word event" (*Wortgeschehen*).[65] God's saving word, that is to say, comes into effective action here and now, bringing to expression in the hearer faith such as found expression in Jesus.

The parables of Jesus in particular have received illuminating exposition in terms of this new insight; it is in them, according to Fuchs, that the "most significant expression" of the message of God appears, for in them Jesus enters the world of his hearers' experience and establishes a common understanding with them.[66] Two pupils of Fuchs have carried forward this aspect of his thought: Eta Linnemann, who in her *Gleichnisse Jesu* (1961; E.T. *Parables of Jesus,* 1966) emphasizes the rôle of the hearer in the situations in which the parables were told, and Eberhard Jüngel, who in his *Paulus und Jesus* (1962) propounds the thesis that the parables convey the same message as Paul does in his teaching about justification by faith.

It may be asked if the new hermeneutic, for all its advance on Bultmann, succeeds in doing justice to the whole New Testament message – for example, to the emphasis on God's unfolding purpose in salvation-history or on the rôle of Jesus as the fulfiller of the past and the Amen to the promises that went before. It may be suggested, too, that it remains more relevant to the believing individual (albeit in his entering into a fellowship of love with his neighbour) than to the believing community, not to speak of the reconciled universe of the future. But if the new hermeneutic is viewed not as *the* way of interpreting scripture but as one useful way among others (including the classical historico-critical methods), then it can yield results of positive value.

6. GOSPEL CRITICISM

The twentieth century has seen little advance in the source criticism of the Synoptic Gospels. It is still the general view that Mark was a principal source of Matthew and Luke, who also were able to draw upon a collection of sayings of Jesus set in a minimum of narrative framework – the collection commonly designated Q. This two-source hypothesis has been elaborated, e.g. by B. H. Streeter, who propounded a four-source hypothesis in *The Four Gospels* (1924) and by Wilhelm Bussmann who, in *Synoptische Studien* ii (1929), distinguished two sources in the Q material – one written in Greek and the other in Aramaic. Attempts to revive the belief in the priority of Matthew over Mark raise more difficulties than they solve.[67]

Where the Fourth Gospel is concerned, there is a strong tendency to detach its testimony from the Synoptic tradition. Rudolf Bultmann, in *Das Evangelium des Johannes* (1941; E.T. *The Gospel of John,* 1971), distinguishes two main sources – one consisting of revelatory discourses (*Redenquelle*) and the other a book of "signs" (*Semeiaquelle*) – together with a good deal of redactional material. P. Gardner-Smith, in *Saint John and the Synoptic Gospels* (1938), argued for John's independence of the Synoptic Gospels; this case was persuasively developed by C. H. Dodd in *The Interpretation of the Fourth Gospel* (1953) and especially in his *Historical Tradition in the Fourth Gospel* (1964). If the historical tradition of this Gospel is an independent witness for the events of Jesus' ministry, the implications are far-reaching, and special importance attaches to those points at which the Markan and Johannine traditions coincide.

There is a general impression that the determination of written sources has gone as far as the evidence permits, and where it is inconclusive other forms of criticism have been invoked to carry us farther back.

Tradition criticism presses the quest for sources back beyond such written sources as may be discerned. Where there is reason to believe that a period of oral transmission preceded the first writing down (as is most probable where the gospel story is concerned), it endeavours to trace the course of this transmission. Whereas in many areas where tradition criticism is most fruitfully employed the period of oral transmission covered many generations or even centuries, its usefulness in New Testament interpretation is limited by the brevity of this period, extending over a few decades at most.

Form criticism is one of the most serviceable tools for reconstructing the pre-literary tradition. It classifies the material according to the various "forms" represented in its contents and examines these in order to discover how they were handed down and what their successive life-settings were until they took their present shape and position. H. Gunkel, E. Sievers and S. Mowinckel had applied form-critical methods to various parts of the Old Testament; E. Norden had applied them to classical and Hellenistic subjects – notably in his *Agnostos Theos* (1913) – and Allan Menzies of St. Andrews had applied them to Mark's record, without using the explicit terminology of form criticism, in *The Earliest Gospel* (1901). His work must be borne in mind when Martin Dibelius's *Die Formgeschichte des Evangeliums* (1919),[68] K. L. Schmidt's *Der Rahmen der Geschichte Jesu* (1919) and Rudolf Bultmann's *Die Geschichte der synoptischen Tradition* (1921)[69] are hailed as the pioneer essays in this field.

With the aid of tradition criticism and form criticism the exegete's task is undertaken in three stages as he works back from (*a*) interpretation of our canonical Gospels and their written sources through (*b*) interpretation of the tradition lying behind these to (*c*) the reconstruction of the preaching about Jesus or of the preaching of Jesus himself.[70]

An over-concentration on tradition and form criticism, however, like an over-concentration on source criticism, can easily obscure the important work of the evangelists themselves. Just as a study of Shakespeare's sources and other traditional antecedents would never be allowed to replace the study of Shakespeare in his own right, so the critical methods just mentioned should never replace the study of the Gospels as finished products. Granted that the evangelists delivered what they themselves had received by tradition and otherwise, how did they, as individual authors, use the material which they received? What particular interests led to their arranging that material as they did?

Wrede, as has been said, took these questions seriously as he tackled the problem of the messianic secret, and Menzies, for all his interest in the state of the pre-Markan tradition, gave careful consideration to Mark's "lively" treatment of his materials.[71] In more recent years the study of the intention of the several evangelists has received the designation "redaction criticism". The rise and progress of redaction criticism has been recorded by Joachim Rohde in *Die redaktionsgeschichtliche Methode* (1966; E.T. *Rediscovering the Teaching of the Evangelists,* 1968). Important German studies in redaction criticism are Hans Conzelmann, *Die Mitte der Zeit* (1954; E.T. *The*

Theology of St. Luke, 1960), Willi Marxsen, *Der Evangelist Markus* (1959; E.T. *Mark the Evangelist,* 1969) and G. Bornkamm, G. Barth and H. J. Held, *Überlieferung und Auslegung im Matthäusevangelium* (1960; E.T. *Tradition and Interpretation in Matthew,* 1963). Due mention should be made of a series currently being published by the Paternoster Press, Exeter, the contributors to which are also contributors to the present symposium: I. H. Marshall, *Luke: Historian and Theologian* (1970), and R. P. Martin, *Mark: Evangelist and Theologian* (1972), have already appeared, and companion volumes are in preparation by G. N. Stanton on *Matthew* and by S. Smalley on *John (John: Evangelist and Interpreter,* 1977).

7. THE NEW QUEST OF THE HISTORICAL JESUS

The main purpose of Gospel criticism, as of New Testament interpretation, must be a closer acquaintance with Jesus, and with the historical Jesus at that. The significance of the exalted Christ lies in his identity with the crucified Jesus.

The title of a study by J. M. Robinson, *A New Quest of the Historical Jesus* (1959), is plainly meant to echo the title of Albert Schweitzer's great work, but it is also meant to imply that today's quest is different in character as well as later in time than the "old quest". The new quest marks a reaction from the extremely negative assessment of the importance of history to the gospel found in Rudolf Bultmann's work. This negative assessment has been undergirded with an apostolic text in Paul's words about no longer knowing Christ "after the flesh" (2 Cor. 5:16), but in those words Paul is not concerned with the historical Jesus. In Bultmann's eyes, any appeal to history is precarious, for it is liable at any moment to be overthrown by further historical research or discovery; it is also illegitimate, being as much a denial of the gospel of justification by faith as is any other form of justification by works. But a Jesus whose identity and significance can be neither proved nor disproved by history is an insubstantial basis of faith, and some of Bultmann's colleagues have asked why he adheres so tenaciously and, as they see it, so illogically to the historical Jesus – Jesus the crucified – when, on his premises, some other figure or phenomenon might equally well present the challenge and elicit the response of that liberating decision which leads into authentic existence. Jesus, on this showing, is little more than the unknown *x* which triggers off this spiritual release.[72]

Some of Bultmann's most distinguished pupils have sought to find a way out of this impasse. Günther Bornkamm has written a full-length study of *Jesus von Nazareth* (1956; E.T. *Jesus of Nazareth,* 1960) which finds no such hiatus as Bultmann postulated between the ministry of Jesus and the preaching of the primitive church. Whereas Bultmann placed the shift from the old age to the new between Jesus and Paul, Bornkamm places it between John the Baptist and Jesus – which is where, according to one early strand of gospel tradition, Jesus himself placed it (Luke 7:28; 16:16).

Still more positive is Eduard Schweizer's assessment in *Jesus Christus*

(1968; E.T. *Jesus,* 1971) which, while not in itself a study of the historical Jesus, devotes one chapter (entitled "Jesus: the man who fits no formula") to this subject and concludes that the chief christological motifs found throughout the New Testament "go back, in fact, to Jesus himself".[73]

In 1953 Ernst Käsemann gave a lecture at a reunion of Marburg old students on the problem of the historical Jesus (published in ZTK 51 (1954), pp. 125ff.; E.T. in *Essays on New Testament Themes,* 1964, pp. 15ff.), in which he called for a reopening of the question which their revered teacher was thought to have closed and argued that it was necessary to work out what could be known about the historical Jesus if they were not to end up in a new docetism.

> If he can be placed at all, it must be in terms of historical particularity. . . . For to his particularity there corresponds the particularity of faith, for which the real history of Jesus is always happening afresh; it is now the history of the exalted Lord, but it does not cease to be the earthly history it once was, in which the call and the claim of the Gospel are encountered.[74]

To much the same effect Ernst Fuchs finds the key to the continuity between the historical Jesus and the Christ of the apostolic preaching in faith – in faith seen as a "language occurrence".

> We formerly endeavoured to interpret the historical Jesus with the help of the primitive Christian kerygma; today we endeavour rather to interpret this kerygma with the help of the historical Jesus – the two lines of investigation are mutually complementary.[75]

The New Testament as a whole bears witness to one and the same Jesus – incarnate, crucified, and exalted as Lord over all. To grasp, to share and to perpetuate this witness is the interpreter's task. One way forward in the prosecution of this task is certainly pointed out by the new quest of the historical Jesus.

Finally, two quotations will sum up the moral of this chapter. First, from my old teacher Alexander Souter:

> It can never cease to be of moment to the real lover of Scripture what was thought of its meaning by any patient investigator in any country or in any age.[76]

Next, from Johann Albrecht Bengel:

> Apply thyself wholly to the text; apply the text wholly to thyself.[77]

NOTES

1. Justin, *Second Apology* 10.
2. Irenaeus, *Haer.* i. 12. 2–4.
3. Hippolytus, *Ref.* v. 8.29.
4. Hippolytus, *Ref.* v. 9. 6.
5. Cf. D. de Bruyne, "Prologues bibliques d'origine marcionite", Rev. Ben. 24 (1907), pp. 1ff.; A. von Harnack, "Der marcionitische Ursprung der ältesten Vulgata-Prologe zu den Paulusbriefen", ZNW 24 (1925), pp. 205ff.
6. R. M. Grant, *A Short History of the Interpretation of the Bible* (London 1965), p. 55.

7. F. F. Bruce, *Tradition Old and New* (Exeter 1970), p. 116.
8. R. P. C. Hanson, *Allegory and Event* (London 1959), p. 360.
9. Cf. A. Souter, *The Earliest Latin Commentaries on the Epistles of St. Paul* (Oxford 1927).
10. Augustine, *Quaestiones Evangeliorum* ii. 19.
11. Augustine, *De doctrina christiana* i. 36. We can scarcely recognize as seriously-meant exegesis his misuse of "Compel them to come in" (Luke 14:23) to authorize the coercion of the Donatists (*Epistle* 93.5).
12. B. Smalley, *The Study of the Bible in the Middle Ages* (Oxford 1952[2]), p. 64.
13. Cf. M. Deanesly, *The Significance of the Lollard Bible* (London 1951).
14. M. Luther, *Werke*, Weimarer Ausgabe ii. 279.
15. W.A. vii. 838.
16. M. Luther, *On the Bondage of the Will*, ed. and tr. J. I. Packer and O. R. Johnston (London 1957), p. 69 = W.A. xviii. 604f.
17. W.A. xviii. 608.
18. W.A., *Deutsche Bibel* vi. 10.
19. Preface to Epistle of James (W.A., *Deutsche Bibel* vii. 384f.).
20. W.A., *Deutsche Bibel* vi. 2.
21. J. Calvin, *The Epistles of Paul the Apostle to the Galatians, etc.*, tr. T. H. L. Parker (Edinburgh 1965), pp. 24f.
22. In the C.T.S. edition of Calvin's *Commentary on Genesis*, i (Edinburgh 1847), pp. 71f., attempts to find the Trinity in *'elohim* are described as "violent glosses" and "absurdities"; that the translator-editor was not too happy about this language may be inferred from his copious footnotes to Calvin's exposition of Gen. 1:1.
23. He continues with a *caveat*: "His *Institutes*, so far as respects Commonplaces, I give out to be read after the Catechism as a more extended explanation. But here I add – with discrimination, as the writings of all men ought to be read." Cited from C. Bangs, *Arminius: A Study in the Dutch Reformation* (New York 1971), pp. 287–288. (The original is in a letter to Sebastian Egbertsz, in P. van Limborch and C. Hartsoeker, *Praestantium ac eruditorum virorum epistolae ecclesiasticae et theologicae* (Amsterdam 1704[3]), no 101.) I am indebted for this reference to Dr A. Skevington Wood.
24. P. Schaff, *History of the Christian Church* (1882–1910), vii, p. 211.
25. W. G. Kümmel, *The New Testament: The History of the Investigation of its Problems*, E.T. (London 1972), p. 27.
26. Arethas (*c.* 850 – *c.* 945), metropolitan of Cappadocian Caesarea; his commentary on the Apocalypse was an amplified reissue of the work of his predecessor Andrew (*c.* A.D. 600).
27. J. Owen, *Works*, ed. W. H. Goold, xvi (London 1853), p. 347.
28. W. G. Kümmel devotes a chapter of *The New Testament: The History of the Investigation of its Problems* to "English Deism and its Early Consequences" (pp. 51–61).
29. A. Schweitzer, *The Quest of the Historical Jesus*, E.T. (London 1910), p. 48.
30. G. Tyrrell, *Christianity at the Cross-Roads* (London 1913), p. 44.
31. T. W. Manson, "The Failure of Liberalism to interpret the Bible as the Word of God", *The Interpretation of the Bible*, ed. C. W. Dugmore (London 1944), p. 92.
32. Quoted in T. and T. Clark's Prospectus to the English translation of the Meyer Commentary (Edinburgh 1873).
33. A. A. Hodge, Preface to revised edition of C. Hodge, *Commentary on the Epistle to the Romans* (New York 1886), p. iv.
34. This essay, "Die Christuspartei in der korinthischen Gemeinde", has been reissued in F.C. Baur, *Ausgewählte Werke in Einzelausgaben*, ed. K. Scholder (Stuttgart-Bad Cannstatt 1963), i (*Historisch-kritische Untersuchungen zum Neuen Testament*), pp. 1ff. E. Käsemann's introduction to Vol. I is worthy of special attention.
35. Cf. L. Perlitt, *Vatke und Wellhausen* (Berlin 1965), the first part of which studies the course of the philosophy of history in the later eighteenth and earlier nineteenth centuries.
36. C. K. Barrett, "Joseph Barber Lightfoot", *The Durham University Journal* 64 (1972), p. 203.

37. *Essays and Reviews,* by F. Temple and others (London 1861[4]), pp. 358f.
38. Ibid., p. 373.
39. Ibid., p. 377.
40. Ibid., p. 391.
41. *The Messianic Secret,* tr. J. C. G. Greig (London: James Clarke).
42. *The Mysticism of Paul the Apostle,* E.T. (London 1931), p. 113.
43. *The Kingdom of God and the Son of Man,* E.T. (London 1943), p. 59.
44. "Das innerweltliche Reich Gottes in der Verkündigung Jesu", *Theologische Blätter* 6 (1972), pp. 120ff.; E.T. "The This-Worldly Kingdom of God in our Lord's Teaching", *Theology* 17 (1928), pp. 258ff.; and "Jesus as Teacher and Prophet" in *Mysterium Christi,* ed. G. K. A. Bell and A. Deissmann (London 1930), pp. 53ff.
45. *Parables of the Kingdom* (London 1935), p. 198.
46. *Parables of the Kingdom,* p. 75.
47. R. H. Fuller, *The Mission and Achievement of Jesus* (London 1954), p. 49.
48. *The Apostolic Preaching and its Developments* (London 1936), pp. 46f.
49. *The Interpretation of the Fourth Gospel* (Cambridge 1953), p. 447, n. 1.
50. J. Jeremias, *The Parables of Jesus,* E.T. (London 1954), p. 159.
51. Ibid.
52. O. Cullmann, *Christ and Time,* E.T. (London 1951), pp. 139ff.
53. See E. Yamauchi, *Pre-Christian Gnosticism* (London 1973).
54. See R. Bultmann, "Die Bedeutung der neuerschlossenen mandäischen und manichäischen Quellen für das Verständnis des Johannesevangeliums", ZNW 24 (1925), pp. 100ff.; *The Gospel of John,* E.T. (Oxford 1971), pp. 7ff. *et passim.*
55. K. Lake, *The Earlier Epistles of Paul* (London 1911), p. 215.
56. F. J. Foakes Jackson and K. Lake, *The Beginnings of Christianity,* Part I, vol. i (London 1920), p. vii.
57. A. Harnack, *Luke the Physician,* E.T. (London 1907); *The Acts of the Apostles,* E.T. (London 1909); *Date of the Acts and of the Synoptic Gospels,* E.T. (London 1911); *Ist die Rede des Paulus in Athen ein ursprünglicher Bestandteil der Apostelgeschichte?* (Leipzig 1913); W. M. Ramsay, *The Historical Geography of Asia Minor* (London 1890); *The Church in the Roman Empire* (London 1895[4]); *Luke the Physician and Other Studies . . .* (London 1908); *St. Paul the Traveller and the Roman Citizen* (London 1920[14]); cf. W. W. Gasque, *A History of the Criticism of the Acts of the Apostles*, (Tübingen 1975; Grand Rapids 1975).
58. H. Küng, *The Structures of the Church,* E.T. (London 1965), pp. 142ff.
59. Cf. E. Käsemann, "Das Interpretationsproblem des Epheserbriefs", TLZ 86 (1961), pp. 1ff. (a review article on Schlier's commentary, which had originally been designed for the Meyer series).
60. R. Bultmann, "Das Problem der Hermeneutik", in *Glauben und Verstehen* ii (Tübingen 1952), pp. 211ff.; E.T. "The Problem of Hermeneutics" in *Essays Philosophical and Theological,* tr. J. C. G. Greig (London 1955), pp. 234ff.
61. R. Bultmann, "New Testament and Mythology"; E.T. in *Kerygma and Myth,* ed. and tr. R. H. Fuller (London 1953), pp. 1ff.; cf. *Jesus Christ and Mythology,* E.T. (London 1960).
62. R. Bultmann, "Ist voraussetzungslose Exegese möglich?" in *Glauben und Verstehen* iii (Tübingen 1960), pp. 142ff.; E.T. "Is Exegesis without Presuppositions Possible?" in *Existence and Faith,* ed. and tr. S. M. Ogden (London 1961), pp. 289ff.
63. M. Heidegger, *An Introduction to Metaphysics,* E.T. (Oxford 1959), pp. 146ff.; E. Fuchs, *Marburger Hermeneutik* (Tübingen 1968), pp. 79ff.
64. E. Fuchs, *Studies of the Historical Jesus,* E.T. (London 1964), pp. 207ff.
65. G. Ebeling, *The Nature of Faith,* E.T. (London, 1966), pp. 182ff.; cf. his *Introduction to a Theological Theory of Language,* E.T. (London 1973).
66. E. Fuchs, *Studies of the Historical Jesus,* pp. 125f.
67. Cf. B. C. Butler, *The Originality of St. Matthew* (Cambridge 1950); W. R. Farmer, *The Synoptic Problem* (New York 1964).
68. E.T. *From Tradition to Gospel* (London 1934). The third German edition (1959) was edited by G. Bornkamm and supplied with an appendix by G. Iber.

69. E.T. *The History of the Synoptic Tradition* (Oxford 1963), based on the third German edition (1958).
70. Cf. H. Conzelmann, *An Outline of the Theology of the New Testament,* E.T. (London 1969), p. 98.
71. A. Menzies, *The Earliest Gospel* (London 1901), p. 33.
72. Cf. H. Braun's discussion of "The Meaning of New Testament Christology", E.T. in J Th. Ch. 5 (1968), pp. 89ff. (These words were written before Professor Bultmann's death on July 30, 1976.)
73. E. Schweizer, *Jesus,* E.T. (London, 1971), p. 51.
74. E. Käsemann, *Essays on New Testament Themes,* E.T. (London 1964), pp. 46f.
75. E. Fuchs, *Zur Frage nach dem historischen Jesus* (Tübingen 1960), p. vii.
76. A. Souter, *The Earliest Latin Commentaries on the Epistles of St. Paul* (Oxford 1927), p. 7.
77. J. A. Bengel, *Novum Testamentum Graecum* (Tübingen 1734), preface.

CHAPTER III

PRESUPPOSITIONS IN NEW TESTAMENT CRITICISM

Graham N. Stanton

Why do the conclusions of New Testament scholars differ so widely? Anyone who begins to read books about the New Testament soon becomes aware that competent scholars defend with equal vigour and sincerity widely differing approaches to the New Testament. The variety of viewpoints often causes great perplexity both to theological students and to the church at large. Occasionally bewilderment leads to abandonment of serious historical critical study of the Scriptures in favour of a supposedly simple and direct "devotional" approach. Theological students are prone to the temptation to regard a listing of scholarly viewpoints and names in support of a particular opinion as serious exegesis.

As many parts of this book show, there is an on-going discussion about critical methods. But this hardly accounts for the extent to which scholarly conclusions differ; there is now considerable agreement among Protestant and Roman Catholic scholars about the appropriate tools and methods to be used in exegesis. The presuppositions adopted either consciously or unconsciously by the interpreter are far more influential in New Testament scholarship than disagreements over method.

The question of presuppositions in interpretation arises in all historical studies, in literary criticism, and also in scientific studies.[1] Historians frequently differ considerably in their assessment of the same source material. Literary critics are no more likely than New Testament scholars to reach agreement about the interpretation of ancient or modern literature. But there are, as we shall see, some questions which arise in a particularly acute form only in connection with the interpretation of the Bible.

As soon as we recognize the importance of presuppositions in all scholarly inquiry, we are bound to ask whether it is possible to abandon them in the interests of scientific rigour. If not, which presuppositions should be allowed to affect interpretation, and which not? Behind these questions lurk philosophical problems about the nature of knowledge; indeed, the task of philosophy can be defined as "the logical analysis of presuppositions."[2] A discussion of presuppositions has even wider implications: it is only a slight exaggeration to claim that the history of the church is the history of the interpretation of Scripture; the whole of church history revolves around the presuppositions adopted in study of the Bible in different times and in different circumstances.[3]

Although discussion of presuppositions has frequently continued alongside scholarly study of the New Testament since the time of F. D. Schleiermacher, it has recently become much more prominent, particularly in association with the new hermeneutic.[4] As C. E. Braaten stresses, renewed interest in hermeneutical philosophy has encouraged exegetes to become self-conscious about their presuppositions.[5]

Presuppositions are involved in every aspect of the relationship of the interpreter to his text. Our theme is so wide and has so many implications that we cannot attempt to cover all aspects of it.[6] We shall discuss first some of the prejudices and presuppositions which are, or have been, involved in exegesis of the New Testament. An examination of presuppositions must be the first step taken in scientific interpretation. This is no easy task; for it is so hard to see the spectacles through which one looks and without which one cannot see anything clearly at all. We can attempt to do little more than underline the wide variety and all-pervasiveness of presuppositions at work in interpretation; a full-scale critique of various major theological positions is obviously not possible here. We shall then consider whether or not exegesis can be undertaken without presuppositions, for an allegedly neutral unbiased approach has often been appealed to in the past, and will always seem to be an attractive possibility. Finally, we shall discuss presuppositions which cannot be dispensed with and which ought to be involved in interpretation; in particular we shall discuss the interpreter's pre-understanding.

I. *Prejudices and Presuppositions*

"Prejudice" and "presuppositions" are often used loosely as synonyms. Although the two words cannot be completely separated, it may be useful to distinguish between the personal factors which affect the judgment of the interpreter (prejudices) and the philosophical or theological starting point which an interpreter takes and which he usually shares with some others (presuppositions).[7]

An interpreter's work is always affected by human foibles and fallibility. Prejudice arises in all scholarly disciplines. The individual's personality will play a part in his work, even though this will usually be an unconscious influence; an optimist and a pessimist may well assess a literary or a historical document differently. Historians are usually well aware that their own political standpoint cannot be discounted; sometimes a particular political stance is taken quite deliberately. Cultural factors are also important; the interpreter may be so conditioned by his environment that he is almost automatically biased in one direction or else he is quite unable to consider all the alternative approaches.

Scholarly politics should not be neglected as a factor in interpretation. Younger scholars are often under considerable pressure to publish their results as quickly as possible; short cuts are sometimes taken, awkward evidence ignored, and hypotheses all too often become proven results. Scholars rarely criticise the work of colleagues and friends as rigorously as other work.[8] There may be subtle pressures from a publisher with an eye on his market and, in the case of the biblical scholar, from various official or denominational quarters.

The New Testament scholar's interest in original results often leads to an over-emphasis on the distinctive theological perspective of different parts of the New Testament.[9] Recent redaction criticism of the gospels provides several examples of this.[10] There is no doubt that Matthew and Luke speak with different accents; both evangelists have modified and re-shaped the sources at their disposal. But a number of scholars assume too readily that a fresh theological outlook is the only factor at work.[11]

These varied pressures must be taken seriously. But they are not necessarily negative factors to be avoided at all costs. Without debate and without scholarly pressures advance would be slower. If all idiosyncratic features were to be eliminated from an individual performer's interpretation of a Beethoven sonata, how much poorer we should be! Hence different conclusions which arise from the prejudice of the individual interpreter are not necessarily undesirable; they are bound to arise, even where similar presuppositions are shared.

The interpreter must beware of and attempt to allow for the prejudice which may influence his judgment. But, as Gadamer has strongly stressed, a completely detached and unbiased stance is impossible: "Even a master of historical method is not able to remain completely free from the prejudices of his time, his social environment, his national position etc. Is that to be taken for a deficiency? And even if it were, I regard it as a philosophical task to reflect as to why this deficiency is never absent whenever something is done. In other words I regard *acknowledging what is* as the only scholarly way, rather than taking one's point of departure in what should be or might be."[12] Here, Gadamer overstates his case in debate with an opponent, E. Betti. But his main point is valid, even though he comes close to making a virtue out of a necessity. If an individual's prejudice is so deep-seated that, in effect, a verdict is passed before the evidence is even considered, then, surely, prejudice negates the possibility of understanding a text.

II. *The Effects of Presuppositions*

A brief perusal of the history of the interpretation of Scripture is sufficient to confirm that the classical creeds of Christendom and particular doctrinal presuppositions have exercised a profound influence on interpretation right up to the present day.[13] Interpretation of the Bible has often involved little more than production of proof texts to support an already existing doctrinal framework. Later theological reflections have often been read back, often unconsciously, into the New Testament documents. W. Wrede saw the history of New Testament scholarship in the eighteenth and nineteenth centuries as the constant struggle of historical research to cut itself loose from dogmatic prejudgments.[14] The impact of doctrinal convictions on historical and exegetical studies can also be seen in Jewish scholarship; J. Neusner has recently argued that in this respect Jewish scholarship is 150 years behind New Testament research. Neusner shows that the rabbinic traditions have often been used for apologetic purposes by both Jewish and Christian scholars who have failed to study them from a rigorously historical perspective.[15]

It is hardly necessary to list examples of the profound effect theological presuppositions have had on exegesis. But we must take time to illustrate this important point briefly before we consider whether or not it is possible to avoid the impact of presuppositions.

The parables of Jesus have always been central in hermeneutical discussion; this is not surprising since the meaning of a parable is rarely made explicit in the gospels, but it is left for the hearer or interpreter to discover for himself. Hence presuppositions can influence exegesis of the parables even more easily and strongly than other parts of the Bible. Allegorical interpretation of the parable of the Good Samaritan was all but universal in the early church and in the middle ages, and it has persisted until modern times.[16] Origen's interpretation is a good example of allegorical exegesis. For Origen (who lived from *c.* 185–*c.* 254 A.D.), the man who fell among thieves is Adam. As Jerusalem represents heaven, so Jericho, to which the traveller journeyed, is the world. The robbers are man's enemies, the devil and his minions. The priest stands for the law, the Levite for the prophets. The good Samaritan is Christ himself. The beast on which the wounded man was set is Christ's body which bears the fallen Adam. The inn is the Church; the two pence, the Father and the Son; and the Samaritan's promise to come again, Christ's Second Advent.

Why will this simply not do? Such an interpretation presupposes that the original hearers of the parable were already completely familiar with a systematically organised summary of "classical" Christian doctrine. This is the presupposition which unlocks the meaning of the parable; if one does not have the key, the parable remains a mystery. In allegorical exegesis of this kind, the text becomes a coat-hook on which the interpreter hangs his own ideas; the exegete can draw from the parable almost whatever he likes.[17] Interpretation becomes an "in-game".

Not surprisingly, the two pence given by the good Samaritan to the inn-keeper provided plenty of scope for imaginative exegesis. Some of the early fathers suggested that they represented the Old and the New Testaments, others the two commandments of love, or faith and works, or virtue and knowledge, or the body and blood of Christ; less frequently, the promise of present and future life, or historical and anagogical interpretation, or a text and its interpretation were mentioned.[18] We have chosen an extreme example in order to underline as clearly as possible the impact which presuppositions, particularly doctrinal presuppositions, always have on interpretation.[19]

Ian Paisley's strident attack on the New English Bible illustrates the same point. Paisley explicitly adopts a doctrinal standpoint from which he judges the New English Bible: "The Shorter Catechism, that great little compendium of Biblical Theology".[20] Paisley argues that the translators of the NEB have with diabolical cunning deliberately attacked a number of cardinal Christian doctrines; their presuppositions have influenced their translation of the text.[21] Most of Paisley's criticisms are patently absurd. But one cannot suppose that while his own presuppositions are clearly stated, the translators of the NEB have managed to eliminate their own presuppositions and have simply translated the text with sound scholarly methods. For all translation involves interpretation and interpretation without any presuppositions is, as we shall argue later, an unattainable goal.

The history of life of Jesus research provides further confirmation of the impact of presuppositions on historical research and on exegesis. Albert Schweitzer introduced his survey of scholarly lives of Jesus with the observation that there is no historical undertaking which is more personal in character than the attempt to write a life of Jesus.[22] And the position has hardly changed since Schweitzer's day: once the assumptions and presuppositions of the author are known, it is not difficult to predict the main outlines of his portrait of Jesus.[23] C. E. Braaten notes cynically but correctly that nothing makes an onlooker so skeptical of New Testament scholarship as observing the frequency with which there occurs a convenient correspondence between what scholars claim to prove historically and what they need theologically.[24]

Presuppositions in New Testament exegesis are as frequently philosophical as doctrinal, though a sharp distinction is impossible. The miracle stories in the gospels and in Acts provide an example of the interplay of philosophical and doctrinal presuppositions. The interpreter's prior decision about the possibility or impossibility of miracle is bound to influence his conclusions about the historicity of the miracle stories even more than his literary analysis of the traditions; doctrinal or theological presuppositions will influence his assessment of their significance for Christology.[25] Existential exegesis also involves philosophical and theological presuppositions.

R. Bultmann's comment is apposite: "Every exegesis that is guided by dogmatic prejudices does not hear what the text says, but only lets the latter say what it wants to hear."[26] Neither the conservative nor the radical scholar can claim to be free from presuppositions. But this does not mean that the interpreter must attempt to become a neutral observer; on the contrary, empathy with the subject matter of the text is an essential presupposition. Before we take up this point in more detail, we must examine briefly the alternative approach: presuppositionless exegesis.

III. *Presuppositionless Exegesis?*

Once the close relationship between the interpreter's own assumptions and convictions and his exegetical and theological results is appreciated fully, the attraction of interpretation which does not read into the text what is not there becomes apparent.[27] Is it possible to set aside completely one's own presuppositions, and to approach the text from a neutral detached viewpoint with an agreed historical critical method and so reach scientific, objective results quite untainted by dogma? Can we, for example, locate the "pure" facts of the life and teaching of Jesus behind the early church's interpretation of him?

This possibility has frequently teased Biblical scholars. Indeed, as confidence in the historical critical method grew in the nineteenth century, so too did the appeal of presuppositionless exegesis. In 1860 Benjamin Jowett claimed that the interpretation of Scripture had nothing to do with any opinion of its origin; the meaning of Scripture was one thing, the inspiration of Scripture was another.[28] Although "spectator" exegesis is associated particularly with the latter half of the nineteenth century and the first decades of the twentieth, it has continued to be championed by a few scholars. E. Stauffer, for example, claimed that in his attempt to write what he called a history of Jesus, the evangelists' interpretation of Jesus, the interpretation offered by the dogmas of the church, even his own personal interpretation of Jesus were barred.[29] No doubt the aim seemed to some to be laudable, but the results were disappointing. Stauffer's own prejudices and assumptions were clearly revealed on almost every page.

Whenever scholarly results diverge strongly, and whenever influential "schools" of exegesis arise which are heavily dependent on particular presuppositions, a supposedly neutral uncommitted approach will always seem to offer an attractive way forward. Secure, firmly established results will always appeal to many scholars and laymen, however meagre the results turn out to be.

Nor may we suppose that whereas exegetical or theological judgments are very much at the mercy of presuppositions, historical and literary questions need not be open to the distortion of the interpreter's standpoint. An historian cannot approach either an ancient or a modern text without asking particular questions of his sources; behind his questions lurk his presuppositions.

A completely detached stance is not even possible in textual criticism; whenever the textual evidence is ambiguous the scholar's decision will be influenced, however indirectly, by his own presuppositions. The Jerusalem Bible provides an interesting reminder that doctrinal presuppositions are at work in textual criticism, even when least expected. At John 1:13 all the Greek manuscripts have a plural verb: it is those who believed in the name of Jesus who were born, not of blood nor of the will of the flesh nor of the will of man, but of God. A weakly attested variant has a singular verb: the verse then refers to Jesus who was born, not of blood nor of the will of the flesh . . . but of God. The variant is almost certainly not original; it is more likely that a reference to the virgin birth has been introduced rather than removed by an early scribe. The scholarship which lies behind the Jerusalem Bible is generally of a high standard, but in this case preference for a most unlikely variant would seem to stem ultimately from a desire to find within the New Testament a further strand of evidence which supports the Virgin Birth.

Bernard Lonergan has recently called presuppositionless exegesis "the Principle of the Empty Head". "On this view," he writes, "the less one knows, the better an exegete one will be . . . Anything over and above a re-issue of the same signs in the same order will be mediated by the experience, intelligence, and judgment of the interpreter." [30] This is surely correct. It is possible to minimise the influence of presuppositions; it is not possible to begin to interpret a text without approaching it from a particular angle – and behind the choice of that initial stance from which one asks questions of a text lie presuppositions.

The attempt to interpret the New Testament from a neutral detached standpoint with methods which were assumed to be strictly scientific has largely been abandoned. At the height of its popularity this approach had its own widely shared assumptions, those of classical liberalism.

IV. *Pre-understanding and the Text*

Although R. Bultmann launched a series of attacks on the assumptions of nineteenth century scholars and developed his own distinctive understanding of the role of presuppositions in interpretation, it was Karl Barth who took the first decisive step in a new direction in interpretation, with the publication of his commentary on Romans. The brief preface, written in 1918, is a powerful and moving theological statement. It begins: "Paul spoke as a son of his own time to his own contemporaries. But there is a much more important truth than this: Paul speaks as prophet and apostle of the Kingdom of God to all men of all times." [31] At the beginning of the twentieth century almost all New Testament scholars took it for granted that the task of exegesis was to establish as exactly and as fully as possible what the text meant in its own time. For Barth the more important and dangerous question was the present meaning of the text. [32] The preface continues, "The reader will detect for himself that it has been written with a sense of joyful discovery. The mighty voice of Paul was new to me, and if to me, no doubt to many others also." Barth had no desire to reject the historical critical method as such; he states this explicitly in the preface to his commentary as well as in later writings. [33] For Barth the historical critical method was the starting point in exegesis, though, as many of his critics have maintained with not a little justification, Barth himself frequently paid only lip-service to his own principle.

The interpreter does not observe the text from a safe distance; interpretation means confrontation with the text – and this means the confrontation of blind and sinful man with the sovereign and gracious God. In the light of recent scholarly preoccupation with hermeneutics and with presuppositions in particular, it is surprising that Barth did not comment explicitly in much greater detail on the relationship of the interpreter to the text. [34]

R. Bultmann quickly joined forces with Barth (though in later years they disagreed on many basic theological issues). Bultmann and Barth both insisted that exegesis which merely interprets the text in its original historical situation cannot uncover the meaning of the text. In an important essay published in 1950 Bultmann discussed the interpreter's presuppositions at some length. He stressed that presuppositionless exegesis is impossible; understanding is continually informed by a definite way of asking questions of the text, and this includes a pre-understanding of the subject matter of the text.[35]

In a second essay on the same theme Bultmann insists that the one presupposition which cannot be dismissed is the historical method of interrogating the text. The interpreter must pay attention to the meaning of words, to the grammar, to the style and to the historical setting of the text.[36] But the most important part of the essay is Bultmann's exposition of the interpreter's pre-understanding (*Vorverständnis*). If history is to be understood at all, then some specific perspective is always presupposed. "Can one understand economic history without having a concept of what economy and society in general mean? . . . Only he who has a relation to music can understand a text that deals with music."[37] This is surely correct. It is not surprising that Bultmann's notion of pre-understanding has been extremely influential in recent theological writing. The so-called new hermeneutic takes this aspect of Bultmann's work as one of its main starting points.

If one accepts that the interpreter must have a pre-understanding of the subject matter of his text, one is driven to the conclusion that there can never be a definitive interpretation of a text. "The understanding of the text," insists Bultmann, "remains open because the meaning of the Scriptures discloses itself anew in every future . . . Since the exegete exists historically and must hear the word of Scripture as spoken in his special historical situation, he will always understand the old word anew. Always anew will it tell him who he, man, is and who God is . . ."[38] Here we have one answer to the problem with which we began: the variety of conclusions reached by scholars committed to the historical critical method. If exegesis cannot be conducted at a safe distance from the text, from a neutral perspective, then there are bound to be a variety of interpretations, since the questions asked of the text by different scholars or readers will differ.

If each interpreter must approach the text with his own pre-understanding, we are bound to ask which kinds of pre-understanding are valid and which are not. Bultmann himself insisted that the historian must be "self-conscious about the fact that his way of asking questions is one-sided and only comes at the phenomenon of the text from the standpoint of a particular perspective. The historical perspective is falsified only when a specific way of raising questions is put forward as the only way – when, for example, all history is reduced to economic history."[39] Bultmann did not always put this sound theoretical principle into practice. His own particular way of asking questions of the text from an existentialist perspective became not just one approach among many others, but was elevated to a commanding height from which the whole New Testament landscape was surveyed.[40]

But even if Bultmann was inconsistent himself, he did quite rightly insist that the interpreter's pre-understanding is not in any sense to be regarded as definitive for it must be open to modification by the text.[41] This is a most important point to which we shall return in a moment.

V. *Possible Safeguards*

If it is not necessary for the interpreter to lay aside his own preliminary understanding of the subject matter of the text, have we not succumbed yet again to the tendency of Christian scholars right through history to read the New Testament through their own doctrinal spectacles? There are important safeguards against this threat, but no guarantees that it will be avoided.

The first is that the interpreter who is aware of the danger is more likely to avoid it than one who is not. Hence the importance of the history of exegesis for the theologian. Such a study underlines the need to refrain from allowing a doctrinal framework to dominate the text; it also reminds one that the Word of God must be heard anew in every generation. The latest exegesis or the latest theological insight is not the first time that new light has been shed on the text – nor will it be the last.

The second safeguard is the historical critical method. This at once rules out, for example, fanciful allegorical exegesis. The current flight from careful scholarly historical study of the Bible is surely only a passing fashion. The meaning of the Scriptures must not be restricted to what the text seems to be saying to me today. The critical methods used by biblical scholars (and discussed in later chapters in this book) are a fence which keep the interpreter's doctrinal assumptions or convictions in check. The methods themselves must be open to constant scrutiny and reappraisal lest they too become a framework which locks the text rigidly into one position.

The third safeguard is even more important. The interpreter must allow his own presuppositions and his own pre-understanding to be modified or even completely reshaped by the text itself. Unless this is allowed to happen, the interpreter will be unable to avoid projecting his own ideas on to the text. Exegesis guided rigidly by pre-understanding will be able to establish only what the interpreter already knows.[42] There must be a constant dialogue between the interpreter and the text. The hermeneutical circle is not only unavoidable but desirable.[43] Indeed, one must go still further: the text may well shatter the interpreter's existing pre-understanding and lead him to an unexpectedly new vantage point from which he continues his scrutiny of the text. Once the text is given priority and once the interpreter ceases to erect a barrier between himself and the text, he will find that as he seeks to interpret the text, the text will, as it were, interpret him. When this happens, the authority of Scripture is being taken seriously; God's Word is not a dead letter to be observed coldly but a Word which speaks to me in my situation.

This important hermeneutical principle helps us to see in a new light a problem which often arises in discussions of the exegete's presuppositions. Must the interpreter share the convictions and faith of the New Testament writers, or can the New Testament be interpreted by a non-Christian? Many would want to affirm that since the New Testament documents were written by men deeply and passionately committed to the person of Jesus Christ, the faith of the original writers must be shared by the interpreter. For if full understanding includes not only what the text meant, but also what it means now, faith must be necessary if the intention of the text is to be exposed.

Some, on the other hand, would want to stress that many parts of the New Testament were written to awaken faith, not to confirm it. The parables of Jesus do not presuppose that the hearers share Jesus' standpoint, for many of them are deliberately designed to break through the defences of those who listened. Many parts of the gospel traditions were used primarily in the missionary preaching of the early church. Luke almost certainly wrote his two volumes for interested but uncommitted readers; the Fourth Gospel is evangelistic in intention. Surely it is legitimate for the interpreter to stand where the original readers or hearers stood: they did not necessarily share the convictions of the writer or speaker. Hence, it might be argued, we must not insist that the text can be understood fully only from the standpoint of faith.

How is this dilemma to be resolved, for both positions can be defended cogently? We cannot suggest that while the parts of the New Testament which were written originally to Christian believers can be understood fully only in the light of faith, the "evangelistic" sections do not require any such prior commitment. The New Testament cannot be divided up neatly into these two categories.

If, as we have argued, interpretation involves *dialogue* with the text, to ask whether or not the interpreter must be a Christian believer is, in a sense, to ask the wrong question. It would be a valid and important question if it were possible for the interpreter to isolate himself from the text in the safety of a detached position, for in that case, even if he claimed to be working without any presuppositions, his own convictions and understanding would be the spectacles through which the text would *always* be viewed. But, as we have stressed, "spectator" exegesis is both impossible and undesirable. Once exegesis is seen as an on-going dialogue between the interpreter and the text, the interpreter's starting point becomes less important than his willingness and readiness to run the risk that the pre-understanding with which he comes to the text may well be refined or completely renewed: he must be prepared to be interpreted by the text. That is the necessary presupposition with which he must attempt to operate.

The exegete cannot allow either his own personal bias or prejudice or his pre-understanding to dominate the text. They cannot be avoided completely, but they must be no more than a door through which the text is approached. The text is prior: the interpreter stands before it humbly and prays that through the scholarly methods and the questions with which he comes to the text, God's Word will be heard afresh. This is the exciting task to which the interpreter is called. But it is also a dangerous task: God's Word sweeps away my comfortably secure presuppositions; it is a Word of judgment as well as of grace.

NOTES

1. The standard work is H. -G. Gadamer, *Wahrheit und Methode* (Tübingen 1973[3]; E.T. *Truth and Method,* London 1975). In both the second (1965) and the third editions (1973), Gadamer interacts with his critics and with the recent literature. For a useful summary and critical discussion, see E. D. Hirsch, *Validity in Interpretation* (New Haven 1967), especially pp. 245ff.

2. A. Nygren, *Meaning and Method: Prolegomena to a Scientific Philosophy of Religion and a Scientific Theology* (London 1972), pp. 160ff.

3. Cf. G. Ebeling's lecture, *Kirchengeschichte als Geschichte der Auslegung der Heiligenschrift,* Tübingen 1947); reprinted in G. Ebeling, *Wort Gottes und Tradition* (Göttingen 1964), pp. 9–27; E.T. *The Word of God and Tradition* (London 1966), pp. 11–31.

4. See J. M. Robinson, "Hermeneutic Since Barth" in J. M. Robinson and J. B. Cobb (ed.), *The New Hermeneutic* (New York 1964), pp. 1–77.

5. C.E. Braaten, *History and Hermeneutics* (London 1968), p. 52.

6. This chapter should be read in close conjunction with F. F. Bruce's preceding chapter "The History of New Testament Study" and A. C. Thiselton's discussion of "The New Hermeneutic" in chapter XVI.

7. Cf. A. Nygren, op. cit., pp. 187ff.

8. Cf. for examples, W. R. Farmer's discussion of the history of synoptic source criticism, *The Synoptic Problem,* (New York and London 1964), esp. pp. 94ff. and pp. 287ff.

9. This danger is, however, less serious than the widespread assumption that all the writers of the New Testament speak with the same voice.

10. See S. S. Smalley's discussion of redaction criticism in chapter XI; also M. D. Hooker, "In his own Image?" in *What About the New Testament*? ed. M. Hooker and C. Hickling (London 1975), pp. 28–44.

11. I have argued elsewhere that some of the alterations Luke makes to his sources are not theological (as several scholars have supposed) but stylistic. G. N. Stanton, *Jesus of Nazareth in New Testament Preaching* (Cambridge 1974), pp. 31–66.

12. *Wahrheit und Methode* (3rd ed. 1973), pp. 483f. (E.T. pp. 465f.). I have used J. M. Robinson's translation, *The New Hermeneutic,* op. cit., p. 76.

13. Doctrinal presuppositions have also exercised a profound influence on interpretations of church history!

14. See R. Morgan's interesting discussion of W. Wrede, *The Nature of New Testament Theology* (London 1973), esp. p. 22.

15. J. Neusner, *The Rabbinic Traditions about the Pharisees before 70* (Leiden 1970), Vol. III, pp. 320ff.

16. For valuable detailed studies, see W. Monselewski, *Der barmherzige Samariter: eine auslegungsgeschichtliche Untersuchung zu Lukas 10, 25–37* (Tübingen 1967), and H. G. Klemm, *Das Gleichnis vom Barmherzigen Samariter: Grundzüge der Auslegung im 16./17. Jahrhundert* (Stuttgart 1973).

17. Not all allegorical exegesis is as fanciful as the example given. I do not accept that all traces of allegory in the parables must stem from the early church rather than from Jesus himself.

18. For the details and the references, see H. G. Klemm, op. cit., p. 22f., n.23 and W. Monselewski, op. cit., pp. 45ff.

19. For a discussion of the influence of presuppositions on recent interpretation of the parables, see N. Perrin, "The Modern Interpretation of the Parables and the Problem of Hermeneutics", *Interpretation* 25 (1971), pp. 131–148.

20. Ian R. K. Paisley, *The New English Bible: Version or Perversion?* (Belfast, no date), p. 6.
21. Paisley concentrates largely on the judgment of the NEB translators in an area with which he himself is not familiar: textual criticism.
22. *The Quest of the Historical Jesus* (London 1953³), p. 4.
23. See, for example, R. Slenczka's discussion, *Geschichtlichkeit und Personsein Jesu Christi* (Göttingen 1967). See also H. K. McArthur's useful collection of excerpts from a wide range of recent writing on the life of Jesus, *In Search of the Historical Jesus* (New York 1969).
24. *History and Hermeneutic,* p. 55.
25. For a useful discussion, see H. van der Loos, *The Miracles of Jesus* (Leiden 1965).
26. "Is Exegesis without Presuppositions Possible?", English translation in *Existence and Faith,* ed. S. M. Ogden, (London 1961 and 1964), p. 343. Page references are to the 1964 paperback edition.
27. Cf. K. Frör's discussion, *Biblische Hermeneutik* (Munich 1967³), pp. 51ff.
28. "On the Interpretation of Scripture", in *Essays and Reviews* (1860), pp. 350f. I owe this reference to C. W. Dugmore (ed.), *The Interpretation of the Bible,* (London 1944), p. vii. cf. the essay by T. W. Manson in the same volume, pp. 92–107.
29. *Jesus and His Story* (London 1960), p. 13.
30. B. J. F. Lonergan, *Method in Theology* (London 1972), p. 157.
31. *Der Römerbrief,* 1st ed. 1919; E. T. *The Epistle to the Romans* (London 1933), pp. 1f.
32. I have oversimplified Barth's position for the sake of clarity. Elsewhere Barth insists that the interpreter is dealing not so much with the text *per se* as with the "reality" which lies behind the text.
33. See, for example, *Church Dogmatics* I/2 (E.T. Edinburgh 1956), pp. 464ff. and 722ff.
34. For more detailed discussions, see G. Eichholz, "Der Ansatz Karl Barths in der Hermeneutik" in *Antwort: Karl Barth zum siebzigsten Geburtstag* (Zollikon- Zürich 1956), pp. 52ff.; F.-W. Marquardt, "Exegese und Dogmatik in Karl Barths Theologie", *Die kirchliche Dogmatik,* Registerband (Zürich 1970), pp. 651ff.
Verstehen II (Tübingen, 1952), pp. 211–235: E.T. *Essays Philosophical and Theological* (London 1955), pp. 236-261.
36. "Is Exegesis without Presuppositions Possible?" *Existence and Faith,* p. 344. Bultmann insists that "the historical method includes the presupposition that history is a unity in the sense of a closed continuum of effects in which individual events are connected by the succession of cause and effect ... This closedness means that the continuum of historical happenings cannot be rent by the interference of supernatural transcendent powers . . ." Bultmann's main point is that historical science as such can neither prove nor disprove that God has interfered in history; "it can only leave every man free to determine whether he wants to see an act of God in a historical event that it itself understands in terms of that event's immanent historical causes."(ibid., p. 345). Bultmann does not wish to deny that God has acted in history.
37. Ibid., p. 347. Similarly, "Das Problem", op. cit., p. 218f.
38. "Is Exegesis without Presuppositions Possible?", op. cit., p. 351.
39. Ibid., p. 346.
40. So also, among many others, C. E. Braaten, op. cit., p. 134, and A. Nygren, op. cit., pp. 200ff. (cf. also pp. 131ff. and 299ff.).
41. "Is Exegesis without Presuppositions Possible?" op. cit., p. 347f.
42. Cf. D. O. Via, *The Parables* (Philadelphia 1967), p. 50.
43. On the hermeneutical circle, see A. C. Thiselton's discussion below, p. 316.

PART TWO

The Use of Critical Methods in Interpretation

CHAPTER IV

SEMANTICS AND NEW TESTAMENT INTERPRETATION

Anthony C. Thiselton

I. *Semantics and Theories of Meaning*

1. INTRODUCTION

Semantics is the study of meanings; but not simply the meanings of words. What is at issue is the varied meanings and kinds of meaning which belong both to words and to sentences as they occur within a context that is both linguistic and extra-linguistic. John Lyons comments in his *Structural Semantics,* "Any meaningful linguistic unit, up to and including the complete utterance, has meaning in context. The context of the utterance is the situation in which it occurs . . . The concept of 'situation' is fundamental for semantic statement . . . Situation must be given equal weight with linguistic form in semantic theory".[1] It will be seen that this is not very far from the traditional concerns of New Testament exegesis, in which the aim is to discover and interpret the meaning of an utterance in relation to its historical and literary context. Semantics, however, also raises explicit questions about such issues as synonymy, multiple meaning, types of semantic opposition, kinds and degrees of vagueness and ambiguity, change of meaning, cognitive and emotive factors in meaning, and so on.

The relevance of semantics to biblical interpretation was demonstrated for the first time, but demonstrated decisively, with the publication in 1961 of James Barr's epoch-making book *The Semantics of Biblical Language.* Since that time there have been other attempts to apply principles of semantics, or at least of linguistics, to biblical interpretation, including most recently the very different approaches of Erhardt Güttgemanns, René Kieffer, John Sawyer and K. L. Burres.[2] Although the study of semantics can be approached from the side of philosophy as well as linguistics, James Barr and in practice all these writers draw their insights exclusively from linguistics. Indeed the claim which will be put forward here is that in spite of his obvious knowledge of more recent writers, the fundamental inspiration behind Barr's contribution is the figure of Ferdinand de Saussure whose famous *Cours de linguistique générale* was published posthumously in 1915. Apart from some brief attempts by the present writer, perhaps the only studies, to date, to draw on more philosophical work in the service of biblical interpretation are those of D. D. Evans and, less directly, O. R. Jones.[3]

If semantics is so important to New Testament interpretation, why have we had to wait until after 1961 for its insights and potentialities to become apparent? Either, it seems, the exegete can manage very well with only his traditional questions about vocabulary and grammar; or else, it seems, some convincing explanation is needed of why biblical scholars have been slow to avail themselves of its insights.

2. THE INHIBITING EFFECTS OF TRADITIONAL ASSUMPTIONS ABOUT LANGUAGE

Part of the answer to this question is suggested by Stephen Ullmann's description of semantics as "the youngest branch of modern linguistics".[4] The earliest hints of a fully modern semantics came towards the end of the nineteenth century with the work of Arsène Darmesteter and more especially Michel Bréal.[5] Semantic study at this period, however, was seriously hampered by a number of mistaken assumptions, some of which still find their way into the outlook of some interpreters of the New Testament even today.

These false assumptions include the following:

(1) that the *word, rather than the sentence or speech-act,* constitutes the basic unit of meaning to be investigated;[6] (2) that questions about *etymology* somehow relate to the real or "basic" meaning of a word; (3) that language has a relation to the world which is *other than conventional,* and that its "rules" may therefore be prescriptive rather than merely descriptive; (4) that *logical and grammatical structure* are basically similar or even isomorphic; (5) that meaning always turns on the relation between a word and the object to which it *refers*; (6) that the basic kind of language-use to be investigated (other than words themselves) is the *declarative proposition* or statement; and (7) that language is an *externalization,* sometimes a merely imitative and approximate externalization, of inner concepts or ideas. Commenting only on three of these assumptions, Max Black writes, "Until comparatively recently the prevailing conception of the nature of language was straightforward and simple. It stressed communication of thought to the neglect of feeling and attitude, emphasized words rather than speech-acts in context, and assumed a sharp contrast between thought and its symbolic expression."[7] While such assumptions held sway, semantic enquiries could not advance beyond an elementary point.

An especially disastrous assumption for semantics was logico-grammatical parallelism.[8] When interest grew in eighteenth and nineteenth-century linguistics in the relation between language-structure and national character, the effects of this error were particularly unfortunate. Supposed differences of conceptual thought were based on arbitrary differences of grammar.

The influence of such a view persists in biblical studies in a work such as

T. Boman's *Hebrew Thought Compared with Greek,* and we shall trace some of the ways in which James Barr rightly criticizes it. On the other hand, once we recognize that logical function, or meaning, is not wholly determined by grammar, huge questions in New Testament interpretation are opened up. Is Bultmann correct in claiming, for example, that what looks like an objective declarative statement, "God will judge men at the last day", really *means* an imperative: "act responsibly in the present . . ."? Certainly in every-day speech I may use an indicative to function as an imperative. If I exclaim, "This is poison", I *may* be making a declarative descriptive statement. But I may also be uttering an urgent imperative, "Quick! Fetch a doctor"; or giving a warning, "Look out! Don't drink this"; or even uttering a reproach, "You forgot to put sugar into my coffee." [9] The meaning of the words depends on their setting or non-linguistic situation, even more than upon grammar. Yet on the basis of the traditional view, "this is poison" is simply a statement, for "is" is a third person singular present indicative form in grammar.

The traditional view received two death-blows, one from linguistics and one from philosophy. From the direction of linguistics, Saussure pointed out the arbitrary character of grammatical forms. [10] More sharply and decisively still, in his philosophical discussion of logic Russell showed in his Theory of Descriptions that "the apparent logical form of a proposition need not be the real one." [11] Denoting phrases such as "the present king of France" or "the author of *Waverley*" cannot be reduced to simple referring expressions. "Denoting phrases never have any meaning in themselves." [12] The linguistic form "a round square does not exist" does not logically make an assertion about some non-existent entity called a round square; it is a *negation* of the statement, "an *x* exists which is such that 'round' and 'square' can be predicated of it simultaneously." The linguistic form of the expression conceals its logical function. But once this principle is accepted, the New Testament interpreter should be extremely cautious about making too much of such maxims as "this word is in the indicative, therefore it is a statement"; or "this verb is an imperative, therefore it expresses a command." Whether it *is* a command depends on the whole context and situation in which it is uttered. Thus, we shall be cautious about reading too much into the fact that, for example, an imperative or an indicative features in a particular verse. In Phil. 3:1 and 4:4, for instance, "rejoice in the Lord" (*χαίρετε ἐν κυρίῳ*) is admittedly a second person plural present imperative. On this basis Karl Barth writes that rejoicing "must" take place, because it is "expressed as an imperative", and W. Hendriksen insists that we are bidden "to rejoice *in obedience to a command*".[13] But, firstly, it is possible that *χαίρετε* is a form of greeting, which is no more a command than "how do you do?" is a question. On the basis of grammar, one can imagine an exegete interpreting "how do you do?" as a call to self-examination! When Judas greets Jesus with a betraying kiss in Mt. 26:49, *χαῖρε* means simply "hello", and certainly not "rejoice". In Phil. 3:1 and 4:4 F. W. Beare translates the word "Farewell".[14] Secondly, even if we insist, after examining the historical and literary setting (which Barth and Hendriksen fail to do), that χαίρετε still means "rejoice", the fact that it occurs in the imperative is no guarantee that it must be understood as a "command". If I cry "Help!" in the imperative, or "Lord, save me", this is a plea; if someone tells me, "enjoy yourself", but in the end I spend a miserable afternoon, this need not be "disobedience to a command".

The task of Bible translation also reveals the utter impossibility of remaining wedded to the idea of logico-grammatical parallelism. In I John 2:26, for example, the writer states "I have written this to you (ταῦτα ἔγραψα ὑμῖν) concerning those who would mislead you." But ἔγραψα, although it is an "indicative" (I have written) does not serve primarily to *describe* the action of writing here; it in fact signals the end of a topic. So the *New English Bible* sensibly renders it, "*So much for* those who would mislead you."

In Bible translation, the rejection of logico-grammatical parallelism stems not only from structural linguistics (discussed in II.2), and from a recognition of the conventionality of grammatical form (discussed in II.3), but also from the influence of Noam Chomsky's type of "transformational" generative grammar (discussed in III). Eugene A. Nida and William L. Wonderly accept the principle of transformation in terms of "*kernel*" sentences as an *axiom* of Bible translation.[15] Thus the complex R. S. V. sentence in Eph. 1:7 "... we have redemption through his blood, the forgiveness of our trespasses" is analyzed into four "kernel" sentences: (1) (God) redeems us; (2) (Christ) died (or shed his blood); (3) (God) forgives (us); and (4) we sinned. The "quasi-kernel" structure is now: "we sinned. But Christ died; therefore God redeems us and he forgives us." *Today's English Version* then renders this: "by the death of Christ we are set free, and our sins are forgiven"; whilst the *New English Bible* has: "in Christ our release is secured and our sins are forgiven through the shedding of his blood." Neither *grammatical* structure follows the Greek at all closely. Whether such a handling of the text is justified cannot be determined without carefully examining the issues which are discussed in the remainder of this essay.

3. WORDS AND MEANINGS

Genuine advances in semantics were decisively inhibited all the while the *word* was viewed as the basic unit of meaning. But in some types of exegesis the assumption still lurks in the background that words are the basic carriers of meaning, whilst sentences convey the exact sum of the semantic values of their verbal components. A virtue is made out of the method of moving over a text "word by word". Side by side with this is often the assumption that exhaustive interpretation must proceed by way of *analysis,* atomizing language into ever-smaller and smaller units. Such an approach may seem to be connected with a theory of "verbal" inspiration, but is in reality based, rather, on ignorance about the nature of language. As Saussure has shown decisively in one way, and Wittgenstein decisively in another, the meaning of a word depends not on what it is in itself, but on its relation to other words and to other sentences which form its context. Dictionary-entries about words are rule-of-thumb generalizations based on assumptions about characteristic contexts. Admittedly these comments will be qualified in due course; for words do indeed possess a stable core of meaning without which lexicography would be impossible, and there is also a legitimate place for word-study. Nevertheless, the most urgent priority is to point out the fallacy of an atomizing exegesis which pays insufficient attention to context.

This should heighten our appreciation of the value of all technical work in biblical studies which seeks to shed light on the historical and literary contexts of utterances. In a valuable article John F. A. Sawyer compares the emphasis placed on "context of situation" in linguistics with the account taken of situation, setting, or *Sitz im Leben* in form criticism.[16] Indeed he goes as far as to claim, "The relation between *Gattung* and *Sitz im Leben* in Old Testament literary theory is potentially more important for *semantic* theory (my italics) than a number of situational theories put forward by the professional linguistician from Bloomfield to Firth."[17] Thus the necessity and value of standard techniques in New Testament studies is not simply a question which can be decided on theological grounds alone. Because biblical language *as language* can only be understood with reference to its context and extra-linguistic situation, attention to the kind of question raised in critical study of the text is seen to be necessary on purely *linguistic* grounds. To try to cut loose "propositions" in the New Testament from the specific situation in which they were uttered and to try thereby to treat them "timelessly" is not only bad theology; it is also bad linguistics. For it leads to a distortion of what the text *means*. This point will emerge with fuller force when we look at the structural approach of Ferdinand de Saussure (below, II.2).

There are also other inbuilt limitations in the traditional approach to language. For example, a persistent pre-occupation with descriptive assertions or "propositions" tends to flatten out the distinctive contributions of biblical poetry, metaphor, parable, and apocalyptic, reducing it all to the level of discursive "units of information". A consideration of the issues discussed in the remainder of this essay, however, will show that a "mechanical" emphasis on verbal and propositional forms is not only pre-critical in terms of Biblical studies, it is also obsolete in terms of *semantics*, violating virtually every modern insight into the nature of meanings.

II. *Some Fundamental Principles in Saussure and Modern Linguistics and their place in the work of James Barr*

Ferdinand de Saussure (1857–1913) is rightly regarded as the founder of modern linguistics. He viewed language as a social and structured system, thereby preparing the way for a structural semantics. We may trace the outlines of his thought under four headings: (1) the contrast between synchronic and diachronic methods of language-study; (2) the structural approach to language; (3) the connexion between structuralism and conventionality, with its implications about the relation between language and thought; and (4) the basic contrast between *langue,* the language system, and *parole,* actual speech. All four principles are fundamental for semantics, and three, at least, feature prominently in the work of James Barr.

1. SYNCHRONIC AND DIACHRONIC APPROACHES TO LANGUAGE

By "diachronic" linguistics Saussure means the study of language from the point of view of its *historical evolution* over a period of time. By "synchronic" linguistics he means "the relations of co-existing things ... from which the intervention of time is excluded ... the science of *language-states (états de langue) ... Synchrony* and *diachrony* designate respectively a language-state and an evolutionary phase."[18] Saussure's point is not, as is occasionally thought, that one of these methods is right and the other wrong, but that the two methods are fundamentally *different,* and perform different tasks. Certainly of the two, synchronic linguistics has priority both in importance and in sequence of application. But as long as the two methods are kept distinct, each has its own role to play.

During the nineteenth century comparative philology had become the centre of interest in linguistics, and much energy went to the formulation of *laws of development,* such as Grimm's law and Verner's law, which could account for the phenomena of language-change in terms of general scientific principles.

It is against this background that Ferdinand de Saussure voiced his protest, "The linguist who wishes to understand a state (*état de langue*) must discard all knowledge of everything that produced it and ignore diachrony. He can enter the mind of the speakers only by completely suppressing the past."[19] Saussure illustrates the principle from chess. To understand the *state* of a game it is unnecessary and irrelevant to know how the players arrived at it. A chess problem is simply set out by describing the state of the board.

During the years between Saussure and Barr, the priority of synchronic description became a fundamental and universally accepted principle in semantics; and the distinction between synchronic and diachronic perspectives has become an axiom in linguistics.[20] In particular this principle strikes at etymologizing in semantics. Many writers, including a number of biblical scholars, believe that the etymological meaning of a word is somehow its "basic" or "proper" meaning. As James Barr comments, "We hear from time to time that 'history' 'properly' means 'investigation' (Greek *ἱστορία*) or that 'person' 'basically' means 'mask' (Latin *persona*)."[21]

But can an etymological meaning based on diachronic investigation, or even inference, concerning the long distant past be the "real" meaning of a word from the point of view of synchronic enquiry? The English word "nice" is said to be derived from the Latin *nescius,* ignorant. Is "ignorant" the "basic" meaning of "nice"? When Englishmen say "Good-bye" do they "properly" mean "God be with you"? "Hussy" is etymologically a doublet of "housewife", but can it be said on this basis that if I were to call someone a hussy I "properly" meant only "housewife"?[22] As James Barr rightly asserts, "The main point is that the etymology of a word is *not a statement about its meaning but about its history*."[23] Hundreds of words diverge from or even (like "nice") oppose their etymology.

We may admit that in lexicography, etymological considerations may occasionally be of value, as, for example, in cases of homonymy, when two distinct words of different meanings have the same lexical form. But biblical scholars have not been content to restrict their study of etymology to such cases. As a general principle Edmond Jacob declares, "The first task of the Hebraist in the presence of a word is to recover the original meaning from which others were derived."[24] The very arrangement of the Hebrew lexicon of Brown, Driver, and Briggs may seem to encourage such a procedure. Some writers, says J. Barr, have even interpreted the word "holy" in terms of an *English* etymology. Contrary to actual usage in Hebrew and Greek, they take its "basic" meaning to be that of "healthy" or "sound". But in practice, Barr insists, this is only "a kind of opportunist homiletic trick" whereby "holy" may be thought to lose some of its less attractive and more challenging features.[25] Norman Snaith certainly goes to the Hebrew, rather than to the English, for the meaning of "Blessed is the man . . ." in Psalm 1:1. But he claims that "happiness of" or "blessed" is related by etymology to the idea of "footstep", or "going straight ahead". Hence, supposedly, "this shows how apt is the use of the first word . . . The happy man is the man who goes straight ahead." Barr observes, "There is not the slightest evidence that these associations were in the mind of the poet, and indeed some of them were almost certainly unknown and unknowable to him."[26]

When we come specifically to the New Testament, it will be seen that it can be seriously misleading to base the meanings of words on their use in Plato or in Homer, let alone on their etymologies. For example, it is sometimes suggested, as Barr points out, that *λειτουργία* "means" a work (*ἔργον*) performed by the people (*λαός*) perhaps through a priestly or kingly representative. But at least by the time of Aristotle the word had simply become a generalized one for any kind of "service" or "function".[27] Sometimes interpreters seek to read too much into a dead metaphor. Thus "to show compassion" (*σπλαγχνίζομαι*) is said to be a matter of one's innermost being, since *σπλάγχνα* means "internal organs". But the metaphor is no longer any more a live force than when we speak of "losing heart". Similarly, it is sometimes claimed that *ὑπηέτης* in 1 Cor. 4:1 "literally" means the under-rower (*ὑπό* + *ἐρέσσω*) of a ship.[28] But the word has become a dead metaphor meaning simply "servant" or "assistant"; no more than "dandelion" "literally" means *dent de lion* or "lion's tooth". Occasionally someone even uses diachronic investigation in a way that leads to sheer anachronism, as when we are told that "witness" (*μαρτύριον*) means "martyrdom"; or, worse still, that *δύναμις* in the New Testament "properly" means "dynamite"!

Neither Saussure nor Barr rules out diachronic linguistics as illegitimate. Indeed it may be helpful to use diachronic study to demonstrate that the meaning of a Greek word has *changed* in between Plato and the New Testament. It is proper to trace the historical evolution of a term and its changing semantic value, provided that two factors are borne in mind: firstly, that synchronic description is the pre-requisite of diachronic study at every separate stage; secondly, that adequate attention is paid to the phenomenon of semantic change. David Crystal sums up the point made by Saussure: "Both are subjects in themselves, with different procedures of study and largely different aims. Neither excludes the other . . . But . . . a synchronic description is pre-requisite for a proper diachronic study." [29]

2. THE STRUCTURAL APPROACH TO LANGUAGE

In his introduction to the English edition of Saussure's work, W. Baskin, his translator, comments, "Saussure was among the first to see that language is a self-contained system whose interdependent parts function and acquire value through their relationship to the whole." [30] In Saussure's own words, "Language is a system of interdependent terms (*les termes sont solidaires*) in which the value (*la valeur*) of each term results solely from the simultaneous presence of the others." [31] He adds, "Within the same language, all words used to express related ideas limit each other reciprocally . . . The value (*la valeur*) of just any term is accordingly determined by its environment."[32] Words or other linguistic signs have no "force", validity, or meaning, independently of the relations of equivalence and contrast which hold between them.

Once again Saussure illustrates the point with reference to chess. The "value" of a given piece depends on its place within the whole system. Depending on the state of the whole board when one piece is moved, resulting changes of value will be either nil, very serious, or of average importance. A certain move can revolutionize the whole game, i.e. radically affect the value of all the other pieces. "Exactly the same holds for language."[33]

This brings us to a major pair of categories which are fundamental and central in modern linguistics, namely to *syntagmatic and paradigmatic relations*. A linguistic unit, Saussure pointed out, is related to the rest of the system within which it functions in two distinct ways. Firstly, it has a *linear* relationship with other words or units with which it is chained together. "Combinations supported by linearity are *syntagms*." [34] In the phrase "a crown of thorns", the word "crown" stands in syntagmatic relationship to "a" and "of thorns"; just as in the phrase "God is righteous", "righteous" has a syntagmatic relation to "God is". From a semantic viewpoint, if "eat" stands in syntagmatic relationship to "bread", "meat" and "cheese" but not to "water", "tea" or "beer", this contributes to establishing its *meaning,* as the ingestion of solid food.

The *paradigmatic* relation was called by Saussure an *associative* relation, although writers in linguistics prefer the former term. This is the relation between a word or linguistic unit and another such unit which is *not* present in the actual utterance, but which might have been chosen *in its place*. In the phrase "a crown of thorns" the words "laurel" or "gold" could have been slotted in, in place of "thorns". Thus "thorns" stands in a paradigmatic relation to "laurel", "gold", "silver", and so on. In "God is righteous", the word "righteous" stands in paradigmatic relation to "good", or "merciful". This principle is so important that John Lyons states that one of the two "defining characteristics" of modern structural linguistics is the axiom that "linguistic units have no validity independently of their paradigmatic and syntagmatic relations with other units."[35]

The relevance of this principle to New Testament interpretation has been conclusively demonstrated by Erhardt Güttgemanns and by Kenneth L. Burres.[36] Güttgemanns, for example, shows how the meaning of "righteousness" in Romans turns partly on its syntagmatic relations to "of God" (*Θεοῦ*) and "on the basis of faith" (*ἐκ πιστέως*). Burres discusses the meaning of "reveal" (*ἀποκαλύπτω*) partly in terms of its syntagmatic or "syntactic" relations to "righteousness of God", "wrath of God", and other phrases; partly in terms of its paradigmatic or "paratactic" relations to *φανερόω* and its two-way relations (e.g. in 1 Cor. 14:6) to *γνῶσις* and *προφητεία*. The aim in the case of Burres' work is to build up a semantic field of terms relevant to the semantic value of "reveal" in Paul.

The notion of paradigmatic relations is connected with the semantic axiom that meaning implies *choice*. For example, "pound" (weight) draws part of its meaning from the fact that it functions to *exclude* ton, stone, ounce, or dram. It also draws part of its meaning from its syntactic relation to butter, cheese, or apples. On the other hand, "pound" (money) draws part of its meaning from its paradigmatic relation to 50p, 100p or £5; and part of its meaning from its syntagmatic relation to "pay me a" or "change for a". Thus Güttgemanns examines the paradigmatic relations of "righteousness of God" to "power of God" and "wrath of God", as well as its syntagmatic relations to "on the basis of faith" and "on the basis of law". Similarly the meaning of *κατὰ σάρκα* depends not only on its syntagmatic relation to *'Ισραήλ* ("earthly" Israel) or *σοφοί* (wise according to "human standards"); but also on its paradigmatic relation to *κατὰ πνεῦμα* (spirit).

Saussure's notion of "associative fields", which depends largely on paradigmatic relations, thus provides a way into the task of mapping out a semantic field. K. L. Burres uses both syntagmatic and paradigmatic relations to map the semantic field surrounding Paul's uses of words meaning "to reveal".[37]

In view of the importance of the field, Barr and Burres each supports Trier's point that a word has meaning not autonomously or independently but "only as part of a whole" (*nur als Teil des Ganzen*); only within a field (*im Feld*).[38] All the same, criticisms about words as units of meaning should not be taken too far. No less an authority than G. Stern has written: "There is no getting away from the fact that single words have more or less permanent meanings, that they actually do refer to certain referents, and not to others, and that this characteristic is the indispensable basis of all communication."[39] Or as Stephen Ullmann puts it, more moderately, "There is usually in each word a hard core of meaning which is relatively stable and can only be modified by the context within certain limits."[40] Word-studies, then, are not to be dismissed as valueless.

When James Barr ruthlessly criticizes many of the articles in G. Kittel's multi-volume *Theological Dictionary of the New Testament,* it might be tempting to imagine that he is mainly attacking the method of word-study. But word-study *as such* is not his main target of criticism. His real complaint is against what he calls "*illegitimate totality transfer*".[41] This occurs when the semantic value of a word as it occurs in *one context* is *added* to its semantic value in *another context*; and the process is continued until the *sum* of these semantic values is then *read into a particular case.*

Barr illustrates this fallacy with reference to the meaning of ἐκκλησία, church, in the New Testament. "If we ask 'What is the meaning of ἐκκλησία in the New Testament?' the answer may be an adding or compounding of different statements about the ἐκκλησία in various passages. Thus we might say (a) 'the Church is the Body of Christ' (b) 'the Church is the first instalment of the Kingdom of God' (c) 'the Church is the Bride of Christ', and other such statements."[42] In *one* sense Barr concedes, this is the "meaning" of "church". But it is certainly *not* "the meaning of 'church' *in Matt. 16.18.*" Yet preachers and expositors often lump together the meanings of words drawn from various different contexts, and "expound" them as the meaning of the word in a given verse. Barr quite successfully shows, for example, that this error is committed by Grundmann in his article on αγαθός "good", in Kittel's *Dictionary.*

This error stands in complete contrast to the principles elucidated in modern linguistics after Saussure by Eugene A. Nida and by Martin Joos in particular. Nida asserts, "The correct meaning of any term is that which contributes least to the total context."[43] For example we might define the semantic values of "green" in several ways: as a colour, as meaning inexperienced, as meaning unripe, and so on. Similarly, we might define "house" as a dwelling, lineage, and a business establishment. But as soon as we place "green" and "house" in syntagmatic relation to each other, we minimize the semantic values of each, so that "green" can only be a colour, and "house" only a dwelling. In the case of "greenhouse" the contribution of "green" almost disappears. Yet if "green house" were a phrase in the New Testament, we could imagine an expositor exploring the supposed "richness" of each term separately, and then adding together the components into one great theological compound. On the other hand Martin Joos calls it "semantic axiom number one" that in defining a word it must be made to "contribute least to the total message desirable from the passage where it is at home, rather than e.g. defining it according to some presumed etymology or semantic history."[44] Nida concludes "Words do not carry with them all the meanings which they may have in other sets of co-occurences."[45] Thus in a balanced comment on the whole question of word-meaning R. H. Robins adds that words may be convenient units about which to state meanings "*provided that* it is borne in mind that words have meaning by virtue of their employment in sentences . . . and that the meaning of a sentence is not to be thought of as a sort of summation of the meanings of its component words taken individually." [46]

3. CONVENTIONALITY IN LANGUAGE AND ITS CONNEXION WITH STRUCTURALISM

Saussure was certainly not the first to show what he called "the arbitrary nature of the sign" in language. "No-one", he writes, "disputes the principle of the arbitrary nature of the sign, but it is often easier to discover a truth than to assign to it its proper place." What was distinctive about Saussure's assessment was, firstly, that he described it as the very first principle in language-study, which "dominates all the linguistics of language; its consequences are numberless." [47] Secondly, the far-reaching effects of this principle on the relationship between language and thought, or between words and concepts, emerge clearly only against the background of structuralism. Saussure's structural approach, we have seen, calls in question a semantics which is based entirely on the word as a unit of meaning. This now enables us to expose what Barr has called the one word/one concept fallacy, and also to challenge the drawing of inferences about national "thought" made on the basis of linguistic distinctions which turn out to be arbitrary.

There are everyday phenomena in language which make it clear that the relations between language and the world depend in many respects on arbitrary or conventional factors rather than on "nature" or even logic. These include *homonymy* (when two words of different meanings have the same form, e.g. "he *left* me", as against "turn *left*"); *polysemy* (when one word has multiple meanings, e.g. "*board* and lodging", "*board* of directors", "*board* from the floor"); *opaqueness* in vocabulary (e.g. in contrast to the transparent meanings of onomatopoeia); and diachronic *change* in language.[48] Saussure, however, points simply to the very basic fact of differences both in vocabulary and in grammar between different languages, when logically the same semantic value is involved. The relation between the French word *soeur* and a sister is no more "natural", "inner" or "logical" than it is in the case of the German *Schwester* or the English *sister*. Similarly, in terms of grammar, in the sentence *ces gants sont bon marché,* "these gloves are cheap", *bon marché* functions logically or semantically as an adjective, but is not an adjective from the arbitrary viewpoint of grammar. [49] (We have already referred, in philosophy, to the parallel observations of Russell about such phrases as "the present King of France", or "a round square"). Further, in terms of morphology, *bon marché* is composed of two words which correspond to the one word "cheap". Even the limits of the word as a unit have an arbitrary element. In Latin and in Greek *amo* and φιλῶ or ἀγαπῶ must be translated by two words in English and in German, "I love," and "*ich liebe*". Saussure concludes, "The division of words into substantives, verbs, adjectives, etc., is not an undeniable linguistic reality." [50]

We have already noted some of the fallacies involved in logico-grammatical parallelism. The other side of the coin is the equally misguided attempt to draw inferences about the distinctive thought of a people, for example, about "Hebrew thought" or "Greek thought", on the basis of its grammatical categories. Eugene A. Nida writes, "The idea that the Hebrew people had a completely different view of time because they had a different verbal system does not stand up under investigation. It would be just as unfounded to claim that people of the English-speaking world have lost interest in sex because the gender distinctions in nouns and adjectives have been largely eliminated, or that Indo-Europeans are very time conscious because in many languages there are tense-distinctions in the verbs. But no people seems more time-orientated than the Japanese, and their verbal system is not too different from the aspectual structures of Hebrew. Furthermore, few peoples are so little interested in time as some of the tribes in Africa, many of whose languages have far more time distinctions than any Indo-European language has." [51]

J. Pedersen, T. Boman, and G. A. F. Knight are among the many Biblical scholars who have made pronouncements about "Hebrew thought" on the basis of grammatical categories. Knight, for example, asserts, "the Hebrew almost invariably thought in terms of the concrete. There are few abstract nouns in the Hebrew language." [52] T. Boman argues, again mainly on the basis of a grammatical and morphological investigation of linguistic categories, that Israelite thinking is "dynamic, vigorous, passionate" while "Greek thinking is static, peaceful, moderate, and harmonious." [53] For example, he claims that even stative verbs in Hebrew express an activity rather than portray a static state of affairs. Some of his most extreme arguments occur in connexion with quantity and number. The so-called "concept of number" is arrived at in Greek and in modern thinking in terms of visual representation. But the distinctive "concept" in Hebrew is evident from the "meaning" of the word "*two*": "*Shenayim* comes from the verb *shanah* – double, repeat, do for the second time. Thus the Hebrews form the concept of number not, as we do, through visual perception, but through frequent repetition of the same motion." [54] Similarly, the two words for "small" come from verbal forms meaning "to diminish", "to become less"; and the word *min* which expresses "more than" in comparative degree really means "away from". Boman actually concludes "Number or quantitive variety is thus not something spatial and quantitive but dynamic and qualitative."[55] When Saul is said to be "taller than" all the people, he dynamically towers over and "away from" the others!

But not only is this to argue on the basis of a supposed logico-grammatical parallelism; it is also to compound this particular error with further arguments of a diachronic or even etymological nature, and to ignore the role of context in semantics. If, for example, *min* means "away from" in *many* contexts, its context *in a comparison* restricts its semantic value to "more than". On the one hand, Boman's method flies in the face of structuralism; on the other hand, as Barr concludes, "Boman's kind of interpretation of language . . . depends to a great extent on the logico-grammatical unclarities of the older grammar, and evaporates with the stricter method of modern linguistics." [56] This is not to say that all of Boman's conclusions are wrong. For sometimes, as Barr admits, he expresses an insight which may have independent value as an *exegetical* observation. [57] Barr does not dispute that Hebrew uses of language may *sometimes* be more "dynamic" than Greek or English near-equivalents. The error, however, is to attempt to base such conclusions on dubious linguistic arguments which ignore structuralism and conventionality in language, and Barr has performed a valuable service in subjecting this approach to systematic criticism.

This brings us to a fundamental principle in semantics, about the relationship between language and "concepts". Commenting on claims made about the Hebrew or Greek "mind" or "way of thinking", David Crystal makes a crucial observation. He writes, "One often hears statements of the form 'Language X has a word for it, but Y has not, therefore X can say something Y cannot', or 'X is a better language than Y.' This fallacy stems from the misconception . . . that the unit of translation-equivalence between languages is the word . . . *The fact that Y has no word for an object does not mean that it cannot talk about that object; it cannot use the same mechanical means to do so, but it can utilize alternative forms of expression in its own structure for the same end.*" [58]

The implication which is made by the vast majority of writers in linguistics is that, in John Lyons' words, "No language can be said to be intrinsically 'richer' than another – each is adapted to the characteristic pursuits of its users." [59] The number of classifications under which "life" or "the world" could be described is virtually infinite. The distinctions which already exist within a given language, then, reflect only those that have hitherto in the past been of importance for that particular culture. But they do not absolutely *determine* the limits of what can be said in the future, for example by a creative thinker within that culture, or by a translator. This is not entirely to deny that there may be *some* element of truth in the well-known hypothesis of B. L. Whorf, based on the outlook of Wilhelm von Humboldt, that the structure of a language may influence a culture in terms of its thought. For, firstly, the translation or expression of certain ideas may be made *easier or more difficult* by the presence of this or that distinction, or lack of distinction, already to hand in a language. Secondly, *habits* of language-*use* make certain ways of thinking easier or more difficult in the sense shown by Wittgenstein. But difficulty does not mean impossibility. The weaknesses of the Whorf hypothesis have been demonstrated by Max Black, among others in several discussions. [60] Even so-called primitive languages are, as Edward Sapir admits (in the words of David Crystal) "not better or worse; only different." [61]

Biblical scholars, however, have been quick to draw far-reaching conclusions about Hebrew or Greek "thought" on the basis of vocabulary-stock. John Paterson, for example, makes the far-fetched statement that the ancient Israelite was "economical of words", because "Hebrew speech has less than 10,000 words while Greek has 200,000. Thus a word to the Hebrew was something . . . to be expended carefully." He was a man of few words, for "He knew there was power in words and that such power must not be used indiscriminately." [62] I have tried to expose the fallaciousness of this whole approach in the study to which I have referred on the supposed power of words in the biblical writings.

James Barr has little difficulty in citing and criticizing what he calls "arguments of the 'the Greeks had a word for it' type which so proliferate in Biblical theology." [63] For example, J. A. T. Robinson writes, "If we ask why it was that the Jews here (i.e. in language about "flesh" and "body") made do with one word (*basar*) where the Greeks required two (*σάρξ* and *σῶμα*) we come up against some of the most fundamental assumptions of Hebraic thinking about man." The difference in vocabulary-stock shows, according to Robinson, "that the Hebrews never posed, like the Greeks, certain questions the answer to which would have forced them to differentiate the 'body' from the 'flesh'." [64] Barr comments, "This statement could not have been written except in a total neglect of linguistic semantics." [65] It may be that this criticism should be softened in the light of the half truth represented by the Whorf hypothesis. But the main force of Barr's criticism is undoubtedly correct.

Barr also criticizes the methodological procedure of Kittel's *Theological Dictionary of the New Testament* according to which in effect, "the *lexical*-stock of N.T. Greek can be closely correlated with the *concept*-stock of the early Christians." [66] The *Dictionary* is a dictionary, in practice, of *words;* but it purports to be a "*concept*-history" (*Begriffsgeschichte*). Thus a contributor writes not about "the Greek word –" but "the Greek concept –". The temptation to which this leads is to commit the "illegitimate totality transfer" (which we described and discussed in II, 1). Since words and concepts do not necessarily correspond with each other isomorphically, such ambiguity of terms can only be misleading, and the confusion becomes still worse when some German scholars use *Begriff* to mean both "concept" and "word".

4. *LANGUE* AND *PAROLE*

The distinction between *langue* and *parole,* so important for Saussure, has been taken up in connexion with the form criticism of the gospels by Erhardt Güttgemanns. According to Saussure, language (either *langue* or, in a different sense *langage* cf. *Sprache*) must not be confused with speech or actual speaking (*parole*; cf. *sprechen*). *Langue* "is both a social product of the faculty of speech and a collection of necessary conventions that have been adopted by a social body to permit individuals to exercise that faculty." It is inherited within the community; and is "the sum of word-images stored in the minds of all individuals . . . a *storehouse* filled by the members of *a given community* . . . Language is not complete in any (individual) speaker, it exists perfectly only within a collectivity." *Langue* is thus the language-system which, as it were, waits in readiness for acts of speech. By contrast, *parole* is "the executive side of speaking . . . an individual act".[67]

Parole, the actual concrete act of speaking on the part of an individual, is the only object directly available for study by the linguist, although from its study he draws inferences about the structure of a *langue.* In his work on form-criticism E. Güttgemanns stresses the sociological and communal character of a *langue,* in contrast to the individual origin of *paroles.*[68] The *paroles* of the individual are objectified in written forms, for only an individual can do the actual writing. On the other hand the written *paroles* reflect the *oral* tradition of the *langue* of the community. One of Güttgemanns's points is that just as *langue* should not be confused with *parole,* so the "laws" which apply to the growth of oral traditions should not be made to apply to forms which already have been committed to writing by individuals. He believes that traditional form criticism in Germany has not been careful enough in keeping apart (1) written forms, individual speech, *parole*; and (2) oral forms, the language of the social community, *langue.*

One consequence of Saussure's distinction between *langue* and *parole* is of interest to the New Testament interpreter. We have already stressed in connexion with paradigmatic relations (in II.2) that "meaning is choice." The interpreter cannot know how much significance to attach to an author's use of word *x* until he also knows *what alternatives were available* to him at the same time. It is often said, for example, that the choice of ἀγαπῶ and ἀγάπη to mean "love" in the New Testament is especially significant because Christian writers chose them in preference to ἐρῶ and ἔρως and also to φιλῶ and φιλία. Supposedly *agapē* is a discerning and creative love; *erōs* is a passionate love which seeks self-gratification; whilst *philia* is a more general word for solicitous love or kindly inclination. But before we can say with certainty that a New Testament writer "chooses" to use ἀγάπη we must first establish whether the other two words for love were genuinely live options in the contexts concerned. It is not enough to ask whether different words for "love" might be available in first-century Greek in general. In this respect a lexicon may even be misleading. We must also ask: what words for love were available for use in the linguistic repertoire of the New Testament writer in question? Words may perhaps exist in Greek of which he is unaware, or for which he has a personal dislike for any of a variety of reasons. It would then be thoroughly misleading to argue that he has chosen word *x* as against *these.*

III. *Other Basic Tools in Field Semantics, Linguistics and Philosophy*

1. TOOLS IN FIELD SEMANTICS; TYPES OF OPPOSITION AND SYNONYMY

We have already seen the principle laid down by J. Trier that a word has meaning "only as part of a whole . . . it yields a meaning only within a field" (*nur im Feld gibt es Bedeutung*). Following the implications suggested by Saussure's structuralism, the task of the semanticist, as Trier saw it, was to set up lexical systems or sub-systems (*Wortfelder*) in terms of semantic relations of sameness or *similarity* of meaning (synonymy); of opposition or *incompatibility* of meaning (antonymy or complementarity); and of a special kind of *inclusiveness* of meaning (hyponymy) as where one word expresses a class ("furniture") to which the items belong ("chair", "table"). In broad outline this describes the programme of field semantics.[69]

E. A. Nida has suggested that more use should be made of the methods of field semantics in Biblical lexicology. He writes, "Quite new approaches to lexicology must be introduced . . . Critical studies of meaning must be based primarily upon the analysis of *related meanings of different words,* not upon the *different meanings of single words.*"[70] According to the traditional method, the lexicographer would take a word such as "run", for example, and distinguish in terms of its syntagmatic relations (1) running along the road; (2) running a business; (3) a run on the bank; and so on. But the method in field semantics would be to compare "run" in the first sense with words to which it stood in paradigmatic relation, such as "walk", "skip", "crawl"; and to compare "run" in the second sense with "control", "operate" and "direct". In this way a "field" very much like Saussure's "associative field", or system of paradigmatic relations, may be constructed.

The traditional attention to syntagmatic relations in lexicology is in fact *complementary* to newer methods. In New Testament Greek, a traditional lexicon-entry under πνεῦμα for example, would distinguish between (1) wind or breath; (2) men's spirit; (3) the Spirit of God; and (4) spirit-beings. The "field" approach would examine the first category in relation to ἄνεμος, πνέω and λαῖλαψ; the second category in relation to σάρξ, ψυχή, σῶμα, and so on. A diagram will illustrate how the two approaches can be complementary.

Katz and Foder put forward a comparable system of lexicology, in which they call the first explanatory term (noun) a *grammatical* marker; the second set of terms (e.g. human, divine) *semantic* markers; and the third set of subdivisions within the semantic markers (e.g. mind, breath) semantic *distinguishers*. I have then added Greek words which *commence* the construction of a semantic field.

We must now look more closely at different types of *opposition*. In a whole book devoted to the subject C. K. Ogden lists some twenty or so examples, most of which involve a distinctive type of semantic opposition.[71] The basic distinction, however, is between what he calls opposition by cut and opposition by scale. The sharpest type of opposition by cut is the relation of two-way exclusion known as *complementarity*. The denial of the one

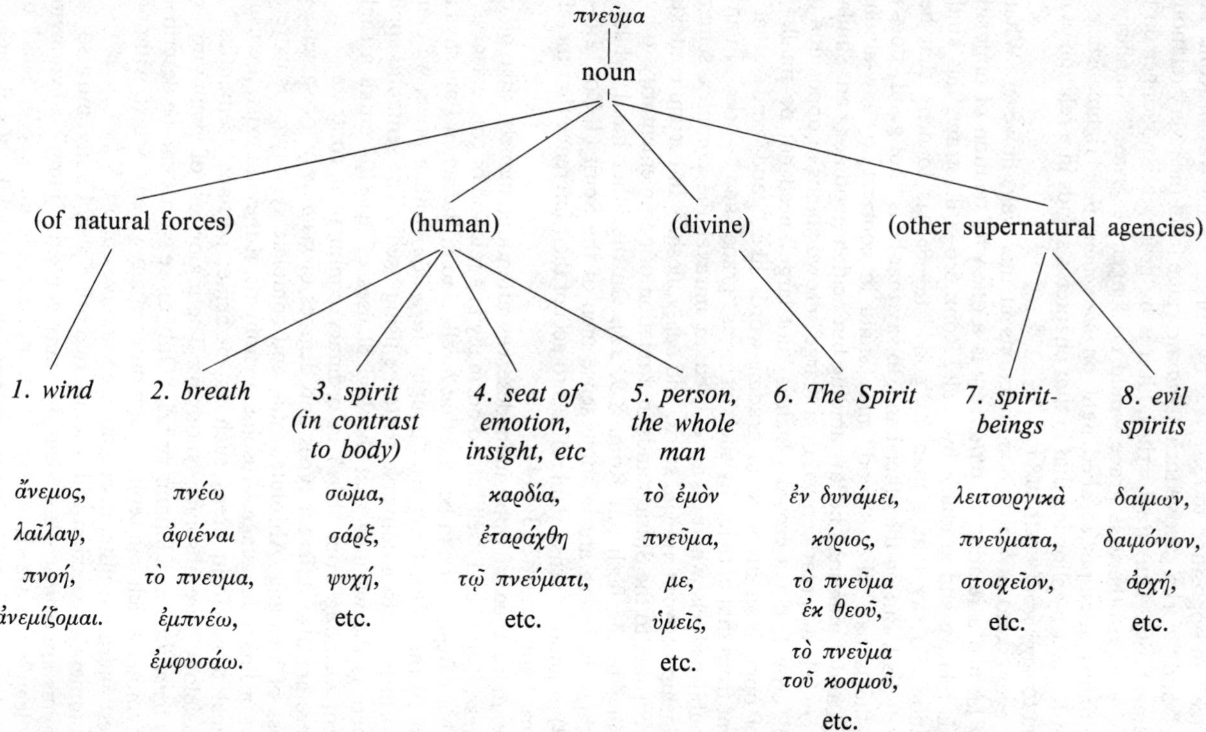
πνεῦμα
noun
(of natural forces)
(human)
(divine)
(other supernatural agencies)
1. wind
ἄνεμος,
λαῖλαψ,
πνοή,
ἀνεμίζομαι.
2. breath
πνέω
ἀφιέναι
τὸ πνευμα,
ἐμπνέω,
ἐμφυσάω.
3. spirit (in contrast to body)
σῶμα,
σάρξ,
ψυχή,
etc.
4. seat of emotion, insight, etc
καρδία,
ἐταράχθη
τῷ πνεύματι,
etc.
5. person, the whole man
τὸ ἐμὸν
πνεῦμα,
με,
ὑμεῖς,
etc.
6. The Spirit
ἐν δυνάμει,
κύριος,
τὸ πνεῦμα
ἐκ θεοῦ,
τὸ πνεῦμα
τοῦ κοσμοῦ,
etc.
7. spirit-beings
λειτουργικὰ
πνεύματα,
στοιχεῖον,
etc.
8. evil spirits
δαίμων,
δαιμόνιον,
ἀρχή,
etc.

involves the assertion of the other, and vice versa. Paul sets the word χάριτι "by grace", in opposition to ἐξ ἔργων "by works" in this way in Rom. 11:6. "Grace" and "works" derive their *semantic* value from their very relation of complementarity. Thus Paul writes, "if it is by grace, it is no longer on the basis of works; otherwise grace would no longer be *grace*." Similarly E. Güttgemanns attempts to shed light on δικαιοσύνη θεοῦ righteousness of God, in Rom. 1 by showing that in that chapter it stands in a relation of opposition to ὀργὴ θεοῦ, wrath of God.[72]

Not every kind of opposition functions in this way, however. What is strictly termed a relation of *antonymy* is a one-way relation of opposition which is relative and gradable by scale. Rom. 5:6–8 illustrates this kind of opposition. To say that a man is "good" (ἀγαθός) is to deny that he is positively bad. But on the other hand, to say that he is "not good" does not entail "he is bad". For "good" may stand in contrast to "law-abiding" (δίκαιος) and a man may be law-abiding but neither good nor bad. Similarly in the gospels a "great" crowd or a "large" crowd stands in opposition to a "small" crowd; but a crowd which is "not large" need not be small. The type of opposition involved in grading-words like "good" and "great" is different from that entailed by such terms as "grace" and "works". In an article published elsewhere I have tried to unravel the complex semantic relationship between πνεῦμα, spirit, and σάρξγ, flesh.[73] In certain contexts to live according to the Spirit stands in a relation of complementarity to living according to the flesh (cf. Rom. 8:9, 12). On the other hand, whilst the Corinthian believers are in some sense men of the Spirit (1 Cor. 2:6–16; 12–14) in another sense Paul refuses to accept their inference that therefore they are "not fleshly" (3:1–4).

One more type of opposition deserves attention, namely that of *converseness*. "Buy" and "sell" stand normally in a relation of converseness, for if *a* buys *x* from *b*, it can be said that *b* sells *x* to *a*. But when Paul says in 1 Cor. 6:19 that Christians are "bought" (ἀγοράζω) with a price, we cannot transform this into a converse sentence using "sell". The semantic application here is the warning that theological uses of ἀγοράζω entail a slightly different *meaning* from "buy" in ordinary commercial contexts.

There are also different types and degrees of *synonymy*, or sameness or likeness of meaning. Absolute, total, and complete synonymy is extremely rare in ordinary language. Absolute synonyms, if they do exist, are usually technical terms from areas such as medicine; perhaps "semantics" and "semasiology" are absolute synonyms. The major test of synonymy is *interchangeability*. S. Ullmann writes, "Only those words can be described as synonymous which can replace each other in any given context, without the slightest alteration either in cognitive or emotive import."[74]

A moment's reflection will disclose two principles. Firstly, most so-called synonyms are *context-dependent*. In many contexts "jump" is synonymous with "leap"; but we do not say "that noise made me leap." "Sick" often means the same as "ill"; but we do not talk about a bird of sick omen, nor say that we are ill of repeating the same thing. Similarly in New Testament

Greek *καινός* and *νέος* are clearly synonymous when both mean "new" as applied to the "covenant" (*διαθήκη*, e.g. cf. Heb. 8:8 with Heb. 12:24); but a writer would not presumably speak of *καινὸν φύραμα* (dough) or of a young man as *καινός*. It could be misleading, then, to answer "yes" or "no" to the simple question: are *καινός* and *νέος* synonyms? The semanticist will ask, rather: in what kinds of context, if any, are they synonymous?

Secondly, many words are synonymous with others at a cognitive level, but not in emotive terms or in terms of register. We might write to "decline" an invitation, but hardly to "reject" it; yet it is difficult to see any great difference between them in cognitive scope. "Decease" is more formal and professional than "death"; whilst "passed on", "popped off", "was called to higher service" and "kicked the bucket" all have their own special overtones. Similarly in certain contexts Mark's *κράβαττος*, mattress, may be cognitively synonymous with Matthew and Luke's *κλίνη*, bed; but the colloquial overtones of Mark's word are deemed inappropriate by Matthew and Luke. Sometimes similar actions or attitudes can be described by terms suggesting overtones of moral approval or blame. Thus Bertrand Russell begins his well-known "emotive conjugations" as follows: "I am firm, you are obstinate, he is pig-headed; . . . I have reconsidered, you have changed your mind, he has gone back on his word." "Reasoning" in the New Testament can be alluded to with overtones of disapproval (*διαλογισμός*) or either neutrally or with approval (cf. *νόημα, νοῦς*).

Three further comments may be made about synonymy. Firstly, another test of context-dependent synonymy can be provided by antonymy. "Wide" is a synonym of "broad", for example, in contexts in which "narrow" would be applicable: a narrow plank or a narrow road. But we do not talk about a narrow accent; only of a broad one. "Deep" and "profound" thought stand in opposition to "shallow" thought; but the opposite to a deep voice is a high one. Secondly, synonymy may be explored in diachronic linguistics. Sometimes over a period of many years two words may move more closely together in meaning, and if they become total synonyms one may eventually disappear. David Clines has shown in an unpublished study that this happens to *ἀγαθός* and *καλός*. In classical Greek they are distinct, *ἀγαθός* being reserved mainly for moral goodness; in New Testament Greek they are usually synonymous; in modern Greek *ἀγαθός* has disappeared. Sometimes, however, the procedure may be reversed, and what were once synonyms may develop in different directions. Thirdly, synonymy raises questions of style. Many writers call on similar terms, for example, simply to avoid repetition of the same word.[75] In such contexts similar terms may become more clearly synonymous. It is likely that this is the case, for example, with *ἀγαπῶ* and *φιλῶ* in John 21:15–17.

2. TYPES OF VAGUENESS AND METAPHOR

Certain kinds of vagueness are useful and desirable. Language would be impoverished if we could never talk about "furniture", but only about chairs and tables; or never talk about something's being "red", without specifying whether we mean crimson or scarlet; or never talk about "flowers" without explicating whether we mean tulips, roses, or a mixture of both. When the New Testament interpreter comes across a superordinate term like *κακία*, badness, *it is a mistake to insist on a greater degree of precision than that suggested by the text.* I have argued this point in two articles, one with reference to the applications of the parables, the other with reference to the meaning of *σάρξ* in 1 Cor. 5:5.[76]

One type of vagueness is due to lack of *specificity,* of which superordinate terms supply some, but not all, examples. A skilful politician may retain universal support, for example, if he promises to "take steps" to meet a crisis; he loses some votes if he is forced to specify *what* steps.

Another type of vagueness is due to lack of a clear *cut-off* point on a scale. Words like "urban", "warm", and "middle-aged" are very useful, not least because they are *not* quantified precisely like "above 60°F." or "between 39 and 61 years old."

A third type of vagueness is that of *polymorphous* concepts, which are of special interest in philosophy. The meaning of a word of this type cannot be given in generalizing terms, but only as different meanings apply by way of example in different contexts. Ludwig Wittgenstein, Gilbert Ryle and others, insist that we cannot say in general what "thinking" *is*; only give examples of the application of the term in specific situations. G. E. M. Anscombe examines the logic of "intention" in this way; and A. R. White underlines the polymorphous character of "attention". What attending *is* depends on what we are attending *to.* It seems likely, to my mind, that *πίστις*, faith, has this polymorphous character, especially in Paul. Depending on the situation or context it may involve intellectual assent, or practical obedience; it may stand eschatologically in contrast to sight; or mean a Christ-centred appropriation of God's gift. To try to overcome this so-called ambiguity by offering a generalizing definition is to invite misunderstanding about what "faith" means.

Too often in biblical interpretation exegetes have looked for exactness where the author chose vagueness. *Must* the "horrifying abomination" in Mark 13:14 refer specifically to the violence of the zealots, or to a statue of Titus, or to Caligula or Hadrian? Must "Son of man" be robbed of an ambiguity which may have commended the term to Jesus? Might not the New Testament writers have wished to keep some ideas open-ended no less often than we do?

We must also glance briefly at *metaphor,* which is not unrelated to questions about vagueness. A live metaphor presupposes a well-established use of language (often popularly called the "literal" meaning) and then extends this use in a way that is novel or logically odd. The aim of this extension is twofold. Firstly, it sets up a tension which is intended to provoke the hearer into some reaction; secondly, it provides a model, or picture, or frame of reference, according to which the hearer now "sees" the point in question in a new way. It should be stressed, however, that this happens only when a metaphor is genuinely "live". Most metaphors very soon become dead metaphors. This is one crucial difficulty confronting the New Testament interpreter about biblical metaphors. The well-known metaphor of the Christian's armour in Eph. 6:14–17 has become dead metaphor, or even a mere analogy or simile, because a term like "sword of the spirit" has itself become an established use of language. Sometimes a new translation will recapture some force by replacing an old metaphor by a new but closely-related one. Thus "gird up the loins of your mind" in 1 Pet.1:13 becomes "stripped for action" in the NEB. On the other hand "anchor of the soul" (Heb. 6:19), "fed you with milk" (1 Cor. 3:2) and "living stones" (1 Pet. 2:5) still retain an element of their original tension without alteration.

The interpreter has to steer a very careful path between evaporating the *force* of a metaphor by total explication, and leaving its meaning open to doubt. If a metaphor is already dead even in the New Testament, no harm is done by erring on the side of clarity. Thus "hand of the Lord" (Acts 11:21) becomes "the Lord's power" in *Today's English Version;* and "pass from me this cup" (Luke 22:42) becomes "free me from having to suffer this trial" in the Spanish *Version Popular*. But it is a different matter when the metaphor is a live one. It is difficult to justify, for example, the rendering of Paul's "put on Christ" (Gal. 3:27) by "take upon themselves the qualities of Christ himself" (*Today's English Version*). A metaphor is to make the hearer think for himself, often by means of some deliberate ambiguity. It gives us something as a model for something else without making explicit in exactly what way it is supposed to be a model.[77] We could say of metaphor what F. Waismann says of poetry: "Its mission is to break through the wall of conventional values that encloses us, to startle us into seeing the world through fresh eyes."[78] If metaphor is eliminated or turned into simile, as W. L. Wonderly recommends as a "basic technique" of popular Bible translation, this entire dimension is lost.[79]

The literature on metaphor is extensive.[80] It should warn us against ever talking about Biblical metaphors as "mere" metaphors, as if to imply that metaphorical language is somehow inferior to non-metaphorical discourse. But it is also evident from this range of literature that there are different types of metaphors with different purposes; and that the line between metaphor and non-metaphor is not in fact a line but a continuous scale, passing through "dead" metaphor and merely figurative language such as metonymy or synecdoche. Robert Funk and Sallie TeSelle have argued that the parables of Jesus function as metaphor; and in theology, especially with reference to Bultmann, it is crucial to distinguish between metaphor and myth.

3. SOME EFFECTS OF RECENT APPROACHES IN LINGUISTICS

Ideally a comprehensive discussion of the present subject would include an examination of transformational grammar with special reference to the work of Noam Chomsky. However, in practice this area is far too complex and technical to allow for a brief summary in a few paragraphs. Our aim in this section, therefore, must be more modest. We shall attempt to describe and evaluate only the uses to which this approach has been put at the hands of those engaged in Bible translation. This concerns especially the work of Eugene A. Nida, who speaks enthusiastically of the insights of transformational grammar, and in particular draws on the technique of reducing the surface structure of stretches of language to its underlying kernels.

Nida and Taber write, "One of the most important insights coming from 'transformational grammar' is the fact that in all languages there are half a dozen to a dozen basic structures out of which all the more elaborate formations are constructed by means of so-called 'transformations'. In contrast, back-transformation, then, is the analytic process of reducing the surface structure to its underlying kernels."[81] We have already illustrated this principle by noting certain kernel forms behind Eph. 1:7. Nida and Taber further cite the example of Eph. 2:8, 9: "For by grace you have been saved through faith; and this is not your own doing, it is the gift of God – not because of works lest any man should boast." This can be reduced to seven kernel sentences: (1) God showed you grace; (2) God saved you; (3) you believed; (4) you did not save yourselves; (5) God gave it; (6) you did not work for it; (7) no man should boast.[82] The kernel sentences may in principle undergo further transformation in terms of what Chomsky calls "deep structure", but whilst this is of interest in theoretical linguistics Nida and Taber question its practical value for the Bible translator. The translator's task, they suggest, is firstly to reduce utterances to kernel sentences by "back-transformation" (if necessary making explicit any elements that are still ambiguous), and then at the end of the process to re-formulate the kernels into a linguistic structure which best accords with a native speaker's understanding in the receptor language.

One merit of this approach is to demonstrate, once again, the arbitrariness of surface-grammar and the fallacy of assumptions about logico-grammatical parallelism. The surface-grammar of the final translation may not necessarily correspond to the surface-grammar of the original Greek. In this respect, translation is a creative task and not merely a mechanical one.

We must also note, however, that the contrast between surface grammar and deep grammar is used as a means of eliminating certain types of *ambiguity*. As long ago as 1924, Otto Jespersen noted the fundamental difference in structure between two such superficially parallel phrases as "the doctor's arrival" and "the doctor's house". The reason for the difference is that, in Chomsky's terms, "the doctor's arrival" derives from the transform "the doctor arrived", which has the form NP/Vi (noun phrase/intransitive verb); whilst "the doctor's house" derives from the transform "the doctor has a house", which has the form NP/Vt//N[a] (noun phrase/transitive verb//noun in the accusative).[83]

This example of transformational techniques is already employed, by implication, in New Testament exegesis and in traditional grammar. The traditional contrast between "objective genitive" and "subjective genitive" is usually explained in what amounts to transformational terms. In 1 Cor. 1:6, for example, the phrase "the testimony of Christ" (τὸ μαρτύριον τοῦ Χριστοῦ) is, as it stands, ambiguous. If it is subjective genitive it derives from the transform "Christ testified", in which "Christ" is subject; if it is objective genitive it derives from the transform "Paul testifies to Christ", in which "Christ" is (indirect) object. Similarly, as the phrase stands, "love of God" (ἡ ἀγάπη τοῦ Θεοῦ) in 1 John is ambiguous, and has to be interpreted as deriving either from the transform "God loves . . ." (subjective genitive), or from ". . . loves God" (objective genitive). It is a regular manoeuvre in *Today's English Version* to remove ambiguity of this kind by clearly reflecting one particular transform. Thus "light of the world" (Mt. 5:14) becomes "light for the world" (objective genitive, from "lights the world"); and "the promise of the Holy Spirit" (Acts 2:33) becomes "the Holy Spirit, as his Father had promised" (objective genitive, from the transform "the Father promised the Holy Spirit", excluding the alternative transform "the Holy Spirit promised").

Transformational grammar often seeks to make explicit elements of meaning which are implied, but not expressed, in a sentence. Chomsky comments, "Surface similarities may hide distinctions of a fundamental nature . . . It may be necessary to guide and draw out the speaker's intuition in perhaps fairly subtle ways before we can determine what is the actual character of his knowledge." [84] This principle is of positive value in Bible translation, provided it is recognised that, once again, translation inevitably becomes *interpretation*. Sometimes it is possible that this technique of making linguistic elements explicit goes further than the text allows. Thus it is questionable whether *Today's English Version* is justified in translating καὶ ἰδὼν ὁ Ἰησοῦς τὴν πίστιν αὐτῶν as "Jesus saw *how much* faith they had" (Mark 2.5). The R.S.V. simply has "when Jesus saw their faith". But presumably the translators of *Today's English Version* would claim to be making explicit what *they judged* was implicit in the text.

One further point arises from this principle of making linguistic elements explicit. It demonstrates that *statistical* statements about word-occurrences may often be superficial or even misleading guides to the occurrence of actual concepts. K. L. Burres makes this point about "boasting" in Rom. 3:27.[85] The text reads: "Then what becomes of our *boasting*? It is excluded. On what principle? On the principle of works? No, but on the principle of faith." In this form of the text "boasting" occurs once only. But if we allow a transformational analysis to unpack occurrences which are implicit but functionally operative, Burres suggests that we now have: "Then what becomes of our *boasting?* Our *boasting* is excluded. On what principle is our *boasting* excluded? Is our *boasting* excluded on the principle of works? No. Our *boasting* is excluded on the principle of faith". "*Boasting*" now occurs five times.

Although Nida succeeds in demonstrating points of value in transformational approaches for Bible translation, however, I still have hesitations about certain uses of these techniques. Firstly, in spite of Nida's obvious awareness of the problem, the translator must be on guard against thinking of semantic equivalence simply in cognitive terms. If "decease", departure from this life", and so on, could all be transformed into the kernel sentence "he dies", it would be easy to overlook the emotive, cultural, or religious overtones of meaning which may have been important in the original utterance. Nida would no doubt agree that every effort must be made not to lose sight of this problem. Indeed he and Taber stress this very point in a chapter entitled "Connotative Meaning". Secondly, the notion of kernel sentences comes too near for comfort to Wittgenstein's earlier notions in the *Tractatus* about elementary propositions. We cannot attempt to evaluate the theories of the *Tractatus* in this essay, but it is not irrelevant to point out that in his later writings Wittgenstein expressed his own deep dissatisfaction with theories of meaning which are arrived at in this way. Theories about a "universal" grammar of objects, events, abstracts and relations are too reminiscent of the theory of language which Wittgenstein first propounded and then rejected. These criticisms do not invalidate this whole approach, but they perhaps call for caution over the ways in which it is used.

IV. *A Concluding Example of Semantic Exploration: Justification by Faith*

By way of conclusion I shall try to show how a particular set of problems in New Testament interpretation may be solved, or at least made to look very different, by explorations into questions of semantics and logic. Since hitherto we have been looking mainly at tools which have been forged in general linguistics, I shall conclude by glancing at some possibilities which emerge against the background of linguistic philosophy. Beginning with the contrast between descriptive and evaluative language-uses, I shall draw on Wittgenstein's notion of "seeing as", on his idea of the "home" setting of a language-game, and on the concept of analycity or "grammaticalness" in his own sense of the term. I shall apply these notions to three standard problems raised by justification in Pauline thought.[86]

1. How can the Christian be both "righteous" and yet also a sinner? E. Käsemann speaks of the "logical embarrassment" of this doctrine, and F. Prat exclaims, "How can the false be true, or how can God declare true what he knows to be false?"[87] Various answers have been put forward: for example, that *dikaióō* (δικαιόω) means to make righteous, rather than to count righteous; that "righteousness" refers only to God's acting as champion, to vindicate the oppressed; that the "righteousness" of God means his saving power; or that "being made righteous" means "put into a right relation with God", without special reference to ethics or to ethical status.[88] For reasons which cannot be discussed here, I do not think that any of these approaches is entirely satisfactory. The "paradox" remains that the Christian is a sinner, but that God regards him as if he were righteous.

2. Is justification present or future? Many passages indicate that it is a present reality (Rom. 5:1, 9; 9:30; 1 Cor. 6:11); but in Gal. 5:5 Paul states

unambiguously that believers "wait for the hope of righteousness" in the future. Many interpreters of Paul, following Weiss and Schweitzer, believe that it "belongs strictly speaking" to the future, but is also effective in the present.

3. How can Paul place "faith" in contrast to "works" when it is not, as Whiteley puts it, "another kind of work"; it is not a species of the same genus?[89] It is not as if "having faith" were a trump card which could be played if one had run out of "good works".

Taking these three problems together, I shall now make three suggestions about the semantics, or logic, of Paul's language.

(1) In speaking of the believer as *iustus et peccator* we are not dealing with two sets of descriptive assertions which may be true or false; we are dealing with two different *evaluations* or *verdicts* each of which is valid within its own frame of reference. Whereas two mutually exclusive *assertions* stand in a relation of contradiction or perhaps "paradox", this is a misleading way of describing the logical relation between two competing evaluations. If one man claims "*x* is black", and another man claims, "*x* is white", one of them must be wrong. But if one claims "*x* is satisfactory" or "*x* is fast" and the other claims "*x* is unsatisfactory" or "*x* is slow", each may be a valid assessment *in relation to a different frame of reference.* In particular, Wittgenstein examines the phenomenon of "seeing *x* as *y*".[90] A man may see a puzzle-picture, now as a series of dots, now as a face. He may see a drawing of a cube now as a glass cube, now as an open box, now as a wire frame, now as three boards forming a solid angle. What is seen remains the same; but how it is seen depends on its function within a system or frame of reference provided by the viewer. If a thing can be "seen as" more than one possible thing, there must be more than one possible frame of reference within which it can be viewed. Donald Evans argues this point about "onlooks", in which we "look on" *x* as *y.*[91] In Pauline thought the Christian is "seen as" or "looked on" as righteous or as a sinner, because he can stand within two alternative frames of reference.

(2) These two frames belong, respectively, to eschatology and to history. In the context of history, in terms of what he is in this world and of what his past has made him, the Christian remains a sinner. Justification is strictly a matter of the future, when he will be acquitted at the last judgment. Nevertheless the eschatological frame is the decisive one because it corresponds with future reality, and it can be brought forward and appropriated in the present by faith. In this sense, justification becomes a present reality, for it is granted "apart from the law" (Rom. 3:21, cf. Gal. 2:16; Phil. 3:9). In as far as the believer is already accorded his eschatological status, viewed in that context he is justified. In as far as he still lives in the everyday world, he remains a sinner who awaits future justification. History and eschatology each provide a frame or logical context in which a different verdict on the Christian is valid and appropriate. In Wittgenstein's sense of the "home" setting of a language-game, eschatology is the home setting in which the logic of justification by faith receives its currency.

(3) We are now in a position to see that "justification" and "faith" have an internal, "grammatical", or analytical relation to each other in this setting. "Faith", in the context of justification (certainly not in all contexts in Paul) means the acceptance of this future-orientated onlook as being effectively relevant in the present. The verdict which, for external history, will be valid only at the judgment day is valid *for faith* now. From an external viewpoint, justification remains future; but faith involves stepping out of that purely historical frame of reference. In this sense, faith for Paul is not as remote from Heb. 11:1 ("faith is the substance of things hoped for") as it is often imagined to be. But if this is true, faith may now be seen not as a merely external means which somehow "procures" justification, but as *part of what justification is and entails.* In Wittgenstein's terms, to say "justification requires faith" is to make an analytical statement about the *grammar* or *concept* of justification. It is like saying, "Green is a colour", or "Water boils at 100°C."[92] It does not so much state a condition, in the sense of *qualification* for justification, as state something more about what justification involves and *is*.

I have deliberately concluded with a speculative example suggested by the philosophical side of semantics. Many of the insights drawn from linguistics offer largely negative warnings to the New Testament interpreter, urging him to proceed with rigour and with caution, and challenging a number of cherished assumptions. A number of insights drawn from philosophers, however, seem to offer fresh perspectives sometimes of a more positive nature.[93] In this essay we have also noted philosophical contributions to the study of synonymy and metaphor. Both sides, however, offer indispensable contributions to the interpreter of the New Testament in so far as he is concerned with language and meanings. He can ignore their methods and conclusions only at his own peril.

NOTES

1. John Lyons, *Structural Semantics. An Analysis of Part of the Vocabulary of Plato* (Oxford 1963), pp. 23–4. Cf. C. K. Ogden and I. A. Richards, *The Meaning of Meaning* (London 1923), pp. 306–7; cf. pp. 308–36, and also Stephen R. Schiffer, *Meaning* (Oxford 1972), pp. 1–5.

2. J. Barr, *The Semantics of Biblical Language* (Oxford 1961); E. Güttgemanns, *Studia Linguistica Neotestamentica. Gesammelte Aufsätze zur linguistischen Grundlage einer Neutestamentlichen Theologie* (Beiträge zur evangelischen Theologie Bd. 60; Münich 1971); R. Kieffer, *Essais de méthodologie néotestamentaire* (Lund 1972); J. F. A. Sawyer, *Semantics in Biblical Research, New Methods of Defining Hebrew Words for Salvation* (London 1972) and Kenneth L. Burres *Structural Semantics in the Study of the Pauline Understanding of Revelation* (unpublished Ph.D. Dissertation Northwestern University, Evanston, Illinois, 1970; University Microfilms Xerox, Ann Arbor, Michigan 71–1810). Cf. also the journal edited by Güttgemanns, entitled *Linguistica Biblica: Interdisziplinäre Zeitschrift für Theologie und Linguistik,* and published in Bonn: see also the discussions of Barr's work in: G. Friedrich "Semasiologie und Lexicologie", in TLZ 94 (1969) cols. 801–16, especially cols.

803–7; cf also T. Boman, ibid., 87 (1962), cols. 262–5; D. Hill, *Greek Words and Hebrew Meanings. Studies in the Semantics of Soteriological Terms* (Cambridge 1967); J. Barr "Common Sense and Biblical Language", in *Biblica* 49 (1968), pp. 377–87; and especially K. Arvid Tangberg, "Linguistics and Theology: an Attempt to Analyse and Evaluate James Barr's Argumentation . . .", in *The Bible Translator* 24 (1973), p. 301–10. For other articles involving semantics see G. B. Caird "Towards a Lexicon of the Septuagint" in JTS 19 (1968), pp. 453–75.

3. For my articles see notes 9, 48, 73, 76, 86. For D. D. Evans see n. 91 and for O. R. Jones see n. 93.

4. S. Ullmann, *The Principles of Semantics,* (Oxford 1957[2]), p. 1.

5. A. Darmesteter, *La vie des mots étudiée dans leur significations* Paris, 1895[5]) especially in pp. 138–48 on synonymy; and M. Bréal *Semantics, Studies in the Science of Meaning* (London 1900), especially chapters 14 and 15 on polysemy.

6. "Probably all mediaeval philosophers, all the 16th and 17th century authors, and later Johnson and Mill, and still later Frege . . . Meinong, Russell . . . and Wittgenstein (in their earlier work) – all of them *de facto* constructed theories of meaning of *names,* and tried, with varying success, to extend them to all linguistic expressions, above all to sentences. In doing so they were motivated by the belief that the meaning of a sentence . . . is a function of the meanings of its components." J. Pelc, *Studies in Functional Logical Semiotics of Natural Language* (The Hague 1971), p. 58.

7. M. Black, *The Labyrinth of Language* (London 1968), p. 9.

8. S. Ullmann, *The Principles of Semantics,* p. 16.

9. I have used this example in A. C. Thiselton, "The use of Philosophical Categories in New Testament Hermeneutics", in *The Churchman* 87 (1973), p. 96.

10. F. de Saussure, *Cours de linguistique générale* (édition critique par R. Engler; Wiesbaden 1967, 3 fascicles), fasc. 2, pp. 147–73 and 303–16; cf. E.T. *Course in General Linguistics* (London 1960, ed. by C. Bally et al.), p. 67–78, and 134–9.

11. Cf. L. Wittgenstein, *Tractatus Logico-Philosophicus* (London 1961), 4.0031; and B. Russell, "On Denoting", in *Mind* 14 (1905) pp. 479–93.

12. B. Russell, loc. cit., p. 480.

13. K. Barth, *The Epistle to the Philippians* (London 1962), p. 121; and W. Hendriksen, *Philippians* (London 1962, rp. 1973), p. 192 (his italics). Similarly cf. J. J. Muller, *The Epistles of Paul to the Philippians and to Philemon* (Grand Rapids 1955), p. 140.

14. F. W. Beare, *The Epistle to the Philippians* (London 1959), pp. 100 and 145–6. Cf. W. F. Arndt and F. W. Gingrich, (W. Bauer) *A Greek-English Lexicon of the New Testament and Other Early Christian Literature* (Chicago 1957), p. 882.

15. E. A. Nida, *Towards a Science of Translating* (Leiden 1964), especially pp. 9–10 and 60–63 and chapters 8–10; and W. L. Wonderly, *Bible Translations for Popular Use* (London 1968), pp. 50–55 and 149–172.

16. J. F. A. Sawyer, "Context of Situation and Sitz im Leben. Some Questions concerning Meaning in Classical Hebrew", in *Proceedings of the Newcastle on Tyne Philosophical Society* 1 (1967), p. 137–47. Similarly, cf. the important work of Erhardt Güttgemanns, *Offene Fragen zur Formgeschichte des Evangeliums* (Beiträge zur evangelischen Theologie, 54; Munich 1971[2]) p. 44–68; 174–7; *et passim.*

17. J. F. A. Sawyer, loc. cit., p. 140.

18. F. de Saussure, *Course in General Linguistics,* pp. 80–81; cf. *Cours de linguistique générale,* p. 177–8.

19. F. de Saussure *Course in General Linguistics,* p. 81 (Édition critique p. 181–2).

20. E.g. J. Lyons, *Introduction to Theoretical Linguistics,* pp. 45–50; S. Ullmann, *The Principles of Semantics,* pp. 144–52; A. Martinet *Elements of General Linguistics* (London 1964), p. 37f; David Crystal, *Linguistics, Language and Religion* (London 1965), pp. 57–9; and K. L. Burres, *Structural Semantics in the Study of the Pauline Understanding of Revelation,* p. 36–40.

21. J. Barr, op. cit., p. 108.

22. Some of these examples, and many more, are suggested by S. Ullmann, *Semantics,* pp. 97–9, and *Principles of Semantics,* pp. 171–257.

23. J. Barr, op. cit., p. 109 (my italics).
24. E. Jacob, *Theology of the Old Testament* (London 1958), p. 159.
25. Ibid., p. 113.
26. Ibid., p. 116; cf. N. Snaith, "The Language of the Old Testament", in *The Interpreter's Bible* (Nashville 1952) vol. 1, p. 224.
27. J. Barr, op. cit., p. 149–51.
28. As in C. Hodge, *The First Epistle to the Corinthians* (London 1958), p. 64.
29. D. Crystal, op. cit., p. 58.
30. F. de Saussure, *Course in General Linguistics,* p. xii.
31. Ibid., p. 114, and *Cours de linguistique générale* (édition critique) fasc. 2, p. 259 col. i (Baskin's translation has not been without criticism).
32. F. de Saussure, (*Course in General Linguistics,* p. 166 (édition critique, pp. 261–262).
33. Ibid., p. 89; cf. p. 110.
34. Ibid., p. 123.
35. J. Lyons, *Introduction to Theoretical Linguistics,* p. 75. Similarly, cf. R. H. Robins, *General Linguistics. An Introductory Survey* (London 1964), p. 47–50; David Crystal, *Linguistics* (London 1971), pp. 163–6; and Herbert E. Brekle, *Semantik. Ein Einführung in die sprachwissenschaftlich Bedeutungslehre* (Munich 1972), p. 81–8.
36. E. Güttgemanns, *Studia linguistica neotestamentica,* especially pp. 75–93; and K. L. Burres, op. cit., p. 59–123.
37. K. L. Burres, op. cit., p. 107–23 and 222–307; cf. especially charts 5–7 on pp. 282–3, 291 and 294–7.
38. Trier, *Der Deutsche Wortschatz im Sinnbezirk des Verstandes* (Heidelberg 1931), p. 6.
39. G. Stern, *Meaning and Change of Meaning. With Special Reference to the English Language* (Göteborgs Högskolas Arsskrift, 38, Gothenburg 1931), p. 85.
40. S. Ullmann, *Semantics,* p. 49.
41. Ibid., p. 218.
42. Ibid.
43. E. A. Nida "The Implications of Contemporary Linguistics for Biblical Scholarship", in JBL 91 (1972), p. 86 (cf. pp. 73–89).
44. M. Joos "Semantic Axiom Number One" in *Language* 48 (1972), p. 257 (cf. pp. 258–65, in which Joos acknowledges his indebtedness for this approach to Stern).
45. E. A. Nida, loc. cit., p. 86.
46. R. H. Robins, *General Linguistics,* p. 22.
47. F. de Saussure, op. cit., p. 68 (cf. édition critique, p. 152–3).
48. Cf. A. C. Thiselton, "The Supposed Power of Words in the Biblical Writings", JTS 25 (1974), pp. 283–299; J. Lyons, *Introduction to Theoretical Linguistics,* pp. 4–8, 59–75, 272 and 403; S. Ullmann, *Semantics,* pp. 80–115; L. R. Palmer, op. cit., p. 175–8; E. A. Nida, *Towards a Science of Translating* (Leiden 1964), pp. 46–51; P. Naert, "Arbitraire et nécessaire en linguistique", in *Studia Linguistica* (1947), pp. 5–10.
49. F. de Saussure, op. cit., p. 109.
50. Ibid., p. 110.
51. E. A. Nida, "The Implications of Contemporary Linguistics for Biblical Scholarship", loc. cit., p. 83.
52. G. A. F. Knight, *A Biblical Approach to the Doctrine of the Trinity* (Edinburgh 1953), p. 8.
53. T. Boman, *Hebrew Thought compared with Greek* (London 1960), p. 27.
54. Ibid., p. 165.
55. Ibid.
56. J. Barr, op. cit., p. 67; cf. pp. 46–88.
57. E.g. Boman's remarks about practical atheism in Psalm 14:1, op. cit., p. 48–9.
58. D. Crystal, *Language, Linguistics and Religion,* p. 144 (my italics).
59. J. Lyons, *Introduction to Theoretical Linguistics,* p. 45.
60. Cf. M. Black, *The Labyrinth of Language,* pp. 63–90; and "Linguistic Relativity. The Views of Benjamin Lee Whorf", in *Philosophical Review* 68 (1959), p. 228–38; cf. also S. Ullmann, "Words and Concepts" in *Language and Style* (Oxford 1964), pp. 212–28.

61. D. Crystal, *Linguistics,* p. 72; cf. p. 49.
62. J. Paterson, *The Book that is Alive. Studies in Old Testament Life and Thought as Set Forth by the Hebrew Sages* (New York 1954), p. 3.
63. J. Barr, op. cit., p. 35; cf. pp. 21–45.
64. J. A. T. Robinson, *The Body, A Study in Pauline Theology* (London 1952), pp. 12 and 13.
65. J. Barr, op. cit., p. 35.
66. Ibid., p. 207; cf. pp. 206–19.
67. F. de Saussure, op. cit., pp. 9 and 13–14 (my italics); cf. H. E. Brekle, *Semantik,* pp. 50–54.
68. E. Güttgemanns, *Offene Fragen zur Formgeschichte,* pp. 50–54.
69. Cf. J. Trier, op. cit., 6ff. I am not concerned to draw too careful a distinction between the "linguistic field" (*sprachliches Feld*) of Trier and the "semantic field" (*Bedeutungsfeld*) of Ipsen or Porzig. For the distinction see S. Ullmann, *The Principles of Semantics,* pp. 156–69; cf. also J. Lyons, *Structural Semantics,* pp. 44–50.
70. E. A. Nida, "The Implications of Contemporary Linguistics for Biblical Scholarship", loc. cit., p. 85 (my italics). cf. also E. Güttgemanns, *Offene Fragen zur Formgeschichte des Evangeliums,* pp. 54–7.
71. C. K. Ogden, *Opposition. A Linguistic and Psychological Analysis,* (Bloomington 1967²), especially p. 65–90. On the three most basic types of opposition, however, see J. Lyons, *Introduction to Theoretical Linguistics,* pp. 460–70.
72. E. Güttgemanns, *Studia Linguistica neotestamentica,* pp. 87–93. On antithesis in Paul see especially Norbert Schneider, *Die rhetorische Eigenart der paulinischen Antithese* (Tübingen 1970); J. Nélis, "Les Antitheses litteraires dans les épîtres de S. Paul", in *Nouvelle Revue Théologique* 70 (1948), pp. 360–87; J. Weiss, "Beiträge zur Paulinischen Rhetorik" in *Theologische Studien Bernhard Weiss* (Göttingen 1897), pp. 165–247; and Willard H. Taylor, *The Antithetic Method in Pauline Theology* (unpublished doctoral dissertation for Northwestern University; Evanston, Illinois, 1959).
73. A. C. Thiselton, "The Meaning of *Σάρξ* in 1 Corinthians 5.5: A Fresh Approach in the Light of Logical and Semantic Factors", in SJT 26 (1973), p. 204–28.
74. S. Ullmann, *The Principles of Semantics,* pp. 108–9; cf. pp. 110–14, and *Semantics,* pp. 141–55 and J. Lyons, *Introduction to Theoretical Linguistics,* p. 446–53. From the philosophical side cf. W. P. Alston, op. cit., pp. 44–7; J. Searle, op. cit., p. 5–12, N. Goodman, "A Note on Likeness of Meaning", in *Analysis* 10 (1950), pp. 115–8; and other contributions in *Analysis* by Rollins and Thomson, in 11 (1951), pp. 18–19, 38–45, and 12 (1952), pp. 73–6.
75. See S. Ullmann, *Semantics,* pp. 152–3.
76. A. C. Thiselton "The Parables as Language Event. Some Comments on Fuchs's Hermeneutics in the Light of Linguistic Philosophy" in SJT 23 (1970) especially pp. 450–58 and 461–7; and "The Meaning of *Σάρξ* in 1 Cor. 5:5", op. cit., especially pp. 207–8, 217–18 and 227–8.
77. W. P. Alston, *Philosophy of Language* (Englewood Cliffs, N.J. 1964), op. cit., p. 102.
78. F. Waismann, "The Resources of Language", in M. Black (ed.), *The Importance of Language* (Englewood Cliffs, N.J. 1962), p. 116.
79. W. L. Wonderly, op. cit., pp. 121–8.
80. The following selection is of special value: W. P. Alston, *Philosophy of Language,* pp. 96–106; Mary A. McCloskey, "Metaphor", in *Mind* 73 (1964), pp. 215–233; C. S. Lewis, "Bluspels and Flalansferes", and O. Barfield, "Poetic Diction and Legal Fiction", both in M. Black (ed.), *The Importance of Language,* pp. 36–50, and 51–71; J. Pelc, *Studies in Functional Logical Semiotics of Natural Language,* pp. 142–94; C. M. Turbayne, *The Myth of Metaphor* (New Haven 1962); Marcus B. Hester, *The Meaning of Poetic Metaphor. An Analysis in the Light of Wittgenstein's Claim that Meaning is Use* (The Hague 1967), especially pp. 114–92; M. Black, *Models and Metaphors* (New York 1962), pp. 25–47; and J. de Waard, "Biblical Metaphors and their Translation", in *The Bible Translator* 25 (1974), pp. 107–116; cf. also V. Heylen "Les Métaphores et les métonymies dans les Epîtres Pauliniennes", in ETL 8 (1935), pp. 253–90.

81. E. A. Nida and C. R. Taber, *The Theory and Practice of Translation* (Leiden 1969), p. 39. Cf. also E. A. Nida, *Towards a Science of Translating.*
82. E. A. Nida and C. R. Taber, op. cit., pp. 53–4.
83. N. Chomsky, *Aspects of the Theory of Syntax* (Cambridge Mass. 1965, rp. 1970), p. 21. Cf. also J. Lyons, *Chomsky* (London 1970), pp. 47–82, and *Introduction to Theoretical Linguistics,* pp. 247–69.
84. N. Chomsky, op. cit. p. 24. Cf. pp. 179–82, on "deletion".
85. K. L. Burres, op. cit., p. 105.
86. A.C. Thiselton, "On the Logical Grammar of Justification in Paul", paper read at the Fifth International Congress on Biblical Studies (September 1973), forthcoming in *Studia Evangelica.*
87. E. Käsemann, *New Testament Questions of Today* (London 1969), p. 171; and F. Prat, *The Theology of St. Paul* (London 1945), vol. 2, p. 247.
88. L. Cerfaux, *The Christian in the Theology of Paul* (London, 1967), pp. 391–400; P. Stuhlmacher, *Gerechtigkeit Gottes bei Paulus* (Göttingen, 1965) J. A. Ziesler, *The Meaning of Righteousness in Paul* (Cambridge 1972); R. Bultmann, *Theology of the New Testament,* vol. 1 (London 1952) pp. 270–85; and other standard discussions.
89. D. E. H. Whiteley, *The Theology of St. Paul* (Oxford, 1964), p. 164 cf. G. Bornkamm, *Paul* (London 1972), pp. 141–6.
90. L. Wittgenstein, *Philosophical Investigation s,* sect. 74, and II, xi, pp. 193–214; *The Blue and Brown Books,* pp. 163–74; and *Zettel,* sects. 195–235. (cf. especially *Zettel,* sect. 228).
91. D. D. Evans, *The Logic of Self-Involvement,* (London 1963), pp. 124–41.
92. L. Wittgenstein, *Philosophical Investigations,* sects. 248–52; and *On Certainty* (Oxford 1969), sects. 292–3 and 604.
93. A. C. Thiselton, "The Supposed Power of Words in the Biblical Writings" and "The Parables as Language Event", op. cit., pp. 438–9. Cf. O. R. Jones, *The Concept of Holiness* (London 1961) and D. D. Evans, op. cit.

CHAPTER V

QUESTIONS OF INTRODUCTION

D. Guthrie

I. *General Considerations*

In approaching any writing there are various preliminary questions which an exegete must settle before he can decide on the right approach to the interpretation of the text. There are five main considerations, all of which are in some respects dependent on one another. These are (1) Background, (2) Date, (3) Destination, (4) Integrity and (5) Authorship. While the first four are important, this essay will be devoted mainly to the fifth since this in the past has tended to have more influence over interpretation than the rest. Some initial comments must, however, be made on the others since they frequently affect problems of authorship.

1. BACKGROUND

If an attempt is made to place any writing in its context, attention to background is essential. Hence any information available about first century life is useful to the exegete. It goes without saying that knowledge of eastern customs and ways of thought is indispensable for a right interpretation of a group of writings whose setting is essentially oriental. This is no less true for the Epistles than for the Gospels. It involves some understanding of Judaism, Hellenism and paganism. The discovery of the Dead Sea Scrolls has contributed to the interpretation of the New Testament almost wholly in this area of background. New light has been cast on the relationship between Judaism and Hellenistic thought which has particularly affected the approach to John's Gospel. It can no longer be interpreted as a wholly Hellenistic production. Similarly increasing knowledge of Gnosticism and its precursors has provided a better understanding of some of the New Testament books, particularly Colossians.

Some warning must be issued against a wrong use of background material. The existence of parallels is not in itself proof of common ground. The most notable example of the use of such a wrong method is to be seen in the *religionsgeschichtlich* school, which played down the uniqueness of the New Testament text to such an extent that its true perspective became lost. Care must also be taken to ensure that any background material appealed to is contemporary with the writings being examined and not of considerably later date, as has happened, for instance, in certain cases in the use of Mandaic materials.

2. DATE

In many of the New Testament writings precise dating is impossible simply because insufficient information is available. But in most cases an appropriate dating is possible by taking into account available background material and historical allusions which contain time-elements. The importance of dating for exegesis may be illustrated by the following example. If the Epistle to the Colossians is dated in the time of fully developed Gnosticism in the second century the interpreter of its Christology and of its allusions to the heresy will be obliged to take this into account. But its meaning and purpose will be different if, on the contrary, first century Gnosis is in mind. Moreover, dating has an immediate effect on determination of authorship, for if Colossians is dated in the second century, Pauline authorship is immediately ruled out. But this raises the problem as to which should be established first, to which the most satisfactory solution is a *via media* which sees both as complementary problems, but in which the weighting must be in favour of authorship.

3. DESTINATION

This consideration may be treated from two points of view: on the one hand concern about the geographical location of the readers, and on the other hand concern about their character. Although geography has little effect on exegesis, it is not entirely unimportant. The destination of the Pauline letters may be cited as an example. Although in all cases this is specified, there are questions, for instance, about the precise destination of Ephesians. If this letter is regarded as a circular, to what extent would this affect the exegesis? It would seem to be very little affected since the background is so general. But many New Testament books have no clear indication of destination (e.g. the Gospels, and such Epistles as James, I John, Hebrews and Jude). In some cases our understanding of obscure statements in the text might well be elucidated if more information were available, but the exegete can work only with the data he has. Although it might help if we knew the specific group to whom Hebrews was sent, it is possible without this knowledge to interpret it in a broadly satisfactory way.

Of more importance is the character of the readers, as far as this can be ascertained. The exegete needs to decide to what extent statements in the text are of purely local or of general significance. The Corinthian Epistles are a case in point. Some of the advice given by Paul regarding women in 1. Corinthians, for instance, may be due to the local background. It would be questionable exegesis in such cases to assume that a general principle is necessarily being given, although it is usually possible to extract some general teaching from the specific example. Moreover, the circumstances of the original readers were conditioned by contemporary customs (e.g. the wearing of veils by women) and this must clearly be taken into account in considering the modern relevance of the passage. Another important consideration is the extent to which Gnosis lies behind the texts. The exegete will look for it particularly in those books which are thought to have been sent to destinations where Gnostic influences are known to have been active.

4. INTEGRITY

Where a writing is claimed to be composed of several originally disconnected fragments, its integrity may then be at stake and the exegesis affected. As an example 2 Corinthians may be cited. If the exegete comes to the text believing, for instance, that it consists of four separate fragments, he will not attempt to trace any unifying thread of thought or any structure. Indeed in this case it is usually as exegetes that scholars claim to discover different emphases in the separate parts. But those who approach the book as a unity will be more inclined to absorb the apparent differences within an overall understanding of the epistle. Thus differences in interpretation are bound to result.

II. *Authorship*

In varying degrees, all authors impress their personal characteristics on their respective texts. Adequate interpretation of what is written cannot be divorced from considerations of authorship. The more that is known about the author, the greater the possibility that his words will be correctly understood. In the field of New Testament exegesis this at once poses problems, since for many of the books no certain data are available about the writers. It raises the question whether exegesis of anonymous books needs to proceed on different lines from exegesis of books where the author is well known.

Another problem which arises as a direct result of the application of criticism to New Testament writings is the evaluation of the effects of theories of pseudonymity on the exegesis of a text. We need to discuss, for instance, whether interpretation is affected by the exegete's adoption of a pseudonymous theory of authorship for any of Paul's epistles. Before this question can be answered, many factors must be examined, including the first century approach to pseudonymity and the validity of literary devices.

1. THE VALIDITY OF AUTHOR-CRITICISM

A cursory glance at the history of criticism is sufficient to demonstrate the importance of authorship in critical enquiry. The pre-critical period, with its emphasis on the divine origin of scripture, was not greatly interested in questions of human authorship. The historical background was considered to be irrelevant in view of the dogmatic approach to the text. As soon as a critical approach was adopted it became of first importance to consider who wrote the words which were the subject of exegetical examination. The earliest serious critical examination which resulted in the rejection of the traditional authorship of a New Testament writing was Schleiermacher's examination of 1 Timothy.[1] Since he came to the conclusion that Paul was not the author of this Epistle, he was obliged to interpret it as a pseudonymous letter. His example was soon followed by Eichhorn[2] who applied the same methods to all three Pastoral Epistles. This movement away from traditional ascriptions and from the claims made in the texts themselves soon spread still further with Baur[3] and his school. It is noticeable that challenges to traditional ascriptions of authorship went hand in hand with rejection of authority. In other words, the earlier critics never supposed a category in which authorship could be challenged and authority maintained. Baur considered only four Pauline Epistles to be genuine, which at once implied that the rest were of lesser calibre. His view of authorship strongly affected his exegesis of the Epistles, although it should be noted that his assessment of authorship was governed by his prior reconstruction of the history.

Since Baur's time the history of criticism has shown a constant interest in problems of authorship. Holtzmann[4] followed in the tradition which considered that historical background was of utmost importance to the exegete. In the twentieth century, reaction against the possibility of reconstructing the historical background, typified in the work of Bultmann[5] and his associates, has lessened detailed attention to authorship, but has certainly not eliminated it. There are many assumptions made without discussion on the basis of earlier views which have survived in the course of the development of criticism. Hence many modern exegetes approach the text from the point of view of non-authenticity, with the result that interpretations resting on acceptance of authenticity are not even discussed.

In order to illustrate this latter point some examples will be cited. In his approach to the Gospels as books which mainly contain the theological creations of the early church, Bultmann[6] does not discuss authorship. In the strictest sense the writers take on the role of compilers or editors of the units of tradition and not the role of authors. Exegesis loses sight of the personal contribution of the writer. It is this impersonal side of Bultmann's method of interpretation which has caused the development of redaction criticism,[7] with its restoration of the importance of the individual. Many redaction critics, however, consider that the author is two stages removed from the original events, the first stage being the development of units of tradition and the second the shaping of these units into a theological whole.[8] None of these approaches looks at the Gospels in the same light as those which give weight to traditional views of authorship. For instance, if Matthew, an apostle, was the author of the Gospel attributed to his name, the exegete will clearly approach the Gospel from a different point of view.[9] There will be more inclination to treat his record as historically correct than if some unknown compiler, with his own specific theological viewpoint, had written it.[10] A similar difference is seen in approaches to the book of Acts, for clearly an exegete who regards the book as written by a reliable historian will have a different assessment of its statements from one who regards the book as an essentially theological composition.[11] This latter point illustrates a problem that could arise among those who share a common theory of authorship. Acceptance of Lucan authorship does not necessarily imply acceptance of his work as history rather than theology, which shows that more is needed than the identification of the author.[12] For many New Testament books information regarding the character of the author is nevertheless restricted to deductions from the contents of the books themselves, or else scattered material in traditions which may or may not be correct. The exegete could wish that as much information existed about all the New Testament authors as exists for the apostle Paul, but in most cases the data are scanty.

In considering the validity of author-criticism some attention must be given to the implications of tradition on the subject. Are there evidences from patristic sources that early Christians attached much importance to questions of authorship? The answer to this question falls into two sections – a consideration of any comments on the significance of authorship in approaching exegesis and a consideration of statements of authorship without comment. The latter evidence is much more prevalent than the former. There are certain comments which suggest the importance of authorship, as when Tertullian[13] asserts that the four gospels come either from apostles or from their pupils, an assertion which clearly shows that authorship weighed heavily with him in his approach to the books. Indeed, this statement shows the important connection between authorship and apostolicity in his mind. Irenaeus[14] makes a similar statement about the authors of the gospels, Mark being described as "the disciple and interpreter of Peter", Luke as "the follower of Paul" and John as "the disciple of the Lord". These statements suffice to show the significance attaching to authorship, but the question remains whether early and uncritical comments of this nature have any relevance for the modern exegete. Many scholars rule them out as guesses. Yet the strong persistence of belief in apostolic authorship demands explanation. The early patristic writers may, of course, be treated as too naive to deserve serious consideration, or their opinions may be regarded as valid data for an approach to the text. The most reasonable approach is to subject their comments to serious examination and where justifiable to regard their evidence as reliable data which must be given weight in resolving the historical background. Where there are no sound reasons for suspecting the validity of patristic comments on authorship, to ignore such evidence would not be in harmony with sound critical principles.[15]

The close connection between traditional comments on authorship and apostolicity has been mentioned above, but this raises the most important problem of all – that of apostolicity itself. What importance did apostolic origin have for authoritative Christian literature? Could any writing be regarded as authoritative that was not known to have come from an apostolic source? While the evidence on this theme is not conclusive, there are many indications that apostolic authorship was generally regarded as a guarantee of the authority of the writing. The preponderance of apocryphal books purporting to come from apostolic sources suggests the importance of supposed apostolic origin among those producing this kind of literature.[16]

There needs to be a right appreciation of the relationship between apostolic authorship, apostolic content and authority. Apostolicity is more to be identified with apostolic content than with authorship. If the New Testament is based on what was generally recognized as apostolic doctrine, problems arise when critical enquiry pronounces against apostolic authorship. In that case either the book in question must be placed on a different level from the rest, or else the early Christian basis for canonicity must be revised. The latter course is the one generally followed, in which case even books of pseudonymous origin can be placed alongside authentic apostolic books.[17] Yet the problem of authority is not so easily settled in this way, especially where writings claim some specified author, a claim which is then believed to be inaccurate. It cannot be disputed that more authority rests with literature which is known to be apostolic than with writings whose origin is confidently declared to be non-apostolic. The Pastoral Epistles are a good example of this difference. Those who dispute their genuine Pauline origin generally regard them as second century productions which can practically be disregarded in the reconstruction of the development of thought in the apostolic age.[18] They are certainly not in that case given the same weight exegetically as if they are treated as the actual words of the apostle. Even those theories which propose that the content of these Epistles is Pauline but not by Paul cannot escape the dilemma over the authority of the writings, for secondary writings in the Pauline tradition have less validity than primary apostolic documents. This discussion leads naturally into a consideration of the relationship between apostolicity, anonymity and pseudonymity.

2. APOSTOLICITY, ANONYMITY AND PSEUDONYMITY

Whenever a theory is proposed which denies the genuineness of the ascription to a particular author, the problem of pseudonymity arises. Whenever traditional ascriptions to books which give no claim to specific authorship are rejected, the problem is one of anonymity. In both cases apostolicity is ruled out unless the term is comprehensive enough to include works in the apostolic tradition which were not written by apostles. The questions raised are not purely academic. What grounds are there for the view that if pseudonymity was an accepted literary convention, pseudonymous works attributed to apostles would carry the same authority as genuine writings? The main problem here is to discover to what extent it can be demonstrated that pseudonymity was a literary convention for writings of the type found in the New Testament. Even if this could be established it would still be difficult to prove that such works were received on the same footing as genuine works.

Our first consideration must be the problem of anonymity. There are some instances, notably the epistle to the Hebrews, where specific authorship appears to have been attributed to an originally anonymous letter. In this case it cannot be supposed that the letter loses any authority by being declared anonymous. Those patristic writers who questioned the Pauline ascription did not dispute its canonicity, although the hesitation over it in the West may have been due to its unknown origin.[19] It is significant that Origen,[20] while disputing the Pauline authorship, nevertheless recognized the apostolic content.

The case of Hebrews has led some to suppose that the key to an understanding of pseudonymity is to be found in anonymity. K. Aland,[21] for instance, maintains that since the real author was believed to be the Holy Spirit, anonymity was natural. The human author was but the vehicle through whom the Spirit spoke. Under this theory ascriptions of authorship are seen as a retrograde step, a movement to put too much stress on the human agent. In this case anonymity and pseudonymity would be regarded as normal, whereas clear claims to authorship would be seen as abnormal. Indeed, Aland goes as far as to maintain that the anonymous authors not only believed themselves to be under the Spirit, they actually were.[22] If this thesis is correct, it would almost make author-criticism irrelevant for exegesis, since whatever the method of production the text can be regarded as the message of the Spirit. Yet such a theory needs careful examination to establish its validity.

The first point to notice is that the Pauline Epistles, which may reasonably be regarded as among the earliest group of writings in the New Testament, are not anonymous and that Paul was certainly conscious of being under the inspiration of the Spirit.[23] Aland attempts to escape from the difficulty by maintaining a distinction between letters and epistles.[24] By excluding the former and concentrating on the latter, he dispenses with an examination of the writings of Paul which would prove an embarrassment for his theory. The Christian message was, in fact, communicated powerfully by the personality of this man. If this factor is not given full weight, any exegesis of the text must be strongly affected.

The second serious weakness in Aland's position lies in his conception of the activity of the Spirit. The New Testament shows the Spirit to be the Spirit of truth, which at once rules out all methods of deception. If the Spirit used pseudonymous methods the only acceptable hypothesis would be that the method was so universally acknowledged that no-one would have questioned its validity as a justifiable means of Christian communication. But this is too big an assumption to accept without evidence. It calls for some statement regarding the prevalence of an attitude towards pseudonymous writings in the first century world.

Pseudonymity was certainly prevalent among both Jews and Greeks during this period. But the widespread use of assumed names does not prove that it was necessarily acceptable. In respect of the Jewish apocalypses, for instance, although these were invariably ascribed to venerable names, there is no evidence that this pseudepigraphic form was ever officially accepted. Indeed, these works were not included at any stage in the Hebrew canon.[25] On the other hand they enjoyed considerable popularity and it is difficult to believe that many, if any, of the original readers supposed that the pseudonyms were real. When ante-diluvian patriarchs are purported to write apocalypses, it is evident enough that the motive could not have been to deceive. But there is no suggestion that the apocalypses were ever regarded as authoritative by official Judaism. Moreover these Jewish works bear no relation in form to the New Testament epistles and even in respect of the Apocalypse of John the parallels are slight.[26] There are similarly no close parallels in Greek literature to the supposed New Testament epistolary pseudepigrapha, which forms a major obstacle to the view that this kind of literature was an accepted convention. In fact epistolary pseudepigraphy is the most difficult form to produce, with the result that the makers of pseudepigrapha avoided the form.[27] Such works as 3 Corinthians and the Epistle to the Laodiceans are so obviously not genuine that they must be regarded as conspicuous failures as effective pseudonymous works. Since, therefore, no real parallels can be found to the epistolary form, those who advance hypotheses which posit epistolary pseudepigrapha cannot claim that this was an established convention and this must clearly affect their approach to exegesis. If, for instance, Ephesians is considered to be non-Pauline, the interpretation of the meaning of the Epistle must differ from an understanding of it as a Pauline Epistle.[28] It is not simply that an adequate explanation is necessary for the pseudonym, but the words themselves lose in weight of authority when they are reduced to the utterance of an anonymous man who has had to take cover under the pseudonym. The suggestion that this is a sign of his modesty is unconvincing.[29] The church in Asia took a very different view of the presbyter who "for love of Paul" composed *The Acts of Paul.*[30] There would of course be less difficulty if the writer had been in close touch with Paul and was reproducing faithfully the apostle's ideas in his own way, but even in this case a pseudonymous letter could not bear the same weight as one personally written by the apostle.

3. METHODS OF DETERMINING AUTHORSHIP

One of the problems for the New Testament exegete is the fact that methodology in relation to the examination of authorship has been piecemeal, each exponent determining his own principles of criticism. What weighs heavily with one seems slight or even irrelevant to another. In these circumstances there is only one satisfactory course of action and that is for the exegete to delineate the methods he has adopted in reaching his conclusions. Clearly the scope of this article is too restricted to give anything more than a brief indication of the lines along which a constructive methodology might proceed.

(1) Where more than one writing is attributed to the same author, it is possible and desirable to compare the language and thought to verify

whether the same author could have written both works. But great care must be taken in implementing this method. Literary parallels are notoriously difficult to decide either as a proof of borrowing or of dissimilar authorship. It is not a sound principle of criticism to maintain that a man who wrote a document A could not have written document B if the only grounds for this conclusion are a varied use of the same terms or the use of different terms to express the same idea. In fact the only justification for such a conclusion is when document A plainly contradicts document B, although even here care must be taken to ensure that the contradiction is real and not merely apparent.

(2) Arising out of this is the deduction from use of sources as to the character of the author. Arguments, for instance, based on the assumption of what an apostolic author would or would not use are invalid because of the lack of any supporting evidence. One might hold that an apostle would not use or quote a non-apostolic source and another might see no reason to exclude such a possibility. In the long run the decision one way or the other is quite arbitrary and cannot form a valid basis for criticism.

(3) An approach to authorship on the basis of stylistic data would seem to present a more objective basis, but again difficulties arise because of the indefinable qualities of a man's style. Before style can be used as a reliable test of authorship it is necessary to determine what its characteristics are. Do these, for instance, reside in the peculiar or most striking words which an author uses, or do they reveal themselves in the unconscious patterns with which he employs common words? Are sentence structures a sure guide to distinctive style? Do authors have any kind of norm from which they rarely deviate? Obviously if the last question could be answered in the affirmative this would provide an objective test which could be relied on to lead to an effective conclusion. Certain linguistic statisticians have made this assertion, but their methods need careful assessment. Is it demonstrable that every author has a statistical norm in such matters as word-frequencies or sentence lengths from which they do not deviate beyond what might be expected from standard deviations? To be able to maintain this position with any confidence it would be necessary for extensive examination to be made among a wide variety of known authors.[31] Until this has been done evidence of this kind must be received with the greatest reserve. Even if a tendency towards a statistical norm for authors could be established, it would still be difficult, if not impossible, to apply the test where the extant literature does not provide adequate samples, which is certainly the case with many of the New Testament Epistles. The older emphasis on the number of hapaxes used in each writing as a means of comparing authors[32] is equally difficult unless a thorough demonstration can be made of the extent to which any author may be reasonably expected to enlarge his vocabulary. If no certain method of comparing style can be established, it must remain an inconclusive tool in the hand of the exegete for determining authorship.

(4) Another matter of some importance is doctrine. If in two accounts claiming the same author one brings into prominence a range of doctrines

which are absent from the other, can this legitimately be regarded as evidence that they could not have come from the same author? The problem resolves itself into a discussion of the extent to which an author may be expected to reflect his characteristic ideas in all that he writes. The problem obviously cannot be resolved without reference to the purposes of each writing. What may be expected for one purpose may not obtain for another. It is not self-evident, for example, that Paul will write in the same way to a Christian church which he has never visited as to a close associate. It would be natural to suppose that the former would contain a fuller exposition of his ideas than the latter. Nevertheless the question must be faced whether a creative thinker like Paul could ever write in a non-creative way. In the end a decision on this can only be subjective. No-one is in fact entitled to say that a book must be non-authentic because some characteristic doctrine is lacking, for this would mean tying down the personal freedom of the author within too narrow limits. It may as reasonably be deduced that authors do not necessarily reflect their characteristic doctrines in all their writings.

(5) Because every author writes in a historical situation, an examination of the historical background of the writing together with an examination of historical data known about the supposed author is a valid methodology in order to decide whether one excludes the other. If, for instance, historical background suggests a second century date whereas the author ascription denotes a first century date, only two explanations are possible. Either the ascription is incorrect or else the historical background must be re-examined. The latter course may, in fact, be the more reasonable, especially where there is room for difference of opinion in the identification of the historical allusions. A case in point is the Colossian letter, where the supposed second century background of Gnosticism reflected in the heresy is being fast abandoned as a ground for non-Pauline authorship because of the undoubted existence of pre-Gnosticism in the first century. Additional knowledge of Gnosticism has led to a re-appraisal of the place of this type of evidence in disputing the Pauline origin of this epistle.[33] The same might be said about the various allusions to persecutions in the New Testament. It is impossible in these cases to be certain to which period of church history these indecisive references belong and it is certainly precarious to argue from what might have been to what is. This could be illustrated from I Peter where the references to persecutions might refer to Trajan's time, but cannot be proved to do so.[34]

(6) The preceding considerations might suggest that no positive approach to authorship is possible, but this would not give the full picture. In cases where the New Testament text does not give an author's identity, there are no means of arriving at a conclusion without relying on external evidence (as, for instance, in the case of Luke-Acts). For the remainder the self-claims of the books themselves must be given adequate weight. It would seem to be a fair principle of criticism to allow the claims to stand until they are dislodged by being shown to be untenable. This means that such claims should be given the benefit of the doubt where challenges to them fall short of

positive proof. In these cases also due weight must be given to external tradition.

NOTES

1. *Über den sogenannten ersten Brief des Paulus an den Timotheus* (Berlin 1807).
2. *Historische-Kritische Einleitung in das Neue Testament* (Leipzig 1812)III.315.
3. *Die sogenannten Pastoralbriefe* (Stuttgart (1835).
4. *Einleitung in das Neue Testament* (Freiburg 1885).
5. Cf. for instance, Bultmann's approach to history in his *The History of the Synoptic Tradition* (E.T., Oxford 1958[2]).
6. Emphasis on units of tradition has made emphasis on authorship irrelevant.
7. In writings of scholars like Marxsen, Conzelmann and Bornkamm. See the article on redaction criticism, ch. XI.
8. Clearly authorship becomes important in discussions of the theological moulding, but even here the theology is more important than the personal characteristics of the author.
9. A comparison between the approach of G. Bornkamm and R. V. G. Tasker in his *The Gospel according to St. Matthew* (London, 1961) illustrates this point.
10. An unknown compiler could, of course, produce an authentic work, but anonymity makes it more difficult to establish authenticity (cf. Hebrews).
11. An exegete like E. Haenchen continually refers to "Luke" but does not mean Paul's companion, whereas F. F. Bruce fully accepts the Lucan authorship and interprets the book accordingly. See E. Haenchen, *The Acts of the Apostles* (Oxford 1971), and F. F. Bruce, *The Acts of the Apostles* (London 1952).
12. Lucan authorship may be said to corroborate other evidences of authenticity since Luke must have had access to much first-hand material.
13. *C. Marcion* iv.2.
14. *Adv. Haer.* iii.1.
15. E.g. it is not sound criticism when all the statements of a particular author are discounted because on some issue he expresses a naive opinion.
16. Cf. E. Hennecke, *New Testament Apocrypha* (ed. W. Schneemelcher and R.M. Wilson; London 1963, 1965).
17. Those who regard pseudonymity as an acceptable literary device claim that this places books of such origin in the same category as books which advertise their true authorship.
18. Consider, for instance, the dating of F. D. Gealy in his exegesis of these epistles in *The Interpreter's Bible* (New York 1955), Vol. II, pp. 351ff. in which a post-Marcion period places them in a secondary category.
19. The earliest evidence comes from Tertullian (*De Pudicitia*) who placed Hebrews below the apostolic epistles. His acceptance of Barnabas as author clearly influenced him in his decision.
20. Cf. Eusebius, H.E. vi.25.
21. JTS ns. 12, (1961), pp. 39–49, reprinted in SPCK *Theological Collections* 4 (London 1965), 1–13.
22. Aland considers that in those days the Christian writers were regarded as pens moved by the Spirit.
23. Those times when Paul draws attention to his own opinion (as for instance in I Cor.7:12) suggest that he is generally conscious of speaking from God. His whole emphasis on the work of the Spirit supports this view.
24. Op. cit., pp. 3, 4.
25. At the meeting of elders at Jamnia they were not considered canonical and at no stage subsequent to this.
26. A parallel exists in the title, but in form and content John's apocalypse differs in a marked way from the Jewish apocalypses. His is not pseudonymous, does not contain a survey of past history and moves on a higher plane (i.e. is more spiritual).

27. Cf. my article on epistolary pseudepigraphy in my *New Testament Introduction* (London 1970), pp. 671ff. For a general discussion of canonical pseudepigrapha, cf. B. M. Metzger, JBL, 91 (1972), pp. 3–24.
28. A comparison between C. L. Mitton, *The Epistle to the Ephesians* (Oxford 1951), and F. Foulkes, *The Epistle of Paul to the Ephesians* (London 1963), will demonstrate this.
29. Cf. Mitton, op. cit.
30. According to Tertullian, *De Baptismo* 17.
31. A.Q. Morton, who has advocated this view, has based his conclusions on a restricted amount of evidence and cannot claim to have established a general principle (cf. *Paul the Man and the Myth* (London, 1966), by A. Q. Morton and J. McLeman).
32. Cf. P. N. Harrison's approach in *The Problem of the Pastorals* (Oxford 1921).
33. Cf. R. M. Wilson's treatment in his *Gnosis and the New Testament* (Oxford 1968).
34. Cf. the different approaches of F. W. Beare, *The First Epistle of Peter* (Oxford 1958), and C. E. B. Cranfield, *The First Epistle of Peter* (London 1950).

CHAPTER VI

THE RELIGIOUS BACKGROUND

John W. Drane

It ought to be self-evident to every reader of the New Testament that one of the most important tools in the understanding of its message is a proper appreciation of the religious background to its thought. Jesus himself and his disciples, along with almost all the writers of the New Testament, were Jews, and most of the early churches embraced people with very diverse religious backgrounds. We cannot get very far through the New Testament without encountering the representatives of various religions, whether it be the Pharisees and Sadducees of the gospel traditions or the enigmatic representatives of pagan religious thought who are mentioned in the Pauline letters and Acts. It is therefore essential for the student of the New Testament to be thoroughly familiar with the background of religious thought against which it was written.

I. *The Sources*

This religious background to the New Testament writings comprises three main elements:

1. THE OLD TESTAMENT

The Old Testament is of crucial importance for a correct understanding of the message of the New Testament. On almost every page of the New Testament we are reminded of the fact that the coming of Jesus was the decisive conclusion to a long history of religious experience. He was the promised Messiah of the Old Testament (Mk. 14:61f.), and his coming was the fulfilment of the ancient prophecies (Lk. 4:21). Even relatively trivial incidents in his life and work could be seen in this light (Mt. 2:16–23), and though it was not generally apparent at the time, even the events of his death and resurrection were later seen as the fulfilment of Old Testament predictions (Acts 2:22–36).[1]

Not only could Jesus' own life, death and resurrection be seen in the context of the Old Testament, but the new life of the Christian church could also be interpreted in terms of Old Testament categories. St. Paul had no doubt that because of their relationship to Jesus the Christ, even Gentile

Christians could be described as "sons of Abraham", heirs of the promises made in the Old Testament to God's chosen people (Gal. 3:29). On almost every page of St. Paul's correspondence, Old Testament figures are taken up and reinterpreted, while even small details of his language can often conceal an allusion to some Old Testament event. Even such a cosmopolitan church as that at Corinth could be expected to have their Christian faith thoroughly grounded in the Old Testament (cf. 1 Cor. 10:1ff.).

2. CONTEMPORARY JUDAISM

The Judaism of the first century A.D. was no doubt more complex than people often suppose,[2] but three main strands appear to have had an important influence on the faith of the first Christians:

(a) *The Pharisees* and their beliefs almost certainly exercised an important influence on the development of New Testament theology. Though to the first evangelist they were the arch-enemies of Jesus and his followers (Mt. 22–23), St. Paul could boast more than once of his upbringing and education as a Pharisee (Phil. 3:5; cf. Gal. 1:13f.). Though his attitude to the Old Testament Torah shows that he had cast aside many of the most cherished beliefs of the Pharisees, it is certain that he continued to be deeply influenced by what he had learned from his Pharisaic teachers. At his trial before Agrippa (Acts 26:4–8), as before the Sanhedrin at a previous trial (Acts 23:6–10), the author of Acts depicts him appealing to the belief in the future resurrection which he shared with the Pharisees – and we can see from his own treatment of this very subject in 1 Cor. 15 how deeply indebted he was to the traditions of his fathers.[3]

(b) *Qumran* doctrines have also played their part in helping us to understand the religious background of the New Testament. Though we must reject outright any theories that Christianity was derived from the Qumran community, there are many points of contact. One of the most spectacular reversals of scholarly opinion in recent years has come about largely because of the discovery that the dualism of the Qumran scrolls bears a certain resemblance to that of the Fourth Gospel. As a result of this, the Fourth Gospel can now be seen in a completely new light, both historically and theologically,[4] while some scholars are suggesting a much earlier date for it than has hitherto been proposed.[5]

(c) *Hellenistic Judaism* must also be taken into account. This was the kind of Judaism that developed among the Jews of the Diaspora, as they tried to accommodate their ancestral faith to the requirements of a different situation. Its most eloquent exponent was Philo of Alexandria, a contemporary of Jesus and St. Paul, who set himself the task of interpreting the Old Testament in terms of Greek philosophy. In order to do this, he had to allegorize almost the whole of the Old Testament, thus removing it from the realm of the truly historical, but in the process he claimed to have proved that Moses had anticipated all that was best in classical Greek philosophy! The thought of Philo and those who followed him is often an important consideration in the interpretation of Pauline theology. In Gal. 4:21–31, for instance, Paul uses the allegory of Sarah and Hagar to prove his theological points, and the question naturally arises whether Paul was using the same method as the Alexandrian Jews, and if so whether he did it with the same presuppositions in mind. The answer to this question will give us an important insight into St. Paul's attitude towards the Old Testament, and his understanding of Jesus in Old Testament categories.

3. HELLENISTIC THOUGHT

The other main area of religious thought that provided a backcloth to the early church is the religion of the Hellenistic world. By New Testament times, the cults of the old Greek gods had lost their former power and the main religions of the Roman empire were the mystery cults and various forms of what later became known as Gnosticism. Both these systems were concerned with the provision of a personal salvation for the individual. Generalization in this area of study is always a hazardous business, but we shall perhaps not go too far wrong if we distinguish the Mysteries from Gnosticism by saying that the former claimed to provide a personal salvation by magic, whereas the latter did it by more philosophical-theological means. This distinction is not a very clear-cut one, but in this it merely reflects the confusion of the Hellenistic world, where men were willing to grasp any straw that held out the slightest support for their future spiritual security.

What we know of these Hellenistic religions has come from two main archaeological finds. From about 1850 large quantities of papyri were discovered in Egypt, many of them containing accounts of the magical religious observances of the Hellenistic world. These were gathered together and published by Adolf Deissmann as *Licht vom Osten* in 1908.[6] These magical papyri shed a great deal of light on the popular superstitions of Hellenism. None of the papyri as such can be dated earlier than the Christian era, and most of them are from the second to the sixth centuries A.D. But there is plenty of other evidence for the widespread practice of magic in New Testament times. This includes cursing tablets, magical amulets and magicians' apparatus, some of it dating from the pre-Christian era.[7] The Gnostic religion is known to us through the accounts of Christian forms of Gnosticism given by the early church Fathers, and also through a vast quantity of MSS discovered at Nag Hammadi in Egypt about 1945.[8] This collection, written in Coptic, includes sayings attributed to Jesus but not contained in the canonical gospels (e.g. *The Gospel of Thomas*), along with more speculative and philosophical Gnostic treatises. These MSS are still in the process of being edited and published by scholars, but so far none has come to light from a pre-Christian period.

II. *The Use of Background Materials*

How can we use such varied materials? There are two main points at which such comparative materials can be a help to the exegete:[9]

1. THE USE OF SIMILAR LANGUAGE

A quick reading of the comparative texts soon reveals that the same terminology often occurs in several different contexts. Take the idea of "knowledge", for instance, which runs like a metallic thread through the fabric of all the materials enumerated above. An uncritical approach to the subject might lead us to suppose that in all these religious texts it has one and the same meaning, and so there will be no difficulty in deciding its meaning in the New Testament. But in fact, there is great variety even among the non-Christian sources. "Knowledge" is a prominent theme in the Old Testament, where knowledge of God is the prerogative of those who live in close covenant fellowship with him;[10] and in the Qumran scrolls "knowledge" is the possession of the religious elite of the community.[11] In the writings of Philo and the Gnostics, on the other hand, knowledge (*γνῶσις*) is something secret that can be obtained only by the soul to which esoteric religious truths have been revealed.[12]

In view of these distinctions of emphasis, we can see that the meaning of *γνῶσις* in the New Testament is a matter for careful exegesis of the text. What we must do is to make a careful analysis of the use of the word as it occurs in all the relevant religious contexts, and then to compare the different uses. As often as not, we will discover that the New Testament concept, though having some relationship to Jewish or Hellenistic religious thought, is in a distinctive class of its own, and the Christian meaning of a given word will usually be determined by the eschatological fact of Christ.[13]

The importance of exercising due caution in dealing with linguistic terms is now generally recognised, though in the early days after the discovery of the Hellenistic magical texts some extravagant statements were made on the flimsy basis of common terminology. In 1913, Wilhelm Bousset wrote the first edition of his important book, *Kyrios Christos,*[14] in which he suggested that since the first Gentile Christians were accustomed to hailing their pagan gods as *κύριος,* they instinctively worshipped the Christian Jesus by using the same word – though the practice went far deeper than that, for the word itself carried with it a multitude of theological associations, which were also transformed into beliefs about Jesus.[15] Consequently, when the New Testament writers refer to Jesus as *ὁ κύριος* they are demonstrating their theological isolation from the historical Jesus, and their close association with the pagan theology of the Hellenistic world. Far from being the guardians of the truth revealed once and for all by Jesus the Christ, the apostles were religious plagiarists of the worst sort, attempting to conceal the rags of a discredited Jewish apocalyptist beneath the rich robes of Hellenistic deity.

No-one today would accept this kind of argument in its entirety, for it is now seen that in his enthusiasm for newly discovered sources of information Bousset ignored the important semantic problems involved in transferring a set of ideas from one culture to another. No doubt the early Christians thought of Jesus as in some way a superior counterpart to their pagan "lords", but the evidence does not allow us to go much beyond that.[16] James Barr has gone so far as to suggest that it is a linguistic impossibility for isolated words to convey theological meaning from one context to another, and though his judgment may well be too sweeping, it is a timely reminder that if linguistic comparisons are to mean anything a very complex analysis is called for.[17]

2. THE USE OF RELIGIOUS MYTHOLOGY

The next question that arises is this: if several religious sources describe their deity in similar ways, doing similar things in the same contexts, what are the possible relationships between them? In the case of the New Testament, this has resolved itself into two main issues, concerned with the miracle stories of the synoptic gospels and the Christology of the Pauline churches.

(a) *Miracle Stories.* It was recognised from the very start that the synoptic miracle stories had a certain similarity to the magical performances of wizards and "divine men" in the Hellenistic world. There is ample evidence for that in the New Testament itself (Mt. 7:22; 1 Jn. 4:1; cf. 2 Thes. 2:9; Rev. 13:13ff.), and at a later date Clement of Alexandria used the similarity as an argument to advance the claims of the Christian faith: Gentiles, he said, had no reason to deny the miracles accredited to Jesus, since their own religious traditions contained miracles of a similar nature (*Strom.* vi.3). There were also miracle stories told of the Jewish rabbis,[18] though most scholars have failed to discern any meaningful relationship between these and the synoptic traditions.[19] It is more usual to treat the gospel miracles as stories that describe Jesus after the pattern of the familiar figure of Hellenistic magic.[20] Nor is there any good reason for us to dispute the general validity of this assertion. In a world thoroughly permeated with the superstitious and the magical, where magicians and miracle-workers were two a penny,[21] it is no surprise that the early Christians should soon have realised the apologetic value of the miracle traditions. For people who had previously followed the local *magus,* it was important to know that Jesus had exercised a more powerful form of supernatural power. In the traditions themselves, Jesus was often portrayed doing the very same things as the Hellenistic magician claimed to be able to do. The exorcism of demons, coupled with magical methods of healing, like the use of spittle, were the stock-in-trade of the Hellenistic wonder-worker.[22]

Some recent studies have emphasised again the importance of this aspect of the synoptic traditions. R. P. Martin argues that one of the purposes of Mark's gospel was to tone down these magical associations that were so clear in the miracle stories. In the face of a Docetic Christology that had arisen in the Gentile churches from a misunderstanding of Pauline teaching, Mark edited the miracle traditions to exclude the possibility of misunderstanding. He wanted to avoid the impression that Jesus was very closely allied with the commonplace magic of Hellenism, hoping that this would sweep the ground from under the feet of would-be Docetists.[23] J. M. Hull reaches somewhat different conclusions after his analysis of the synoptics. According to him, Mark portrays Jesus acting in precisely the ways expected of the Hellenistic "divine man", while in Luke the contrast between the magic of Jesus and that of his opponents is brought out very clearly, and in Matthew Jesus is portrayed not so much as a miracle worker as a teacher of faith.[24]

Can we go further, and suppose that the synoptic miracle stories are pagan myths applied to the Christian Jesus? The earlier form critics often thought so, but they tended to make pronouncements about such historical questions on quite inadequate grounds.[25] The fact that the gospel traditions have the same "form" as the Hellenistic stories proves nothing except that the first Christians were fully aware of the apologetic requirements of the moment, and presented their material accordingly.

In dealing with such a vast subject, we need to decide each case on its own merits,[26] but there are a number of guidelines that may be noted briefly here:

(i) The purpose of the magical performance in Hellenistic religion was usually to coerce the gods to do as the "holy man" wanted.[27] The magical papyri contain the incantations, prayers and rituals to be used to this end. Each circumstance could be dealt with in a particular way, so that with increasing pressure being brought to bear, the god was finally forced to submit to the will of the magician. There is no parallel to this in any of the New Testament miracles. Jesus does not operate in order to pressurize God into acting on his behalf – indeed, on one crucial occasion there is a definite emphasis on Jesus' submission to the will of God (Mk. 14:32ff.). Nor is there any record of Jesus using the kind of spells, incantations or magical apparatus that are described in the papyri.

(ii) It is unlikely that it would have been possible to credit Jesus with miraculous powers if he had not in fact possessed such powers in one form or another. Both the rabbinic and the Hellenistic miracle stories had been evolved over a long period of time, but with the gospel traditions the situation was quite different, for the traditions were reduced to writing within the lifetime of eyewitnesses of the events they purport to describe. This does not necessarily mean that Jesus actually thought of himself as a magician after the Hellenistic model, though we can have no doubt that the early Christians were being faithful to their Lord and Master when they so portrayed him.[28]

(iii) The miracles play a theological part in the gospels that is unparalleled both in pagan and in later Christian sources.[29] They are eschatological events, portraying the coming of the Kingdom and themselves being a part of the salvation brought by Jesus. In them God's action in Christ is revealed, his power is made manifest, and men are called to faith and repentance. This is quite different from the purposes of either Hellenistic or rabbinic magic.[30]

(b) *Christology*. Some scholars have gone further, and have argued that the Christology of the early church was largely dependent on an earlier Hellenistic doctrine. It has often been urged that there was in the Hellenistic world, specifically in Gnostic circles, a widespread myth of a Primal Man, who took upon himself the appearance (though not the reality) of material form, descending to save the souls of men, in much the same fashion as the Christian Jesus is said to have done.[31] Thus, the pre-existence of Jesus as a divine figure, his true involvement in material flesh, his death, resurrection and ascension are all nothing more than a projection of pagan religiosity through the befuddled minds of the apostles onto the pages of the New Testament.

This suggestion founders on the fact that there is no evidence for such a myth in pre-Christian times, though there is plenty of evidence for it from the second century onwards.[32] This highlights another basic consideration to be applied in the comparison of religious texts, for it is all too easy to compare texts from quite different ages, and so to arrive at misleading conclusions. The fact that comparative dating of materials has caused so much confusion in this area of study draws our attention to another problem in utilising non-Christian sources to interpret the New Testament, for in this field, as perhaps in no other, the attitude of every scholar is bound to be determined by his own presuppositions, and particularly his answer to the question: Is there such a thing as the supernatural?

The scholar who answers that question negatively must regard the whole concept of deity as the New Testament presents it as nothing more than an elaboration of pagan religious mythology. Since Jesus can have been no different from any other man, the true message of the New Testament is not one we can readily understand today in its own terms. It was essentially an existential message, related to the thought-patterns and ideas of ancient man, who in a vague way believed in miracles, though in fact what he thought he believed in only existed as a mythological hangover from his religious past. According to this view, the concept of miracle was an invention of unsophisticated man, designed to answer questions which at that stage of his development were incapable of any other explanation. Consequently, if we find ancient records like the New Testament which appear to relate incidents in which the miraculous took place, it must be explained as a reflection of an unsophisticated stage in the development of humanity. Since Greek pagans were at the same stage of development as the New Testament Christians, the miraculous elements of the New Testament and the pagan miracles are all of a piece, and are nothing more or less than variant forms of the same irrelevant phenomenon.

To the scholar who does accept the possibility of the miraculous, the question is seen in a different light. He will take his starting point from the assumption that there is no *a priori* reason why miracles should not happen.

Nor indeed is there any *a priori* reason why Jesus should not have been divine, as he evidently claimed to be. Beginning as they do from completely different premises, it is not surprising that supernaturalists reach quite different conclusions from naturalists. For the supernaturalist, it is possible that Jesus was divine and that miracles could take place. Whether in fact Jesus was divine and did perform miracles is something that needs to be established by the norms of historical and literary investigation. In this enquiry no investigator has the right to impose his own preconceived ideas onto the New Testament texts (nor indeed onto the Hellenistic or rabbinic texts), but we all need to be aware of our presuppositions, and to make due allowance for them.

From this brief survey we can see that the benefits of a judicious use of other religious texts in the exegesis of the New Testament are many. The main advantage is a simple one: we are enabled to view the New Testament writings from the perspective of men and women of the first century. This is something we take for granted today, but it is fundamental to our whole modern understanding of the New Testament. If we did not know about the paganism of Hellenism we would be unable to understand most of the New Testament. If we knew nothing about contemporary Judaism, we could hardly begin to exegete the synoptic traditions and much of St. Paul's writings. Used wisely, these materials can add a basic dimension to our comprehension of the New Testament. Used indiscriminately, they can lead us up many a blind alley. But no reader of the New Testament can say they are irrelevant.

NOTES

1. Cf. B. Lindars, *New Testament Apologetic* (London 1961), pp. 32–137.
2. W. Förster, *Palestinian Judaism in New Testament Times* (E.T. Edinburgh 1964).
3. W. D. Davies, *Paul & Rabbinic Judaism* (London 1970[3]), pp. 303ff. At the same time, we cannot understand the ideas that Paul was opposing without taking into account the Gnosticising background of the Corinthian correspondence: cf. W. Schmithals, *Gnosticism in Corinth* (E.T. Nashville 1971), pp. 155–159.
4. Cf. J. H. Charlesworth (ed.), *John and Qumran* (London 1972).
5. After a survey of the present debate on the Fourth Gospel, A. M. Hunter is willing to date it as early as A.D. 80. Cf. his *According to John* (London 1968). J. A. T. Robinson is willing to support an even earlier date; see his book, *Redating the New Testament* (London 1976).
6. E.T. *Light from the Ancient East* (London 1927).
7. For a comprehensive account of all this material, see J. M. Hull, *Hellenistic Magic and the Synoptic Tradition* (London 1974), pp. 5–15, 20–44.
8. For an account of their discovery, cf. J. Doresse, *The Secret Books of the Egyptian Gnostics,* (E.T. London 1960).
9. See B. M. Metzger, "Methodology in the Study of the Mystery Religions", in *Historical and Literary Studies,* (Leiden 1968), pp. 1–24 (originally in *Harvard Theological Review,* 48, 1955, 1–20).
10. According to N. H. Snaith, *The Distinctive Ideas of the Old Testament* (London 1944),

p. 9, knowledge of God was the one feature of Old Testament religion that distinguished it from other ancient religions.

11. Cf. W. D. Davies, *Christian Origins and Judaism* (London 1962), pp. 119–144. F. F. Bruce, *Second Thoughts on the Dead Sea Scrolls* (Exeter 1966), pp. 115f.

12. Cf. Philo, *Somn.* II.226.

13. The kind of study required is exemplified in J. Dupont, *Gnosis* (Louvain/Paris 1949).

14. E.T. Nashville 1970.

15. Op. cit., pp. 119–152.

16. For a full discussion of this particular example, see J. G. Machen, *The Origin of Paul's Religion* (London 1921), pp. 293–317; V. Taylor, *The Names of Jesus* (London 1953), pp. 38–51. In a recent discussion of the christology of the early church, M. Hengel argues that there is little value in considering the Hellenistic parallels at all, and suggests that its true background is to be found in Judaism and the Old Testament (*The Son of God*, E.T. London 1976).

17. J. Barr, *The Semantics of Biblical Language* (London 1961).

18. For the value of rabbinic parables, cf. P. Fiebig, *Jüdische Wundergeschichten des neutestamentlichen Zeitalters unter besonderer Berücksichtigung ihres Verhältnisses zum Neuen Testament* (Tübingen 1911). SB *in loc.* cite a number of rabbinic parallels, while R. Bultmann often refers to them in his *History of the Synoptic Tradition* (E.T. Oxford 1972), pp. 209–244.

19. According to Fiebig (op. cit.) the rabbinic parallels are the only ones worth taking seriously, for they at least share the monotheism of the New Testament traditions, whereas the Hellenistic parallels are usually polytheistic. But Dibelius has argued on form-critical grounds that the rabbinic miracle stories are quite different from their Christian counterparts and from the Hellenistic stories. Rabbinic miracles fall into two formal types: "theodicy legends", designed to show God's interest in the keeping of the Law, and "personal legends", designed to enhance the reputation of the wonder-worker. Since there is no formal analogy to these types in the New Testament, he argues that there can have been no real relationship (*From Tradition to Gospel,* E. T. Greenwood 1971, pp. 133–151). On this whole question of Hellenistic and Rabbinic parallels, cf. L. Sabourin, "Hellenistic and Rabbinic 'Miracles' ", *Biblical Theology Bulletin* 2 (1972), pp. 281-307.

20. Cf. H. D. Betz, "Jesus as Divine Man", in *Jesus and the Historian,* ed. F. T. Trotter (Philadelphia 1968), pp. 114–133.

21. According to Petronius, *Sat.* 17, in Rome "the gods walk abroad so commonly in our streets that it is easier to meet a god than a man."

22. Cf. Hull, op. cit., pp. 61–72. Dibelius, op. cit., pp.81-103

23. R. P. Martin, *Mark: Evangelist and Theologian* (Exeter 1972), pp. 175f, 214ff.

24. Op. cit., pp. 142–145.

25. See p. 160.

26. For this kind of study, cf. H. van der Loos, *The Miracles of Jesus* (Leiden 1968[2], Supplement to Nov.T IX).

27. Hull, op. cit., pp. 42ff.

28. "We can perhaps venture to suggest . . . that Jesus did not think of himself as a magician . . . But to the early Christian the myth of the magus was helpful in various ways; it drew attention to certain aspects of the salvation of Christ in a manner which no other myth was able to do." (Hull, op. cit., p. 145).

29. Jesus and his followers were often portrayed as Hellenistic magicians in the second century and many of the apocryphal gospels describe miracles that are clearly borrowed from Hellenistic magical traditions. Compared with these, the New Testament traditions are remarkable for their constraint and their recognition that the portrayal of Jesus as a master-magician was not the final judgment on his significance. Cf. Hull, op. cit., pp. 1–4.

30. Cf. R. H. Fuller, *Interpreting the Miracles* (London, 1963), pp. 39–45. A. Richardson, *The Miracle Stories of the Gospels* (London 1941), pp. 38–58.

31. Cf. inter alia R. Bultmann, *The Gospel of John* (E.T. Oxford 1971), p. 102 n. 1.

32. For a full discussion of this theory, see E. M. Yamauchi, *Pre-Christian Gnosticism* (London 1973), pp. 163–169.

CHAPTER VII

HISTORICAL CRITICISM

I. H. Marshall

I. *Aims and Method*

By "historical criticism" is meant the study of any narrative which purports to convey historical information in order to determine what actually happened and is described or alluded to in the passage in question. The phrase "what actually happened" is by no means free from difficulties of interpretation, but a common-sense view of it will suffice us in the present discussion.

Historical study may be undertaken in order to throw light on an obscure narrative by determining more precisely the nature of the events to which it bears witness. In his useful study of the matter G. E. Ladd illustrates how the meaning of various statements in the New Testament becomes apparent to the modern reader only when they are placed within their historical context.[1] In John 4:6 Jesus is said to have sat at the well near Sychar at "the sixth hour". If this detail is "historical" (i.e. refers to what actually happened), it must have been remembered and recorded because it conveyed some significant information to the original readers, but for the modern reader it is a mere, empty time note without some elucidation. A knowledge of Jewish chronology enables us to state that the equivalent time in modern terms was probably noon.[2] If so, the detail indicates that this was the hottest time of day, and helps us to understand why Jesus felt tired from his journey and thirsty.[3] Here we see how a mixture of historical skills – a knowledge of ancient chronology and insight into normal human feelings – may be used to illuminate the verse in question so that the modern reader may gain from it the full meaning which the author intended to be grasped by his original readers.

Alongside this task of *elucidation* a second aim of historical criticism is to *test the historical accuracy* of what purports to be historical narrative. In the Acts of the Apostles several pieces of local colour, e.g. the various titles given to magistrates, have been shown to be accurate by the production of confirmatory evidence from inscriptions and other ancient documents. It is well known that Sir W. M. Ramsay began his archaeological researches in Asia Minor with the belief that Acts was a tendentious second-century document. The evidence which he discovered led him to the verdict that Luke was a first-class historian, and he devoted the rest of his life to further researches designed to find confirmatory evidence for the historical truth of the NT.[4]

The problems that arise in pursuing these two aims are obviously those of applying historical science to the NT. This method consists in the careful scrutiny of any given narrative by itself and in comparison with whatever other sources of information are able to shed any light on it and the incidents which it records. The marks of the good historian are consequently that he possesses a good knowledge of all the sources which may be relevant, that he is adept at probing into their reliability and establishing what is historically probable, and that he is capable of framing a historical hypothesis which will successfully account for what the sources say. He interrogates the texts in order to construct a picture of the event which they reflect, a picture which will be in itself historically coherent and which will also serve to explain the wording of the sources. His tools include the various types of criticism discussed elsewhere in this volume, and he uses them to work back from the historical narrative to its possible sources and so to the incident which gave rise to them. We say "incident", but it should be remembered that various historical situations may have influenced the narration of the story at different stages in its transmission, and these need to be taken into account by the historian.[5]

It will be clear that many factors enter into the historian's reconstruction of the past, and that he cannot always arrive at certainty. Too often the sources are fragmentary and opaque, too often the original events are too complex for any source to reproduce them fully, too often several reconstructions of what happened are possible. The historian is frequently reduced to reasoned conjectures and assessments of comparative probabilities.

II. *Historical Problems in the New Testament*

The process of historical study often suggests that events did not happen exactly as they are reported in a particular source. So far as the New Testament is concerned such conclusions can arise in a number of ways.

1. DISCREPANCIES BETWEEN PARALLEL NARRATIVES

Comparison of different accounts of the same incidents in the NT may lead to the conclusion that two or more of them cannot simultaneously be true. For example, the order of events in Mt. 8 is quite different from the order of the same events in Mk. In Mt. the healing of a leper (Mt. 8:1–4) precedes the healings of Peter's mother-in-law and of the crowds in the evening (Mt. 8:14–17), but in Mk. the order is the reverse (Mk. 1:40–45, 29–34); again the crossing of the lake and stilling of the storm occur in Mt. 8:23–27 long before the teaching in parables in Mt. 13, but in Mk. 4 the teaching in parables occurs just before the crossing of the lake. It is clear that one or both narratives cannot be in chronological order.

In the same way parallel accounts of the same incidents may differ from each other. In Mt. 21:40f. Jesus reaches the climax of the parable of the wicked husbandmen by asking what the owner of the vineyard will do to his tenants. The question is answered by the audience, and then Jesus replies by quoting Ps. 118:22f. In Lk. 20:15–17, however, Jesus answers his own question, and the audience replies, "God forbid", before Jesus goes on to cite the Psalm. Both accounts of the conversation cannot simultaneously be literally true.[6] Or did Jesus allow or forbid the use of a staff to the Twelve when he sent them out on their missionary travels (Mt. 10:10; Mk. 6:8)?

2. COMPARISON WITH NON-BIBLICAL MATERIAL

Exactly the same kind of problems can arise when the NT narratives are compared with evidence from secular history, both in written accounts and in archaeological records. There is still no completely satisfactory solution to the problem arising from Luke's statement that Quirinius was in office as governor of Syria and conducted a census at the time of the birth of Jesus *before* the death of Herod (Lk. 2:1f.; cf. Mt. 2:1) when compared with Josephus' statement that Quirinius was governor and held the census several years *after* Herod's death (Josephus, *Antiquities* 17:135; 18:1f.)[7]

3. HISTORICAL IMPROBABILITIES

Some narratives contain incidents which appear to be inherently improbable. This can happen with ordinary, everyday events. One of the most serious attacks on the historicity of the Gospel of Mark came from W. Wrede who argued that the whole series of commands to keep the deeds and teaching of Jesus secret were incapable of being carried out, and hence unhistorical: how, for example, could Jairus and his wife have kept the cure of their daughter secret (Mk. 5:43) after her death had already been publicly announced?[8]

4. SUPERNATURAL OCCURRENCES

The suggestion of improbability is all the stronger when the stories contain miracles, visions of heavenly beings and prophetic knowledge of the future. The problem here has two sides.

On the one hand, there is scepticism regarding the possibility of such events. Some scholars reject the supernatural out of hand. Others, while theoretically preserving an open mind, act in accordance with Hume's principle: while miracles are rare occurrences, it is not rare for witnesses to be mistaken, especially in an era when superstition abounded and modern scientific knowledge was lacking. Every apparent example of the supernatural must therefore be scrutinised with care for the possibility of a natural explanation. Behind this attitude lies the belief that ancient history should be regarded as continuous in character with modern history, so that the one can be interpreted on the analogy of the other. Since (it is said) the supernatural is unknown today, it cannot be admitted into explanations of the past.[9]

On the other hand, it is argued that even if a person believes in the supernatural as a private individual, he cannot as a historian allow supernatural explanations of events. To do so would be to abandon the ordinary principle of natural cause and effect in history and to allow a place to the irrational. This procedure would put an end to historical method, since historical method, like scientific method, must proceed on the basis of natural causation. To accept the supernatural would mean giving up the usual methods of establishing historical probability and leave no firm basis for historical investigation, since no grounds would exist for preferring one account of an event to another.

The result of these considerations is that many scholars feel bound to explain the events behind the NT in natural terms and to refuse to allow any place to the supernatural as a possible category of interpretation.

5. CREATION AND MODIFICATION OF MATERIAL IN THE EARLY CHURCH

What appears to be a historical narrative can sometimes be explained as the product of the inventive faculty of a community or individual. Scholars applying the method of tradition criticism often assert that in the case of the so-called pronouncement stories the original element is simply the saying ascribed (correctly or incorrectly) to Jesus: these sayings were remembered because they were important for the early church, and it was the early church which invented the settings for such isolated and context-less sayings. Much attention has been devoted to tracing the development of traditions, and whenever an element in a story or saying appears to reflect a particular interest of the church or the predilection of an Evangelist the temptation is to argue that the church or Evangelist *created* the element (rather than that they *preserved* it because of its inherent value to them). What appears to be historical can thus often be explained as historical fiction, and the genesis of a narrative may be explained more plausibly in terms of the motives which animated the mind of its creator than in terms of a purported historical event reported in it.

6. LITERARY GENRE

The historian needs to ask whether any narrative which is a *prima facie* historical account has been assigned to its correct literary genre. A historical narrative may turn out to be a historical novel. Did the writers of the Gospels intend them to be taken as historical documents in the sense that they are in their entirety reliable accounts of events as they actually happened? It could be that the significance of Jesus was too great to be expressed within the limits of a historical narrative: do we therefore fall into the error of reading as history what was never intended to be so understood? What, for example, is the historical status of the temptations in the wilderness? Have the NT writers woven event and interpretation together in such a way that interpretation may appear in the guise of historical event? Was the story of the tearing of the temple veil (Mk. 15:38) intended to be a historical account or a piece of symbolism (to signify the opening up of the presence of God to all believers)?

7. INSUFFICIENT EVIDENCE

A final question concerns the amount of evidence needed to demonstrate that an event took place. Suppose that we have a single narrative of some event, with no confirmatory evidence from other sources: is that report adequate as a basis for belief, especially if the event is unusual or supernatural? Only Jn. 11 tells us of the raising of Lazarus: is that sufficient evidence to justify us in believing that such a stupendous event occurred despite its miraculous nature and despite the silence of the other Gospels? What is adequate evidence? Is it possible to prove historically that salient events in the life of Jesus occurred? There is surely a distinction between being able to say that a certain event (e.g. that there was a person called Jesus of Nazareth) took place with a probability approaching certainty and merely being able to say that there is no evidence that an event did not take place. If the events in question are said to be the basis for religious faith, then the question is manifestly of crucial importance.

III. *The Legitimacy of Historical Study*

It is not surprising that many people feel worried if the application of the historical method leads to the conclusion that certain events described in the NT either did not take place as they are recorded or cannot be established above a low degree of probability. The discovery of errors is not a problem in the same kind of way in the study of some secular history. Nobody is particularly disturbed by finding errors in Josephus and having to make allowance for them, however inconvenient this may be to the student of Jewish history. No problem of religious faith arises. The matter is more worrying for the Christian believer whose faith includes the belief that the Bible is in some sense true and reliable. He has come to the study of the NT with this working presupposition. It may not be superfluous to observe that at least he is (or should be) aware of the existence of this presupposition, and also that, if he is intellectually honest, he must be prepared to test its validity. It may also be worth observing that the contrary belief (namely, that the Bible is not reliable) is every bit as much a presupposition, and indeed from one important point of view a much less likely one, since there is a good case that the Bible does claim to be a reliable revelation of God and that this claim is a justifiable one.[10]

What, then, is to be the Christian believer's attitude to historical study? Many students have been tempted to conclude that there must be something wrong with a method which leads to such alarming conclusions, and therefore to pronounce the method illegitimate. But in reality the Christian cannot deny the *legitimacy of historical criticism.* If he is correct in his presuppositions, then the effects of such criticism should be ultimately to confirm the historicity of the NT.

In fact anybody who tries to understand the NT or to defend its historicity against sceptics by any kind of reasonable argument is already practising the historical method. He may try to argue that he personally does not need any historical proof of the truth of the NT because this is a matter of faith and not of proof, but this is not so. Not only does he need to practise it in order to overcome the arguments of sceptics and give an apologetic for Christianity (insofar as this can be done by historical argument); he also needs it in order to elucidate the historical statements made in the NT. There *are* problems of interpretation in the NT that cannot be solved apart from historical study, and it does no good to ignore them and try to move on straight to a spiritual or devotional exposition of a passage.[11] There are, for example, two *prima facie* different datings of the crucifixion in the Synoptic Gospels and John: it is impossible to study the Gospels seriously and avoid trying to discover *when* Jesus was crucified and *why* the Gospel records differ on so important a date. Historical criticism is both legitimate and necessary.

There is a deeper sense in which it is necessary. It must be practised in order to throw light on *the nature of the truth which is to be ascribed to the NT*. The answer to this question can be determined only by applying historical criticism to the actual phenomena. Two examples will illustrate the point.

First, as was indicated above, the *form* of a narrative must be taken into account in order to determine whether or not it was meant to convey historical truth. The parables of Jesus are related as if they were stories of real events. But nobody would claim that there *must* have been a historical good Samaritan or prodigal son in order that these two stories may be "true". The parabolic form does not demand the historicity of the story.

Second, the *aims* of the author must be considered. He may not have wished to give more than a summary of an event. Matthew so abbreviates the story of Jairus' daughter that one gains the impression that she had already died before Jairus first approached Jesus (Mt. 9:18), but according to Mark at this point she was only *in extremis,* and not until later did Jairus learn that she had died (Mk. 5:23, 35; cf. Lk. 8:42, 49). What Matthew reports is, therefore, *not* what actually happened, and it stands in contradiction to the report of Mark. But when Matthew's method of abbreviation (possibly in order to make room for additional material elsewhere in his Gospel) is taken into account, it is seen that he was not concerned with detailed accuracy, and he should not be faulted for what he was not trying to do. In the same way a first-century audience would not have expected the brief accounts of the various sermons in Acts to be *verbatim* accounts of what was actually said, any more than we would expect the same of brief newspaper reports of parliamentary speeches (as opposed to detailed reports in *Hansard*).

These examples indicate that the *prima facie* impression which may be gained by an untutored or naive modern reader of the NT can be wrong, and that historical criticism is needed in order to clarify what the NT intends to teach. Belief in the "truth" of the Bible cannot be a substitute for historical study. We may wish that this was the case, that God had given us a Bible that would be instantly and correctly understandable by any modern man. But he has not done so, just as he has not given us a Bible with a guaranteed text (instead of one that has to be determined by the techniques of textual criticism) or in a modern *lingua franca* (instead of having to be laboriously translated into many different human tongues). The Bible needs interpretation, and historical criticism is part of that process. This is not, of course, to say that the Bible is hopelessly obscure until the scholars have done their work on it; its broad meaning is clear enough, but the details of interpretation need scholarly skill.

IV. *The Implications of Inspiration*

The previous section attempted to show that our understanding of the historical truth of the NT must be formulated in the light of historical criticism – and that in this light some of the apparent difficulties in regarding the NT as historically reliable disappear. We must now stress the converse point, that the process of historical criticism must take place in the light of the doctrine of biblical inspiration. For example, John Calvin was not insensitive to the existence of historical problems in the NT, and did not brush them aside. He observed the problem caused by the different datings of the crucifixion in the Synoptic Gospels and John. Let it be noted that there is nothing wrong in establishing such a discrepancy. (If conservative scholars have been slow to look for such things, it has usually been because they have been too busy looking for answers to problems turned up by their more sceptical colleagues). What is wrong is to stop at this point. So Calvin goes on to seek a solution to the discrepancy in terms of the Jewish calendar. He looks for a solution to the problem which will not sacrifice the historical accuracy of the NT authors. He attempts a *harmonization* in the light of historical knowledge.[12]

This sort of procedure is surely legitimate. If any particular event has been described by several witnesses, it is fair to expect that they will be in agreement, although allowance must be made for errors of observation and memory. A full picture can be gained only by piecing together several testimonies from different points of view. We would have a one-sided and wrong view of the chronology of the passion if we had only one of the sources in question.

Nevertheless, harmonization of the Gospels has aroused much adverse comment. There may be only one original written source (as in passages where two Synoptic writers are dependent on the third), so that differences between parallel accounts may be due to the growth of tradition or to independent editorial revision. This objection has some force, but is not decisive. For, first, it ignores the evidence of continuing oral traditions which may have preserved features omitted from the written sources used by the Evangelists.[13] Second, the work of the later Evangelist may be an "exegesis" of his source through which features which were played down or obscured in the source but were nevertheless latent in it may be brought out more clearly: *Tendenz* is not necessarily the fruit of creative imagination. It is true that much misapplication of harmonization has brought the process into disrepute. The theory which harmonizes the two accounts of the healing of the centurion's servant by arguing that the centurion came to Jesus himself (Mt. 8:5–13) *and* sent two deputations of friends to him, the latter of whom repeated the centurion's own message *verbatim* (Lk. 7:1–10)[14] is rightly to be rejected as too great a strain on credulity. Harmonization is legitimate, but only when the hypotheses necessary to establish harmony are not more unlikely than the hypothesis of non-historical reporting in one or more of the sources.

A conservative outlook may thus lead the critic to a more earnest reckoning with the possible historicity of his sources and hence to the discovery of historical material which may otherwise have gone undetected. Simple loyalty to the truth is all that should be required to lead to such effort – the willingness to check each and every theory, and to take nothing for granted. But the history of NT interpretation shows that where the conservative has not played his part the sceptic has often been content with inadequate solutions to problems, and has not tested them carefully in the light of the possibility that "*Die Bibel hat doch Recht*".[15] Historical criticism must press on beyond what may be a superficial solution of a given solution in terms of the error of the source to a deeper solution which may be able to resolve the apparent error in the light of a more exact knowledge of the historical situation.

V. *Conservatism and Scepticism*

Such an attitude may well seem to have certain weaknesses. First, *conservative scholars may often seem unduly reactionary in their refusal to accept hypotheses which depend on the presence of errors and contradictions in the NT*. Thereby they appear to have precluded the possibility of fruitful research. For example, conservative scholars have never been very happy about the dismemberment of the Epistles to the Corinthians, especially the view of Hausrath that 2 Cor. 10–13 forms part of an earlier Epistle than 2 Cor. 1–9, since this means that the various fragments have been erroneously joined together in the wrong order. It could be argued that by this obstinate refusal to accept an "assured result" of criticism they have prevented themselves from entering into a fruitful discussion of the historical development of the Corinthian church or of Paul's own thought. But two comments are in order. First, recent study suggests that earlier conservatives may well have been right in their hesitation (whatever their grounds for it); one solution to the enigma of 2 Corinthians that finds increasing favour at present regards 2 Cor. 10–13 as posterior to 2 Cor. 1–9 and forming part of a later Epistle.[16] Second, if the historical evidence demands the dismemberment of the Epistle, and if there is no doctrinal reason why this should be regarded as illegitimate, then modern scholars should not be bound by the attitudes of an earlier generation.

What this illustration demonstrates is not that the historical method is wrong – for it is only by the application of it that a better solution to the problem can be found – but rather that the conservative is right to insist on the element of conjecture in many proposed solutions and therefore to be sceptical towards them.

This raises the possibility of another weakness in our approach. How far should scepticism be carried? After all, the basis for the newer view of 2 Corinthians may be no better founded than the old, even if it is a more congenial solution. Is the conservative sufficiently sceptical with regard to conservative solutions to problems? Indeed – and this is the crucial point – *ought he not to adopt an approach of methodological scepticism towards the NT text itself*? The conservative, it may be argued, is prepared to adopt the principle of historical criticism only up to a point; he refuses to apply to the text that wholesale scepticism and questioning attitude which is the mark of the historian.[17]

This description of the conservative attitude is correct; what is debatable is whether it represents an illegitimate, unhistorical approach to the text. It is surely one thing to interrogate a text minutely in order to discover all that it really says or implies; it is quite another to disbelieve every statement that it makes until it can be proved to be true. It is at this point that a clear distinction emerges between the so-called conservative and radical viewpoints. The position adopted by the sceptical historian is thoroughly unrealistic – as he would soon realise if he attempted to apply it to all the ordinary statements made to him by other people in the course of everyday life.[18] If we have a narrative that purports to be historical from a writer whose general content is known to be reliable, it is more reasonable to accept it as reliable until satisfactory evidence is produced against it. *In the absence of contrary evidence belief is reasonable.*[19] When a scholar finds that his general belief in the reliability of the NT is confirmed by the available historical evidence, he has every right to protest that methodological scepticism is unjustified.[20]

One important special factor in this connection is the *question of the supernatural.* The conservative scholar accepts the possibility, and indeed the probability, of the supernatural. "If the universe is dominated by a Spirit, miracles are possible; if by a Spirit that is Love, probable; and if that Spirit has become incarnate, this miracle would make further ones very probable indeed."[21] As a Christian historian he cannot rule the supernatural out of court in his attempt to furnish a historical account of the phenomena behind the NT. To do so would be to provide a naturalistic explanation of what, as a Christian, he believes to be supernatural; it would indeed be to explain away that on which his belief in the supernatural rests. The historian who believes in the possibility of the supernatural cannot divorce his faith from his historical judgment.

But this attitude does not condemn him to a non-historical approach. Historical judgment has to be exercised on the quality of the evidence and the nature of the event to which it bears witness. What appeared miraculous to the contemporaries of Jesus may in some cases be better explained in terms of insights derived from psychosomatic medicine. The nature of the evidence may be such that an account of the miraculous is not to be taken at its face value.[22] Nevertheless, if the historical critic is convinced of the reality of the incarnation, he will be prepared to account for certain events as miraculous without any sense of incongruity or lack of historical sense. It has been sufficiently demonstrated by W. Pannenberg that there can be cases where the historian can admit the supernatural without in any way abandoning the principles of historical method.[23]

VI. *Conclusion*

The argument so far has attempted to show that the application of the historical method leads to the elucidation of the NT and the resolution of the historical problems which it contains. A scepticism towards solutions to historical problems which postulate the unreliability of the NT documents is justified by its results. It is sensible to adopt an attitude of scholarly caution towards historical conjectures, whether they tend towards disproving or confirming the historicity of the NT narratives.

These points, however, do not remove the possibility of discovering intractable historical difficulties in the NT. There may be a stage at which the difficulties involved in explaining away an apparent historical error are greater than those caused by accepting the existence of the error. Theories which attempt to harmonise the narratives of Easter morning by postulating several different visits by the women to the tomb seem much more improbable than those which allow for a certain amount of confusion in the narratives,[24] just as there came a point when the pre-Copernican solution to the movements of the planets, though mathematically possible, broke down under the weight of the number of epicycles which more accurate observation of the heavens made it necessary to postulate, and the simpler Copernican system became much more probable. More generally, one may ask whether there is a stage when the number of alleged historical difficulties for which there is as yet no solution must lead the conservative scholar to conclude that the absolute historical reliability of the NT is a mirage: is there a point at which faith becomes sheer credulity? On more than one occasion Calvin himself notes the indifference of the Evangelists to details of times and sequences:[25] was the Spirit less concerned about such matters than we are?

It is certainly impossible to practise the historical method without concluding that on occasion the correct solution to a difficulty lies in the unhistorical character of a particular narrative. Several cases of this kind have been cited above, but in many of them we have claimed that to establish that a particular statement is unhistorical is not to establish the presence of an error which would call in question the reliability of the NT writer. Very often the reader may be demanding a kind of historical truth from the narrative which it was never intended to provide.

We must of course sympathise with the ordinary reader of the Bible at this point. He may well argue that if what the text says did not happen, then it is in error, and that to explain the text in terms of an abbreviated narrative or an interpreted narrative or even as a piece of symbolism is illegitimate. But sympathy is not an argument for dispensing with reason. The ordinary reader may not be able to recognise when unusual literary categories are being intentionally and properly used by the NT writers any more than the average reader of the Greek NT is likely to detect the presence of the odd examples of prose and verse rhythms that can be found in it by a person trained to do so.[26]

When all this is said, however, there will still remain cases of apparent historical error which cannot be explained away with the knowledge at present at our disposal. There is a difference of opinion among scholars of a conservative inclination regarding these. Some scholars are prepared to allow that a Bible which is infallible in its doctrinal statements may nevertheless contain inaccurate historical statements in matters that do not affect its doctrinal affirmations: the truth of the incarnation is not affected if one or both of the genealogies assigned to Jesus are not accurate in every detail. Others would disagree, and claim that, even if no solution is *known* at present, nevertheless a solution *exists* and will one day become known. So far as doctrine is concerned, these two views obviously differ, although not perhaps as much as their proponents may think. In practice, however, they are not so very different, for where the former group of scholars admit *real* error, the latter group must admit *apparent* error. What is important is that scholars of both persuasions are equally committed to the search for truth – God's truth – and both are required to be humble and cautious in their statements regarding the phenomena in the NT. Both groups can and must work together in a spirit of mutual understanding instead of yielding to their respective tendencies to regard the others as beyond the pale or as dangerous heretics. Only through mutual cooperation and discussion are we likely to come to a resolution of these as yet unsolved problems.

NOTES

1. G. E. Ladd, *The New Testament and Criticism* (London 1970), pp. 171–194.
2. Most commentators agree that John reckoned the hours of the day from 6.00 am.
3. It has been argued that John used a different system of chronology (see N. Walker, "The Reckoning of Hours in the Fourth Gospel", Nov. T 4 (1960), pp. 69–73; also however, J. E. Bruns, "The Use of Time in the Fourth Gospel", NTS 13 (1966–67), pp. 285–290).
4. W. W. Gasque, *Sir William Ramsay: Archaeologist and New Testament Scholar* (Grand Rapids 1966).
5. V. A. Harvey, *The Historian and the Believer* (London 1967).
6. In the account in Mk. 12:9f. the crowds do not intervene at this point.
7. The case against Luke's reliability is presented most fully and strongly by E. Schürer, *The History of the Jewish People in the Age of Jesus* Christ (175 B.C. – A.D. 135), revised edition by G. Vermes and F. Millar, (Edinburgh 1973), Vol. I, pp. 399–427. In defence of Luke see E. Stauffer, *Jesus and his Story* (London 1960).
8. W. Wrede, *The Messianic Secret* (Cambridge 1971). See, however, J. D. G. Dunn, "The Messianic Secret in Mark", Tyn. B. 21 (1970), pp. 92–117.
9. R. Bultmann, *Existence and Faith* (London 1961).
10. J. I. Packer, *"Fundamentalism" and the Word of God* (London 1958); J. W. Wenham, *Christ and the Bible* (London 1972).
11. It is unfortunately the case that all too frequently evangelical scholars ignore these questions and give the impression that they do not exist.
12. J. Calvin, *A Harmony of the Gospels* (Edinburgh 1972), Vol. III, pp. 126f. Calvin's solution may not be acceptable; our point is simply that he did look for a solution which would do justice to all the evidence. The modern scholar is required to find a better solution in the same kind of way.
13. Some such theory appears to be necessary in order to explain (for example) the agreements of Matthew and Luke with each other against Mark in the so-called "triple tradition"; cf. T. Schramm, *Der Markus-Stoff bei Lukas* (Cambridge 1971).
14. N. Geldenhuys, *Commentary on the Gospel of Luke* (London 1950), pp. 220f.
15. The title of a well-known popular book by W. Keller, translated as *The Bible as History* (London 1956).
16. F. F. Bruce, *1 and 2 Corinthians* (London 1971); C. K. Barrett, *2 Corinthians* (London 1974). To be sure, this theory still requires that 2 Corinthians be regarded as a compilation.
17. See especially V. A. Harvey, op. cit.
18. Such ordinary statements form historical data. If the historian, bidding farewell to a departing friend, were to stop to question such a statement as "Hurry up and get off the train; the signal is at green", he would be taken where he did not wish to go.
19. This principle obviously does not commit us to believing any cock-and-bull story simply because it sounds plausible. It operates in the area where a writer may reasonably be regarded as attempting to convey historical fact.
20. We would thus align ourselves with those scholars who insist that it is not the authenticity of sayings attributed to Jesus that needs to be demonstrated (so N. Perrin, *Rediscovering the Teaching of Jesus* (London 1967), p. 39), but rather it is the inauthenticity that needs to be demonstrated: a saying attributed to Jesus can be accepted as authentic until it is shown not to be authentic (C. Colpe, TDNT VIII, pp. 432, 434f.; W. G. Kümmel, *Die Theologie des Neuen Testaments* (Göttingen 1969), pp. 22–24; J. Jeremias, *New Testament Theology* (London 1971), Vol. I, p. 37).
21. T. E. Jessop, cited by A. M. Hunter, *The Work and Words of Jesus* (London 1950), p. 59.
22. For example, in view of the evidence given by Mk. 5:1–20, it is highly unlikely that Matthew's description of the healing of *two* Gadarene demoniacs (Mt. 8:28–34) is to be regarded as historical; even N. Geldenhuys, hardly a radical critic, suggests the possibility that "Matthew, after his fashion, conflates two incidents here" (Op. cit., p. 258).

23. W. Pannenberg, *Jesus – God and Man* (London 1968), p. 109; cf. D. P. Fuller, *Easter Faith and History* (Grand Rapids 1964), p. 251; R. J. Sider, "The Historian, the Miraculous and Post-Newtonian Man". SJT 25 (1972), 309–319.
24. This is not to say that the narratives are necessarily irreconcilable, but that so far nobody has produced a convincing hypothesis.
25. J. Calvin, op. cit., I, p. 168.
26. F. Blass, A. Debrunner and R. Funk. *A Greek Grammar of the New Testament* (Chicago 1961), paras. 487, 488.

CHAPTER VIII

SOURCE CRITICISM

David Wenham

I. *The Justification for Source Criticism*

In the prologue to his gospel the author of Luke/Acts refers to many people before him who had "undertaken to compile an account of the things that have been fulfilled among us" (1:1). It is reasonable to infer from this that he knew some of these earlier writings, and it seems likely that he would have been influenced by them to a greater or lesser extent in the writing of his own gospel. There is nothing comparable to Luke's prologue in the other gospels, but it may be surmised that the other evangelists would have been in a similar position to the author of Luke/Acts, at least if their gospels are rightly dated after A.D. 50 or 60. It is not likely, despite the claims of some, that the highly literate Christian community of the first century will have studiously refrained from putting into writing traditions of the life and teaching of Jesus for the first thirty years of its existence, however much it expected the imminent end of the present age.

A case for source criticism might be made out on such *a priori* grounds, but the decisive evidence for the use of sources in the New Testament lies in the New Testament documents themselves. Not only are there dislocations [1] and apparent duplications [2] in the documents which suggest that the gospels, for example, have undergone a more complex editorial process than is often imagined; but much more important and much less ambiguous evidence is provided by the striking phenomenon of agreement between the synoptic gospels in certain passages. [3] The agreement is too close to be explained as the accidental convergence of independent accounts, and the only adequate explanation is either in terms of a common source lying behind the different accounts or in terms of mutual dependence. [4]

Source criticism is needed to explain this sort of evidence, and it has not been displaced either by form criticism, which tries to explain how a story or saying was used in the oral tradition of the church before being incorporated into a source, or by redaction criticism, which seeks to analyse the New Testament writers' use of their sources. The form critic in fact needs the insights of source criticism, since he must trace the literary history of the traditions as far back as he can before speculating about the oral period; and so does the redaction critic, since he can comment reliably on an author's editorial tendencies only if he knows what sources the author was using.

II. *The Methods of Source Criticism*

1. WHERE THERE ARE TWO OR MORE OVERLAPPING TRADITIONS

The search for sources is an easier and much less speculative enterprise when the critic has several parallel traditions to analyse, such as the three synoptic gospels, than when he has only one. Given such a situation his procedure will be (a) to note the evidence internal to the documents themselves, i.e. the areas of overlap and the points of difference in the different traditions,[5] (b) to note any relevant external evidence, e.g. the statements of the early church fathers about the writing of the gospels, and (c) to propose and test different possible explanations of the evidence for comprehensiveness and simplicity. Comprehensiveness is important, since simplicity is no virtue if any substantial part of the evidence is not accounted for; but simplicity is also a significant criterion, since almost any theory can be made comprehensive if sufficient modifications and exceptions are allowed.[6]

(a) *Explaining the internal evidence.* So far as internal evidence is concerned, the basic grist to the critic's mill is the combination of agreement and disagreement in the parallel documents; in the case of the gospels this includes agreement and disagreement in wording, order, contents, style, ideas and theology.

(i) *Wording.* The extensive verbal agreement of Matthew, Mark and Luke in various passages seems to most people to point to some sort of literary connexion, direct or indirect, between the synoptic gospels.[7] When it comes to asking more precisely about their relationship to each other, it is observed that the three gospels have a very considerable amount of material where they all run parallel to each other, and that in this so-called Triple Tradition Matthew and Luke agree frequently with Mark's wording (and also with his order) either together or independently, but rarely with each other against Mark.[8] It has usually been concluded from this that Mark stands mid-way between Matthew and Luke. Thus, for example, Matthew and Luke may be thought to have used Mark and not to have known each other; or Mark may be supposed to have conflated Matthew and Luke, always following them when they agree together and normally following one or the other when they disagree; or Mark may be thought to have used Matthew, and Luke may be thought to have used Mark.

These and other hypotheses make sense of the phenomenon in question, and to try to narrow down the number of options on the basis of the evidence of the wording is not easy, much of it being difficult to handle.

Thus it is particularly difficult to explain the different levels of agreement in the different parts of the tradition, for example in the Q material, i.e. in the passages where Matthew and Luke have parallel material which is not found in Mark. Some think that the fact that Matthew and Luke agree closely sometimes and very loosely at other times is explicable if they were using a single common source; others prefer to think in terms of a number of tracts of Q material. Deciding between such alternatives is not easy, since the evangelists were not simply copyists and scissors-and-paste editors, but individuals with minds of their own and also very probably with some knowledge of oral traditions of the life and teaching of Jesus.[9] The critic therefore has to ask himself whether his knowledge of the evangelist's style and interests suggests that a particular difference can be explained as an editorial alteration by one evangelist or the other, and/or whether one or other of the evangelists may not have diverged from his written source under the influence of some oral tradition. Very often the answer will not be at all obvious.

(ii) *Order*. The conclusion that Mark stands mid-way between Matthew and Luke is suggested by the agreements and disagreements of Matthew, Mark and Luke in the ordering of their common material; but the significance of the phenomenon of order is in other respects less clear. For example, it has long been observed that the Q material is differently arranged in Matthew and Luke; in Matthew it is distributed through the gospel, in Luke it is found in two main blocks (6:20–7:35; 9:57–13:34). This seems to some to exclude the idea of Luke having known and used Matthew, making something like the document Q indispensable, since it is unreasonable to think of Luke extracting the Q sayings from their Matthean setting and then grouping them together artificially. Others on the other hand find the postulated Lukan editing quite intelligible: Luke was using Mark as his main source, and it was his deliberate policy not to confuse and conflate Mark and his other sources.

Weighing such opinions is difficult, and the disagreement of scholars over such points illustrates the precariousness of arguments about what seems credible and incredible. The danger is that in pronouncing something incredible a scholar will merely reveal his own lack of imagination and his own lack of sympathy with the situation in which the evangelist was writing.

(iii) *Contents – omissions, doublets, misunderstandings*. A comparison of the contents of the different gospels tends to confirm what was said about Mark being mid-way between Matthew and Luke in the Triple Tradition; but does it help us go further in excluding other hypotheses?

Some would wish to argue for Marcan rather than Matthean priority on the grounds that Mark could not have known Matthew and have left out so much valuable material, e.g. the Sermon on the Mount. But this is very much the sort of argument that has already been criticised, being based on assumptions about "what I would have done if I were the evangelist". In fact it is not really so difficult to suppose that Mark might have omitted large tracts of Matthew's teaching material, if, for example, his aim was primarily to write a gospel for the Gentile unbeliever. And even if this was not his aim, it remains true that omissions may well be explicable in terms of an editor's particular interests. The point can be reinforced in this case by two observations: (1) that the problem of omissions exists in one form or another on almost any theory of synoptic origins. Thus, if Luke used Mark, his "Great Omission" of Mark 6:45–8:26 must be explained. (2) That there is reason to believe that Mark omitted material that he might have included whether or not his was the first gospel.[10] It is an attractively simple but quite unlikely assumption that the first evangelist included in his gospel all that he knew of Jesus' life and teaching.

Arguments about supposed omissions or insertions of material may have more force, if it can be shown that the insertion or omission corresponds with some sort of break or disjointedness in the sequence of the narrative.[11] Unfortunately, however, the evidence rarely points unambiguously in one direction, and it will often be arguable that the smoother fuller version of a story is a later writer's revision of the earlier dislocated text.

A rather similar argument is that based on supposed doublets in a gospel, which may be taken to suggest the use of two sources. In Matthew, for example, the accusations that Jesus cast out demons by the prince of demons comes twice (9:34; 12:24), and this is simply explained via the hypothesis that Matthew found the saying both in Q (cf. Lk. 11:15) and also in Mark (3:22). But arguments about doublets are not always quite as simple as they may look. It is not always easy, in the first place, to be sure that two similar stories or saying are in fact the same: there can be no doubt that Jesus did and said the same or similar things on many different occasions, and there is no reason for assuming that the early church could have retained in the tradition only one saying or action of a particular type (e.g. one feeding of the multitudes). A second point to reckon with is the fact that an author may quite possibly repeat himself without this necessarily indicating the use of more than one source.[12]

Like suspected doublets, supposed misunderstandings are a possible but not very reliable means of detecting the use of sources. If it can be shown that something appearing in one document has been misunderstood or misplaced in a second document, then this evidently assists the critic who wishes to decide which of the two documents is secondary. The problem is to identify clear-cut examples.[13]

(iv) *Style.* Source critics have made a lot of the differences of style between the Synoptic Gospels. Thus Mark's has been judged the most primitive gospel, because his Greek is supposedly of a poor standard, containing numerous Aramaisms,[14] and also because he includes the sort of vivid irrelevant details that an eyewitness might be expected to include in a life of Jesus whereas Matthew and Luke omit such things as superfluous.[15]

Unfortunately arguments such as these, at least in the way that they are usually presented, are not at all cogent. An author's style depends very much on the author, and, unless he is copying a source closely and suppressing his own style, an author whose Greek is poor or colloquial or Aramaizing will use that sort of Greek whether or not he is using a source. Mark, for example, was the sort of writer to use *καί* repeatedly, whether he was writing with or without a source.[16] So far as Mark's vivid touches go, both common sense and a study of the development of the gospel tradition in the early church[17] suggest that such things are as likely to have been added into the tradition as omitted from it.

A different and potentially much more convincing argument from style depends on the possibility of detecting differences in style within a particular work according to whether or not a source was being used at a particular point. It has been argued, for example, that Matthew's way of using the Old Testament changes when he begins to run parallel to Mark and that he uses the LXX to a much greater degree in his so-called Marcan quotations than elsewhere,[18] and a different argument from style has recently been proposed on the basis of the statistical analysis of the gospels.[19] These arguments as they have been put forward so far may not be convincing, but the method being tried is one that could prove fruitful.

To say that arguments from style are frequently unsuccessful is not to say that they can never be of any value. In particular instances it may be possible to urge that stylistic peculiarities in one account and not in a parallel account point to a particular relationship. It is, however, important not to claim too much for the evidence and to remember, for example, that on occasion a later gospel may have the most primitive form of a tradition.

(v) *Ideas and theology*. Attempts have been frequently made to try and put the gospels into some sort of chronological order according to their particular ideas or theology. Thus Mark has been thought to have the most primitive account of Jesus' visit to Nazareth, since he speaks of Jesus being *unable* to do miracles (except that he healed a few sick people) (6:5); Matthew here simply and more reverently says that Jesus did not do many miracles (13:58); he does not ascribe any inability to the Lord. Mark later speaks of the disciples failing to understand Jesus' prediction of his death and resurrection (9:32); Matthew speaks of their "grieving exceedingly" (17:23), implying that they understood at least something.

This is another argument that sounds attractive, but which is not in fact as simple as it sounds. 1. It is often hard to be sure that a supposed difference in outlook is a real one; in the case cited, for example, Mark could well have substituted his account of Jesus' visit to Nazareth for Matthew's without intending anything very significant by his alterations. 2. It is not usually easy to tie down a particular idea of theology or outlook to a particular period in early church history. One cannot, for example, say simply that Matthew's gospel is the most Jewish and therefore the most primitive; nor can one assume that a high Christology is always a late Christology.[20]

3. It is a mistake to suppose that the evangelists will simply have mirrored the ideas of the church and of the time in which they lived. If Mark shows a particular interest in the disciples' failings and weaknesses, this does not prove that he was writing in a period before the apostles had come to be revered and respected, but more probably that he saw some particular value in describing the disciples' weaknesses; if he did, then it is quite likely that this would have come across – like his literary style – whether he was using sources or not.

(b) *The external evidence.* The limitations of the arguments based on the internal evidence make the potential importance of the external evidence greater. There has in recent years been a tendency to neglect the statements of the church fathers relating to the writing of the gospels, partly perhaps because critics concluded on internal grounds that Mark was the first gospel, thus contradicting the unanimous testimony of the fathers and casting doubt on their reliability as witnesses. But if, as many believe, the Synoptic Problem is a much more open question than previous generations of scholars have thought, then the external evidence, which is admittedly not very extensive and not always clear in its implications, must again be taken seriously.

2. WHERE THERE ARE NO OVERLAPPING TRADITIONS

Source criticism may be a difficult art when the critic has several parallel traditions to compare; it is even more difficult when he has only one tradition to work with. But this has not deterred scholars from making the attempt, and there are a number of supposedly tell-tale signs that the critic will look for which may indicate the use of sources.

(a) *Breaks and dislocations of the sequence.* First, there are from time to time awkward breaks and apparent dislocations in the narrative sequence which are explicable if it is supposed that the author was trying to weave into a single account material drawn from a number of different sources. Thus in John 14:31 Jesus says "Rise, let us go hence", as though the previous discourse were over and as though he were about to go out to Gethsemane and to his death; but then the discourse resumes and three full chapters elapse before Jesus finally goes out. One possible explanation of this is that the evangelist was working with a number of tracts of material which he has not wholly integrated.

The success of the critic's search for sources via dislocations depends on the original author's lack of success in integrating his sources, and will therefore be of little use if the original writer was competent as an editor. It also depends on the critic's ability to interpret dislocations in the text accurately. Critics, whether source, form or redaction critics, are sometimes unimaginative in their treatment of documents, making much of apparent dislocations or incoherences and not allowing that the New Testament writers might periodically have expressed themselves loosely and with something less than absolute precision. If an argument for sources is to be cogent, it must be clear that the phenomenon in question is really significant and that the source critical explanation is superior to others that are possible.

(b) *Stylistic inconsistency.* Stylistic inconsistency within a document is a second sign pointing to the possible use of sources. For example, Luke's birth narratives are very Hebraic; and, although a possible explanation may be that Luke was a versatile author who chose his style to suit his material, it is probably simpler to postulate the use of sources at this point, whether oral or written.[21]

(c) *Theological inconsistency.* If it can be shown that a particular passage or verse contains theological ideas that are quite untypical of, or better still contradictory to, the theology of the writer as it is expressed elsewhere, then it may reasonably be argued either that the material is an interpolation or that it is material taken by the author from a source and not properly assimilated. Scholars have claimed to have detected this sort of inconsistency in Mark, for example in Mark 4, where they have identified what they regard as two inconsistent views of the purpose of parables side by side in the same chapter.[22] The difficulty with this sort of argument lies in identifying genuine and significant inconsistencies. Presumably the authors of the documents themselves were not conscious of letting serious inconsistencies through, and the question in each case is, therefore, whether the original author was correct in assuming no inconsistency or whether the modern critic is correct in detecting certain contradictions.

(d) *Historical inconsistencies.* Historical inconsistencies in a document, for example, doublets, are a fourth possible clue that may indicate that the author is using sources.[23] But for the difficulty of this sort of argument see our earlier discussion of doublets.

III. *Learning from Source Criticism*

1. THE HISTORY OF THE BIBLICAL TRADITIONS

The Christian's knowledge of the historical events that are fundamental to his faith derives from the New Testament, and so the study of the history of the New Testament documents is ultimately of the greatest relevance to him. It may strengthen his convictions about those events, as also his belief in the inspiration of Scripture; or it may do the opposite. The Christian will be encouraged by source criticism if it leads him to conclude that the evangelists used primitive written sources in writing the gospels; the importance of sources will be especially great if the author of the gospel (or of Acts) is not thought to have been an eyewitness of the events he records. If on the other hand source criticism were to indicate that the evangelists' only sources were vague and unreliable folk traditions transmitted over a long period of time, this would be disturbing to the believer.

The mistake should not be made, however, of thinking that an author cannot be trusted where no source can be detected. The limitations of the source critic's methods have been made clear, and it cannot be assumed that it will always be possible to identify the use of written sources, still less of oral sources, especially if the author was a competent editor. Whether or not any of the evangelists are thought to have been eyewitnesses of the events they describe, it is virtually certain that they will all have been familiar with many of the traditions they record long before they wrote them down, and the fact that such traditions may be recorded in the language and style of the evangelist in question is scarcely surprising and proves nothing about the reliability of the tradition.

2. THE METHODS AND OUTLOOK OF THE NEW TESTAMENT WRITERS

When it can be firmly established what sources were used by any particular writer, the modern reader can learn a lot from the writer's use of his sources, for example about the writer's method of writing. The fact that Matthew and Luke agree so extensively with Mark and especially closely in the words of Jesus indicates, if it is accepted that Mark was their source, that they were concerned to preserve the received tradition and that they did not feel free to write the story of Jesus just as they pleased in accordance with their own theology.

The other side to this coin is the divergence of the gospels at numerous points, which suggests to some that the evangelists were not worried about precision in historical details. Thus Luke has Jesus heal blind Bartimaeus on the way into Jericho whereas his source Mark has the miracle on the way out of the city, and it may well be concluded from this that Luke's concern was not with the precise location of such events. If this is the correct conclusion, then clearly it is a complication for the Christian wishing to use and defend the gospels as documents that are historically trustworthy. To assert that one or more of the evangelists was reliable on the major historical and theological questions but that he felt free over historical details may be necessary and may be compatible with a high view of Scriptural authority, but it is less straightforward than maintaining that the evangelists were faithful in large and small points alike.[24]

Whether the divergences between the gospels do in fact demand that we take the more complicated view is uncertain. It was observed earlier that the evangelists will have been familiar with many of the traditions which they record in their gospels long before they found them in the document that was their main written source, which means that a writer's departures from his main source are not necessarily his own improvisations, and that the possibility of harmonizing the divergent accounts should not be too quickly ruled out.[25] Once this is realised and allowance is made (a) for the fact that different witnesses and narrators of an event will always view the event from different perspectives, (b) for stylistic variation, (c) for the interpretative work of the individual evangelist bringing out the meaning of the original event or saying for a particular church situation, the number of divergences that appear to demand the hypothesis that the evangelists were unconcerned for accuracy in detail will not be very great.[26]

A source critical analysis allows the critic to say something about a writer's method of writing, and also about his particular interests and ideas. Although the redaction critic may be able to detect certain dominant motifs in a writing even when he is uncertain about the sources used by its author, his task is made immeasurably easier when he can compare the writing with the source lying behind it. Thus, for example, when Matthew is compared with Mark, Matthew is seen to have a particular emphasis on the Jewish people; but in order to say whether this was a definite Matthean interest or *Tendenz* or not, we need to know what his sources were. If Mark was his source, the answer would presumably be yes; but if some very strongly Jewish traditions of the Jerusalem church were his main source, the answer might conceivably be the opposite.[27]

Since it will from time to time throw light on what the author or authors intend in a particular passage, source criticism is important for biblical exegesis in general and not just for redaction criticism in particular. Difficulties of interpretation, for example, may be cleared up when a document is compared with its source and when it is seen how a tradition is used by different writers;[28] and a source critical analysis is of obvious value to the exegete wishing to make sense of apparently divergent versions of the same tradition and wishing to avoid an arbitrary choice between the versions or an uninformed harmonization. But as well as bringing benefits, source criticism may raise problems for the expositor, if it suggests that a biblical writer has departed significantly from his source. For example, the expositor may find himself having to choose between preaching on a source critic's reconstruction of a word of Jesus and the supposed misunderstanding or creative reinterpretation of that saying found in the gospels. He may perhaps learn something about how the biblical tradition may be applied to different audiences, but there are difficult questions that arise in this situation regarding the authority of the different versions of the saying. The problem arises, however, only if the source critic finds himself forced to conclude that the later writer has departed significantly from the original meaning.

3. THE EARLIEST PERIOD OF CHURCH HISTORY

Our knowledge about what happened to the traditions of the life and teaching of Jesus before the gospels were written is sadly lacking; but if it can be demonstrated that collections of sayings such as Q or the postulated parable collection lying behind Mark 4 were in existence from an early date, this is evidence of the first importance for the historian. Through an examination of the form and contents of such documents he may also be able to discover something of the interests and ideas and theology of the authors and so of the churches where the documents were compiled and first circulated.[29] This is, however, no easy task when one is dealing with complete and extant documents; it is still harder when the sources have first to be reconstructed.

NOTES

1. E.g. one explanation of the awkwardness in Mk. 4:10–13 is that the evangelist was working with a source in which verses 11, 12 were not present.
2. Compare Mt. 9:32–34 and 12:22–24.
3. Compare for example Mt. 21:23–27; Mk. 11:27–33; Lk. 20:1–8; or Mt. 8:8f. and Lk. 7:6f.
4. The agreements of 2 Peter and Jude demand the same explanation. For a similar phenomenon in the Old Testament compare the parallelism between the books of Kings and Chronicles.
5. The use of a synopsis, which sets out the relevant texts in parallel, is essential for this, and the underlining in different colours of the points of agreement and disagreement will help the student to appreciate the meaning of the so-called Synoptic Problem. (Cf. F. C. Grant *The Gospels Their Origin and their Growth* (London 1957), pp. 41ff.) The best known synopses of the gospels in Greek are *Synopsis Quattuor Evangeliorum,* ed. K. Aland (Stuttgart 1964[3]), and *Synopsis of the First Three Gospels,* eds. A. Huck, H. Lietzmann, F. L. Cross (Oxford 1959).
6. The solution to the Synoptic Problem which has commanded most support for some 50 years or more is the Two Source Theory. According to this view, Mark's gospel was the first of our gospels to be written. Matthew and Luke used Mark as one of their main sources, but they also made use of a sayings source which is no longer extant and which is known as "Q" (from the German word *Quelle* meaning "source"). Sometimes Q is thought of as oral material rather than as a written source. Although this has been the generally accepted solution of the problem for some time, there have always been dissentients. See W. R. Farmer's history of *The Synoptic Problem* (New York 1964).
7. For the view that the agreements can be adequately explained in terms of oral tradition see, for example, B. F. Westcott, *Introduction to the Study of the Gospels* (London, 1895[8]). It is certainly easy for us to underestimate the powers of memory that some had in the ancient world. Cf. B. Gerhardsson, *Memory and Manuscript* (Uppsala, 1961).
8. Dissentients from the Two Source Theory observe that the agreements of Matthew and Luke against Mark are not so rare or so minor as is often thought.
9. A citation of Papias in Eus. H.E. iii, 39, 4, shows that there was a living oral tradition in the early church even after the gospels were written.
10. See the possible hints of omissions in 4:1, 33; 12:1, 38. If it is admitted that Mark knew Q, then Mark's omissions were extensive.
11. J. Chapman argues that Mark shows signs of disjointedness at certain points where he omits something that Matthew includes. See his *Matthew Mark and Luke* (London 1937). E. De Witt Burton lists the following criteria for identifying the second of two documents known to be directly related: (1) misunderstandings of one by the other; (2) insertions breaking the sequence of thought or symmetry of plan in the other; (3) clear omissions destroying the connection in the other; (4) insertions that can be explained according to a writer's aim and the omission of which by the other could not be explained; (5) the opposite of 4; (6) alterations conforming to the general method or tendency of the other. (*Some Principles of Literary Criticism and Their Application to the Synoptic Problem,* Chicago 1904).
12. A simple, though not typical, example is the overlap at the end of Luke and the beginning of Acts; it is quite intelligible that Luke might have gone back over ground covered in volume 1 at the beginning of volume 2.

13. G. M. Styler claims that Herod's grief at John the Baptist's death is out of place in Mt. 14:9, since Matthew has given the impression that Herod wished to kill John; Matthew has taken the expression from Mark's account in which it makes good sense. (Excursus on "The Priority of Mark" in C. F. D. Moule's *Birth of the New Testament* (London 1966 [2]), p. 229). Styler's observation is an interesting one, but the expression is not unintelligible if Matthew is read for itself apart from Mark.
14. On whether Mark's is the most Semitic gospel see E. P. Sanders, *The Tendencies of the Synoptic Tradition* (Cambridge 1969) p. 254.
15. See, for example, Mark's description of the 5000 in 6:39, 40.
16. H. G. Jameson, *The Origin of the Synoptic Gospels* (Oxford 1922), pp. 91f. and B. C. Butler, *The Originality of St Matthew* (Cambridge 1951), pp. 116f., argue for Matthean priority on the basis of style, claiming that it is very hard to imagine Matthew producing his elegant, well-ordered and often poetic gospel on the basis of Mark.
17. Cf. Sanders, op. cit., *passim.*
18. See R. H. Gundry, *The Use of the Old Testament in St. Matthew's Gospel* (Leiden 1967), pp. 150f.
19. A. M. Honoré, Nov.T 10 (1968), pp. 95–147.
20. It is usual to date most of the Pauline corpus with its high Christology before the first of the gospels.

It is surprisingly difficult to date any of the material in the gospels. A phrase like that in Mt. 27:8, "That field was called the field of blood up to today", suggests *prima facie* a date before the destruction of Jerusalem; but it is not impossible to avoid that implication.
21. So E. E. Ellis, *The Gospel of Luke* (London 1966), p. 28. Something similar may be said about the Aramaic flavour of parts of the early chapters of Acts.
22. Compare v.33, supposedly the primitive view, with vs. 11, 12 and 34, supposedly Mark's view.
23. A. Harnack argued that two sources lie behind Acts 2–5, in which the apostles are twice arrested and put in custody and twice brought before the Jewish authorities. For discussion of his view see J. Dupont, *The Sources of Acts* (E.T. London 1964), pp. 35f.
24. Luke's detailed accuracy in parts of Acts is well attested, and his prologue does not suggest that he was interested only in the broad sweep of events and not in the details.
25. It also means that an evangelist will often have had a way of checking his main source and of confirming it.
26. On Luke's location of the healing of Bartimaeus see J. N. Geldenhuys, *Commentary on the Gospel of Luke* (London 1950), pp. 467f.
27. The critic's analysis of 2 Peter and Jude will be affected in some respects at least if he belives that Jude was the source of 2 Peter rather than that 2 Peter was the source of Jude or that a common source lies behind both of them.
28. Mark's *προφήτευσον* in 14:65 is explained in Matthew and Luke, though whether rightly or wrongly may be debated.
29. The same point would apply to other New Testament books apart from the gospels. If, for example, Bultmann's theory that a gnostic source lies behind 1 John and that this has been edited by an ecclesiastical redactor were to be accepted, this would evidently be of interest to the historian of early Christian doctrine.

APPENDIX

SOURCE CRITICISM ILLUSTRATED

For an example of the source critic's task and the potential value of his work the student may examine Mt. 12:1–8 and its parallels (Mk. 2:23–28; Lk. 6:1–5) with the aid of a synopsis of the gospels in Greek.

1. *The source critic's task*

This passage is part of the so-called triple tradition, and Matthew, Mark and Luke overlap extensively, notably in Mt. 12:3, 4 and parallels. Compare Mt.'s *οὐκ ἀνέγνωτε τί ἐποίησεν Δαυίδ, ὅτε ἐπείνασεν καὶ ἱ μετ᾽ αὐτοῦ; πῶς εἰσῆλθεν εἰς τὸν οἶκον τοῦ θεοῦ καὶ τοὺς ἄρτους τῆς προθέσεως ἔφαγον* with Mark and Luke. As well as agreements between all three gospels, there are agreements of Matthew and Mark against Luke (e.g. in various minor points of grammatical construction in Mt. 12:1–2 and parallels; also of Mark and Luke against Matthew (e.g. *ἐγένετο* Mk. 2:23 and parallels, *ἔδωκεν* v.26, *καὶ ἔλεγεν αὐτοῖς* v.27); most modern critics would want to treat Mark here as elsewhere as the source of Matthew and Luke. But there are complications, notably in the agreements of Matthew and Luke against Mark, e.g. positively in the use of the words *ἐσθίειν* (Mt. 12:1 and parallels) and *μόνος* (Mt. 12:4 and parallels), and in the order of words in the expression *Κύριος γάρ ἐστιν τοῦ σαββάτου ὁ υἱὸς τοῦ ἀνθρώπου* (Mt. 12:8 and parallels), and negatively in the omission of several Marcan phrases, including most strikingly the whole of Mark's verse 27. These agreements of Matthew and Luke against Mark raise difficult questions for the source critic. Is their agreement perhaps coincidental? Certainly Matthew and Luke might both independently have omitted Mark's *ἐπὶ Ἀβιαθὰρ ἀρχιερέως* since Mark's dating of the incident in question is problematic and apparently mistaken; but can all the other agreements be equally simply explained? If not, then one alternative view is that Matthew and Luke had a common non-Marcan source at this point; Mark's verse 27 (which is introduced by his characteristically vague imperfect phrase *καὶ ἔλεγεν αὐτοῖς*) could then be regarded as a Marcan interpolation into the context. Whether this view or another is correct is not important for our argument at present; the example is cited simply to illustrate the sort of data which the source critic seeks to interpret.

2. *The value of source criticism*

If some sort of answer can be given to the source critical questions, of what value is that answer? First, it will help us to understand something of the history of the gospel traditions and of the evangelists' method of writing. If, for example, it is concluded that Mark's verse 27 is a saying imported into the context by Mark, then this is a piece of evidence which supports the view that Mark's gospel is in part at least arranged topically not chronologically; it may also be seen as evidence confirming the view that gospel traditions (or some of them) circulated in the early church without any particular historical context.

Second, it should help us to understand something of the evangelists' redactional concerns. If it is concluded that Mark was Matthew's primary source here, then his omission of Mark's radical saying about the sabbath being made for man is striking, as is his addition of the saying about the priests working on the sabbath and his quotation (for the second time in his gospel, cf. 9:13) of Hosea 6:6, "I desire mercy not sacrifice". (His change in the order of Mark's verse 28 may also be regarded as significant.) Matthew may be thought among other things to be reacting against the possible antinomian tendency of Mark's verse 27 and to be showing that Jesus' concern was not for the abolition of the law, but for its proper interpretation. Conversely if Mark's verse 27 is his own addition to the tradition (whether the saying goes back to Jesus or not), then this may tell us something significant about Mark's liberal view of the law (cf. also Mk. 7:19).

Thirdly, answering the source critical questions may help us decide about some of the difficult points of interpretation in the different gospels. For example, some scholars have wanted to take Mark's verses 27 and 28 very closely together, interpreting the one by the other. Thus it has been suggested on the one hand that the *ἄνθρωπος* referred to in verse 27 is really the *υἱὸς τοῦ ἀνθρώπου* of v.28, i.e. it is Jesus himself who is the man for whom the sabbath was made; it has been suggested on the other hand that the *υἱὸς τοῦ ἀνθρώπου* of v.28 is really the *ἄνθρωπος* of v.27 and that the Son of man who is lord of the sabbath is not Jesus in particular, but man in general. Whether either of these views is to be recommended is doubtful on any source critical hypothesis; but if the source critic were able to establish that Mark's verse 27 is the evangelist's interpolation and that Mark's source had his verse 28 following on from his verse 26, then this would be an additional, though still not decisive, argument to be weighed on the side of those who want to take verses 27 and 28 separately. Similarly in Matthew: his train of thought in verses 5–8 is not immediately straightforward, and verse 8, for example, does not at first sight appear to follow very well from verse 7. Now if the source critics who say that Matthew used Mark as a source are correct, this disjointedness is simply explained. Matthew has added his own material in verses 5–7, and verse 8 is as a result left hanging. It is not necessary on this hypothesis – and indeed it may be a mistake – to try by ingenuity to interpret Matthew's verses 5–8 as a coherent unity. If on the other hand Matthew is regarded as the oldest form of the tradition, then it will at least be reasonable to see if sense can be made of the sequence as it stands. Answering source critical questions may help the exegete in this sort of way to interpret the gospel texts accurately.

CHAPTER IX

FORM CRITICISM

Stephen H. Travis

Form criticism of the New Testament has two aims – to classify the various New Testament books according to their literary genre (German *Gattungsgeschichte*), and to analyse the smaller units of traditional material according to the "form" or "shape" they have assumed during the oral, preliterary period. The German word *Formgeschichte* ("form-history") is often used in a broader sense with reference to attempts to trace the development of units of tradition during the oral period and thus to make historical value-judgments on the material. But this is, strictly speaking, the function of "tradition criticism", which is treated elsewhere in this volume. My contribution will be confined to the more purely analytical aspect of form criticism, and to units of tradition in the Gospels.[1]

I. *Some Axioms of Form Criticism*

Form-critical methods were first applied systematically to the Gospels by three German scholars – K. L. Schmidt, M. Dibelius and R. Bultmann.[2] In order to understand how the method works, we must now list some of the axioms from which form criticism proceeds.

(1) The Synoptic Gospels are "popular" or "folk" literature rather than literary works in the classical sense. And the evangelists, according to Dibelius, "are only to the smallest extent authors. They are principally collectors, vehicles of tradition, editors."[3] Although both these claims are regarded by more recent scholars as over-statements, they are important because they emphasize that the evangelists were not historians employing modern methods of research, but receivers and transmitters of traditions cherished by Christian communities.

(2) Between the time of Jesus' ministry and the writing of the Gospels there was a period when the sayings of Jesus and stories about him were communicated orally among Christians. Even though "Q" may have existed as a document as early as A.D. 50, the church continued to set great store by oral tradition until well into the second century. Thus Papias stated: "I supposed that things out of books did not profit me so much as the utterances of a voice which lives and abides" (Eusebius, H.E. III.39.4).

(3) During this oral period the traditions about Jesus circulated as in-

dependent units. It can hardly have been otherwise, since the acts and sayings of Jesus would be recounted by preachers and teachers *as occasion demanded.* We cannot imagine the apostles giving a series of lectures in the temple precincts on the life of Jesus. Rather they would use some particular story or word of Jesus to bring home some point in the course of their preaching. This is why when we look, for example, at Mk. 2:1–3:6 we find a collection of short paragraphs (known as *pericopae*), each complete in itself and with no essential connection with what precedes or follows.

However, there are exceptions to this general rule. All three early form critics agreed that some joining up of pericopae had taken place before Mark compiled his Gospel. But this was normally on a *topical* basis, for example the "controversy stories" in Mk. 2:1–3:6, and the "miracle stories" in Mk. 4:35–5:43. Only very rarely is there reason to believe that such groupings of traditions preserved memory of the *chronological* order of events – the most famous example of this being the insertion of the story of the woman with the haemorrhage into the story about Jairus' daughter (Mk. 4:21–43), which is probably due to recollection that "this is how it actually happened."[4]

The major exception to the rule about independent pericopae is the Passion Narrative, where the paragraphs are joined together in a continuous story.[5] From early times the Passion Story may have been recounted as a whole, both in worship and in apologetic to outsiders. For such a connected account was necessary in order to answer the question, "How could Jesus have been brought to the cross by people who were blessed by his signs and wonders?"[6]

(4) During the oral stage these "units of tradition" assumed particular *forms* according to the function which they performed in the Christian community. Form critics recognize certain forms or categories in the gospel tradition – such as "pronouncement-stories" and "miracle-stories" (see below) – and insist that these distinctive forms are no creation of accident or free invention, but are determined by the setting in which they arose and the purpose for which they were used. The technical term for this setting is *Sitz im Leben* ("life-situation"). Just as information about the qualities of a particular toothpaste will be told in a distinctive manner by an advertisement, but in a quite different manner by a scientific report, so stories about Jesus acquired different forms or shapes according to their *Sitz im Leben.* Thus form critics claim the ability to deduce the *Sitz im Leben* of a gospel pericope from its form. If we find several pericopae with the same form, we may assume that they all had the same *Sitz im Leben,* i.e., they all performed the same function in the church's life, whether it be worship or apologetic or catechesis or some other function.[7]

It is important to understand that for form critics "*Sitz im Leben*" is primarily a "*sociological*" term, denoting a whole "area" or function of the community's life (e.g., worship, or missionary preaching). Only in a secondary sense is it applied (as often by Bultmann) to the *particular* historical situation which gave rise to a *particular* story or saying. Thus, for example,

Bultmann might say that the pericope about paying taxes to Caesar (Mk. 12:13–17) had its *Sitz im Leben* (in the general, "sociological" sense) in the apologetic of the Palestinian church, while its *Sitz im Leben* (in the specific sense) was the problem about whether Christians had obligations to Caesar as well as to God.[8] A further refinement of this "specific" sense is the distinction made between the life-situation of the early church where a piece of tradition was created or transmitted (*Sitz im Leben der alten Kirche*) and the historical situation in the life of Jesus where the piece of tradition originated (*Sitz im Leben Jesu*).[9]

II. *The Various Forms*[10]

A form critic's main purpose, then, is to classify the gospel pericopae according to their forms, and to assign them to their respective *Sitze im Leben*. Apart from the Passion Narrative, Dibelius found five main categories. I shall now list them, noting some variations suggested by other scholars.

1. PARADIGMS

These are brief episodes which culminate in an authoritative saying of Jesus, or sometimes in a statement about the reaction of onlookers. A typical "pure paradigm" is Mk. 3:31–35:

> And his mother and his brothers came; and standing outside they sent to him and called him. And a crowd was sitting about him; and they said to him, "Your mother and your brothers are outside, asking for you." And he replied, "Who are my mother and my brothers?" And looking around on those who sat about him, he said, "Here are my mother and my brothers! Whoever does the will of God is my brother, and sister, and mother."

Dibelius also cites as "pure paradigms" Mk. 2:1–12, 18–22, 23–28; 3:1–5, 20–30; 10:13–16; 12:13–17; 14:3–9. He also speaks of "less pure paradigms" – pericopae including extraneous features, such as names of characters in the story, which are not found in the pure paradigms. These include Mk. 1:23–27; 2:13–17; 6:1–6; Lk. 9:51–56; 14:1–6.

Dibelius believed that paradigms attained this shape in order to serve as examples or illustrations in the preaching of the early missionaries. Hence their name (Greek *paradeigma* = "example"). His list of five characteristic features of the paradigms shows how ideal they would be for this purpose: (1) independence from the literary context; (2) brevity and simplicity – we are told nothing of biographical interest about the participants, who act merely as foils for the saying of Jesus; (3) religious rather than artistic colouring; (4) the word of Jesus is made to stand out clearly as the climax of the narrative (as in a "punch-line" joke); (5) the pericope ends with a thought useful for preaching – either a word or act of Jesus or the reaction of the onlookers.[11]

Dibelius' location of the *Sitz im Leben* of the paradigms in early Christian preaching has been criticized by Bultmann as too narrow. He prefers the term "*apophthegm*" for pericopae of this type, and subdivides them into *controversy-dialogues* (e.g. Mk. 3:1–6), *scholastic dialogues* (e.g. Mk. 12:28–34), which arose from the needs of polemic and apologetic, and *biographical apophthegms* (e.g. Lk. 9:57–62), which purport to contain information about Jesus and were used as "edifying paradigms for sermons".[12] V. Taylor has criticized the terminology of both Dibelius and Bultmann, and claims – with some justification – that his term "*pronouncement-story*" is simpler and puts the emphasis in the right place.[13]

2. TALES (NOVELLEN)

These are stories of Jesus' miracles which, unlike paradigms, include details betraying "a certain pleasure in the narrative itself",[14] and which Dibelius therefore attributed to a special class of story-tellers and teachers (for whose existence there is no New Testament evidence, unless these stories are themselves evidence). The stories may be subdivided into exorcisms (e.g. Mk. 5:1–20; 9:14–29), other healing miracles (e.g. Mk. 1:40–45; 5:21–43) and nature miracles (e.g. Mk. 4:35–41; 6:35–44, 45–52). All the stories follow the same basic pattern: (1) a description of the disease or situation to be remedied; (2) a statement of the cure or solution achieved by Jesus; (3) a statement of the results of the miracle – either the effects on the person healed or the reaction of the onlookers. This is a natural pattern for any story of this kind, shared by Jewish and pagan miracle-stories, as well as by TV adverts for vitamin pills and medicated shampoos.

In these tales, says Dibelius, there is "a lack of devotional motives and the gradual retreat of any words of Jesus of general value", and "didactic applications altogether fail."[15] Thus, in contrast to the paradigms, they were not formed for the purpose of illustrating sermons. Rather, their *Sitz im Leben* was their use by the story-tellers "to prove the miracle-worker was an epiphany of God, and this was done by the Tale as such apart from inclusion in a sermon." They were used especially in a Hellenistic setting to demonstrate Jesus' superiority over rival gods and miracle-workers.[16]

Bultmann, who calls these narratives "miracle-stories", does not endorse Dibelius' belief in a special class of story-tellers, but agrees with him that these stories were formed for propaganda and apologetic purposes.[17]

3. LEGENDS

Dibelius took over this term from its application in later Christian centuries to "legends of the saints". It does not necessarily imply that what is recorded is unhistorical – though that may often be the case, in the opinion of Dibelius, and particularly of Bultmann, who treats these pericopae under the heading "historical stories and legends". What is important is the purpose of these narratives. They are "religious narratives of a saintly man in whose works and fate interest is taken". And they arose in the church to satisfy a twofold desire: the wish to know something of the virtues and lot of the holy men and women in the story of Jesus, and the wish which gradually arose to know Jesus himself in this way.[18]

Thus there are legends about Jesus (e.g. Lk. 2:41–49; 4:29f), Peter (e.g. Mt. 14:28–33; 16:13–23), Judas (Mt. 27:3–8) and other characters. In narratives like this the characters are not simply foils for some word of Jesus, as in paradigms – they become real people and are presented as examples to follow.

4. MYTHS

Myths are narratives which depict "a many-sided interaction between mythological but not human persons" – the supernatural is seen breaking in upon the human scene.[19] Only three narratives are listed in this category: the baptismal miracle (Mk. 1:9–11 and parallels), the temptations (Mt. 4:1–11 and parallel), the transfiguration (Mk. 9:2–8 and parallels). Bultmann does not use the term "myth" to denote a category, but includes these three narratives among the "historical stories and legends".

5. EXHORTATIONS

Exhortations (*Paränesen*) is Dibelius' term for the teaching material in the Gospels. Their *Sitz im Leben* is catechesis. Formally, the sayings of Jesus may be divided into maxims, metaphors, parabolic narratives, prophetic challenges, short commandments, and extended commandments including some kind of motive clause (e.g. Mt. 5:29f, 44–48; 6:2–4).

Bultmann's treatment of the sayings of Jesus is more extensive. He divides them according to *content* into three groups: (1) *logia* or wisdom sayings; (2) prophetic and apocalyptic sayings; (3) laws and community regulations. *Formal* characteristics cut right across these categories, provoking B. S. Easton to ask: "What *formal* difference is there between the 'logion' – Whosoever exalteth himself shall be humbled – the 'apocalyptic word' – Whosoever shall be ashamed of me, the Son of Man shall be ashamed of him – and the 'church rule' – Whosoever putteth away his wife and marrieth another committeth adultery?"[20] On grounds of *form* rather than content, Bultmann was able to isolate only two main types: "I-sayings" in which Jesus speaks of himself, his works and his destiny (e.g. Mt. 5:17; Mk. 10:45); and "Parables". His analysis of the parabolic material is particularly illuminating.[21]

III. *Some Limitations of Form Criticism*

We must now mention some limitations of form criticism as it has hitherto been practised, and some questions which it has not yet answered satisfactorily.

(1) How many of the forms or categories commonly referred to by form critics have in fact been satisfactorily established? We can agree that the

"paradigms" and "tales" are distinctive types (though the names "pronouncement-story" and "miracle-story" are more meaningful in English), and that parables are a particular form within the sayings tradition. But what of the rest? Dibelius' "myths" are classified by their content, not by their style or form. On grounds of form alone, the temptation story in Mt. 4:1–11 would more naturally be described as a controversy dialogue (it is not very different from Mk. 10:2–9; 11:27–33 or 12:18–27), and is in fact so described by M. Albertz.[22] Similarly the "legends", though they may have certain typical features in common, can hardly be said to have a common form or shape. "What common form can be perceived in the stories of the Confession of Peter, the Entry into Jerusalem, the Transfiguration, and Jesus in the Temple at the age of twelve?" asks Redlich.[23] He therefore calls such pericopae "form-less stories", and Taylor for similar reasons speaks simply of "stories about Jesus". Most of the discourse material, too, refuses to be categorized according to form. Bultmann's categories, for instance, "do little more than describe stylistic features; they do not denote popular forms into which an individual or a community unconsciously throws sayings."[24]

Admittedly, too sharp a distinction must not be drawn between form and content – they do influence each other. Thus it is legitimate to speak of miracle-stories as a distinctive form – even though "miracle" is a designation of *content* – because all miracle-stories are told in the same basic form. But to describe "legends" or "myths" as forms, when no common shape is discernible in the various examples adduced, is not form criticism. Thus R.H. Lightfoot, who did much to introduce form-critical methods into Britain, admits that we may have to be content with the form critics' success in distinguishing and classifying two types of story, paradigms and miracle-stories – and no others.[25]

Furthermore, even these two types are not as distinct as is sometimes suggested. Compare, for example, Mk. 3:1–6 (the man with the withered hand – a "pure paradigm" according to Dibelius), Mk. 10:46–52 (Bartimaeus – a "less pure paradigm") and Mk. 5:25–34 (the woman with the haemorrhage – a "tale"). Is there really as much difference between them as Dibelius' classification would suggest? Since Mk. 3:1–6 so obviously contains a "didactic motive" (which according to Dibelius a "tale" does not have), Dibelius classes it as a paradigm, saying that the healing is only incidental.[26] Yet the pericope concludes not with the saying about the sabbath, but with the miracle and its effect on the Pharisees. "The plain fact", comments A. Richardson, "is that we have here a miracle-story which is something more than what the form critics have decided that a miracle-story ought to be."[27] To take another example, Mk. 1:29–31 is a perfect little healing-story following the pattern of description of the illness, the cure and the results. Yet it betrays none of the "delight in the narrative itself" which Dibelius regards as a feature of his "tales". Is it because it does not fit his theory that he nowhere discusses it in *From Tradition to Gospel*?

In fact there are many pericopae in the Gospels which do not fit neatly into categories, but are of "mixed type". Bultmann makes a virtue out of this problem, claiming that "it is no objection to the form-critical approach, but rather a demonstration of its fruitfulness, to find that one piece of the tradition is seldom to be classified unambiguously in a single category". It is difficult to see how this can be reconciled with his statement about the *Sitz im Leben* earlier on the same page: "The proper understanding of form-criticism rests upon the judgment that the literature in which the life of a given community ... has taken shape, springs out of quite definite conditions and wants of life from which grows up a quite definite style and quite specific forms and categories." [28] When dealing with a living tradition, we must certainly resist excessive systematization; but the more we resist systematization, the more we undermine form criticism itself. [29]

This question about how far it is possible to establish fixed and clear-cut "forms" does have exegetical implications. Thus, for example, many scholars assert that Mk. 2:19b–20 is an addition by the early church to the pronouncement-story about fasting in vv. 18–19a. Part of their argument for this is that vv. 18–19a so clearly form a perfect paradigm or controversy dialogue that the extra sayings of Jesus can hardly have stood there originally. [30] But what if the definition of a paradigm, from which this conclusion is drawn, is too rigid and doctrinaire? Similarly with parables, it is too readily assumed that Jesus could not have included allegorical traits in his teaching, and that a parable *must* have been designed originally to have only one point, so that a second point must be an addition by the church. [31]

(2) The assumption that there was an "oral period" before any of the gospel material came to be written down has been questioned by H. Schürmann. He suggests that during Jesus' ministry his disciples may have written notes on main aspects of his teaching. [32]

(3) How did the traditions about Jesus arise and how did they develop? These are questions which form criticism has not taken seriously enough. Dibelius and Bultmann wrote confidently about the "laws of tradition", giving the impression that these were well-proven laws of the development of oral tradition which could be scientifically applied both to biblical narratives and to extra-biblical material. Their main contention was that traditions develop from the simple to the more complex – hence, in general, legends were regarded as later creations than paradigms. But in fact no one has thoroughly examined these "laws of tradition", and there is no agreement on this matter among the experts on "folk tradition". [33] E. P. Sanders has shown that in the manuscript tradition and the apocryphal gospels there are developments *both* from the simple to the more complex, *and* from the complex to the simpler. [34] The situation is not straightforward.

Moreover, H. Riesenfeld and B. Gerhardsson have contended that the transmission of traditions by the early Christians must be understood on the analogy of transmission of traditions by the Jewish rabbis. Since the rabbis' concern was to transmit accurately the traditions as they received them, we should assume that the Christian churches were similarly concerned for accurate transmission, rather than being the "creative communities" which form critics often imagine them to have been.[35] Although this thesis has been widely criticized, its insistence that the transmission of Christian traditions should be understood in the light of the way Jewish traditions were transmitted in the first century deserves serious attention.[36]

This question of how the traditions about Jesus developed has bearing on the problem of "doublets" in the Gospels, among which we may note the following:

The parable of the talents/pounds	(Mt. 25:14–30; Lk. 19:12–28)
The miraculous draught of fishes	(Lk. 5:1–11; Jn. 21:4–14)
The anointing of Jesus	(Mk. 14:3–9 = Mt. 26:6–13; Lk. 7:36–50; Jn. 12:1–8)
The feeding of the 5000/4000	(Mk. 6:30–44; 8:1–10)
The healing of the centurion's servant/nobleman's son	(Mt. 8:5–13 = Lk. 7:1–10; Jn. 4:36–54)

The usual form-critical approach to such doublets is that divergent traditions have developed from one original story. But since form criticism itself involves the assumption that different stories of the same type have come to be told in a similar way to each other, is it not also possible that two originally different stories have assimilated features from each other in the course of transmission? The answer to this question may not be the same in each case, but it is a question which ought to be considered.

A similar question could be asked about parables with more than one "moral" attached to them (e.g. Lk. 16:1–9; or the different applications of the parable of the lost sheep in Mt. 18:10–14 and Lk. 15:3–7). Must we assume that this is always the result of development in the church, rather than of development in *Jesus' mind*?[37] Is it not likely that Jesus would use similar stories on separate occasions to drive home different points, just as Paul does with his athletic metaphor or his imagery from slavery?

(4) The concern to draw parallels with extra-biblical material can sometimes distort rather than help exegesis. This is the fault of many form critics' approach to the miracle-stories. Noting formal parallels with stories of Hellenistic "divine men" and miracle-workers, they have underplayed the didactic purpose of the miracle-stories and regarded them as quite distinct from the proclamation of Jesus as bringer of the kingdom of God.[38] This is ironical when we observe that Bultmann, for example, regards as genuine sayings of Jesus Mt. 11:4–6 and 12:28, where Jesus clearly relates his miracles to his message of the kingdom.[39] It is quite misleading to suggest that the miracle-stories have "no didactic motive". In Acts 3:1ff, often in John's Gospel, and in the paradigms involving a miracle, we see miracles used as springboards for teaching. And Richardson has shown how suitable many of the miracle-stories are, not just to exalt Jesus as a wonder-worker, but to point to various aspects of the Christian message.[40]

IV. *Some Insights of Form Criticism*

We have seen that form criticism has limitations, and that there are some questions it has left unanswered. But there are also real gains for our understanding of the New Testament, including the following.

(1) Form criticism has helped us, however tentatively, to penetrate into the "tunnel period" between A.D. 30 and 50, before any of our New Testament documents were written down. For instance, it has given us clues about methods of preaching and teaching among the early Christians, and about their debates with Jewish opponents.

(2) The search for the *Sitz im Leben* of a tradition is an aid to exegesis. Once we can discover how and why a particular story was used in the early church, we shall have a surer way of knowing how we should use it to speak to our own situation. It is true that suggested *Sitze im Leben* are often only tentative, and frequently scholars disagree about the life-situation of a particular pericope.[41] So we must beware of claiming too much. It is true that the quest for a *Sitz im Leben* involves a circular argument – "The forms of the literary tradition must be used to establish the influences operating in the life of the community, and the life of the community must be used to render the forms themselves intelligible."[42] But the method is not thereby invalidated, since all advances in historical precision involve a certain circularity of method. Also, the evidence of the Acts and Epistles provides some external check on any postulated life-situation. Despite these difficulties, therefore, form criticism has drawn valuable attention to the question of the *Sitz im Leben*. "In this way the gospels can be to us . . ., within limits which need to be carefully guarded, a mirror of the hopes and aspirations, the problems and the difficulties, of the early church."[43]

(3) Linked with this is the emphasis that the early Christians preserved stories and sayings of Jesus not because of mere antiquarian interest, but because they were *useful* for worship, preaching, teaching or some other situation. And this helps us to understand why the Gospels ought not to be regarded as biographies of Jesus. Independent pericopae, transmitted because of their practical value to the church, tell us less about Jesus' inner development than about what he meant to the church.[44] This may well mean that we can expect to deduce from the Gospels only the barest of chronological outlines of Jesus' life.[45]

(4) An understanding of the form of a pericope is often of major importance for its accurate exegesis. Attention has already been drawn to the exegetical value of understanding the parable form – and the dangers of applying this too rigidly.[46] Another example of form-analysis guiding exegesis is K. Koch's study of the beatitudes in Mt. 5:3–12. He shows that these "blessings" follow the pattern of "apocalyptic blessings" in the Old Testament and Jewish literature, rather than the quite different type of blessings found in Old Testament wisdom-sayings. On *formal* grounds, therefore, it can be established that these beatitudes are not speaking of general worldly

well-being, but should be related to Jesus' eschatological teaching – and the *content* confirms this impression.[47]

(5) Form criticism draws attention to the presence of the "gospel in a nutshell" in each pericope. "It was probably to the light thrown by the historical traditions on these great themes [of life and death, judgment and salvation, etc.], even more than to their historical interest, that the traditions themselves owed their preservation; and if form criticism can show once more the vital connexion in this respect between the gospels and the Gospel, it will have proved its value."[48] This insight can be overdone – plainly, the message contained in one pericope is of limited meaningfulness to the hearer unless he can relate it to an overall impression of Jesus which he has derived from other pericopae. But it points the interpreter of the Gospels in the right direction: to the authoritative and saving message contained in the gospel tradition.

V. *What Now?*

Form criticism is not merely something to be studied as an aspect of modern theology. Since an appreciation of form is necessary for the understanding of *any* literature, form criticism will remain a basic tool for exegesis of the Gospels. And so the work goes on, as scholars seek to build on the insights of their predecessors and to correct the weaknesses of earlier studies. More recent trends have included attempts to discern behind the Fourth Gospel some of the same basic forms as have been found in the Synoptics;[49] and to throw light on Gospel pericopae by comparing them with Jewish forms known to us from rabbinic literature.[50] If all this makes the study of the Gospels more complicated, it can also make such study more fruitful.

NOTES

1. On tradition criticism see Ch. X by D. R. Catchpole. On the study of literary genres (*Gattungsgeschichte*) and of units of tradition in the Epistles and Revelation, see R. P. Martin (Ch. XIII).

2. Schmidt's book, *Der Rahmen der Geschichte Jesu* ("The Framework of the Story of Jesus", Berlin 1919), has never been translated into English. Dibelius's book, *Die Formgeschichte des Evangeliums,* also appeared in 1919, but the English translation, *From Tradition to Gospel* (London 1934; reprinted 1971), is based on the much enlarged second German edition (Tübingen 1933). Bultmann's *History of the Synoptic Tradition* (Oxford 1963) is a translation of the third German edition (1958) of *Die Geschichte der synoptischen Tradition* (originally published Göttingen 1921).

3. *From Tradition to Gospel,* pp. 3–6.

4. But Bultmann believes that the insertion is made simply to provide the time lapse necessary between the statement that Jairus' daughter is "at the point of death" (v. 23) and "your daughter is dead" (v. 35) (*History of the Synoptic Tradition,* p. 214).

5. Bultmann only partly agrees (op. cit., p. 275).

6. Schmidt, op. cit., p. 305.

7. For typical statements, see Dibelius, op. cit., pp. 13f; Bultmann, op. cit., p. 4.
8. See Bultmann, op. cit., pp. 26, 48.
9. But H. Schürmann has denied the appropriateness of applying the term to a particular historical situation and has insisted on the sociological meaning ("Die vorösterlichen Anfänge der Logientradition", in *Der historische Jesus und der kerygmatische Christus: Beiträge zum Christusverständnis in Forschung und Verkündigung,* ed. H. Ristow and K. Matthiae (Berlin 1962), p. 351).
10. There is no space to discuss these in detail. Apart from the books of Dibelius and Bultmann, see the summary of their classification of forms in E. V. McKnight, *What is Form Criticism?* (Philadelphia 1969), pp. 20–33, as well as the discussions in V. Taylor, *The Formation of the Gospel Tradition* (London 1933), and E. B. Redlich, *Form Criticism: its Value and Limitations* (London 1939).
11. Dibelius, op. cit., pp. 24–26, 37–69. For some illustrations of how these stories may have been used by the early preachers, see G. R. Beasley-Murray, *Preaching the Gospel from the Gospels* (London 1965[2]), pp. 11ff.
12. Bultmann, op. cit., p. 61.
13. Op. cit., p. 30.
14. Dibelius, op. cit., p. 70. There are some pericopae including accounts of healings which nevertheless are classified as paradigms because the centre of interest is not the healing itself but the pronouncement of Jesus which follows from it (e.g. Mk. 1:23–27; 2:1–12; 3:1–6).
15. Op. cit., p. 79.
16. Op. cit., pp. 95f.
17. Bultmann, op. cit., p. 368.
18. Dibelius, op. cit., pp. 104, 115.
19. Op. cit., p. 271.
20. *The Gospel Before the Gospels* (New York 1928), p. 74.
21. For details see Bultmann, op. cit., pp. 166–179, 188–192.
22. *Die synoptischen Streitgespräche* (Berlin 1921), pp. 41–48.
23. Op. cit., p. 180.
24. Taylor, op. cit., p. 31.
25. *History and Interpretation in the Gospels* (London 1935), p. 43.
26. Op. cit., p. 55.
27. *The Miracle-Stories of the Gospels* (London 1941), p. 77.
28. Op. cit., p. 4.
29. Cf. P. Benoit, "Reflections on 'Formgeschichtliche Methode' ", in *Jesus and the Gospel,* Vol. I (London 1973), pp. 24f.
30. See, e.g. D. E. Nineham, *The Gospel of St Mark* (Harmondsworth 1963), pp. 103f.
31. For a criticism of these assumptions see J. A. Baird, *Audience Criticism and the Historical Jesus* (Philadelphia 1969), pp. 167f. For recent criticisms of this doctrinaire denial that Jesus intended an allegorical interpretation of the Parable of the Sower, see B. Gerhardsson, "The Parable of the Sower and its Interpretation", NTS 14 (1967–68), pp. 165–193; C. F. D. Moule, "Mark 4:1–20 yet once more", in *Neotestamentica et Semitica,* Studies in Honour of Principal Matthew Black, ed. E. E. Ellis and M. Wilcox (Edinburgh 1969), pp. 95–113; J. Drury, "The Sower, the Vineyard, and the Place of Allegory in the Interpretation of Mark's Parables", JTS 24 (1973), pp. 367–379.
32. Op. cit., pp. 342–370.
33. See Baird, op. cit., and literature cited there. Also E. Güttgemanns, *Offene Fragen zur Formgeschichte des Evangeliums* (Munich 1971[2]).
34. E. P. Sanders, *The Tendencies of the Synoptic Tradition* (Cambridge 1969).
35. H. Riesenfeld, *The Gospel Tradition and its Beginnings* (London 1957); B. Gerhardsson, *Memory and Manuscript: Oral Tradition and Written Transmission in Rabbinic Judaism and Early Christianity* (Lund and Copenhagen 1961).
36. A valuable critique is that by W. D. Davies, "Reflections on a Scandinavian Approach to the Gospel Tradition", in *The Setting of the Sermon on the Mount* (Cambridge 1964), pp. 464–480. Gerhardsson replied to his critics in *Tradition and Transmission in Early Christianity* (Lund and Copenhagen 1964).

37. See Baird, op. cit., pp. 166–168.
38. See, e.g., Dibelius, op. cit., p. 80; Bultmann, op. cit., p. 241.
39. Bultmann, op. cit., pp. 128, 162.
40. Op. cit., *passim*. See further L. J. McGinley, *Form Criticism of the Synoptic Healing Narratives* (Woodstock, Maryland 1944); W. Nicol, *The Semeia in the Fourth Gospel* (Leiden 1972).
41. For a good example of this see S. Neill, *The Interpretation of the New Testament, 1861–1961* (London 1964), pp. 247f.
42. Bultmann, op. cit., p. 5.
43. R. H. Lightfoot, *The Gospel Message of St Mark* (London 1950), p. 102.
44. This can of course be asserted without denying (as many form critics do deny) that the early Christians were interested in the historical Jesus and able to transmit accurately information about his earthly life. See G. N. Stanton, *Jesus of Nazareth in New Testament Preaching* (Cambridge 1974).
45. For an attempt to establish the reliability of the Marcan outline see C. H. Dodd, "The Framework of the Gospel Narrative", in *New Testament Studies* (Manchester 1953), pp. 1–11; and D. E. Nineham's criticisms in "The Order of Events in St Mark's Gospel – an Examination of Dr Dodd's Hypothesis", in *Studies in the Gospels,* Essays in Memory of R. H. Lightfoot (Oxford 1955), pp. 223–239. G. E. Ladd has a balanced discussion in *The New Testament and Criticism* (London 1970), pp. 165–168.
46. See notes 21 and 31.
47. Koch, *The Growth of the Biblical Tradition* (E.T. London 1969), pp. 6–8; cf. pp. 17f, 28f.
48. Lightfoot, *The Gospel Message of St Mark,* p. 105.
49. See, e.g., B. Lindars, *Behind the Fourth Gospel* (London 1971).
50. See D. Daube, *The New Testament and Rabbinic Judaism* (London 1956), pp. 55–201; and B. Gerhardsson, *The Testing of God's Son (Matt. 4:1–11 and par.)* (Lund 1966).

CHAPTER X

TRADITION HISTORY

David R. Catchpole

The German word *Traditionsgeschichte* is often translated into English as "tradition criticism", but this term suffers from the same defects as the term "form criticism" when that stands for *Formgeschichte.* For *Geschichte* does not mean "criticism" but rather, in this context, "meaningful process" and "changeful movement". In New Testament study, therefore, the term "tradition criticism" would be better abandoned and replaced by the term "tradition history", interpreted in the sense of an on-going process of development in the form and/or meaning of concepts or words or sayings or blocks of material. The pattern, the limits and the range of such a development may of course vary. One example would be the evolution in the thought of a given writer, as for instance the use of the term "head" for an unspecified member of the body of Christ in the earlier Pauline letters (e.g. 1 Cor. 12:21) but its application to Christ alone in later Pauline letters (e.g. Col. 1:18; Eph. 4:15). Another example would be the idea suggested by some that "Son of man" is a term used by Jesus without implying any equation between himself and that figure, while at a subsequent stage in the traditional process the identification is established. As to the range of the overall tradition-historical development, the most widely used is that which stretches from the historical Jesus via the Aramaic-speaking/Palestinian Jewish-Christian community and the Hellenistic Jewish-Christian community through to Gentile Christianity.[1]

It follows from this summary that "tradition history" includes "redaction criticism/history". The latter term, which in the case of the gospels stands for the refashioning and editing of material by the theologically active evangelist, is only a special case of the former. But as such it draws attention to evidence within the text which permits comparisons and contrasts between different versions. This demonstrates the fact of development and indicates certain tendencies within the transmission process, with the result that tradition-historical study as such is protected from any charge of imposing an alien pattern upon the text. That is, we are not limited to dependence upon *a priori* presuppositions or the making of statements about what may conceivably have happened; we can repeatedly see with our eyes what actually did happen. So tradition history, as an idea, can be tested by the evidence provided by redaction criticism, its special case.

But tradition history stretches much further. It is not simply concerned with the interaction of a man and his sources but also with the process of development in material which, though related, does not have that relationship structured by direct literary dependence. Thus, for instance, redaction criticism is concerned with the use made by Matthew and Luke of the earlier Markan and Q versions of the parable of the mustard seed (Mk. 4:30–32, and par.). In this way it contributes evidence of one stage of tradition history. But the latter will also be concerned with how a postulated original form of the parable may have developed into those variant forms which underlie the Markan and Q versions. Similarly, redaction criticism is concerned with the use made by John of, for example, his sources underlying John 2:13–22, but tradition history as a whole includes this and also the process which has produced the variant forms of the material in John's sources and in Mark 11:15–18, 27–33; 14:58.

If the relationship between redaction criticism and tradition history is so close, it is just the same in respect of form criticism. The work of the pioneers of form criticism,[2] and indeed already before them D. F. Strauss and the Tübingen school of the 19th century, makes this plain. For as soon as the post-Easter churches are seen creatively at work inside the gospel traditions; as soon as variations in outlook among those early churches are appreciated; as soon as distinct concepts and traditions are assigned to various sources and settings; as soon as history-of-religions parallels are invoked to this end; just so soon has form history become, in fact, tradition history. So it is not too much to say that the totality of the application of the historical-critical method can be described as tradition-historical criticism.

As with other areas of New Testament study, so in this attempt to reconstruct a tradition-historical scheme, important questions about methods and criteria for decisions are raised. It is necessary to ask about the criteria for deciding whether or not given traditions belong to one and the same tradition-historical development. It is also necessary to ask about criteria for determining the setting of any given material in the mission of Jesus or in the life of a post-Easter community. And at every stage questions therefore arise about implications concerning historicity or otherwise. A few examples may perhaps help in exposing the issues.

I. *Post-Easter Material*

Firstly, there seems to be some relationship between Luke 22:27: "I am among you as the servant", and Mark 10:45: "The Son of man came not to be served but to serve and to give his life as a ransom for many", and also 1 Timothy 2:5: ". . . the man . . . who gave himself as a ransom for all". Powerful arguments have been put forward by J. Jeremias in favour of locating Mark 10:45 within Palestinian tradition, while 1 Timothy 2:5 has "a more pronounced Greek flavour in every word".[3] But what about Luke 22:27? This saying is not in a direct literary relationship with Mark 10:45 but, if it emerges that the variations between the Lukan and Markan forms are typical of the sort of fluctuation shown by the gospel tradition as a whole, it would appear likely that some non-literary relationship exists between the two. Now in view of its less advanced theological content, Luke 22:27 is unlikely to be a later form of Mark 10:45, but it could very easily be, as often suggested, an earlier form. And if it does turn out that these forms are neither unrelated nor explicable in terms of a "Jesus might have said it twice" argument, we shall not only have here the raw material of a tradition-historical development but also find ourselves confronted by evidence that gospel sayings cannot without more ado be taken as *ipsissima verba* of Jesus.

Secondly, there are marked divergences in the wording of Peter's confession, "You are the messiah" (Mk. 8:29). Matthew has in addition the term "the Son of the living God", and Luke the extra words "of God". How should the variation be explained? A harmonizing additive approach would produce the form, "You are the messiah of God, the Son of the living God", but this would immediately run into difficulties. Firstly, the overloaded wording is awkward, and all the more so if we add extra wording from the parallel in John 6:69: "the holy one of God".[4] Secondly, it is hard to envisage the evangelists reducing the wording of Peter's statement and scaling down his acclamation of Jesus as *ex hypothesi* they did. More likely is the view that Matthew and Luke have added phrases which amount to their own commentary on the idea of messiahship. But in that case we reduce drastically the likelihood that their additions are historical, and again we find ourselves involved inexorably in the tradition-historical enquiry.

Thirdly, to argue that a phrase here or a nuance there is unhistorical would not worry many who would, however, be seriously disturbed by the idea that any sayings are as a whole inauthentic. In other words, the fact that a saying is in the gospel tradition at all is for those persons a sufficient guarantee that it goes back substantially to Jesus. But since we are compelled to include in a discussion of tradition history an examination of the criteria for authenticity, this approach must be examined. And when it is examined the actual contents of the gospel tradition suggest (in the view of the present writer, though on this, as on all controversial topics, opinions would be divided[5]) that this approach has serious flaws, and correspondingly that allowance needs to be made for a greater degree of post-Jesus creativity within that tradition.

Take, for instance, Matthew 18:17: "If he (the offending brother) refuses to listen to the church, let him be to you as a Gentile and a tax collector." This saying has in mind a disciplinary purification of the community, which is somewhat discordant with the message of the two parables of the wheat and the tares (Mt. 13:24–30), and the dragnet (Mt. 13:47f).[6] Moreover, the saying presupposes an audience which is Jewish and which also depreciates and excludes Gentiles and tax collectors.[7] This seems most unlike the historical Jesus. The exclusion of the Gentiles was hardly his approach: quite the contrary, he announced in word (Mt. 8:11f.) and action (Mk. 11:15–17) their acceptance and continually held them up as those whose example the Jews should follow in responding to the appeal or word of God (Lk. 7:9; 10:12–14; 11:31f). And what applies to the Gentiles applies even more forcefully to the tax collectors. It was their inclusion, their joyful participation in his fellowship meals, their genuine repentance, which Jesus was prepared to defend with vigour and in the teeth of scathing criticism (Lk. 7:34; 15:1f; Mk. 2:15–17).[8] So it appears to be unlikely that Matthew 18:17 is authentic: indeed, it seems to represent a later acceptance of attitudes which Jesus himself had resisted.[9]

Similar issues are raised by Matthew 23:2f: "The scribes and the Pharisees sit on Moses' seat; so practise and observe everything they say to you . . .". Such a saying undergirds Pharisaic traditional teaching with Mosaic authority,[10] and accepts Moses as the final court of appeal. Far from making any distinction between law and tradition,[11] this saying belongs to the same rabbinic outlook as that expressed in, for instance, Peah 2:6: "Nahum the Scrivener said: 'I have received a tradition from R. Measha, who received it from his father, who received it from the *zugoth,* who received it from the prophets as a *halakah* given to Moses from Sinai" (cf. Aboth 1:1). But the historical Jesus does not seem to have adopted so conservative an attitude to either tradition or law: indeed, it is probable that the combined effect of the evidence in Mark 7:15, 10:2–9, the traditions underlying Matthew 5:21–48, and Luke 9:60[12] is that Jesus authoritatively declared the will of God and proceeded on that basis to evaluate certain laws, but not that he set about deducing the will of God directly from the law. In that case, we would have to ask whether an alternative post-Easter setting is available for Matthew 23:2f. In view of the Pharisaic membership and theological influence within the church, which is attested in Acts 15:5; 21:20 (cf. Gal. 2:4f, 12), the answer might not be hard to reach.

We therefore conclude that the gospel tradition itself compels us to engage in tradition-historical enquiry. In looking to the gospels as sources for the sayings and actions of Jesus we can hardly avoid attributing to the later post-Easter stage both the redaction of material, and, on occasion, its creation. But we still have to discuss the validity of two related arguments which are often used in order to restrain tradition-historical work. The first takes the form of a denial of differences between parallel traditions in the interests of a harmonistic uniformity and in heavy reliance on the hypothesis of eyewitness testimony. The second maximizes the differences and argues for the separate distinctness of the incidents or settings or sayings concerned. These arguments and approaches to the text must be taken seriously and submitted to the test of the text itself in order that the problems of method which they raise may have justice done to them. We shall, therefore, take some relevant examples and, in so doing, hope not only to assess these approaches but also to illustrate the tradition-historical method in action.

II. *Unique Sayings and Incidents*

In principle there is of course every likelihood that Jesus did say certain things twice though in variant forms, and also that certain sorts of incident did occur more than once. The question is whether the actual phenomena of the tradition are adequately accounted for in every case by the invocation of such a principle. We can, I believe, see the guidelines for the use of the tradition-historical method emerging specially clearly in cases where a unique and unrepeated (and often unrepeatable) situation is in involved. This uniqueness can be grounded in either literary or historical considerations.

1. AN EXAMPLE OF LITERARY CONSIDERATIONS.

The New Testament contains several passages which presuppose an equation: Jesus = Wisdom. This is the case in the pre-Pauline material in Philippians 2:6–11 and Colossians 1:15–20, as well as in the Johannine prologue.[13] In the fourth gospel, indeed, this equation is presumed not only in sayings about Jesus but also in sayings of Jesus (see especially 4:14; 6:35). But what about the synoptic tradition?

In Matthew 11:2–19 = Luke 7:18–35 a long section of material common to both gospels is climaxed in a saying about wisdom. For Matthew "wisdom is justified by her works" (11:19), but for Luke "wisdom is justified by all her children" (7:35). It is the relationship between Jesus and wisdom in the developing tradition which here concerns us. It must, first, be quite clear that the literary setting of each version of the saying proves that the same saying is under consideration. That is, "Jesus might have said it twice" is not a viable option. Secondly, we clearly have to choose between the two rather than to amalgamate them[14] if we are to avoid producing a theologically confused hybrid version. Thirdly, the identity of the "children of wisdom" in the Lukan strand is already made plain by the word *πάντων* which negatively precludes John and Jesus (7:33f) and positively takes up *πᾶς ὁ λαὸς . . . . . . καὶ οἱ τελῶναι* in 7:29. The link between 7:29 and 7:35 is reinforced by the common use of *δικαιοῦν*. For Luke, John and Jesus are the messengers of wisdom, and the people at large and the tax collectors are her children.[15] It is probable that Luke's understanding is broadly in line with that of Q (even though the *πάντων* of 7:35 is typical of his style and is probably his own editorial insertion), for 7:29f contains un-Lukan features and is probably substantially drawn from Q.[16] At the Q stage it probably did not include *πᾶς ὁ λαός* but did refer to prostitutes, in view of Matthew 21:32 which is related to Luke 7:29f and in view of Luke's addition of 7:36–50 immediately afterwards:[17] the latter passage, which centres on "a woman which was a sinner", may well have been introduced at this point in reminiscence of the Q form of Luke 7:29. Be that as it may, Q like Luke saw John and Jesus as wisdom's messengers,[18] and those who responded to their missions as wisdom's children. This usage of the "children of wisdom" idea is of course in line with the Old Testament tradition of wisdom's children as those who listen attentively to her teaching (Pr. 8:32f; Ecclus. 4:11; 15:2).

This reconstruction depends, however, on the Matthaean reference to wisdom's "works" being secondary. But this is indeed extremely likely. For Matthew 11 as a whole exhibits a uniform pattern of concern with "works". This is the case in 11:2 where the words *τὰ ἔργα τοῦ Χριστοῦ* are unlikely to have been omitted by Luke if they stood in Q, and therefore are attributable to Matthew.[19] This is also the case in 11:20–23 which Matthew has added after 11:2–19, and in which Jesus reproves unrepentant cities who have witnessed but rejected his mighty works.[20] So the form of Matthew 11:19 is the product of the evangelist's intervention, and this intervention has significant theological overtones. Above all, the correlation between *τὰ ἔργα τοῦ Χριστοῦ* and *τὰ ἔργα τῆς σοφίας* automatically intensifies the rapprochement between Jesus the messiah and wisdom. This rapprochement is not yet a straight equation, in view of *αὐτῆς* (Mt. 11:19).[21] But it is a rapprochement which we can, as it were, see growing closer before our eyes as Matthew brings together some traditions which view Jesus as the person sent by, but not the same as, wisdom,[22] and others (for example, Mt. 11:28–30[23]) where the equation has probably already been established.[24] All the more interesting, incidentally, is Luke's determined faithfulness to the less developed christological viewpoint.

Here then is a case where literary setting puts us on the track of a divergence in the tradition of one and the same saying, and consequently on the track of an extended tradition-historical development. In the process, not only are important questions about method posed and answered, but also important restraints imposed on any attempt to construct too neat a sequence in terms of time and place. By this I mean the following: (a) While Q and Luke are witnesses to the existence of a christology which does not go beyond the view that Jesus is a messenger of Wisdom to the "Jesus = Wisdom" equation, Matthew is a witness to the survival of both schemes in one and the same community without the more developed pattern obliterating the less developed one. (b) With pre-Pauline material acting as a witness to the remarkable earliness of the stage at which the "Jesus = Wisdom" scheme was constructed, it is important to see that schemes later in time can still be more primitive in content. Tempting though it must have been to make the synoptic Jesus claim pre-existence or agency in creation as did the pre-Pauline material, and later indeed the Johannine Jesus, the first three evangelists still hold back. (c) Luke (a Gentile Christian) and Q (belonging perhaps to a Hellenistic Jewish Christian environment) have in common the view that Jesus was simply a messenger of Wisdom; Matthew's community stands at the point of convergence of this and the more developed view. Therefore we have to learn to live with a greater degree of raggedness at the edges and a less neat evolutionary process than would emerge if we envisaged a straight and consecutive development from Jesus to the Aramaic-speaking and Hellenistic Jewish-Christian outlooks and ultimately to the Gentile Christian position. Not only were the early communities mixed in membership (as the Pauline correspondence also demonstrates), but they were also communities within which spectrums of membership probably varied in theology.

2. AN EXAMPLE OF HISTORICAL UNIQUENESS.

The visit of Mary Magdalene to Jesus' tomb on the first Easter morning is a case in point this time. Since it is an unrepeated occurrence there is in principle the possibility that the different accounts may form a tradition-historical sequence. This is, incidentally, by no means ruled out if the traditions prove capable of harmonization, for the differing perspectives of the various traditions could still form such a sequence; but it is positively required if, as D. F. Strauss[25] argued with characteristic vigour long ago, harmonization proves impossible.

Now the timing of the visits of Mary to the tomb in Mark 16:1–8 and John 20:1f. means that they represent one and the same event, and the content of each tradition reinforces this view. The incident in John 20:1f. could not have happened *before* the Mark 16:1–8 one, for it would be absurd for the women to speculate about how the stone might be moved away (Mk. 16:3) if it had already been seen to be moved (John 20:2); equally, it would be absurd for the women to set out to anoint a body (Mk. 16:1) which was already known by at least one of them to be no longer there (Jn. 20:2). But the John 20:1f. incident could not have happened *after* the Mark 16:1–8 one, for the words of Mary (Jn. 20:2), "They have taken the Lord out of the tomb and we do not know where they have laid him", far from presupposing the angelic message announcing resurrection (Mk. 16:6), show that "the thought of a resurrection did not enter her head".[26] Attempts to achieve a harmony between the traditions have certainly been made. Thus Z. C. Hodges has argued for a decision by Mary not to tell of the angelic vision,[27] but this falls foul of Luke 24:23, not to mention Matthew 28:9f., and it also leaves us wondering why at the later stage Mary is still consumed with anguish and grief and still genuinely convinced that the body has been stolen (Jn. 20:11, 13). For similar reasons, D. Guthrie has suggested that Mary set out for the tomb and then, seeing the stone moved, rushed back to the disciples and left her companions to see and hear the angel.[28] But this attempt at harmonization only produces disharmony with Luke 24:9f. It therefore seems to respect the intentions and the contents of each tradition rather more if we accept that one and the same event has been presented by means of divergent traditions, and that the forms and functions of each must be determined within the tradition-historical process.

To determine these forms and functions means taking into account a number of possibilities, and to decide between these means a more protracted investigation than we can accommodate here. Suffice to mention two possibilities: (a) If John 20:3–10 were treated as separable and then removed from the narrative, John 20:1f., 11ff. could then be taken as one unit which has been remodelled to accommodate the intervening passage.

This underlying unit with its reference to Mary and the angels could then be taken as parallel to, but later in composition than, Mark 16:1–8. Since this latter passage may itself have been subject to editorial modification – for instance, an intrusion may have occurred with verse 7, or even with verses 1, 4, 5, 7 and 8b,[29] or with some other combination – the tradition-historical sequence might consist of a primary pre-Markan unit which was then modified by literary means into the present Markan unit (with or without a lost ending!), which in turn developed, but not by direct literary intervention, into the Johannine form.[30] The theological and apologetic considerations which were in force at each stage would then need to be uncovered. (b) Alternatively, it could be that John 20:11–14a, a passage which plays little part in the chapter as a whole, is itself an editorial bridge passage based on general acquaintance with synoptic data and leading to the appearance of Jesus to Mary, an event presented in a separate and self-sufficient unit of tradition in Matthew 28:9f. In this case, John 20:1f. might also represent a separate independent unit complete in itself,[31] which could then be correlated with Mark 16:1–8 as a whole. If so, one possibility worthy of consideration is that John 20:1f. is more or less the earliest form of the tradition,[32] and a form which is uninfluenced by post-Easter convictions and unhampered by the historical-critical objections[33] often felt to be involved in Mark 16:1–8. On this showing the tradition-historical sequence would be from John 20:1f. to the pre-Markan form, and then to Mark, and then to the versions of Matthew and Luke.

Here then is another example of the tradition-historical enquiry in action. Certainly there is room for legitimate difference of opinion among scholars as to the actual pattern of the tradition-historical development, but there can be no doubt that the content of the gospel tradition itself demands that the attempt to discover one be made.

III. *Which Community?*

The attempt to establish criteria by means of which traditions might be attributed to Jesus, to the Palestinian community, to Hellenistic Jewish-Christian communities or to Gentile Christian communities, is beset with formidable difficulties and is probably incapable of producing firm results. In part this is due to the nature of contemporary Judaism, and in part to the nature of primitive Christianity. To the degree that we do know something of each we can detect an extremely fluid and flexible situation in both, and to the degree that we do not know enough about each any observations are bound to be tentative. Again and again it is apparent that it is easier to replace old certainties with new uncertainties than to produce assured results, and it is as well to be open about this. Perhaps a few observations along this line may help.

(1) The distinction between Palestinian and Hellenistic Judaism cannot be treated as absolute. Long-established "Hellenistic" influence inside Palestine is a firm datum by the time the Christian movement begins. One

has only to recall the non-Palestinian origin of prominent Jewish leaders (e.g. the high priest Ananel or the great Hillel, both of whom came from Babylon), or the movements of distinguished rabbis in and out of Palestine (e.g. Joshua ben Perahjah in b.Sanh. 107b), or the wide adoption of non-Semitic loan-words, or the occurrence of so-called Hellenistic terminology and thought forms at Qumran, or the existence of a Hellenistic synagogue in Jerusalem (Acts 6:9).[34] The openness of the channels of communication is also suggested by the evidence of the hold kept by the Jerusalem authorities on the Diaspora (Acts 9:2; 28:21). It is not to be thought that all influence of "Hellenistic" thinking was shaken off with the dust of a person's feet when he crossed the frontiers of Palestine. And if Judaism is not susceptible to division into totally separate and water-tight compartments, it is not to be thought that nascent Christianity could be. For the varied phenomenon of Judaism was the most prominent feature of the circumstances within which the growing Christian church developed, and theological development was, in part at least, a response to circumstances.

(2) Distinctions between one sort of community and another may have been less significant than distinctions within communities. And while internal distinctions are likely to have brought about creative interaction between varieties of emphasis and even confrontation and controversy, there are clear signs in the gospels of processes of accommodation and conciliation. Not that such processes were bound to be successful, but the fact that they were necessary confirms that different views could be maintained within a single community. An example of this is the rigorist tendency which emerges in material like Matthew 5:18f. (cf. the comments above on Mt. 23:2f.), a point of view which is preserved rather than suppressed by both Q and Matthew, and even in a reduced form by Luke (Lk. 16:17).[35] Yet in all these documents material of this sort is set alongside other material whose perspective is different. This is a particularly illuminating issue because the spectrum of opinion existing within the Matthaean (non-Palestinian Jewish?) community seems to mirror the spectrum existing within the early Jerusalem community. That the leadership could safely stay in Jerusalem after a persecution dispersed those who were "liberal" in the matters affecting law and temple (Acts 8:1) strongly suggests that they were inoffensively conservative and advocates of a Matthew 5:18f.-type position. The judgment we make on the relative faithfulness to Jesus of the apostles and of the Stephen group will have a big influence on our decision about the authenticity of Matthew 5:18f., but for the present it is enough to note that the pre-persecution period in Jerusalem was one when differing outlooks co-existed inside one Christian community. The upshot is consequently that it is more advisable to speak of variant theological schemes or developing trends than to allocate the different patterns to separate slots.

(3) There is no automatic means of deciding whether material containing Semitisms belongs to Jesus or to the Aramaic-speaking communities. Equally, the absence of Semitisms or, say, the use of the LXX does not demonstrate a non-Semitic or non-Jesus point of origin. Any writer may

reformulate tradition in his own language or idiom, and he may equally adjust scriptural quotations and allusions to conform to the received biblical text in use in his own community. But the existence of tradition is not thereby disproved.

To sum up, Christianity was born into an exceptionally varied world of thought, and itself responded – indeed, within a missionary context, could not but respond – to that variety. It could no more preserve a compartmentalized character than the environment did. As far as tradition-history is concerned, the text of the New Testament permits us to reconstruct developments and successive stages of theological reflection, but not to be too confident about assigning these successive developments to specific areas or times.

IV. *Suggested Criteria for Sayings of Jesus*

The criteria for distinguishing Jesus-material from later church developments are still vigorously debated,[36] and uncertainty about this fundamental issue of method is in no small way the cause of the marked variation in the conclusions of various scholars, and ultimately the cause of the pessimistic declaration that "faith cannot and should not be dependent on the change and uncertainty of historical research."

The criterion of dissimilarity has been formulated in a particularly clear-cut manner by R. H. Fuller: "Traditio-historical criticism eliminates from the authentic sayings of Jesus those which are paralleled in the Jewish tradition on the one hand (apocalyptic and Rabbinic) and those which reflect the faith, practice and situations of the post-Easter church as we know them outside the gospels."[37] It will be noticed that this lays down dissimilarity as a *necessary* condition, and takes material *outside* the gospels as the primary data for the life of the church. But these are two of a range of considerations which call the dissimilarity criterion in question. Firstly, the deceptive simplicity of this test should not mask the fact that at most it can produce the distinctive Jesus but cannot guarantee the characteristic Jesus. And since there can be no assurance, nor indeed any likelihood, that Jesus overlapped in no way with contemporary Judaism and contributed nothing to primitive Christianity, the distinctive Jesus can hardly be the historical Jesus.[38] Secondly, by separating the "distinctive Jesus" (who is wrongly assumed to be the historical Jesus) from what functions as the "characteristic community", it is a necessary presupposition of the method that the community members must have regarded authentic Jesus-material as neither vital nor important, since they did not ground their life and faith upon it. In effect, Easter becomes the point of discontinuity. But that is very doubtful since (a) H. Schürmann has rightly drawn attention to the pre-Easter beginnings of the community based upon a response to Jesus and his words, and the consequent sociological continuity,[39] and (b) whatever else Easter was not, it certainly was about the vindication of Jesus, his pre-Easter cause and his pre-Easter words. Thirdly, it is not possible to salvage continuity by proposing, for example, an evolution from pre-Easter implicit christology to post-Easter explicit christology.[40] For if the post-Easter community members were correct, as is suggested, to regard Jesus as the messiah on the basis of what he had said and done, it follows that such implications must have been intended deliberately by Jesus, and that the disciples could just as easily have drawn the correct inference before Easter. Fourthly, the gospels themselves belong to the living experience of the communities, and it is highly doubtful whether anything at all within them can fail to represent the standpoint of some one community.[41] As a consequence, the dissimilarity principle should logically produce one and only one result. That is, concerning the historical Jesus we know absolutely nothing. In view of the truly radical nature of this result which the dissimilarity criterion inevitably constructs, it is not surprising to see that its continued existence in principle has had to be allied to its tacit abandonment in practice. Thus: (a) R. H. Fuller declares that in the authoritative Ἀμήν "Jesus pledges his whole person behind the truth of his proclamation. This formula has certainly been added secondarily to some of Jesus' sayings, as a synoptic comparison will show. But it cannot be doubted that it was characteristic of the historical Jesus."[42] But surely secondary additions imply that the word figures in community theology, and that consequently what Fuller says cannot be doubted can, and indeed by the criterion of dissimilarity should, be doubted. (b) H. Conzelmann has analysed and assessed sayings which refer to "the Father", "my Father", and "your Father".[43] None of the first group, he suggests, goes back to Jesus. Nor do any of the second group, though somewhat surprisingly he writes: "If the form of address goes back to Jesus. . . ." In the third group, Conzelmann with obvious reserve allows that Matthew 5:48; 6:32 and 23:9 may go back to Jesus. But with much greater, and therefore rather surprising, confidence he then affirms: "There is no doubt that Jesus designated God as 'Father'." But surely again, by the criterion of dissimilarity, there must be some doubt. References to "Father" should be treated as inauthentic because of their overlap with Judaism, and references to "Abba" should be treated as inauthentic because of their overlap with Aramaic-speaking and Pauline Christianity, as attested by Romans 8:15 and Galatians 4:6.[44] (c) N. Perrin has argued that the coming of the kingdom is an authentic element in Jesus' preaching, and has used the dissimilarity criterion to ground such an argument, first of all, on the verbal distinction between the kingdom's "coming" (so, Jesus) and its "being established" (so, Judaism); secondly, on the Jesus-tradition's use of the "kingdom" as "a comprehensive term for the blessings of salvation", which is only rarely paralleled in Judaism; thirdly, its application to "the final act of God in visiting and redeeming his people".[45] But while the distinction between Judaism and Jesus in respect of the future coming of the kingdom is probably over-emphasized here, it is the impossibility of distinguishing Jesus from the church on this point which jeopardizes the argument. Indeed Perrin appears to be aware of precisely this Achilles' heel in his thesis, when he writes: "A reasonable explanation is that usages of 'Kingdom of God' characteristic of the teaching of Jesus and not of the early Church live on in the synoptic tradition. This does not mean, of course, that even in the Kingdom sayings the tradition suddenly becomes historically reliable. If the Church had not had her own use for the sayings, she would not have preserved them, and if they could not have been made expressive of his purposes, no evangelist would have used them."[46] It is that last sentence which makes the fatal concession. For once it is allowed that the coming of the kingdom is indeed a theme of early Christian theology – and who can doubt that "May your kingdom come" (Mt. 6:10 = Lk. 11:2) is the church's prayer, even though it involves all three features listed by Perrin? – then there are only two options open: *Either* accept a line of continuity from Jesus to the church, which rules out the criterion of dissimilarity, *or* apply the criterion of dissimilarity, which rules out the line of continuity. If the second option is chosen, yet more material drops out of the authentic Jesus-tradition. And we are left to move step by step with inexorable certainty, but surely with increasing disquiet, to the truly radical conclusion mentioned above: that is, concerning the historical Jesus we know absolutely nothing.

The criterion of multiple attestation, i.e. whether or not a saying occurs in more than one independent strand of gospel tradition, cannot be tested independently of the assessment of the dissimilarity test. For traditions which are unrelated in literary terms could still emerge as an independent but common response to similar problems or insights. But if the logical possibility of a line of continuity from Jesus to the church is accepted, multiple attestation may have a part to play. For it can suggest that a deep impression has been made by a particular saying or theme, or that an earlier archetype exists behind the various forms, an archetype which is closer in time to the beginnings of the tradition. Even here, of course, the tradition-historical enquiry must at some stage take over, as the examples quoted earlier demonstrate. The same necessity is clearly indicated by the variations within multiple attestation in the cases of, for example, the traditions of the anointing (Mk. 14:3–9; Lk. 7:36–50; Jn. 12:1–8) or the saying about blasphemy against the Spirit (Mk. 3:28f; Mt. 12:31f. = Lk. 12:10). One must also add in connection with multiple attestation that using it can only produce eccentric results if it is taken to mean the laying down of a necessary condition.

The criterion of coherence also lacks the force to operate as a primary test, for it depends upon the existence of material which is already proved to be authentic, and with which other material may cohere. It can, however, prove useful in such circumstances. Thus, if a series of features of "Son of man" sayings can be shown to be among features of Jesus' mission in such a way that the only extra element in those sayings is the actual term "Son of man" itself, it is bound to be extremely difficult to dismiss all such "Son of man" sayings as inauthentic.[47] On the negative side, suggestions of a lack of coherence have to be used with caution, for, as M. D. Hooker and R. S. Barbour have pointed out, there is a risk of supposing incoherence when in fact there is paradox.[48] But equally, one must be alive to the risk of too freely invoking paradox in such a way as to attempt to reconcile the irreconcilable.

The problems which emerge during any critical examination of criteria might suggest that there is no future for the enquiry except in pessimism or even agnosticism. But this would, I believe, be more sceptical than is necessary, though it must be conceded that any reconstruction of the content of Jesus' message or the shape of his mission will involve much that is tentative.

Dissimilarity is, as already noted, a doubtful tool when the relationship between Jesus and the post-Easter churches is under scrutiny. It also has some drawbacks in respect of a discussion of his relationship with Judaism, in view of the incompleteness of our knowledge of Judaism. But even though our understanding of Judaism must remain open to modification and supplementation, we can do no more than work from what we actually do know. And if we do that we can begin by taking account of that gospel material which, after the tradition-historical investigation has got as far as establishing the earliest form of the tradition, marks a deviation from the basic principles of Judaism. Now certainly that earliest form may represent the outlook of some person or community after Easter. But if there is no reason to suppose that anything intrinsic to Easter as such has created the tradition, we are bound to ask what decisive impulse may have led to such a new development and deviation from Judaism. And the most probable answer to that question is Jesus. It is important to be clear about what we are doing. That is, dissimilarity is not being regarded as necessary. It is merely being taken as a starting-point in the discussion of the relationship between the tradition and Judaism, and it is at the same time being supplemented by considerations of evolutionary continuity (not dissimilarity) in the relationship between Jesus and the churches. As an example one could take legal material. Mark 7:15 is a saying widely regarded as radical vis-à-vis the law.[49] It could theoretically be the product of Pauline influence, in view of the comparable outlook expressed in Romans 14:14. But instead of arguing that this deviation from the law is a post-Easter construction (which a consistent use of the dissimilarity criterion in a necessary sense should oblige us to do), we ask what could have moved Mark and Paul to take such a view. The most probable answer is Jesus, so that behind this material there can be heard his *ipsissima vox*. By the same method one could confidently attribute radical positions on divorce and discipleship (1 Cor. 7:10b, 11b; Mk. 10:2–9; Lk. 16:18 and Mt. 8:22 = Lk. 9:60) to Jesus. With multiple attestation (used positively rather than actually required) adding strength to the argument that in these sayings critical of law and tradition we do hear his voice, we have confidence in a wide range of gospel material which expresses this position. And we are, incidentally, working forward by this means to a position which stands some chance of explaining adequately post-Easter phenomena. That is a substantial advance.

To this modified use of the dissimilarity test there can be added considerations of coherence. That is, we assess next the material whose most primitive form coheres with the theological presuppositions and explicit affirmations in the material already secured as authentic tradition. Again there are admittedly margins for error at every stage of the process, but this argumentation is not unique in that respect. Certainly coherence can lead too far, and should only be operated on the basis of a clear understanding of what sort of documents the gospels are. And, of course, there must also be a coherence of the context presupposed by a tradition with the context of Jesus' mission, as well as a coherence of content. But at least the use of coherence, after dissimilarity to Judaism has been explored, does offer certain advantages: (a) It allows for the incorporation of other material reflecting similarity between Jesus and Judaism. (b) It allows for the continuity between Jesus and some at least of the post-Easter Christian developments. And, as we have seen, no collection of criteria which prohibits in advance such factors can hope to do justice to the historical Jesus as he was in himself and as he participated in the development of events and ideas of his time.

All this is but the beginning of a process which is arduous and exacting. The suggestions above are but guidelines, and the implementation of them is just as certain to allow room for judgment by the individual, and therefore room for disagreement between individuals, as any other suggestions. For this we must settle, even if it seems by comparison with older but, in view of the character of the gospels, unrealistic certainties to be unsettling. But it does at least have the merit of recognizing that the gospels do belong to Jesus and also to the churches. For Jesus this means that he is seen as not merely *historisch,* a figure of the past, but also one whom we can see within the developing tradition as truly *geschichtlich,* that is, a person whose relevance is explored and exploited ever and again in places far removed from Galilee and Jerusalem and in times long after A.D. 30.

NOTES

1. Particularly clear examples of the method in action on the basis of such a scheme can be found in H. E. Tödt, *The Son of Man in the Synoptic Tradition* (E.T. London 1965); R. H. Fuller, *The Foundations of New Testament Christology* (London 1965); F. Hahn, *The Titles of Jesus in Christology* (E.T. London 1968).
2. See R. Bultmann, *The History of the Synoptic Tradition* (E.T. Oxford 1963), p. 4.
3. *New Testament Theology I: The Proclamation of Jesus* (E.T. London 1971), pp. 293f.
4. The equivalence of Mark 8:29 and John 6:69 is widely recognised. Cf. R. E. Brown, *The Gospel according to John I–XII* (London 1966), pp. 301–303.
5. See, for example, note 11 on p. 348.
6. J. Jeremias, *The Parables of Jesus* (E.T. London 1963), pp. 224–227.
7. Cf. also Mt. 5:46f.
8. O. Michel, *τελώνης* TDNT 8 (1972), pp. 103–105; J. Jeremias, *Theology I,* pp. 113–118.
9. This conclusion is in no way prevented by the argument that the saying is authentic and was spoken by Jesus prophetically (cf. Jn. 14:26) with a view to a period after his death. Leaving aside the substantial number of questions begged by such an argument, it is sufficient to note here that Jesus would hardly have authorized the post-Easter churches to ig-

nore or reject the principles for which he campaigned so determinedly during the pre-Easter period.

10. E. Klostermann, *Das Matthäusevangelium* (Tübingen 1927[2]), p. 181; R. Hummel, *Die Auseinandersetzung zwischen Kirche und Judentum im Matthäusevangelium* (München 1966), pp. 31f.

11. It is argued by N. B. Stonehouse, *The Witness of Matthew and Mark to Christ* (London 1944), pp. 196f, that such a distinction is present in Mt. 23:4, 16ff, 23f, and therefore in 23:2f. However, this does not do justice to the word *πάντα* (Mt. 23:3), cf. G. Strecker, *Der Weg der Gerechtigkeit,* (Göttingen 1966[2]), p. 16. Moreover, the tendency of Matthew to act as a conciliator between various divergent theological positions (see p. 169f. for another example of this in his treatment of "wisdom" material) without smoothing out the differences rules out any such limitation of Mt. 23:2f, which should therefore be allowed its full force.

12. On this material, see H. Merkel, "Jesus und die Pharisäer", NTS. 14 (1967–68), pp. 194–208; M. Hengel, *Nachfolge und Charisma* (Berlin, 1968), pp. 3–17; H. Merkel, "Markus 7, 15 – das Jesuswort über die innere Verunreinigung", ZRGG 20 (1968), pp. 340–363; D. R. Catchpole, "The Synoptic Divorce Material as a Tradition-historical Problem", BJRL 57 (1974–75), pp. 92–127.

13. On Phil. 2:6–11, see D. Georgi, "Der vorpaulinische Hymnus Phil. 2:6–11", in E. Dinkler (ed.). *Zeit und Geschichte* (Tübingen 1964), pp. 263–293; R. P. Martin, *Carmen Christi* (Cambridge 1967); E. Käsemann, "A Critical Analysis of Philippians 2:5–11", JTh.Ch. 5 (1968), pp. 45–88. On Col. 1:15–20, E. Schweizer, "The Church as the Missionary Body of Christ", NTS 8 (1961–62), pp. 1–11. On the Johannine prologue, R. E. Brown, *The Gospel according to John I–XII,* pp. 519–524; R. Schnackenburg, *The Gospel according to St. John* (E.T. London 1968), pp. 481–493; E. Käsemann, *New Testament Questions of Today* (London 1969), pp. 138–167.

14. So, rightly, R. V. G. Tasker, *Gospel according to St. Matthew* (London 1961), p. 119.

15. H. Schürmann, *Das Lukasevangelium I* (Freiburg 1969), p. 423.

16. Schürmann, op. cit., pp. 420f. D. Lührmann, *Die Redaktion der Logienquelle,* (Neukirchen 1969), pp. 27f, argues that Luke 7:29f. comes from Q (cf. Mt. 21:32), but that Luke has altered its position and substituted it for Mt. 11:12f. which did occur in its present position in Q. He argues that there is no particular reason why Matthew should have inserted 11:12f., and that the special Matthaean interpretation appears first in 11:14f. (drawing upon Mark 9:13 and drawing out Mt. 11:10 = Lk. 7:27). However, the themes of prophecy, the kingdom and John which are common to Mt. 11:11 and 11:12f. are sufficient to explain why Matthew should insert 11:12f. at this point, while elsewhere in Q material Matthew shows a tendency to move material around (cf. Mt. 8:11f.) more than Luke does.

17. Schürmann, op. cit., p. 423.

18. Lührmann, op. cit., p. 99; otherwise, U. Wilckens, *σοφία* TDNT VII (1971), p. 515, who thinks an equation between Jesus and wisdom is already achieved in Q.

19. Lührmann, op. cit., pp. 29f.

20. Mt. 11:20–23 cannot originally have belonged with 11:2–19 since the persons addressed are different. The link word *τότε* between the two blocks is typical of Matthaean editorial work.

21. That single word *αὐτῆς* must restrain the tendency (cf. M. J. Suggs, *Wisdom, Christology and Law in Matthew's Gospel* (Harvard 1970), p. 58) to treat Matthew's redaction as thorough-going and complete even to the point of saying that "Jesus is Sophia incarnate". In fact he has not quite got that far.

22. On the Q tradition's view of Jesus as Wisdom's representative, see G. N. Stanton, "On the Christology of Q", in B. Lindars and S. S. Smalley (edd.), *Christ and Spirit in the New Testament* (Cambridge 1973), pp. 27–42, esp. 36–38.

23. U. Wilckens, op. cit., pp. 516f; H. D. Betz, "The Logion of the Easy Yoke and of Rest", JBL 88 (1967), pp. 10–24.

24. The results obtained here can be confirmed and strengthened by a similar study of Mt. 23:34 = Lk. 11:49, where Wisdom's rôle as sender of the prophets and others (as in Q) is taken over by Jesus according to Matthaean redaction. Cf. Suggs, op. cit., pp. 13–29.

25. *The Life of Jesus Critically Examined* (E.T. London 1973), pp. 709–718.

26. L. Morris, *The Gospel according to St. John* (London, 1972), p. 831.
27. "The Women and the Empty Tomb", *Bibliotheca Sacra* 123 (1966), pp. 301–309, esp. pp. 305f.
28. *Jesus the Messiah* (Glasgow 1972), p. 359.
29. Thus, L. Schenke, *Auferstehungsverkündigung und leeres Grab* (Stuttgart 1969[2]), pp. 54f.
30. Thus, C. F. Evans, *Resurrection and the New Testament* (London 1970), pp. 120–124.
31. At the pre-Johannine stage material now present in John 20:1f. may have led directly into the story of Peter's visit to the tomb. Cf. G. Hartmann, "Die Vorlage des Osterberichte in Joh. 20", ZNW 55 (1964), pp. 197–220.
32. So, P. Benoit, "Marie-Madeleine et les Disciples au Tombeau selon Joh 20:1–18", in W. Eltester, (ed.) *Judentum, Urchristentum, Kirche* (Berlin 1964), pp. 141–152.
33. For a summary of these specific problems, cf. Evans, op. cit., pp. 75–79.
34. Abundant evidence of this very open situation is readily accessible in J. Jeremias, *Jerusalem in the Time of Jesus* (E.T. London 1969); M. Hengel, *Judaism and Hellenism* (E.T. London 1974).
35. For the view that Mt. 5:19 stems from Q, see H. Schürmann , "Wer daher eines dieser geringsten Gebote auflöst . . .", repr. in *Traditionsgeschichtliche Untersuchungen zu den synoptischen Evangelien* (Düsseldorf 1968), pp. 126–136.
36. See N. Perrin, *Rediscovering the Teaching of Jesus* (London 1967), pp. 15–53; M. D. Hooker, "Christology and Methodology", NTS 17 (1970–71), pp. 480–487; id., 'On using the Wrong Tool', *Theology* 75 (1972), pp. 570–581; J. Jeremias, *New Testament Theology,* I, pp. 1–41; R. S. Barbour, *Traditio-historical Criticism of the Gospels* (London 1972), pp. 1–27; D. G. A. Calvert, "An Examination of the Criteria for Distinguishing the Authentic Words of Jesus", NTS 18 (1971–72), pp. 209–219.
37. *The Foundations of New Testament Christology* (London 1965), p. 18; cf. E. Käsemann, "The Problem of the Historical Jesus", *Essays on New Testament Themes* (E.T. London 1964), pp. 34–37; N. Perrin, op. cit., p. 39; H. Conzelmann, "Jesus Christus", RGG III, p. 623.
38. Cf. W. G. Kümmel, "Das Problem des geschichtlichen Jesus in der gegenwärtigen Forschungslage", in E. Grässer (ed.), *Heilsgeschehen und Geschichte* (Marburg 1965), p. 403; M. D. Hooker, "Christology", pp. 481f., who also rightly points out the limitations of our knowledge of both Judaism and Christianity.
39. "Die vorösterlichen Anfänge der Logientradition", *Untersuchungen,* pp. 39–65.
40. Thus, Käsemann, op. cit., pp. 37–45.
41. It is worth pondering the comment of G. Bornkamm, *Jesus of Nazareth* (E.T. London 1960), p. 14: "We possess no single word of Jesus and no single story of Jesus, no matter how incontestably genuine they may be, which do not embody at the same time the confession of the believing congregation, or are at least embedded therein."
42. Op. cit., pp. 104f.
43. *An Outline of the Theology of the New Testament* (E.T. London 1969), pp. 102–106.
44. R. S. Barbour, op. cit., p. 17, draws attention to the fact that *Abba* is "as characteristic of the prayers of the early Church as one could wish", but argues that those who accept authenticity in spite of the dissimilarity criterion probably do so largely because it is neither christological in the narrow sense nor kerygmatic. One can only note that the criterion of dissimilarity is not usually proposed with the intention to limit its application to christology and kerygma. It is hard to draw back from the main conviction that the process does indeed involve inconsistency.
45. Op. cit., pp. 54–63.
46. Op. cit., p. 62.
47. This approach can be seen in the article of I. H. Marshall, "The Synoptic Son of man sayings in Recent Discussion", NTS 12 (1965–66), pp. 327–351.
48. M. D. Hooker, "Christology", p. 483; R. S. Barbour, op. cit., pp. 9f.
49. See n.12.

CHAPTER XI

REDACTION CRITICISM

Stephen S. Smalley

New Testament critics in the last century were preoccupied with the sources of the Gospels, chiefly the synoptic Gospels. At the beginning of this century they turned their attention to the first stages in the history of the Gospel tradition, to the original form of the teaching of Jesus.[1] Tradition criticism, as we have seen, was a special case of form criticism. Today, in a relatively new approach to the analysis and study of the Gospels, the centre of interest in New Testament criticism is moving from source criticism and form criticism to an examination of what happened at the final stage in the composition of the Gospels. Redaction criticism (*Redaktionsgeschichte*) has come to birth.[2]

These critical methods belong together, and any sharp distinctions drawn between them must necessarily therefore be artificial. They arise out of each other, and can be used to complement each other in the study of Gospel origins. It is important to recognize this as we consider redaction criticism on its own.

What is redaction criticism? The term "redaction" in Gospel criticism describes the editorial work carried out by the evangelists on their sources when they composed the Gospels.[3] It has been suggested by Ernst Haenchen[4] that "composition criticism" would better describe the study of this process. In fact, however, "redaction" and "composition" criticism, although close together, are strictly speaking different disciplines. One (redaction criticism) is the study of the observable changes introduced by the Gospel writers into the traditional material they received and used. The other (composition criticism) examines the *arrangement* of this material, an arrangement which is motived by the theological understanding and intention of the evangelists. And some scholars expand the term "composition" in this context to include the construction of wholly new sayings by the Gospel writers, which are then (so it is claimed) attributed by them to Jesus.[5] It is possible that in the future composition criticism will need to be distinguished from redaction criticism, just as redaction criticism is currently distinguished from form criticism. But meanwhile, and for convenience, the term "redaction criticism" can be understood as the detection of the evangelists' creative contribution in all its aspects to the Christian tradition which they transmit.

Why is it necessary at all in the study of the Gospels to move beyond form criticism into redaction criticism? Since both disciplines are concerned with the editing and shaping of the tradition about Jesus, although at different stages, need they be separated? The answer to these questions is straightforward. There is an important difference between the approaches of form criticism and redaction criticism in the method used and the conclusions reached, as well as in the fact that they are concerned with different stages in the history of the Christian tradition.

Form criticism (especially in its older versions) tends to view the Gospels as collections of material which originated as independent units (an assumption that itself needs qualification), and the evangelists as little more than "scissors and paste" men who gathered these units together with a special interpretative slant in mind. Redaction criticism, on the other hand, looks at the Gospels as complete documents, and sees the evangelists as individual theologians (even "authors") in their own right. Form criticism deals with the origins of the Gospel tradition, redaction criticism with its later stages.

Redaction criticism thus builds on form criticism, in the sense that form-critical method enables us to detect the work of the evangelists themselves more clearly. The newer discipline of redaction criticism moves away from form criticism, however, in that it sets out to discover the theological uniqueness of the evangelists *in relation to their sources*. To this extent redaction criticism is not a real part of form criticism. But once the two have been separated, it is important to notice that redaction criticism does not then become simply a study of "the theology" of the evangelists.[6] It is rather a consideration of the creative way in which these writers have handled their sources at the final stages of composition.

Any saying or narrative in the Gospels may have taken shape originally in three basic "settings" (*Sitze im Leben*): first in the teaching of the historical Jesus, then in the life of the early church, then in the thought of the evangelists.[7] In the third setting, the Gospel writers' own understanding, a new and decisive forward movement in the transmission of the Gospel tradition becomes apparent. From the moment when the Gospels as such come to birth, the oral period of the Christian tradition fades out, and individual writers (perhaps in the context of a "school" or even church) take over from an otherwise anonymous community. By looking carefully at the individual comments of the evangelists, their editorial links and summaries, and generally at the selection, modification and expansion of the material they use (when Matthew or Luke, for example, is compared with Mark), it is possible to discover how each writer understood and *interpreted* (as well as edited) the tradition he received. This is redaction criticism.[8] We shall consider the practice, the presuppositions and the implications of this method after a brief glance at its history.

I. *How it arose*

Redaction criticism came to the fore after the second world war, and is associated in the first place with the names of three prominent German New Testament scholars: Günther Bornkamm, Hans Conzelmann and Willi Marxsen.[9] These critics worked independently of each other on the three synoptic Gospels, Matthew, Luke and Mark respectively. It was Marxsen who gave the common approach which resulted from these studies the German name of *Redaktionsgeschichte.*[10]

Günther Bornkamm's work on the Gospel of Matthew marks the rise of redaction criticism. As a pupil of Rudolf Bultmann, he proceeded from form-critical assumptions to the further stage of analyzing Matthew's own theological outlook and intention as this is to be discerned in his handling of traditional material. In two articles which were later included in the volume now translated as *Tradition and Interpretation in Matthew,*[11] Bornkamm set out his conclusions about the first evangelist and his work. The earlier essay[12] is a study of the episode of the stilling of the storm in Matthew 8:23–27, and attempts to show how Matthew treated the source from which he derived this pericope (Mk. 4:35–41). The new context and presentation given to the incident, Bornkamm claims, reveal the independent meaning it has for the evangelist. The miracle thus becomes to him "a kerygmatic paradigm of the danger and glory of discipleship".[13] The other essay of Bornkamm[14] deals with the construction of the discourses of Jesus in Matthew, and discusses the extent to which these are controlled by the evangelist's own understanding of the church, the end, the law, Christ himself, and the inter-relation of all four. Together, these two studies reflect Bornkamm's dominant conviction that Matthew is a distinctive redactor; an "interpreter of the tradition which he collected and arranged".[15]

Hans Conzelmann's work as a redaction critic has been concerned mainly with Luke-Acts. His book *Die Mitte der Zeit,* first published in 1954, and translated into English as *The Theology of St. Luke,*[16] marks a watershed in Gospel studies and an important advance in the method of redaction criticism itself; for it is an analysis of Luke's unique role as a theologian. Perhaps Dr. Norman Perrin goes too far when he concludes that as a result of Conzelmann's work, "Luke the historian becomes a self-conscious theologian, and the details of his composition can be shown convincingly to have been theologically motivated."[17] Not everyone would dismiss so easily the historical basis from which Luke writes in both his Gospel and Acts.[18] But undoubtedly Conzelmann has helped us to discern Luke's special contribution to a proper understanding of the biblical history of salvation (*Heilsgeschichte*), which is presented and developed by the third evangelist in three distinct stages: the periods of Israel, Jesus and the church. The problem which Luke answers by this scheme, with its greater degree of "realized" eschatology, is alleged to be the so-called delay of the parousia.[19] However we view some of Conzelmann's assumptions and final conclusions, he has at least helped us to see more clearly than ever the extent to which history and theology, not one or the other, co-exist in Luke-Acts.

The third redaction critic in chronological order whose pioneering work in this field must be mentioned is Dr. Willi Marxsen, whose book *Der Evangelist Markus* (1959 [2]) [20] contains four studies of the second Gospel which use the redaction-critical method. Like Bornkamm, and indeed Conzelmann, Marxsen accepts the method and conclusions of form criticism as a basis for his work. But once more, like them, he goes beyond this to emphasize the important contribution made by Mark himself when he collected together the independent units of the evangelic tradition and wrote them up into a Gospel as such, characterized by his own theological outlook.[21] That outlook is seen particularly, Marxsen claims, in Mark's treatment of such features as the tradition about John the Baptist and the geographical references in his narratives. (Galilee, for example, is "obviously the evangelist's own creation".[22]) Throughout, Marxsen sees the second evangelist as a theologically motivated redactor, whose doctrinal interpretations become clearer when the use by Matthew and Luke of the Marcan tradition and its interpretations is considered.

One of Marxsen's more important contributions to the whole discussion of redaction criticism is his clarification of the threefold setting of all Gospel material (in the teaching of Jesus, in the life of the early church and in the writing and intention of the evangelists), of which mention has already been made. In this as in many other ways, Marxsen laid down methodological precedents which other redaction critics have followed.[23]

These three scholars, Bornkamm, Conzelmann and Marxsen, have been succeeded by others in redaction-critical studies of the synoptic Gospels. For Matthew, Bornkamm has been followed (among others) by Gerhard Barth and H. J. Held, both pupils of his.[24] (Two other pupils, H. E. Tödt[25] and F. Hahn,[26] have also used this method in the more general area of New Testament christology.) For Mark, Marxsen has been followed among others by the two English-speaking writers J. M. Robinson[27] and E. Best,[28] and by the Swiss scholar E. Schweizer.[29] And for Luke, Conzelmann has been followed by H. Flender.[30] Redaction criticism has not been applied so frequently to the study of St. John's Gospel as to the Synoptics, but a start has been made in the work of J. L. Martyn,[31] B. Lindars[32] and W. Nicol.[33]

II. *How it works*

An example of redaction criticism at work may help to clarify the purpose and value of this method, as well as its results.[34] Before we begin, it will be useful to spend a moment longer recapitulating the principles of redaction criticism. We can then see these at work in our example.

The best way of examining the distinctive contribution of any evangelist to his sources is to investigate the precise method by which he has brought together and handled the materials available to him.[35] This means looking carefully at the "seams" by which the sources are joined together, the summaries, modifications, insertions and omissions made, and in general the selection and arrangement of the material. It may also be illuminating to consider the evangelist's vocabulary, his theological standpoint (especially as this is discernible from his christology and his use of titles for Jesus), and finally the introduction and conclusion to his Gospel. These lines of approach will not necessarily be of equal value or yield equally important results; but together they will provide a firmly based method by which to carry out any redaction-critical investigation.

We will confine our present sample to the Gospel of Matthew, and consider in this light first the Gospel as a whole, then a pericope within it, and finally a single logion. The method of redaction criticism, we hope to show, can be used in each case for the purpose of understanding and illuminating the evangelist's approach. Each example, moreover, will reveal the way in which source criticism, form (tradition) criticism and redaction criticism belong together and can be used together in the study of the Gospels.

1. THE GOSPEL OF MATTHEW

One view of the problem of the four Gospels[36] will suggest that the writer of Matthew has composed his Gospel by editing the sources Mark, Q and M. But we can see that by the selection and arrangement of his material he has imposed his own understanding and interpretation of the kerygma on the underlying tradition with which he is working. This gives rise, for example, to Matthew's characteristic christology (Jesus as both king and servant; cf. Mt. 1:1; 12:15–21, *et al.*), his attitude towards the law (transcended and yet remaining in force; cf. 5:38f.; 5:17–20, *et al.*), and his presentation of the gospel itself (exclusive but also universal; cf. 15:24; 8:5–13, *et al.*).[37] In general, the evangelist works with the theme of fulfilment in mind. Evidently he writes to present Jesus as the Christ, the Messiah who has absorbed the functions of Moses and gone beyond them.[38] Taking full account of the character of his over-all redaction, therefore, we can hazard a guess at the position and needs of his audience. It is possible that he wrote for a cell-type Jewish-Christian group under pressure from orthodox Jews for alleged antinomianism, and that this accounts for some of the distinctive Matthean ambivalences of which we have just taken note.[39]

2. A PERICOPE FROM MATTHEW

The same technique can be applied to one section of the first Gospel, with similarly illuminating results. Take, for example, the account of the transfiguration in Matthew 17:1–8. Source-critical analysis tells us (on one view, at least) that this comes from Mark 9:2–8. Redaction criticism reveals, by a comparison of the two narratives, the editorial changes which Matthew has made and further study may suggest the theological reasons for these modifications.

Matthew handles his Marcan source for the transfiguration individually, and in line with the theological understanding evident throughout his Gospel. First, he presents Jesus "after the manner of Moses".[40] For example, he alters Mark by referring to Moses before Elijah, thus making the Mosaic reference more emphatic (Mt. 17:3). He adds to the description of the actual transfiguration the detail that the face of Jesus "shone like the sun" (verse 2), recalling the appearance of Moses after receiving the law on Sinai (Ex. 34:29–35). He alone of the synoptic evangelists describes the cloud which over-shadowed the group on the mountain as "bright" (*φωτεινή* verse 5), thus reminding his readers of the Shekinah glory in the Israelite wilderness. Matthew also draws attention to the fact that after the transfiguration Jesus remains alone after Moses and Elijah have disappeared; he adds in verse 8 *αὐτὸν (μόνον)* to the Marcan version. Jesus is now seen as the unique teacher (verse 5b) and also the new Moses.

But, as W. D. Davies points out,[41] although the new Moses/new exodus theme is undoubtedly present here and elsewhere in Matthew, it is ultimately restrained. For Matthew sees clearly that Jesus in his uniqueness finally supersedes Moses. At the climax of the transfiguration narrative, for example, Matthew adds to the words of the *bath qol* in Mark 9:7 ("This is my beloved Son;[42] listen to him"), the phrase "with whom I am well pleased". This echoes Isaiah 42:1 as well as Psalm 2:7,[43] and reminds us not only of Matthew's particular (servant) christology, but also of his individual soteriology, since this redaction suggests that Jesus was the one destined to bring law to the nations (as in Is. 42:4). Thus the first evangelist's motivation in his report of the transfiguration is not merely one of reverence, despite his mention of the disciples' "awe" immediately after the command of God to listen to his Son has been heard.[44] He writes out of a particular christological understanding, and with the needs of a particular audience in mind.

3. A SAYING IN MATTHEW

The method of redaction criticism may also be used, finally, for the examination of individual logia within the Gospel of Matthew. We may consider briefly, as one instance, the *crux interpretum* Matthew 16:16. Peter's confession at Caesarea Philippi, according to Matthew's account, reads "You are the Christ, the Son of the living God." Mark (8:29) has "You are the Christ", and Luke (9:20) "(You are) the Christ of God."

One explanation of these variations is to say that Matthew has simply expanded Mark. (This assumes, of course, that Peter did not make different confessions on the same occasion.) In that case, the expansion was either the result of a Q tradition containing both elements of the confession (Christ and Son of God), and reflected in the Lucan version, or due to a straightforward explanatory redaction on Matthew's part.[45] Knowing his approach as we do, it need not surprise us if Matthew at such an important moment as this should heighten as well as deepen his christology, and remind his readers of the real and exalted status of the central figure in his Gospel.[46]

III. *Some Presuppositions*

The critical method we have been reviewing, and illustrating in terms of Matthew's Gospel, rests on a number of presuppositions. It is important to recognize these, and to be aware of the fact that the conclusions of redaction criticism (like those of form criticism) are to some extent subjective, and should not therefore be accepted uncritically. We shall consider two major presuppositions belonging sometimes to redaction criticism.

(1) Form criticism relies, as we have seen elsewhere, on the so-called "traditio-historical" approach, which can involve two basic assumptions about the sayings of Jesus. The first is that the christology of the New Testament, including the Gospels, does not spring from the authentic teaching of Jesus himself, but from the response to Jesus made by the first Christians. The second is that the genuine teaching of Jesus preserved by the evangelists (a relatively small deposit) can be isolated from the large quantity of material created in the early church by identifying and removing the additions made to that teaching at various stages of the church's development.

The traditio-historical approach is also used in redaction criticism, which (as we have seen) stems from form criticism. In this case, the same basic assumptions are sometimes made. The only difference is that the whole process is now used to investigate the additions made by the evangelists to the already interpreted tradition they received, in the final stages of writing their Gospels. And the conclusion, we are not surprised to learn, may now be that any saying of Jesus which *could* have been created by the evangelists, or shaped by them, *was* so created or shaped. It is possible to recognize the particular contribution of each Gospel writer, it is further claimed, once their own way of thinking, as distinct from that of earlier Jewish and Hellenistic Christianity, has been identified. To recover the authentic words of Jesus these different layers, beginning with the one for which the evangelists themselves were responsible, can simply be stripped off.[47]

Clearly these assumptions are open to question if they are to serve as the only basis for the conclusions of the redaction critics. No one doubts that an important influence was exercised on the formation of the Gospel tradition and the final composition of the Gospels by the background of the authors as well as their audience. But the presuppositions about the basic nature of the Christian tradition and its transmission which have been mentioned are, as we have seen elsewhere, suspect.[48]

(2) There is a tendency on the part of some who use the method of redaction criticism to assume that the special contribution of the evangelists can be discovered only when they depart from their received sources, or do not depend on them at all, rather than when they reproduce them without alteration. This assumption leads Norman Perrin, for one, to conclude that redaction on the part of the evangelists involves something *other* than preserving the historical tradition about Jesus. For Perrin, the "old way" of regarding a

narrative in the Gospels as historical (he uses Mk. 8:27–9: 1 par. as his main sample), is set over against a redaction-critical approach to it.[49] But the use of the Christian tradition as it stands, without editorial shaping, may be just as much an indication of the evangelist's theological outlook. In such a case we must assume that the tradition expressed his intention and understanding so clearly that alteration was unnecessary.[50] We do not need, that is to say, to equate "redaction" in the Gospels with unhistorical theologizing. It can involve the use of sources as they stand.[51]

IV. *Some Implications*

Provided that we are aware of the hazards inherent in the method of redaction criticism, especially when sceptical and subjective presuppositions form a starting-point, it can prove to be a very useful aid to the understanding of the Gospels. It is not intended, and should not be used, as an end in itself, or simply as an academic exercise. On the contrary when it is properly used it has many advantages, as we shall see, and some far-reaching implications for any reading of the Gospel material. Three of these must now be mentioned.

1. THE JESUS OF HISTORY DEBATE

First, redaction criticism impinges on the "Jesus of history" debate.[52] The "new quest" for the historical Jesus has made us aware that any search for the central figure of the Jesus tradition must be allied neither to the extreme of history alone nor to that of faith alone; it must maintain a balance (as the evangelists do) between them both.

The method of redaction criticism is clearly of importance to this question of Christian origins. For we are bound to recognize that the Gospels were written from within a circle of faith, by those who in a particular first-century environment became convinced that Jesus of Nazareth was the Christ of God, and that he had risen from the dead. Inevitably, therefore, the evangelists reported the Jesus tradition from their own understanding, and coloured it with their own outlook.

Such a view, when honestly advanced, affects the Christian faith at its central point. Have we any reason to suppose that the evangelists' redacted version of the tradition about Jesus is at all historical? If they redacted part, could they not have redacted all of it; leaving us with a picture of Jesus which is interpretative and therefore informative, but essentially an unhistorical product of the human imagination? How do we know, in fact, that any continuity exists between the Jesus of history and the Christ of faith?

The suggestion that no continuity of this kind exists largely depends for its validity on the assumption that the evangelists themselves were unaware of the distinction between history and faith, and were prepared to disregard the former completely in the interests of the latter. We are not, in fact, compelled to believe that this was the case.[53] If the Gospel writers were, on the contrary, sensitive to what was historical and what was kerygmatic (as there are real grounds for supposing),[54] it is unlikely that they would have treated their traditional sources for the words and works of Jesus with anything but respect. All the more would respect have been shown by the evangelists, indeeed, if (as is probable) eyewitnesses were still around. These considerations lead us to the second implication of the redaction-critical method to be considered.

2. THE AUTHORITY OF THE GOSPELS

The second implication arises out of the first, and in many ways it has been anticipated. Redaction criticism has an obvious bearing on the issue of the authority of the Gospels (and indeed of the New Testament generally). If the evangelists have redacted their tradition, can we be sure that the Gospels are not (as the followers of Bultmann would say) simply products of the early church, which have been written in the light of the post-Easter situation to meet the demands and answer the questions of that day?

In answer to this important challenge, three points may be made briefly. These are in addition to the suggestions offered in the previous section in support of an historical rather than an existential approach to the Gospel tradition.

(a) First, although we now recognize the theological content of all four Gospels, it is becoming increasingly clear that theology and history belong together (as we have noticed) at all stages in the transmission of the Jesus tradition. So far from abandoning one or the other, all the evangelists apparently drew out the theological implications of the history which they recorded. This can be illustrated very easily from the contemporary debate on the Fourth Gospel, with its discovery that there is a greater element of reliable, historical tradition in John (its high theological content notwithstanding) than criticism ever previously allowed.[55]

(b) Secondly, as we have seen, the redactional element in the Gospels is not necessarily opposed to the historical and traditional. Redaction can mean the use of the tradition as it stands, without any redactional editing. An example of this may be found in an early section of Mark's Gospel (2:1–3:6).[56] Form criticism tells us that here Mark has assembled originally independent units of material, the primary setting of which in the teaching of Jesus was probably unknown to the evangelist as it is lost to us. Redaction criticism then shows us how Mark has interpreted these incidents according to his own theological understanding of the person and work of Jesus. The key to this is to be found in the concept of authority; for the authority of Jesus here is constantly questioned and constantly vindicated (2:6f., 10f., *et al.*). Indeed this (a significant comment on Mark's christology) is the only link in a collection of pericopes, each of which could otherwise stand anywhere in the Jesus tradition. But while we can in this way discover Mark's specialized approach to his material, we are also made aware of the fact that his contribution lies not in altering the tradition (which mostly consists of evidently primitive "pronouncement stories" suiting his theological purpose) but in combining its separate elements and providing for them a context and therefore a particular meaning.[57] The authenticity and authority of the tradition at this point are thus not diminished by the Marcan redaction, but increased.[58]

(c) Thirdly, it may be suggested that in order to establish the authority of the sayings of Jesus (at least), we are not necessarily confined by the Gospels themselves to the pre-resurrection logia. The word of the risen Jesus spoken through the evangelists can still be authoritative. To this extent the editorial activity of the evangelists can be regarded as a medium of revelation rather than an obstacle to it.

As an illustration of this point, we may consider the famous saying of Jesus about divorce in Matthew 5:32 and 19:9 (= Lk. 16:18; cf. Mk. 10:11f.). Only the Matthean version of this logion contains the exceptive clause *παρεκτὸς λόγου πορνείας* (19:9, *μὴ ἐπὶ πορνείᾳ*), and the question of the origin of this phrase therefore naturally arises. (Even in Paul the prohibition of divorce remains absolute; see 1 Cor. 7:10–13.)

One view is that Matthew has carried out a straight redaction, reflecting his accommodation to the Christian legislation of his day. As there was hardness of heart in Israel (Mk. 10:4f.), so there could be in the new Israel. But equally Matthew may be making explicit what was assumed by Jesus and the other evangelists, that divorce was made necessary by Jewish law when sexual irregularity was discovered among partners before or after marriage. Betrothed couples could separate when unfaithfulness was suspected, as in the case of Joseph and Mary (Mt. 1:19); and strict Hebrews insisted on divorce when marriage within the forbidden degrees of kinship was uncovered.

In any case Matthew is reporting and upholding the principle laid down by Jesus, that marriage is a God-given ordinance within creation, and therefore to be regarded as hallowed. But his explanatory redaction, we can now see, draws out for his readers both the importance of the original teaching of Jesus, and also the sole but inevitable grounds for departing from it – grounds which were already recognised and accepted by the Jews. In no case may we claim that Matthew's redaction weakens the authority of the teaching he preserves, or departs from the mind of Christ.[59]

In the light of all that has been said, it is possible to take account of the fact that the Gospel writers have redacted their basic tradition, and still come to the Gospels with confidence in their essential authority and trustworthiness. For the redaction of the Jesus tradition in accordance with the perspectives of the writers and the community surrounding them does not remove the discoverable historical basis on which that tradition rests. Nor does it prevent the post-Easter words of Christ from being heard and transmitted.[60]

3. THE INTENTION OF THE EVANGELISTS

The final implication of redaction criticism for the study of the Gospels concerns the intention of the evangelists. Again, this question arises out of some of the issues already discussed in detail.

The work of redaction critics such as Bornkamm, Marxsen and Conzelmann has helped us, as we have seen, to appreciate the theological themes and concerns which motivated the evangelists when they wrote their Gospels. Just as form criticism enables us to detect the shaping of individual sayings of Jesus or pericopes about him in the course of their transmission, so redaction criticism makes it possible to uncover this process of shaping in each of the Gospels as a whole.

This point can be developed in one further direction. By examining the theological perspective of an evangelist, and the way he has selected and used his material, it is also possible to suggest why he wrote his Gospel in the first place. We have already applied this test to Matthew. The aim of the other Gospels may be similarly investigated. On the basis of a redaction-critical approach it may be guessed that Mark wrote his Gospel for would-be or present disciples, to supplement Paul's kerygma;[61] that Luke's intention was the kerygmatic and didactic presentation of gospel history for the benefit of mostly non-Christian Gentile readers;[62] and that John wrote for an audience that was in the end as wide as it could be, to enable his readers to "see" that Jesus was the Christ, the revealing and glorified Word of God, and so to live.[63] Broadly speaking the intention in each case is evangelistic, but redaction criticism focuses attention on the precise interpretation and therefore presentation of the kerygma by the four writers, which gives their theology its individual character.[64] In fine, we no longer need to spend time trying to "harmonize" the Gospels. Their differences, uncovered by the redaction critical approach, stand as a positive pointer to the distinctive outlook of their writers, and their unique understanding of and witness to the Jesus tradition.

V. *Some Conclusions*

Our discussion of redaction criticism as a method of studying the Gospels has made one point clear at least. It has both advantages and disadvantages.

We may summarize the disadvantages as follows. (1) The traditio-critical criteria on which the redaction method normally depends are often open to question because of the assumptions involved in them. (2) It is too often presupposed that redaction on the part of an evangelist means "composition", in the sense of invention. This is unwarranted. (3) Redaction critics are at times too subtle and subjective in their approach to the Gospels, and in their assessment of the evangelists' motives and methods. This is the reason for the wide variation in their results; although this need not surprise us with a discipline still in its infancy.[65] Caution is obviously needed in the analysis of any editorial activity, particularly when, as in the case of the Gospels, we are not always sure who the "editor" is, or the exact nature of his sources.[66]

On the other hand, there are positive advantages to be gained from using this approach. (1) It treats the Gospels whole, and is a useful method for discovering the exact contribution of the evangelists to their traditions. In this way it is an extremely fruitful aid to exegesis, which helps us to perceive more clearly the evangelists' many-sided witness to Christ. (2) It also helps us to see precisely how the evangelists handled their sources, with or without shaping them. (3) We can also detect more easily by this method the intention of the Gospel writers, and see the reason for the existence of four variations on one theme; four Gospels illuminating one gospel from different stand points.

Clearly we must use redaction criticism in any serious study of the Gospels. But we must use it with care. It is not a question of redaction *or* history in the New Testament, but both. If we accept that, the method of *Redaktionsgeschichte* can be a positive aid to understanding the four Gospels, and using them intelligently for Christian preaching and teaching. By this method also further light can be thrown on the crux of the whole matter, the origins of Christianity itself.

NOTES

1. See P. Benoit, *Jesus and the Gospel,* vol. 1 (E.T. London 1973), pp. 11–45.

2. The flowering of redaction criticism was in fact anticipated long ago by New Testament scholarship in both Germany and the English-speaking world. F. C. Baur, for example, in *Das Markusevangelium nach seinem Ursprung und Charakter* (Tübingen 1851), saw Mark as a (non-historical) late compilation dependent on Luke and Matthew, written to reconcile the differences, reflected in the other Synoptists, between the Gentiles and the Jews. Early in this century W. Wrede's study of Mark, *Das Messiasgeheimnis in den Evangelien* (Göttingen 1901; E.T. *The Messianic Secret,* Cambridge and London 1971), suggested that the so-called "messianic secret" in Mark was a dogmatic intrusion and not an historical account. Cf. also the latter part, on "the editing of the traditional material", of R. Bultmann's form-critical study, *Die Geschichte der synoptischen Tradition* (Göttingen 1958[3]), pp. 347ff., esp. 393–400 (E.T. *The History of the Synoptic Tradition,* Oxford 1963, pp. 321ff., esp. 368–74). From England, the work of R. H. Lightfoot, in his famous Bampton Lectures for 1934 (published as *History and Interpretation in the Gospels,* London 1935) foreshadows redaction-critical method. We also have redaction criticism under another name, no doubt, in the work of B. W. Bacon (e.g. *Studies in Matthew,* London 1931), N. B. Stonehouse (e.g. *The Witness of Luke to Christ,* London 1951), P. Carrington (e.g. *According to Mark: A running commentary on the oldest Gospel,* Cambridge 1960) and A. M. Farrer (e.g. *St. Matthew and St. Mark,* London 1966[2]). See J. Rohde, *Rediscovering the Teaching of the Evangelists,* (E.T. London 1968), pp. 31–46.

3. The method of redaction criticism can also be applied to the study of other parts of the New Testament, notably Acts and Revelation.

4. E. Haenchen, *Der Weg Jesu* (Berlin 1968[2]), p. 24.

5. So N. Perrin, *What is Redaction Criticism?* (London 1970), p. 66. See the whole section on "Redaction and Composition", pp. 65–7.

6. Dr. Ernest Best's redaction-critical essay, *The Temptation and the Passion: The Markan Soteriology* (Cambridge 1965), falls into this trap in its declared aim of "understanding the Markan theology", and by taking Mark himself to be essentially an "author and theologian" (see pp. xi f.).

7. Among form-critical scholars, J. Jeremias in *Die Gleichnisse Jesu* (Zürich 1947), p. 15 (E.T. *The Parables of Jesus,* London 1963[2], p. 23), distinguishes usefully between the original context of a dominical discourse (in this case the parabolic teaching) and its subsequent setting. See also C. H. Dodd, *The Parables of the Kingdom* (London 1936[2]), pp. 111–53.

8. See further R. H. Stein, "What is *Redaktionsgeschichte?*", JBL 88 (1969), pp. 45–56, for a useful historical survey, and an explanation of the method. See also on the discipline in general D. Guthrie, *New Testament Introduction* (London, 1970[3]), pp. 214–9; and J. Rohde, op. cit.

9. N. Perrin, op. cit., p. 25, points out that just as the work of three German theologians gave rise to the method of *Redaktionsgeschichte* after the second world war, so the work of three other German theologians (K. L. Schmidt, M. Dibelius and R. Bultmann) gave rise to the method of *Formgeschichte* after the first world war. We have already noticed, however, that this method in its final form was anticipated in the work of F. C. Baur, R. H. Lightfoot and others (see note 2).

10. W. Marxsen, *Der Evangelist Markus* (Göttingen 1959[2]), p. 11; E.T. *Mark the Evangelist* (New York and Nashville 1969), p. 21. The subsequent page references are to the English edition.

11. G. Bornkamm, G. Barth and H. J. Held, *Überlieferung und Auslegung im Matthäusevangelium* (Neukirchen 1960; E.T. *Tradition and Interpretation in Matthew,* London 1963) = *Tradition.* The subsequent page references are to the English edition.

12. G. Bornkamm, "The Stilling of the Storm in Matthew", in *Tradition,* pp. 52–7.

13. Ibid., p. 57.

14. G. Bornkamm, "End-Expectation and Church in Matthew", in *Tradition,* pp. 15–51.

15. Ibid., p. 49. See also J. Rohde, op. cit., pp. 11–13, 47–54.

16. H. Conzelmann, *Die Mitte der Zeit* (Tübingen 1964[5]; E.T. *The Theology of St. Luke,* London 1960). The subsequent page references are to the English edition.

17. N. Perrin, op. cit., p. 29.

18. See, for example, C. K. Barrett, *Luke the Historian in Recent Study* (London 1961), pp. 9–26; also I. H. Marshall, *Luke: Historian and Theologian* (Exeter 1970), esp. pp. 21–76.

19. H. Conzelmann, op. cit., esp. pp. 131f. But see S. S. Smalley, "The Delay of the Parousia", JBL 83 (1964), pp. 42–7. On Conzelmann's work generally, see J. Rohde, op. cit., pp. 154–78.

20. See note 10. For a study of Mark's theological (esp. christological) activity as a clue to the nature of "Gospel" as such, see N. Perrin, "The Literary *Gattung* 'Gospel' – Some Observations", Exp.T 82 (1970–71), pp. 4–7.

21. W. Marxsen, op. cit., pp. 18–23, *et al.*

22. Ibid., p. 59.

23. See further J. Rohde, op. cit., pp. 113–40; also N. Perrin, *What is Redaction Criticism?*, pp. 33–9.

24. See *Tradition,* pp. 58ff. Note also E. Schweizer, *Das Evangelium nach Matthäus* (Göttingen 1973; E.T. *The Good News according to Matthew,* London 1976); J. D. Kingsbury, *Matthew: Structure, Christology, Kingdom* (London 1976).

25. Cf. H. E. Tödt, *Der Menschensohn in der synoptischen Überlieferung* (Gütersloh 1963[2]; E.T. *The Son of Man in the Synoptic Tradition,* London 1965).

26. Cf. F. Hahn, *Christologische Hoheitstitel: Ihre Geschichte im frühen Christentum* (Göttingen 1964[2]; E.T. *The Titles of Jesus in Christology,* London 1969). Note also R. H. Fuller, *The Foundations of New Testament Christology* (London 1965), for a similar theological approach in this area from beyond Germany; and cf. the useful review article of this book by I. H. Marshall, "The Foundations of Christology", in *Themelios* 3 (1966), pp. 22–34.

27. J. M. Robinson, *The Problem of History in Mark* (London 1957).

28. E. Best, *The Temptation and the Passion.*

29. E. Schweizer, *Das Evangelium nach Markus* (Göttingen 1967; E.T. *The Good News According to Mark,* London 1971; the subsequent page references are to the English edition). Cf. also for studies in Markan redaction, D. Blatherwick, "The Markan Silhouette?", NTS 17 (1970–71), pp. 184–92; R. H. Stein, "The Proper Methodology for Ascertaining a Markan Redaction History", Nov.T 13 (1971), pp. 181–98; F. Neirynck, *Duality in Mark:*

Contributions to the Study of the Markan Redaction (Louvain 1972); R. P. Martin, *Mark: Evangelist and Theologian* (Exeter 1972), esp. pp. 84–162.

30. H. Flender, *Heil und Geschichte in der Theologie des Lukas* (München 1965; E.T. *St. Luke: Theologian of Redemptive History,* London 1967). Cf. also I. H. Marshall, *Luke: Historian and Theologian* (Exeter 1972).

31. J. L. Martyn, *History and Theology in the Fourth Gospel* (New York 1968); also id. "Source Criticism and *Redaktionsgeschichte* in the Fourth Gospel", in D. G. Miller and D. Y. Hadidian (ed.), *Jesus and Man's Hope,* Vol. 1 (Pittsburg 1970), pp. 247–73. Cf. also M. Wilcox, "The Composition of John 13:21–30", in E. E. Ellis and M. Wilcox (ed.), *Neotestamentica et Semitica: Studies in Honour of Matthew Black* (Edinburgh 1969), pp. 143–56.

32. B. Lindars, *Behind the Fourth Gospel* (London 1971); id., *The Gospel of John* (London 1972).

33. W. Nicol, *The Semeia in the Fourth Gospel: Tradition and Redaction* (Leiden 1972).

34. See also N. Perrin's redaction-critical analysis in *What is Redaction Criticism?*, pp. 40–63.

35. Cf. R. H. Stein, "The Proper Methodology for Ascertaining a Markan Redaction History", loc. cit.

36. In these days of the "new look" on John, this is a more acceptable description of the inter-relation of the Gospels than "the synoptic problem". See S. S. Smalley, "The Gospel of John in Recent Study", *Orita* 4 (1970), pp. 42f.

37. Cf. the study of Matthew's theology in D. Hill, *The Gospel of Matthew* (London 1972), pp. 60–72.

38. Cf. W. D. Davies, *The Setting of the Sermon on the Mount* (Cambridge 1964), pp. 92f.

39. So C. F. D. Moule, "St. Matthew's Gospel: Some Neglected Features", in F. L. Cross (ed.), *Studia Evangelica* 2 (TU 87, Berlin 1964), pp. 91–9, esp. 92–4.

40. Cf. W. D. Davies, op. cit., p. 56.

41. Ibid. For this whole section, see pp. 50–6.

42. *Οὗτός ἐστιν ὁ υἱός μου ἀγαπητός* may also mean (as in RSV[mg]) "This is my Son, my (or the) Beloved".

43. Cf. the *bath qol* in Mt. 3:17, at the baptism of Jesus.

44. In Mark, the mention of the disciples' reaction is made after the transfiguration and subsequent vision; in Luke, it comes after the descent of the cloud. Notice, however, the use of *Κύριε* in Mt. 17:4 (Mark has *'Ραββέι* and Luke *'Επιστάτα*).

45. For another explanation of the conjunction of "Christ" and "Son of the living God" in Mt. 16:16, see O. Cullmann, *Petrus, Jünger-Apostel-Märtyrer: Das historische und das theologische Petrusproblem* (Zürich 1952), pp. 190–206 (E.T. *Peter: Disciple, Apostle, Martyr,* London 1962², pp. 176–91). As always when using the method of redaction criticism, the source-critical presuppositions involved (in this case, the use of Mark by Matthew) will to some extent affect the conclusions reached.

46. See further G. M. Styler, "Stages in Christology in the Synoptic Gospels", NTS 10 (1963–64), pp. 404–6. Despite his heightened christology, Matthew does not give to this incident the same climactic significance as Mark.

47. On the other side see B. Gerhardsson, *Memory and Manuscript* (Uppsala 1961), esp. pp. 324–35. Gerhardsson argues for the place and importance of (Jewish-Christian) tradition in the primitive transmission of the Gospel material.

48. For a critique of the assumptions involved in the tradition-historical approach, see further D. Guthrie, op. cit., pp. 208–11: also I. H. Marshall, "The Foundations of Christology", loc. cit., pp. 29–34. See also D. R. Catchpole's article in this volume.

49. N. Perrin, *What is Redaction Criticism?,* p. 40.

50. See I. H. Marshall, *Luke: Historian and Theologian,* pp. 19f.

51. The dangers involved when redaction critics base their conclusions on presuppositions such as those outlined, are highlighted in Dr. Norman Perrin's work, *Rediscovering the Teaching of Jesus* (London 1967). Using the redaction-critical approach, Perrin formulates three stringent and questionable criteria for establishing the authentic elements in the teaching of Jesus (dissimilarity, coherence and multiple attestation), and on this foundation

reaches the doubtful conclusion that the parables of Jesus in their earliest form, the kingdom of God sayings and the tradition of the Lord's Prayer can be accepted as a genuine part of the dominical teaching, but little else. For a critique of Perrin's general method, and its results, see M. D. Hooker, "Christology and Methodology", NTS 17 (1970–71), pp. 480–7. The commentary by Barnabas Lindars, *The Gospel of John,* important as it is, exemplifies the likelihood of subjectivity in redaction criticism. See further G. N. Stanton's article in this volume.

52. See F. F. Bruce's article in this volume.

53. Against e.g. N. Perrin, *Rediscovering the Teaching of Jesus,* pp. 234–48.

54. See further C. F. D. Moule, *The Phenomenon of the New Testament: An Inquiry into the Implications of Certain Features of the New Testament* (London 1967), pp. 43–81, for a positive discussion of the continuity between the Jesus of history and the Lord of faith.

55. See, *inter alios,* J. A. T. Robinson, "The New Look on the Fourth Gospel", in K. Aland (ed.), *Studia Evangelica,* Vol. 1 (TU 73, Berlin 1959), pp. 338–350, reprinted in J. A. T. Robinson, *Twelve New Testament Studies* (London 1962), pp. 94–106; also S. S. Smalley, "New Light on the Fourth Gospel", *Tyn. B* 17 (1966), pp. 35–62.

56. This passage is part of a complete section of the Gospel, Mark 1:1–3:6.

57. The saying in Mk. 2:20 (with its mention of the bridegroom being taken away) is probably an exception, and may derive from a later setting. For Mark's redactional use of this verse, see R. P. Martin, op. cit., pp. 184–8. See also the treatment of this passage (sceptical, however, in the form-critical conclusions on which it is based) in E. Schweizer, op. cit., pp. 59–77.

58. It is possible that the "assembly" in Mk. 2:1–3:6 was wholly or in part pre-Markan (see V. Taylor, *The Formation of the Gospel Tradition,* London 1935[2], pp. 177–81), in which case we cannot be sure about the redactional interests which guided this early *Sammler.* But even if the collection were pre-Marcan, it is likely that Mark took it over unchanged because it fitted his interests so exactly.

59. See further on this passage D. Hill, op. cit., pp. 124f., 280f.; also R. Bultmann, op. cit., E.T. pp. 132, 148.

60. On the general issue of New Testament authority, see R. E. Nixon's article in this volume.

61. Cf. R. P. Martin, op. cit., pp. 140–62, esp. 161f.

62. As it happens, T. Schramm's study, *Der Markus-Stoff bei Lukas: Eine Literarkritische und Redaktionsgeschichtliche Untersuchung* (Cambridge 1971) sounds a note of caution in the use of *Redaktionsgeschichte* for discovering the intention of Luke. See also C. H. Talbert, "The Redaction Critical Quest for Luke the Theologian", in D. G. Miller and D. Y. Hadidian (ed.), op. cit., pp. 171–222.

63. Cf. S. S. Smalley, "Diversity and Development in John", NTS 17 (1970–71), pp. 289f.

64. See further, C. F. D. Moule, "The Intention of the Evangelists", in A. J. B. Higgins (ed.), *New Testament Essays* (Manchester 1959), pp. 165–79; reprinted in C. F. D. Moule, *The Phenomenon of the New Testament,* pp. 100–14.

65. This is clear from the most cursory reading of J. Rohde's book, *Rediscovering the Teaching of the Evangelists.*

66. Cf. C. F. D. Moule, "The New Testament", in F. G. Healey (ed.), *Preface to Christian Studies* (London 1971), pp. 50f.

PART THREE

The Task of Exegesis

CHAPTER XII

HOW THE NEW TESTAMENT USES THE OLD

E. Earle Ellis

I. *The Character of New Testament Usage*

1. GENERAL

Old Testament phraseology in the New Testament occurs occasionally as the idiom of a writer whose own patterns of expression have been influenced by the Scriptures (1 Thess. 2:4; 4:5). Most often, however, it appears in the form of citations or intentional allusions or reminiscences. Dr. Hartman suggests three reasons for an author's citation of another: to obtain the support of an authority (Mt. 4:14), to call forth a cluster of associations (Mk. 12:1f.), and to achieve a literary or stylistic effect (Tit. 1:12). He rightly observes that an allusion sometimes can be discerned only after the total context of a passage has been taken into account.[1]

As might be expected in Greek writings, citations from the Old Testament are frequently in agreement with the LXX, the Greek version commonly used in the first century. But they are not uniformly so, and at times they reflect other Greek versions, Aramaic targums, or independent translations of the Hebrew text.[2] Apart from the use of a different text-form, a citation may diverge from the LXX because of a lapse of memory. However, this explanation is often less probable than has been supposed in the past.[3] More frequently, as will be detailed below, citations diverge from the LXX because of deliberate alteration, i.e. by *ad hoc* translation and elaboration or by the use of a variant textual tradition, to serve the purpose of the New Testament writer. The variations, then, become an important clue to discover not only the writer's interpretation of the individual Old Testament passage but also his perspective on the Old Testament as a whole.

2. INTRODUCTORY FORMULAS

Formulas of quotation, which generally employ verbs of "saying" or "writing," correspond to those found in other Jewish writings, e.g. the Old Testament,[4] the Qumran scrolls,[5] Philo and the rabbis.[6] They locate the citation with reference to the book or writer or, less frequently, the story ("in Elijah," Rom. 11:2; "at the bush," Mk. 12:26). At times they specify a particular prophet (Acts 28:25), a specification that on occasion may be important for the New Testament teaching.[7] When one book is named and another cited, the formula may represent an incidental error or, more likely, the cited text may be an interpretation (Mt. 27:9)[8] or elaboration (Mk. 1:2) of a passage in the book named.

Introductory formulas often underscore the divine authority of the Old Testament, not in the abstract but within the proper interpretation and application of its teaching. Thus, the formula "Scripture (γραφή) says" can introduce an eschatological, i.e. "Christianized" summation or elaboration of the Old Testament (Jn. 7:38; Gal. 4:30), and γραφή can be contrasted to traditional interpretations (Mt. 22:29). That is, it implies that the revelational, "Word of God" character of Scripture is present within the current interpretation. In the words of Renée Bloch, Scripture "always concerns a living word addressed personally to the people of God and to each of its members. . . ."[9] The formula "it is written" can also have the intended connotation of a specific and right interpretation of Scripture (Rom. 9:33; 11:26) even though the connotation may not always be true (Mt. 4:6).

Sometimes an explicit distinction between reading Scripture and knowing or hearing Scripture may be drawn. It is present in the story of the Ethiopian eunuch (Acts 8:30) and, implicitly, in Jesus' synagogue exposition at Nazareth (Lk. 4:16f., 21). It may be presupposed, as it is in rabbinical writings, in the formula "have you not (οὐκ) read?"[10] That is, "you have read but have not understood." This formula is found in the New Testament only on the lips of Jesus and usually within a Scriptural debate or exposition.[11]

A few formulas are associated with specific circles within the Christian community. The nine λέγει κύριος ("says the Lord") quotations probably reflect the activity of Christian prophets.[12] The ἵνα πληρωθῇ ("that it might be fulfilled") quotations, found especially in the Gospels of Matthew and John, may have a similar origin.[13] Both kinds of quotations contain creatively altered text-forms that facilitate an eschatological re-application of the Old Testament passages, similar to that found in the Qumran scrolls,[14] to the experiences and understanding of the early church. This is a kind of activity recognized in first century Judaism to be appropriate to prophets as well as to teachers.[15]

Somewhat similar are the πιστὸς ὁ λόγος ("faithful is the word") passages in the Pastoral letters.[16] They appear to be instructions of Christian prophets (cf. 1 Tim. 4:1, 6, τοῖς λόγοις τῆς πίστεως) and/or inspired teachers, used by Paul in the composition of the letters. Although they do not contain Old Testament quotations, some of these "faithful sayings" may refer to the exposition of the Old Testament.[17] They appear to arise out of a prophetic circle engaged in a ministry of teaching.

3. FORMS AND TECHNIQUES IN QUOTATION

(a) *Combined quotations* of two or more texts appear frequently in a variety of forms: a chain of passages (Rom. 15:9–12), a commentary pattern (Jn. 12:38–40; Rom. 9–11) and composite or merged citations (Rom. 3:10–18; 2 Cor. 6:16–18). With the exception of the last type these patterns were commonly employed in Judaism.[18] They serve to develop a theme and perhaps exemplify the principle in Dt. 19:15 that two witnesses establish a matter. Sometimes (Rom. 10:18–21), in the fashion of the rabbis, they bring together citations from the Law, the Prophets and the Writings. Such combinations usually were formed in conjunction with catchwords important for the theme (e.g. "stone," "chosen" in 1 Pet. 2:6–9).

(b) *Testimonia.* Citations "testifying" to the messiahship of Jesus were of special interest to the early church. Sometimes they appear as combined quotations (Heb. 1), combinations that possibly lie behind other New Testament citations.[19] Such "testimonies" were primarily thematic combinations for instructional and apologetic purposes and, as the *testimonia* at Qumran indicate (4Qtest), some may have circulated in written form during the apostolic period. However, the hypothesis that they were collected in a pre-canonical "testimony book," used by the Church in anti-Jewish apologetic,[20] is less likely.

The "testimonies" apparently presuppose a worked-out christological understanding of the particular passages and are not simply proof texts randomly selected. The earliest Christians, like twentieth century Jews, could not, as we do, simply infer from traditional usage the "Christian" interpretation of a biblical word or passage. Proof texts standing alone, therefore, would have appeared to them quite arbitrary if not meaningless.

According to a thesis of C. H. Dodd[21] the "testimony" quotations were selected from and served as pointers to larger Old Testament contexts that previously and as a whole had been christologically interpreted. For example, Mt. 1:23 in citing Is. 7:14 probably has in view the total section, Is. 6:1–9:7, as the additional phrase "God with us" (Is. 8:8, 10 LXX) and the frequent use of Is. 6–9 elsewhere in the New Testament indicate. Dodd correctly perceived that the *testimonia* were the result of "a certain method of biblical study" (p. 126). But what precisely was that method? It may well have included, as Dodd thought, a systematic christological analysis of certain sections of the Old Testament. Beyond this, however, the method probably corresponded to a form and method of scriptural exposition used in contemporary Judaism and known to us as midrash.

4. QUOTATION AND MIDRASH

(a) The Hebrew term "midrash" has the meaning "commentary" (cf. 2 Ch. 13:22; 24:27), and in the past it has usually been associated with certain rabbinic commentaries on the Old Testament. Recently it has been used more broadly to designate an activity as well as a literary genre, a way of expounding Scripture as well as the resulting exposition.[22] Thus, "the house of midrash" (Sirach 51:23) was a place where such exposition was carried on (and not a library of commentaries). According to Miss Bloch (op. cit., note 9) the essence of the midrashic procedure was a contemporization of Scripture in order to apply it to or make it meaningful for the current situation. It can be seen, then, in interpretive renderings of the Hebrew text (= implicit midrash), e.g. the Greek LXX[23] and the Aramaic targums, as well as in more formal "text + exposition" pattern (= explicit midrash), e.g. the rabbinic commentaries.[24] Both kinds of midrash appear in first-century Judaism in the literature of the Qumran community.

(b) In the use of the Old Testament by the New, implicit midrash appears in double entendre, in interpretive alterations of Old Testament citations and in more elaborate forms. The first type involves a play on words. Thus, Mt. 2:23 cites Jesus' residence in Nazareth as a "fulfilment" of prophecies identifying the Messiah as a *Ναζωραῖος* (= ?Nazirite, Jud. 13:5, 7 LXX) or a *netzer* (= branch, Is. 11:1; cf. 49:6; 60:21).[25] Possibly the double meaning of "lift up" in Jn. 3:14; 12:32ff., i.e. hang and exalt, alludes to an Aramaic rendering (*z^ekaph*) of Is. 52:13, which carries both meanings; the terminology is clarified in the Synoptic Gospels where Jesus prophesies that he is to "be killed and rise" (Mk. 8:31; cf. Lk. 18:31).[26] A similar double entendre may be present in Acts 3:22–26 where "raise up" apparently is used both of Messiah's pre-resurrection ministry and of his resurrection.

The second type can be seen in Rom. 10:11:

> For the Scripture says, "Everyone (*πᾶς*) who believes on him shall not be put to shame."

The word "everyone" is not in the Old Testament text; it is Paul's interpretation woven into the citation and fitting it better to his argument (10:12f.). Similarly, in the citation of Gen. 21:10 at Gal. 4:30 the phrase "son of the free woman" is substituted for "my son Isaac" in order to adapt the citation to Paul's application. More elaborate uses of the same principle will be discussed below.

More complex forms of implicit midrash occur (1) in making a merged or composite quotation from various Old Testament texts, altered so as to apply them to the current situation, and (2) in the description of a current event in biblical phraseology in order to connect the event with the Old Testament passages. Contemporized composite quotations appear, for example, in 1 Cor. 2:9; 2 Cor. 6:16–18. The use of Scriptural phraseology to describe and thus to explain the meaning of current and future events is more subtle and reflects a different focus: the event appears to be of primary interest and the Old Testament allusions are introduced to illumine or explain it. This kind of midrash occurs, for example, in the Lucan infancy narratives, in Jesus' apocalyptic discourse and his response at his trial and in the Revelation of St. John.[27]

In the infancy narratives the Annunciation (Lk. 1:26–38) alludes to Is. 6:1–9:7 – e.g. 7:13f. (27, *παρθένος, ἐξ οἴκου Δαυίδ*); 7:14 (31); 9:6f. (32, 35) – a section that C. H. Dodd has shown to be a primary source for early Christian exegesis.[28] It probably also alludes to Gen. 16:11 (31); 2 Sam. 7:12–16 (32, ?35, *υἱὸς Θεοῦ*); Dan. 7:14 (33b); and Is. 4:3; 62:12 (35, *ἅγιον* κληθήσεται). The Magnificat (1:46–55) and the Benedictus (1:68–79) appear to be formed along the same lines. It is probable that family traditions about the events surrounding Jesus' birth were given this literary formulation by prophets of the primitive Jerusalem church.[29]

The response of our Lord at his trial (Mk. 14:62 par) is given by the Gospels in the words of Ps. 110:1 and Dan. 7:13. It probably represents a summary of Jesus' known response, a summary in biblical words whose "messianic" exegesis either had been worked out in the Christian community or, more likely, had been taught to the disciples by Jesus. That Jesus made use of both Ps. 110:1 and Dan. 7:13 in his preresurrection teaching is highly probable.[30]

The apocalyptic discourse (Mk. 13 par), which also includes the use of Dan. 7:13, apparently consists of a midrash of Jesus on certain passages in Daniel, a midrash that has been supplemented by other sayings of the Lord and reshaped by the Evangelists and their predecessors "into something of a prophetic tract" linked to the Church's experiences. In the course of transmission the midrash "lost many of its once probably explicit associations with the OT text".[31] If this reconstruction is correct, it shows not only how teachings of Jesus were contemporized in a manner similar to the midrashic handling of Old Testament texts but also how our Lord's explicit midrash was modified so that the Old Testament references, although not lost, were largely assimilated to the current application. The process is much more thoroughgoing than is the case in the composite quotations cited above.

These examples suggest that implicit midrash sometimes presupposes and develops out of direct commentary on the Old Testament, i.e. explicit midrash. We may now turn to that form of the early Christian usage.

(c) Explicit midrash in the New Testament has affinities both with the *pesher* midrash at Qumran and with certain kinds of midrash found in rabbinic expositions. The ancient expositions of the rabbis are preserved in sources that date from several centuries after the New Testament writings.[32] However, in their general structure they provide significant parallels for early Christian practice since (1) it is unlikely that the rabbis borrowed their methods of exposition from the Christians and (2) similar patterns may be observed in the first-century Jewish writer, Philo.[33] They probably originated not only as "sermon" or "homily" but also as "commentary," that is, not only as the complement of the synagogue worship but also as the product of the synagogue school.[34] The type of discourse that finds most affinity with New Testament expositions is the "proem" midrash.[35] As used in the synagogue, it ordinarily had the following form:

The (Pentateuchal) text for the day.
A second text, the proem or "opening" for the discourse.
Exposition containing additional Old Testament citations, parables or other commentary and linked to the initial texts by catch-words.
A final text, usually repeating or alluding to the text for the day.

The general outline of this pattern, with some variation, occurs rather frequently in the New Testament. Without the text for the day, it appears in Heb. 10:5–39:

5–7	– Initial text: Ps. 40:7–9.
8–36	– Exposition containing additional citations (16f., 30) and linked to the initial text by catchwords: *θυσία* (8, 26), *προσφοράν* (8, 10, 14, 18), *περὶ ἁμαρτίας* (8, 18, 26), *ἁμαρτία* (17).
37–39	– Final text and application alluding to the initial text with the verbs *ἥκειν* and *εὐδοκεῖν*: Is. 26:20; Hab. 2:3f.

The pattern is expressed more specifically in Rom. 9:6–29:

6f.	– Theme and initial text: Gen. 21:12.
9	– A second, supplemental text: Gen. 18:10.
10–28	– Exposition containing additional citations (13, 15, 17, 25–28) and linked to the initial texts by the catch-words *καλεῖν* and *υἱός* (12, 24ff., 27).
29	– A final text alluding to the initial text with the catchword *σπέρμα*.

A less complex form occurs in 1 Cor. 1:18–31. Here the second, supplemental text has been merged with the initial text; and the final text, the only subsequent citation, does not allude to the opening text:

18–20	– Theme and initial texts: Is. 29:14 and 19:11f.; cf. 33:18.
20–30	– Exposition linked to the initial and final texts by the catchwords *σοφός* (26f.), *σοφία* (21f., 30), *μωρός* (25, 27), *μωρία* (21, 23), *καυχᾶσθαι* (29).
31	– Final text. Cf. Jer. 9:22f.

In 1 Cor. 2:6–16 the initial texts are a composite and highly interpreted quotation:

6–9	– Theme and initial texts. Cf. Is. 64:4; 65:16, LXX.
10–15	– Exposition linked to the initial and final texts by the catchwords *ἄνθρωπος* (11, 14; cf. 13), *ἰδεῖν* (11f.), *γινώσκειν* (11, 14).
16	– Final text and application: Is. 40:13.

Instead of a composite quotation the initial text of the commentary at Gal. 4:21–5:1 is itself a summary of a Genesis passage, an implicit midrash introducing the key word *ἐλευθέρα*. It is probably Paul's summation, but it might have been drawn from a Genesis midrash similar to Jubilees or to the Qumran *Genesis Apocryphon*:[36]

21f.	– Introduction and initial text. Cf. Gen. 21.

23–29 – Exposition with an additional citation, linked to the initial and final texts by the catchwords ἐλευθέρα (22, 23, 26, 30), παιδίσκη (22, 23, 30, 31) and *ben*/υἱός=τέκνον (22, 25, 27, 28, 30, 31).

30ff. – Final text and application, referring to the initial text: cf. Gen. 21:10.

The pattern in 2 Pet. 3:5–13 is similar, although less clear. As in Gal. 4, the initial "text" is a selective summary of a section of Scripture:

5f. – Initial text (with eschatological application). Cf. Gen. 1;6.

7–12 – Exposition (with an additional citation: 8) linked to the initial and final texts by the catchwords οὐρανός (5, 7, 10, 12), γῆ (5, 7, 10), ἀπόλλυμι (6, 9, cf. 7). Cf. ἡμέρα (7, 8, 10, 12).

13 – Final text and applications.[37] Cf. Is. 65:17.

The above examples show how a composite, interpreted citation and an interpretive summary of a larger section of Scripture may serve as the "text" in a midrash. The use of short, explicit midrashim as "texts" in a more elaborate commentary-pattern is only an extension of the same practice. One instance of this appears in 1 Cor. 1:18–3:20,[38] which is composed of the following sections, all linked by catchwords, e.g. σοφία, μωρία:

1:18–31 – Initial "text."
2:1–5 – Exposition/Application.
2:6–16 – Additional "text."
3:1–17 – Exposition/Application.
3:18–20 – Concluding texts: Job 5:13; Ps. 94:11.

The synoptic Gospels also display exegetical patterns similar to those in the rabbis.[39] Mt. 21:33–44 corresponds to an ancient form of a synagogue address:[40]

33 – Initial text: Is. 5:1f.

34–41 – Exposition by means of a parable, linked to the initial and final texts by a catchword λίθος (42, 44, cf. 35; Is. 5:2, *saqal*); cf. οἰκοδομεῖν (33, 42).

42–44 – Concluding texts: Ps. 118:22f.; Dan. 2:34f., 44f.[41]

In Lk. 10:25–37[42] appears a somewhat different pattern, called in the rabbinic writings the *yelammedenu rabbenu* ("let our master teach us"), in which a question or problem is posed and then answered. Apart from the interrogative opening it follows in general the structure of the proem midrash (see above, p. 203):

25–27 – Dialogue including a question and initial texts: Dt. 6:5; Lev. 19:18.

28 – A second text: Lev. 18:5.

29–36	– Exposition (by means of a parable) linked to the initial texts by the catchwords πλησίον (27, 29, 36) and ποιεῖν (28, 37a, 37b).
37	– Concluding allusion to the second text (ποιεῖν).

Mt. 15:1–9 is similar:[43]

1–4	– Dialogue including a question and initial texts: Ex. 20:12; 21:17.
5–6	– Exposition/application linked to the text and/or the dialogue by the catchwords τιμεῖν (4, 6, 8), παράδοσις (3, 6), cf. ἐντολή/ἔνταλμα (3, 9).
7–9	– Concluding text: Is. 29:13.

Compare also Mt. 19:3–8:[44]

3–5	– Question, answered by the initial texts: Gen. 1:27; 2:24.
6	– Exposition linked to the initial text by the catchwords δύο, σὰρξ μία.
7–8a	– Additional citation (Dt. 24:1), posing a problem, with exposition.
8b	– Concluding allusion to the (interpolated!) initial text (ἀπ' ἀρχῆς).

As the Gospels uniformly attest, debates with scribes, i.e. theologians, about the meaning of Scripture constituted an important part of Jesus' public ministry. They were certainly more extensive than the Gospel accounts although they may have followed the same general pattern. In any case a *yelammedenu* pattern known and used by the rabbis is the literary form often employed by the Gospel traditioners.[45] In the rabbinical writings the pattern is usually not a dialogue but the Scriptural discourse of one rabbi. In this respect the exegetical structure in Rom. 9–11 is closer to the rabbinic model than are the Gospel traditions.[46]

Certain differences between rabbinic and New Testament exegesis should also be noted. Unlike the usual rabbinic practice the New Testament midrashim (1) often do not have an initial text from the Pentateuch, i.e. do not employ the sabbath text of the synagogue lectionary cycle. (2) They often lack a second, proem text. (3) They often have a final text that does not correspond or allude to the initial text. (4) They have an eschatological orientation (see below, p. 209f.). Nevertheless, in their general structure they have an affinity with the rabbinic usage that is unmistakable and too close to be coincidental.

(d) A kind of exposition known as the *pesher* midrash appears in the Qumran writings, e.g. the commentary on Habakkuk. It receives its name from the Hebrew word used in the explanatory formula, "the interpretation (*pesher*) is." This formula and its apparent equivalent, "this is" (*hû'h*), sometimes introduce the Old Testament citation (CD 10:16) or, more characteristically, the commentary following the citation. Both formulas occur in the Old Testament,[47] the latter translated in the LXX by the phrase *οὗτος (ἐστίν)*.

Besides the formula, the Qumran *pesher* has other characteristics common to midrashic procedure. Like the midrashim discussed above, it apparently uses or creates variant Old Testament text-forms designed to adapt the text to the interpretation in the commentary. It also links text and commentary by catchwords. It is found, moreover, in various kinds of commentary patterns: anthology (4Qflor), single quotations (CD 4:14) and consecutive commentary on an Old Testament book (1QpHab).

More significantly for New Testament studies, the Qumran *pesher,* unlike rabbinic midrash but very much like early Christian practice, is both charismatic and eschatological. As *eschatological exegesis,* it views the Old Testament as promises and prophecies that have their fulfilment within the writer's own time and community, a community that inaugurates the "new covenant" of the "last (*'ahᵃrit*) days,"[48] and constitutes the "last (*'ahᵃrôn*) generation" before the coming of Messiah and the inbreaking of the kingdom of God.[49]

This characteristic feature, the *pesher* formula combined with an eschatological perspective, appears in a number of New Testament quotations:

> "In Isaac shall your seed be called" (Gen. 21:12). That is (τοῦτ' ἔστιν)... the children of the promise are reckoned for the seed. For this is (οὗτος)the word of promise, "... for Sarah there shall be a son" (Gen. 18:10).
>
> Rom. 9:7–9

> Do not say in your heart, "who shall ascend into heaven" (Dt. 30:12), that is (τοῦτ' ἔστιν) to bring Christ down....
>
> Rom. 10:6–8

> "On account of this shall a man leave father and mother and be joined to his wife, and the two shall be one flesh" (Gen. 2:24). This is (τοῦτο ... ἐστίν) a great mystery ... for Christ and the Church.
>
> Eph. 5:31f.

> It is written, "Abraham had two sons...." (cf. Gen. 21). These are (αὗται ... εἰσιν) two covenants....
>
> Gal. 4:22–24

> All our fathers were under the cloud.... But with many of them God was not pleased, for they were destroyed in the desert (cf. Ex. 13f.; 16f.; Num. 20; 14). These things (ταῦτα) happened as types for us....
>
> 1 Cor. 10:1–5, 6f.

> They were all filled with the Holy Spirit and began to speak in other tongues.... This is (τοῦτό ἐστιν) what was spoken by the prophet Joel, "I will pour out my spirit ..." (Joel 2:28).
>
> Acts 2:4, 16f.

> Jesus Christ of Nazareth.... This is (οὗτός ἐστιν) "the stone that was rejected by you builders, which has become the head of the corner" (Ps. 118:22).
> Acts 4:10f.

The Qumran *pesher* is regarded by the community as *charismatic exegesis,* the work of inspired persons such as the Teacher of Righteousness and other wise teachers (*maskilim*). The Old Testament prophecies are understood, as they are in the book of Daniel (9:2, 22f.; cf. 2:19, 24), to be a "mystery" (*raz*) in need of interpretation (*pesher*), an interpretation that only the *maskilim* can give.[50]

(e) From midrash to *testimonia:* "Words lifted from their scriptural context can never be a testimonium to the Jewish mind. The word becomes a testimonium for something or other after one has brought out its meaning with the aid of other parts of Scripture."[51] With this perceptive observation J. W. Doeve goes beyond the thesis of C. H. Dodd, mentioned above (p. 201), to contend that "testimony" citations in the New Testament are derived from midrashim, i.e. expositions of those particular Old Testament passages.

In support of Doeve are several examples of a "Christian" interpretation of a text that is established in an exposition and presupposed elsewhere in a "testimony" citation of the same text.[52] (1) The exposition in Acts 2:17–35 and that underlying Mk. 13 (see above, p. 203) apply Ps. 110:1 and Dan. 7:13, respectively, to Jesus. This interpretation is presupposed in the use of the verses at Mk. 14:62. (2) Heb. 2:6–9 establishes by midrashic procedures that Ps. 8 is fulfilled in Jesus; in 1 Cor. 15:27 and Eph. 1:20, 22 this understanding of Ps. 8 (and Ps. 110) is presupposed. (3) Acts 13:16–41 is probably a (reworked) midrash in which 2 Sam. 7:6–16 is shown to apply to Jesus.[53] This interpretation of 2 Sam. 7 is presupposed in the *testimonia* in Heb. 1:5 and 2 Cor. 6:18.

The midrashic expositions in these examples are not, of course, the immediate antecedents of the cited *testimonia* texts. But they represent the kind of matrix from which the "testimony" usage appears to be derived. They show, furthermore, that the prophets and teachers in the early church were not content merely to cite proof texts but were concerned to establish by exegetical procedures the Christian understanding of the Old Testament.

We may proceed one step further. Rabbinic parables often are found in midrashim as commentary on the Old Testament texts. Christ's parables also occur within an exegetical context, e.g. in Mt. 21:33–44 and Lk. 10:25–37 (see p. 205f.); and elsewhere, when they appear independently or in thematic clusters, they sometimes allude to Old Testament passages.[54] Probably such independent and clustered parables originated within an expository context from which they were later detached. Their present context, then, represents a stage in the formation of the Gospel traditions secondary to their use within an explicit commentary format.

II. *The Presuppositions of New Testament Interpretation*

1. GENERAL

To many Christian readers, to say nothing of Jewish readers, the New Testament's interpretation of the Old appears to be exceedingly arbitrary. For example, Hos. 11:1 ("Out of Egypt I called my son") refers to Israel's experience of the Exodus; how can Mt. 2:15 apply it to Jesus' sojourn in Egypt? In Ps. 8:4ff. the "son of man" (*ben-'adam*) given "glory" and "dominion" alludes to Adam or to Israel's king;[55] how can Heb. 2:8f. and 1 Cor. 15:27 apply the text to Jesus? If Gen. 15:6 and 2 Sam. 7 are predictions of Israel's future, how can New Testament writers refer them to Jesus and to his followers, who include Gentiles as well as Jews?

As has been shown above, the method used to justify such Christian interpretations of the Old Testament represents a serious and consistent effort to expound the texts. The method itself, of course, may be criticized. But then, our modern historical-critical method also is deficient: although it can show certain interpretations to be wrong, it can achieve an agreed interpretation for virtually no biblical passage. "Method" is inherently a limited instrumentality and, indeed, a secondary stage in the art of interpretation. More basic are the perspective and presuppositions with which the interpreter approaches the text.

The perspective from which the New Testament writers interpret the Old is sometimes stated explicitly, sometimes it can be inferred from their usage. It is derived in part from contemporary Jewish views and in part from the teaching of Jesus and the experience of the reality of his resurrection. Apart from its christological focus, it appears to be governed primarily by four factors: a particular understanding of history, of man, of Israel and of Scripture.

2. SALVATION AS HISTORY

Jesus and his disciples conceive of history within the framework of two ages, this age and the age to come.[56] This perspective appears to have its background in the Old Testament prophets, who prophesied of "the last (*'aḥᵉrit*) days" and "the day of the Lord" as the time of an ultimate redemption of God's people and the destruction of their enemies.[57] It becomes more specific in the apocalyptic writers, who underscored the cosmic dimension and (often) the imminence of the redemption and, with the doctrine of two ages, the radical difference between the present time and the time to come. This point of view is clearly present in the message of the Baptist that "the kingdom of God is at hand" and that the one coming after him, Jesus, would accomplish the final judgment and redemption of the nation (Mt. 3:2, 10ff.).

The two-fold consummation of judgment and deliverance that characterized the teaching of apocalyptic Judaism becomes, in the teaching of Jesus and his disciples, a two-stage consummation. As "deliverance" the kingdom of God that Judaism expected at the end of the age is regarded as already present in the person and work of Jesus.[58] As "judgment" (and final deliverance) the kingdom awaits the second, glorious appearing of Messiah.[59] This perspective may be contrasted with that of Platonism and of apocalyptic Judaism as follows:

```
Platonism
(and Gnosticism):       Eternity
                           ↑
                          Time

                   This Age        Age to Come (Kingdom of God)

Judaism:         C                 P
                 |———————————————————————————————————————————→
New              C                 P
Testament:       |        † ↑– – – –↓– – – – – – – – – – – – →
```

Platonic and later Gnostic thought anticipate a redemption from matter, an escape from time and history at death. The Jewish hope includes a redemption of matter within time: The present age, from creation (C) to the coming of Messiah (P), is to be succeeded by a future age of peace and righteousness under the reign of God. The New Testament's modification of Jewish apocalyptic rests upon the perception that in the mission, death and resurrection of Jesus the Messiah the age to come, the kingdom of God, had become present in hidden form in the midst of the present evil age, although its public manifestation awaits the parousia (P) of Jesus. Thus, for Jesus "the kingdom of God does not culminate a meaningless history, but a planned divine process." [60] Equally, for the New Testament writers faith in Jesus means faith in the story of Jesus, the story of God's redemptive activity in the history of Israel that finds its high-point and fulfilment in Jesus.

For this reason the mission and meaning of Jesus can be expressed in the New Testament in terms of a *salvation history* "consisting of a sequence of events especially chosen by God, taking place within an historical framework."[61] Although the concept *οἰκονομία* as used in Eph. 1:10 represents this idea, that is, a divinely ordered plan, the term "salvation history" does not itself occur in the New Testament. The concept is most evident in the way in which the New Testament relates current and future events to events, persons and institutions in the Old Testament. That relationship is usually set forth as a typological correspondence.

3. TYPOLOGY

(a) Typological interpretation expresses most clearly "the basic attitude of primitive Christianity toward the Old Testament." [62] It is not so much a system of interpretation as, in the phrase of Dr. Goppelt, a "spiritual perspective"[63] from which the early Christian community viewed itself. As a hermeneutical method it must be distinguished from τύπος ("model," "pattern") as it is widely used in the Greek world.[64]

Only occasionally using the term τύπος, typological interpretation appears, broadly speaking, as *covenant typology* and as *creation typology*. The latter may be observed in Rom. 5, where Christ is compared and contrasted with Adam, "a type (τύπος) of the one who was to come" (5:14). The former appears in 1 Cor. 10 where the Exodus events are said to be "types for us", to have happened "by way of example" (τυπικῶς) and to have been written down "for our admonition upon whom the end of the ages has come" (10:6, 11). Covenant typology accords with the Jewish conviction that all of God's redemptive acts followed the pattern of the Exodus;[65] it is, then, an appropriate way for Jesus and his community to explain the decisive messianic redemption. More generally, covenant typology approaches the whole of Old Testament as prophecy. Not only persons and events but also its institutions were "a shadow of the good things to come."[66]

New Testament typology is thoroughly christological in its focus. Jesus is the "prophet like Moses" (Acts 3:22f.) who in his passion brings the old covenant to its proper goal and end (Rom. 10:4; Heb. 10:9f.) and establishes a new covenant (Lk. 22:20, 29). As the messianic "son of David," i.e. "son of God," he is the recipient of the promises and ascriptions given to the Davidic kings.[67]

(b) Because the new covenant consummated by Jesus' death is the occasion of the new creation initiated by his resurrection, covenant typology and creation typology may be combined. As the "eschatological Adam" and the "Son of man," i.e. "son of Adam,"[68] Jesus stands at the head of a new order of creation that may be compared and contrasted with the present one. This combination in Paul and Hebrews finds its immediate background in the resurrection of Jesus.[69] But it is already implicit in Jesus' own teaching, e.g. his temple saying, his promise to the robber and his teaching on divorce.[70] It is probably implicit also in his self-designation as the Son of man (Mk. 14:62), a designation that is derived from Ps. 8:4 and Dan. 7:13f., 27. The Son of man in Ps. 8 refers not only to Israel's (messianic-ideal) king but also to Adam;[71] likewise the Son of man in Dan. 7 is related not only to national restoration but also to a new creation.[72] In apocalyptic Judaism also Israel was associated with Adam and the new covenant with a renewed creation.[73] Jesus and his followers shared these convictions and explained them in terms of the mission and person of Jesus.

(c) The Old Testament type not only corresponds to the new-age reality but also stands in antithesis to it. Like Adam Jesus is the representative headman of the race; but unlike Adam, who brought death, Jesus brings forgiveness and life.[74] Jesus is "the prophet like Moses" but, unlike Moses' ministry of condemnation, that of Jesus gives righteousness.[75] Similarly, the law "is holy, just and good" and its commandments are to be "fulfilled" by the believer;[76] yet as a demand upon man it can only condemn him.[77] One may speak, then, of "synthetic" and of "antithetic" typology to distinguish the way in which a type, to one degree or another, either corresponds to or differs from the reality of the new age.[78]

(d) Since the history of salvation is also the history of destruction,[79] it includes a *judgment typology*. The flood and Sodom, and perhaps the A.D. 70 destruction of Jerusalem, become types of God's eschatological judgment;[80] the faithless Israelite a type of the faithless Christian;[81] the enemies of Israel a type of the (Jewish) enemies of the Church[82] and, perhaps, a type of Antichrist.[83]

(e) In a brilliant and highly significant contribution to New Testament hermeneutics Leonard Goppelt has set forth the definitive marks of typological interpretation.[84] (1) Unlike allegory, typological exegesis regards the words of Scripture not as metaphors hiding a deeper meaning (*ὑπόνοια*) but as the record of historical events out of whose literal sense the meaning of the text arises (pp. 18f., 243ff.). (2) Unlike the "history of religions" exegesis, it seeks the meaning of current, New Testament situations from a particular history, the salvation-history of Israel. From past Old Testament events it interprets the meaning of the present time of salvation and, in turn, it sees in present events a typological prophecy of the future consummation (pp. 235–248). (3) Like rabbinic midrash, typological exegesis interprets the text in terms of contemporary situations, but it does so with historical distinctions that are lacking in rabbinic interpretation (pp. 31–34). (4) It identifies a typology in terms of two basic characteristics, historical correspondence and escalation, in which the divinely ordered prefigurement finds a complement in the subsequent and greater event (p. 244).

In a masterly essay[85] Rudolf Bultmann rejected Goppelt's conclusion that salvation history was constitutive for typological exegesis and sought to show that the origin of typology lay rather in a cyclical-repetitive view of history (cf. Barnabas 6:13). Although Judaism had combined the two perspectives, the New Testament, e.g. in its Adam/Christ typology, represents a purely cyclical pattern, parallels between the primal time and the end time.

However, Professor Bultmann (pp. 369f.), in interpreting the New Testament hermeneutical usage within the context of the traditional Greek conception,[86] does not appear to recognize that the recapitulation element in New Testament typology is never mere repetition but is always combined with a change of key in which some aspects of the type are not carried over and some are intensified. Exegetically Goppelt made the better case and established an important framework for understanding how the New Testament uses the Old.

4. OTHER PRESUPPOSITIONS

(a) In agreement with the Old Testament conception, the New Testament views *man as both individual and corporate existence*. It presents the corporate dimension, the aspect most difficult for modern Western man to appreciate, primarily in terms of Jesus and his church.[87] For the New

Testament faith in Jesus involves an incorporation into him:[88] It is to eat his flesh (Jn. 6:35, 54), to be his body (1 Cor. 12:27), to be baptized into him (Rom. 6:3), or into his name (1 Cor. 1:13; Acts 8:16), to be identified with him (Acts 9:4f.), to exist in the corporate Christ (2 Cor. 5:17) who is the "tent" (Heb. 9:11) or "house" (2 Cor. 5:1) in the heavens, God's eschatological temple.

Corporate existence can also be expressed as baptism "into Moses" (1 Cor. 10:2), existence "in Abraham" (Heb. 7:9f.) or "in Adam" (1 Cor. 15:22) and, at its most elementary level, the unity of man and wife as "one flesh" (Mt. 19:5; Eph. 5:29ff.). It is not merely a metaphor, as we are tempted to interpret it, but an ontological statement about who and what man is. The realism of this conception is well expressed by the term "corporate personality."[89]

The corporate extension of the person of the leader to include individuals who belong to him illumines the use of a number of Old Testament passages. It explains how the promise given to Solomon (2 Sam. 7:12–16) can be regarded as fulfilled not only in the Messiah (Heb. 1:5) but also in his followers (2 Cor. 6:18) and, similarly, how the eschatological temple can be identified both with the individual (Mk. 14:58; Jn. 2:19ff.) and corporate (1 Cor. 3:16; 1 Pet. 2:5) Christ. It very probably underlies the conviction of the early Christians that those who belong to Christ, Israel's messianic king, constitute *the true Israel.*[90] Consequently, it explains the Christian application to unbelieving Jews of Scriptures originally directed to Gentiles[91] and, on the other hand, the application to the church of Scriptures originally directed to the Jewish nation.[92]

Corporate personality also offers a rationale whereby individual, existential decision (Mk. 1:17; 2 Cor. 6:2) may be understood within the framework of a salvation history of the nation or the race. These two perspectives are considered by some scholars to be in tension[93] or to be mutually exclusive.[94] However, in the words of Oscar Cullmann,[95] the "now of decision" in the New Testament is not in conflict with the salvation-historical attitude but subordinate to it: "Paul's faith in salvation history creates at every moment the existential decision." For it is precisely within the context of the community that the individual's decision is made: Universal history and individual history cannot be isolated from one another.[96]

The history of salvation often appears in the New Testament as the history of individuals – Adam, Abraham, Moses, David, Jesus; yet they are individuals who also have a corporate dimension embracing the nation or the race. The decision to which the New Testament calls men relates to them. It is never a decision between the isolated individual and God but is, rather, a decision to "put off the old man" and to "put on the new man," to be delivered from the corporeity "in Moses" and "in Adam" and to be "immersed in" and to "put on" Christ, i.e. to be incorporated into the "prophet like Moses" and the eschatological Adam of the new creation in whom the history of salvation is to be consummated.[97]

(b) The early Christian prophets and teachers explain the Old Testament by what may be called *charismatic exegesis* or, in the words of L. Cerfaux,[98] "spiritual interpretation." Like the teachers of Qumran, they proceed from the conviction that the meaning of the Old Testament is a "mystery" whose "interpretation" can be given not by human reason but only by the Holy Spirit.[99] On the basis of revelation from the Spirit they are confident of their ability to rightly interpret the Scriptures.[100] Equally, they conclude that those who are not gifted cannot "know" the true meaning of the word of God.[101]

This view of their task does not preclude the New Testament writers from using logic or hermeneutical rules and methods. However, it does disclose where the ultimate appeal and authority of their interpretation lie. Correspondingly, an acceptance of their interpretation of Scripture in preference to some other, ancient or modern, also will rest ultimately not on the proved superiority of their logical procedure or exegetical method but rather on the conviction of their prophetic character and role.

NOTES

1. L. Hartman, "Scriptural Exegesis in the Gospel of Matthew and the Problem of Communication," *L'evangile selon Matthieu,* ed. M. Didier (Gembloux 1972), pp. 131–152, 134.
2. Cf. E. E. Ellis, *Paul's Use of the Old Testament* (Edinburgh 1957), pp. 11–16, 150–152; R. H. Gundry, *The Use of the Old Testament in St. Matthew's Gospel* (Leiden 1967), pp. 9–150; K. Stendahl, *The School of St. Matthew* (Lund 1969 (1954)), pp. 47–156.
3. Cf. Ellis, *Paul's Use,* pp. 14f.
4. E.g. 1 Ki. 2:27; 2 Ch. 35:12.
5. E.g. 1 QS 5:15; 8:14; cf. J. A. Fitzmyer in NTS 7 (1960–61), pp. 299–305.
6. E.g. Philo, *de migr.* 118. Cf. Ellis, *Paul's Use,* pp. 48f.
7. E.g. Mk. 12:36; cf. R. T. France, *Jesus and the Old Testament* (London 1971), pp. 101f., 163–169.
8. Cf. J. W. Doeve, *Jewish Hermeneutics in the Synoptic Gospels and Acts* (Assen 1954), pp. 185f.; Gundry, *Matthew,* p. 125n.
9. R. Bloch, "Midrash," *Dictionnaire de la Bible: Supplément* (Paris) 5 (1957), 1266. Cf. B. B. Warfield, *The Inspiration and Authority of the Bible* (Philadelphia 1948), p. 148: "Scripture is thought of as the living voice of God speaking in all its parts directly to the reader;" M. Barth, "The Old Testament in Hebrews," *Current Issues in New Testament Interpretation,* ed. W. Klassen (New York 1962), pp. 58ff.
10. Cf. D. Daube, *The New Testament and Rabbinic Judaism* (London 1956), pp. 423–436.
11. Cf. Doeve, *Hermeneutics,* pp. 105f., 163f. Cf. Mt. 12:3, 5; 19:4.
12. Ellis, *Paul's Use,* pp. 107–112.
13. Stendahl, *School,* pp. 163, 200f.: "Matthew's formula quotations give evidence of features of text interpretation of an actualizing nature, often closely associated with the context in the gospel." "(They) seem to us . . . to be a decisive indication that we must postulate a School of Matthew."
14. Cf. Ellis, *Paul's Use,* pp. 139–47. See notes 48, 49.
15. Cf. E. E. Ellis, "The Role of the Christian Prophet in Acts," *Apostolic History and the Gospel,* ed. W. W. Gasque (Exeter 1970), p. 58; "'Wisdom' and 'Knowledge' in I Corinthians," Tyn.B 25 (1974), pp. 93–96.

16. Cf. G. W. Knight, *The Faithful Sayings in the Pastoral Epistles,* (Kampen 1968).
17. Tit. 1:9, 14; 3:5f., 8; 1 Tim. 2:13–15; 3:1a.
18. For the practice in classical literature cf. F. Johnson, *The Quotations of the New Testament from the Old* (London 1896), pp. 92–102. On merged citations, see below, p. 202f.
19. Cf. Ellis, *Paul's Use,* pp. 98–107; P. Prigent, *L'épitre de Barnabé I–XVI et ses sources* (Paris 1961).
20. So, J. Rendel Harris, *Testimonies,* 2 vols. (Cambridge 1916, 1920).
21. C. H. Dodd, *According to the Scriptures* (London 1952), pp. 78f., 107f., 126.
22. Cf. E. E. Ellis, "Midrash, Targum and New Testament Quotations," *Neotestamentica et Semitica,* edd. E. E. Ellis and M. Wilcox (Edinburgh 1969), pp. 61–99; M. P. Miller, "Targum, Midrash and the Use of the Old Testament in the New Testament," *Journal for the Study of Judaism* 2 (1970), pp. 29–82.
23. E.g. in Is. 9:11 (12) "Aramaeans and Philistines" becomes in the LXX the contemporary "Syrians and Greeks." In agreement with Bloch, G. Vermes (*Scripture and Tradition in Judaism* (Leiden 1961), p. 179) characterizes the LXX and targums as a "re-writing of the Bible" in which contemporary interpretations are woven into the text. He distinguishes two purposes for such midrash, to eliminate obscurities in the biblical text and to justify current beliefs and practices from the Scripture. Cf. his "Bible and Midrash," *Cambridge History of the Bible I,* ed. P. R. Ackroyd (Cambridge 1970), p. 221. On other midrashic elements in the LXX and targums cf. D. W. Gooding in JTS 25 (1974), pp. 1–11.
24. A. G. Wright (*CBQ* 28, 1966, 105–38, 517–57) prefers to restrict the use of the term to explicit midrash. On the continuing problem of defining the relationship of targum and midrash cf. R. Le Déaut in *Biblical Theology Bulletin* 4 (1974), 18–22; Ellis, "Midrash, Targum," pp. 63f; A. Diez-Macho in *Revue des Sciences Religieuses* 47 (1973), 171–175.
25. Cf. H. H. Schaeder in TDNT 4 (1967/1942), pp. 878f.; Stendahl, *School,* pp. 198f.; for the various interpretations, Gundry, *Matthew,* pp. 97–104.
26. Cf. M. Black in BJRL 45 (1963), 315ff.
27. In Revelation no formal quotations occur, but almost 70% of the verses contain allusions to the Old Testament.
28. See note 21.
29. See E. E. Ellis, *The Gospel of Luke* (London 1974[2]), pp. 27ff., 67f. Lk. 1:5–2.40 is a literary unity and reflects a Hebraic source or sources that were composed in part, at least, from the perspective of a narrator in Jerusalem (e.g. 2:38). The New Testament evidence for the presence in the Jerusalem church of the Virgin Mary and of the brothers of Jesus (Gal. 1:19; Acts 1:14; 12:17; 15:13; 21:18) is not without significance for this matter, even if their presence in diaspora churches also is attested (1 Cor. 9:5; Epiph., *Panarion* 78, 11, 2).
30. On the use of Ps. 110:1 by Jesus cf. D. M. Hay, *Glory at the Right Hand; Psalm 110 in Early Christianity* (Nashville 1973), p. 110 (on Mk. 12:35–37); France, *Jesus,* pp. 101ff.
31. So, L. Hartman (*Prophecy Interpreted* (Lund 1966), pp. 235–52, 242), who identifies the original midrash with Mk. 13:5b–8, 12–16, 19–22, 24–27. His acute analysis is largely persuasive.
32. E.g. W. G. Braude, *Pesikta Rabbati,* 2 vols. (New Haven 1968). He dates the expositions in this seventh century collection from third and fourth century Palestinian rabbis.
33. Cf. P. Borgen, *Bread from Heaven* (Leiden 1965), pp. 59–98.
34. In Judea, apparently, the synagogue served in the pre-destruction period primarily for the study of Scripture and only later as a center of worship. Cf. J. W. Bowker, "Speeches in Acts," NTS 14 (1967–68), pp. 96–99 and the literature cited there.
35. Cf. Pesikta Rabbati 33:7: Text (Is. 51:12) + Second Text (Hos. 6:1) + Exposition (with parable and application, linked verbally to the second text) + Additional Text (La. 1:13) + Concluding Text (Is. 51:12). Also: Pesikta Rabbati 44:7. For Acts 2 and 13 cf. Bowker ("Speeches," pp. 96–111) and Doeve (*Hermeneutics,* pp. 168–86); for Jn. 6:31–58, Rom. 4:1–22, Gal. 3:6–29 cf. Borgen (*Bread,* pp. 37–52); for 1 Cor. 1:18–3:20, Rom. 1:17–4:25 cf. E.E. Ellis ("Exegetical Patterns in I Corinthians and Romans," in *Grace upon Grace, Essays in Honor of L. Kuyper,* ed. J. I. Cook (Grand Rapids 1975) pp.137–42).
36. Cf. Ellis, "Midrash, Targum," p. 63. A somewhat different pattern appears in 1 Cor. 10: Implicit Midrash (1–5, cf. Ex. 13f.; Nu. 14; 20) + Application (6) + Additional Text (Ex.

32:6) + Exposition/Application, alluding to the preceding midrash and other texts (8–13). Such midrashic summaries also appear to form the "texts" on which the letter of Jude makes its commentary, e.g. Jude 5 (Nu. 14), 6 (Gn. 6), 7 (Gn. 19), 14f. (1 Enoch 1:9; cf. Gn. 5:22). This is, in effect, midrash on midrash. One can, thus, understand how Jude and others could use an interpretation of biblical material, e.g. 1 Enoch, as a "text" without necessarily regarding the book of Enoch *eo ipso* as Scripture. The targums provide an analogy in Jewish practice: they set forth an interpretation of Scripture for the synagogue hearers without themselves being given the status of Scripture.

37. The application following the final quotation, which appears in a number of the examples above, has a parallel in Philo and the rabbis. Cf. Philo, *leg. alleg.* III, 75b–76; *Sacr. Abel.* 87b; Borgen, *Bread,* p. 53; E. Stein, "Die homiletische Peroratio . . .," *Hebrew Union College Annual* 8–9 (1931–32), pp. 353–71, 368; cf. Pesikta Rabbati 5:4; 9:2; 22:1.

38. See note 35 and, for the structure of 1 Cor. 1:18–31; 2:6–16, above p. 204.

39. Cf. E. E. Ellis, "New Directions in Form Criticism," *Jesus Christus in Historie und Theologie. Festschrift für H. Conzelmann,* ed. G. Strecker, (Tübingen 1975), pp. 299–315; B. Gerhardsson, *The Testing of God's Son* (Lund 1966) (on Mt. 4:1–11). Cf. also J. A. Sanders in *Essays in Old Testament Ethics,* ed. J. L. Crenshaw (New York 1974 pp. 247–271) (on Lk.

40. So SB IV, 173 citing Mek Exod. 19:2 (69b). See note 35.

41. As Is. 5:1f. appears in the Gospels, the phrase "cleared it of stones" is lacking; but it was probably in the original form of the midrash. Here the gospel tradition tends to reduce the Old Testament references. Luke curtails them further and the Gospel of Thomas (65f.) eliminates them altogether. On the dependence of Thomas on canonical Luke (here) cf. E. E. Ellis in ZNW 62 (1971), p. 102; (in other sayings) cf. H. Schürmann in BZ 7 (1963), pp. 236–260. Otherwise: H. Montefiore and H. E. W. Turner, *Thomas and the Evangelists* (London 1962), pp. 62ff.

42. On the original unity of the pericopes, Mt. 21:33–44 and Lk. 10:25–37, cf. Ellis, "New Directions," pp. 309–315. Cf. further J. D. M. Derrett, *Law in the New Testament* (London 1970), pp. 208–227 = NTS 11 (1964–65), pp. 22–37; B. Gerhardsson, *The Good Samaritan* (Lund 1958), p. 28.

43. D. Daube (*The New Testament and Rabbinic Judaism* (London 1956), p. 143) regards the passage, Mt. 15:1–20 as an original unity, "one whole from the outset," with a close parallel in structure to Gn. Rabba 8:9 (on Gn. 1:26) and Nu Rabba 19:8 (on Nu. 19:2). Even so, Mt. 15:1–9 remains an original literary unity, relatively self-contained, and the midrash from which the rest of the passage proceeds.

44. A more complex stating of a problem is found in Mt. 22:23–33 = Mk. 12: 18–27, the Sadducees' question about the resurrection.

45. For the Gospels, as the above examples indicate, the forms in Matthew are at times clearer and closer to the Jewish, rabbinical patterns, i.e. presumably more primitive; those in Mark are at times broken and somewhat dissipated. This raises questions about the source criticism of the Gospels that cannot be discussed here.

46. Cf. the midrash in Rom. 9:13, 14–23 (Ellis, "Exegetical Patterns," pp. 140f.).

47. Cf. Is. 9:14.; Ezk. 5:5; Zc. 1:10; 5:6; Dn. 4:21 (24); 5:25f.; at Qumran, 4Qflor 1:2f., 11f., 14; IQpHab 3:1ff. Cf. E. E. Ellis, 'Midrashic Features in the Speeches of Acts' *Mélanges bibliques en hommage au B. Rigaux,* ed. A. Descamps (Gembloux, 1969), pp. 306–309. For the use of the formula in the rabbinic literature cf. W. Bacher, *Die Proömien der alten jüdischen Homilie,* (Farnborough (Eng.) 1970 (1913), p. 17; *Exegetische Terminologie der jüdischen Traditionsliteratur* (Darmstadt 1965 (1899, 1905)), pp. 173f., 177f.

48. Je. 31:31; 1QpHab 2:3–6; cf. CD 6:19; 8:21; 19:33; 20:12f.; 1 Cor. 11:25; Heb. 8:7–13.

49. CD 1:12; 1QpHab 2:7; 7:2; 4QpIsa[a] 8; Mk. 13:30; cf. Mt. 4:14–17; Acts 2:17; I Cor. 10:11.

50. Cf. 1QpHab 7:1–8; 1QH 12:11ff.; R. N. Longenecker, *Biblical Exegesis in the Apostolic Period* (Grand Rapids 1974), pp. 41–45; F. F. Bruce in *Neotestamentica et Semitica,* ed. E. E. Ellis and M. Wilcox (Edinburgh 1969), pp. 225ff.; O. Michel, *Paulus und seine Bibel,* (Darmstadt 1972[2]), pp. 215ff.; H. C. Kee, "The Function of . . . Quotations . . .

in Mark 11–16", in E. E. Ellis and E. Grässer (ed.), *Jesus und Paulus* (Göttingen 1975), pp. 179–82.
51. Doeve, *Hermeneutics,* p. 116.
52. Cf. Ellis, "Midrash, Targum", pp. 65–69; "Exegetical Patterns", p. 137 (cf. 1 Cor. 1:31 with 2 Cor. 10:17); Michel, *Paulus,* p. 213. Somewhat different perhaps is Hab. 2:4; it appears with Gn. 15:6 = Rom. 4:3 as the initial text of a midrash, Rom. 1:17–4:25, and is apparently interpreted in terms of the exposition of the same text in Gal. 3:6–29.
53. See note 35.
54. E.g. Mk. 4:1–22 (on Je. 4:3); Lk. 15:3–6 (on Ezk. 34:11).
55. Cf. F. Delitzsch, *The Psalms* (Grand Rapids 1949 (1871)), pp. 154–157; (re the king) A. Bentzen, *Fortolkning . . . Salmer,* (Copenhagen 1939, cited in H. Ringgren, *The Faith of the Psalmists* (Philadelphia 1963), p. 98.
56. E.g. Mt. 12:32; Mk. 10:30; Lk. 20:34f.
57. Nu. 24:14; Is. 2:2; Dn. 10:14; Ho. 3:5; Am. 5:18ff.; Mi. 4:1; Zc. 14; cf. Hg. 2:9; G. Kittel and G. von Rad, TDNT 2 (1964/1935), pp. 697, 944f.; U. Luz, *Das Geschichtsverständnis des Paulus* (München 1968), pp. 53ff.
58. Cf. Lk. 7:19–22; 11:20–22, 31 par; Rom. 14:17; Gal. 1:4; Col. 1:13; O. Cullmann, *Christ and Time* (London 1952), pp. 81–93; *Salvation in History* (London 1967), pp. 193–209; Luz, *Paulus,* p. 5.
59. Cf. Lk. 11:2; 21:27; 22:16, 28ff.; Mt. 25:31.
60. Cullmann, *Salvation,* pp. 233, 236.
61. Ibid., p. 25. Cf. F. F. Bruce, "Salvation History in the New Testament," *Man and his Salvation,* ed. E. J. Sharpe (Manchester 1973), pp. 75–90; W. G. Kümmel, *Promise and Fulfilment* (London 1957), p. 148: . . . "the New Testament message itself is abrogated if a timeless message concerning the present as a time of decision or concerning the spiritual nearness of God replaces the preaching of the eschatological future and the determination of the present by the future. For this would result in a complete degeneration of Jesus' message that man . . . is placed in a definite situation in the *history* of salvation advancing toward the end, and the figure and activity of Jesus would lose their fundamental character as the *historical* activity of [God] . . ."
62. W. G. Kümmel, "Schriftauslegung," RGG V, 1519.
63. "pneumatische Betrachtungsweise." L. Goppelt, *Typos: Die typologische Deutung des Alten Testaments im Neuen* (Darmstadt 1969 (1939)), pp. 183, 243f. An English translation is forthcoming from Eerdmans Publishing Co., Grand Rapids, Mich. USA.
64. Cf. Luz, *Paulus,* p. 53.
65. D. Daube, *The Exodus Pattern in the Bible* (London 1963); G. von Rad, *Old Testament Theology,* 2 vols. (London 1960), 1965, II, 272.
66. Heb. 5:1–10; 9:9; 10:1; Col. 2:17; cf. Mt. 7:11; Jn. 3:14f.; 6:32. Heb. 8:5 (cf. 9:24; Acts 7:44, reflecting Ex. 25:40, reverses the usual typological imagery and identifies *τύπος* with the heavenly model for which the Old Testament institutions were "anti-types." Like John (6:31–39; 14:1–3) and unlike Philo, Hebrews incorporates the vertical typology into the horizontal, two-age schema by identifying the "heavenly" with the age to come, that is, with the ascended and *coming* Jesus. Cf. Heb. 9:24–28; 10:37; L. Goppelt, TDNT 8 (1972), p.258; Rev. 21:2; Gal. 4:25f.: "present Jerusalem . . . Jerusalem above." See also C.T. Fritsch, "*TO ANTITOΠON*", *Studia Biblica [for] T. C. Vriezen,* ed. W. C. van Unnik (Wageningen 1966), pp. 100–110.
67. 2 Sa. 7:12ff.; Ps. 2; 16; 110; Am. 9:11f.; cf. Jn. 7:42; Acts 3:25–36; 13:33ff.; 15:16ff.; 1 Cor. 15:25; Heb. 1:5; E. Lohse, TDNT 8 (1972), pp. 482–487. Re Moses cf. J. Jeremias, TDNT 4 (1967/1942), pp. 856–873. Re Son of God cf. M. Hengel, *The Son of God* (London 1976), pp. 42–5.
68. Ps. 8:4, *ben-'adam*; 1 Cor. 15–27, 45; Eph. 1:21f.; Heb. 2:5–10; cf. Lk. 3:38; Acts 6:14; 7:44, 48.
69. Cf. also 1 Pet. 3:21f.; Rev. 2:7, 26f.
70. Mk. 14:58 (*ἀχειροποιητός*); 15:29; Lk. 23:42f. ("kingdom," "Paradise"); Mt. 19:4–9; cf. Lk. 16:16–18.
71. See note 55. Cf. W. Wifall, "Gen. 3:15. . .", CBQ 36 (1974), p.365; The Yahwist has

presented Israel's prehistory within a "Davidic" or "messianic" framework.
72. Dn. 7:14 ("dominion," "glory"); cf. M. Hooker, *The Son of Man in Mark* (London 1967), pp. 17ff., 24–30, 71.
73. Dn. 7:13f., 27; Test. Levi 18; 2 Baruch 72–74; 1QS 4:22f.; CD 3:13–20; 4:20; 1QH 6:7f., 15f.; 17:12–15; 1Q34; cf. Is. 43; 65:22.
74. 1 Cor. 15:22; Rom. 5:12, 15.
75. Acts 3:25; 2 Cor. 3:6–9.
76. Gal. 5:14; Rom. 7:12; 13:8: "Love" (Lev. 19:18) is not a substitute for the commandments (Ex. 20) but a means and guide by which they are interpreted and fulfilled. Cf. Heb. 10:1.
77. 2 Cor. 3:6; cf. Gal. 3:10–13. The failure to distinguish, among other things, between the law as an expression of God's righteousness, which it ever continues to be, and the (works of) law as a means of man's salvation, which it is not and never was, leads G. Klein (*Rekonstruktion und Interpretation* (München 1969), p. 210 = *Evangelische Theologie* 24 [1964], 155) to the totally misguided conclusion that for Paul Moses, the giver of the law, is "the functionary of anti-godly powers . . . [and] the historical realm based on him is not merely profaned but flatly demonized." Cf. C. E. B. Cranfield, "St. Paul and the Law", SJT 17 (1964), pp. 43–68; 'Notes on Rom. 9:30–33", in E. E. Ellis and E. Grässer (ed.), *Jesus und Paulus* (Göttingen 1975), pp. 35–43.
78. Luz, *Paulus,* pp. 59f. E.g. Abraham represents synthetic typology (i.e. his faith) but not antithetic (i.e. his circumcision, Gal. 3). Moses and the Exodus can represent both (Heb. 11:28f.; 1 Cor. 10:1–4, 6–10; 2 Cor. 3:9); so can Jerusalem (Gal. 4:25f.; Rev. 11:8; 21:2). The old covenant, i.e. the law, more often represents antithetic typology.
79. Cullmann, *Salvation,* pp. 123; cf. 127–135.
80. Lk. 17:26–30; 2 Pet. 2:6; Jude 7 (δεῖγμα); Mt. 24:3.
81. 1 Cor. 10:6–11; Heb. 4:5, 11.
82. Rev. 11:8; 17:5; cf. Rom. 2:24; Gal. 4:29.
83. 2 Th. 2:3f.; Rev. 13:1–10.
84. Goppelt, *Typos.* Cf. Cullmann, *Salvation,* pp. 127–135; J. C. K. von Hoffman, *Interpreting the Bible* (Minneapolis 1972 (1880)). Alternative approaches have been advocated by R. E. Brown (*The Sensus Plenior of Sacred Scripture* (Baltimore 1955)), by the existentialist theologians (e.g. M. Rese, *Alttestamentliche Motive in der Christologie des Lukas* (Gütersloh 1969), p. 209; A. Suhl, *Die Funktion der alttestamentliche Zitate . . . im Markusevangelium* (Gütersloh 1965), pp. 162–186) and by A. T. Hanson (*Jesus Christ in the Old Testament* (London 1965), pp. 6f., 172–178), who believes that "the real presence of the pre-existent Jesus" best explains, for the most part, this area of New Testament exegesis. Cf. also his *Studies in Paul's Technique and Theology* (London 1974), pp. 149–158. Whether *sensus plenior* is only a kind of allegorical interpretation, as J. L. McKenzie thinks (JBL 77, 1958, pp. 202f.), will depend upon the criteria used; cf. R. E. Brown, CBQ 25 (1963), pp. 274ff. Hanson's view does not pose an absolute alternative to typological interpretation, as he admits (p. 177); it also does not appear to do justice to certain aspects of the two-age, apocalyptic framework of New Testament thought. The setting of existential decision in opposition to salvation history (Suhl) is, in my judgement, a false dichotomy. See below, pp. 213.
85. R. Bultmann, "Ursprung und Sinn der Typologie als hermeneutische Methode," TLZ 75 (1950), cols. 205–212 – *Exegetica* (Tübingen 1967), pp. 369–380.
86. See note 64.
87. Mk. 14:22ff.; Col. 1:24; J. A. T. Robinson, *The Body,* London 1952; R. P. Shedd, *Man in Community* (London 1958); Ellis, *Paul's Use,* pp. 88–98, 126–135; B. Gärtner, *The Temple and the Community in Qumran and in the New Testament* (Cambridge 1965), pp. 138–142.
88. Even the phrase "in faith" appears to denote at times a sphere of existence, i.e. "in Christ." Cf. Acts 14:22; 16:5; 1 Cor. 16:13; 2 Cor. 13:5; Col. 1:23; 2:7; 1 Tim. 1:2; 2:15; Jas. 2:5; 1 Pet. 5:9. On baptism, however, cf. L. Hartman, "Baptism 'into the name of Jesus,'" *Studia Theologica* 28 (1974), pp. 24–28, 35f.
89. H. W. Robinson, *Corporate Personality in Ancient Israel* (Philadelphia 1964 (1935)); cf. *Deuteronomy and Joshua* (The Century Bible) (Edinburgh 1907) p. 266. Cf. J. Pedersen,

Israel (London 1959 (1926), I–II, pp. 263–296, 474–479; III–IV, pp. 76–86; A. R. Johnson, *The One and the Many in the Israelite Conception of God* (Cardiff 1961), pp. 1–13. J. W. Rogerson (JTS 21, 1970, pp. 1–16) suspects that Robinson's concept may have been derived from a current theory about primitive man's thought. The theory may have stimulated Robinson's work, just as current psychological theory may have stimulated a recognition of the psychosomatic unity of man in Scripture. But it is hardly responsible for the exegetical conclusion that has been established with considerable probability by Robinson, Pedersen, Johnson and others. To set that aside one needs a more persuasive explanation of the texts, a task that Rogerson does not attempt.

90. Cf. Ellis, *Paul's Use,* pp. 136–139; Lk. 19:9; Acts 3:22f.; 15:14ff.; Rom. 9:6; Gal. 6:16; Phil. 3:3; Heb. 4:9; Rev. 2:14. Otherwise: J. Jervell, *Luke and the People of God,* (Minneapolis 1972), pp. 41–69; P. Richardson, *Israel in the Apostolic Church* (Cambridge 1969).

91. E.g. Acts 4:25ff.; Rom. 8:36; 9.25; 10:13; cf. M. Simon, *Verus Israel* (Paris 1964[2]), pp. 104–24; W. Gutbrod, TDNT 3 (1965/1938), pp. 384–388; H. Strathmann, TDNT 4 (1967/1942), pp. 50–57.

92. E.g. 2 Cor. 6:16ff.; Heb. 8:8–12; 1 Pet. 2:9f. The Qumran sect views itself similarly. In 1QM 1:2 the Jewish "offenders" are included among the pagan enemies. Cf. 1QpHab 2:1–4; 4Qtest 22, 29f.

93. E. Dinkler, "Earliest Christianity," *The Idea of History in the Ancient Near East,* ed. R. C. Denton (New Haven 1955), p. 190.

94. Klein, *Rekonstruktion,* pp. 180–204.

95. Cullmann, *Salvation,* p. 248.

96. Luz, *Paulus,* p. 156.

97. Eph. 4:22ff.; 1 Cor. 10:2; 15:22, 45; Gal. 3:27; Acts 3:22ff.

98. P. Auvray *et al., L'Ancient Testament et les chrétiens* (Paris 1951), pp. 132–148.

99. 1 Cor. 2:6–16. See notes 15, 50.

100. Cf. Mt. 16:17; Mk. 4:11; Rom. 11:25f.; 12:6f.; 16:25f.; 1 Cor. 2:12f.; Eph. 3:3–6; 2 Pet. 3:15f.

101. Mt. 22:29; 2 Cor. 3:14ff.

CHAPTER XIII

APPROACHES TO NEW TESTAMENT EXEGESIS

Ralph P. Martin

I. *Different Ways of Interpreting the New Testament*

Exegesis means interpretation and as we apply the term to the books of the New Testament we may begin with a provisional definition of the task. To practise exegesis in regard to the New Testament literature is to enquire what was the meaning intended by the original authors. The process is one of uncovering that meaning, and the technique is known as heuristics, i.e. the study which explains how to discover the sense of a passage of Scripture. This is to be the interpreter's primary aim, requiring that his approach to Scripture be one of honest enquiry and a determined effort to find out the intended meaning of the author for his day.

But this approach, expressed in a way which at first glance commends itself as straightforward and full of commonsense, both proceeds with some assumptions which ought to be acknowledged openly and conceals several hidden pitfalls. We can notice these as we set down some of the different ways in which the approach to the interpretation of the New Testament has been understood.

1. THE DOGMATIC APPROACH

Under this heading we refer to a view of the New Testament Scripture which sees it as an arsenal of proof-texts to be arranged, without much regard given to their literary form, historical context, theological purpose, or even their best translation into modern English, to form a network of probative evidence.

Seen in this light, the meaning of Scripture is atomized by being regarded as contained in key-words or key-phrases or isolated single verses treated without respect to their neighbouring context. Little attention is paid to the teaching of the passage or book in which the individual texts appear. There is obvious danger in this method. It misuses the text of Scripture by appealing to a truncated part (a verse) instead of to the larger, more intelligible unit (a paragraph or longer section, according to the writer's purpose). It cannot escape the charge of subjectivism when isolated verses are chosen because of their apparent suitability to "prove a point". And it is forgetful of God's providence in conveying his word to men not in fragmented or situation-less dicta, but in the total context of the historical milieu of an ancient people (Israel, the early church) and through the medium of a set of languages which make use of non-prescriptive modes of expression. Failure to recall this last point turns the New Testament into a legal code or a set of cold facts, like a telephone directory.

On a different level another version of the dogmatic approach is evident in those instances in church history when an ecclesiastical authority has imposed an interpretation on Scripture. To give one example, the Council of Trent gave clear directive about the meaning of Jesus' eucharistic words to the disciples in the upper room.

> He said in plain, unmistakable words that he was giving them his own body and his own blood. . . .
>
> These words have their proper and obvious meaning and were so understood by the Fathers.[1]

This ruling by the Magisterium indicates an authoritative appeal to one, highly particularized interpretation of Scripture and its use as a dogmatic instrument to establish church teaching. Again, as with the previous discussion about Protestant proof-texting, Scripture has assumed the character of a law-book.

2. THE IMPRESSIONISTIC APPROACH

The impressionistic approach may seem to be the exact antithesis of the method just described. Its main characteristic is a way of approaching the New Testament Scripture in which the reader equates the message of the passage before him with the thoughts which fill his mind as he reads. The exercise is one of gaining impressions from the text which has its function in exciting and engendering a series of "thoughts", triggered by the verses in question. This is a popular treatment of the Bible with some recent evangelical young people's groups, for example the Jesus people.[2]

There can be no doubt that this approach is open to grave objection. It is a treatment of Scripture which is at the mercy of human feelings; it fails to submit to some objective control in a recognition of the plain sense of the text, set in its historical context. Therefore it overlooks the reality that Scripture comes to us in historical dress and requires that we respect its contextual setting in the day in which it was first given. Moreover, the approach ignores the fact, only too painfully obvious, that the Bible is not an easy book to understand and its study demands our full attention and the mental discipline of concentrated effort to grasp the import of the words before us if we are to penetrate to their true meaning. It is a counsel of despair to turn away from serious Bible study because it is difficult, in preference for the easy way of impressionism.

3. THE GRAMMATICO-HISTORICAL METHOD

The grammatico-historical method has everything to commend it as an antidote to both of the approaches mentioned. It takes seriously God's revelation which he has been pleased to communicate in verbal form in the pages of holy Scripture. The New Testament is the word of God in the words of men.[3] For that reason, the reader begins his enquiry into the meaning of a passage with a conscious endeavour to know what the words (Gr. *grammata*) meant in their historical setting. And that means that he will strive to gain understanding of the text through the language-form which any specific passage employs. Certain corollaries follow from this appreciation of what Scripture is and how God has been pleased to make it available to his people. For one thing, there is the problem of the best text of the New Testament in the original Greek. The student will want to satisfy himself, as far as he is able, that either the Greek Testament in front of him or the translation based upon it is the "best". By that word is meant that it is as close to the original autographs as it is possible to get through the science of textual criticism. The transmission of the New Testament text has been affected by the contingencies of historical circumstances and, since we do not possess the original autographs for inspection, it is incumbent upon us that we use all the means available to recover the text which stands nearest to the original.

The other matter is the ascertaining of the meaning of the Greek words and their translation equivalents in our native language. For this we need the help of grammar books, lexicons, dictionaries and concordances. To be sure, there will also be a residue of places where the grammatical or syntactical sense is unclear. The first epistle of John contains several instances of this ambiguity and it is uncertain (e.g. at 1 John 4:17) exactly how the prepositional phrases, dependent clauses and adverbial expressions fit together as the author originally intended. Several permutations and combinations are possible.[4]

Then, the clothing of God's saving revelation of himself in historical events and their interpretation means that the present-day student must take history seriously and be alive to the setting of Scripture's story as far as the New Testament is concerned in the world of first century Graeco-Roman society. Luke's notice in his gospel (3:1f.) shows the evangelist's purpose in describing the historical framework in which the gospel events took place. This anchoring of the saving message in history is of immeasurable importance. It was appreciated by the early Christians in their refusal to evacuate the gospel of its historical content and to cut it loose from its historical moorings – a refusal which led them to oppose gnostic influences as heretical (cf. 2 Pet. 1:16ff.).

Furthermore, the grammatico-historical method enters a needed protest against an inordinate desire for relevance which marks out the impressionistic approach. According to the aim of the latter, the reader professes a desire to study and to heed only those parts of Scripture which have an easily convertible theological and spiritual value and whose application to life stands out most obviously. This proclivity to accept only parts of the Bible as relevant and spiritually valuable has been severely criticized in recent years, notably by J. Barr.[5]

This is a tendency, however, to be held in check as we pay due recognition to the demands of the grammatico-historical requirements. They include the reminder that the scope of the Bible covers the entire range of life and offers a comprehensive world-view which is distorted if we choose to narrow it to our personal interests at any given moment of our Christian experience. A true corrective is supplied by our resolve to treat the whole corpus of Scripture with serious intent and to hear what its total witness may be by the rigorous and disciplined application of a method which seeks to elucidate the message in its original setting and in its literal sense.

4. THE MEANING FOR THE TWENTIETH CENTURY

The question is now raised whether a Christian reader of the New Testament can remain content with a line of study which sets its aim only at the ascertaining of the first century meaning. Granted that this is a legitimate and necessary starting-point, must we not press on to enquire about the meaning of the text for ourselves today? This second stage of enquiry is the determining of the true transition point needed to move from "What did the text mean?" to "What does the text say and how do I understand it for myself today?" The issue was first pinpointed by W. Dilthey when he drew the distinction between explanation and understanding.[6]

At this point we should notice an approach to the interpretation of the New Testament which regards as totally unsatisfactory any attempt to stay with the first century meaning of the text. This is *the existentialist approach,* which is more fully described and criticized later in this book (pp. 294–300). It will be sufficient to mention here its main emphasis since it is regarded as the most serious rival to the view which has just been mentioned.

Its starting principle is the acceptance of the thesis stated by H.-G. Gadamer (in his *Wahrheit und Methode* Tübingen 1973[3]) that a modern reader is bound to understand the meaning of an ancient author in a way different from the one which that author intended. This barrier led Gadamer to enunciate the principle that interpretation inevitably includes translation from one situation to another, and that the modern interpreter should ask what the text is saying to him in his situation. Basically the approach of existential hermeneutics is: Granted that the text meant such-and-such to its first writer and his readers, what does the text mean to me today even though I cannot share the presuppositions of that ancient situation and am separated by a barrier of world-view and culture from that old-world scene? Put otherwise, this method of exegesis asks, What would the ancient author have meant by his words if he had been living in our contemporary situation and how does he speak to us today? We can hear his message by taking what we think to be *his* meaning given long ago and bringing it over (trans-lating) into our frame of reference. The chief exponent of this way of looking at and listening to Scripture is E. Fuchs. See further pp. 308ff.

But it would be wrong to imagine that this method has gained general currency outside a limited constituency. Opponents of Bultmann (e.g. O. Cullmann, whose teaching on salvation history is based on the priority of the grammatico-historical method), insist that we must listen to what the New Testament meant to its first readers and give that our obedience however unpalatable and "strange" its message may be. Writing from within the Bultmannian school, E. Käsemann objects that the existential exegetical method may lead to serious distortions of what the New Testament is all about and set up a new norm by which the New Testament message is required to be tested.[7]

One important way of bridging the gap between the poles of reading the New Testament in order to ascertain the first century meaning and arriving at the contemporary application of that message is the approach known as the seeking of *sensus plenior*. By this term is meant the deeper meaning of the text, a meaning not apparently intended by the author but seen to be intended by God when we have regard to the further light which is shed on the text by developing revelation.[8]

A good example of this method is the exegesis of Old Testament "Messianic" prophecies (e.g. Is. 7:14) which yield their full meaning to the Christian believer when he reads them in the light of interpretation given by the New Testament writers (e.g. Mt. 1:23). There is much value in this approach inasmuch as the New Testament itself encourages its readers to see larger fulfilments of what appeared only in embryo or in part in the Old Testament revelation (Heb. 1:1–3). But some firm control is needed, and the principle of *sensus plenior* is misused if it opens the door to the notion of a tandem relationship between Scripture and tradition (even in the modified form suggested by Y. M.-J. Congar[9]) or suggests that the later church has power to sanction as authoritative for Christian doctrine ideas and dogmas which are held to be latent in Scripture and subsequently elevated to the status of "articles of belief".[10] The criteria by which we may decide what constitutes *sensus plenior* are (a) an authorization in the New Testament which gives warrant to the "fuller sense" to be accorded to an Old Testament passage. This credential would have the effect of placing the Old Testament teaching in a wider context, and making it germane for the history of salvation (e.g. the Immanuel prophecies in Isaiah). Then (b) the New Testament's "larger fulfilment" should be congruous with the literal sense. Examples of the possible homogeneity of two passages may be given in the prophetic psalms 2 and 110 where the original setting in the Israelite monarchy is capable of wider and deeper application to "great David's greater Son".

A more cautious way of framing the interrelation between the Old Testament preparation for Christ and the fulfilment in the New is in terms of *typology*.[11] According to this method the emphasis is shifted from the *words* in the Old Testament passages which are thought to contain hidden truth (which later became clarified through further revelation) to *events* or *things* described in the Old Testament which are the subject of interpretative commentary in the New. Thus we are encouraged to see in a series of historical happenings (the Passover, the manna, the bronze serpent) and persons (Adam, Melchizedek, Moses, David) the types (for the word *typos* see Rom. 5:14 and for the adverb *typikōs* see 1 Cor. 10:11) of the later events in the ministry of Jesus and the explications of the ways in which his person and work were understood.

5. SALVATION HISTORY

This brings us to consider the method which goes right to the heart of the Christian concern with Scripture, particularly the New Testament. We may express it in terms of *salvation history*.[12] Scripture is the record of God's redeeming acts and their interpretation, directed to his people and calculated to evoke their response in obedience, love and service. The latter part of that statement is important since it is sometimes objected that when "salvation history" is narrowly conceived as a recital of dramatic events of God's redemption it allows no room for the Wisdom literature in the Old Testament, or (say) the hortatory sections in Paul or the Epistle of James in the New Testament. But these portions in the hortatory sections in Paul or in the Epistle of James are to be classified under man's total response to the grace of God and his salvation. The response is as wide-ranging as the revelation of God and covers the whole of life.

Yet even with this caveat it still remains true that the multiform character of the New Testament does not permit us to erect a "canon within the canon" to the exclusion of some parts of the corpus which do not apparently relate to the person and place of Jesus Christ. We may want to give emphasis to those parts of the New Testament which (as Luther said) "present Christ bright and clear" and so which "promote Christ". And in our study of any given passage we should do well to begin with the question of what the section may have to say to us about Jesus Christ as the focus of God's saving purpose for the world and the church. But we may have to admit in all candour that the christological teaching is absent in any given section (e.g. James). However, we shall place an appropriate value on that passage and see it in the total perspective of the New Testament. In this case, it will have something to say to us as we enquire why it was that James raised the objection that "faith without works is dead", perhaps in the context of a misunderstanding of Paul's teaching of *sola gratia, sola fide* and of a travesty of his gospel which turned freedom from the law into antinomianism and libertinism (as in Rom. 3:8; 6:1ff.).

The important guiding principle is that we should seek to begin with the text in its original setting and try to ascertain all we can about the occasion of its teaching. Then we shall be in a good position to read off the application (if any) of that teaching for our situation. Isolated verses taken from their context should be handled with caution (though there is no denying that the Lord of the Scripture may speak to his people in exceptional ways, however much we may wish to hedge about the random method of Bible selection and indicate its hidden pitfalls to the unwary). More safety is found in the sense of a larger unity of Scripture – a paragraph, a whole incident or a book of the New Testament. The recognition that the passage had a message for its readers long before we set eyes on it will save us from presumption and arrogance (as though the Scripture were written primarily for our sakes: see 1 Cor. 14:36). This salutary reminder is an effective answer to both dogmatism and impressionism.

The rigorous application of the grammatico-historical method will place a check on any tendency either to personal idiosyncrasy in wanting to read into the text what we wish it would say or a spiritualizing of the Bible which allows its message to float in an undefined vacuum and untethered to the historical events of the process of God's activity in salvation. That activity is located in the time-and-space framework of the history of Jesus Christ and the apostolic church; and whether we like it or not we are shut up to this segment of world history for the locus of redemption and its inspired interpretation. The New Testament both tells the story and supplies the key to the story. For that reason it remains the indispensable source of our knowledge of God and his ways with men.

II. *Some Principles of Exegesis*

We turn now to consider some principles of interpretation which should be kept in view as we approach any given passage. First, the principles will be stated in the form of questions; then, we shall devote the remainder of the essay to some illustrations of the type of literature which is found in the New Testament.

1. LITERARY FORM

We may first ask the general question, what is the literary form (technically known as *genus litterarium*) of the several New Testament documents? The twenty-seven books of the New Testament are not written in the same genre and it is important to know the chief classifications of the New Testament "library" of books. One question regarding classification has to do with the precise type of writing known as "gospel". Is it an attempted "Life of Jesus" on the analogy of contemporary parallels in the ancient world (such as Plutarch's *Lives*)? Or does the first Christian Gospel (usually taken to be Mark) fall into no category for which antiquity can produce a parallel? If so, is this unique literary type of writing the way we should classify the later Gospels (*e.g.* Luke) which both follow Mark's general outline and add features of a more "biographical" nature which are not found in Mark?

A similar question has to be faced in regard to the segment of the New Testament literature which goes under the caption of "letters". Are they pieces of private correspondence between (say) Paul and the churches? Or were they composed consciously for publication and so fall into the category of "epistles" (as Deissmann once suggested in his well-known discussion of the two classes of epistolary writing in the hellenistic world)? According to the decision taken in this matter, questions touching the manner of Paul's composition, i.e. whether his letters were "occasional writings" composed in the urgency of the moment or carefully constructed discourses arranged with regard to some well-attested literary forms of the day and showing evidence of a polished style, will have to be considered. Either way, there is the problem set by the possibility that Paul may have used a scribe to take down his oral messages. Indeed the existence of an amanuensis is seen in Romans 16:22. Then, it becomes a matter of some importance to know how much freedom Paul gave to a man such as Tertius and whether the forms of speech and the actual words used are Paul's own or whether he permitted his scribe to fill in the skeleton he suggested and gave the final product his approval when he came to append his signature. The latter method of scribal freedom is found in our knowledge of writing methods in the Graeco-Roman world.[13]

2. BACKGROUND

We can now turn to consider the literary problems presented by a given text or passage in one of the books of the New Testament by asking, what do the words mean in their obvious background? Sometimes this background will be clearly the Old Testament as when the text is written in conscious imitation of the poetry of the Old Testament psalms or in a Septuagintal style or with the use of expressions which are identifiable as Semitic (e.g. hyperbole, gnomic or pithy sayings, liturgical formulas). At other times, the setting will be that of the Graeco-Roman world, as evidenced by snatches of hellenistic philosophy, lines from the Greek theatre or the use of language which is seen in the non-literary papyri.[14]

3. CULTURAL SETTING

What is the cultural setting of the passage and how is it illumined by knowing something of the customs, traditions, folk-lore of the people who play a part in the narrative or who were the audiences for whom the sayings or the writing were intended?[15] At a deeper level, we shall need to enquire about the religious and theological milieu in which the people of the story stood and to learn something of the presuppositions (e.g. cosmological ideas, belief in evil spirits) which informed those religious beliefs.

4. THEOLOGICAL PURPOSE

Above all, we must ask what is the theological purpose of the author and how does he express it.[16] Underlying our attempted exegesis will be the desire to learn what theological motivation (called a *Tendenz*) has inspired the writer. Only in this way can we hope to appreciate the meaning which he intended in his recording (say) of a parable of Jesus or a piece of descriptive narration or a statement of religious conviction. This does not imply that we think that the New Testament writers had an ulterior motive in their presentations. But it does insist that no New Testament author wrote without some definite purpose in view. Sometimes the purpose is openly declared (e.g. Lk. 1:1–4; Jn. 20:31; Col. 2:2–4; 1 Tim. 1:3ff.; 1 Jn. 2:1, 7, 12; 5:13) and at other times it has to be teased out of the overall writing of the author as well as discovered by a close inspection of the contextual setting of his individual verses.

Another matter which is raised sometimes acutely for the modern reader of the gospels emerges from the recognition that these evangelists were also theologians in their own right. It was not their purpose simply to reproduce the life and teaching of Jesus in a detached and neutral way. They were men of Christian faith who wrote to confirm the faith of their readers and quite probably to refute some erroneous teaching which had appeared in the churches. The implicit refutation of docetism which lies in the background of John's Gospel with its full stress on Jesus' humanity is a case in point.

Many students, however, find problems with another part of this understanding of the gospel tradition. Source criticism has shown more or less conclusively that the evangelists used materials from the traditions they took over, and redaction criticism has added the supplementary consideration that the evangelists were not simply transmitters of that tradition but the first commentators on it. Their work as editors implies that they adapted and shaped the tradition in order to bring it into line with their own theological purpose. It is this study of the pre-history of the gospel records which causes some important questions to be asked. Specifically, it is asked whether our exegesis is concerned with recovering "what actually happened" in the story and "what Jesus really said" by pressing behind the gospel data which include (in this view) the evangelists' interpretations and editorial work. An example is the way in which many modern scholars treat the parables of Jesus. We are faced with a recoverable setting of the stories in Jesus' own ministry. But in addition the text both contains a transposed setting in the life and activity of the early church and evinces a certain embellishment to make the original message of Jesus relevant to life situations in the later church. The question at issue is how much concern should the modern exegete show about these adaptations and modifications which are attributable to the early church's interest.

As a general principle – and we may refer to other sections of this book to discuss the points in detail – we may concede that our interest should be a double one. In so far as we can press back to recover the *ipsissima verba* of Jesus, or at least to catch the overtone of his *ipsissima vox* which may or may not be the same thing,[17] we must do so. For by this route of enquiry we are assured of being in touch with the historical centre of our faith, the earthly Jesus as he walked and talked in Palestine. But it is a serious mistake to think that we should discard as worthless the testimony of the early Christians which has become woven, often inextricably, into the narrative. That interpretative evidence has its own value as a witness, at once inspired and authoritative, to what the first Christians believed and taught about their Lord or how they responded to the original version of his teaching. To that extent both strata of the gospel tradition have their distinctive roles to play and they should not be set in antithesis.

Nor is it it a wise course to overlook the way in which several parts of the New Testament were written against diverse backgrounds. An example of this feature might be given in the use of the terms "faith" and "works" in Paul and James. Neither writer is saying exactly the same thing by these words. Conceivably, as we have mentioned, James is correcting a defective understanding of Paul's teaching on the part of his followers. Or we can cite the important place given to "righteousness" in Matthew's gospel which looks as though the term there is a conscious rebuttal of the false notion of "righteousness by faith" in the hands of some misguided Christians who turned Paul's teaching into antinomian licence by supposing that Gentile Christians were free to live as they pleased (see Rom. 3:31; 6:1ff.; Gal. 5:13–15; 2 Pet. 2:17–22 in the light of 2 Pet. 3:16).[18]

In effect, this caution means that every section of the New Testament must be interpreted in the light of the larger context of the overall purpose and plan of the book of which it forms a part, and according to the purpose for which it was intended. Often the purpose of individual verses can only be known as we see the fuller purpose of the book or the epistle, and (paradoxically) the specific reason for writing is found in the sum of the individual verses. This is the hermeneutical circle in which the modern interpreter finds himself.[19]

An example of this inter-relation of the whole and the parts is the book of the Revelation. Starting from the premise (which in turn is deducible from an examination of the chapters of the book) that this book of the New Testament belongs to the literary genre of apocalyptic (see later, p. 234f.), we may state that its primary purpose is that of the encouragement and strengthening of the afflicted people of God as they undergo trial and persecution. This conclusion is borne out by an inspection of individual verses (e.g. 2:10; 13:10; 14:12) and thus it becomes a principle which helps us to interpret the message of the whole book.

III. *Literary Forms and Styles*

We turn now to pass under review specimen *exempla* of the chief literary forms which are found in the New Testament. Obviously some choice will have to be made in this selection; and what governs that choice is the need to single out such material as requires some comment if we are to be helped in the task of exegesis. The literary forms, then, will not be discussed in their own right as examples drawn from ancient literature but rather as data contributing to a fuller appreciation of Scripture as God's word to man. That word was written in the style and manner of a first century writing. Our task is to throw some light on the literary usages which the New Testament writers employed as an aid to a clearer exegesis.

1. GENRE

The literature of the New Testament falls into four categories as we classify it according to its literary genre: gospel, acts, epistle and apocalypse.

(a) The literary type of "acts" need not detain us for the purposes of our discussion. The term *πράξεις* is known to have been applied to some biographical works in antiquity but the author of the writing *ad Theophilum* does not use the word. He uses *λόγος* for his first volume (Acts 1:1) and he calls the work of predecessors in that field by the title of "stories", *διηγήσει*. The canonical title of "The Acts of the Apostles" was added later to the second volume in the Lucan corpus and it seems "if anything an effort to describe the contents rather than the form".[20] The later apocryphal Acts get their name from the Lucan model, and in both instances there does not seem to be any adherence to a stereotyped literary form in the choice of this title.

(b) The term "gospel" is restricted in the New Testament to the activity and substance of the early Christian preaching. "To preach the gospel" (Mk. 1:14; 1 Cor. 1:17; Gal. 1:11) is a common expression. The New Testament invariably connects "gospel" (i.e. the announcement of good news) with verbs of speaking and responding, and never with verbs of writing and reading. Even where the meaning is slightly ambiguous (2 Cor. 8:18, AV) there is no indication that the early Christians thought of the gospel as a written composition. "Evangelist" in this period meant a herald, a proclaimer of good news, and not a scribe busy with his reed-pen.

One of the earliest designations of the gospel records was "memoirs" (Justin Martyr), but this term did not remain in vogue. Instead, the Christians of the second and third centuries coined the title "Gospels" for these books.[21]

The reason for this is important, and provides a vital key to a reading of the "gospels" today. No Christian "biographer" thought that he was preserving by his literary records the memory of Jesus, which might otherwise lapse and be forgotten. To imagine this is to overlook the Christian belief in the risen Lord whose living presence was assured to the church in every generation. It is true that Christians may well have desired a permanent account of Jesus' earthly life, words and activity, especially since his first followers were being removed from the scene by death with the passing of the first generation. But it still remains a factor of considerable importance in our understanding of primitive Christianity that the church's thought and life were not oriented to the past as though the believers were harking back to some lost "golden age" when Jesus was here among men. His living presence was vouchsafed by the Spirit and was made a present reality as often as they acted upon his promise (Mt. 18:20; 28:19, 20) and broke bread "in remembrance of" him (1 Cor. 11:24f.).

So the first account of Jesus' ministry (the outline of it may be seen in skeletal form in Acts 10:37–41) boldly carried as its title: Beginning of the gospel of Jesus Christ, Son of God (Mark 1:1). Consistently thereafter through Mark's account the term "gospel" refers to the content of the proclaimed message which was designed to tell the story of God's saving action in Jesus and of the human response to it. In this way the "gospels" received their name because they gave the substance of the "gospel", declared in Romans 1:16 to be God's power to salvation for all who believe.

This, we may submit, is the first principle of gospel interpretation. We place a high value on these four books because they contain the essence of the saving events which formed the bedrock of the apostolic gospel. They are kerygmatic (i.e. announcing the good news and calling for a decision in regard to it) in nature and evangelical in design (i.e. intended to lead to faith in Jesus Christ, according to Jn. 20:31). They are historical in the way in which they root the life-story of Jesus in the world of first century Judaism and the times of Graeco-Roman civilization, but it is history with a distinct bias.

The history of Jesus is reported from a particular and individualistic perspective in order to show the kerygmatic side of that history. That means that the separate sections (the *pericopae*) and the gospels seen as whole books were intended to direct their readers' faith to a living person, once localized in Galilee and Jerusalem but now set free from all earthly limitation, and exalted as Lord of heaven and earth as the one in whom alone salvation is to be found. We might describe this history as salvation-history or perhaps better as "interpreted history", that is, history angled in such a way as to bring out the present significance of Jesus as the living Lord, accessible to all who call upon him, and as the exemplar of faith who trod a road of victory through suffering which his followers in every age are bidden to take. This last mentioned feature of the gospel story suggests to A. N. Wilder that the truest genre of the Christian gospels is re-enacted history centred on a faith-story in which Christ is recalled as a pattern of meaning or orientation for the believer.[22] The element of "mimesis" or re-enactment implies that history is recalled not as a record of the past valuable for its own sake but in order to contemporize Christ who comes out of the past to greet his people in the present.

(c) The major part of the New Testament corpus as regards size falls into the category of "epistle".[23] As early Christianity spread across the Mediterranean basin and churches were formed in different localities it became necessary for lines of communication to be extended between the various centres. In this way the role played by epistolary correspondence assumed an importance spoken of by Polycarp in his description of Paul's contact with the Philippians:

> During his residence with you he gave the men of those days clear and sound instruction in the word of truth, while he was there in person among you; and even after his departure he still sent letters which, if you will study them attentively,

will enable you to make progress in the faith which was delivered to you (*To the Philippians* 3:2).

The fact of apostolic instruction by letter has produced a type of writing for which there are no ancient parallels. "The letter of Christian instruction was in fact almost as distinctive a Christian contribution to literary types as the written gospel." [24]

While this statement may be true in the strict sense of letters composed for a didactic purpose, the format and style of Paul's letters follow conventional patterns known to us from methods of letter-writing in the hellenistic world. There were four parties involved: the author, the secretary, the messenger, and the recipient. Three questions are important as they impinge upon the exegetical task of understanding the New Testament epistles.

First, the two types of correspondence described by Deissmann need to be borne in mind. He distinguished between an epistle, which is a conscious literary effort intended for publication, and a letter, which is private in character, written for a specific occasion and of ephemeral duration. If we accept this distinction, it seems that the New Testament pieces of correspondence without exception fall into the former category. Many signs in the epistles point in this direction. (*a*) Paul and Peter compose in a carefully thought-out style, the evidence for which we shall see later. John's first epistle contains recurring patterns of thought which have bewildered the commentators but the overall impression is that John is pursuing certain lines of pastoral counsel with deliberate intention. (*b*) Apostolic authority runs through the major epistles of Paul showing that he was conscious of his teaching office as "apostle to the Gentiles". This is true even in those parts of Pauline correspondence which are usually regarded as his "tender" pastoral letters (Philippians: see 1:1; 2:12; 3:17) and private communications (the note to Philemon is addressed to the church in his house, verse 2, and speaks of Paul as an ambassador, verse 9). (*c*) Paul intends that his letters will be read out in assemblies of Christian worship (1 Thes. 5:27) and will circulate among other Christian groups as they are sent on from the addressees (Col. 4:16). (*d*) He has in his mind's eye a picture of the church assembled for public worship as he writes (1 Cor. 5:1ff.; Col. 2:5) and in greeting one part of the church in his epistle he takes into account also the wider company of the church in every place (1 Cor. 1:2). This vision of an "ecumenical" church (as in 1 Pet. 1:1, 5:9; Jas. 1:1) enforces the belief that these epistles are all "catholic" inasmuch as their scope reaches out to embrace the Christian brotherhood in the world. Perhaps the only exceptions to this rule are 2 and 3 John, which seem to be individual.

Secondly, Paul and Peter both make reference to a scribe (Rom. 16:22; 1 Pet. 5:12); and this has raised the question of how much liberty these men were allowed in the actual composing of the epistles. O. Roller's thesis has been mentioned. According to this, letter-writing in the ancient world was left to professionals who took down in shorthand the substance of the author's thought and later, at their leisure since transcribing was a laborious business, wrote up the letter. Then the completed letter was presented to the author for final approval and signature. In this way Roller reconstructed the manner in which some of Paul's epistles came into being. But he also maintains that there is evidence for Paul's activity in writing the whole letter, as in Colossians 4:18 where no scribe is mentioned. But this is offset by other pieces of evidence, notably in the places where he seems to be adding his final words (Gal. 6:11), appending his autograph (Col. 4:18), or supplying a signature as a proof of authenticity (2 Thes. 3:17). It has been claimed that the mark of his revising hand is apparent in (e.g.) 2 Cor. 8:23f. with its broken syntax and in a sentence which has no main verb.

The "secretary hypothesis" has been invoked to account for the excellent literary style of 1 Peter as well as the unusual features of word usage and style in the Pastoral epistles.[25] Certainly 1 Peter 5:12 gives more information than do the Pauline letters about the status of the scribe, though it is premature for some scholars to conclude on the strength of this that "the vocabulary and style are not decisive criteria for settling its authenticity" since the secretary *ex hypothesi* took part in the composition of an epistle.[26] W. G. Kümmel has entered some important caveats regarding this theory, namely that frequent breaks and interruptions in the flow of the epistles (e.g. Phil. 3:1f.) show that these are due to pauses in dictation and that the scribe is writing the letter directly from Paul's lips. Also he appeals to a consistency of language throughout the Pauline homologoumena, which suggests that even with scribal assistance it is the real Paul whose personality and teaching comes through the various pieces of his correspondence.[27] On the other hand, Roller objects that Paul's style is "mixed" and runs into that of his amanuensis.[28]

Thirdly, there is a matter which offers more tangible help in the task of Pauline exegesis. This is the apostle's custom of using a form of epistolary thanksgiving in the opening section of his epistles. The investigation of P. Schubert[29] called attention to the use by Paul of the formula, "I thank God for . . ." or "I thank God upon . . ." The two points which this discussion established were (*a*) that as a consistent rule Paul uses the construction of the verb and the preposition ἐπί with the dative case as a way of introducing the cause for which thanks are offered; and (*b*) that, in the epistles, the thanksgiving period introduces "the vital theme of the letter" or "the epistolary situation". This discussion throws considerable light on the exegesis of Philippians 1:3 and makes very probable the interpretation that Paul is thanking God for all the remembrance the Philippians have had of him, i.e. by their support of his ministry and sending of gifts to him. See Moffatt's translation. This view, if accepted, disposes of the objection often brought against the unity of the Philippian letter that Paul would not have waited until chapter 4 to say "Thank you" for the gift brought by Epaphroditus. On this reading of the text, his opening word is one of acknowledgement and it introduces the "epistolary situation" of the letter.

J. T. Sanders has pursued this line of enquiry and maintains that the epistolary thanksgivings are borrowed from the liturgical prayers of the community after the model of the Qumran community's Hymns.[30] This *hodaya* formula expressing thankfulness to God reflects Paul's conscious sense of oneness with the worshipping body of Christ,[31] and both in his use of *hodaya* (I thank God) and *beracha* (Blessed be (God)) he is drawing upon the liturgical vocabulary of the churches which in turn was modelled on Jewish prayer forms (1 Macc. 4:30–33; Genesis Apocryphon col. 20, lines 12ff.) and later set the pattern for early Christian liturgies (e.g. Polycarp, *Mart.* 14; Didache, 9, 10; Acts of Thomas; 1 Clement 59–61; Apostolic Constitutions 7).[32] The upshot of this investigation is to demonstrate that Paul's prayer-speech and his requests for the communities were not as spontaneous and *ad hoc* as is sometimes thought, but that he was consciously following Jewish patterns as a framework into which he fitted his exposition of the Christian gospel. And all this served a didactic purpose in that he intended to teach the congregation by means of the liturgical formularies which were the common property of the churches. The importance of this conclusion will be apparent when we come to consider Paul's use of Christian hymns in his epistles.

(d) The fourth literary genre is apocalyptic. The presence of this type of Jewish material is found in the synoptic apocalypses (Mark 13; Matthew 24; Luke 21), 2 Thessalonians 2 and the book of Revelation. It is a necessity for an understanding of these passages that the Old Testament and intertestamental background should be appreciated (e.g. Is. 24–27; Zc. 9–14; Joel 2, 3 and especially the section of Dan. 7–12 in the canonical Old Testament; and such specimens of "apocalyptic" literature as Enoch, Baruch, 4 Ezra and the Assumption of Moses which came out of the period of the two centuries before Jesus and possibly span his lifetime).[33]

The similarities of the New Testament apocalypses to the Jewish counterparts are important to notice, even if there are important differences. In the area of likeness, there are the obvious features that both examples of this genre of literature share a common religious purpose, namely (*a*) to strengthen the faith of God's people under trial and in anticipation of the decisive intervention of God which will be the dénouement of history and the ushering in of the rule of God over all the world; and (*b*) to express this message of consolation and hope against a background of dualism[34] in which, according to the time-scheme of the two ages, this age is one of wickedness and persecution for the saints of God and the age to come is one of triumph and vindication. There is, then, a double vision in apocalyptic writing. Through the historical circumstances of the clash of earthly powers[35] the reader is meant to see the nature of the real engagement between God and evil in the universe.[36]

Because the seer's vision includes both the earthly and the heavenly worlds the language he uses is circumscribed, since he can only describe events ostensibly set in the heavenly region in a language appropriate to the earthly scene (e.g. what does Rev. 12:7 mean, if literally applied to the upper world?). This is the problem of communication which the apocalyptist solves by his recourse to the language of symbolism, the use of imagery, the employment of mythological forms and anthropomorphisms. The book of

Revelation is replete with examples of all these accommodations (e.g. symbolic values attached to numbers in the descriptions of 7:4; 11:3; 12:6 and 20:3; the imagery of colour in ch. 4 and ch. 17; mythological ideas of the dragon and the serpent in 12:7, which are interpreted for the reader in 20:2; and pictures of the celestial Christ dressed in human form 1:13–16; 19:11–16). Unless we recognize the dramatic quality of this writing and recall the way in which language is being used as a vehicle to express religious truth, we shall grievously err in our understanding of the Apocalypse, and mistakenly try to interpret its visions as though it were a book of literal prose and concerned to describe events of empirical and datable history. To attempt the latter course is to run into all manner of problems of interpretation. More seriously it leads to a distortion of the essential meaning of apocalyptic and so misses the great value of this part of the New Testament as a dramatic assertion in mythopoetic language of the sovereignty of God in Christ and the paradox of his rule which blends might and love (see 5:5, 6: the Lion is the Lamb).

2. HYMNIC AND POETIC FORMS

One distinct advantage of reading the Old Testament in a modern version is that one is able to see at a glance which parts of the text are cast in poetic and hymnic style. The canonical Psalms are the obvious illustration, but by no means are poetry and hymnody restricted to these psalms. Judges 5 is possibly the earliest example of poetry in the Hebrew Bible, and the song of Miriam (Ex. 15) is set in quasi-hymnic form.

(a) The reader of the New Testament needs the same guidance to show him at a moment's glance what are the poetic portions of the literature. The more apparent examples come in Luke 1, 2 which preserve some early canticles doubtless treasured in the Jewish Christian community, and possibly forming part of their liturgical worship. These are the *Magnificat* (Lk. 1:45–55), the *Benedictus* (Lk. 1:68–79), and the *Nunc Dimittis* (Lk. 2:29–32). All the Latin titles are drawn from the opening words of the poetic pieces. Examples of Hebrew poetic forms [37] are to be seen in these canticles. Synonymous parallelism appears in Luke 1:46, 47:

My soul magnifies the Lord,
and my spirit rejoices in God my Saviour.

And to recognize this usage is to avoid the mistake of trying to distinguish anthropologically between "soul" and "spirit" in this text. The two terms are used synonymously.

(i) Antithetical parallelism shines through a later verse of the *Magnificat* (1:52). There is a good example of this feature in Luke 2:14. In the angelic jubilation known as the *Gloria in Excelsis* the two lines are set in direct contrast, corresponding to the two spheres of acknowledgement:

To God in the highest, glory!
Peace to his people on earth!

Two additional comments may be made on this snatch of Advent celebration. It contains a specimen of chiasmus; the lines cross in their agreements and so form a diagram represented by the Greek letter *chi* (χ). So the phrase "in the highest (heaven)" matches the corresponding antithesis of "on earth" but it is set at a different place on the lines, so forming a cross. There are several other places in the New Testament where chiasmus has been suspected,[38] from the isolated cases in the gospels (e.g. Matt. 7:6[39]) to the elaborate attempt to construct Colossians 1:15–20 in chiastic form.[40]

The other element in Luke 2:14 which comes to light when we have regard to its literary formulation is the sense of Greek *ἐν ἀνθρώποις εὐδοκίας* which is decided by this construction. Apart from the textual difficulty, it cannot now be doubted that the meaning is "Peace on earth to men to whom God shows his mercy", and not "to men who have goodwill" or "all those pleasing him" (The Living Bible). The emphasis must lie on God's activity which unites the two spheres of heaven and earth and so "reconciles" them – a theme which runs through the hymnic confessions of Colossians 1:15–20 and 1 Timothy 3:16 where the chiastic device is pressed into the service of a profound theological interpretation of the restoring work of the cosmic Redeemer.

Antithetical parallelism produces one notable type of sentence which has been closely studied in recent research. This is the form known as "Sentences of Holy Law"[41] and these are all variations of the legal principle of *lex talionis*. The basic form is seen in 1 Corinthians 3:17:

If anyone destroys the temple of God,
God will destroy him.

This is both antithesis, and chiasmus, and expresses in memorable style the apocalyptic judgment formula: destruction to the destroyer. It is the application of this "law" which accounts for the summary verdict pronounced on Ananias and Sapphira (Acts 5:1–11). From this initial premise Käsemann launches into a full discussion of the role of charismatic prophets and apostolic authority in the New Testament church and throws some light on the eschatological dimension which is presupposed in many prescriptive standards (e.g. in the Gospels, Mark 8:38; in Paul, 1 Cor. 14:37; in the Apocalypse, Rev. 22:18f.).

(ii) The Hebrew custom of setting two lines side by side, or two stichos in the same line, is called by the Latin term *parallelismus membrorum;* and there are several examples of this feature in Paul and Peter. The device plays a significant theological role, when the early Christians developed the christological scheme of setting side by side the two stages of Christ's "existence". He was described as Man by his incarnation; and as exalted Lord by his enthronement to God's presence. The formula for this is given as *κατὰ σάρκα/κατὰ πνεῦμα.* Examples are seen in Romans 1:3ff:

Born of the family of David on his human side,
Appointed Son of God from the resurrection of the dead
by the power of holy spirit

and, at greater length, in 1 Timothy 3:16 and 1 Peter 3:18–22. The verse 1 Peter 1:20 is an example of a *parallelismus membrorum,* which utilizes the themes of pre-existence/incarnation, and employs the good classical form of contrast μὲν. . . δὲ. . .):

Foreknown before the world's foundation,
Revealed at the end of time for your sake.

One or two fragments of credal formulation apply the same form to a statement of soteriology, as in 1 Corinthians 15:3bff.:

Christ died for our sins
according to the Scriptures;
Christ was raised on the third day
according to the Scriptures

or Romans 4:25:

Who was handed over on account of our trespasses,
But raised in proof of our justification.

(iii) This last mentioned verse also incorporates an Old Testament feature of considerable exegetical value. It is the "divine passive".[42] There are excellent grounds for believing that this mode of expression, i.e. using the passive voice of a verb to denote the hidden action of God as the agent responsible for the activity, was characteristic of Jesus' way of speaking. A feature which began as a reverential way of avoiding the use of the sacred name of God was picked up in the apocalyptic literature and used as a concealed way of expressing divine secrets; and it became customary, with an extended usage, on Jesus' lips. He uses it over 100 times (Jeremias, p. 11) and some of the best examples are Matthew 5:4: "Blessed are those who mourn, for God will comfort them", or Luke 12:7: "All the hairs of your head are numbered (by God)." These are fairly obvious illustrations, once we grasp the principle involved. A less clear case, but with equal theological weight, is in Mark 1:14: "Now after John had been handed over (by God to his fate), Jesus came . . ."[43] where Mark's intention is to suggest a deliberate parallel between John's fate and the destiny of the Son of man who will at last be delivered by God into the hands of sinners (Mk. 9:31, 14:41). In a similar vein we should understand Romans 4:25 and 1 Corinthians 11:23: "The Lord Jesus on the night when he was handed over (to his fateful destiny by God) . . ."[44]

(iv) Snatches of hymnody based on the Old Testament model are seen in the Apocalypse of John. Scattered through the series of visions are songs of the heavenly world (Rev. 4:11; 11:17, 18; 14:7; 15:3, 4). While these lines are placed on the lips of the heavenly worshippers, it is likely that in their form they betray the influence of the synagogues of the Greek-speaking world of the Dispersion.[45] The most illustrious example of these instances, however, is the ejaculation which became embedded in the Christian liturgy of the later church. From the opening words of Revelation 4:8 it is known as the *Ter Sanctus* – the Thrice Holy:

Holy, holy, holy is the Lord God Almighty,
Who was and is and is to come.[46]

(b) Poetic and hymnic forms were more consciously adopted and made the vehicle of theological expression in the era when the church moved out into the hellenistic world. Three prime examples of this style of writing are seen in the Pauline corpus. In each case there are good grounds for thinking that Paul is quoting from some independent source and using a piece of Christian liturgy (in some cases suitably edited by him) to enforce a point of teaching.

(i) 1 Timothy 3:16

The chief literary feature here is the use of antithesis to express two stages of Christ's existence. These are denoted, as we have seen, by the terms: flesh/spirit (cf. 2 Cor. 5:16 for the formula).

Since the pioneering work of E. Norden,[47] other literary forms have been detected in this short, creed-like statement. The authority for these forms is the rhetorian Quintilian in his *Institutio Oratoria*. The repetition of the verb at the beginning of each line and in the same grammatical form produces a species of rhythm known as *parison* and *homoioptoton* (*Inst. Or*. ix. 3. 76, 78). In the first couplet the verbs have the same syllabic length (5 beats) and this leads to *isocolon* (*Inst. Or*. ix. 3. 80). Moreover, the phrases which close the lines of the couplet:

ἐν σαρκί (in the flesh)
ἐν πνεύματι (in the spirit)

have a similar sound in their ending and this device is known as *homoioteleuton* (*Inst. Or*. ix. 3. 77). These poetic forms make the short verse one of the most precious instances of a literary piece in the entire New Testament.[48]

(ii) Ephesians 5:14

This single verse provides another good example of Greek poetic structure. The text of this baptismal chant divides into three lines (a feature unfortunately overlooked by RSV) and there is a swinging trochaic rhythm which cannot be reproduced exactly in English. The nearest we get to it is offered in the translation:

Awake, O sleeper,
From the grave arise.
The light of Christ upon you shines.

Even that rendering fails to capture the assonance of the final syllables of lines i and ii:

ὁ καθεύδων
ἐκ τῶν νεκρῶν

which employs the device of *homoioptoton*. It is interesting that it was precisely this triplet-form which was used in the initiation chants of the hellenistic mystery cults (especially the Attis formula[49]) and in the Hermetic literature.

(iii) Philippians 2:6–11

This text yields to the same literary analysis. Since Lohmeyer's study [50] this passage has been recognized as hymnic in form and capable of division into strophes. Lohmeyer postulated six such stanzas. Later attempts to improve on this arrangement produced a three strophe hymn in which the device of *parallelismus membrorum* was utilized and a tacit acceptance was given to Aristotle's judgment that a perfect literary composition requires "a beginning, a middle and an end" (*Poetics* 1450b 26). This is held to correspond to the three states of Christ: pre-existent, incarnate, enthroned. [51] The permanent contribution of Jeremias is that, in his view, the entire hymn is built up in couplets, though his analysis suffers from some weaknesses. Yet another proposal is to discard the notion of a hymn set in stanzas and to see the passage as structured in the form of a set of antiphonal couplets. [52] When this is done, the several rhetorical and lyrical features which we observed in respect of 1 Timothy 3:16 are also seen to be present in this *carmen Christi;* and the same is true in regard to Colossians 1:15–20 which has been subjected to scrutiny with a view to discovering items of poetic structure such as metrical quantity and syllabic length. According to Ch. Masson, there are patterns of metre in Colossians 1:15–20 which are the result of the regular sequence of syllables and stresses. If his case could be regarded as plausible, this hymn to the cosmic Christ would be the nearest approximation in the New Testament to a Greek poem, with both rhythm and rhyme. But his case has not convinced many readers. [53]

(iv) Some comments on New Testament hymns

It may be thought that the classification of parts of the New Testament according to the basic patterns of poetic and hymnic form is an interesting exercise but nothing more. This is not so; and at least three consequences follow from our conclusion that these passages are set in lyrical form.

First, we are introduced to the worshipping life of the apostolic church and reminded that the church which meets us in the pages of the New Testament is a worshipping company of believing men and women. This is clear from the descriptions in the Acts of the Apostles (1:42; 2:42, 46; 4:31; 5:12, 42; 13:1–3; 20:7–12) as well as from the statements of Paul in his letters (notably 1 Cor. 10–14). Since the post-Pentecostal church and the Pauline mission churches still retained the first flush of enthusiastic experience and the dynamism of a new-found awareness of God, it is not unexpected that this new life imparted by faith in the exalted Lord by the Holy Spirit and expressed in a "conquering newborn joy" would find an outlet and vehicle in religious song. [54] For the modern reader it is a fact of some importance that our study of the documents of the early church is not simply a piece of academic research or an investigation of principles and practice of Christian belief and behaviour in a clinically detached and "scientific" way. Rather we are reading the literature of a highly charged religious movement, which was conscious of living in days of God's special grace and which reflected that awareness of the divine presence and power in an uprush of spiritual energy. The literary deposits of that activity are to be seen in the fragments of creed-like hymns and confessions which lie just beneath the surface of the literature and which put us into touch with pulsating life in the apostolic communities.

Then, we see that much of the hymnic language is poetic and suggestive of deep spiritual reality rather than prosaic and pedestrian. The early Christians, giving vent to their deepest emotions as these were stirred by God's Spirit (as we learn from 1 Cor. 14:13ff., 26ff.; Eph. 5:19 and Col. 3:16: it has been maintained that glossolalia was a form of rhapsodic prayer-speech "sung with the spirit"), were seeking to interpret their understanding of God's salvation in Christ in a way which defied rational and coherent statement. Hence they had recourse to the language of symbol and "myth". Examples of the symbolism used in the hymns will come readily to mind, e.g. the imagery of light and darkness; Christ is likened to the sun which banished gloom and the shadows; the totality of the universe is summed up in phrases such as "every knee should bow, in heaven and on earth and under the earth" (Phil. 2:10), or "thrones or dominions or principalities or authorities" (Col. 1:16). Exegetical questions which are raised by these sonorous descriptions are more satisfactorily negotiated if we remember that Paul's language is consciously poetic. Otherwise, we shall be hard pressed to say exactly what is meant by demonic forces located in subterranean regions or to explain how Christ's death on the cross of Calvary in Jerusalem at a specific time in history affected the astral deities which hellenistic man thought of as controlling his fate and destiny. Paul is dealing with very real problems – specifically the overthrow of evil and the relaxing of the grip which planetary powers exercised over his readers when they were still victims of bad religion under the tyranny of "the elemental spirits of the universe" (Col. 2:8, 20); but he is couching his thought-forms in a language which his fellow-believers would appreciate and learn from; and in some cases he is borrowing concepts and terms from his opponents' vocabulary, and either arguing *ad hominem* for the sake of his churches or disinfecting the terms by placing them in his own frame of reference. This is very noticeable in Colossians 1:15–20. See the references given in footnotes 53 and 58.

This brings us to the vexed question of "myth". Some scholars deny outright that the New Testament makes use of myth at all, and there are substantial grounds for this conviction.[55] Myth is set in antithesis to truth, and the New Testament is shown to be exclusively concerned with the record of "divine fact with all the weight of historical reality" (Stählin, loc. cit., p. 786). There is no denying the force of the assertion that if "myth" means non-historical make-believe or fairy tales or the product of the human inventiveness, there is no evidence that the writers interpreted the gospel in this way. Quite the opposite, as the Pastoral Epistles (1 Tim. 1:4, 4:7; 2 Tim. 4:4) make clear. But if the term "myth" is differently defined and regarded as a language-form needed to express in human terms and with human analogies the transcendent world of God and angels and spirits, then it seems that we *must* have recourse to pictorial and mythopoetic language. The issue is whether, to avoid confusion, we should use a new term or at least qualify the word "myth".[56] Within this restricted definition we should recognize that Paul and John do use the scaffolding of the story of the heavenly Redeemer who "comes down" from the high God and returns thither after his mission of redemption (Phil. 2:6–11; Jn. 3:31; 6:62). But it is not the use of the framework which is important nor the presence of a kinetic imagery to denote the "movements" of katabasis and anabasis which is vital. Both writers utilize the first century "stage props" and simply use the "myth" to their own ends by re-casting it in terms of a human life of the earthly Jesus whose feet stood firmly on Palestinian soil and who tasted the bitterness of human misery and endured death before his exaltation to the rank of cosmic Lord. The "evangelical" content which is fitted into the "mythical" framework really destroys it. There is thus a "mythoclastic" element in the New Testament.[57]

Thirdly, this discussion brings us to the great contribution to exegesis offered by a study of these "hymns to Christ". They are set in a polemical context as part of the apostolic concern to defend the gospel against false christological notions and to ward off heretical attacks on the infant churches. Paul in particular makes appeal to the common deposit of Christian teaching in these hymns with a view to showing how the churches should remain steadfast; and he enforces his teaching by supplementing the "received text" of the hymns and modifying it to his own purpose. This is very probably the case with Colossians 1:15–20 where Paul has edited an already existing hymn to bring it into line with his teaching.[58] A simpler case is seen in Philippians 2:8 where most modern commentators see Paul's hand in the insertion of *θανάτου δὲ σταυροῦ* (even the death of the cross) to emphasize that Jesus' obedience to death meant a death on a cross and so a death of atoning value (Gal. 3:13).

3. LITURGICAL EXPRESSIONS

Several words and phrases in the New Testament belong to the actual liturgical vocabulary of primitive times. They are most easily recognized by the simple token that in the Greek of the New Testament they have been allowed to remain in their original Semitic form, sometimes with a Greek interpretative translation to accompany them. The most interesting examples are Abba, Amen, Hosanna, Hallelujah and Maranatha.

'Abba was Jesus' favourite name for God. While it was the child's title for his earthly parents (meaning "dear father"), there is no evidence that the pious Jew, either in private prayer or in the synagogue liturgy, ever used this precise form for invoking God.[59] Instead he used a variant form such as *'Abi* or *'Abinu* ("My Father, Our Father"); but *'Abba* was avoided because

it was thought to be too daring and presumptuous for a mortal to call upon God in this familiar way.

The wonder of this address to God is that Jesus used it as part of his filial obedience (Mk. 14:32–9) and taught his disciples to use it in their approach to God (Lk. 11:2). Undeniably there is no mistaking in this word the *ipsissima vox* of Jesus; and so much of his characteristic teaching about God as Father is expressed in this caritative form of the word for father. That it quickly was seized upon and passed into the worshipping life of the Gentile churches is seen from Paul's use of the exact word (in Rom. 8:15; Gal. 4:6) where he regards the invoking of God as *'Abba* as the sign of the Spirit's presence and the hallmark of the new life in Christ.

'Amen is known from the Old Testament times as a vocal response made by people as they endorsed the words of the speaker (*e.g.* Ne. 8:6). The verb underlying the cry means "to be firm, true" and is connected with the verb "to believe". It has a place in the synagogue service when the congregation replies to the precentor's call or the minister's prayers, and it serves to endorse the worship or the prayer as something the people believe and accept. There are many examples of this usage in the New Testament, usually at the close of doxologies or ascriptions of praise (e.g. Rom. 1:25, 9:25, 11:36; Eph. 3:21; 1 Tim. 1:17, 6:16; Heb. 13:21; 1 Pet. 4:11 *et al.*). It belongs too to the scenario of the heavenly sanctuary and its worship (Rev. 5:13, 14), though as we indicated this probably reflects the worship of the Asia Minor churches and is extrapolated from a liturgy with which John and his readers were already familiar.

There are two special instances of the use of Amen in Paul's epistles, which take on a distinct significance. First, in 2 Corinthians 1:20ff., the language is rich in liturgical overtones. Paul is probably alluding to baptism under the figure of a seal applied by the Spirit. The thought is: As God is faithful in fulfilling his pledge to give the Spirit to all who trust him, and confess Christ in baptism, and we attest his faithfulness with our Amen, so we as apostolic messengers can be relied on to keep faith with Christian people and not to play false.

At 1 Corinthians 14:16 Paul is describing the scene at a worship assembly at Corinth and points to the need for intelligibility in the service so that an outsider who comes into the room and hears the church at prayer may not be utterly confused but may know when to express his agreement (by saying "Amen") with the prayer of thanks. It is shown by this incidental allusion that Amen was in common use among the Pauline churches as the worshipper's assent to what he heard from the lips of his fellow-believers.

Special interest attaches to Jesus' use of the single or double *'Amen* placed as a preface to his public and private teaching. As with *'Abba,* this exact formulation is unique; and by the stringent criterion of eliminating from the records all that has parallels in Judaism and early Christianity,[60] the logia which contain this usage manage to survive. In the gospels the prefacing Amen (now to be taken as adverbial and meaning "certainly") is found only on Jesus' lips (familiarly in the Johannine "verily, verily") and in all the strata of gospel tradition.[61] The fact that it is retained in its Semitic form before the Greek λέγω ὑμῖν shows that the evangelists attached importance to it. Its purpose was to draw attention to the vital words of Jesus who in turn adopted the formula as One standing in the prophetic succession (the prophets used "Thus says Yahweh" as a claim to an inspired utterance) and going beyond them in his sublime authority to override the law of Moses and to utter oracles in his own name as God's unique Son and messenger.[62]

Hosanna is a Jewish ejaculation meaning "Save now!" and is addressed as a petition to God the Saviour (Ps. 118:25). Other references to the Hebrew expression (*hoši'an na'*) are in 2 Samuel 14:4 and 2 Kings 6:26, but these are non-significant for our purpose since they are cries addressed to men.

Psalm 118 was used at the Feast of Tabernacles and the Passover, and at the former celebration branches of trees were carried by the pilgrims and waved. These branches took their name from the festival and were called "hosannahs". This looks to be the most natural setting for the incident of Mark 11:1–10 and par.[63] In view of the evangelist's silence as to what the cry was intended to mean it is uncertain whether we should take it as an appeal for God's aid or as a greeting or benediction addressed to Jesus. However, the word soon found a place in Christian liturgy. In Didache 10:6 there is a strange snatch of liturgical dialogue in the form of a versicle and a response. To the invitation –

> May Grace come, and let this world pass away,

the congregation's reply is:

> Hosanna to the God of David![64]

Hallelujah is another Hebrew ascription of praise (meaning "Praise be to Jah", Israel's covenant God). It is found in the New Testament at Revelation 19:1, 6 as a song of triumph to celebrate the victory of the heavenly host.

Maranatha is a more decisive term, since it has considerable christological interest. In the context of 1 Corinthians 16:22 it voices the appeal of the community for the coming and presence of the Lord, and most likely the *Sitz im Leben* of the word falls in the dialogue pattern of versicle and response at the eucharistic service. These are the two conclusions reached by J. A. T. Robinson following suggestions made by H. Lietzmann and G. Bornkamm,[65] viz.

(a) that in 1 Corinthians 16:20–24 the language is "not merely of epistolary convention, but of one worshipping community to another, the converse of the saints assembled for Eucharist" and (b) that in this pericope there can be traced the remains of the earliest Christian liturgical sequence which we possess, and which is pre-Pauline in origin.

These conclusions are now generally accepted;[66] and with this confidence in a *sententia recepta* we can proceed to draw out some indications of the ways in which exegesis is helped.

The meaning of the Aramaic expression *Maranatha* is a matter of some debate since a decision about the division of the composite word affects its sense.[67] Most commentators agree that it should be divided as *Maranâ thâ* with the translation, "Our Lord, come" (cf. Rev. 22:20; Didache 10:6: both contexts require an imperative) and this settles the nature of the expression as a petition for the Lord's coming. In the light of the eucharistic setting of the passage in 1 Corinthians 16 the cry seems to be one of invitation that the risen Christ will come to meet his people at his table and be present with them as they celebrate in his name.[68] But an eschatological "coming" is not excluded (cf. 1 Cor. 11:26), and probably is the dominant theme of the cry.[69]

The christological meaning of *Maran* (our Lord) is also a controverted issue. The title cannot refer to God the Father (as was suggested years ago by some German scholars[70]), nor can it be placed in any other original setting than the Aramaic-speaking Palestinian church (against Bousset who wanted to locate it in a bilingual region of the hellenistic communities of Antioch, Damascus or even Tarsus).[71] It is now accepted that, on linguistic and ideological grounds, this watchword is embedded in Palestinian Christianity and represents a species of early christological belief.[72]

But even with this admission it still becomes a question of debate whether the term means that the early Jewish Christians offered cultic veneration of Jesus (as Cullmann insists)[73] or whether this is no more than an expression of hope that he will return as Lord-Son of man (so Fuller).[74] It is hard to accept the attenuated significance given in the latter view, and when Fuller writes that "even in the later Hellenistic church the exalted Jesus was never the direct object of worship", the significance of such texts as Acts 7:56–60; Romans 9:5 and Pliny's report of Christian worship as *carmenque Christo quasi Deo dicere* has been overlooked.

Maranâ thâ stands as a monument to Christian belief in Jesus' present lordship and the hope of the parousia. It places him on the side of God in a unique way by appropriating a title which properly belongs to God and shows that, from its inception, the Christian church has felt no incongruity in confessing one God (1 Cor. 8:6) and in the same breath in hailing Jesus as *Deus praesens,* God-with-us.

4. FIGURES OF SPEECH AND LITERARY DEVICES

In this section we shall include a variety of literary forms which the reader of the New Testament is likely to encounter and which need some brief comment.

(a) *Wisdom Sayings and Parables*

We have already mentioned that much of the gospel speech-forms is derived from Old Testament precedents, and this is only to be expected since both Jesus and his hearers stood in that tradition. Jesus himself was regarded as "teacher" and "prophet", and more than one aspect of his recorded teaching is modelled on the wisdom literature of the Jewish people.

The most elemental "form" in this background is the *mašal,* a word which contains several shades of meaning. It stands for an aphorism used to express succinctly some proverbial wisdom, a legal axiom, a philosophy of living or a rule for conduct. The teaching of Jesus offers examples of all these:

Matthew 6:34:	Do not allow tomorrow's troubles to affect you today.
Mark 8:38:	Whoever disowns me will be disowned.
Luke 12:48:	All who have great privileges have great responsibilities.
Mark 2:27:	The sabbath day is for man's benefit not the other way round.

Sometimes the *mašal* takes on the form of another Old Testament nuance, namely a riddle. Examples from the great sermon are: Matthew 5:13 (How can you season salt once it has lost its tang?); 6:27 (Can you increase your height by worrying over it?); 7:16 (Can you pick figs off a thistle bush?). These are conundrums drawn from experience. Some of the *m*e*šalim*, however, are given to awaken interest at a deeper level and to set the enquirer or the audience thinking about God and his kingdom and the meaning of life. These are the "dark sayings" which needed Jesus' interpretation (Mk. 4:11, 34); and often the disciples were utterly bewildered (Mk. 8:17; 9:6, 11; 10:10, 24; and the upper room sayings in John's gospel). J. Jeremias points out that this type of saying was original with Jesus and could not have been invented by the church which was interested in explanations, not riddles.[75]

When the *mašal* is extended into a larger story or comparison drawn from a life-situation, it forms a parable. The rabbis told parables and illumined their teaching with analogies drawn from everyday life.[76] But the parables of Jesus are in a class by themselves for many reasons:[77] (*a*) they are not fables which make animals their main characters, nor do trees or bushes speak (as in Jdg. 9:8–15; 2 Ki. 14:9; Ezk. 17:3–8, 31:3–14); (*b*) little use is made of extensive allegory (as in Enoch 85–90 where the history of Israel is told in great detail by means of speaking animals: cf. the use of animals and reptiles in Dn. and Rev.). Mark 12:1–11 is the closest the parables of Jesus get to the allegorical form; (*c*) the chief part of Jesus' parables is not the tale as such so much as the "punch-line" which usually comes at the climax of the story (cf. 2 Sa. 12:1–7 which ends on the note of a rapier thrust, You are the man!); and (*d*) Jesus used parables not to amuse or to gain a hearing but to proclaim the kingdom as a present reality. In that sense his words were performative of the grace of God which his message of the kingdom brought with it (see Luke 15 especially). Where this message was refused. his words took on judgmental force and were "weapons of warfare" (Jeremias[78]) attacking Pharisaic pride (Lk. 18:9) as well as announcing the presence of the kingdom. Above all (*e*) Jesus' parables were calculated to make the hearers feel that they were involved in the action of the story. The parable brings home to the listener the "existential" dimension of Jesus' teaching and confronts him here and now with a situation from which he cannot escape but which forces him to take sides. See Mark 4:24, 25.

(b) *Gematria*

A device that is likely to cause some trouble to the present-day interpreter is known as *gematria*. Since neither Hebrew nor Greek had separate characters for numerals, the letters of the alphabet were used by being given a numerical value. When the letters were added together a sum total was reached; and by reversing this procedure and using the aggregate number as a cipher it was possible to convey a message in a cryptic way. The most obvious case is Revelation 13:18 where after the lurid description of the beast which came out of the earth to embark on a persecuting rampage against the saints the seer remarks to the reader: "Here is the key; and anyone who has intelligence can work out the number of the beast. The number represents a man's name, and the numerical value of its letters is six hundred and sixty-six" (NEB). The commentaries should be consulted for a full discussion of this text. Solutions begin with the simplest idea that 666 falls short of the "perfect" number of 777 just as the numerical addition of the letters for the name "Jesus" in Greek is 888. The message then is that Jesus' name is supreme, while the name of "Man" (generically considered) means a persistent falling short.[79] A popular view sees here a concealed allusion to Nero Caesar who is referred to in the image of the beast with a mortal wound (13:3, 15). If this name is written in Hebrew characters and the vowel letter (*yôdh*) omitted, the sum of the letters is 666; if the Latin form of the name is examined, it yields 616; this is a variant reading of the text of 13:18. But this seems to be a complicated method of arriving at a solution, however much it may be conceded that the myth of *Nero redivivus* as an epitome of the church's enemy appears to underlie the Apocalypse's message to the Asian churches. There is an even more intricate solution offered by E. Stauffer who takes the five names by which the emperor Domitian was known, and uses the first letters of those titles in Greek. In this way the total of 666 is produced.[80] This idea has the merit of setting the Apocalypse in the reign of Domitian where the early fathers placed it and where it finds its most natural background. But there are difficulties. It is obvious therefore that this verse has not yet yielded its secret.

The other instance of *gematria* is easier to see. In Matthew's birth list (ch. 1) the account of Jesus' ancestry has been set into the framework of selective periodization with groups of fourteen names built around king David. This is artificially contrived, as we can see from a counting of the names; and it leads to the suspicion that the evangelist is deliberately using the name David with its numerical value of fourteen (Hebrew characters *daleth-waw-daleth* add up to 14) to set the pattern for this roll-call (1:17)[81] and so to prove that Jesus is "great David's greater Son".

(c) *Greek Rhetorical Forms*

Greek rhetorical forms, in addition to those we mentioned earlier, are further represented by some passages in which Paul is the speaker.[82]

They include Acts 17:22ff. (Paul's address on Areopagus) where the speech falls into clearly defined sections corresponding to the rhetorician's model of *exordium* (verse 22), *narratio* (verse 23), *divisio* (verses 24ff.) and *conclusio* (verses 29ff.); and Romans 2, 3 which contain several direct questions as though Paul were addressing a hostile audience. This is the device of *diatribe* by which a speaker or writer enters into imaginary debate with an interlocutor, raising points which he would make and objections he would voice, which are then answered and refuted.[83] There are other brief examples of this in Paul (1 Cor. 9 and 15:35, 36) and the influence of this Cynic-Stoic method of argumentation has been traced in James, especially 2:2f.[84]

Paul's versatility as a writer is seen in the epistle to the Romans. He can move with agility from the employment of a hellenistic debating style such as *diatribe* to a careful piece of exegesis based on the Old Testament. His exegesis follows the rabbinic principle of *g^ezerah šawah* and such illustrations as the "light and the heavy". These are two principles of exegesis which Hillel included in his list of seven (the *middoth*).

The principle of "analogy" (Heb. *g^ezerah šawah,* lit. "similar decision") states that when the same word or phrase is found in two passages of the Old Testament, one can be used to illumine the other. This is Paul's key to the Christian use of Genesis 15:6 adopted in Romans 4.[85]

The principle of *a minori ad maius* (which is what the Hebrew, translated literally "light and the heavy," means) is also seen in Romans (at 5:15; 8:32).

Perhaps these final *exempla* are themselves a parable, for they remind us that Paul's exegetical methods are as varied and suggestive as the often unexpected turns in his thought; and such versatility will put us on our guard against reading Scripture without regard to its literary style and cultural setting, and encourage us to bring as lively a mind to the interpretation of Scripture as was employed, on its human side, in composing it.

NOTES

1. Denzinger and Schönmetzer, *Enchiridion Symbolorum* (1963) 1637, quoted by R. E. Brown, *The Jerome Biblical Commentary* (London 1968) 71:87.

2. Cf. R. M. Enroth, E. E. Ericson, Jr., C. B. Peters, *The Jesus People.* Old-Time Religion in the Age of Aquarius (Exeter/Grand Rapids, 1972), p. 167.

3. For an elaboration of this statement, see G. E. Ladd, *The New Testament and Criticism* (London/Grand Rapids, 1967), ch. 1.

4. I owe this example to Dr. J. P. Kane.

5. J. Barr, *Old and New in Interpretation* (London 1966), pp. 192–96: "One of the theological functions of biblical interpretation is that it must expand our conceptions of what is relevant and introduce new perceptions. Any attempt to judge relevance at the beginning of our study must only perpetuate the value systems we previously accepted. Where this is so, the relevance conception works like tradition in the negative sense" (p. 193).

6. For the place of Dilthey, see later, pp. 313–315. See too the discussion in R. Kieffer, *Essais de méthodologie néo-testamentaire* (Lund 1972), pp. 46–50, who distinguishes between the text's "sens" and its "signification" and insists rightly that the two must be kept separate: "Nothing can be more disastrous for investigation of the 'sens' (explanation) of our text than to announce vigorously certain propositions which spring from an interpretation required by the 'signification' (understanding) of that text" (p. 50). For a comment on the New Testament problems seen in this light we may refer to W. Marxsen, *Introduction to the New Testament* (Oxford 1968), p. 27 and more fully in his *The New Testament as the Church's Book* (Philadelphia 1972).

7. See a critique of Fuchs and Ebeling in P. J. Achtemeier, *Theology Today* 23 (1966), pp. 101–19.

8. For a discussion of this definition of *sensus plenior* see R. E. Brown, *The Sensus Plenior of Sacred Scripture,* Baltimore 1955), especially pp. 92f. supplemented by the same writer's articles in CBQ 25 (1963), pp. 262–85 and ETL 43 (1967), pp. 460–69.

9. Y. M.–J. Congar, *Tradition and Traditions* (E.T. London 1967), especially pp. 63f. This view of regarding tradition as having an interpretative function in bringing out truth from the Scripture in a complementary way has been justly criticized by R. P. C. Hanson, *Tradition in the Early Church* (London 1962), pp. 239–45. Cf. EQ 40 (1968), pp. 79ff.

10. Congar cites the Immaculate Conception of Mary, Papal Primacy and Infallibility, the Assumption of Mary as dogmas which the Magisterium has decreed "either come from, or are based on, Scripture" (op. cit., p. 64 n. 2).

11. See G. W. H. Lampe and K. J. Woollcombe, *Essays on Typology* (London 1957); and the several contributions to *Essays on Old Testament Interpretation* ed. C. Westermann (London 1963).

12. For this term, see O. Cullmann, *Salvation in History* (London 1967).

13. For many of these questions we may refer to the study of G. A. Deissmann, *Light from the Ancient East* (New York 1927), O. Roller, *Das Formular der paulinischen Briefe* (Stuttgart 1933), and B. Rigaux, *The Letters of St. Paul* (Chicago E.T. 1968). For a discussion of Roller, see C. F. D. Moule, BJRL 47 (1964–5), p. 449.

14. See the chapters in the present volume, written by J. W. Drane and E. E. Ellis, on the backgrounds of the New Testament writers.

15. To take a well-known illustration. Methods of shepherding in Eastern lands differ from what are customary in rural districts in the Western countries. The meaning of John 10 is greatly enhanced by a reading of George Adam Smith's description of "the grandeur of the shepherd's character" (*The Historical Geography of the Holy Land* (London 1966 ed.), p. 210.

16. For the meaning of redaction criticism, which is concerned to investigate the Gospel writers' theological interest, see S. S. Smalley's essay in the present volume.

17. See the distinction drawn by J. Jeremias, *New Testament Theology,* (London 1971), Vol. I, ch. 1.

18. For this view of Matthew's stress on the validity of the law and the call to a higher righteousness see G. Barth, "Matthew's Understanding of the Law" in *Tradition and Interpretation in Matthew* by G. Bornkamm, G. Barth and H. J. Held (London 1963), pp. 159ff.

19. See R. S. Barbour, *Traditio-Historical Criticism of the Gospels* (London 1972), p. 19. See also J. I. Packer, "Biblical Authority, Hermeneutics and Inerrancy" in *Jerusalem and Athens: Critical Discussions on the Philosophy and Apologetics of Cornelius van Til*, ed. E. R. Geehan (Philadelphia 1971), pp. 146ff.

20. H. J. Cadbury, *The Making of Luke-Acts* (London 1958 ed.), pp. 135ff. (p. 136).

21. The reasons for the development of this term are mentioned in my book *Mark: Evangelist and Theologian* (Exeter 1972), ch. 1.

22. A. N. Wilder, *Early Christian Rhetoric* (London 1964), pp. 36f.

23. See now W. G. Doty, *Letters in Primitive Christianity* (Philadelphia 1973).

24. E. J. Goodspeed, *The Formation of the New Testament* (Chicago 1926), p. 25.

25. See J. N. D. Kelly, *The Pastoral Epistles* (London 1963), pp. 25ff., who argues that the linguistic and literary features of these letters may be accounted for on the supposition that Paul employed a new secretary at this juncture in his life, "a Hellenistic Jewish Christian, a

man skilled in rabbinical lore and at the same time a master of the higher *koinē*".
26. So A. Wikenhauser, *New Testament Introduction* (Dublin 1958), p. 348.
27. W. G. Kümmel, *Introduction to the New Testament* (London 1966), pp. 178.
28. O. Roller, *Das Formular der paulinischen Briefe*, p. 148.
29. P. Schubert, *Form and Function of the Pauline Thanksgivings* (Berlin 1939), pp. 71–82.
30. J. T. Sanders, "The Transition from Opening Epistolary Thanksgiving to Body in the Letters of the Pauline Corpus", JBL 81 (1962) pp. 348ff. See the forthcoming study of P. T. O'Brien on "Pauline Thanksgivings". See too H. Boers, NTS 22 (1975–76), pp. 140–158.
31. This conclusion has been demonstrated by L. G. Champion, *Benedictions and Doxologies in the Epistles of Paul* (Oxford 1934).
32. These are the chief data discussed by J. M. Robinson in "Die Hodajot-Formel in Gebet und Hymnus des Frühchristentums", *Apophoreta: Festschrift für E. Haenchen* (Berlin 1964), pp. 194–235.
33. See for details D. S. Russell, *The Method and Message of Jewish Apocalyptic* (London 1964).
34. Dualism is taken to be *the* characteristic of apocalyptic by C. E. Braaten, *Christ and Counter-Christ* (Philadelphia 1972).
35. In the case of the synoptic apocalypses, it is the series of events prior to and including the outbreak of the first Jewish war with Rome, A.D. 66–73; in the Revelation it is the conflict between the church in Asia Minor and the emperor cult in the time of Domitian, A.D. 90–96.
36. For this understanding of a double vision, see Karl Heim, *Die Königsherrschaft Gottes* (Stuttgart 1948), pp. 55f. (as quoted by C. E. B. Cranfield, "Mark 13", SJT 6 (1953), p. 300): "But all this (i.e. the destruction of Jerusalem and the events connected with it) is for Him only a *Transparent* standing in the foreground, through which He beholds the last events before the End of the world, in which all this will at last come to its real fulfilment." See too the use of Heim made in Daniel Lamont, *Christ and the World of Thought* (Edinburgh 1934), especially ch. 16: Ethic and Apocalyptic.
37. For these forms see the discussion by K. Koch, *The Growth of the Biblical Tradition* (New York 1969), pp. 91–100, and T. R. Henn, *The Bible as Literature* (London 1970), pp. 128ff.
38. See the full study by N. W. Lund, *Chiasmus in the New Testament* (Chapel Hill 1942). This work needs to be supplemented by the more recent investigations, e.g. of E. Schweizer in TDNT 6, pp. 416f. There is a critique of aspects of Lund's book in J. Jeremias, "Chiasmus in den Paulusbriefen" ZNW 49 (1958), pp. 145–56.
39. For the Semitic background of this logion see M. Black, *An Aramaic Approach to the Gospels and Acts* (Oxford 1967[3]), pp. 200–2. Cf. G. Schwarz, "Matthaus vii 6a. Emendation und Rückübersetzung", Nov.T 14.1 (1972), pp. 18–25.
40. E. Bammel, "Versuch zu Col. 1:15–20", ZNW 52 (1961), pp. 88–95. The clearest example is in verses 16c and 20:

a *τὰ πάντα*	b *καὶ διαὐτοῦ*
b *δἰ αὐτὸν καί*	a *τὰ πάντα*

But there is objection to the systematic way Bammel applies this method, voiced by H.–J. Gabathuler, *Jesus Christus. Haupt der Kirche-Haupt der Welt* (Zürich/Stuttgart 1956), pp. 118–21.
41. E. Käsemann's essay carries this title in his *New Testament Questions of Today* (London 1969), pp. 66–81. For a discussion see K. Berger, "Die sog. 'Sätze heiligen Rechts' im N.T.", Th.Z 28 (1972), pp. 305–330.
42. See J. Jeremias, *New Testament Theology,* Vol I, pp. 9ff. and W. Popkes, *Christus Traditus; Eine Untersuchung zum Begriff der Dahingabe im Neuen Testament* (Zürich/Stuttgart 1967).
43. See Popkes, op. cit., pp. 144: "Subjekt des Geschehens kann letztlich nur Gott sein . . ." It is wrong to translate: After John had been delivered *into prison.*
44. J. Jeremias, *The Eucharistic Words of Jesus* (London 1966[2]) pp. 112.
45. See A. Hamman, *La Prière 1: Le Nouveau Testament* (Tournai 1959).
46. See W. D. Maxwell, *An Outline of Christian Worship* (Oxford 1936), pp. 8f. But see W. C. van Unnik, "1 Clement and the 'Sanctus'", VC 5 (1951), pp. 204–48.

47. E. Norden, *Agnostos Theos.* (Stuttgart 1923), pp. 254ff., 272.
48. J. Schmitt, *Jésus ressuscité dans la prédication apostolique* (Paris 1949), p. 100 speaks of "un rythme hiératique". For a full study of this hymn see R. H. Gundry, "The Form, Meaning and Background of the Hymn Quoted in 1 Timothy 3:16", in *Apostolic History and the Gospel,* Essays presented to F. F. Bruce (ed. W. W. Gasque and R. P. Martin, Exeter 1970), pp. 203–22.
49. See the data displayed in H. Schlier's commentary, *Der Brief an die Epheser* (Düsseldorf 1957), p. 241.
50. E. Lohmeyer, *Kyrios Jesus* (Heidelberg 1926).
51. So J. Jeremias, "Zur Gedankenführung in den paulinschen Briefen", in *Studia Paulina in honorem J. de Zwaan* (ed. J. N. Sevenster and W. C. van Unnik, Haarlem 1953), pp. 154.
52. See R. P. Martin, *Carmen Christi: Philippians ii. 5–11* (Cambridge 1967), pp. 36ff. and *idem, The Epistle to the Philippians* (New Century Bible) (London 1976), pp.109–112.
53. Ch. Masson, *L'épitre de S. Paul aux Colossiens* (Neuchâtel 1950), pp. 105. Cf. C. F. D. Moule, *The Epistles to the Colossians and to Philemon* (Cambridge 1957), p. 61: "Arguments based on rhythm, parallelism, and supposed strophic arrangement are precarious enough at the best of times, and most of all when there is no recognizable quantitative metre by which to judge." See a discussion of the literary background of Colossians 1:15–20 in R. P. Martin, *Colossians and Philemon* (New Century Bible) (London 1974), pp. 61–66.
54. See A. B. Macdonald, *Christian Worship in the Primitive Church* (Edinburgh 1934) for an elaboration of this thesis.
55. G. Stählin, in TDNT 4, pp. 781ff. See too C. K. Barrett, "Myth and the New Testament", Exp.T 68 (1956–57), pp. 345–8, 359–62. For a consideration of the meaning of "myth" in the New Testament, see J. D. G. Dunn's contribution to the present volume.
56. T. R. Henn, op. cit., p. 19 borrows the term "mythologem" in place of "myth" from G. C. Jung and C. Kerényi, *Introduction to a Science of Mythology* (New York 1951).
57. To use the expressive word of A. N. Wilder, *Early Christian Rhetoric* (London 1964), p. 129.
58. For details see my essay in *Reconciliation and Hope* (Exeter 1974), pp. 104–124.
59. This is a conclusion maintained in the several works of J. Jeremias, most recently in his *New Testament Theology,* Vol. I, pp. 61–8.
60. See for this criterion D. R. Catchpole's essay in the present volume.
61. See J. Jeremias, op. cit., p. 35. One example may suffice. Luke 4:24: "Amen, I say to you that no prophet is accepted in his own locality."
62. Therefore the occurrence of *ἐγὼ δὲ λέγω ὑμῖν* in the Sermon on the Mount is highly significant as Jesus displaces Moses' authority. See E. Käsemann, "The Problem of the Historical Jesus", *Essays on New Testament Themes* (London 1964), pp. 37f.
63. Though a case has been made (by F. C. Burkitt, JTS o.s. 17 (1915), pp. 139–52) for the dating of the Entry into Jerusalem at the Feast of Dedication (based on the incident of 2 Macc. 10:8); and this setting at a time when nationalist feelings were running high has suggested to J. S. Kennard (JBL 67 (1948), pp. 171–76) that the crowd's cry had definite political overtones. For the development of the meaning attached to the word, see E. Werner, " 'Hosanna' in the Gospels", JBL 65 (1946), pp. 97–122.
64. For the textual question here, see J.-P. Audet, *La Didaché. Instructions des Apôtres* (Paris 1958), pp. 62–7, Audet supports the reading. "Hosanna to the house of David", and argues that the liturgical prayers of Did. 9, 10 belong to a special breaking of bread service modelled on a Jewish precedent (op. cit., pp. 422f.). For the later liturgical usage of Hosanna, see J. A. Jungmann, *Missarum sollemnia* ii (Vienna 1949), pp. 161–67 (E.T. *The Mass* (New York 1951), pp. 379–84).
65. J. A. T. Robinson, "The Earliest Christian Liturgical Sequence?" JTS n.s. 4 (1953), pp. 38–41, reprinted in *Twelve New Testament Studies* (London, 1962), pp. 154–7. H. Lietzmann, *Mass and Lord's Supper* Fasc. i (Leiden 1953) pp. 186f., 192f. and G. Bornkamm, "Das Anathema in der urchristlichen Abendmahlsliturgie", TLZ 75 (1950), cols. 228f., reprinted in *Das Ende des Gesetzes: Paulusstudien* (Munich 1961), pp. 123–32.
66. But see C. F. D. Moule, "A Reconsideration of the Context of *Maranatha*" NTS 6

(1959–1960), pp. 307–10 who revives E. Peterson's view that *maranatha* is part of the *anathema*-formula which acts as a ban. So in 1 Corinthians 16:22 the term is not a eucharistic invocation but a formula to sanction the "fencing of the table" preliminary to the eucharist.
67. See K. G. Kuhn, TDNT 4, pp. 467–9.
68. So O. Cullmann, *Early Christian Worship* (London 1953), pp. 13f.
69. So H. Conzelmann, *History of Primitive Christianity* (Nashville 1973), p. 51; "The Supper turns the gaze toward the advent of the Lord; hence he is begged, 'Come!' – i.e., 'Come soon!' "
70. For example, R. Bultmann, *Theology of the New Testament* (E.T. London 1952), Vol. I, p. 52.
71. W. Bousset, *Kyrios Christos* (E.T. Nashville 1970), p. 129. Bousset's position was vigorously opposed by A. E. J. Rawlinson, *The New Testament Doctrine of the Christ* (London 1926), pp. 231–7.
72. R. H. Fuller, *The Foundations of New Testament Christology* (London 1965), pp. 156ff.
73. O. Cullmann, *The Christology of the New Testament* (London 1959), p. 214; cf. F. F. Bruce, " 'Jesus is Lord' " in *Soli Deo Gloria. New Testament Studies in Honor of William Childs Robinson* (Richmond 1968), pp. 31f.
74. R. H. Fuller, ibid.; S. Schulz, "Maranatha und Kyrios Jesus", ZNW 53 (1962), p. 138 argues that the *maranatha* formula did not acclaim Jesus as divine Lord who was present, but prayed for his coming as Son of man and judge.
75. J. Jeremias, *New Testament Theology,* Vol. I, p. 31.
76. See R. A. Stewart, "The Parable Form in the Old Testament and the Rabbinic Literature", EQ 36 (1964), pp. 133–47.
77. See M. D. Goulder, "Characteristics of the Parables in the Several Gospels", JTS n.s. 19 (1968), pp. 51–69.
78. J. Jeremias, *The Parables of Jesus* (London 1954), p. 19.
79. L. Morris, *The Revelation of St. John* (London 1969), p. 174.
80. E. Stauffer, "666", *Coniectanea Neotestamentica* 11 (1947), pp. 237 ff.
81. See G. H. Box, "The Gospel Narratives of the Nativity", ZNW 6 (1905), p. 85; and M. D. Johnson, *The Purpose of the Biblical Genealogies* (Cambridge 1969), pp. 223ff.
82. Other specimens are discussed by J. Weiss, *A History of Primitive Christianity* (New York 1937), pp. 399–421 and J. Nélis, *Nouvelle Revue Théologique* 70 (1948), pp. 360–87. See too the examination of rhetorical figures in Galatians by H. D. Betz, NTS 21 (1974–75), pp. 353–79. Included here may be the few allusions in the New Testament to the world of Greek literature. In Acts 17:28 Paul's reference to "For we are also his offspring" comes from his fellow-Cilician Aratus (*Phainomena* 5), and the earlier part of his statement, "For in him we live and move and have our being" is apparently drawn from a poem of Epimenides the Cretan. In Titus 1:12 the same Cretan poet is cited in a complete hexameter. Cleanthes' *Hymn to Zeus* also contains a reminiscence of the Aratus quotation.

In 1 Corinthians 15:33 the Athenian comic poet Menander (4th cent., B.C.) is quoted as the author of the moral tag, Bad friends ruin the noblest people (JB), from his play *Thais.*
83. See R. Bultmann, *Der Stil der paulinischen Predigt und die kynisch-stoische Diatribe* (Tübingen 1910).
84. Cf. M. Dibelius – H. Greeven, *Der Brief des Jakobus* (Göttingen 1957), pp. 120–22.
85. See J. Jeremias, "Zur Gedankenführung", *Studia Paulina,* pp. 149ff., on rabbinic exegesis in Romans 4.

CHAPTER XIV

EXEGESIS IN PRACTICE: TWO SAMPLES

R. T. France

This chapter is intended to bring the reader down to earth. Many theoretical points have been made in the preceding pages, and many ideals expressed, with carefully selected examples to illustrate the points at issue. But in practice the exegete, be he professional or amateur, is seldom concerned with carefully selected sample verses, but with the actual New Testament text in its entirety. He finds himself faced with the task of determining the meaning not of the odd word or phrase here and there, but of a whole connected passage, which may involve quite complex thought-patterns. He soon finds himself forced, whether he likes it or not, to read the individual words and phrases *in their context*.

This chapter will consist, then, not of lists of rules for correct exegesis, but of an attempt to interpret two actual New Testament passages as a whole (Matthew 8:5–13 and 1 Peter 3:18–22). The passages have been chosen to represent two quite different literary genres, which between them raise many of the problems of method which confront the exegete in practice. We shall not stop to point out at every juncture precisely what methods are being employed. It is for the reader to notice where and how the various techniques of textual criticism, literary criticism, lexical study, study of religious or literary background, etc. are brought into play. These various techniques will not occur in any logical order, but as the passages themselves require them. That is how exegesis must work in practice: it is the passage in front of us that itself dictates the methods to be used.

Only a few preliminary points need to be made before we turn to the selected passages:

(1) We are taking "exegesis" to mean the discovery of what the text means in itself, i.e. the original intention of the writer, and the meaning the passage would have held for the readers for whom it was first intended. This is *exegesis* proper. The further step of *application* of this original meaning to our own situation is strictly a separate discipline (see the chapter by J. E. Goldingay). It is, of course, a necessary step if our study of the New Testament is to be any more than mere antiquarianism, and in practice the exegete is likely to have the contemporary relevance of the text in mind from the start. But the two stages must not be confused, and short cuts must be avoided. Exegesis proper should be as far as possible an objective discipline,

and it is the essential prerequisite for any more existential application of the message of the New Testament. It is with *exegesis,* in this sense, that this chapter is concerned.

(2) Exegesis is seldom a simple case of black and white, where all honest scholars must inevitably reach the same conclusion. The exegesis offered in this chapter is not presented as the last word on the passages concerned. The reader will probably disagree at several points. But this is essentially an essay in *method.* Where the reader disagrees with the proposed exegesis, he should ask himself whether the author has adopted the wrong method to solve this particular problem, or whether he is using the right method, but using it wrongly. Both are, of course, entirely possible!

(3) This chapter presents exegesis as essentially a "do-it-yourself" pursuit. The author believes that no serious exegete should be content merely to follow where some revered commentary or version leads. He should satisfy himself whether the job has been properly done. But this does not mean the abolition of all commentaries, lexica, concordances and versions, leaving the exegete closeted alone with his Greek text (or, ideally, with the original manuscripts!). It will be very clear, particularly in the second passage below, how much the author has in fact leaned on commentaries and works of reference. The exegete needs information, and much of what he needs will not be found in the pages of the New Testament itself. He needs guidance on critical, lexical, textual and other principles. He needs to be aware of the range of suggestions which have been offered on the point at issue. But, in the last resort, the conclusion must be his own. He must weigh the evidence, and decide between the options for himself. If he shirks this responsibility, he is not an exegete.

Without more ado, then, we turn to the two selected passages, trusting that the discussion will throw up most of the major principles and methods which must govern the practice of exegesis. The reader should note how the various methods of study mentioned in preceding chapters are worked out in practice.

I. *Matthew 8:5–13*

This passage has been chosen as an example of a pericope in the Synoptic Gospels where a comparison with the treatment of the same material by another evangelist may help to throw light on the special concerns of the writer, i.e. where exegesis is aided by critical, particularly redaction-critical, considerations.

The incident of the healing of the centurion's servant is recorded only in Matthew and Luke.[1] It may thus be loosely referred to as "Q material"; but a few minutes with a synopsis will reveal that the relation between the two accounts is anything but an exact equivalence. There is nearly verbal equivalence in the dialogue in verses 8b–10 (Lk. 7:6b, 7b–9), but for the rest, while the essential features of the story are the same, they are told in a very different way. Matthew is short and to the point, but includes verses

11–12, a Q saying which Luke records in a quite different context (13:28–29), and which was therefore presumably preserved independently, and inserted here by Matthew because he found it relevant in the context.[2] Luke, on the other hand, is more leisurely and colourful in his telling of the story, including extra detail about the centurion's Jewish sympathies, and in particular the account of his having approached Jesus through his friends, rather than in person as in Matthew's version. Other differences in detail will be mentioned in our discussion of the passage.

Convinced advocates of Q as a single document are therefore reduced to believing that Q preserved the dialogue, with perhaps a brief indication of the narrative setting, and the evangelists were left to supply the details from oral tradition. Those who in any case find a unitary Q hard to swallow find here further evidence for an oral tradition which preserved significant sayings with great fidelity, perhaps jotting them down to aid memory, but was less concerned with the verbatim form of the narrative.

At any rate, the significant point is that what mattered to the early Christians in this incident was primarily the dialogue to which it led. Doctrinaire form-critics will therefore label it a pronouncement-story or apophthegm, rather than a miracle story; those less worried about exact labelling may be inclined to ask why it should not be both![3] But it is certainly not *just* a miracle story: attention is focused on the sayings about authority and faith.

Apart from questions of exact wording and emphasis, the only significant factual discrepancy between the two accounts is the question whether the centurion approached Jesus through his Jewish friends (Luke) or in person (Matthew). Which is the original version? Has Luke added the messengers to emphasise the centurion's humility (see esp. Lk. 7:7a), or has Matthew abbreviated the story by omitting what he regarded as an inessential detail? Here commentators differ, their conclusions depending often on their presuppositions about the "laws of tradition", whether oral material tends to lose inessential details in transmission, or to be elaborated in the interest of story-telling. It must be remembered, however, that it is almost certainly not a question of either evangelist sitting down with a written account of the event in front of him and deliberately either abbreviating or expanding it. It is a question of an orally preserved story which each tells in his own way, including just so much detail as he feels is necessary to make his point. Matthew, as we shall see, is concerned to emphasise the *faith* of the centurion, and for this purpose the messengers are irrelevant. Luke, on the other hand, also wishes to indicate his *humility,* and here the sending of the messengers is significant. Thus to the question whether there actually were any messengers or not, we should probably answer "yes", but we should be missing the point if we therefore accuse Matthew of falsification. His deliberate abbreviation is a valid literary device to throw the emphasis clearly onto the central theme of the story, the centurion's faith. His omission makes no significant difference either to the miracle, or to the crucial dialogue. If anything, it high-lights the latter.

What we have been sketching in this last paragraph is the contribution of redaction-criticism to exegesis in this particular case. A comparison of the handling of the story by the two evangelists has alerted us to Matthew's primary intention in telling the story, to teach about faith. This insight is clearly going to be important in our detailed exegesis.

VERSE 5

Capernaum needs little comment. A Bible dictionary will tell us that it was one of the leading towns of Galilee, a prosperous lake-side community, which was Jesus' base for much of his Galilean ministry. This latter fact accounts for the centurion's awareness of Jesus' healing power: it was, no doubt, the talk of the town.

A Bible dictionary will also supply details about centurions. They were the backbone of the Roman army, the N.C.O.s on whom discipline depended, responsible and respected officers. There were no Roman legions stationed in Palestine, but Herod Antipas had under his control a small force of auxiliaries. These were all non-Jewish troops, drawn largely from the area of Lebanon and Syria. The centurion was, therefore, certainly not a Jew, though Luke makes much of his sympathy for the Jewish religion. It is as the believing Gentile that he finds his significance in Matthew's account. (Is this perhaps another reason for Matthew's omission of the Jewish friends, to avoid blurring the sharp Jew/Gentile contrast which is a prominent feature of his version of the story, coming into sharp focus in his addition of verses 11–12? Luke is concerned only with the man's character, Matthew also with his nationality.)

VERSE 6

This verse raises two points of translation, both of some importance for exegesis. The first is the centurion's address to Jesus, *κύριε* (repeated in verse 8). Should this be translated "Lord", or, as in Moffatt, NEB, Jerusalem Bible, "Sir"? In other words, is it just a polite form of address, or does it imply more? AG tell us that *κύριε* is "a form of address to respected pers. gener.". MM show that in secular Greek, apart from its use of a god, it certainly involves an acknowledgement of superiority, particularly in addressing a higher official. But when used as a form of address to Jesus, the precise connotation of such a flexible word obviously cannot be determined by the dictionary, but by what the context tells us of the person's attitude to Jesus. The centurion, as we shall see in verses 8–9, regards Jesus as a superior authority, and a worker of miraculous healing, so "Sir" seems a bit weak. On the other hand, there is no indication that he attributes to Jesus any divine status, as "Lord" might well imply. However it be translated, *κύριε* should be regarded as acknowledging the superiority of Jesus, but cannot be pressed into an indication of the centurion's christological understanding.

More important is the word *παῖς* which can mean either "child" or "servant". Traditionally it has always been translated "servant", but this is based on Luke, who has used the unambiguous term *δοῦλος* (as well as *παῖς* in 7:7). But was this what Matthew meant? Bultmann[4] pronounces, "Unquestionably *παῖς* in Matt. 8:6 is to be understood as child: *δοῦλος* in Lk. 7:2 is an error in reproduction." Like many of Bultmann's "unquestionable" pronouncements, this is not supported by any argument. The exegete should be on his guard against unsupported dogmatic assertions, by however august an authority! What is the evidence?

Παῖς occurs 24 times in the New Testament (see concordance). In only *one* of these does it mean "son" (Jn. 4:51); in eight other cases it clearly means "child", but without implying any relationship to the speaker or to a character in the narrative. In four cases it refers to a "servant" of a man, and in eight cases to a "servant" of God.[5] Thus if *παῖς* in Matthew 8:6, 8, 13 means the centurion's "son", it would be agreeing with the only use of the word by John against all the other New Testament uses (which are in fact all in Matthew and Luke-Acts). MM also show that both "child" and "servant" were common meanings in secular Greek, but apparently not "son". In Matthew, outside this passage, there are three uses in the sense of "child" (not "son"), and two in the sense of "servant", one of which (14:2) is closely parallel to the sort of "retainer" envisaged here. Thus there seems no reason for driving a wedge between Matthew and Luke at this point, or for doubting that Matthew is using *παῖς* in exactly the same sense that Luke does in 7:7, where it is parallel to *δοῦλος* in 7:2.[6] Some commentators (e.g. Lohmeyer, Schlatter) suggest that while *δοῦλος* was the formal, official term for a slave, *παῖς* was used for a slave who was held in personal friendship (see Lk. 7:2, *ἔντιμος*). The use of "boy" for servants in colonial days may be roughly parallel.

Matthew does not emphasise, as Luke does, the centurion's fondness for his servant, which would be remarkable, but not unparalleled, in non-Jewish circles. He is not so interested in the man's character as in his faith. His kind-heartedness, as well as his friendly relations with the Jewish community, are irrelevant to this purpose, and only what is necessary to the story is retained.

VERSE 7

This apparently straight-forward verse in fact poses a significant problem. It all turns on the punctuation: are the words of Jesus a promise, or a question? Greek manuscripts bore no punctuation marks, and such questions frequently arise. Often they are of considerable exegetical importance. Sometimes linguistic considerations help to provide an answer. More often we are entirely dependent on the context.

The one striking linguistic feature is the very prominent *ἐγώ*. Greek does not usually include personal pronouns in addition to the person indicated by the verb-inflection unless there is need to emphasise the person. When the pronoun comes first in the sentence, the emphasis is unmistakable. So if these words are treated as a statement, the ἐγώ is a puzzle. It looks either redundant, or uncharacteristically pompous – "I myself will come and heal him." (One is reminded of Longfellow's "I myself, myself! behold me!")

But if this is a question, the emphatic ἐγώ has a real function: "Shall *I* come and heal him?" H.-J. Held[7] regards this as an "astonished or indignant question". It is usually explained on the basis of the racial distinction. For a Jew to enter a Gentile's house was to contract defilement (see Acts 10–11). In fact there is no record of Jesus ever entering a Gentile house, or even touching a Gentile to heal him. His two healings of Gentiles were done by a word, at a distance. Such an apparent reluctance, on racial grounds, would be closely parallel to Jesus' harsh reply to the Syro-Phoenician woman (Mt. 15:24, 26), and the two stories are so closely parallel at many points that this analogy supports an apparent reluctance on Jesus' part in Matthew 8:7, rather than the ready response indicated by punctuating as a statement.

Even if the racial overtone be doubted, an interrogative punctuation makes the dialogue flow more smoothly. The centurion has not, in verse 6, made any formal request, but simply presented the situation. Jesus' question is then drawing out the logical implication: "So you want *me* to come and heal him?" The centurion's deprecatory reply in verse 8 then follows naturally.

If then we accept that verse 7 is a question, what is its implication? The parallel with the story of the Syro-Phoenician woman is illuminating here. Jesus is testing the faith of the supplicant by an apparent refusal (or at least reluctance). In each case, faith triumphs over this obstacle, proving stronger than the racial barrier, and in each case Jesus then effects the cure in explicit response to this faith. Such a build-up to the story gives added point to Jesus' amazement at the centurion's faith (verse 10), that it is able to see beyond racial distinctions, and this leads on naturally to the universalistic pronouncement of verses 11–12. Thus even this question of punctuation proves to have implications for the meaning of the story: the recognition of a question in these words of Jesus, and the implication of a testing of the centurion's faith, introduces already that contrast between Jewish racialism and the faith of the Gentile which is Matthew's concern here and at several points in his gospel. Luke significantly does not record this question, with its apparent reluctance, nor the parallel story of the Syro-Phoenician woman.

VERSE 8

Is the centurion's deferential reply (notice κύριε again) due to a consciousness of racial distinction, and a respect for Jesus' scruples about entering a Gentile home (so many commentators), or is the thought more of his personal unworthiness in contrast with the greatness of Jesus? The whole of his reply in verses 8–9 says no word about race; apparently his faith is such that the concept is irrelevant to him. His words are all concerned with the supreme *authority* of Jesus, and his ability to heal. In the face of such authority he both feels his personal unworthiness to receive Jesus, and regards a personal visit as unnecessary, since a word will be enough. Thus the context suggests that his feeling of unworthiness is personal, not racial.

This argument from context is reinforced by the Greek word used, ἱκανός, which means at root "sufficient", and thus suggests considerations of character rather than status. A concordance will reveal similar uses, such as Matthew 3:11; 1 Cor. 15:9; 2 Cor. 2:16, all of which are concerned with personal worthiness or adequacy. Hence Rengstorf concludes, "It denotes the impression made by the person of Jesus upon the Gentile centurion . . . He is not thinking of the ritual uncleanness which Jesus as a Jew would incur by entering a non-Jewish house. What he has in view is the majesty and authority of Jesus which lift him above everything human, especially in the non-Jewish sphere . . . On the lips of the centurion the οὐκ εἰμὶ ἱκανός is thus a confession of the Messiahship of Jesus." [8] The word "messiahship" seems misconceived, but the exegesis of ἱκανός is both lexically and contextually sound.

In the request for healing by a mere word, uttered at a distance, we are shown the extent of the centurion's faith.[9] No such cures had yet been performed, as far as our records go. The centurion had heard of Jesus' healing work, perhaps seen it, but his faith goes beyond the evidence of his senses. The only other such healings recorded are that of the Syro-Phoenician woman's daughter, and of the nobleman's son in John 4. The *word* was a normal part of the healing process, but it was usually uttered to the patient in person. The next verse goes on to make explicit the unlimited power with which the centurion credited Jesus.

VERSE 9

The centurion's confession of faith is one of the two key pronouncements in the story. Its main drift is clear: he likens Jesus' authority to that of the army officer, who need only speak the word to receive instant obedience. So Jesus need only speak the word, and the healing will be accomplished. [10]

There is, however, some dispute as to how exactly the comparison is made. The text as usually printed gives the centurion two contrasting observations, (1) that he is under authority (and so must obey orders), and (2) that he has soldiers under him, who must obey him. So he knows his place in a chain of authoritative command. There is, however, evidence of a variant reading, particularly in the old Syriac version (never an authority to be treated lightly), which would substitute for ὑπὸ ἐξουσίαν something like ἐν ἐξουσίᾳ or ἐξουσίαν ἔχων, thus eliminating the idea of subordination, and restricting the comparison entirely to the authority exercised by the centurion himself.[11] There are, however, good reasons why the reading "under authority" (which is undisputed in Luke) should have been altered to "in authority": firstly, a tidy-minded scribe would be likely to take this simple means of eliminating a contrasting element and reducing the whole verse to a single point of comparison; secondly, the mention of the centurion's subordination might cause embarrassment if it was felt that there must be exact correspondence at every point – to whom was Jesus "under authority"?

If then we accept the reading "under authority", is not this last point a problem, particularly in view of the phrase καὶ γὰρ ἐγώ . . .? Must this not mean, "For I too (like you) am a man under authority . . .", and therefore make Jesus a mere man, and a subordinate at that? However, an examination of the uses of καὶ γάρ listed in AG (under γάρ) shows many cases where it means simply "for" or, better, "for indeed", and where there is no room for the meaning "also".[12] So here the translation "For I indeed am a man under authority . . ." would be permissible, without drawing the direct comparison between the status of the centurion and that of Jesus. Moreover, even if one were to insist on the meaning "For I *too* am . . .", which is perhaps the more natural translation when ἐγώ follows directly after καὶ γάρ, it is not legitimate to restrict the point of comparison to the first clause only ("under authority"), when in fact it is the issuing, not the obeying, of orders which is the main theme of the verse. The καὶ γάρ governs the whole sentence, not just its first words. The point could be made by paraphrasing, rather tendentiously, "For even I too, set as I am within a chain of authority, know what it is to give orders . . ."

The minor points of text and translation covered in the last two paragraphs are, of course, quite inessential for a basic exegesis of the passage. The main point of the verse is beyond doubt, the assertion of Jesus' absolute authority by analogy with that of a military commander. But the exegete is not on this account entitled to ignore the incidental details, particularly where these have given rise, as in this case, to doctrinal embarrassment.

VERSE 10

This is the second key pronouncement, the point to which the whole narrative has been building up. The punch-line is introduced by the statement that Jesus was "amazed" by what he heard. The concordance will show that θαυμάζω is a verb which is not used lightly. In particular, it is used only twice of Jesus himself, here and at Mark 6:6. Here the object of his amazement is faith, there it is unbelief. Good material for the preacher, this!

The saying is introduced by ἀμὴν λέγω ὑμῖν, the mark of a solemn, emphatic pronouncement. It is often singled out as one of the characteristic rhetorical devices of Jesus, as a teacher of unique authority, since no other Jewish teacher of the time is known to have used the phrase. A statement thus introduced is to be carefully noted.

The pronouncement is concerned with *faith*. This, as we have seen, is the focal point of the story for Matthew, and it is clinched in the peculiarly Matthean "As you believed let it be done for you" of verse 13. Faith here is a practical confidence in Jesus' power to heal, based on a conviction of his supreme authority: so much we may infer from the centurion's saying in verses 8–9 which gives rise to Jesus' commendation. It would be quite inappropriate to the narrative situation to ask whether this was saving, justifying faith in the Pauline sense, or whether it involves a doctrinal acceptance of the divinity of Jesus. These are questions derived from later theological development in the New Testament which are certainly anachronistic when applied to the period of Jesus' ministry. Whether they occurred to Matthew in his telling of the story we must consider shortly. But for the original setting of the story and of Jesus' pronouncement, "faith" must be interpreted in terms of its context, as a practical trust based on a conviction of Jesus' power to heal. It involves a recognition that Jesus has a unique authority, and wields supernatural power. Beyond that the context forbids us to go.

It is this unreserved confidence and acceptance of Jesus' authority which amazes him, and calls forth his commendation. Here is none of that suspicion or reservation of judgment which he had met with among his own people. Here is a man who has grasped more fully than any Jew what sort of person Jesus is, and who is prepared to act decisively on that understanding.

And the man is a *Gentile*. Jesus' mission was first of all to Israel. He deliberately restricted his activity during his lifetime to the chosen people, and forbade his disciples for the time being to preach to Gentiles (Mt. 10:5–6; 15:24). Yet here, spontaneously, there appears in a Gentile that very response which his Jewish mission had failed to evoke. It ignores and overrides racial barriers. The importance of this for Matthew we shall see shortly, but for Jesus and his disciples it is of tremendous significance. A whole new horizon has opened up. This incident is a preview of the great insight which came later through another centurion's faith, "Then to the Gentiles also God has granted repentance unto life" (Acts 11:18). The barrier between the chosen people and the rest of mankind is beginning to crumble.

The precise wording of Jesus' saying is slightly different in Matthew from that in Luke. Luke has the familiar "Not even in Israel have I found such faith", but the original Matthean form seems certainly to be, "With no-one in Israel have I found such faith." [13] W. Grundmann calls this a "radikalisierten Form" compared with the Lucan. [14] Instead of a general comparison of the centurion with Israel as a whole, the Matthean form states that not a single individual in Israel reaches his standard. It is thus a more all-embracing condemnation of Israel's unbelief, and leads appropriately to the devastating saying added by Matthew in verses 11–12. The Lucan form could even be construed as a veiled compliment to Israel: "Not even in Israel (where I would most expect it) have I found such faith." But the Matthean form leaves no room for a compliment. His emphasis is, as we shall see, single-mindedly on the rejection of Israel as the chosen race.

VERSES 11–12

This is Matthew's own addition to the story of some words of Jesus almost certainly uttered in a different context, and preserved elsewhere by Luke (13:28–29). The addition by Matthew shows clearly what was for him the main point of the story. It is two-fold: (1) the centurion, by his faith, gives evidence that Gentiles are to find a place in the kingdom of God, and (2) by the same token the Jews who do not have this faith are to be rejected from that kingdom. Thus Matthew sees faith as the means of entry to the kingdom, and race as irrelevant. The days of a chosen race are finished. God's people are now all those who believe, of whatever race.

It may be objected that Matthew is pressing the story too far. There is no mention in the story of *saving* faith, or of entering the kingdom of God. The centurion's faith is simply a practical confidence in Jesus' healing power. Certainly, Matthew is developing the theme beyond the actual narrative context, but is the development illegitimate? Is not the man who recognises in Jesus a uniquely authoritative figure, and whose faith is praised above that of any Jew, rightly taken as a symbol of the coming Gentile church? Matthew is not misunderstanding and allegorizing a simple story; he is drawing the logical conclusion from the key pronouncement which is the focus of that story.

VERSE 11

This verse envisages the Gentiles entering the kingdom. *Πολλοί* does not explicitly mean Gentiles, of course, but in parallelism with the "sons of the kingdom" (verse 12), who are clearly Jews (see below), it could have no other meaning, and the context of Jesus' pronouncement about the centurion's faith in contrast with Israel confirms this.

The words "will come from east and west" echo a recurring Old Testament formula, seen for instance in Psalm 107:3; Isaiah 43:5–6; 49:12. But the significant point is that these are predictions (or retrospective accounts) of God's regathering of dispersed *Jews*. There are similar passages which speak of Gentiles (probably, though the reference could again be to the dispersed Jews) acknowledging and worshipping God in all parts of the earth, but not *coming* (e.g. Isaiah 45:6; 59:19; Mal. 1:11). There are also passages which predict the coming of Gentiles to Jerusalem (e.g. Is. 2:2–3; 60:3–4), but not in the terms used here by Jesus. So it seems that Jesus, in predicting the coming of the Gentiles (itself an Old Testament idea), deliberately does so in words recalling Old Testament hopes of the regathering of *Israel*. Here we see already the idea of the supplanting of the chosen race by others which becomes more explicit as we go on.

The Gentiles are envisaged as gathering for a banquet, *ἀνακλιθήσονται*, literally "recline", is correctly translated "sit at table" by RSV, since it was a common practice in the ancient world to recline on couches by the table rather than to sit on chairs (cf. the disciple *ἀνακείμενος ἐν τῷ κόλπῳ τοῦ Ἰησοῦ* at the Last Supper, Jn. 13:23).[15] This is no ordinary meal, however, but one shared with Abraham, Isaac and Jacob in the kingdom of heaven. Jesus is here taking up a common Jewish eschatological idea, where the joys of the Messianic age are pictured as a banquet. Derived from such Old Testament passages as Isaiah 25:6; 65:13f, this theme was richly embroidered by later Jewish writers, both in the apocalyptic and the rabbinic traditions.[16] It would be tedious to give all the details here, but it is worth mentioning that the presence of Abraham, Isaac and Jacob at the banquet (together with other great Old Testament figures) is specifically mentioned in two rabbinic passages (Pes. 119b; Ex.R. 25:8): there will be a very polite debate about which of them shall "say grace", and in the end the honour will go to David! But the important point is that in these and most of the other relevant passages the banquet is regarded as being for the Jews only: it is "for the children of Isaac on the day when he (God) will receive them into his favour" (Pes. 119b). Sometimes the banqueters are referred to as "the pious", but it is, often explicitly, the pious within Israel who are in mind.

Jesus is, then, deliberately predicting that the eschatological banquet with the patriarchs to which the Jews looked forward as a national right will in fact include Gentiles as well. For a Jew to sit at table with Gentiles meant ritual defilement, and such an idea in the eschatological banquet would be unthinkable. But Jesus is rejecting all racial barriers. Abraham, Isaac and Jacob, the very founders of the Jewish race, will, it is assumed, be happy to sit with Gentiles, with no thought of defilement. Jesus is not predicting the conversion of Gentiles to Judaism – that would have been a very acceptable idea to many in his day. He is envisaging their inclusion in the joys of the kingdom *as Gentiles,* apparently on equal terms with the patriarchs. This is revolutionary stuff! And there is worse to come in verse 12.

VERSE 12

The phrase "sons of the kingdom" would have been readily understood by Jews – to mean themselves! "Sons of . . ." is often used in the sense of "belonging to . . .", "destined for . . .", etc. See e.g. "sons of the bridechamber" (Mt. 9:15); "son of hell" (Mt. 23:15). The Talmud frequently uses the phrase "a son of the age to come" (cf. Lk. 16:8; 20:34–35). So the "sons of the kingdom" are those to whom the kingdom belongs by right. And such was the Jewish estimate of themselves: as children of Abraham, it was their birthright. "According to the popular view in the time of Jesus, Israel's superiority over the Gentiles consisted in the fact that Israel, by virtue of its lineal descent from Abraham, enjoyed the benefits of the vicarious merits of the patriarchs, and the consequent assurance of final salvation. It was the current belief that no descendant of Abraham could be lost." [17]

Yet Jesus not only says that they must share the kingdom with the Gentiles, but that they, the rightful heirs, will themselves be excluded. Literally, his words should mean that *all* Jews are excluded, but Abraham, Isaac and Jacob are clearly not rejected. The point is that racial descent will be irrelevant. To claim to be a son of Abraham will be worthless. John the Baptist had said as much (Mt. 3:9), but no other Jew dared to suggest such a thing. By calling them "sons of the kingdom" Jesus emphasises the paradoxical reversal of roles which will take place when believing Gentiles receive what the Jews regarded as their inalienable right.

This theme of the imminent rejection of Israel as a nation from its status as God's chosen people is a common one in Jesus' teaching, often seen by implication in the way he applies Old Testament passages about Israel to his own disciples,[18] but sometimes quite explicit, as in the parable of the tenants (Mk. 12:1–9), or in Jesus' laments over Jerusalem (Lk. 13:34–35; 23:28–31).[19]

The imagery of "outer darkness", weeping, and gnashing of teeth is all found in Jewish apocalyptic or midrashic sources.[20] The difference here is that it is the "sons of the kingdom" themselves who will be the sufferers, whereas in Jewish apocalyptic it is "the sinners", "the ungodly", and certainly *not* the Jews. Some commentators suggest that the darkness is specifically mentioned in contrast with the bright lights of the banqueting hall, since it is a common apocalyptic theme that the sufferings of the lost will be increased by their being able to see the blessed in Paradise.[21]

Verses 11–12 are designed, then, to express in (for the Jew) the most shocking manner possible the change which is now imminent in the economy of God, when the chosen race will no longer have a special privilege, but the kingdom of God will be for all who believe, from whatever race, while those who do not believe, even though they may be sons of Abraham, will not be able to join their father at the banquet; when "the last shall be first, and the first last."

VERSE 13

Matthew now returns to the narrative, and concludes it with a minimum of words. Yet even in this brief conclusion a comparison with the Lucan version reveals again Matthew's overriding concern – faith. Matthew alone inserts the healing word of Jesus for which the centurion had asked; taking up the theme of verse 10, it focuses on his remarkable faith: "As you have believed let it be done for you." In the Synoptic accounts healing frequently depends on faith; how much more healing at a distance, paralleled only in Matthew 15:21–28 and John 4:46–54. The parallel with Matthew 15:27 is here very close, just as the themes of the two stories have run parallel throughout, both concerned with Jesus' encounter with a Gentile supplicant, both focusing on the trial and the triumph of faith despite the racial barrier, both culminating in healing at a distance. John 4:48, 50 also points out the faith of the father.

CONCLUSION

So a request for healing from a Gentile centurion, which gave rise to a significant dialogue with Jesus about authority and faith, has been taken further by Matthew, both in the details of his telling of the story and particularly by the insertion of an independent saying of Jesus about membership in the kingdom, to provide a more comprehensive piece of teaching on the central importance of faith not only for healing but for salvation, for inclusion in the true people of God for whom his eschatological blessings are reserved. Matthew, the evangelist to the Jews, has a great deal to say on this theme. The healing of the Gentile's servant provides him with an excellent paradigm of the universal application of the work of Jesus, and he makes sure by his telling of the story and in particular by his insertion of Jesus' devastating saying that the message is not missed.

This understanding is the result of a "redaction-critical" exegesis of the pericope in comparison with the Lucan parallel.[22] To ignore, or to try to remove, the differences in treatment would have been to lose a vital part of what Matthew wants to emphasise. As a miracle story alone the pericope is of great value, but Matthew is concerned to teach more than the miraculous power of Jesus, and the modern reader, no less than those for whom Matthew originally wrote, stands to gain much from a recognition of his special emphasis.

II. *1 Peter 3:18–22*

In contrast to Matthew 8:5–13, which was a relatively straightforward narrative-cum-sayings Gospel pericope, we turn now to a concentrated piece of doctrinal-cum-hortatory teaching in a letter. We have deliberately chosen a notoriously obscure passage, so as to see the importance of proper exegetical methods in the clearest possible light. As so often in the New Testament letters, the thought is highly concentrated, and not at all easy to follow in a logical sequence. One thought leads to another, apparently unrelated to the main theme, in a way which leaves the tidy-minded Western reader bewildered. The passage contains one notorious centre of controversy, which involves serious doctrinal implications (the "preaching to spirits" in verse 19), and a fairly obscure piece of typology (the Flood as a type of Christian baptism, verses 20–21). The whole passage has given rise to more monographs, additional notes, and excursuses than almost any other. Yet there is probably no more agreement about its exegesis now than there ever has been.

For such a passage, the generous use of commentaries is obligatory. Only so can the new-comer hope to grasp what are the issues involved, and what the nature of the evidence which has led to such controversy. One commentary is not enough, for few commentators (including, no doubt, the present writer) can resist the temptation to make all the evidence point towards their chosen solution, and to play down or even ignore the less convenient facts. By using several reputable commentaries, the reader will not find an agreed answer, but he will be in a fair position to work towards his own exegesis on the basis of a cautious awareness of the issues, not of blissful ignorance. The availability of several such commentaries is assumed in what follows, and the source of basic information is therefore not usually stated.[23]

It will soon be discovered that "the difficulty of the text lies not in the thought of the author, which is neither odd nor fantastic, but in our ignorance of his background and field of reference."[24] The author of those words continues, "More recent studies in later Jewish apocryphal writings and in early Jewish-Christian literature reveal a whole world of ideas which was powerfully at work, all the more so because simply taken for granted, in the writers of the New Testament. The exegete . . . must try to immerse himself as deeply as possible in the mental atmosphere of the biblical writer, his pre-suppositions, his categories of thought, his literary conventions." [25] In fact, if you are not prepared to dirty your hands in the muddy waters of apocalyptic and rabbinic speculations, much of the New Testament must necessarily remain obscure. To try to understand 1 Peter 3:19–20 without a copy of the Book of Enoch at your elbow is to condemn yourself to failure.

Space does not allow a discussion of the standard questions of literary criticism. We shall assume that the letter was written in the second half of the first century (and probably in the earlier part of it) by Peter or someone closely associated with him (Silvanus, writing on Peter's behalf?) to the churches of the northern part of Asia Minor, whose membership was largely, but not exclusively, Gentile. Its occasion was an outbreak of persecution against the Christians of that area, which, if the letter may be taken as a unity, had already begun, and was causing serious distress. A particular connection of the letter with baptism seems probable, but the precise form of that connection is not clear. Earlier views that it was simply a baptismal liturgy or sermon are now generally discounted, and it is accepted as a genuine letter (or "epistle" in the technical sense).

Thus the overall context of our passage is an encouragement to Christians under persecution. How serious that persecution was is disputed. Many commentators write it off as petty local discrimination against converts to Christianity, stopping far short of martyrdom. Some of the language is very strong for such a situation, particularly when it is recognized that *πάσχω* was often used for dying in persecution (cf. its use for Christ's death in 2:21). The parallel with Christ's "suffering" in 3:17–18 and 4:1 suggests martyrdom, as does the entrusting of their souls to God by those who "suffer" in 4:19. And would the "suffering" of a murderer be less than death (4:15)? Moreover, if we are right in interpreting 4:6 to refer to those who have died since hearing the gospel, a martyrdom context fits the verse best, with its contrast between being "*judged* in the flesh" and "living in the spirit"; the verse reads most naturally as an assurance on the ultimate fate of those already martyred. We shall, therefore, assume a context of persecution in which martyrdom was a real possibility. This, as we shall see, increases the relevance of 3:18 and the sequel.

The immediate context of our passage is concerned with this same theme, giving directions for the Christian's deportment under persecution. In 3:13–17 the Christian is envisaged *vis-a-vis* his persecutors. He may not compromise his loyalty to Christ, but neither must he give them proper cause to punish him: if he must suffer, let it be for his good deeds, not for bad. The same theme of uncompromising loyalty to Christ despite the suffering this may bring is taken up again after our passage, in 4:1–6.

Our exegesis must then be consistent with this context. Verses 18–22 must have something relevant to say to those facing fierce hostility in the name of Christ. It is the fault of many interpretations of the passage that they ignore this requirement, and so accuse the author of inserting an irrelevant doctrinal digression in the middle of his exhortation. The context is not to be thus flouted if the passage will yield *relevant* sense. The importance of this discussion of the context for our exegesis will soon become apparent.

We should notice at this point that many scholars have found in various parts of 1 Peter traces of early Christian hymns or credal formulae, marked by a stylized, rhythmic structure for easy memorization. One such "hymn" is often seen in verses 18 and 22; but the intervening verses are, in comparison, tortuous and prosaic, so that it is not possible to take the whole passage as a hymn. This hymnic or credal origin for verses 18 and 22 is not unlikely, and has a limited importance for exegesis.[26]

VERSE 18[27]

The main drift of this verse, at least up to the penultimate clause, is clear. It is one of the most direct statements in the New Testament of the vicarious significance of the death of Christ. But what is the relevance of such a statement in this context? The obvious answer, given in most commentaries, is that Jesus' death is given as an example of innocent suffering. The persecuted Christians of Asia Minor must be prepared to accept undeserved suffering as their Master did.[28] That such an application is intended cannot be doubted, and the mention that Jesus in his suffering was righteous seems designed to reinforce the lesson. But why then all the emphasis in this verse on the *redeeming* character of Jesus' death? Are his followers called to die for men's sins to bring them to God? Presumably not, unless Peter is here stepping right out of line with the rest of New Testament teaching. Hence the conclusion is generally drawn that Peter, having once mentioned the death of Jesus, is drawn by the attraction of the subject to explore the meaning of that death and its sequel, and forgets the exemplary purpose for which he introduced it.[29] Some would suggest that his use of a set credal formula or hymn leads him to include details from that formula which are irrelevant to his purpose in the context. Then, having indulged his doctrinal interests in a wide-ranging digression, he returns to his theme in chapter 4.

We hope to show more fully as we go on that an exegesis which thus disregards the context is quite inadequate. The emphasis in these verses is on the triumph of Jesus over all opposing powers. This triumph began in his redeeming death, was established through his resurrection, and is now effective through his ascension and sitting at God's right hand. Verse 18 is the beginning of this recital, and its relevance to the context is that the persecuted Christian, facing the powers of evil, may know that these powers are already defeated, that he shares in the triumph of his Master, to whom all powers are subject. The apparent defeat of death was for Jesus the beginning of victory. So it is for the Christian martyr: death leads to resurrection and triumph, because Jesus through his redeeming death has once for all conquered sin and all the powers of evil. This is no digression, but the very foundation of the Christian hope in which the martyr may die. The justification for this overall exegesis will emerge as we go on.

There are several details in the wording of verse 18 which deserve fuller investigation than space permits us here. It is steeped in Old Testament sacrificial ideas. *ἅπαξ* introduces the thought of the decisive, once-for-all nature of Jesus' atonement, stressed so much in Hebrews.[30] *περὶ ἁμαρτιῶν* recalls the technical term for the Old Testament sin-offering as rendered in the LXX.[31] *δίκαιος ὑπὲρ ἀδίκων* continues the sacrificial allusion by reminding of the substitutionary principle, which required an unblemished animal, and also very likely alludes to Is. 53:11, "By his knowledge shall the righteous one, my servant, make many to be accounted righteous." *προσαγάγῃ* introduces the reconciliation aspect of the atonement, reminding us of the *προσαγωγή* mentioned by Paul in Romans 5:2; Ephesians 2:18. The Old Testament background to this term is exegetically very suggestive, especially in a context of sacrificial language, but we cannot explore it here.[32] So verse 18, up to the penultimate clause, concentrates on the death of Jesus, viewed as a decisive, sacrificial, atoning, reconciling act. It is the doctrine of the atonement in a nutshell.

The last clause of verse 18 begins the transition of thought from the death of Jesus to the triumph which followed. The rhythmically balanced phrases, focusing on the two essential events of Easter, seem clearly to come from a traditional formula, and the close formal parallel of 1 Timothy 3:16 (cf. also Rom. 1:3–4) supports this.

The terms "flesh" and "spirit" need careful handling. In the world of Greek philosophy they would mean the material and immaterial "parts" of a man, of which the former dies but the latter survives. Many have automatically read this clause in such terms, without reflecting that such a distinction is foreign to Jewish thought, and that it is in the world of the Old Testament and later Jewish literature that our author moves. Nor is there any reference here to the divine and human natures of Christ: this is the New Testament, not a fifth-century doctrinal work, and the New Testament never speaks of two natures in Christ, let alone using *σάρξ* and *πνεῦμα* to describe them. *σάρξ* in the New Testament denotes the natural human sphere of existence, and *πνεῦμα* in contrast with it denotes the supernatural sphere.[33] The closest parallel to the present use is Paul's careful distinction between two modes of existence, *ψυχικός* and *πνευματικός*, in 1 Corinthians 15:42ff. His distinction there is not between "body" and "soul", but between two types of body, adapted to two different modes of existence. So here the contrast is between Christ's death in the natural sphere, and his risen life in the eternal, spiritual sphere. His earthly life ended, but that was succeeded by his heavenly life. Thus the second phrase does not refer to Christ *disembodied,* but to Christ *risen* to life on a new plane.

The reason for insisting on this is that some commentators have interpreted *ζῳοποιηθεὶς πνεύματι* of something less than, and prior to, the resurrection of Christ, of an intermediate disembodied state. This is to make the clause fit in with an interpretation of verse 19 in terms of a descent of Christ to Hades between his death and resurrection. We shall come to the exegesis of verse 19 shortly, but we must be clear before we do so that the reference of ζῳοποιηθεὶς πνεύματι is to the resurrection of Christ and nothing less, however inconvenient this may prove. An early Christian, reading this formal contrast between Jesus' death and his being "made alive" could not be expected to think of anything other than the resurrection,[34] least of all of so foreign an idea as a disembodied state. Whatever verse 19 may refer to, the last clause of verse 18 refers to the death and resurrection of Jesus.[35]

This last clause has a clear relevance to a persecuted church. Jesus was "done to death" (θανατωθείς is a strong word, with special reference to judicial killing), but this was not the end. It terminated his earthly life (σάρξ), but issued in a new risen life "in spirit". So the Christian facing martyrdom (θανατόω would be very appropriate) may be sure that death is only "in the flesh"; it will be followed by a new risen life. Verses 19 and 22 will go on to show that for Jesus death was the way to triumph, a triumph which his follower can share.

VERSE 19

Here, in these nine words, all the controversy centres. Is this a precursor of the medieval doctrine of the "harrowing of hell"?[36] If not, what is it talking about? Why is it so obscurely worded?

Before we go into detail, it would be as well to observe that Peter presumably wrote to be understood by his readers. What is obscure to us can hardly have been so obscure to them. The problem lies in our not knowing what were the common ideas, the common background of thought, which Peter shared with his readers, and to which therefore he can allude without needing to explain his reference. It is this background of thought which we must try to discover, rather than insist that the verse *must* or *cannot* refer to the harrowing of hell, purgatory, a second chance for the dead, etc. Our own doctrinal predilections are irrelevant: we want to find out what Peter meant, from the meagre words he has provided for us.

Most of the relevant issues will be raised by taking the words of the verse in order, and letting them pose the questions.

(1) Ἐν ᾧ. In what? Most recent versions and commentators say "In the spirit", taking πνεύματι, the immediately preceding noun, as the antecedent.[37] It is doubtful whether anyone would have disputed this rendering, if it did not lead in a direction incompatible with their chosen exegesis. For πνεύματι in verse 18 refers, as we have seen, to Christ's *risen* state. To take ἐν ᾧ as "in the spirit" must therefore mean that verse 19 is talking about an activity of Christ *after* his resurrection. If you are committed to referring it to the period between his death and resurrection, such an interpretation must be avoided. Accordingly some commentators take ἐν ᾧ as a conjunction without specific grammatical antecedent, meaning "when", i.e. in the course of the events mentioned in the preceding clause, *viz.* the death-resurrection sequence. In support of this interpretation they note that

ἐν ᾧ occurs in this sort of sense elsewhere in 1 Peter (1:6; 2:12; 3:16; 4:4). It is to be noted, however, that in none of these cases is there any masculine or neuter noun in the preceding clause which could be taken as the antecedent. Here the presence of an eligible antecedent *immediately* before *ἐν ᾧ* places a strong presumption in favour of its translation as a straightforward relative. Dogmatic considerations apart, it would seem that *ἐν ᾧ* must mean "in the spirit" in the sense of that word in verse 18, i.e. verse 19 must refer to an activity of the *risen* Christ.

(2) *Τοῖς ἐν φυλακῇ πνεύμασιν*. This is the crucial phrase. Who are they? There are two suggested interpretations of *πνεῦμα* here, either as men who have died, or as supernatural powers. *πνεῦμα* in the former sense occurs clearly in the New Testament only in Hebrews 12:23;[38] there is another clear use in the Song of the Three Holy Children 64, and 1 Enoch 22:3–13 has many references to "the spirits of the dead", etc. But in none of these cases is *πνεῦμα* used absolutely: it is always qualified by "of the dead", "of the righteous", etc. If *τὰ πνεύματα* here meant "men who have died", it would be a unique absolute use in this sense. This does not exclude the possibility entirely, but it casts strong doubt on it. Moreover, *ἀπειθήσασιν* in verse 20 would go strangely with this sense: one would expect "spirits of those who disobeyed" rather than "spirits who disobeyed", since on this interpretation they were living men, not spirits, at the time of disobedience.

Πνεῦμα in the sense of a supernatural being, usually evil, is common in the New Testament and contemporary literature.[39] Note particularly the title of God in 1 Enoch as "the Lord of Spirits". Used absolutely, *πνεύματα* would unquestionably be understood in this sense by a contemporary reader, especially one at all familiar with Jewish apocalyptic and other inter-testamental literature. Again, the only obstacle to accepting this meaning of the word is a preconception that verse 19 is about Christ preaching to the dead in Hades. 4:6 is often used to buttress this interpretation, but it should be noted that the word *πνεῦμα* is not used there, and that there is no reason to suppose that the two verses refer to the same event.[40]

The interpretation of *πνεύμασιν* on lexical grounds as referring to supernatural beings is confirmed by the sequel. They are those "who were once disobedient in the days of Noah". Here we step into a whole world of Jewish mythology which is foreign to most modern readers. Jewish apocalyptic and other writings make frequent reference to the passage in Genesis 6:1–4 about the sin of the "sons of God". These are regarded as angelic beings (often called "Watchers"), who, because of this sin, were cast out of heaven and imprisoned, awaiting their punishment at the final judgment. Meanwhile, either in person or through their offspring, they are the source of evil on earth.[41] These fallen angels and their punishment are referred to elsewhere in the New Testament in Jude 6 and 2 Peter 2:4. In the latter passage they are associated with Noah and the Flood, and this connection was commonly made, since the two events are related together in chapter 6 of Genesis. Testament of Naphtali 3:5 specifically states that they were cursed by God "at the Flood", and that the Flood came on their account, and Jubilees 10:5 regards their sin as taking place in Noah's day.

But it is the Book of Enoch which gives the most detailed account of the sin and punishment of the angels, to which it returns again and again. The story is told in great detail in 1 Enoch 6–16, and the prison where the angels are bound is described in 18:12–19:2; 21:1–10. There are further references in 54:3–6, and throughout chapters 64–69. The story is told again in symbolic form in chapters 86–88, and a further reference occurs in 106:13–17. A bare listing of these references is not enough to indicate the extent of the hold which this mythology had on the minds of the authors of the Enochic literature: the exegete who wants to get inside the skin of the writer and original readers of 1 Peter (and of 2 Peter and Jude at least) should read the relevant parts of 1 Enoch in full. As he does so he will discover numerous points of contact with 1 Peter 3:19–20. He will find the fallen angels referred to as *πνεύματα* (15:4, 6, 8), he will find many references to their imprisonment,[42] and he will find their disobedience (21:6 etc.) connected with Noah and the Flood.[43] But most striking of all is the fact that in chapter 12 Enoch is given a commission to go to these fallen angels and proclaim to them their punishment; this mission is the subject of chapters 12–16. Here is a remarkable parallel to Christ's mission in 1 Peter 3:19 (compare *πορευθεὶς ἐκήρυξεν* with Enoch's commission in 12:4, *πορεύου καὶ εἰπε* . . .).[44]

The evidence is more than sufficient to indicate that *τὰ ἐν φυλακῇ πνεύματα* must be the fallen angels who, according to apocalyptic tradition, sinned at the time of Noah, and are in custody awaiting their final punishment. To us the reference is obscure; to a church which knew and prized the Book of Enoch (as the author of Jude so evidently did too) it would need no explanation.

(3) *Πορευθείς*. *Where* did he go to, and *when*? Advocates of a reference here to Christ's going down to Hades between his death and resurrection naturally assume that *πορευθείς* indicates "descended". But it does not say so. Indeed, in verse 22 the very same participle is used of his going *into heaven*. In itself it is neutral. Clearly he went to wherever the spirits were in their prison. And on this point Jewish tradition is divided. A prison under the earth is indicated in Jubilees 5:6, 10 ("depths of the earth"), and this tradition is apparently followed in Revelation 20, where the *φυλακή* of verse 7 is presumably the *ἄβυσσος* of verses 1 and 3.[45] In 1 Enoch 17–18, however, the place is reached by a journey to the furthest west, where heaven and earth join, and there, *beyond* a chasm, he finds the prison in "a place which had no firmament of the heaven above, and no firmly founded earth beneath it", which is described as "the end of heaven and earth" (18:12, 14).[46] The prison of the angels is elevated still further by the rather later 2 Enoch, which locates it in the second of seven heavens (2 Enoch 7:1–3; 18:3–6; cf. also Test. Levi 3:2), using a new cosmology developed in Hellenistic circles, and much valued in late Jewish and early Christian works (see e.g. 2 Cor. 12:2). It has therefore been suggested that 1 Peter 3:19 had this view in mind, and regards Christ as visiting the fallen angels in the course of his

ascension (thus taking *πορευθείς* in the same sense as in verse 22), as he passed through the lower heavens towards the seventh. This is attractive, but the text lacks any suggestion of acquaintance with the seven-heavens cosmology, so we may most prudently record a *non liquet* on the precise location of the prison. The main point to be established is that there is no mention of going down, or of Sheol or Hades (which is *never* called *φυλακή* in biblical literature).[47] Christ went to the prison of the fallen angels, not to the abode of the dead, and the two are never equated.

The question of *when* Jesus made this journey has already been raised with reference to the phrase *ἐν ᾧ*, which we argued must refer to his risen state. Unless there is evidence to the contrary, this journey must therefore be dated at some time after the resurrection. It is tempting to connect it with the use of *πορευθείς* in verse 22 for the ascension, but *πορεύομαι* is a very general and common verb of "going", and its repetition here need not be significant. The precise time, like the precise location, may be left undecided. But what does seem clear is that it was not, as some commentators have suggested, *between* his death and resurrection.[48] This conflicts with the natural meaning of *ἐν ᾧ* and also interrupts the sequence of thought which has already reached the resurrection at the end of verse 18, returns to it at the end of verse 21, and proceeds to the ascension in verse 22. This sequence confirms that verse 19 should be read as a sequel to, not a precursor of, the resurrection.

(4) *Ἐκήρυξεν*. What did Jesus preach (or, more literally, "proclaim") to the spirits in prison? The verb means "to act as herald", and so is essentially neutral as to the content of the message. This neutral use is found in Revelation 5:2.[49] But in the vast majority of New Testament uses it refers to preaching the gospel. Here, where it is used absolutely, it would therefore need strong arguments to disprove that it carries its usual New Testament meaning of preaching the gospel of repentance and forgiveness. That is how the majority of commentators take it.

There are, however, strong arguments against this interpretation in this particular case. (a) In the LXX, whose language is clearly familiar to our author, *κηρύσσω* is used as often of bringing bad news as of good: see e.g. Jonah 1:2; 3:2, 4. (b) Enoch's mission to the fallen angels, which was certainly in the author's mind, as we have seen, was to proclaim judgment; when they plead for mercy he has to refuse it (1 Enoch 13–15, esp. 14:4–5). (c) The statement in verse 22 that all spiritual powers are subject to Christ would cohere better with a proclamation of his victory than with an offer of salvation. (d) The purpose of the letter, to boost the morale of persecuted Christians, would be better served by a mention of Christ's triumphing over evil powers than of an offer of salvation to them. This last point we shall develop further shortly. Meanwhile, these arguments seem to the present writer sufficient to demand here the original neutral meaning of *κηρύσσω*, "to make proclamation"; the reference would then be to an announcement to the fallen angels of his triumph over them and all evil through his death and resurrection, which have placed all spiritual powers under his control (v.22).

We conclude then that 1 Peter 3:19 has nothing to do with a descent of Christ to Hades, or a second chance for the dead, but refers to a tradition not mentioned elsewhere in the New Testament that after his resurrection Christ proclaimed his victory to the fallen angels in the "prison" where they were awaiting their final punishment. Whether the other New Testament writers did not know this tradition, or knew it but had no occasion to mention it in the writings preserved, it was clearly well-known to Peter's readers. It is closely related to the common New Testament theme of Christ's triumph through the cross over Satan, death, and all powers of evil.[50] It shows the all-embracing sovereignty and control of the risen Christ.

And this was a theme of real practical importance to Peter's readers. They might be called to endure the worst that anti-Christian prejudice could inflict. But even then they could be assured that their pagan opponents, and, more important, the spiritual powers of evil that stood behind them and directed them, were not outside Christ's control: they were already defeated, awaiting final punishment. Christ had openly triumphed over them. Here is real comfort and strength for a persecuted church which took very seriously the reality and power of spiritual forces. These brief allusive words of Peter convey the same message of encouragement as Paul's great "more than conquerors" passage in Romans 8:31–39.

It is the greatest strength of the exegesis here proposed that it yields a sense so pastorally relevant to the context of a persecuted church.[51]

VERSE 20

We have already dealt with the disobedience of the spirits in the days of Noah. The mention of God's patience may reflect a current interpretation of Genesis 6:3, that the 120 years referred not to man's life-span, but to the period of grace granted before the punishment should come.[52] The dating of the angels' sin within this period is in agreement with Jewish tradition, as we have already seen.

The mention of the flood now leads to a change of scene; the fallen angels are left behind, and the Flood, once mentioned, becomes the basis for more teaching relevant to the encouragement of persecuted Christians. Two facts are isolated from the story: (1) that few were saved; (2) that they were saved "through water".

That few were saved was of obvious pastoral application. The persecuted Christians must have been painfully conscious of their small numbers and relative feebleness compared to the pagan majority among whom they lived. But Noah and his crew were an even smaller minority: only eight out of the whole wicked population of the world. Yet they were saved, and the world destroyed. If Peter had known the cliché, he might have added, "One with God is a majority"![53]

That they were saved *through water* is the means of transition to the next theme, baptism, of which this water is regarded as a type; verse 21 expounds this typology and its significance for the readers. The precise meaning of "through" is debated: is it local (they passed *through* the water to safety) or instrumental (*by means of* the water)? Both could be true of Noah, though the former is much more obvious: the idea of the water which destroyed the rest of mankind and *from* which Noah escaped being nonetheless the *means* of his salvation (by carrying the ark) is a little whimsical, though certainly not beyond the imagination of a keen typologist. On the other hand, the instrumental sense is much easier when one considers the typological application: the Christian is more easily viewed as saved "by means of" the water of baptism than by passing through it, though the latter is also possible. Probably Peter is deliberately exploiting the ambiguity of the word διά to assist his passage from the Old Testament story to its typological application.[54]

VERSE 21

The first seven words, in which the typological relation is succinctly expressed, are almost impossibly difficult to construe from the grammatical point of view.[55] The main questions are: (1) What is the antecedent of ὅ? (2) Does ἀντίτυπον refer to ὑμᾶς or to βάπτισμα? (3) Assuming that ὅ is the subject, what is the syntactical function of βάπτισμα (or, if βάπτισμα is the subject, where does ὅ fit in!)? Space forbids a discussion of these questions. We shall assume that the antecedent of ὅ is the immediately preceding ὕδατος, that ἀντίτυπον refers to ὑμᾶς and that βάπτισμα is an explanatory addition, in apposition to ὅ (*viz.,* water); this gives the translation, "which (water) now also saves you, the antitype (of Noah and his crew) – that is, baptism." However, a little juggling with the different grammatical possibilities will soon show that the various permutations all yield essentially the same sense, that as Noah and his family were saved through water, so Christians are saved through the water of baptism, the relationship of the latter to the former being described as ἀντίτυπον. Exegetically ἀντίτυπον is the key.

The only other New Testament use of ἀντίτυπος is Hebrews 9:24, where it refers to an earthly sanctuary as a "copy" of the true sanctuary of heaven. But within the same word group we also find τύπος used for the "model" or "pattern" from which such a copy is made (Ac. 7:44; Heb. 8:5 quoting LXX Ex. 25:40), for a moral "example" to be copied (1 Pet. 5:3 and several other uses), and, most significantly for our purpose, for Old Testament figures as "types", prefigurations, of New Testament persons (Rom. 5:14; 1 Cor. 10:6, cf. τυπικῶς in 10:11, though in 1 Cor. 10 the sense of "example" is probably adequate in context). Here we have all the materials for, and probably the actual beginning of, the technical use of τύπος as a hermeneutical term which quickly developed in the Christian church. That typology, by whatever name or none, was widely practised by Christians right from the time of Jesus himself cannot be doubted.[56] Here we have the beginning of its technical terminology.

The essential principle of New Testament typology is that God works according to a regular pattern, so that what he has done in the past, as recorded in the Old Testament, can be expected to find its counterpart in his work in the decisive period of the New Testament. Thus persons, events and institutions of the Old Testament, which in themselves need have no forward reference, are cited as "types", models of corresponding persons, events and institutions in the life of Christ and the Christian church.[57] On this principle, then, as ἀντίτυπον warns us, Peter takes the salvation of Noah in the Flood as a model of the Christian's salvation through baptism. He has thus accomplished another change of scene, from the story of the Flood to Christian baptism, which is startlingly abrupt to the modern reader, but which would seem quite natural to a reader accustomed to typological application of Old Testament narratives. A grasp of the typological principle will go a long way towards dispelling the exegetical obscurity of some parts of the New Testament.

Peter's confident pronouncement that the water of baptism "saves you" is sure to sound an alarm bell in a faithful Protestant mind. Is this a doctrine of baptismal regeneration, an *ex opere operato* view of the sacrament? Two points may be made in this connection. Firstly, such "realist" language concerning the effect of baptism is by no means unparalleled in the New Testament;[58] any view of baptism which finds it a rather embarrassing ceremonial extra, irrelevant to Christian salvation, is not doing justice to New Testament teaching. But, secondly, Peter is very careful to qualify his statement immediately by pointing out the true nature of baptism, involving two aspects, one negative and one positive, which between them effectively allay fears of a "magical" view of the sacrament.

The negative aspect is given in the strange words, "not a removal of dirt from the body". This is certainly not a straightforward way of saying "not the outward act of washing", but that is the meaning assumed by almost all commentators:[59] Peter is defending the true nature of baptism by asserting that the outward act does not bring salvation in itself, but only as it represents a right inward attitude. The words are unusual, but they are certainly not inappropriate to convey the sense of an outward, physical washing, perhaps with reference to the Jewish ritual washing before meals: baptism is not a matter of washing away ritual uncleanness, but a transaction with God in the sphere of συνείδησις.

This brings us to the second, positive, aspect of baptism, and to another very obscure phrase: συνειδήσεως ἀγαθῆς ἐπερώτημα εἰς θεόν. The two key words are clearly συνείδησις and ἐπερώτημα. Etymologically, ἐπερώτημα (which occurs only here in the New Testament) ought to mean "enquiry", "asking a question". That is the almost invariable meaning of the common verb, ἐπερωτάω. In Matthew 16:1 the verb carries the very unusual meaning "request",[60] and on this basis some have translated ἐπερώτημα here as "a *request* (appeal) to God for a good conscience". If the more obvious meaning "enquiry" made any sense here, there would be no need to suggest this translation, which would be unique in the whole of Greek literature, but it is not easy to see how baptism could be viewed as an "enquiry" to God, nor how συνειδήσεως ἀγαθῆς would fit in with this meaning. We are, then, apparently faced with a choice between the regular meaning "enquiry", which makes no sense in the context, and an otherwise unknown meaning, "request", which is at least intelligible, but which introduces a view of baptism, as an act of supplication, for which there is no parallel in the New Testament or the early church.

The solution to this dilemma is found in the papyri, where *ἐπερώτημα* appears as a technical term in legal contracts, signifying the formal question addressed by one party to the other *and* the response, a formal undertaking or pledge. Etymologically, *ἐπερώτημα* would be expected to denote only the first of these, but in fact it is used for the total transaction, and so carries the meaning "pledge", "undertaking", "contract".[61] Here we have a meaning clearly relevant to baptism, where the baptizer puts formal questions to the candidate concerning his beliefs and his moral commitment, and the candidate responds with a "pledge". Such a form of baptism is attested very early in the Christian church, and may well be referred to in the New Testament.[62] Most recent commentators accordingly accept the meaning "pledge".

The genitive preceding *ἐπερώτημα* could be related to it either as subjective ("pledge proceeding from a good conscience") or objective ("pledge to maintain a good conscience"). The latter seems more consistent with the New Testament view of baptism as a transition from the old life to the new: it looks *forward* to a life of obedience, rather than being based on an already good conscience.

The precise meaning of *συνείδησις* is never easy to define. It is certainly much wider than "conscience", as even its other uses in this letter (2:19; 3:16) will show. A long discussion in TDNT[63] concludes that in the "Post-Pauline Writings" *συνείδησις ἀγαθή* is "a formula for the Christian life" in all its aspects. Commentators suggest "disposition" or "attitude" as translations for *συνείδησις* here, with sometimes an element of "loyalty" or "sense of duty".[64] Thus the total meaning of the phrase before us will be a pledge to God of a life loyally devoted to his service. The contrast with the preceding negative clause is thus very strong: the saving significance of baptism does not lie in the external, physical act of washing, but in the moral and spiritual commitment to God which it symbolizes.

The verse concludes with an unexpected addition, "through the resurrection of Jesus Christ". The connection of baptism with the resurrection of Christ is expounded by Paul in Romans 6:1–11. It is a uniting with Christ in his death and resurrection, leading to a sharing of his risen life. Some such idea is probably the connection of thought leading Peter to reintroduce the resurrection in his argument here. It erodes still further any mechanical idea of the efficacy of baptism, by adding another aspect of its spiritual significance. Not only is baptism an act of commitment by the candidate: it is also a uniting with the risen Christ giving him the power to live up to his commitment.

We have now examined verse 21 in detail to see just what Peter is saying about the nature of baptism, and why he regards it as the antitype of the

Flood. But why did he mention baptism at all? Was he simply carried away by the fascination of typology, so that, having mentioned the Flood, he could not resist pointing out its typical significance? And then, realizing that he might have laid himself open to misunderstanding, did he feel obliged to qualify his statement that baptism "saves" before he could return to his theme? Or is this perhaps a deliberate turn in the argument, introduced because it was relevant to his readers' situation, and not just an academic digression? We have so far eschewed the suggestion of irrelevant academic theorising; must we admit it here?

If, as many scholars believe, the whole letter is closely connected with baptism, either as incorporating parts of a baptismal liturgy or sermon, or as written for the occasion when baptism was to be administered, here is an obvious explanation for the "digression" of verse 21. But has it no relevance to the overall theme of the Christian under persecution? These were men whose faith was costly, and who were in dire need of assurance that the salvation for which they faced persecution was a reality. Just as Luther was to return in times of doubt and despair to the assurance "baptizatus sum", so Peter reminds his readers of what their baptism means. It marks them out as God's chosen few who, like Noah, will be saved though all around mock them and perish. Their baptismal pledge commits them to unswerving loyalty to God whatever the consequences. And their baptism is a symbol of their being united with the risen Christ, who in his resurrection has triumphed over all the powers of evil. It is a reminder, in fact, of all that they stand for, and of the strength in which they stand, the victory of the risen Christ. It is, properly understood, a real assurance of salvation, and as such is intensely relevant to a persecuted minority. This is no academic digression.

VERSE 22

The last phrase of verse 21 has brought Peter back to the theme of the end of verse 18 and of verse 19, the triumph of the risen Christ. This theme he now concludes with an exultant description of Christ's ascension and sitting at God's right hand with all powers subject to him. The language used is based on Psalm 110:1, and has many parallels in the New Testament. It poses no serious exegetical problems. Verse 19 has shown the victory of Christ over the fallen angels; verse 22 rounds out the picture to include the whole range of spiritual powers.[65] To the modern Western reader this may appear no more than a picturesque way of expressing the universality of the dominion of Christ "at the right hand of God". But experience in African society shows that to a community in which evil spirits are a part of everyday concern, and in which securing protection against the powers of evil ranks very high among life's priorities, such a bold assurance is breathtaking. We may be sure that Peter's readers, who were facing the very real onslaught of evil powers through their persecutors, could find real courage from these words.

CONCLUSION

We insisted at the outset that the key to the exegesis of such a passage is its context. The verses both preceding and following our passage are concerned with the Christian's attitude under persecution. It is the exegete's duty to discover why, *in this context,* Peter feels it right to delve into the rather obscure and complicated doctrinal matters dealt with in verses 18–22. It is not good enough to accuse him of exercising his private theological hobby-horses in an irrelevant academic digression set in the middle of a serious piece of pastoral exhortation.

It has been our aim in the detailed exegesis above to keep this context always in mind, and to show how each point introduced is relevant to the readers' situation. We cannot pretend that the passage is plain sailing. The author does have a tendency to jump from thought to thought extremely rapidly, sometimes with little more obvious logical connection than in a game of word-chains. But he does not lose sight of his readers, and each point, however obscurely connected with what precedes, has a practical bearing on the situation of a persecuted church.

We shall attempt to make this clear by concluding with a paraphrase of 1 Peter 3:18–22, along the lines of the exegesis outlined above, adding in brackets the relevance of the various points to the situation of the original readers.

". . . 17. It is better to suffer, if suffer you must, for good deeds than for bad. 18. Because Christ also suffered for no fault of his own when he, the just one, died on behalf of the unjust. (So do not complain if your suffering too is undeserved.) His death was an effective, once-for-all sacrifice to make atonement for (your?) sins, so that you might be restored to fellowship with God. (It is for this faith that you are called to suffer; it is no optional extra, but the only way of salvation; it is worth the cost.) He was put to death (as you may well be), but that was only in the earthly sphere: he has been raised to new spiritual life (as you will be too, if you die for him). (So death was, for Jesus, the way of achievement and victory; do not fear those who can only kill the body.) 19. In the triumph of his resurrection he went to the fallen angels awaiting judgment in their place of confinement, and proclaimed to them the victory won by his redeeming death. (Even the most wicked of spiritual powers have had to recognize the authority of the risen Jesus; whatever the forces against you, they are not his equal.) 20. These were those spirits who rebelled against God in the days of Noah, while God in his mercy was still withholding the punishment of the Flood (as he is now delaying judgment on your persecutors), and the ark was being built, but, when the Flood came, there were few, only eight, who were saved in the ark. (It is nothing new to be a minority standing for God. Noah and his family must have been very conscious of the weight of opposition, but in the end they were saved, and the rest drowned. "Fear not, little flock.") It was through water that Noah and his family were saved, 21. and similarly the water of baptism now saves you, since Noah's experience was a prefiguration of

Christian experience. (So let your baptism be an assurance to you of your ultimate salvation.) Of course, it is not the mere outward washing of the body which is the essence of baptism, but the candidate's commitment to a life of loyal service to God. (Do not forget your pledge. You are committed, and can not go back, however strong the pressure. The ceremony without the commitment is not true baptism, and gives no ground for assurance.) Baptism involves your union with the risen Christ (and hence gives you the power to remain faithful), 22. who has now gone into heaven, where he sits at God's right hand, and all angels and spiritual powers are under his control. (So whom have you to fear? You are on the winning side. Your persecutors, and the spiritual forces which drive them on, can have no ultimate victory. Your Lord reigns!)"

NOTES

1. The vexed question of the relationship of Jn. 4:46–54 to this Synoptic pericope is beyond our scope here. Whether or not the Johannine account refers to the same incident (and this is at least doubtful), it is clearly not derived from the same strand of tradition. See further C. H. Dodd, *Historical Tradition in the Fourth Gospel* (Cambridge 1963), pp. 188–195.

2. In such cases it is, of course, always arguable that Jesus made the same point in similar words on two different occasions. There is no inherent improbability in this suggestion, and many of the parallel traditions in the Gospels may most probably be accounted for in this way. In this particular case, however, the force of the saying is so clearly in line with the emphasis Matthew is concerned to bring out by his handling of the rest of the narrative (as the discussion below hopes to show) that it seems more probable that he was responsible for its insertion at this point.

3. See S. Travis above, pp. 157–159.

4. *The History of the Synoptic Tradition* (E.T. Oxford 1963), p. 38, n. 4.

5. Five of these refer to Jesus, and derive from *'ebed* in Is. 42ff: one (Mt. 12:18) is an actual quotation of Is. 42:1. So here the meaning "servant" is certain. The others are in Luke and Acts referring to David and to Israel as God's *παῖς*.

6. T. W. Manson, *The Sayings of Jesus* (London 1949), p. 64 argues that the original meaning was "son", on the assumption that Jn. 4:46–54 refers to the same incident. This involves the improbable supposition that the *δοῦλος* of Lk. 7:8 is a different person from the *παῖς* of 7:7 (and, presumably, the *δοῦλος* of 7:2!).

7. G. Bornkamm, G. Barth, and H.-J. Held, *Tradition and Interpretation in Matthew* (E.T. London 1963), p. 194.

8. TDNT 3, p. 294, *s.v. ἱκανός*. This article is a good illustration of the direct exegetical usefulness of TDNT at many points.

9. Note Matthew's addition of *μόνον*, emphasising the miraculous element in the cure requested.

10. Many commentators press the analogy further: the commander represents Jesus; whom then do the soldiers represent? To whom is Jesus envisaged as issuing commands? To this question there can be only one answer – the powers of illness, the demons or spirits to whom the servant's paralysis is supposed to have been attributed. But was this a right question to ask? Must we expect point-for-point correspondence? The point of the analogy lies in the authority which achieves its end by a mere word of command. There is no mention of spirits or demons in this story, or indeed in any story of the healing of *paralysis*. (Acts 8:7 deliberately distinguishes between exorcism of spirits and healing of paralysis.) Good exegesis does not require pressing every comparison or parable to the point of full allegorical correspondence.

11. G. Zuntz argued strongly for this reading in JTS 46 (1945), pp. 183ff; cf. J. Jeremias,

Jesus' Promise to the Nations (E.T. London 1958), p. 30 n.4, arguing that ὑπὸ ἐξουσίαν is a mistranslation of the original Aramaic phrase "*in* authority"; also M. Black, *An Aramaic Approach to the Gospels and Acts* (Oxford 1967[3]), p. 159, supporting the same reading on grounds of parallelism.

12. E.g. Lk. 1:66; 22:37; Jn. 4:23; 1 Cor. 5:7; 11:9; 12:13, Heb. 5:12; 12:29.

13. Many MSS have substituted the Lucan wording, as frequently happens in Synoptic passages, but a large number of the most reliable early MSS and versions preserve this text.

14. *Das Evangelium nach Matthäus* (Berlin 1971[2]), p. 252.

15. Some commentators (e.g. Lohmeyer, Schlatter) suggest that the reclining in itself indicates a banquet in contrast to an ordinary meal (where one would sit). But ἀνακλίνομαι and κατακλίνομαι seem to be more widely used in the New Testament, including the very informal meal of the five thousand (Mk. 6:39), and the meal at the house of Simon the Pharisee whose lack of due ceremony Jesus particularly noted (Lk. 7:36ff).

16. Details of these expectations may be found by consulting SB (under Mt. 8:11, where one is referred to a long excursus in Vol. IV/2 on Jewish ideas of heaven and hell), or, more briefly, by looking up δεῖπνον in TDNT. McNeile's commentary refers one to a useful treatment in G. Dalman, *The Words of Jesus* (E.T. Edinburgh 1902), pp. 110–113.

17. J. Jeremias, *Jesus' Promise to the Nations* (E.T. London 1958), p. 48.

18. For details see R. T. France, *Jesus and the Old Testament* (London 1971), pp. 60–67.

19. Cf. ibid., pp. 67–74. See further Tyn.B 26 (1975), pp. 53–78.

20. See examples quoted by W. C. Allen, *The Gospel according to S. Matthew* (Edinburgh 1907), p. 78. SB give further examples: see under Mt. 8:12 for references to relevant sections of the Excursus in Vol. IV/2.

21. The Lucan parallel (13:28–29) brings this aspect out more clearly with its use of ὄψεσθε.

22. The discussion of the pericope by H.–J. Held, op. cit., pp. 193–197, provides a valuable example of the redaction-critical approach and its positive contribution to exegesis.

23. The following provide a representative cross-section of good recent commentaries in English: E. G. Selwyn, *The First Epistle of St. Peter* (London 1947[2]); F. W. Beare, *The First Epistle of Peter* (Oxford 1970[3]); B. Reicke, *The Epistles of James, Peter, and Jude* (New York 1964); J. N. D. Kelly, *The Epistles of Peter and of Jude* (London 1969); E. Best, *1 Peter* (London 1971).

24. W. J. Dalton, *Christ's Proclamation to the Spirits: a study of 1 Peter 3:18–4:6* (Rome 1965), p. 7. This detailed study by a Jesuit scholar is a fine example of painstaking, responsible and independent exegesis. A few hours with this book would richly repay the serious student, not only as a contribution to his understanding of this text, but as an example of how the job should be done.

25. Ibid., p. 9.

26. See above, pp. 235–241 on such hymns in the N.T.

27. There are several uncertainties about the text of this verse, but none of them affects the exegesis significantly. Whether or not ὑπὲρ ὑμῶν, ὑπὲρ ἡμῶν, or just ἡμῶν is added after περὶ ἁμαρτιῶν matters little: the thought is of Christ dying for sins, without restriction to any one group. Similarly, whether ὑμᾶς or ἡμᾶς is read, it is Christians in general who are clearly thought of as being brought to God. The variants ἔπαθεν/ἀπέθανεν might seem more significant, but in fact it is not doubted that if ἔπαθεν is read it must refer in this context to the *death* of Christ, as in 2:21, so the reference is the same whichever verb is read.

28. Compare the similar sequence of thought in 2:18–21a, leading to 2:21b–25.

29. Cf. Mk. 10:45, where Jesus' death, introduced as an example of selfless "service", is then described in terms of its redemptive purpose, which presumably the disciples are not called to imitate.

30. Heb. 9:25–28; cf. 7:27; 9:12; 10:10.

31. See e.g. Lev. 5:6–7; Ezk. 43:21; Ps. 39:7 (Heb. 40:7; EVV 40:6). The LXX form is singular, περὶ ἁμαρτίας but the plural is used in this technical sense in Heb. 5:3; 10:26 (cf. 1 Jn. 2:2; 4:10), and would be so understood by a reader familiar with the LXX.

32. See TDNT I, pp. 131–134.

33. Among many discussions of these and related terms, see the relevant articles in TDNT and W. J. Dalton, op. cit., pp. 124–134.

34. ζῳοποιεῖν is not in fact used elsewhere of Christ's resurrection; but it is used frequently of believers being raised to eternal life, in Rom. 8:11 in explicit parallel with the resurrection of Jesus.
35. The datives σαρκί and πνεύματι are usually, and rightly, taken as "datives of reference", meaning "as to the flesh", "as to the spirit". *Πνεύματι* alone could be taken as instrumental, "made alive *by* the spirit", but it would make little sense to speak of Jesus being "put to death *by* the flesh", and the two balancing phrases may be assumed to have the same grammatical structure.
36. The doctrine is already well developed in the *Odes of Solomon* 42, probably written in the second century, so it is not *a priori* impossible that it appears in the New Testament.
37. Selwyn argued against this on the ground that nowhere else in the New Testament does a relative depend on a dative of reference. Kelly replies with reason that the ancient commentators took it that way, and Greek was their native language!
38. In Lk. 24:37, 39 it means a "ghost", probably regarded as man's angelic counterpart or "double"; cf. Acts 12:15. In Lk. 23:46 (cf. Acts 7:59) it is in a quotation from Ps. 31:5, where "my spirit" probably means simply "myself".
39. For some New Testament examples of the absolute use see Mt. 8:16; 12:45; Lk: 10:20; Ac. 23:8–9.
40. Note also that the verb in 4:6 is εὐαγγελίζομαι, not, as here, κηρύσσω, which we shall argue has a quite different meaning in this context. 4:6 is probably to be interpreted with reference to Christians who have died: "This is why the gospel was preached to those (who are now) dead . . ."
41. See e.g. Jubilees 5:1–11; 10:1–13; 2 Baruch 56:10–13. For further references see W. J. Dalton, op. cit., pp. 169–170.
42. See esp. δεσμωτήριον in 18:14; 21:10, and the whole idea of bonds in chapter 10.
43. See the sequence from chapter 6 to chapter 10, and within chapters 65–67; and esp. 106:13–17.
44. So remarkable is the parallel that some have proposed an emendation of 1 Peter 3:19 to read ἐν ᾧ καὶ Ἐνωχ τοῖς . . ., the name of Enoch having been lost from the text because of its similarity in sound to ἐν ᾧ καί. This emendation has even found its way into the translations of Moffatt and Goodspeed. It finds little support today, simply because a narration of *Enoch*'s mission intrudes without justification into the context here, where Christ is the subject both of verse 18 and of verse 22. But the suggestion is evidence of how irresistibly this verse recalls the Enoch literature to those who are acquainted with it.
45. Cf. also 2 Pet. 2:4, ταρταρώσας, though it is questionable whether the word need still convey the classical Greek view of Tartarus as a *subterranean* dungeon.
46. There is also a mention of the fallen angels being *on earth,* in the Lebanon region: 13:9.
47. See W. J. Dalton, op. cit., pp. 157–159.
48. Other New Testament evidence for such a journey is very precarious, the only likely references being Ac. 2:27, 31 (where Jesus' being in Hades simply means being dead – cf. Mt. 12:40), and Eph. 4:9, which can also be interpreted of the "descent to earth" of the incarnation. Rom. 10:7 is a hypothetical suggestion which is mentioned only to be rejected.
49. Cf. Lk. 12:3; Ac. 15:21; Rom. 2:21; Gal. 5:11.
50. E.g. Lk. 10:17–18; Jn. 12:31; 1 Cor. 15:24–28; Eph. 1:20–22; Col. 2:15.
51. B. Reicke, p. 111, takes the application further, and suggests that Christ is still being presented here as an example: as he preached even to the very powers of evil, so they should be prepared to preach to their persecutors. This application would depend on taking κηρύσσω in the sense of "preach the gospel".
52. So Targum Onkelos *ad loc.* Note that 1 Enoch 9:11 also refers to God's patience before the Flood, with reference to the sin of the angels.
53. For attempts to find symbolic meaning in the number eight (which interestingly is mentioned also in 2 Pet. 2:5 in the same connection) see the commentaries of Reicke and Kelly. Reicke takes it of the *totality* of the church, Kelly of the eighth day, the day of resurrection and of baptism. Such numerical symbolism seems to be largely a matter of taste! In context the more obvious significance is to stress how *few* they were.
54. So e.g. Beare and Kelly.

55. So difficult that even the cautious Hort proposed to emend a text which is very firmly supported in the MSS by accepting Erasmus' conjecture of ᾧ for ὅ (for which there is *no* early MS support), thus contravening all the accepted canons of textual criticism!
56. For typology in the teaching of Jesus, see R. T. France, op. cit., pp. 43–80; for Paul see E. E. Ellis, *Paul's Use of the Old Testament* (Edinburgh 1957), pp. 126–135.
57. The subject is well treated by G. W. H. Lampe and K. J. Woollcombe, *Essays on Typology* (London 1957), pp. 9–38; more briefly, R. T. France, op. cit., pp. 38–43.
58. See e.g. Jn. 3:5; Rom. 6:3–4; Gal. 3:27; Col. 2:12; Titus 3:5.
59. The oddity of the language used has caused W. J. Dalton, op. cit., pp. 215–224, to suggest that the phrase refers not to an act of washing but to the Jewish rite of circumcision, commonly regarded as the removal of uncleanness. His case is well argued, but there remains the difficulty of explaining why it would be relevant to mention circumcision at this point to a largely Gentile readership, and the question whether such readers could be expected to recognize such a cryptic way of referring to circumcision.
60. The simple verb *ἐρωτάω* often carries this meaning, but the only other use of the compound *ἐπερωτάω* in this sense seems to be LXX Ps. 136:3.
61. See MM *s.v.*; cf. G. C. Richards, JTS 32 (1931), p. 77.
62. Rom. 10:9; 1 Tim. 6:12. Ac. 8:37, which clearly illustrates the point, is not the original reading, but is a Western gloss already known by Irenaeus towards the end of the second century.
63. TDNT 7, pp. 898–919.
64. See esp. 2:19 for this last element.
65. For lists of spiritual beings comparable to the three-fold list here cf. Rom. 8:38; 1 Cor. 15:24; Eph. 1:21; Col. 1:16. Such lists are found also in Jewish writings: see SB on Eph. 1:21.

PART FOUR

The New Testament and the Modern Reader

CHAPTER XV

DEMYTHOLOGIZING – THE PROBLEM OF MYTH IN THE NEW TESTAMENT*

James D. G. Dunn

The subject of myth is a vast and complex one. To do it justice one would require an all-embracing competence in such diverse fields as early Greek literature and drama, the comparative study of religion, anthropology, psychoanalysis and the philosophy of history. It is important, however, that the problem of myth in the NT – that is whether there is myth in the NT, and if so what the NT exegete does with it – should not be tackled on too narrow a front, but rather should be set in the wider context of the investigation and treatment of myth in other disciplines. We shall first therefore briefly examine the concept of myth in general (I); we should then hopefully be in a better position to evaluate the various claims made over the past 150 years or so that mythological thinking and particular myths have decisively influenced the NT writers in their presentation of the salvation event of Jesus Christ – particularly the key contributions of D. F. Strauss (II), the History of Religions school (III) and R. Bultmann (IV).

I. *The Problem of Definition*

The basic problem of myth is the problem of definition. There are two questions here: (1) What is myth? Is the word "myth" a hold-all for a wide diversity of meanings, or should its use be restricted as a narrowly defined technical term – clearly marked off, for example, from legend and saga, folk tale and fairy tale, symbol and analogy? (2) What is the function of myth; what does myth do? Or, as I prefer to put the question, What is the *truth* of myth? Does one remain at the level of explicit statement and story? Or is the truth of myth *implicit* – a subconscious and unintended disclosure of the nature of man and his world?

(1) What is myth? "There is no one definition of myth, no Platonic form of a myth against which all actual instances can be measured."[1] The problem of definition extends back to the original usage of the word μῦθος. In terms of etymology it means simply "word" or "story". And in early Greek literature its meaning can range from a "true story", "an account of facts", and so "fact" itself, to an invented story, a legend, fairy story, fable or poetic creation.[2] But in later Greek thought *mythos* came to stand in antithesis both to *logos* (rational thought) and *historia,* and so came to denote "what

cannot really exist". In a western Europe conscious of its Graeco-Roman heritage it was inevitable that this sense of "myth" should be determinative, so that in the 19th century "myth" usually meant anything that was opposed to reality. For the same reason it was probably inevitable that the term should become attached primarily to the ancient stories of the Greeks – the stories of Prometheus, Perseus, Heracles, etc. – so that the "classical" (and still popular) meaning of myth is a fabulous, untrue story about gods (or demi-gods) set at the dawn of time or in a timeless past.

In the 19th and 20th centuries however the concept of myth has been thrown back into the melting pot, and its meaning and the precise demarcation of its meaning are the subject of a vigorous and ongoing debate. In his recent essay on the subject W. Pannenberg distinguishes three main competing views.[3] (a) "Myth" as used by anthropologists and comparative religionists – that is, myth as a story whose subject is the primal age and whose function is to provide a basis for the present world and social order in that primordial time – what M. Eliade calls "archetypal history". "Myth narrates a sacred history; it relates an event that took place in primordial time, the fabled time of the 'beginnings'."[4] (b) Myth as defined originally by C. G. Heyne – myth, that is, as a primitive conceptual form, the "mode of conception and expression" in the childhood of the human race, exposing the structure of primitive consciousness as yet untouched by modern science; such mythical thought has been rendered obsolete by modern science. As we shall see, it is this concept of myth which has dominated the debate about demythologizing within NT hermeneutics.[5] (c) Myth as poetry, myth as belonging to a sphere where it is judged by standards other than that of its understanding of the world, myth as symbol and drama able to awake feeling, "invite thought" and evoke response.[6]

When we turn to the problem of myth in the NT we must bear in mind this diversity of meaning of the word "myth" and not permit any one definition to determine and answer the problem from the outset.

(2) What is the truth of myth? The paradox of a word which could mean both "fact" and "invented story" did not escape the Greeks, and the problem of the truth content of myth was one which tested the finest minds of the ancient world as it does today. Above all we should mention Plato. Plato was openly critical of traditional myth, though he allowed that the best of them, even if false (*ψεῦδος*) had a value in teaching children.[7] More important, he recognized that mythical thought was an indispensable complement to rational thought (*logos*). "Myth carries the lines of *logos* organically beyond the frontiers of conceptual knowledge . . . It arises when there is need to express something which can be expressed in no other way."[8]

In the modern discussion about the truth of myth many answers have been proposed. The following are probably the most important. (a) The dominant view among anthropologists at the turn of the century (E. B. Tylor, J. G. Frazer, etc.) was that myth only tells us something about primitive man, how he speculated about the heavens and the annual cycle of nature and fertility, how he handled his fears of the unknown (particularly death and beyond), how he conceptualized the mysterious in his present experience (gods, demons, spirits), how he sought to control and manipulate these powers by ritual magic, and so on. (b) Closely associated with the first was the view that myth fulfilled a *legitimation* function: that myth originated from ritual and its truth lay in legitimizing the cult (W. Robertson-Smith), or the broader idea of "charter myth" – a story used to assert and justify a tribe's rights, loyalties and beliefs and lacking any deeper meaning (B. Malinowski).[9] (c) More recently the recognition of the importance of dreams in psychoanalysis has led to the understanding of myth as the expression of the subconscious, the archetypal images rising from the depths of man often drawing on the psychic heritage of centuries and so telling us something about man as he is. "Myth is the natural and indispensable intermediate stage between unconscious and conscious cognition." "Myths are original revelations of the preconscious psyche, involuntary statements about unconscious psychic happenings." [10] (d) Somewhat analogous is the structuralist definition of the French anthropologist C. Lévi-Strauss who holds that the true "message" of myth is nothing to do with content as such; myth is rather a piece of algebra about the workings of the human mind in the abstract. Lévi-Strauss believes that the structure of all myths is identical with that of the human mind: human thought is a process of binary analysis; so myth is a model whereby the binary divisions in society, the contradictions in man's view of the world (between village and jungle, malë and female, life and death, earth and sky, etc.) can be resolved and overcome. In a phrase, myth reveals man striving to create order out of the contradictions in which he finds himself involved.[11] (e) A fifth understanding of the truth of myth may be termed the poetic view – myth as the expression of a whole area of human experience and awareness, of (universal) values and truths, that can only be presented in symbolic language, what K. Jaspers calls "the cipher language of myth"[12] – myth as the poet's awareness of a "moreness" to life than eating, sleeping, working, loving, without wishing or attempting to define that "moreness" except by means of evocative images and symbols.[13] (f) A sixth view is that at least some myth is the expression of distinctively religious experience, that ultimately myth is not merely man's response to what he thinks of as divine, but is itself somehow revelatory of the divine. Thus "stories about gods" may not always simply be the expression of primitive, unscientific conceptualization but may rather in the first instance be the product of religious consciousness, "the vestibule at the threshold of the real religious feeling, an earliest stirring of the numinous consciousness".[14] So too the "which came first?" controversy in the myth-ritual debate may be wrongly conceived, since the roots of both myth and ritual may lie in primitive man's attempts to express an irreducibly religious experience. Or in Jung's words.

> "No science will ever replace myth, and a myth cannot be made out of any science. For it is not that 'God' is a myth, but that myth is the revelation of a divine life in man. It is not we who invent myth, rather it speaks to us as a Word of God." [15]

The primary problem of myth is therefore the problem of definition. As we narrow the focus of discussion to the NT, we must constantly ask of those who postulate the presence of myth in the NT, What kind of myth? Myth in what sense? Above all we must bear in mind that mythical thinking can move on different levels: myths as consciously invented stories intended merely to give pleasure or to serve a legitimation function; myths as primitive conceptualizations of reality now *wholly* superseded by the advance of scientific investigation, though perhaps still retaining a power to evoke and move particularly by their repetition in the cult;[16] myth as a veiled window into the reality of man, whether into the structure of his mind or into the depths of his collective subconscious, or as an expression of his values and aspirations;[17] myth as man's conscious or unconscious perception of a "beyondness" in his experience of reality, which comes to him with the force of inspiration or revelation, which can be expressed only by means of symbol and image and analogy, and which may neither uncritically nor unscientifically be taken as *prima facie* evidence of an ontological reality which is "larger" and more complex than our scientific investigations have so far recognized.[18] If myth or mythological thinking is present in the NT we must not *assume* that it moves only on one level and not another, but must always ask, What is the function, what is the truth of this myth? in each individual instance.

II. *The Problem of Miracle – D. F. Strauss*

Is there myth in the NT? Insofar as NT writers take up the question the answer is a blunt and unequivocal No! The word itself is found only five times (1 Tim. 1:4; 4:7; 2 Tim. 4:4; Tit. 1:14; 2 Pet. 1:16) and in every case the writers completely repudiate myth. For these writers myths are invented and untrue stories, whether Hellenistic speculations about divine emanations or more Jewish speculative interpretations of OT stories. Myth is unreal, untrue, unhistorical, in contrast to the reality, truth and historicity of the gospel. What is rejected here, however, is only one *genre* of myth. The question of whether other levels of myth and of mythological thinking are present in the NT is neither posed nor answered.

Subsequent attempts to wrestle with the problem at this deeper level reveal something of its complexity. I am referring here to the long and respected tradition of biblical interpretation by means of allegorizing. For by turning to allegory the allegorizer expresses his dissatisfaction with the obvious meaning of the biblical text (it is unedifying, outmoded, or whatever) and seeks for a deeper meaning. That is to say, he treats the biblical narrative as a type of myth whose literal meaning can be disregarded and whose truth can be extracted by the methods of allegorical exegesis. This was certainly the way Philo used the OT. So too the Alexandrians (particularly Origen), even though they rejected the charges of opponents that the biblical accounts are in fact myths, nevertheless by using allegorical interpretation treated the Bible in effect as a collection of myths.[19]

In the 19th century the problem of myth re-emerged with disconcerting sharpness as the problem of miracle; or to be more precise, with D. F. Strauss myth was given a central and positive role in the NT as the decisive answer to the problem of miracle. For much of the 18th and 19th centuries the question of miracle stood at the storm centre of theological debate. For many the truth of Christianity stood or fell with the historicity or otherwise of the biblical miracles[20] – not unnaturally since for centuries Christian apologetic had presented the miracles of the Bible as sure proof of the supernatural origin of and divine approval for Christianity. But post-Enlightenment man, with his growing scientific knowledge of the cosmos and his high regard for the perspicacity and sufficiency of reason, found the very concept of miracle less and less satisfactory: the laws of nature, the chain reaction of cause and effect, could not be violated and suspended in the way "miracle" supposed; God would not work in such an arbitrary and unreasonable manner. Miracle ceased to be an aid to apologetic and became instead an embarrassment and a problem.

This is Strauss's starting point for his minute investigation of the events of Jesus' life.[21] Since miracles are incompatible with natural law (and with reason) they are incompatible with history; and since miracles are incompatible with history, then the Gospels are not historical records. What is the status of the Gospel narratives then? Strauss's answer is simple: they are *myths*. What does Strauss mean by myth? As his negative assessment of the Gospels shows the influence of post-Enlightenment rationalism, so his positive assessment shows the influence of German idealism. For Strauss myth is the expression or embodiment of an *idea;* it is the form in which the idea is apprehended.[22] In the case of the Gospels, myth is the expression of the first Christians' idea of Christ – an idea shaped partly by Jewish expectations concerning the Messiah and partly by the "particular impression which was left by the personal character, actions and fate of Jesus". It was this idea of Christ which gave rise to the accounts of miracles in the Gospels; the miraculous element in any recorded event was created out of or by the idea.[23] Some of these accounts are *pure* myths – that is, they have no historical foundation whatsoever: for example, the cures of the blind, the feeding of the 5,000, and the transfiguration, which all grew out of the disciples' belief that Jesus was Messiah, the one greater than Moses and Elijah according to Jewish expectation.[24] Others are *historical* myths – that is, a historical fact overgrown with mythical conceptions culled from the idea of Christ: for example, "Peter's miraculous draught of fishes [Luke 5.1–11] is but the expression about the fishers of men [Mark 1.17] transmuted into the history of a miracle"; and underlying the now mythically presented baptism of Jesus is the historical event itself.[25] In a word, myth is an invented, symbolical scene.

Strauss's contribution to our subject has been epochal and is still fundamental to the modern programme of demythologizing. His painstaking scrutiny of individual narratives, his careful analysis of what the miracle intended by the evangelist would have involved, and his ruthless exposure of the shifts and artifices to which rationalist explanations of Gospel miracles resorted, is without equal in NT scholarship.[26] It is largely due to Strauss that more recent debates on the historical Jesus have focused on the teaching of Jesus rather than on his "works". Perhaps above all, Strauss showed the importance of starting with the text as it stood, and of respecting the purpose of its author; against those who played down or explained away a Gospel miracle he insisted that where the writer intended to narrate a miracle his intention must be taken seriously. Furthermore, he showed that there are other considerations to be taken into account than simply those of historicity: the *idea* of Jesus cherished by early Christianity, or, as we would say now, their *faith* in the risen Jesus, must have influenced their representation of the historical Jesus; simply to ask after the historicity of this or that episode or detail may be to miss the author's point.[27]

At the same time, Strauss's basic statement of the problem of "miracle" and his use of "myth" cannot escape criticism. In effect he works with the equation: miracle = story of unnatural/unhistorical event = myth = idea. But does the equation hold?

(1) To define miracle as "a transgression of a law of nature . . ." (Hume),[28] or even to judge an event "irreconcilable with the known and universal laws which govern the course of events" (Strauss) begs too many questions about natural law. Of course the "law" of cause and effect is axiomatic in all scientific investigation – inevitably so – and its operation can be easily recognized in such a relatively simple case as one billiard ball striking another. But whenever we are dealing with human relationships or the relation between the physical world (especially the body) and the psyche (including such unquantifiables as temperament, will-power, purpose) the matter is more complex. What is and what causes a decision? What is the scientific explanation of love and does it begin to do its subject justice? Is the pleasure and uplift I experience at hearing Beethoven's Eroica Symphony merely the effect of certain sound waves on my ear drum? And so on. The "chemistry of human relationship" raises the question of other or complementary causes which are less determinable than (other) "natural laws". Such considerations become all the more important when one is discussing the impact of a charismatic figure such as Jesus.[29] And if this line of reasoning were pursued it would also become possible to postulate divine activity in a "miracle" even though the closed weft of history and the continuum of cause and effect as it presents itself to objective observation is left undisturbed.[30]

Consequently, we must question any definition of miracle which sets God as cause over against the natural world in a dualistic way, so that any effect attributed to God must be described in terms of "violation" or "intervention". For all the sophistication of our understanding of the universe how far in fact have we passed beyond the threshold of knowledge of reality in all its complexity and depth? After all, at the time Strauss was writing his *Life of Jesus,* Michael Faraday was only beginning to recognize the nature of electro-magnetic waves with his talk of "lines of force" and conception of a sort of cosmic cobweb of electrical forces – a comparatively recent discovery in the history of scientific investigation. What other sources of energy and "lines of force" (particularly in relation to the human personality) have we yet to discover simply because we have not yet been able to conceptualize and measure them? I think here, for example, of such parapsychological phenomena as telepathy and levitation, claims concerning which have been made for centuries and yet have still been too little investigated.[31] Perhaps after all reality consists of a sort of intermeshing of physical, psychical *and spiritual* forces in a cosmic pattern of which only a few threads at present are visible, not least in the human being himself, so that, for example, the concept of "demon-possession" regains in status as the first century's recognition of the complex forces (not least spiritual) which bear upon the human personality (to put it no more strongly). Such a conceptualization of reality can be maintained without lapsing into pantheism or denying the "otherness" of God.[32]

(2) Moving to the other end of Strauss's equation, it is evident that there are two central characteristics of his concept of myth: myth is the narrative of an *unhistorical* event; myth is the embodiment of an *idea*. These two characteristics are the two sides of the one coin: where an account is unhistorical (evidenced by historical improbabilities and inconsistencies) there is a mythical idea; where there is myth (evidenced for instance by poetic form or messianic ideas) there is no history. Idea (myth) and history are mutually exclusive.

But this dualism between history and idea (or as we would say today, between history and faith) is too sharp.

(a) Are all accounts of miracles to be explained as inventions to embody ideas? What, we might ask, are the ideas which created the stories of miracles attributed to the other Galilean(?) charismatics, Honi the Circle-Drawer (1st century B.C.) and Hanina ben Dosa (1st century A.D.)?[33] Perhaps these stories testify to nothing more than the imgination of the story tellers of the Galilean bazaars and market places. But more likely they testify to some sort of historical feats on the part of Honi and Hanina which gave rise to their reputations. So too with Jesus. For the earliest Christians the most probable source for many of the accounts of Jesus' miracles would be the recollections of episodes in Jesus' ministry circulating in Galilee and among his first admirers and disciples.[34]

(b) Are history and idea (faith) mutually exclusive? No doubt post-Easter faith is discernible at many points in the miracle stories (see note 27), but has it created the whole, or is it merely hindsight? Strauss himself recognized that Jesus' role as an exorcist cannot be disputed on historical or literary grounds,[35] but in his view historical improbability tells against the historicity of other cures attributed to Jesus.[36] Yet he fails to take account of the fact that Jesus himself appealed to a much wider range of healings, and that it was Jesus who saw them as evidence of the presence of the blessings of the end-time (Matt. 11:5/Luke 7:22).[37] Idea and history are here united by Jesus himself! If we took this point in conjunction with the considerations marshalled above (p. 290f.) and pursued the argument at greater length than this paper permits, even the so-called nature miracles would become much less clear cut in terms of strict historical improbability,[38] and in particular the possibility would begin to gain in strength that the transformation in Jesus' mode of existence which we call "resurrection" was not so much an exception to natural law as a paradigm of the inter-relationship of physical and spiritual, a partial glimpse of the overall pattern of persons and things.

(c) The logic of Strauss's dualism between history and idea is worked out to its conclusion when Strauss attempts to reduce christology to the idea of God-manhood, an idea embodied in Christ but only mythically not historically, an idea realized only in (an idealized view of) Humanity.[39] Here Strauss's Hegelian idealism comes to full flower, only to wither before the blast of man's inhumanity to man, since he has so completely cut it off from the one historical root that could give it sustenance.

All this does not demonstrate the historicity of any one miracle attributed to Jesus. But hopefully enough has been said to show that Strauss's flight from history at this point was premature, and that his posing of the problems of miracle and myth in the NT was inadequate. "Myth" (in Strauss's sense) and "miracle" are not synonymous.

III. *The Influence of Jewish and Hellenistic Myths*

At the turn of the century the problem of myth in Christianity was posed in a new form by the History of Religions school.[40] Already at the time of Strauss the growing awareness of other religions had brought home the significance of the fact that in laying claim to various miracle stories Christianity was not at all unique. Even before Strauss the conclusion had been drawn that if these other stories are to be judged unhistorical myths, the same verdict cannot be withheld from the biblical accounts of creation, virgin birth, etc. But in the latter part of the 19th century and early 20th century various influential scholars came to the conclusion that not only did Christianity have its own myths, but in fact Christianity had been significantly influenced at its formative stage by particular myths of other religions; indeed, the plainly mythical thinking of other systems had decisively shaped Christian faith and worship at key points. The chief sources of influence were thought to be the myths of Jewish apocalyptic, of Gnosticism and of Hellenistic mystery religions.

(1) Jewish apocalyptic thought can justifiably be labelled mythical – particularly its concept of an end-time and new age qualitatively different from this age (restoration of primeval paradise, Zion's glory, etc.) and its portrayal of the end in terms of cosmic catastrophe (slaying the dragon of chaos, stars falling from heaven, etc.).[41] And it would be hard to deny that Jesus was influenced by apocalyptic thought or that apocalyptic thought had a constituent part in the theology of the early church (Mark 13 pars; and 2 Thess. 2:1–12; Rev. 4–21).[42] But in what sense is Jewish and Christian apocalyptic mythical? Certainly the language of apocalyptic is not

to be interpreted literally or pedantically, as is clear from the apocalyptists' use of symbol and cipher (e.g. the "great beasts" and "seventy weeks" of Dan. 7; 9: "that which restrains" and "the breath of his mouth" of 2 Thess. 2; "the lamb" and the beast with the number 666 of Rev. 5; 13).[43] Yet to describe apocalyptic hopes merely as invented stories created to comfort believers in time of crisis would be unjust. Rather are they inspired visions of the future born of confidence in God alone. Thus, for all the mythical character of its language (for example, the primeval dragon myth in Rev. 12ff, as in Isa. 27:1; 51:9f),[44] the general point can be made with some force that apocalyptic embodies a dissatisfaction with the present and an insight into or revelation of future reality as God's which is integrally and irreducibly Christian. How else, after all, can hope which is neither rooted in nor dependent on the present world express itself?[45]

(2) The debate about the influence on NT thought of Gnostic motifs, particularly the pre-Christian Gnostic redeemer myth[46] is long and complex.[47] It must suffice here to note that already there was speculation concerning the Primal Man at the time of the earliest NT writings (Paul), that this speculation is properly described as mythical (myth in the sense of an account of "archetypal history"), and that Paul's Adam Christology shows Paul's awareness of it and indeed may not unjustly be described as part of that first century speculation – though Paul's contribution is distinctively Christian (1 Cor. 15:44ff; cf. Phil. 2:6ff).[48] Perhaps also Paul's description of the body of Christ in cosmic terms (Eph. 1:10, 23) owes something to gnostic-type thought. Of course Paul has no intention of reducing Christ to a symbol expressive of community or to a cosmic idea, though what he conceives to be the ontological reality of Christ underlying this image is not easy to determine. So too if there is anything that can properly be called a "divine man" christology, related to Primal Man speculation, which can be said to have influenced the presentation of Jesus as a miracle worker by the opponents of Paul in 2 Cor. and the earlier collections of miracle stories used by Mark and John,[49] then the point to note is that all three NT writers provide a sharp corrective by emphasizing that the character of the gospel is determined by the suffering and death of Jesus.

(3) A central element in many of the major mystery cults at the time when Christianity came to birth was the (variously represented) myth of the god who dies and rises again – the myth deriving ultimately in most cases from the annual cycle of the earth's fertility. The History of Religions school claimed that initiation to the cult was conceived as an identification of the initiate with the god in his dying and rising again, and consequently maintained that Hellenistic Christianity was strongly influenced by the mysteries, particularly in its theology of baptism.[50] This interpretation of the mysteries and hence of their potential influence on Christian thought has been strongly and justifiably challenged;[51] however, the fact remains that the more we interpret Paul's view of the sacraments in terms of a conveying or bestowing of grace or Spirit, the less easy is it to deny the influence on Paul of the mythical thought of Gnosis or the mysteries.[52]

The impact of the History of Religions school on the problem of myth in the NT has been considerable and lasting. Indeed the parallels between the Jesus depicted by NT faith and the Jewish and Hellenistic myths were thought by some to be so striking that they concluded that Jesus himself was a mythical construct, nothing more than an amalgam of Jewish messianic and apocalyptic hopes with the Hellenistic myth of the dying and rising god.[53] The artificiality and special pleading of such attempts is their own condemnation. On the contrary, the parallel between Christian faith and these Jewish and Hellenistic mythical formulations breaks down precisely at this point. By applying the same sort of (mythical) language to a *historical* individual the NT writers in effect demythologize it. This is true even of the more history-conscious Jewish apocalyptic: Son of man ceases to be merely a man-like figure (Dan. 7:13 – in contrast to the beast-like figures, 7:2–12) and becomes Jesus of Nazareth; similarly Joel's apocalyptic hope (including the "wonders in heaven" and "moon turned to blood") is taken to be fulfilled by the events of the first Christian Pentecost (Acts 2:16–21). The contrast is even sharper with the Hellenistic myths. Sallust said of the Attis myth: "This never happened, but always is." [54] In direct antithesis, the NT writers proclaim, "This *did* happen" (Jesus' life, death and resurrection) and only thereby can the redemption for which the Jewish and Hellenistic world longed come to historical realization for man now and hereafter. Thus, even if the same sort of mythical language has been used to describe the "Christ event" and Christian experience and hope of salvation in the NT, the point to be noted is that by its reference to Jesus the Hellenistic, unhistorical myth has been broken and destroyed as myth in that sense.[55] The parallels between myth-type language in the NT and the particular myths of Hellenistic religion and philosophy should not blind us to its particular function and thus distinctive truth within NT Christianity. It is this function and truth which it is the task of demythologizing to uncover.[56]

IV. *The Problem of Objectifying God – R. Bultmann*

Despite the sharpness of the challenge posed by Strauss and History of Religions scholars like J. Weiss, W. Heitmüller and W. Bousset, the dominant theology at the turn of the century (Liberal Protestantism) had been largely able to shrug off the problem of myth. In the last analysis myth in the NT was of little consequence since it did not touch the heart of the gospel proclaimed by Jesus. The problem of miracle could be ignored since Jesus himself assigned nothing of critical importance to his miraculous deeds. The problem of Hellenistic influence on Paul could be ignored by emphasizing the gap between Jesus and Paul. Even the problem of apocalyptic influence on Jesus could be set aside since apocalyptic was only the shell and husk of Jesus' message which could be stripped off to uncover a kernel of timeless moral truth untouched by myth.[57] Rudolf Bultmann destroyed this comfortable position by denying that gospel and myth could be distinguished in this fashion. For Bultmann the kerygma is expressed *through* myth, not alongside it or inside it. The gospel is not somehow separate and distinct from myth; rather it is embodied in the mythical language of the NT. To discard the myth is to discard the gospel. With Bultmann therefore the problem of myth seems to threaten the gospel itself, and posed in these terms it touched many raw nerves, sparking off a debate which has as yet produced no large scale consensus.

Bultmann's whole work has in effect been addressed to different aspects of this problem,[58] but it was his 1941 lecture which set the present debate in motion.[59] Here, although his summary statements of the problem are over-simplified and confusing, his understanding of myth is fairly clearly that of C. G. Heyne (see above p. 286): viz. myth is a primitive, pre-scientific conceptualization of reality. There are two key characteristics of myth in this sense: it is incapable of abstract thought and it lacks understanding of the true causes of natural and mental processes.[60] Evidently in Bultmann's view NT thought can be described as mythical because it evinces these characteristics: for example, it represented the other worldly in material, spatial terms, the cosmos as a three storied structure (underworld, earth, heaven); and it attributed mental disorders to demons who were everywhere on earth and causation of events to spiritual powers who controlled the lower reaches of heaven. In the 20th century we no longer conceive reality in such terms; with the development of scientific knowledge we cannot: "it is no longer possible for anyone seriously to hold the New Testament view of the world" (p.4).[61]

The problem is, however, that the gospel in the NT is expressed in these terms – Jesus' healings as a victory over demons, his death as a triumphing over the powers, his "ascension" as a literal going up (from second to third floor), his "parousia" as a literal coming on clouds from above back down to earth, and so on. What is to be done? We cannot simply cling to the first century world view – that "would mean accepting a view of the world in our faith and religion which we should deny in our every day life" (p. 4). Nor can we reject the myth while preserving the gospel unscathed (pp. 9f, 12). The correct solution, argues Bultmann, is to *demythologize* it – that is, *not* to *eliminate* the myth, but to *interpret* it.

But to demythologize one must have some insight into the truth of the myth in question. Such an insight Bultmann claims, though the claim itself is presented in arbitrary manner and on the basis of the undeclared assumption that mythological thinking (*all* mythological thinking?)[62] is concerned with precisely the same questions as Bultmann himself.

> "The real purpose of myth is not to present an objective picture of the world as it is, but to express man's understanding of himself in the world in which he lives. Myth should be interpreted not cosmologically, but anthropologically, or better still, existentially . . . The importance of the New Testament mythology lies not in its imagery but in the understanding of existence which it enshrines" (pp. 10f.).

Yet though he fails to justify his starting point he does attempt to justify his procedure. Demythologizing is not simply a matter of reading Heidegger's existentialism into the NT. On the contrary, the criterion for determining the truth of NT myth is "the understanding of human existence which the New Testament itself enshrines" (p. 12).[63] Nevertheless, while he does justify his claim that demythologizing must involve interpretation in existential terms, it is the "*only* in existential terms" implicit in his starting point which leaves him most vulnerable to criticism.

In the second part of the essay he elaborates the NT "understanding of existence", principally from Paul. And lest his presentation of "the life of faith" should appear no different from the existentialist philosopher's talk of "authentic existence",[64] he goes on to insist, again in rather arbitrary manner, that the possibility of such authentic life becomes *actual* (as distinct from remaining *theoretical*) only through "the event of Jesus Christ" (pp. 22–33). This does not mean however that he has retreated once more into the language and thought forms of the NT. For when he goes on to talk of the saving event of cross and resurrection it becomes fairly clear that he is talking in fact of the *proclamation* of cross and resurrection as saving event, about saving event in the here and now of existential encounter with the kerygma:

> "To believe in the cross of Christ does not mean to concern ourselves with a mythical process wrought outside of us and our world, or with an objective event turned by God to our advantage, but rather to make the cross of Christ our own, to undergo crucifixion with him' (p. 36). 'The real Easter faith is faith in the word of preaching which brings illumination" (p. 42).[65]

Similarly, in an essay given over to an investigation of the christological confession of the World Council of Churches, Bultmann maintains that so far as the NT is concerned statements about Jesus' divinity "are not meant to express his nature but his significance."[66]

The questions raised by all this are legion, and I have already criticized Bultmann's setting up of the problem at several points; but here we have space to take up only three issues.

(1) The real problem for Bultmann is not the problem of mythological language as such, but the problem of any language which *objectifies* God (hence the title to this section). It is the problem of what to do with language which speaks as though God was an object, as though God's activity consisted in objective acts within the space-time complex which were therefore open to historical investigation and so to verification or falsification, so that faith would become dependent on the findings of historical and scientific research.[67] That this was the real problem of NT mythology for Bultmann was already evident in the 1941 essay,[68] but it became more explicit in his subsequent restatements of the problem: "Mythological thought . . . objectifies the divine activity and projects it on to the plane of worldly happenings"; "myths give to the transcendent reality an immanent this-worldly objectivity"; "mythological thinking naively objectifies the beyond as though it were something within the world."[69] It is because mythological language is objectifying language and so threatens faith that demythologizing is necessary.

For the same reasons demythologizing is possible only in terms of existentialist interpretation; only the language of existential encounter enables Bultmann to speak of God's activity without objectifying it. God acts now; faith recognizes God acting in the existential encounter of the word of the cross which addresses me as a word of God, as a word of grace. It is by wedding faith firmly to the kerygma alone that Bultmann seeks to deliver faith from the vagaries of historical criticism and from myth. Hence his claim at the end of the 1941 essay: "It is precisely its immunity from proof which secures the Christian proclamation against the charge of being mythological" (p. 44). So too his claim at the end of his later discussions: "Demythologizing is the radical application of the doctrine of justication by faith to the sphere of knowledge and thought. Like the doctrine of justification, demythologizing destroys every longing for security." [70]

But can we equate the problem of myth in the NT so completely with the problem of objectifying God? And if existentialist interpretation is really addressed to the latter problem does it provide such a theologically satisfying answer to the former problem as Bultmann claims? These two questions provide the cues for my other two comments.

(2) What is NT myth? In the 1941 essay Bultmann defined mythology as "the use of imagery to express the other worldly in terms of this world and the divine in terms of human life, the other side in terms of this side" (p. 10 n. 2). This definition was rightly criticized since its concept of myth is too all-embracing:[71] in particular the definition confuses myth and analogy and in effect makes it impossible to speak of God at all.[72] Bultmann recognized this and subsequently attempted to defend the legitimacy of talk of "God as Creator" in terms of analogy.[73] But as soon as one recognizes that "use of imagery to express the other worldly in terms of this worldly" can be legitimate (that is, without objectifying God) – use of metaphor, symbol, analogy – the question arises, How much of the "mythological language" of the NT is in fact metaphor, symbol and analogy? Does the "God-talk" of the NT always imply such a naive and primitive conceptualization as Bultmann assumes? We have already noted how the Acts 2 sermon treats the cosmic spectacle language of Joel 2 as little more than apocalyptic sound-effects. So we must ask whether the NT writers' concept of the cosmos was quite so unsophisticated as Bultmann suggests. For example, the seer of Revelation quite obviously intended his language to be understood symbolically (see above p. 292f.). And if P.S. Minear is right, "the prophet was aware of the danger of absolutizing the relative and of diminishing the inexpressible transcendence of God to the dimensions of his own creation."[74] Paul certainly thought in the current terms of more than one heaven, but how he conceptualized them and whether he considered any language adequate to describe them is another question ("whether in the body or out of the body I do not know, God knows", "unutterable utterances" – 2 Cor. 12:2ff); and though he talked of spiritual powers as real beings in the heavens (e.g. Rom. 8:38; 1 Cor. 2:6, 8; Eph. 6:12), it is clear that for Paul the "powers" which pose the greatest threat to man are the *personifications,* sin, death and law.[75] To take only one or two other

examples: was the talk of Jesus' death as sacrifice, of atonement through his blood, intended as any more than a vigorous metaphor giving a meaningful way of understanding Jesus' death to hearers long familiar with the practice of sacrifice, a metaphor, that is, drawn from the life of the times like the correlative metaphors of cleansing, justification, redemption, adoption, etc? It would certainly be quite justified to argue that the kerygma of the letter to the Hebrews in effect "demythologizes" the sacrificial ritual and the temple by emphasizing the reality of forgiveness and of immediate personal relationship with God in the writer's "here and now".[76]

The issue is of course more complex, but at least the point begins to emerge that much of the "mythological" language of the NT was in fact analogical and metaphorical language – and consciously so – only the analogies and metaphors were the ones appropriate to the age and inevitably took up the language and concepts of the age. But if the beyondness of God was often conceived in terms of "somewhere beyond the frontiers of scientific knowledge", then the fact that first century frontiers of scientific knowledge were not very far advanced does not really touch the metaphorical and analogical value of first century attempts to speak of that beyondness. In short, Bultmann's posing of the problem of myth in the NT is inadequate because the questions, What kind of myth? Myth in what sense? have not been subjected to a sufficiently thorough examination.

(3) What is the truth of NT myth? If demythologizing in existentialist terms is addressed to the problem of objectifying God does it really answer the problem of myth? Does Bultmann's reduction of the "God-talk", Christ-event talk to the kerygmatic encounter of the here and now really uncover the truth of such mythological language as is used in the NT? Paradoxically, while his concept of myth in the NT is too broad (2), his understanding of the truth of myth is too narrow.[77] Bultmann has been attacked here from two sides. He has been attacked by his more radical disciples for the illogicality of his stopping place. If the gospel can be translated so completely into existentialist categories without remainder, why does Bultmann insist on retaining a reference to Christ, and defend so vigorously his right to continue speaking of "God acting in Christ"? If "the self understanding of the man of faith is really the constant in the New Testament",[78] then where does christology properly speaking come in at all? Does Bultmann's flight from history into the kerygma answer the problem of myth since the kerygma is itself mythological; does Bultmann's programme of demythologizing not logically involve "dekerygmatizing" as well?[79] If faith is merely man's possibility of authentic existence, then the realisation of that possibility cannot be tied exclusively to Christ.[80] Why indeed retain the idea of God at all? Does the first century concept of a cosmologically transcendent God not demythologize existentially into the concept of self-transcendence?[81]

These attacks bring out a point which should not be ignored – that Bultmann has always seen his task at this point in terms of Christian evangelism and apologetic (as well as being required by the NT itself). He wishes to affirm the gospel and to "defend" faith by setting it free from the objectification and meaninglessness of first century conceptualizations. "The task of demythologizing has no other purpose but to make clear the call of the Word of God."[82] Hence his initial setting up of the problem in terms of a distinction between kerygma and myth[83] – the heritage of German idealism allowing him to affirm almost as an *a priori* that the kerygma is the truth within the myth, a truth which challenges me today without conflicting with the 20th century scientific world view. Yet it is difficult to see how Bultmann's position can hold before the criticisms of such as Ogden without the arbitrary appeal to faith born of the kerygma to which Bultmann is in fact reduced.[84] But his resort to fideism has obviously proved unsatisfactory to those cited above – and by the very canons to which Bultmann himself appealed when he proposed his programme of demythologizing. Consequently the apologetic stand must be made further to the right.

The criticism of Bultmann from the right has often been expressed in terms of reducing theology to anthropology, which is not altogether unjustified, but forgets that Bultmann added "or better still, existentially" (see above p. 295 and n. 62). The same criticism is better expressed in terms of reducing christology to soteriology,[85] or as the criticism that he has telescoped what faith might wish to affirm regarding the past and the future into the present. On the contrary, Christian faith must make affirmations about Jesus as Jesus, and about past and future including the past and future of Jesus Christ (as well as about God) if it is to retain any meaningful continuity with original Christianity.[86] In particular, it must be said that if the phrase "the resurrection of Jesus" is not attempting to talk about something which happened *to Jesus,* if it merely describes the rise of Easter faith,[87] then it is of no more value than the mystery religions' myth of the dying and rising god, for all that it has been attached to a (once) historical (now dead) figure.[88] In which case, the focus of Christianity must shift from the Christ of faith to the historical Jesus, or Christianity itself reduces to a mystery cult; that is, Christianity becomes a form of *imitatio Christi* moralism (Jesus the first Christian)[89] or a modern vegetation cult (Christ the principle of life, the image of annual rebirth), and whatever grace is experienced through it cannot either legitimately or meaningfully be described as "the grace of God in Christ". Moreover, if "the resurrection of Jesus" is not saying something by way of promise about the present and future of *Jesus* as well as about the present and *future* of believers, then we must also point out that Christianity loses the purpose and hope which originally was one of its crucial and distinctive elements.[90] To be sure, the Fourth Gospel's shift in emphasis from future to past and present ("realized eschatology") can be dubbed a sort of "demythologizing",[91] but only if one recognizes that its realized eschatology does *not* involve a total abandonment of future eschatology (5:28f.; 6:39f., 44, 54; 11:25; 12:48; 14:2f.; 17:24);[92] even for John the truth of the "eschatological myth" includes a still future hope which does not dissolve away in the acids of the demythologizing process. Bultmann fails to realize how much NT myth cannot be demythologized because it is saying something fundamental to the Christian gospel and saying what cannot be expressed in other than mythological terms.[93]

In short, it would appear that because it is addressed primarily to the problem of objectifying God rather than to the wider problem of myth in the NT, Bultmann's programme of demythologizing fails to do justice to the truth of NT mythological language by abandoning the very historical and ontological affirmations about Jesus which that language is able to convey by its very nature as myth. Space forbids the fuller discussion which the subject deserves.

V. *Conclusion*

What is the problem of myth in the NT? It is not reducible to the problem of miracle; the activity of the divine within the world need not be conceived in terms of intervention and suspension of natural laws. It is not reducible to the problem of dependency on other mythological formulations which conceptualize the hoped for deliverance from the frustrations and contradictions of the human condition; when such borrowing does take place the character of the mythological language is transformed by its reference to the historical man Jesus. It is not reducible to the problem of objectifying God; the two problems overlap only in part, and to equate them is to ignore much of the truth of NT myth.

The problem of myth in the NT is that the NT presents events critical to Christian faith in language and concepts which are often outmoded and meaningless to 20th century man. More precisely, the problem of myth in the NT is (1) the problem of how to speak of God at all, the problem of analogy, *compounded* by the fact that many of the NT metaphors and analogies are archaic and distasteful to modern sensibilities (e.g. blood sacrifice); (2) it is the problem of how to speak of God acting in history, *compounded* by the fact that in the first century world the activity of divine beings is often evoked as the explanation for what we now recognize as natural and mental processes, that is, where the natural cause and effect sequence is not recognized and causation is attributed *solely* to the divine *instead* (e.g. epilepsy as demon possession); (3) it is the problem of how to conceptualize the margin between the observable domain of scientific history and "beyond" and how to speak of "passage" from one to the other – *compounded* by the fact that out of date conceptualizations determine certain traditionally important expressions of NT faith about Christ at this point – in particular, the problem that "ascension" (Acts 1:11) and parousia "in clouds" "from heaven" (Mark 13:26; 1 Thess. 4:16) were not merely metaphors or analogies but were intended as literal descriptions, but descriptions which derive from and depend on a first century cosmology which is impossible to us.

The problem is that the faith and hope of the first Christians is not readily distinguishable from this first century language and conceptualization. On the contrary, their faith and hope is expressed *through* that language; it does not have an existence apart from that language. The question then to which demythologizing addresses itself is whether the gospel is forever imprisoned within these first century thought forms, whether it can be re-expressed in 20th century terms. Are we justified in saying that there is a faith and hope which can be expressed in other language and thought forms but which *remains the same faith and hope*? If such first century theologizing as Adam christology, talk of spiritual powers in the heavens and ascension can no longer have the same meaning for us as it had for the first Christians, what meaning should it have?

The problem of myth in the NT is thus a complex one and an adequate answer would require careful exegesis of many different passages. Perhaps I have said enough in the earlier discussions to indicate the broader theological considerations which would guide my own answers, and the following chapter continues the discussion on a somewhat different tack. The point is that each must tackle the problem for himself and no one else can tackle it for him; for in the end of the day it is the problem of how *I* express *my* faith as a Christian. The more one regards the Christ-event and the faith of the first Christians as normative, the more tightly one is bound to the expressions of the faith and hope of these first Christians as the starting point for the elucidation and interpretation of one's own self-understanding and experience of grace. By this I do not mean of course that one must cling to the words themselves as though they were a sort of magic talisman. Rather one must always seek to rediscover afresh the reality of the love and faith and hope which these words expressed, and then seek to re-express that reality in language meaningful to one's own experience and to one's neighbour. The process of demythologizing is therefore a dialectic between me in all my 20th century conditionedness and the faith of the first Christians in all its first century conditionedness. Such a dialectic is not a once-for-all question and answer from one to other, but a continuing dialogue of question and answer where each repeatedly puts the other in question and where one wrestles existentially with the text and with oneself till an answer begins to emerge – an answer which poses a further question in reply. Nor is it a dialogue which involves only my voice and the voice of the past, since it is only part of the wider human search for reality and truth and other voices break in posing other questions and offering other answers. Nor is it a dialogue which can ever reach finality of form or expression since each man's question is peculiarly his own and since 19th century gives way to 20th and 20th begins to give way to 21st and each new generation has its own agenda; rather is it a dialogue which must be taken up ever afresh by each believer and by each believing community. In short, the dialectic of demythologizing is the language of living faith.

NOTES

* I wish to express my thanks to A. C. Thiselton and I. H. Marshall for comments on an earlier draft; also to my colleague R. W. A. McKinney for continual stimulus in many discussions on this and related subjects.

1. G. S. Kirk, *Myth: Its Meaning and Functions in Ancient and Other Cultures* (Cambridge 1970), p. 7.

2. G. Stählin, *μῦθος*, TDNT IV, pp. 766–9; cf. also C. K. Barrett, "Myth and the New Testament", Exp.T 68 (1956–57), p. 345.

3. W. Pannenberg, "The Later Dimensions of Myth in Biblical and Christian Tradition", *Basic Questions in Theology* III (E.T. London 1973), pp. 1–22.

4. M. Eliade, *Myth and Reality,* (London 1964) p. 5; *Encyclopaedia Britannica,* Art. "Myth", Vol. 15, p. 1133. Eliade is criticised by I. Strenski, "Mircea Eliade: Some Theoretical Problems", in A. Cunningham, ed., *The Theory of Myth* (London 1973), pp. 40–78. See also I. G. Barbour, *Myths, Models and Paradigms* (London 1976), pp. 19ff.

5. See also W. G. Kümmel, *The New Testament: The History of the Investigation of its Problems* (E.T. London 1973), pp. 101ff, 121; and see below p. 295. R. A. Johnson, *The Origins of Demythologizing* (Leiden 1974) points out that the work of B. Fontenelle, *De l'origine des fables* (1724) considerably predates that of Heyne (pp. 131–4).

6. Cf. particularly P. Ricoeur, *The Symbolism of Evil* (E.T. New York 1967), discussed by J. Rogerson, *Myth in O.T. Interpretation* (Berlin 1974), chap. 9.

7. Plato, *The Republic* 376–7.

8. Stählin, TDNT IV pp. 774ff. See also R. M. Grant, *The Earliest Lives of Jesus* (London 1961), pp. 121f. J. Creed, "Uses of Classical Mythology", in Cunningham, pp. 7–15.

9. See Kirk, *Myth,* pp. 12–29; also Pannenberg, "Myth", pp. 5ff; further references to the myth-ritual debate in B. S. Childs, *Myth and Reality in the Old Testament* (London 1960), p. 19 n. 2 and discussion in Rogerson, chap. 6.

10. C. G. Jung, *Memories, Dreams and Reflection* (E.T. London 1963), p. 343; Kirk, *Myth,* p. 279. See also C. G. Jung and C. Kerényi, *Introduction to a Science of Mythology* (E.T. London 1951).

11. Kirk, *Myth*, pp. 42–83; Rogerson, p. 105. See further e.g. C. Lévi-Strauss, *Structural Anthropology* (E.T. New York 1963), chap. XI; E. Leach, *Lévi-Strauss* (Glasgow, revised 1974), chap. 4.

12. K. Jaspers, "Myth and Religion", *Kerygma and Myth* II (ed. H. W. Bartsch, E.T. London 1962), p. 145.

13. M. Grant, *Myths of the Greeks and Romans* (London 1962), p. xvii, cites the following appropriate lines:

The intelligible forms of ancient poets,
the fair humanities of old religion, . . .
They live no longer in the faith of reason!
But still the heart doth need a language, still
Doth the old instinct bring back the old names . . .

14. R. Otto, *The Idea of the Holy* (E.T. Oxford 1923), p. 126. Cf. M. Eliade: "For all primitive mankind, it is religious experience which lays the foundation of the World" (*Myths, Dreams and Mysteries* (E.T. London 1960), p. 19).

15. Jung, *Memories,* p. 373; Kirk quotes Jung to similar effect: "The primitive mentality does not *invent* myths, it *experiences* them" (*Myth,* p. 279). See also N. Berdyaev, *Freedom and Spirit* (E.T. London 1935), p. 70.

16. Cf. N. Smart, *The Phenomenon of Religion* (London 1973), ch. 3.

17. Thus, for example, the Gnostic myth reveals man's consciousness of his divided nature (both mind and matter) and its frustrations, and Nietzsche's "myth" of "superman" expresses a certain kind of aspiration, a "will to power".

18. Cf. Pannenberg: "To attribute all phenomena, and especially particularly striking and extraordinary events, to the intervention of gods, neither presupposes ignorance, in every

case, of the true relationship between cause and effect, nor is it comprehensible as the consequence of such ignorance. Rather, such a way of looking at things expresses the basic religious experience which apprehends the individual phenomenon not only in its association with other finite events and circumstances, but with reference to the 'powers' which determine reality as a whole. Without this specifically religious element even an ignorance of true causes would not explain why any event was attributed to a divine power" ("Myth", p. 14 n.32).

19. Stählin, TDNT IV, pp. 790f. See also R. M. Grant, *A Short History of the Interpretation of the Bible* (London revised 1965), pp. 62–8.

20. Cf. L. Feuerbach, *The Essence of Christianity* (1841, E.T. 1854, reprinted, New York 1957): "The specific object of faith is miracle; faith is the belief in miracle; faith and miracle are absolutely inseparable" (p. 126).

21. *The Life of Jesus Critically Examined* (E.T. 1846, 1 vol. 1892, reprinted, London 1973), pp. 39f. The influence of David Hume's still fundamental contribution to the debate is most clearly seen in Strauss's more constructive *New Life of Jesus* (E.T. London 1865): "It is absolutely impossible to conceive of a case in which the investigator of history will not find it more probable, beyond all comparison, that he has to deal with an untrue account, rather than with a miraculous fact" (Vol. I, p. 200).

22. Perhaps his most perceptive definition of myth is to be found in *New Life*, I p. 206: "The myth, in its original form, is not the conscious and intentional invention of an individual but a production of the common consciousness of a people or religious circle, which an individual does indeed first enunciate, but which meets with belief for the very reason that such individual is but the organ of this universal conviction. It is not a covering in which a clever man clothes an idea which arises in him for the use and benefit of the ignorant multitude, but it is only simultaneously with the narrative, nay, in the very form of the narrative which he tells, that he becomes conscious of the idea which he is not yet able to apprehend purely as such". See also the earlier formulation in *Life*, pp. 80ff. For a closer analysis of his concept of myth see P. C. Hodgson's Introduction to the 1973 reprint, pp. xxiii, xxvi, xxxivff.

23. *Life*, pp. 86f.

24. *Life*, §§ 95, 102, 107.

25. *Life*, §§ 71, 51.

26. See also the striking tribute to Strauss by A. Schweitzer, *The Quest of the Historical Jesus* (E.T. London 1910), p. 84.

27. This consideration is particularly relevant in studying the Fourth Gospel; but even in the Synoptics we must note the significance of such redactions as Matt. 13:58 of Mark 6:5f. and Matt. 14:32f. of Mark 6:51f., and of the manner in which Matthew and Luke make different points in narrating the same incident (Matt. 8:5–13/Luke 7:1–10).

28. Much more satisfactory is the definition of R. Swinburne, *The Concept of Miracle* (London 1970): "Miracle is an event of an extraordinary kind, brought about by a god, and of religious significance" (p. 1). His essay is chiefly a critique of Hume's definition on philosophical grounds.

29. See J. D. G. Dunn, *Jesus and the Spirit* (London 1975), ch. 4.

30. Cf. R. Bultmann, *Kerygma and Myth* (ed. H.-W. Bartsch, E.T. London 1953), p. 197.

31. Examples, including several well attested instances of these and other parapsychological phenomena may be found in H. Thurston, *The Physical Phenomena of Mysticism* (London 1952), and C. Wilson, *The Occult* (London 1971).

32. Recent attempts to speak of God while taking full cognisance of modern science in its various disciplines and to do so in an integrated way, include J. V. Taylor, *The Go-Between God* (London 1972), Part One; J. W. Bowker, *The Sense of God* (Oxford 1973); M. Kelsey, *Encounter with God* (London 1974); Barbour, *Myths*. Many have found Karl Heim, *Christian Faith and Natural Science* (E.T. London 1953) helpful; also Teilhard de Chardin, *Le Milieu Divin* (E.T. London 1960).

33. See G. Vermes, *Jesus the Jew* (London 1973), pp. 69–78.

34. E. Trocmé, *Jesus and his Contemporaries* (E.T. London 1973), chapter 7.

35. Strauss, *Life*, §§92–93. See also H. van der Loos, *The Miracles of Jesus* (Leiden 1965), pp. 156–175.

36. Though he wavered on this point in the third edition of *Life;* see Hodgson, pp.xliif.

37. The authenticity of this logion as a word of the historical Jesus has been widely recognized; see e.g. R. Bultmann, *The History of the Synoptic Tradition* (E.T. Oxford, 1963), pp. 23f; R. H. Fuller, *The Foundations of New Testament Christology* (London 1965), pp. 128f. Strauss's own interpretation in *New Life,* I p. 364 is wholly unconvincing: the miracles to which Jesus appeals "are to be understood in a spiritual sense of the moral effects of his doctrine".
38. See e.g. the suggestion of R. Otto, *The Kingdom of God and the Son of Man* (E.T. London 1938), pp. 368–74.
39. Strauss, *Life,* §§148–151. Instead of an individual at the centre of christology Strauss placed an idea – H. Harris, *David Friedrich Strauss and his Theology* (Cambridge 1973), p. 55.
40. See Kümmel, *New Testament,* pp. 245ff.
41. See P. Vielhauer in E. Hennecke and W. Schneemelcher, *New Testament Apocrypha* (E.T. ed. R. M. Wilson, London 1965) Vol. II, pp. 587–90; D. S. Russell, *The Method and Message of Jewish Apocalyptic* (London 1964), 122–7.
42. See particularly K. Koch, *The Rediscovery of Apocalyptic* (E.T. London 1972), chapter 6.
43. J. F. Walvoord, *The Revelation of Jesus Christ* (London 1966), falls into the error of attempting to interpret Revelation literally.
44. Kümmel, *New Testament,* pp. 250ff. See also 1 Pet. 3:19f., Jude 6, 14f.
45. Cf. W. G. Kümmel, "Mythische Rede und Heilsgeschehen im Neuen Testament", *Heilsgeschehen und Geschichte* (Marburg 1965), pp. 161ff.
46. See particularly R. Bultmann, *Theology of the New Testament* Vol. I (E.T. London 1952), pp. 164–83; *Primitive Christianity in its Contemporary Setting* (E.T. London 1956), pp. 162–71, 189–208.
47. See particularly C. Colpe, *Die religionsgeschichtliche Schule* Göttingen 1961); E. Yamauchi, *Pre-Christian Gnosticism* (London 1973); cf. J. W. Drane (p. 123 above).
48. See J. D. G. Dunn, "1 Corinthians 15.45 – Last Adam, Life-giving Spirit", *Christ and the Spirit in the New Testament: Studies in Honour of C. F. D. Moule* (ed. B. Lindars and S. S. Smalley; Cambridge 1973), pp. 129f, 135f; also *Jesus and the Spirit,* ch. 10.
49. See e.g. R. Bultmann, *The History of the Synoptic Tradition* (E.T. Oxford 1963), pp. 241, 371; H. Koester, "One Jesus and Four Primitive Gospels", in J. M. Robinson and H. Koester, *Trajectories through Early Christianity* (Philadelphia 1971), pp. 187–93; R. P. Martin, *Mark: Evangelist and Theologian* (Exeter 1972), chap. VI; E. Trocmé, *Jesus and his Contemporaries* (E.T. London 1973), chap. 7.
50. See e.g. Bultmann, *Theology* I, pp. 140ff, 148ff.
51. For description and critique see particularly G. Wagner, *Pauline Baptism and the Pagan Mysteries* (E.T. Edinburgh 1967).
52. See e.g. E. Käsemann, "The Pauline Doctrine of the Lord's Supper," *Essays on New Testament Themes* (E.T. London 1964), pp. 108ff. But see also Dunn, *Baptism in the Holy Spirit* (London 1970), Part III.
53. See e.g. A. Drews, *Die Christusmythe* (Jena 1910); P. L. Couchoud, *The Enigma of Jesus* (E.T. London 1924); G. A. Wells, *The Jesus of the Early Christians* (London 1971). But see also M. Goguel, *Jesus the Nazarene – Myth or History?* (E.T. London 1926); H. G. Wood, *Did Christ Really Live?* (London 1938).
54. Cited by H. Schlier, "The New Testament and Myth", *The Relevance of the New Testament* (E.T. London 1967), p. 84.
55. Schlier, p. 92. Cf. A. Harnack: "In Christ the principal figure of all myths has become history", cited by G. Miegge, *Gospel and Myth in the Thought of Rudolf Bultmann* (E.T. London 1960), p. 106. To be sure, the concepts of Christ's pre-existence and virginal conception can justifiably be described as "mythical" (cf. Kümmel, *Heilsgeschehen,* p. 155, 165f); but even here we should note that "the idea of the incarnation . . . is contrary to the nature of myth itself" (Pannenberg, "Myth", pp. 71f).
56. O. Cullmann, *Salvation in History* (E.T. London 1967), pp. 139ff.
57. Each of these observations can be illustrated from the classic expression of Liberal Protestantism, A. Harnack's *What is Christianity?* (E.T. London 1901, reprinted 1958); see

particularly Lectures 2, 3 and 10. It is noticeable that Weiss, Heitmüller and Bousset remained firmly entrenched within Liberal Protestantism at this central point; see J. Weiss, *Jesus' Proclamation of the Kingdom of God* (E.T. London 1971), p. 135 (also Introduction pp. 16–24); Kümmel, *New Testament,* pp. 230ff, 255ff, 259ff; Koch, *Apocalyptic,* p. 59.

58. Kümmel, *New Testament,* n. 466; see also Miegge, *Gospel,* pp. 119ff; J. M. Robinson, "The Pre-History of Demythologization", *Interpretation* 20 (1966), pp. 68f; W. Schmithals, *An Introduction to the Theology of Rudolf Bultmann* (E.T. London 1968), p. 250; Johnson, pp. 103–14.

59. "New Testament and Mythology", E.T. in *Kerygma and Myth,* pp. 1–44; subsequent page references in the text are to this essay.

60. Pannenberg, "Myth", p. 9. See also Johnson, pp. 141–151.

61. See also Bultmann, *Jesus Christ and Mythology* (London 1960), p. 37.

62. But see Part I above. K. Barth comments, "What kind of myth is it that recognizes the existence only of the human subject, and so requires an exclusively existentialist and anthropological interpretation?" (*Kerygma and Myth* II, p. 116); see also I. Henderson, *Myth in the New Testament* (London 1952), pp. 30ff – "the non-homogeneous character of the mythical" (p. 52). Bultmann would presumably justify the claim on the grounds that the subject-object distinction and so the possibility of consciously standing apart from the world is a modern development beginning with Descartes (cf. Schmithals, *Bultmann,* pp. 29ff.). Existentialism overcomes this subject-object pattern and so enables post-Cartesian scientific man to get inside pre-Cartesian and particularly NT (mythical) thought. See also F. Gogarten, *Demythologizing and History* (E.T. London 1955), pp. 48–68 – particularly valuable for his warning against an unjustified attack on Bultmann's theology as "subjectivist".

63. See also J. Macquarrie, *An Existentialist Theology* (London 1955), pp. 14–21.

64. "This is what is meant by 'faith': to open ourselves freely to the future" (*Kerygma and Myth,* p. 19).

65. Cf. Bultmann, *Theology* I, pp. 305f. See also Schmithals, *Bultmann,* chapters 6 and 8: "The Christian Easter faith is not interested in the historical question because it is interested in the resurrection of Jesus as saving event, that is as an existential experience" (p. 138). "It is the Word that makes the Jesus-event the saving event"; "apart from this proclamation the Jesus-event is just an ordinary earthly event" (pp. 174, 193).

66. "The Christological Confession of the World Council of Churches", *Essays Philosophical and Theological* (E.T. London 1955), pp. 280f.

67. Here Bultmann acknowledges his debt to his teacher W. Herrmann (*Kerygma and Myth,* pp. 200f); but influential statements on the same theme had been made by Kierkegaard, M. Kähler and of course Barth.

68. See particularly his comments on 1 Cor. 15:3–8 (*Kerygma and Myth* p. 39); and below. Cf. his earlier essay, "What does it mean to speak of God?" (1925), *Faith and Understanding* (E.T. London 1969), pp. 53–65.

69. *Kerygma and Myth,* p. 197; *Jesus Christ and Mythology,* p. 19; "On the Problem of Demythologizing", *New Testament Issues* (ed. R. Batey; London 1970), p. 41; also his reply to H. P. Owen in *The Theology of Rudolf Bultmann* (ed. C. W. Kegley, London 1966) p. 261. See also H. P. Owen, *Revelation and Existence: a Study in the Theology of Rudolph Bultmann* (Cardiff 1957): "Demythologizing would be more accurately called deobjectifying" (p. 15); Schmithals, *Bultmann,* chapter 2; "The basic error of all theology, even of faith itself . . . – God's action is objectified" (p. 141); and particularly Johnson, *Origins,* pp. 14f and *passim,* who notes the important influence of H. Jonas on Bultmann's understanding of myth and of "objectivation" (pp. 114–26, 207–31).

70. *Jesus Christ and Mythology,* p. 84; see also *Kerygma and Myth,* pp. 210f.

71. Miegge, *Gospel,* p. 93.

72. R. W. Hepburn, "Demythologizing and the Problem of Validity", *New Essays in Philosophical Theology* (ed. A. Flew and A. Macintyre; London 1955), pp. 229f; see also e.g. Kümmel, "Mythos im Neuen Testament", *Heilsgeschehen,* p. 221; J. Macquarrie, *The Scope of Demythologizing* (London 1960), pp. 198ff; but see also S. M. Ogden's more sympathetic comments in Kegley, *Bultmann,* pp. 111–6.

73. *Kerygma and Myth,* pp. 196f; *Jesus Christ and Mythology,* pp. 68f; *New Testament*

Issues, p. 42. But see Macquarrie's comment, *Demythologizing,* p. 205 n. 1.
74. P. S. Minear, "The Cosmology of the Apocalypse", *Current Issues in New Testament Interpretation* (ed. W. Klassen and G. F. Snyder; London 1962), pp. 32f; "Certainly we cannot accuse him of holding a naive three-storied idea of the physical world. There is nothing naive about his wrestling with the dilemmas of human existence" (p. 34).
75. Cf. Bultmann, *Theology* I, §§21ff. G. Bornkamm characterizes the heresy which Paul attacks in Colossians as an attempt "to gain access to the gospel by way of myth" – "Myth and Gospel: A Discussion of the Problem of Demythologizing the New Testament Message", *Kerygma and History* (ed. C. E. Braaten and R. A. Harrisville, Nashville 1962), p. 181.
76. Cf. F. F. Bruce, "The Kerygma of Hebrews", *Interpretation* 23 (1969), pp. 9ff.
77. Cf. Barth, *Kerygma and Myth* II, pp. 115f.
78. H. Braun, "The Meaning of New Testament Christology", J. Th.Ch. 5 (New York, 1968), pp. 117f.
79. F. Buri, *Kerygma und Mythos* II (ed. H. W.-Bartsch, Hamburg 1952), pp. 85ff: "The kerygma is a last vestige of mythology to which we still illogically cling" (p. 96). See also Macquarrie, *Demythologizing,* chapter 5.
80. S. M. Ogden, *Christ without Myth* (New York 1961), pp. 76–94, 111–16; Van A. Harvey, *The Historian and the Believer* (London 1967), pp. 139–46; see also Jaspers, *Kerygma and Myth* II pp. 173f.
81. A. Kee, *The Way of Transcendence* (Harmondsworth, 1971), pp. xvi–xxii.
82. *Jesus Christ and Mythology,* p. 43. On Bultmann's concern to remove the *false* skandalon of first century mythology from the gospel, see Schmithals, *Bultmann,* pp. 255f.
83. "Does the New Testament embody a truth which is quite independent of its mythical setting? If it does, theology must undertake the task of stripping the Kerygma from its mythical framework, of 'demythologizing' it" (*Kerygma and Myth,* p. 3). Note also the *a priori* distinction between "the other worldly" and "this world", etc. in the definition on p. 10 n. 2 (cited above p. 297).
84. "The word of preaching confronts us as the word of God. It is not for us to question its credentials" (*Kerygma and Myth,* p. 41); see also his reply to Jaspers, (*Kerygma and Myth* II, p. 190), and Schmithals, *Bultmann,* pp. 193f.
85. See e.g. Barth and R. Schnackenburg in *Kerygma and Myth* II, pp. 91–102, 340–9.
86. This is not to deny that Bultmann wishes to say something about "the historical event of Jesus Christ"; but to describe it only as "the eschatological event . . . only present as address" (Bultmann's reply to Ogden in Kegley, *Bultmann,* pp. 272f) neither meets Ogden's criticism nor says enough about Jesus.
87. "If the event of Easter Day is in any sense an historical event additional to the event of the cross, it is nothing else than the rise of faith in the risen Lord, since it was this faith which led to the apostolic preaching" (*Kerygma and Myth,* p. 42). Barth comments: "The real life of Jesus Christ is confined to the kerygma and to faith" (*Kerygma and Myth* II, p. 101). Similarly Bornkamm: "Jesus Christ has become a mere saving fact and ceases to be a person" (*Kerygma and History,* p. 186).
88. Cf. Kümmel, *Heilsgeschehen,* pp. 157–65, 228f; see also Cullmann, *Christ and Time* (E.T. London 1951, revised 1962), pp. 94–106; *Salvation in History* pp. 136–50; H. Ott, "Rudolf Bultmann's Philosophy of History" in Kegley, *Bultmann,* p. 58 (note Bultmann's response, p. 264).
89. Macquarrie's position in effect in *Demythologizing,* pp. 93, 98f, 224, and in his concept of "Christhood" in *Principles of Christian Theology* (London 1966).
90. Note particularly that 1 Cor. 15:12ff seems to be specifically directed against such a reduction of resurrection hope to the "now" of present religious experience (cf. 1 Cor. 4:8); see Dunn, "1 Corinthians 15:45", pp. 127f. Cf. W. Pannenberg, *Jesus God and Man* (E.T. London 1968), pp. 106ff; J. Moltmann, *The Theology of Hope* (E.T. London 1967), chapter 3. Similar criticism would have to be levelled against Bultmann's reduction of the future imminent expectation of Jesus' own message to the crisis of the eschatological "now" of decision (*Jesus and the Word* (E.T. London 1934, reprinted 1958), pp. 44–7).
91. *Jesus Christ and Mythology,* pp. 33f, 80f.

92. Against Bultmann's arbitrary attempts to attribute such passages to the anonymous "ecclesiastical redactor" – *The Gospel of John* (E.T. Oxford 1971).
93. Kümmel, *Heilsgeschehen,* pp. 156f, 160, 164, 225ff. Cf. Plato's distinction between *mythos* and *logos* above (p. 286); and J. Knox, *The Death of Christ* (London 1959, reprinted 1967), pp. 146ff; also *Myth and Truth* (London 1966), chapters 2 and 3.

CHAPTER XVI

THE NEW HERMENEUTIC

by A. C. Thiselton

I. *Aims and Concerns: How may the text speak anew?*

(1) The approach to the New Testament which has come to be known as the new hermeneutic is associated most closely with the work of Ernst Fuchs and Gerhard Ebeling.[1] Both of these writers insist on its practical relevance to the world of today. How does language, especially the language of the Bible, strike home (*treffen*) to the modern hearer?[2] How may its words so reach through into his own understanding that when he repeats them they will be *his* words? How may the word of God become a living word which is heard anew?

This emphasis on present application rather than simply antiquarian biblical research stems partly from connexions between the new hermeneutic and the thought of Rudolf Bultmann,[3] but also from a pastor's deep and consistent concern on the part of Fuchs and Ebeling, both of whom served as pastors for some years, about the relevance and effectiveness of Christian preaching. Central to Fuchs's work is the question "What do we have to do at our desks, if we want later to set the text in front of us in the pulpit?"[5]

It would be a mistake to conclude that this interest in preaching, however, is narrowly ecclesiastical or merely homiletical. Both writers share an intense concern about the position of the unbeliever. If the word of God is capable of *creating* faith, its intelligibility cannot be said to *presuppose* faith. Thus Fuchs warns us, "The proclamation loses its character when it anticipates (i.e. presupposes) confession."[6] Whilst Ebeling boldly asserts, "The criterion of the understandability of our preaching is not the believer but the non-believer. For the proclaimed word seeks to effect faith, but does not presuppose faith as a necessary preliminary."[7]

Nevertheless the problem goes even deeper than this. The modern hearer, or interpreter, stands at the end of a long tradition of biblical interpretation; a tradition which, in turn, moulds his own understanding of the biblical text and his own attitude towards it. His attitude may be either positive or negative, and his controlling assumptions may well be unconscious ones.[8] The New Testament is thus interpreted today within a particular frame of reference which may differ radically from that within which the text first addressed its hearers. Hence simply to *repeat* the actual words of the New Testament today may well be, in effect, to say something different from what the text itself originally said. Even if it does not positively alter what was once said, it may be to utter "nothing more than just a tradition, a mere form of speech, a dead relic of the language of the past." [9] For never before, Ebeling believes, was there so great a gulf between the linguistic tradition of the Bible and language that is actually spoken today. [10]

Two undue criticisms must be forestalled at this point. Firstly, some may believe that this problem is solved simply by an appeal to the work of the Holy Spirit. Fuchs and Ebeling are fully aware of the role of the Holy Spirit in communicating the word of God; but they rightly see that problems of understanding and intelligibility cannot be short-circuited by a premature appeal of this kind. [11] The New Testament requires hermeneutical translation no less than it obviously requires linguistic translation. This point will become clearer as we proceed.

Secondly, Fuchs and Ebeling do not in any way underestimate the power of the New Testament to interpret itself, and to create room for its understanding. Ebeling insists that hermeneutics "only consist in removing hindrances in order to let the word perform its own hermeneutic function." [12] "Holy Scripture, as Luther puts it, is *sui ipsius interpres*." [13] The "one bridge" to the present is "the Word alone". [14] Similarly Fuchs stresses the importance of Heb. 4:12–13 ("The word of God is living and active, sharper than any two-edged sword") even in the present moment. [15] Indeed it is crucial to Fuch's position, as we shall see, that the New Testament itself effects changes in situations, and changes in men's pre-conscious standpoints. The language of Jesus "singles out the individual and grasps him deep down." [16] "The text is itself meant to live." [17]

The key question in the new hermeneutic, then, is how the New Testament may speak to us *anew*. A literalistic repetition of the text cannot *guarantee* that it will "speak" to the modern hearer. He may understand all of its individual words, and yet fail to understand what is being said. In Wolfhart Pannenberg's words, "In a changed situation the traditional phrases, even when recited literally, do not mean what they did at the time of their original formulation." [18] Thus Ebeling asserts, "The *same word* can be said to another time only by being said differently." [19]

In assessing the validity of this point, we may well wish to make some proviso about the uniquely normative significance of the original formulation in *theology*. The problem is recognized by Fuchs and Ebeling perhaps more clearly than by Bultmann when parallel questions arise in his programme of demythologizing. [20] It is partly in connexion with this problem that both writers insist on the necessity of historical-critical research on the New Testament. [21] At the same time, at least two considerations re-enforce their contentions about the inadequacy of mere repetition of the text from the standpoint of *hermeneutics*. Firstly, we already recognize the fact that in translation from one language to another, literalism can be the enemy of faithful communication. "To put it into another language means to think it through afresh."[22] Secondly, we already have given tacit recognition to this principle whenever we stress the importance of preaching. The preacher "translates" the text, by placing it at the point of encounter with the hearer, from which it speaks anew into his own world in his own language.[23] But this hermeneutical procedure is demanded in *all* interpretation which is faithful to the New Testament. For "God's revelation consisted simply in God's letting men state God's own problems *in their language,* in grace and judgment."[24]

(2) How, then, may the text of the New Testament speak anew? Four sets of considerations are relevant to a positive answer, each of which turns on a given point of contrast.

(a) Firstly, Fuchs and Ebeling draw *a contrast between problems about words (plural) and the problem of the word (singular).* Ebeling laments the fact that too often preaching today sounds like a foreign language.[25] But he adds, "We need not emphasize that the problem lies too deep to be tackled by cheap borrowing of transient modern jargon for the preacher's stock of words. It is not a matter of understanding single words, but of understanding the word itself; not a matter of new means of speech, but of a new coming to speech."[26] Mere modern paraphrase of the New Testament does not answer the problem. The concern is, rather, that the word of God itself should "come to speech" (*das Zur-Sprache-kommen der Sache selbst*), in the technical sense which this phrase has come to bear in the philosophical writings of Martin Heidegger and Hans-Georg Gadamer.[27]

(b) Secondly, hermeneutics in the writings of Fuchs and Ebeling concerns "the theory of understanding", and *must not be reduced "to a collection of rules."*[28] Indeed, because it concerns the whole question of how a man comes to *understand,* Ebeling asserts, "Hermeneutics now takes the place of the classical epistemological theory."[29] This is why hermeneutics cannot be separated from philosophy. Because it concerns "a general theory of understanding", hermeneutics is "becoming the place of meeting with philosophy."[30] Similarly for Fuchs the central question of hermeneutics is: "how do I come to understand?"[31] Yet both writers are concerned not simply with the theory, but with the *practice* of setting understanding in motion. Fuchs suggests an analogy. It is possible, on the one hand, to theorize about an understanding of "cat" by cognitive reflection. On the other hand, a practical and pre-conceptual understanding of "cat" emerges when we actually place a mouse in front of a particular cat. The mouse is the "hermeneutical principle" that causes the cat to show itself for what it is.[32] In this sense biblical criticism and even the traditional hermeneutical "rules" do "not *produce* understanding, but only the preconditions for it."[33]

Admittedly it would not be wholly incorrect to argue that this distinction goes back in principle to Schleiermacher. An illuminating comment comes from the philosopher Heinz Kimmerle, whose research on the earlier writings of Schleiermacher is so important for the new hermeneutic. He writes, "The work of Schleiermacher constitutes a turning point in the history of hermeneutics. Till then hermeneutics was supposed to support, secure, and clarify an *already accepted* understanding (of the Bible as theological hermeneutics; of classical antiquity as philological hermeneutics). In the thinking of Schleiermacher, hermeneutics achieves the qualitatively different function of first of all *making understanding possible,* and deliberately *initiating understanding* in each individual case." [34] This touches on yet another central and cardinal feature of the new hermeneutic. The concern is not simply to support and corroborate an *existing* understanding of the New Testament text, but to lead the hearer or the interpreter onwards *beyond* his own existing horizons, so that the text addresses and judges him *anew*. This fundamental principle will emerge most clearly in connexion with Hans-Georg Gadamer and the wider philosophical background.

(c) The problem of initiating understanding brings us to another concept which is also central in the thinking of Fuchs, namely that of *das Einverständnis.*[35] This is often translated as "common understanding", "mutual understanding" or "agreement", and in one essay as "empathy". Fuchs illustrates this category with reference to the language of the home. Members of a close-knit family who live together in one home share a common world of assumptions, attitudes, and experiences, and therefore share a common language. A single word or gesture may set in motion a train of events because communication functions on the basis of a common understanding. Fuchs explains, "At home one does not speak so that people may understand, but because people understand." [36] The problem of understanding a language, in the sense of "appropriating" its subject matter, "does not consist in learning new words – languages are learned from mothers."[37] So important is this category of *Einverständnis* for Fuchs that in the preface to the fourth edition of *Hermeneutik* he stresses that "all understanding is grounded in *Einverständnis,*" and in a later essay he sums up the thrust of his *Hermeneutik* with the comment, "Ernst Fuchs, *Hermeneutik* (is) an attempt to bring the hermeneutical problem back into the dimension of language with the aid of the phenomenon of 'empathy' (*des Phänomens des Einverständnisses*) as the foundation of all understanding."[38]

Jesus, Fuchs maintains, established a common understanding with his hearers, especially in the language of the parables. Or more accurately, the parables communicated reality effectively because they operated on the basis of this common understanding, which they then extended and reshaped.[39] The hermeneutical task today is to re-create that common world of understanding which is the necessary basis of effective communication of language and appropriation of its truth. Such a task, however, stands in sharp contrast to a merely cognitive and conscious exchange of language. Like Heidegger's category of "world", it is pre-conceptual. "It is neither a subjective nor an objective phenomenon but both together, for world is prior to and encompasses both." [40] It is therefore, for Fuchs as for Gadamer, primarily a "linguistic" phenomenon, reflecting ways in which men have come to terms with themselves and with their world.[41]

(d) Both Fuchs and Ebeling view language as much more than being only a means of information. Ebeling writes "We do not get at the nature of words by asking what they contain, but by asking what they effect, what they set going . . ."[42] In the terminology of J. L. Austin, Fuchs and Ebeling are most interested in the *performative* functions of language, in which "the issuing of the utterance is the performing of an action."[43] The word of God, Ebeling believes, enacts "an event in which God himself is communicated . . . With God word and deed are one: his speaking is the way of his acting."[44] Thus the word of Jesus in the New Testament does not simply provide information about states of affairs. His language constitutes a call or a pledge.[45] He promises, demands or gives.[46] Actually to *make* a promise, or to *convey* a gift is very different from talking *about* promises or gifts. The one is action; the other is mere talk.

In the terminology used by Fuchs, language which actually conveys reality constitutes a "language-event" (*Sprachereignis*), whilst Ebeling uses the term "word-event" (*Wortgeschehen*) in much the same way.[47] Fuchs comments, "The true language-event, for example an offer, shows that, though it sets our thoughts in motion, it is not itself thought. The immediate harmony between what is said and what is grasped is not the result of a process of thought; it takes place at an earlier stage, as event . . . The word 'gets home'."[48] For example, to name a man "brother" performatively is thereby to admit him into a brotherly relationship within the community.[49] In this sense, when the word of God addresses the hearers anew, it is no longer merely an object of investigation at the hands of the interpreter. Fuchs concludes "The text is therefore not just the servant that transmits kerygmatic formulations, but rather a master that directs us into the language-context of our existence."[50] It has become a language-event.

II. *Subject and Object: Understanding as experience*

Two further principles now emerge from all that has been said. The first concerns the interpreter's experience of life, or subjectivity. Ebeling writes, "Words produce understanding only by appealing to experience and leading to experience. Only where word has already taken place can word take place. Only where there is already previous understanding can understanding take place. Only a man who is already concerned with the matter in question can be claimed for it."[51] This is certainly true of a text which concerns history: "It is impossible to understand history without a standpoint and a perspective."[52] Thus there are connexions between the new hermeneutic and Bultmann's discussion about *pre-understanding*.

The second principle concerns the direction of the relation between the interpreter and the text. In traditional hermeneutics, the interpreter, as knowing subject, scrutinizes and investigates the text as the object of his knowledge. The interpreter is active subject; the text is passive object. This kind of approach is encouraged by a notion of theology as "queen of the sciences". But it rests upon, or presupposes, a particular model in epistemology; a model which is exemplified in the philosophy of Descartes. If understanding is viewed in terms of experience rather than knowledge, a different perspective may also be suggested. James Robinson offers an illuminating comment. In the new hermeneutic, he explains, "the flow of the traditional relation between subject and object, in which the subject interrogates the object . . . has been significantly reversed. For it is now the object – which should henceforth be called the subject-matter – that puts the subject in question." [53] Thus Fuchs asserts, "*The truth has us ourselves as its object*." [54] Or even more strikingly, "The texts must translate us before we can translate them." [55]

1. LANGUAGE AND PRE-UNDERSTANDING

It is well known that Rudolf Bultmann, among others, has repudiated the idea that an interpreter can "understand" the New Testament independently of his own prior questions. One cannot, for example, understand a text about economic history unless one already has some concept of what a society and an economy is.[56] In this sense Bultmann rightly insists, "*There cannot be any such thing as presuppositionless exegesis* . . . Historical understanding always presupposes a relation of the interpreter to the subject-matter that is ... expressed in the texts." [57] "The demand that the interpreter must silence his subjectivity . . . in order to attain an objective knowledge is therefore the most absurd one that can be imagined." [58] "Preunderstanding", or a prior life-relation to the subject-matter of the text, implies "not a prejudice, but a way of raising questions." [59]

This principle must not be rejected merely because it has particular connexions with other assumptions made by Bultmann in his programme of demythologizing. Other more moderate scholars including, for example, Bernard Lonergan and James D. Smart, have made similar points.[60] Lonergan rightly asserts, "The principle of the empty head rests on a naive intuitionism . . . The principle . . . bids the interpreter forget his own views, look at what is out there, and let the author interpret himself. In fact, what is out there? There is just a series of signs. Anything over and above a re-issue of the same signs in the same order will be mediated by the experience, intelligence, and judgment of the interpreter. The less that experience, the less cultivated that intelligence, the less formed that judgment, the greater will be the likelihood that the interpreter will impute to the author an opinion that the author never entertained." [61]

In this connexion both Bultmann and the new hermeneutic look back to Wilhelm Dilthey, and even beyond to Friedrich Schleiermacher.[62] Both the later thinking of Schleiermacher after 1819 and also the earlier thinking as rediscovered by Heinz Kimmerle are relevant in different ways to the new hermeneutic. At first sight, Fuchs's central concept of *Einverständnis* seems to relate to the later Schleiermacher's insistence that the modern interpreter must make himself contemporary with the author of a text by attempting imaginatively to re-live his experiences. Especially if we follow the translator who rendered *Einverständnis* as "empathy", this looks like Schleiermacher's procedure of entering into the hopes and fears, desires and aims of the author through artistic imagination and rapport.

We have seen, however, that "mutual understanding" in Fuchs operates at a pre-conscious level. It is not primarily, if at all, a matter of psychology, as it was in the later thought of Schleiermacher. With Manfred Mezger, Fuchs believes that this psychological approach founders on the existential individuality of the "I" who is each particular interpreter.[63] Thus Mezger asserts that we must find "the new place at which this text, without detriment to its historical individuality, meets us. The short cut by which I picture myself as listener in the skin of Moses or of Paul is certainly popular, but it is not satisfactory, for I am neither the one nor the other" (i.e. neither Moses nor Paul).[64] Mezger adds that the way to overcome this problem is "not by treating the particular details with indifference, thus effacing the personal profile of the text, but by becoming aware of the involvement (*Betroffenheit*) which is the same for them as for me, but which is described in a particular way in each instance."[65] He then quotes Fuchs's redoubled warning that the modern listeners "are not the same men to whom the gospel was first proclaimed"; although their concrete situation can nevertheless be "appropriated" today, when the text is accurately translated.[66]

In the earlier writings of Schleiermacher, however, as Kimmerle has shown, hermeneutics are more language-centred, and less orientated towards psychology. Understanding is an *art,* for the particular utterance of a particular author must be understood "in the light of the larger, more universal, linguistic community in which the individual . . . finds himself."[67] "Rules" perform only the negative function of preventing false interpretation. Even on a purely linguistic level the subjectivity of the interpreter has a positive role to play. What we understand forms itself into unities made up of parts. In understanding a stretch of language, we need to understand words in order to understand the sentence; nevertheless our understanding of the force of individual words depends on our understanding of the whole sentence. But this principle must be extended. Our understanding of the sentence contributes to our understanding of the paragraph, of the chapter, of the author as a whole; but this understanding of the whole work in turn qualifies and modifies our understanding of the sentence.

This principle prepares the way for hermeneutics in Heidegger and Gadamer, as well as in Fuchs and Ebeling, and is in fact tantamount to a preliminary formulation of the theory of the hermeneutical circle.[68] It shatters the illusion, as Dilthey later stressed, that understanding a text could be purely "scientific". As Richard Palmer puts it, "Somehow a kind of 'leap' into the hermeneutical circle occurs and we understand the whole and the parts together. Schleiermacher left room for such a factor when he saw understanding as partly a comparative and partly an intuitive and divinatory matter . . ."[69] Still commenting on Schleiermacher but with obvious relevance to Fuchs's notion of *Einverständnis,* Palmer adds, "The hermeneutical circle suggests an area of shared understanding. Since communication is a dialogical relation, there is assumed at the outset a community of meaning shared by the speaker and the hearer. This seems to involve another contradiction: what is to be understood must already be known. But is this not the case? Is it not vain to speak of love to one who has not known love...?"[70] Thus we return to Ebeling's comment, "Words produce understanding by appealing to experience and leading to experience. Only where word has already taken place can word take place. Only where there is already previous understanding can understanding take place."[71]

This helps to explain why the new hermeneutic inevitably involves problems of philosophy.[72] But it also raises theological questions. In one direction, the New Testament cannot be understood without reference to the interpreter's own experiences of life. Thus Fuchs insists, "*In the interaction of the text with daily life we experience the truth of the New Testament.*"[73] In another direction, it raises questions about the relation between exegesis and systematic theology. For the *total* context of any theological utterance is hardly less than Scripture and the history of its interpretation through tradition. In Heinrich Ott's words on the subject, Scripture as a whole constitutes "the 'linguistic room', the universe of discourse, the linguistic net of co-ordinates in which the church has always resided ... Heidegger says, 'Every poet composed from only a single poem ... None of the individual poems, not even the total of them, says it all. Nevertheless each poem speaks from the whole of the one poem and each time speaks it'."[74]

2. THE INTERPRETER AND THE TEXT

All that has been said about the subjectivity of the interpreter, however, must now be radically qualified by the second of the two major principles at present under discussion. We have already noted Fuchs's assertions that the texts must translate us, before we can translate them, and that the truth has "ourselves" as its object. It is not simply the case that the interpreter, as active subject, scrutinizes the text as passive object. It is not simply that the present experience throws light on the text, but that the text illuminates present experience. Ebeling insists, "*The text ... becomes a hermeneutic aid in the understanding of present experience.*"[75] In an important and often-quoted sentence in the same essay he declares (his italics) "*The primary phenomenon in the realm of understanding is not understanding OF language, but understanding THROUGH language.*"[76]

Both Ebeling and especially Gadamer call attention to the parallel between theological and juridical hermeneutics in this respect.[77] The interpretation of legal texts, Gadamer insists, is not simply a "special case" of general hermeneutics, but, rather, reveals the full dimensions of the general hermeneutical problem. In law the interpreter does not examine the text purely as an "object" of antiquarian investigation. The text "speaks" to the present situation in the courtroom, and the interpreter adjusts his own thinking to that of the text. Each of our two principles, in fact, remains equally relevant. On the one hand, the interpreter's own understanding of law and of life guides him in his understanding of the ancient legal texts; on the other hand, that preliminary understanding is modified and moulded, in turn, as the texts themselves deliver their verdicts on the present situation. Even outside the courtroom itself, Ebeling believes that "the man who has no interest in giving legal decisions will be a poor legal historian." [78] Similarly Gadamer asserts, "Understanding the text is always already applying it." [79]

These two principles operate together in Gadamer's version of the hermeneutical circle. We have already noted the idea in Schleiermacher and in Heidegger that we can understand a whole only in the light of its parts, but also that we can understand the parts only in the light of the whole. But Heidegger and especially Gadamer take us a step further. [80] The "circle" of the hermeneutical process begins when the interpreter takes his own preliminary questions to the text. But because his questions may not be the best or most appropriate ones, his understanding of the subject-matter of the text may at first remain limited, provisional, and even liable to distortion. Nevertheless the text, in turn, speaks back to the hearer: it begins to interpret him; it sheds light on his own situation and on his own questions. His initial questions now undergo revision in the light of the text itself, and in response to more adequate questioning, the text itself now speaks more clearly and intelligibly. The process continues, whilst the interpreter achieves a progressively deeper understanding of the text.

In his recently published book the American scholar Walter Wink develops his own particular version of this kind of approach. [81] He criticizes New Testament scholars for failing to interpret the New Testament in accordance with its own purpose, namely "so to interpret the scriptures that the past becomes alive and illumines our present with new possibilities for personal and social transformation." [82] Because of a deliberate suspension of participational involvement, "the outcome of biblical studies in the academy is a trained incapacity to deal with the real problems of actual living persons in their daily lives." [83] The kind of *questions* asked by the New Testament scholar are not those raised by the text, but those most likely to win a hearing from the professional guild of academics. [84] Scholars seek to silence their own subjectivity, striving for the kind of objective neutrality which is not only an illusion, but which also requires "a sacrifice of the very questions the Bible seeks to answer". [85]

Nevertheless, Wink is not advocating, any more than Fuchs, a suspension of critical studies. In order to hear the New Testament *speak for itself*, and not merely reflect back the interpreter's own ideas or the theology of the modern church, the interpreter must allow critical enquiry first to *distance* him from the way in which the text has become embedded in the church's tradition. The text must be heard as "that which stands over against us". [86] Only after this "distance" has first been achieved can there then occur "a communion of horizons" between the interpreter and the text. [87] Thus whilst

Wink acknowledges the necessity for "rigorous use of biblical criticism", his primary concern, like that of Fuchs, is "for the rights of the text".[88]

Hans-Georg Gadamer makes some parallel points. Descartes' theory of knowledge, in which man as active subject looks out on the world as passive object, provides only *one* possible model for the apprehension of truth. This model is more appropriate to the "method" of the sciences than to the art of understanding in hermeneutics. There has always been a tradition in philosophy which stressed the connexion between understanding and *experience.* For example, Vico, with his sensitivity for history, rejected the narrow intellectualism of Descartes' notion of truth, even in the latter's own lifetime. In ancient times the Greek idea of "wisdom" included practical understanding of life as well as intellectual theory.[89] Later, Shaftesbury stressed the rôle of wit, Reid stressed the rôle of common sense, and Bergson stressed the rôle of intuitive insight, as valid ways through which truth could be revealed.[90] It is not simply a matter of discovering theoretical "methods" by which man can arrive at truth. In true understanding, man is grasped *by* truth through modes of experience.[91] A more adequate model than that provided by Descartes is the experience of truth in a work of art, in which something real and *creative* takes place. We shall refer to Gadamer's comments on this in our third section.

One reason why hermeneutics, according to Gadamer, must take account of something more than cognitive "knowledge" (*Erkenntnis*) is that every interpreter already stands within a historical tradition, which provides him with certain presuppositions or pre-judgements (*Vorurteile*).[92] Gadamer insists, "An individual's pre-judgements, much more than his judgements, are the reality of his being (*die geschichtliche Wirklichkeit seines Seins*)".[93] To bring these pre-judgements to conscious awareness is a major goal of hermeneutics, and corresponds to what Walter Wink describes as "distancing". For Gadamer believes that the very existence of a temporal and cultural *distance* between the interpreter and the text can be used to jog him into an awareness of the differences between their respective horizons. The interpreter must cultivate a "hermeneutically trained" awareness, in which he allows the distinctive message of the text to reshape his own questions and concepts.[94]

Once this has been done, the interpreter is free to move beyond his own original horizons, or better, to *enlarge* his own horizons until they come to *merge* or *fuse* with those of the text. His goal is to reach the place at which a merging of horizons (*Horizontverschmelzung*), or fusion of "worlds", occurs.[95] This comes about only through sustained dialogue with the text, in which the interpreter allows his own subjectivity to be challenged and involved. Only in the to-and-fro of question and answer on both sides can the text come to speech (*zur-Sprache-kommen*).[96] Thus in Gadamer's notion of the merging of horizons we find a parallel to Wink's ideas about "fusion" and "communion", and to Fuchs's central category of *Einverständnis.* But this is achieved, as we have seen, only when, firstly, the interpreter's subjectivity is fully engaged at a more-than-cognitive level; and when, secondly, the text, and the truth of the text, *actively* grasps *him* as its object.

III. *The Establishing of New "Worlds" in Language: Heidegger and the Parables*

To achieve a merging of horizons, or an area of shared understanding amounting to *Einverständnis,* involves, in effect, the creation of a new "world". In common with Heidegger's philosophy in both the earlier and later periods, Fuchs believes that man stands within a linguistic world which is decisively shaped by his own place in history, i.e. by his "historicality". But together with the later Heidegger, Fuchs also looks for a *new* coming-to-speech in which the confines and conventions of the old everyday "world" will be set aside and broken through. The language-event, especially the language-event of the parables of Jesus, corresponds to the establishment of a new world through language.

It is difficult to summarize Heidegger's view in a few paragraphs, but we may note the following major themes.

(1) One consequence of man's historicality (his being radically conditioned by his place within history) is that he views objects from the man-centred perspective of his own world. He sees things from the point of view of this relation to his own purposes, seeing them through a kind of grid of egocentric functionalism. A hammer, for example, is not merely a neutral "object" of wood and metal; but a tool which can be used for certain jobs. Thus a hammer is something very different from a broken hammer; although in "neutral" terms of their physical properties the difference would not be very great.[97] Man's language both reveals, creates, and sustains this perspective. Thus in everyday language "time", for example, "has ceased to be anything other than velocity, instantaneousness . . . Time as history has vanished from the lives of all peoples."[98]

(2) Man has lost touch with genuine reality still further by accepting in his intellectual orientation the legacy of Plato's dualism. In Heidegger's words, Western philosophy since Plato has "fallen out of Being".[99] It embodies a split perspective, in which subject becomes separated from object. "Appearance was declared to be mere appearance and thus degraded. At the same time, Being as *idea* was exalted to a suprasensory realm. A chasm . . . was created."[100] Man thus looks out, in the fashion of Plato and Descartes, onto a merely *conceptualized* world, a reality of his own making. He himself, by seeing "reality" through the grid of his own split perspective, becomes the measure of his own knowledge.[101] An example of the evil consequences of this can be seen in the realm of art. Art is divided off into one of the two realms, so that it is *either* a merely "material" thing, in which case it cannot reveal truth; *or* it is conceptualized into "aesthetics" in which case it becomes tamed and emasculated and, once again, unable to reveal truth. By contrast "on the strength of a recaptured, pristine, relation to Being, we must provide the word 'art' with a new content."[102]

(3) The combined effect of these two factors is to lead to circularity and

fragmentation in the use of *language*. The truth of language now depends on an artificial correspondence between man's concepts and what he supposes to be "reality", but which is in fact another set of his own concepts.[103] For everything which he thinks and sees, he thinks and sees through the medium of his own "linguisticality" or language-conditionedness. Thus, Heidegger concludes, "He is always thrown back on the paths that he himself has laid out; he becomes mired in his paths, caught in the beaten track . . . He turns round and round in his own circle."[104]

Fuchs and Ebeling accept the linguistic and hermeneutical problems which Heidegger's diagnosis lays down. Ebeling believes that language has become loosed from its anchorage in reality, to disintegrate into "atoms of speech . . . Everything seemed to me to fall into fragments."[105] This has precipitated "a profound crisis of language . . . a complete collapse of language".[106] Today "we threaten to die of language poisoning." "With the dawn of the modern age . . . the path was clear for an unrestricted development of the mere sign-function of language . . . Words are reduced to ciphers . . . and syntax to a question of calculus."[107] Language has wrongly become a mere "technical instrument".[108] Yet, Fuchs argues, language and reality are bound so closely together that there can be no "reality" *for us* outside this language.[109]

The solution, if it is a solution, offered by Heidegger, and indirectly by Fuchs, is to put oneself in the place at which language may, once again, give voice not to a fragmented set of human concepts, but to undivided "Being". Firstly, this "Being" is not the substantial "beingness" (*Seiendheit*) of human thought; but the verbal, eventful, temporal Being-which-happens (*Sein* or better, *Anwesen*). Echoing Heidegger, Fuchs declares, "Language . . . makes Being into an event."[110] Secondly, when language is once again pure and creative, Heidegger believes, "the essence of language is found in the act of gathering."[111] Before the advent of Plato's dualism, the word (*logos*) was "the primal gathering principle".[112] Where modern Western culture and its idle talk merely divides and fragments, the pure language of Being integrates and brings together. Thus Fuchs writes, "The proclamation gathers (i.e. into a community) . . . and this community has its being, its 'togetherness', in the possibility of its being able to speak the kind of language in which the event of its community is fulfilled . . . *The language of faith brings into language the gathering of faith*."[113]

Once again this notion of "gathering" approaches the idea of sharing a common "world", or achieving *Einverständnis*. But Heidegger, followed by Fuchs, insists that language can achieve this "gathering" only when man accepts the rôle of *listener,* rather than that of subject scrutinizing "object". For Heidegger, this means a silent, receptive waiting upon Being. Language is the "house" or "custodian" of Being (*das Haus des Seins . . . des Anwesens*).[114] Man's task is to find the "place" (*Ort*) at which Being may come to speech.[115] As listeners, whose task is to cultivate a wakeful and receptive openness to Being, Heidegger urges that "we should *do* nothing, but rather wait."[116] The listener must not impose his own concepts of reality onto Being, but should "know how to wait, even for a whole life-time".[117]

Although in principle he is concerned with the word of God rather than the voice of Being, Fuchs does at times seem to identify the two. The word of God relates to "the meaning of Being" (*der "Sinn" des Seins*) and comes as the "call of Being" (*der Ruf zum Sein*).[118] But above all man "listens" in receptive silence and openness to the text of the New Testament. To be sure, critical analysis, as in Wink's and Gadamer's "distancing", is first necessary as a preliminary. In this way, by active critical scrutiny, the interpreter "must in the *first instance* strike the text dead".[119] But *after* this he must wait for God, or Being, to speak "In the tranquillity of faith, where noise is reduced to silence, a *voice* is heard . . . It sings out in Phil. 2.6–11 . . ."[120]

All these principles about language and "world" apply in particular to Fuchs's handling of the parables of Jesus. By means of the image part or picture-half (*Bildhälfte*) of the parable, Jesus creates and enters a "world" which, in the first place, is shared by the hearer. He stands within the hearer's horizons. But everyday conventions and everyday assumptions are then challenged and shattered by the actual message or content-half (*Sachhälfte*). The hearer is challenged at a deep and pre-conceptual level. It is not simply a matter of his assessing certain "ideas" presented to him by Jesus. Rather, "he is drawn over on to God's side and learns to see everything with God's eyes."[121] The parable is both a creative work of *art,* and also a *calling* of love, in contrast to flat cognitive discourse. Thus "Jesus draws the hearer over to his side by means of the artistic medium, so that the hearer may think together with Jesus. Is this not the way of true love? Love does not just blurt out. Instead, it provides in advance the sphere in which meeting takes place."[122]

The difference between entering a "world" and merely assessing ideas is further clarified by Gadamer in his comments on the nature of games and the nature of art. A game creates a special "world" of experience. The player participates in this world, rather than simply observing it, by accepting its rules, its values, and its presuppositions. He yields himself to them, and *acts* on them. It is not a matter of his consciously carrying them in his mind. Hence the *reality* of a game is something shared by the players in the play itself.[123] Such "real-life" experience (*Wirklichkeitserfahrung*) is also involved when one is grasped by a true work of art.[124] It is not a mere set of concepts to be manipulated by a spectator, but a "world" which takes hold of a man as someone who *enters into it*. It is not something presented as a mere object of scrutiny, or source of theoretical concepts.[125]

In his treatment of specific parables, therefore, Fuchs insists that the main point is not simply to convey a conscious "idea". In this sense, he steps away from Jülicher's "one-point" approach. For the "point" or verdict of a parable may come differently to different people. Thus in his work on the Parable of the Unmerciful Servant, Fuchs declares, firstly, that "the parable is not intended to exemplify general ethics."[126] Secondly, the verdict for Israel is "God is harder than you are"; whilst the verdict for the Church is

"God insists upon his indulgence." [127] If these verdicts, however, are turned into merely conceptual generalizations, the result is only a self-contradiction: God is hard and indulgent.

Three principles are especially important for understanding Fuchs's approach to the parables.

(1) The image-part or picture-half of the parable is not merely an illustrative or homiletical device to make a lesson more vivid or memorable. It is a means of creating a common world in which Jesus and the hearer stand together. When Jesus speaks "of provincial and family life as it takes place in normal times", of the farmer, of the housewife, of the rich and poor or the happy and sad, he is not simply establishing a "point of contact" but standing with the hearer in *his* "world". [128] "We find *existentialia* wherever an understanding between men is disclosed through their having a common world." [129]

(2) Conventional everyday presuppositions about life and "reality" may then be challenged and shattered. This is where Fuchs's approach relates closely to Heidegger's verdict about the circularity and "fallenness" of man's everyday concepts and everyday talk. Something new and creative must break in to rescue him; in this case, the creative word and person of Jesus. Thus in the parable of the labourers in the vineyard (Matt. 20: 1–16) at first "we too share the inevitable reaction of the first. The first see that the last receive a whole day's wage, and naturally they hope for a higher rate for themselves." [130] But then comes the shock: "in fact they receive the same . . . It seems to them that the lord's action is unjust." Finally comes the verdict on the assumption which has been brought to light: "Is your eye evil because I am kind?" The word of Jesus thus "singles out the individual and grasps him deep down." For the hearer, by entering the world of the parable, has been drawn into an *engagement* with the verdict of Jesus. "The parable effects and demands our decision." It is *not* simply "the pallid requirement that sinful man should believe in God's kindness. Instead it contains, in a concrete way . . . Jesus' *pledge*." Jesus pledges himself to "those who, in face of a cry of 'guilty', nevertheless found their hope on an act of God's kindness." [131]

The creative language event, therefore, shatters the mould imposed by man's "linguisticality". Even ordinary life, Fuchs suggests, can provide a model of this occurrence: "A new observation can throw all our previous mental images into confusion . . . What has already been observed and preserved in mental images comes into conflict with what is newly observed." [132] This conflict, this clash, demands a decision and re-orientation. Robert Funk illustrates this principle with reference to the parable of the Prodigal Son (Luke 15:11–32). The "righteous" find themselves in the "world" of the elder brother, endorsing his conventional ideas of justice and obligation. "Sinners" participate in the "world" experienced by the prodigal son. Funk writes, "The word of grace and the deed of grace divide the audience into younger sons and elder sons – into sinners and Pharisees. This is what Ernst Fuchs means when he says that one does not interpret the parables; the parables interpret him. *The Pharisees are those who insist on interpreting the word of grace, rather than letting themselves be interpreted by it.*" [133] The judges find themselves judged. Sinners find themselves welcomed. "It is man and not God who is on trial." [134] The same principle operates in the parable of the Great Supper (Matt. 22:2–10; cf. Luke 14:16–24). One group is excluded; the other, embraced. "Each hearer is drawn into the tale as he wills." [135]

Walter Wink applies this approach to the interpretation of the parable of the Pharisee and the Publican (Luke 18.9–14). Most of Jesus' own hearers would at first identify themselves with the Pharisee as the hearer of religious and social status; but "then suffer shock and consternation at the wholly unexpected justification of the publican". [136] This of course raises a major hermeneutical problem, to which both Fuchs and Wink are eager to call attention. The *modern* reader already knows that it is the *Pharisee* who will be condemned. Hence nowadays "a simple descriptive approach wrecks the parable." [137] It must come to speech anew, and not merely be "repeated". For the ending of the parable has now in turn become embedded in the conventional judgements of "religious" man, from which the language-event is meant to free us!

(3) There is not sufficient space to comment adequately on the importance of Christology for Fuchs's understanding of the parables. We must note, however, that he stresses this aspect with special reference to the oneness of word and deed in the ministry of Jesus, and also to the status and rôle of Jesus as one who pronounces God's word in God's stead. God is present in the word of Jesus. Moreover, since Jesus enters the common world of understanding experienced by the hearer, the hearer makes his response to God's word "together with" Jesus. Thus in the parable of the labourers in the vineyard "Jesus acted in a very real way as God's representative" especially in "his conduct . . . and proclamation". Jesus gives us "to understand his conduct as God's conduct". "Jesus' proclamation . . . went along with his conduct." Finally, if I respond in faith," I am not only near to Jesus; in faith I await the occurrence of God's kindness together with Jesus." [138] Similarly, in the parable of the Unmerciful Servant, "God accepted the conduct of Jesus as a valid expression of his will." The hearer "lets Jesus guide him to the mercy of God". "Jesus does not give a new law, but substitutes himself for the law." [139]

This means that as Jesus stands "together with" the hearer, he becomes in some sense, a model for faith. For as the hearer, through the language-event, enters the "world" of Jesus, he finds a new vision of God and of the world which he shares with Jesus. For Fuchs this means especially the abandonment of self-assertion, even to the point of death; which is the repetition of Jesus' own decision to go the way of the cross and way of love. [140] "To have faith in Jesus now means essentially to repeat Jesus' decision." [141] This is why the new hermeneutic has definite connexions with the new quest of the historical Jesus. Fuchs writes, "In the proclamation of the resurrection the historical Jesus himself *has* come to us. The so-called Christ of faith is none other than the historical Jesus ... God himself, *wants to be encountered* by us in the historical Jesus." [142] For the message of Jesus to come-to-speech creatively and liberatingly as language-event presupposes some kind of continuity between his words and his life. Thus Ebeling also concludes, "The kerygma ... is not merely speech about man's existence. It is also a testimony to that which has happened." [143]

IV. *Some Conclusions*

(1) Whilst the new hermeneutic rightly faces the problem of how the interpreter may understand the text of the New Testament more *deeply* and more *creatively,* Fuchs and Ebeling are *less concerned about how he may understand it correctly.* Admittedly they insist on the need for historical-critical study, but rightly or wrongly we receive the impression that this is mainly a preliminary to the real task of hermeneutics. Fuchs and Ebeling are looking at *one* side, albeit a neglected and yet important side, of a two-sided problem. Rather than simply "first" using critical methods, is it not possible *both* to "listen" to the text as subject, and also *alongside this* critically to test one's understanding of it? May not both attitudes be called into play successively and repeatedly as if in dialogue?

It will be suggested, by way of reply, that this is necessarily to surrender a vision of wholeness in exchange for a split conceptualizing perspective in which the text becomes once again, a mere "object" of scrutiny. But whilst we may accept the warning of Heidegger and Gadamer that the subject-object "method" of Descartes is not always adequate, nevertheless conceptualizing thinking must be given *some* place in hermeneutics. Commenting on Heidegger's notion of openness to the call of Being, Hans Jonas points out that thinking "is precisely an effort not to be at the mercy of fate". [144] To surrender one's own initiative in thinking in exchange for a mere "listening" is precisely *not* to escape from one's own conditionedness by history and language, but is to make everything "a matter of the chance factor of the historical generation I was born into". [145] Theologians, Jonas concludes, have been too easily seduced by the pseudo-humility of Heidegger's orientation. The Christian has been delivered from the power of fate, and must use his mind to distinguish the true from the false.

We have already seen that Heidegger, and presumably Fuchs, would regard this as a misunderstanding and short-circuiting of the whole problem of man's "linguisticality". Subject-object thinking, they believe, as well as distancing man from reality also sets in motion a vicious circularity by evaluating one set of human concepts in terms of another. But the New Testament itself, especially Paul, seems to be less pessimistic than Heidegger about the use of reason or "mind" (*nous*). In this respect Heidegger stands nearer to the sheer irrationality of Zen Buddhism. For it is noteworthy that after reading a work of Suzuki's, Heidegger declared "This is what I have been trying to say in all my writings." [146] Moreover the actual practical difficulties of trying to distinguish between the true and the false in "non-objectifying" language are insuperable. They have been exposed, for example, by Paul van Buren in his discussion of Heinrich Ott.[147] Thus, in spite of its emphatic character, there is some justice in the verdict of J. C. Weber, when he insists that in Fuchs's thought "there can be no basis for distinguishing the language of the word of God and the language of Being ... In what way can we know that language does not bring to expression illusion, falsehood, or even chaos? If the criterion of truth is only in the language-event itself, how can the language-event be safeguarded against delusion, mockery, or utter triviality? Why cannot the language-event be a disguised event of nothingness? ... Fuchs's ontology is in danger of dissolving into a psychological illusionism."[148]

(2) *The new hermeneutic is also one-sided in its use of the New Testament and in its relation to the New Testament message.* To begin with, there are large areas of the New Testament which are explicitly concerned with rational argumentation and with the elucidation of theological concepts. Bornkamm, among others, has drawn attention to the rôle of reasoned argument in Paul, and Hebrews also invites consideration in this respect.[149] However, the approach of Fuchs and Ebeling better fits such language-categories as hymns, poems, metaphors, and parables. It is no accident that Fuchs tends to concentrate his attention on the parables, and also on such passages as 1 Cor. 13 and Phil. 2:5–11. This seems to confirm our claim that the new hermeneutic is one-sided. It is tempting to wonder whether if Fuchs were still pastor to a congregation, they would find themselves confronted regularly by the same kinds of passages. This is partly, too, because Fuchs tends to see the "translated" message of the New Testament itself in narrowly selective terms. In the end, almost everything in the New Testament can be translated into a call to love; into a call to abandon self-assertion.

The problem for the new hermeneutic, however, is not only that certain parts of the New Testament take the form of cognitive discourse; it is also that it is frequently addressed to those who *already believe,* and often spoken out of an already existing theological *tradition* in the context of the historical community of the church. But tradition, even *within* the New Testament, is for Fuchs a factor that tends to obscure, rather than clarify, the original proclamation of Jesus, which was to *un*believers. Just as Heidegger wishes to step back "behind" the conceptualizing tradition of Western philosophy, so Fuchs wishes to step back "behind" the tradition of the primitive church.

The consequences of such a move can be seen most clearly in Fuchs's handling of the resurrection of Christ. This may never be seen as a past historical event known on the basis of apostolic testimony. Like Bultmann, Fuchs sees it simply as expressing the positive value of the cross; as expressing, exhaustively and without historical remainder, Jesus's abandonment of self-assertion in the death of the cross. In his attempt to support such a view, Fuchs even claims that Paul made a mistake in 1 Cor. 15:5–8, being driven to ground the resurrection in history only by the exigency of a polemic against the Corinthians.[150] Fuchs can find no room in his hermeneutic for tradition, the church, or history after the event of the cross. The issue is put sharply by P. J. Achtemeier: "The church itself could, and did, become a historical 'security' for faith, thus robbing faith of its announcement of the danger of all such security . . . In this way . . . the new hermeneutic attempts to defend a view of faith based on some portions of the New Testament from a view of faith based on other portions."[151]

Once again, however, these difficulties should not blind us to the positive insights of the new hermeneutic where they occur. Fuchs does make some valid comments on the hermeneutics of the epistles; and from this kind of viewpoint Robert Funk offers some very valuable insights on 1 Cor. 2:2–16 and especially on "Second Corinthians as Hermeneutic". He sees this epistle as "a re-presentation of the kerygma in language that speaks to the controversy in which (Paul) is engaged".[152] The main contribution of the new hermeneutic, however, concerns the parables of Jesus, and here, although many criticisms about exegetical details could be made, the suggestiveness and value of the general approach is clear.

(3) Just as it represents a one-sided approach to the hermeneutical task and also a one-sided use of the New Testament, *the new hermeneutic further embodies a one-sided view of the nature of language.* This shows itself in two ways.

Firstly, like Heidegger whom they follow here, Fuchs and Ebeling fail to grasp that language functions on the basis of convention, and is not in fact "reality" or Being itself. Whilst language admittedly determines, or at least shapes, the way in which reality is perceived and organized in relation to a language-community, effective language-activity presupposes "rules" or conventions accepted by that community. It is an established principle not only of Korzybski's "general semantics", but also of general linguistics since Saussure, that the word is not the thing. Saussure himself described "*l'arbitraire du signe*" as the first principle of language study, and the point is discussed in the chapter on semantics.[153] Opaqueness in vocabulary, polysemy or multiple meaning, change in language, and the use of different words for the same object in different languages, all underline the conventionality of language. But the attitude of Fuchs and Ebeling, by contrast, is close to that which has been described as the belief in "word-magic". Their view is sometimes found especially among primitive peoples. Malinowski comments, "The word . . . has a power of its own; it is a means of bringing things about; it is a handle to acts and objects, not a definition of them . . . The word gives power."[154] Heidegger, of course, would not be embarrassed that such an outlook is primitive; he is concerned with "primal" language.[155] But this does not avoid the problem when Ebeling writes that a language-event is not "mere speech" but "an event in which *God himself is communicated.*"[156]

This is *not* to say that we should reject Ebeling's contrast between a word which speaks *about* reconciliation and a word which actually *reconciles*; between speaking *about* a call and actually *calling*. But in two articles I have tried to show that the sense in which "saying makes it so" is best explained in terms of performative language, and not in terms of word-magic.[157] Furthermore, it should be stressed that, in spite of any appearances to the contrary, Fuchs and Ebeling base their approach on a particular view of language, not on some affirmation of faith about the "power" of God's word.

Secondly, the new hermeneutic has a one-sided concern with imperatival, conative, directive language as over against the language of description or information. Ebeling writes, "We do not get at the nature of words by asking what they contain, but by asking what they effect, what they set going."[158] "The basic structure of word is therefore not statement . . . but appraisal, certainly not in the colourless sense of information, but in the pregnant sense of participation and communication."[159] Here it is important to see exactly what we are criticizing. We are *not* criticizing his concern with function, with communication, with self-involvement. We welcome this. But it is false to make two exclusive *alternatives* out of this, as if description somehow undermined other functions of language. Indeed in my article on the parables as language-event, I have argued in detail, firstly, that not all descriptive propositions function in the same way (some may be open-ended); and secondly that, in Austin's words, "for a certain performative utterance to be happy, certain statements have to be *true*."[160] Amos Wilder presses this kind of point in a different way. He writes, "Fuchs refuses to define the content of faith . . . He is afraid of the word as convention or as a means of conveying information . . . Fuchs carries this so far that revelation, as it were, reveals nothing . . . Jesus calls, indeed, for decision . . . But surely his words, deeds, presence, person, and message rested . . . upon dogma, eschatological and theocratic."[161]

(4) There is some force in the criticism that the new hermeneutic lets "what is true *for me*" become the criterion of "what is true", and that *its orientation towards the interpreter's subjectivity transposes theology too often into a doctrine of man.* We have noted Fuchs's comment that he proposes "a more radical existential interpretation" than even Bultmann. The hermeneutical task, he writes, is "the interpretation of *our own existence* . . . We should accept as *true* only that which we acknowledge *as valid for our own person.*"[162] At the same time, we should also note that there is another qualifying emphasis in Fuchs. He insists, "Christian faith means to speak of God's act, not of . . . acts of man."[163]

Some conservative theologians believe that we are drawn into a man-centred relativism if we accept either the notion of the hermeneutical circle, or Fuchs's idea of "self-understanding" (*Selbstverständnis*). Thus J. W. Montgomery calls for "the rejection of contemporary theology's so-called hermeneutical circle."[164] He writes "The preacher must not make the appalling mistake of thinking, as do followers of Bultmann and post-Bultmann new hermeneutic, that the text and one's own experience enter into a relationship of mutuality . . . To bind text and exegete into a circle is not only to put all theology and preaching into the orbit of anthropocentric sinfulness, but also to remove the very possibility of a 'more sure word of prophecy' than the vagueness of men." [165]

The problem formulated by Montgomery, however, turns on epistemology, or the theory of understanding, and not upon theological considerations alone. To begin with, there are some areas of discussion in which it is possible to distinguish between "Scripture" and "interpretation of Scripture", and others in which it is not. We can and must distinguish between the two, for example, when we are discussing questions about theological method *in principle* and at a formal level. As Ebeling points out, this was important in the Reformation and for Luther. But as soon as we begin to consider a *particular text,* every way of understanding it constitutes an act of interpretation which is related to the experience of the interpreter. This is clear, for example, when we look back on Luther's handling of specific texts. On this level, it is simply philosophically naive to imply that some interpreters can have access to a self-evidently "true" meaning as over against their interpretation of it. Moreover, the interpreter's understanding, as Gadamer rightly insists, is a *progressive* one. In the words of Heinrich Ott, "There is no final black-and-white distinction between 'having understood' and 'not having understood' . . . Understanding by its very nature takes place at different levels." [166] Thus the interpreter is in the position of a student confronted with a new text-book on a new subject. At first his preliminary understanding of the subject-matter is disjointed and fragmentary, not least because he does not yet know how to question the text appropriately. Gradually, however, the text itself suggests appropriate questions, and his more mature approach to it brings greater understanding. At the same time, the parts and the whole begin to illuminate one another. But in all this the interpreter is not merely active subject scrutinizing passive object. The text "speaks" to him as its object, moulding his own questions. The notion of the hermeneutical circle is not, then, a sell-out to man-centred relativism, but a way of describing the *process of understanding* in the interpretation of a text.

The problem of "self-understanding" is often misunderstood. It does not simply mean man's conscious understanding of himself, but his grasp of the possibilities of being, in the context of his "world". It concerns, therefore, his *way of reacting* to life or to reality or to God and not merely his opinions about himself. [167] In one sense, therefore, it is less man-centred than is often supposed. In Ebeling's words, "When God speaks, *the whole of reality as it concerns us* enters language anew." [168] In another sense, however, it is true that a pre-occupation with self-understanding may narrow and restrict the attention of the interpreter away from a wider theological and cosmic perspective. Indeed this underlines precisely the problem of one-sidedness which we have noted in connexion with the task of hermeneutics, with the scope of the New Testament, and with language. We saw, for example, that Fuchs fails to do full justice to the resurrection of Christ.

(5) *The new hermeneutic is concerned above all with the "rights" of the text,* as over against concepts which the interpreter himself may try to bring

with him and impose on it. A "subject-object" scrutiny of the text which takes no account of man's linguisticality tends to tame and to domesticate the word of God, so that it merely echoes back the interpreter's own perspectives. By contrast, the text should challenge him, judge him and "speak" to him in its otherness. But in order that this word may be understood and "strike home", there must also be a common "world", an *Einverständnis,* in which the horizons of the text become fused with those of the interpreter.

Some further strengths and weaknesses of this rejection of mere "knowledge" and "analysis" can be seen when the new hermeneutic is set in the wider context of literary interpretation, of art, and even of educational theory. In the world of literature for example, Susan Sontag argues that interpretation impoverishes, tames, and distorts, a literary creation. "Interpretation makes it manageable, comfortable". Instead of interpreting literature we ought simply "to show *how* it is what it is".[169] Similarly R. E. Palmer sees a further attempt "to transcend the subject-object schema" in the French phenomenological literary criticism of Blanchot, Richard or Bachelard, and in the phenomenological philsophy of Ricoeur or Merleau-Ponty."[170] In the realm of art one could cite the work of Adolph Gottlieb. In education theory it is possible to see both gains and losses in the move away from concerns about "knowledge" and "information", in exchange for an emphasis on participation, engagement and "experience". The pupil will gain from attempts to help him to understand in terms of his own life-experiences; but he may well lose as less stress is laid on the "content" part of instruction.

It is our claim that *both* aspects are important for New Testament interpretation, but that at present there is more danger of neglecting the new hermeneutic than of pressing its claims too far. Although it would be wrong to reduce its lessons simply to a few maxims for preachers, nevertheless it does have something to say about preaching and basic Bible study. For example, it calls attention to the difference between talking about the *concept* of reconciliation or the *concept* of joy, and on the other hand so proclaiming the word of Christ that a man *experiences* joy or reconciliation, even if these concepts are never mentioned. The preacher must concern himself with what his words effect and bring about, rather than simply with what concepts they convey. The gospel must not merely be spoken and repeated; it must also be *communicated.* Similarly in Bible study the student is not only concerned with "facts" and information, but with verdicts on himself. Moreover as he "listens" to the text he will not be content only to use stereotyped sets of questions composed by others, but will engage in a *continuous* dialogue of question and answer, until his own original horizons are creatively enlarged.

The otherness of the New Testament must not be tamed and domesticated in such a way that its message becomes merely a set of predictable religious "truths". Through the text of the New Testament, the word of God is to be encountered as an attack, a judgement, on any way of seeing the world which, in Fuchs's phrase, is not "seeing with God's eyes". The hermeneutical task is a genuine and valid one. Two sets of horizons must be brought together, those of the text and those of the modern interpreter; and this must be done at a more than merely conceptual level. Few questions can be more important than that asked by Fuchs, namely how the text of the New Testament, written in the ancient world, can come alive in such a way as to *strike home* in the present.

NOTES

1. For objections to the customary use of the term, see C. E. Braaten, "How New is the New Hermeneutic?" in *Theology Today* 22 (1965), pp. 218–35, and J. D. Smart, *The Strange Silence of the Bible in the Church* (London, 1970), pp. 37–8; as against James M. Robinson, "Braaten's Polemic. A Reply", in *Theology Today,* loc. cit., pp. 277–82.
2. E. Fuchs, "Zur Frage nach dem historischen Jesus" (*Gesammelte Aufsätze* II; Tübingen 1960), pp. 411–14 and 418; cf. *Studies of the Historical Jesus* (London 1964), pp. 196–8 and 202.
3. E. Fuchs, *Hermeneutik* (Tübingen 1970[4]), p. 281; cf. R. Bultmann, *Essays Philosophical and Theological* (London 1955), p. 14. Cf. further, E. Fuchs, *Hermeneutik,* p. 182, and R. Bultmann, *Faith and Understanding* (London 1969), pp. 286–312.
5. E. Fuchs, *Studies of the Historical Jesus,* p. 8.
6. E. Fuchs, *Studies of the Historical Jesus,* p. 30; cf. Zum hermeneutischen Problem in der Theologie (*Gesammelte Aufsätze* I, Tübingen 1959), pp. 9–10.
7. G. Ebeling, "Non-religious Interpretation of Biblical Concepts" in *Word and Faith,* p. 125.
8. G. Ebeling, *The Word of God and Tradition* (E.T. London 1968), pp. 11–31, especially 26, 28.
9. G. Ebeling, *God and Word* (Philadelphia 1967), p. 3; cf. pp. 8–9.
10. Ibid., p. 4.
11. E. Fuchs, "Proclamation and Speech-Event" in *Theology Today* 19 (1962), p. 354; and G. Ebeling, *Theology and Proclamation* (E.T. Collins, London, 1966), pp. 42 and 100–102.
12. G. Ebeling, *Word and Faith,* pp. 318–19.
13. Ibid., p. 306.
14. Ibid., p. 36.
15. E. Fuchs, *Hermeneutik,* p. 92.
16. E. Fuchs, *Studies of the Historical Jesus,* p. 35.
17. Ibid., p. 193.
18. W. Pannenburg, *Basic Questions in Theology* I (E.T. London 1970) p. 9.
19. G. Ebeling, "Time and Word", in J. M. Robinson (ed.), *The Future of our Religious Past: Essays in Honour of Rudolf Bultmann* (London (1971), p. 265 (translated from *Zeit und Geschichte,* 1964) (my italics). Cf. further, W. G. Doty, *Contemporary New Testament Interpretation* (Englewood Cliffs, N.J. 1972), pp. 34–7.
20. In addition to the previous chapter, see Ian Henderson, *Myth in the New Testament* (London 1952), p. 31, and A. C. Thiselton, "Myth, Mythology". in *The Zondervan Pictorial Encyclopedia of the Bible* (Grand Rapids 1975), vol. 4, pp. 333–343.
21. G. Ebeling, "The Significance of the Critical Historical Method for Church and Theology in Protestantism" in, *Word and Faith,* pp. 17–61; and E. Fuchs, *Hermeneutik,* pp. 159–66, and especially *Studies of the Historical Jesus,* pp. 95–108.
22. G. Ebeling, *The Nature of Faith* (E.T. London 1961), p. 188.
23. E. Fuchs, "Translation and Proclamation", in *Studies of the Historical Jesus,* pp. 191–206; cf. *Hermeneutik,* pp. 249–56, and *Marburger Hermeneutik* (Tübingen 1968), pp.

2–4. Fuchs's approach is related to that of Manfred Mezger. See M. Mezger, "Preparation for Preaching: the Route from Exegesis to Proclamation" in R. W. Funk (ed.) J Th. Ch. 2. *Translating Theology into the Modern Age* (Tübingen 1965), pp. 159–79, especially 166.
24. E. Fuchs, "The New Testament and the Hermeneutical Problem", loc. cit., pp. 135–6. (Fuchs writes almost the whole sentence in italics.)
25. G. Ebeling, *The Nature of Faith,* p. 15, cf. *Introduction to a Theological Theory of Language* (London 1973), pp. 15–80.
26. G. Ebeling, *The Nature of Faith,* p. 16; cf. *God and Word,* pp. 2–3, and E. Fuchs, "The New Testament and the Hermeneutical Problem", loc. cit., p. 125.
27. H. G. Gadamer, *Wahrheit und Methode. Grundzüge einer philosophischen Hermeneutik* (Tübingen 1965[2]) p. 360 (E.T. *Truth and Method* (London 1975), p. 350).
28. G. Ebeling, "Word of God and Hermeneutics", in *Word and Faith,* p. 313.
29. Ibid., p. 317.
30. Ibid.; cf. *The Word of God and Tradition,* p. 9.
31. E. Fuchs, "The New Testament and the Hermeneutical Problem", loc. cit., p. 136.
32. E. Fuchs, *Hermeneutik,* pp. 109–10 ("*die Maus das hermeneutische Prinzip für das Verständis der Katze zu sein . . .*").
33. G. Ebeling, *The Word of God and Tradition,* p. 17.
34. H. Kimmerle, "Hermeneutical Theory or Ontological Hermeneutics" in R. W. Funk (ed.), J Th. Ch. 4, *History and Hermeneutic,* p. 107 (my italics); cf. pp. 107–121.
35. See E. Fuchs, *Marburger Hermeneutik,* pp. 171–81 and 239–43.
36. E. Fuchs, "The New Testament and the Hermeneutical Problem", loc. cit., p. 124; cf. *Marburger Hermeneutik,* p. 176.
37. E. Fuchs, "The Hermeneutical Problem" in J. M. Robinson (ed.), *The Future of Our Religious Past* pp. 267–8 (translated from E. Dinkler (ed.) *Zeit und Geschichte,* p. 357).
38. Ibid., p. 270; German from *Zeit und Geschichte,* p. 360. Cf. *Hermeneutik,* p. 136.
39. E. Fuchs, "The New Testament and the Hermeneutical Problem," loc. cit., p. 126; "Proclamation and Speech-Event", loc. cit., pp. 347–51; *Hermeneutik,* pp. 219–30; *Studies of the Historical Jesus,* pp. 97–9 and 130–66; and *Marburger Hermeneutik,* pp. 231–2. The parables are discussed further below.
40. Richard E. Palmer, *Hermeneutics. Interpretation Theory in Schleiermacher, Dilthey, Heidegger, and Gadamer* (Evanston 1969), p. 139.
41. This point is elucidated below, but for a simple introduction to this aspect of Fuchs's thought, see Paul J. Achtemeier, *An Introduction to the New Hermeneutic* (Philadelphia 1969), pp. 91–100.
42. G. Ebeling, *The Nature of Faith,* p. 187.
43. J. L. Austin, *How to Do Things with Words,* (Oxford 1962) p. 6; cf. *Philosophical Papers* (Oxford 1961), pp. 220–39. Cf. further A. C. Thiselton, "The Parables as Language-Event: Some Comments on Fuchs's Hermeneutics in the Light of Linguistic Philosophy" in *Scottish Journal of Theology* 23 (1970), pp. 437–68, especially 438-9; R. W. Funk, *Language, Hermeneutic and Word of God* New York 1966), pp. 26–8; J. M. Robinson, "The Parables as God Happening" in F. T. Trotter (ed.) *Jesus and the Historian (*Philadelphia 1968), p. 142; and W. G. Doty, op. cit., pp. 39–43.
44. G. Ebeling, *The Nature of Faith,* pp. 87 and 90.
45. E. Fuchs, *Zur Frage nach dem historischen Jesus,* pp. 291 and 293 (cf. *Studies of the Historical Jesus,* pp. 94 and 95).
46. E. Fuchs, loc. cit. (German) pp. 288 and 291 (English, 91 and 93); 224 and 226 (English 36 and 38); and 347 (English 141).
47. Cf. E. Fuchs, *Zum hermeneutischen Problem in der Theologie,* pp. 281–305; *Marburger Hermeneutik,* pp. 243–5; and *Studies of the Historical Jesus,* pp. 196–212; and G. Ebeling, *Word and Faith,* pp. 325–32, and *Theology and Proclamation* pp. 28–31. On the different terminology in Fuchs and Ebeling, James Robinson explains, "*Sprachereignis* and *Wortgeschehen* are synonyms . . . The choice depends on which Bultmannian term serves as the point of departure, *Heilsereignis* or *Heilsgeschehen*" (*New Frontiers in Theology, 2: The New Hermeneutic,* p. 57).
48. E. Fuchs, *Studies of the Historical Jesus,* p. 196 (German, p. 411).

49. Ibid.
50. Ibid., p. 211.
51. G. Ebeling, *Word and Faith,* p. 320.
52. G. Ebeling, *The Word of God and Tradition,* p. 18; cf. E. Fuchs, *Hermeneutik,* pp. 103–26.
53. J. M. Robinson, *New Frontiers in Theology 2: The New Hermeneutic,* pp. 23–4.
54. E. Fuchs, "The New Testament and the Hermeneutical Problem", ibid., p. 143 (his italics).
55. E. Fuchs, "The Hermeneutical Problem", loc. cit., p. 277 ("*die Texte zuvor uns übersetzen müssen bevor wir sie übersetzen können*", in E. Dinkler (ed.) op. cit., p. 365). Cf. G. Ebeling, *Word and Faith,* p. 331.
56. R. Bultmann, "Is Exegesis Without Presuppositions Possible?" in *Existence and Faith* London 1964), p. 347; cf. pp. 342–51. R. Bultmann, "The Problem of Hermeneutics", in *Essays Philosophical and Theological,* pp. 242–3 (cf. pp. 234–61).
57. R. Bultmann, *Existence and Faith,* pp. 343–4 (his italics) and 347.
58. R. Bultmann, "The Problem of Hermeneutics", loc. cit. p. 255.
59. R. Bultmann, *Existence and Faith,* p. 346.
60. Cf. B. J. F. Lonergan, *Method in Theology* (London 1972), pp. 156–8 (cf. 153–266); and J. D. Smart, *The Interpretation of Scripture* (London 1961), pp. 37–64.
61. B. J. F. Lonergan, op. cit., p. 157. A. C. Thiselton, "The Use of Philosophical Categories in New Testament Hermeneutics", *The Churchman* 87 (1973), pp. 87–100.
62. R. E. Palmer, op. cit., p. 94. 96 (cf. F. Schleiermacher, *Hermeneutik und Kritik,* ed. by F. Lucke, p. 29).
63. E. Fuchs, *Hermeneutik,* p. 281 (my italics).
64. M. Mezger, "Preparation for Preaching: The Route from Exegesis to Proclamation", loc. cit., p. 166 (cf. J. M. Robinson, op. cit., p. 59).
65. Ibid.
66. Ibid., pp. 166–7.
67. H. Kimmerle, "Hermeneutical Theory or Ontological Hermeneutics", loc. cit., p. 109.
68. Cf. M. Heidegger, *An Introduction to Metaphysics* (E.T. New Haven 1959, Anchor edn. 1961), pp. 123–38.
69. R. E. Palmer, op. cit., p. 87.
70. Ibid.
71. G. Ebeling, *Word and Faith,* p. 320.
72. Ibid., p. 317.
73. E. Fuchs, "The New Testament and the Hermeneutical Problem", p. 142 (his italics).
74. H. Ott, "Systematic Theology and Exegesis" in his essay "What is Systematic Theology?" in J. M. Robinson and J. B. Cobb Jr. (eds.) *New Frontiers in Theology: I, The Later Heidegger and Theology* (New York 1963), pp. 86 and 87; cf. M. Heidegger, ***Unterwegs zur Sprache*** **(Pfullingen, 1959, 1960[2]) pp. 37–8.**
75. G. Ebeling, *Word and Faith,* p. 33 (his italics).
76. Ibid., p. 318.
77. H.-G. Gadamer, *Wahrheit und Methode,* pp. 307–24, especially p. 311 (E.T. pp. 289–305, 292f.); and G. Ebeling, *Word and Faith,* p. 330.
78. G. Ebeling, loc. cit.
79. H.-G. Gadamer, op. cit., p. 291; cf. pp. 290–95 (E.T. pp. 274–8).
80. H.-G. Gadamer, op. cit., pp. 250–90, especially 250–61 and 275–90 (E.T. pp. 235–74, 235–45, 258–74). Cf. M. Heidegger, *Being and Time* (E.T. London 1962), pp. 188–95.
81. W. Wink, *The Bible in Human Transformation: Towards a New Paradigm for Biblical Study* (Philadelphia 1973).
82. Ibid., p. 2.
83. Ibid., p. 6.
84. Ibid., p. 10.
85. Ibid., p. 3.
86. Ibid., p. 32.
87. Ibid., p. 66.

88. Ibid., p. 62.
89. H. G. Gadamer, *Wahrheit und Methode,* pp. 17–18 (E.T. pp. 20f.).
90. Ibid., pp. 21–4 (E.T. pp. 24–6).
91. Ibid., pp xxvi and 77–105 (E.T. pp. xxvi, 73–99).
92. Ibid., pp. 250–61 (E.T. pp. 233–45).
93. Ibid., p. 261 (E.T. p. 245).
94. Ibid., pp. 282–3 (E.T. p. 266).
95. Ibid., pp. 288–90 (E.T. pp. 270–4).
96. Ibid., p. 345. (E.T. pp. 326f.).
97. M. Heidegger, *Being and Time,* sect 15. pp. 95–102.
98. M. Heidegger, *An Introduction to Metaphysics* (Anchor ed. New York 1961), p. 31.
99. Ibid., p. 30.
100. Ibid., p. 89–90.
101. Cf. M. Heidegger, *Nietzsche* (2 vols. Pfullingen 1961) vol. 2, pp. 148–89 (especially on Descartes).
102. M. Heidegger, *Introduction to Metaphysics,* p. 111; cf. *Unterwegs zur Sprache* (Pfullingen 1959 and 1960), pp. 83–155, especially 86–7; and *Holzwege* (Klosterman, Frankfurt 1963[4]) pp. 7–68. Heidegger's essay "The Origin of a Work of Art" is translated in A. Hofstadter and R. Kuhns (eds), *Philosophies of Art and Beauty* (New York 1964).
103. M. Heidegger *Vom Wesen der Wahrheit* (Frankfurt 1961[4]), pp. 6–13; also rp. in *Wegmarken* (Frankfurt 1967), pp. 74–82.
104. M. Heidegger, *An Introduction to Metaphysics,* p. 132.
105. G. Ebeling, *Introduction to a Theological Theory of Language* (London 1973), p. 71.
106. Ibid., p. 76.
107. G. Ebeling, *God and Word,* p. 2 and 17.
108. G. Ebeling, *Introduction to a Theological Theory of Language,* p. 127.
109. E. Fuchs, *Hermeneutik,* pp. 126–34, and *Marburger Hermeneutik,* pp. 228–32.
110. E. Fuchs, *Studies of the Historical Jesus,* p. 207.
111. M. Heidegger, *An Introduction to Metaphysics,* p. 145.
112. Ibid., p. 108.
113. E. Fuchs, *Studies of the Historical Jesus,* pp. 208–9 (his italics).
114. M. Heidegger, *Unterwegs zur Sprache,* p. 267.
115. Ibid., p. 19.
116. M. Heidegger, *Gelassenheit* (Pfullingen, 1959), p. 37.
117. M. Heidegger, *An Introduction to Metaphysics,* p. 172.
118. E. Fuchs, *Hermeneutik,* p. 71.
119. E. Fuchs, *Studies of the Historical Jesus,* p. 194 (his italics).
120. Ibid., p. 192 (his italics); cf. *Hermeneutik,* pp. 103–7.
121. E. Fuchs, *Studies of the Historical Jesus,* p. 155.
122. Ibid., p. 129.
123. H. G. Gadamer, op. cit., p. 100; cf. pp. 97–115 (E.T. pp. 94, 91–108).
124. Ibid., p. 66–96 (E.T. pp. 63–90).
125. Ibid., p. 98 (E.T. p. 92); cf. A. C. Thiselton, "The Parables as Language-Event", loc. cit., p. 442–5.
126. E. Fuchs, "The Parable of the Unmerciful Servant", in *Studia Evangelica* (Berlin, 1959), p. 487.
127. Ibid., p. 493; cf. pp. 487–94, and *Studies of the Historical Jesus,* pp. 152–3.
128. E. Fuchs, "The New Testament and the Hermeneuticai Problem", loc. cit., p. 126.
129. E. Fuchs, *Studies of the Historical Jesus,* p. 97; cf. *Marburger Hermeneutik,* pp. 171–81.
130. E. Fuchs, *Studies of the Historical Jesus,* p. 33; cf. pp. 32–8 and 154–6.
131. Ibid., p. 33–7.
132. E. Fuchs, "Proclamation and Speech Event", loc. cit., p. 349.
133. R. W. Funk *Language, Hermeneutic and Word of God* (New York 1966), pp. 16–17 (his italics).
134. Ibid., p. 17.

135. Ibid., p. 192; cf. pp. 124–222.
136. W. Wink, op. cit., p. 42.
137. Ibid., p. 43.
138. E. Fuchs, *Studies of the Historical Jesus,* pp. 36–8 (his italics).
139. E. Fuchs, "The Parable of the Unmerciful Servant", loc. cit., pp. 491–2.
140. E. Fuchs *Studies of the Historical Jesus,* pp. 80–82.
141. Ibid., p. 28.
142. Ibid., p. 30–31 (Fuchs's italics).
143. G. Ebeling, *Theology and Proclamation,* p. 38; cf. pp. 32–81 which provides a response to Bultmann.
144. H. Jonas in *The Review of Metaphysics* 18 (1964), p. 216; cf. pp. 207–33.
145. Ibid.
146. Quoted by W. Barrett, "Zen for the West", in N. W. Ross (ed), *The World of Zen. An East-West Anthology* (London 1962), p. 344; cf. p. 284 and D. T. Suzuki, "Satori, or Acquiring a New Viewpoint", ibid., p. 41–7.
147. P. van Buren, *Theological Explorations* (London 1968), pp. 81–105.
148. J. C. Weber, "Language-Event and Christian Faith" in *Theology Today* 21 (1965), p. 455; cf. pp. 448-57.
149. Cf. G. Bornkamm, "Faith and Reason in Paul", in *Early Christian Experience* (London 1969), p. 29–46.
150. Cf. E. Fuchs, *Marburger Hermeneutik,* p. 123–34 and *Glauben und Erfahrung,* p. 216.
151. P. J. Achtemeier, op. cit., pp. 156–7 and 162.
152. R. W. Funk in J. M. Robinson and J. B. Cobb (eds), op. cit. (*The New Hermeneutic*), p. 168; cf. pp. 164–97; cf. also *Language Hermeneutic and Word of God,* pp. 275–305.
153. F. de Saussure, *Cours de linguistique générale* (edn. critique par R. Engler, Wiesbaden 1967), pp. 146–57. Cf. J. Lyons, *Introduction to Theoretical Linguistics* (Cambridge 1968), pp. 4–8, 38, 59–70, 74–5, 272 and 403; S. Ullmann, *Semantics, An Introduction to the Science of Meaning* (Oxford 1958[2]), p. 80–115; and A. C. Thiselton, "The supposed Power of Words in the Biblical Writings", in JTS 25 (1974), pp. 283–299.
154. B. Malinowski, "The Problem of Meaning in Primitive Languages" in C. K. Ogden and I. A. Richards (eds), *The Meaning of Meaning* (London 1946[8]), pp. 489–90.
155. Cf. M. Heidegger, *Existence and Being* (London 1968[3]), p. 291–315; *Wegmarken,* pp. 74–82; and *Unterwegs zur Sprache, passim.*
156. G. Ebeling *The Nature of Faith,* pp. 87 and 183 (my italics).
157. A. C. Thiselton, "The Supposed Power of Words in the Biblical Writings" and "The Parables as Language-Event" loc. cit.
158. G. Ebeling, *The Nature of Faith* p. 187.
159. G. Ebeling, *Word and Faith,* p. 326.
160. J. L. Austin *How to Do Things with Words* (Oxford 1962), p. 45 (his italics); cf. A.C. Thiselton, "The Parables as Language-Event", loc. cit., p. 438.
161. A. N. Wilder, "The Word as Address and Meaning", in J. M. Robinson and J. B. Cobb Jr. (eds), op. cit., p. 213.
162. E. Fuchs, "The New Testament and the Hermeneutical Problem", loc. cit., p. 117 (my italics).
163. Ibid., p. 114.
164. J. W. Montgomery, "An Exhortation to Exhorters", in *Christianity Today* 17 (1973), p. 606; (cf. also his essay in C. F. H. Henry (ed.), *Jesus of Nazareth Saviour and Lord* (London 1966), p. 231–6.
165. Ibid.
166. H. Ott, "What is Systematic Theology?", loc. cit., p. 80.
167. Cf. E. Fuchs, *Marburger Hermeneutik,* pp. 20 and 41–7.
168. G. Ebeling, *The Nature of Faith,* p. 190.
169. S. Sontag, "Against Interpretation", reprinted in D. Lodge (ed.), *Twentieth Century Literary Criticism* (London 1972), p. 656 and 660; cf. pp. 652–9.
170. R. E. Palmer, op. cit., p. 246.

CHAPTER XVII

THE AUTHORITY OF THE NEW TESTAMENT

Robin Nixon

I. *Introduction*

The problems of the interpretation and the authority of the New Testament have always been closely related. It has been possible to profess acceptance of New Testament authority but to use such a system of interpretation that the New Testament itself becomes secondary and its message never bursts out spontaneously and freely but is allowed to run only along carefully guarded canals. So different schools of thought within the church have argued for hundreds of years about the right method to use and about which methods are most true to the New Testament itself. [1] We have now moved into a much more fluid situation in theological debate than there has perhaps ever been before. Previously the lines of battle were more or less clearly drawn. There were accepted norms, even if different interpretation of those norms, and Scripture, church and reason battled with each other for the last word. In the last few years however two particular factors have changed the whole scene. First there is the growth of religious pluralism. This has many implications, and in some cases involves the denial of the uniqueness of Christianity, while in others it means that the Bible or the New Testament are not treated as norms. Related to this is the growth of ecumenism. Even where churches or individual Christians have not been concerned with denominational union schemes, they can no longer fail to be aware that ways of approaching the Bible can no longer run along purely denominational lines. At almost every level of understanding and interpretation denominational boundaries are largely irrelevant and it would be quite anomalous in these days for serious Bible study to be carried out in exclusive groups of, say, Anglicans or Presbyterians.

The second factor is the emergence of a whole range of problems facing the church, because they are also facing humanity, which seem, at least at first sight, alien to the world and the message of the Bible. The whole cast of modern thought tends to be man- and experience-centred and some will go only very reluctantly if at all to God and the objective truths set out in the Bible for help and guidance. Those who do go to the Bible will often find that there is nothing there which can be applied direct to the situation in question. As James Barr has put it:

> "The locus of the authority question has shifted. The critical question is no longer 'What was said back then?' but 'What should we say now?' The centre of the authority crisis . . . lies in the present day . . . The sense of doubt . . . arises from a concentration on that which is closer to the present-day-decision as against that which is more remote."[2]

The importance and difficulty of understanding and applying rightly the authority of the Bible in the situation can readily be appreciated.

The Commission on Faith and Order of the World Council of Churches, at their meeting at Boldern near Zurich in October, 1968, suggested that there were six major question areas which could be divided into smaller or subsidiary questions.[3] They were as follows:

(1) The question of priorities within the Bible itself and its relation to the community which produced it.

(2) The question of diversity within the Bible.

(3) The question raised by changes of world-outlook since biblical times and by our temporal distance from the biblical situation.

(4) The question of relations between past and future in respect to the authority of the Bible.

(5) The question of the relation between biblical authority and other kinds of authority.

(6) Questions of the use, function and application of biblical material.

The purpose of this chapter is to cover approximately the same ground but in a slightly different way. First of all we shall discuss the question of the meaning of authority. Then we shall examine the problems of interpretation and authority within the New Testament, paying special attention to those which arise from the use of the critical methods described in previous chapters. Finally we shall deal with the problems of interpretation and authority today.

II. *The Meaning of Religious Authority*

The whole question of authority has become a major issue in almost every sphere of present-day society. There has been something of a swing in many areas from the objective to the subjective. Attempts have been made to distinguish between "authoritarian" and "authoritative" as epithets for the process involved. The first term would indicate that facts had to be accepted and commands obeyed however unreasonable they might seem simply because the source of authority had said so. The second is taken to mean that facts are accepted and commands obeyed because they commend themselves to those to whom they are addressed. With the spread of education and man's supposed "coming of age" the "authoritative" model has far wider approval in most areas of life today than the "authoritarian".

The meaning of "authority" when applied to the Bible or to other sources of religious information or instruction is likewise taken in different ways.[4] Barr uses the terms "hard" and "soft".[5] He defines "hard" authority as meaning that the Bible has authority before it is interpreted and that that authority is applicable generally. This type of concept has normally been prevalent in the understanding of biblical authority, particularly in the West. This may be partly connected with the Roman legal tradition which has had such a great influence in many aspects of church affairs. "Soft" authority on the other hand suggests that authority comes after interpretation and application and is limited to passages where an authoritative effect had in fact been found. He commends this idea, with its more personal and religious connotation, of a passage that has "spoken to us with authority", as a correct description of the way in which many people in fact become convinced of the authority of the Bible. But he goes on to conclude: "When carried beyond this, however, and given the *logical* status of the *ground* for belief in biblical authority, it is manifestly wrong" (his italics).

The Christian faith is full of situations where complementary truths need to be held together. This is basically because of the involvement of God in human affairs and the possibility of having two levels of explanation of the phenomena. So we can conceive of Christ as divine and human. We can also understand the sacraments as having both a divine objective aspect and also a human subjective one, providing a grace-faith reciprocal. It is not difficult to extend this to the principle of authority. Jesus is referred to as speaking or acting "with authority" (*exousia*) (Mk. 1:22, 27; 2:10 etc.) This authority is something which commended itself to those who encountered him, because he had made no formal claims to divine authority which they had heard and accepted.[6] But for those who have accepted Jesus as God incarnate there will also be an objective authority about his teaching. They will naturally tend to maintain that there is no incompatibility between the two and that his words have authority because his person has authority. The difficulty arises when the teaching of Jesus in some field does not commend itself to the hearer. If he is a believer in Jesus' unique position he will have to choose between the two types of authority. It is at this point that the concept of "soft" authority will be found not to have made sufficient allowance for human sinfulness and blindness and the true way of the disciple is to wrestle with the saying of the master until it can be seen to mean something in his own experience.

The principles which are applied to the authority of Jesus may also be related to the record of the teaching of Jesus which we have in the Gospels and to the New Testament as a whole. It is on the grounds of its relation to some aspect of their spiritual experience that most Christians will begin to accept that the New Testament is authoritative. But once they begin to go deeper into their faith and to study the New Testament further they will find difficult passages which do not immediately ring true. The adoption of the "soft" authority principle would lead to the neglect or rejection of such passages and very likely to the unbalancing and impoverishment of their spiritual lives. But to submit to the "hard" authority of the New Testament does not mean the abdication of the use of the mind. It involves an approach of humble expectation that God can speak through the whole of his word. It implies the willingness to enter into dialogue with the most difficult parts of the text in the expectation that their true meaning will not yield itself lightly either to intellectual understanding or to spiritual experience. The grace-faith reciprocal will be found in the approach to the Scriptures as to the sacraments and what is accepted as the word of God will still need to become the word of God to the one who has ears to hear. If in one sense this may be described as "hard" authority, in another sense it is also something far deeper than that. For the Bible is not just a collection of commands to be obeyed. As the Christian grapples with the text of Scripture he will find that through it the living God encounters him and shapes and guides as well as judging and testing him. To him what is accepted as the word of God will bit by bit become in his experience a word of God directed to him and his situation. It is here that the "New Hermeneutic", rightly used, helps to add a new dimension to some of the rather arid theories of biblical authority which have sometimes prevailed in the past. [7]

III. *Interpretation and Authority Within the Bible*

Any careful student of the Old Testament soon realises that, whatever critical view of the origin and date of its documents is adopted, the material contained in it was written down over a considerable period of time and that what came later very often depended in one way or another on what had come before. There can therefore be discerned in the Old Testament a continuing process of interpretation and application of truths already received in the light of new situations experienced for instance by the prophets. The prophets claimed to speak with authority ("Thus says the Lord") and they both added to the sum of God's revelation and also re-directed the thrust of what others had said or written before. We are justified in seeing in some sense a progressive revelation in the Old Testament and with that goes the implication of the need for continuing re-interpretation within the biblical tradition itself.

The very earliest Christians had as their scriptures simply the Old Testament and it is clear that for all its immense and indeed indispensable value it was not sufficient for the revolutionized situation in which they found themselves. God's revelation in the Old Testament had been partial and piecemeal. His revelation of himself in Christ was complete and final (Heb. 1:1f.). This meant that a whole new way of understanding the Old Testament had to be developed because the person of the Messiah revealed in the human form of Jesus of Nazareth, incarnate, crucified and risen, became the central reference point. [8] It was not said that the Old Testament had no meaning in its original context, but all the stress was now laid on its meaning for those "upon whom the end of the ages has come" (1 Cor. 10:11). To read the Old Testament now was to read it without the veil of misunderstanding or partial understanding that there had been before (2 Cor. 3:12–18). Further things were revealed in Christ which had not been revealed in the Old Testament, but the new treatment of many themes which had been dealt with in the Old Testament indicated a shift in the locus of authority. The Old Testament *per se* no longer had direct authority over the people of God. It was Christ to whom all authority was given in heaven and on earth (Mt. 28:18).

The best known example of the way in which the teaching of the Old Testament was reinterpreted in Christ is to be found in the Sermon on the Mount (Mt. 5–7). In this collection of teaching various precepts of the Law are taken and given a fuller and deeper meaning in the light of Christ. There is a shift from an external authority over actions to an internal one over thoughts and motives. The contrast of "it was said to the men of old" with "but I say to you" makes it plain that the claims of Christ came higher than those of the Old Testament. But the general thrust of the teaching is found in the concept of fulfilment, which involved not the demolition of what had gone before but the giving to it of a new depth of meaning never previously recognized.[9]

A problem is however raised by this. The Sermon on the Mount is presented by Matthew as a collection of sayings of Jesus. Many scholars have questioned the authenticity of some or even all of them. Does such a questioning affect their authority? Some of the issues concerning the *ipsissima verba* of Jesus have been discussed above.[10] While scholars like Jeremias and the Scandinavians Riesenfeld and Gerhardsson have done much in recent years to support the belief that we have a reliable tradition of the teaching of Jesus, others have been more sceptical. While it is important that we should know whether there is a good case for the evangelists' recording faithfully the substance of the teaching of Jesus, it can hardly be claimed that the issue of authority is greatly affected by whether isolated sayings are considered to be *ipsissima verba* of Jesus. It was presumably in the providence of God that the incarnation took place in an age without electronic recording devices and the modern Christian would have been very hard pressed to wade through the millions of words used by Jesus in public teaching had he had access to them. Further in order to understand them he would have to be acquainted with Aramaic (as well as possibly Hebrew and Greek). The attempt by scholars to push back as far as possible to hear the authentic voice of Jesus is a perfectly proper and indeed a praiseworthy one. Yet it must be confessed that we cannot avoid the presence of the New Testament writers as mediators to us of the teaching of Jesus. They, or those who were responsible for their oral or written sources, selected, edited and translated the sayings of our Lord and apart from them we cannot hear his voice at all. If they can be shown to be men of honest intent who were well placed to be in touch with the teaching of the incarnate Jesus, we may feel that they have given us faithfully the general sense of his teaching.[11]

This discussion has led us to the point where we can see that not only do Jesus and the New Testament writers interpret the Old Testament in a new and authoritative way, but that there is a process of interpretation going on within the New Testament itself. If the interpreter in some way has authority, we must ask who the interpreter is? The Christian of New Testament times would not think that it was simply the human agent who recorded the sayings of Jesus or explained them in some other context. He would think of it, when rightly done, as being the work of the risen Jesus through his Holy Spirit. If the word of the Lord Jesus could come in this way to his disciples, its authority could hardly be less than that of the words which he spoke in his Galilean ministry. It is of course a real possibility that the Gospels as well as the Epistles contain such words. Redaction-criticism [12] has reminded us again of the importance of the evangelists and their creative contribution. If they were indeed writing under the inspiration of the Holy Spirit, it makes no difference to the authority of their writings whether their creative editorial role seems to be small, as is probable in the case of Mark, or large, as in different respects it is with the other three evangelists. It would be very naive to think of the evangelists as simply writing down all they know. The problem of the inspiration of the evangelists as creative editors of their material is not substantially different from the problem of the writers of the Epistles as interpreters of the Christ event.

The fact that the early Christians regarded the death and resurrection of Jesus as being central to their faith carries with it the inevitable corollary that explanation of these things after they had occurred could not be given by the incarnate Christ. While scholars disagree how much Jesus taught about these things beforehand, all agree that he could not have explained them fully if only for the reason that the disciples, brought up in Judaism with very different messianic expectations, could not have understood properly. While Jesus apparently gave certain terms and categories (such as "Son of man" and "servant") by which his death and resurrection were to be interpreted, it is the New Testament writers who are left to expound things more fully. What is often implicit in the Gospels, because a Gospel is a special literary form centred round the telling of a story about Jesus of Nazareth, is much more explicit in the Epistles. Can we therefore say that the Epistles are the interpreters of the Gospels? [13] This would be something of a half-truth, particularly when it is remembered that most of the Epistles were probably written before most of the Gospels. It would be better to see the writers of the Epistles as having much greater liberty than the evangelists. They were not bound by the form of the story but were free to apply the truths of the revelation of God in Christ according to the particular needs of their readers or hearers. They could concentrate on systematic doctrinal teaching or on moral and spiritual application according to need. They were also free to refer in a much fuller way to the activity of the risen Christ through his Spirit in the church. Epistle and Gospel were meant to go hand in hand but the former is given no authority over the latter in the canon of the New Testament.

Here we are brought face to face with the problem of diversity within the New Testament. The formation of the canon was a recognition of the fact that there were different interpretations of the Christ event current in the apostolic church. If it were possible to have everything understood "in the flat", then presumably only one Gospel would have been necessary, for in that a full and final interpretation of the ministry, death and resurrection of

Jesus could have been given. Instead of that we have four preserved for us, three of which cover a great deal of the same ground and yet frequently give different emphasis and interpretation, as anyone using a synopsis can soon discover. If we turn to the Epistles we discover what has looked to many scholars like a straight confrontation between the teaching of some of the Epistles of Paul and the Epistle of James. If the extreme ideas of thesis, antithesis and synthesis, which had such currency in some circles in the nineteenth century, have largely been abandoned, there is today an increasing interest in the concept of diversity in the New Testament. The major work in this field has been concerned with the period just after the New Testament[14] but now the questions are being pushed back into the canon itself. It is an observable fact that all spontaneous movements, political or otherwise as well as religious, if they are to endure must acquire some sort of institutional form. It is not therefore surprising to see that the unstructured Christian life of the apostles and earliest disciples in due course developed into the increasingly rigid form of the catholic church. Many Christians have seen this as a process of corruption and decline in which both the word and the Spirit came to be stifled. Lutheran scholars have often gone further than this and have seen in some of the attempts to organize the church in the New Testament the spectre of *Frühkatholizismus* or early catholicism.[15] Against this tendency, which they see particularly prominent in the writings of Luke and in the Pastoral Epistles, they set what they believe to be the authentic New Testament note which is found in the genuine epistles of Paul. It is possible to approach the problem in a more constructive way and to see two approaches to theology and to life in the biblical writings from very early times.[16] The faith of the New Testament can be shown to be greater than any one man's ability to experience and express it fully. A truly balanced Christianity will contain emphasis on word, Spirit and church and even if the resultant product comes out rather differently in different parts of the New Testament it is hard to deny that they are all present in one way or another in all the canonical writings. It is true that the writing of a New Testament theology now requires a proper distinction between the sources and an indication of the differences of emphasis involved, but there is still such a thing as a New Testament theology.[17] Even the division between Palestinian and Hellenistic Christianity may have been greatly exaggerated.[18] It is not really such an exercise in hermeneutical gymnastics as is sometimes suggested to find compatibility as well as diversity between the theology of Paul and that of John or even James.

IV. *Interpretation and Authority Today*

While it is possible to reach a measure of agreement about what happened in biblical times, drawing conclusions from that for application to the situation today is a much more complicated and controversial task. We have to deal with questions about norms, about the status of the canon, about the development of doctrine, about primary and secondary issues, about cultural transposition and about the actual application of the New Testament to the situation of the church and of individuals today.

1. THE IMPORTANCE OF NORMS

Disputes in the past have often been concerned with the use of norms and in particular the way in which the norms of Bible, church and reason have been defined and related to one another. Today there has been a good deal of questioning whether there are or ought to be any norms at all when it comes to the outworking of Christian principles in the modern world. As Barr points out, the ideas of "authority" and "norm" are closely related [19] so that this is one expression of the movement against any external authority. Amongst proponents of the view that the quest for norms is a false trail is D. E. Nineham.[20] In an unpublished paper to the Durham University Lightfoot Society entitled "The Dogma of Normativeness" (a title which he toyed with but did not use for his John Rylands Library lecture) he described the quest for norms as "Judaistic" and therefore an affront to the freedom of the gospel. The standpoint adopted by Nineham is strongly criticized by H. E. W. Turner.

> "The argument that the quest for norms is a false trail in principle ignores the vital importance of the givenness of God. An unmitigated theological pluralism leads at once to a theological relativism which would make all theological statements possible with an equal chance of success or failure. This would mean the end of Christianity as we or anybody else have understood it." [21]

Turner goes on to state that "freedom does not mean unlimited openness and any possible 'Judaism' lies not in the quest for or possession of norms but in certain ways in which they can be used or abused." He refutes Nineham's attempt to force the dilemma, "either unrelated norms or no norms at all," and points out that the givenness of God is a related givenness.

It is certainly difficult to convince those who argue that there are no norms. In the end one can only show that a world-view which makes sense, though not providing slick answers to every problem, and a present religious experience which appears spiritually satisfying are both linked to the historical person and activity of Jesus Christ. Thus he is in some sense a norm for both doctrine and experience and the documents which witness to him and which have always been accepted by his followers are also in some sense at least normative. In the end conviction will only be brought if those who accept this live it out in all aspects of their thought and conduct. The sort of approach which Nineham advocates tends to be much more effective in demolition than in construction.

2. THE STATUS OF THE CANON

If there are to be norms at all in Christian theology, few have ever denied that the Bible should be at least one of them. At times it may have been subordinated to the church or to reason, but it has still been counted as a norm. This means therefore that to certain writings, now ancient, a special status is ascribed and they are collected into a canon which marks them off from other contemporary or later writings. There have in the past been relatively minor disputes about the contents of the canon (Should Esther or 2 Peter go out or should Barnabas or Hermas come in?) but now the whole idea of a canon is under attack. *Is Holy Scripture Christian?* asks C. F. Evans in the provocative title of a book in which he argues that the concept of a holy book may not accord with the faith to which that holy book itself bears witness.[22]

We find this same point being made by Nineham when he quotes an eminent English theologian as referring to "the curse of the canon" and of R. H. Lightfoot's remark to him that the production of the first gospel may have been "the first serious failure of nerve on the part of the infant Church".[23] Nineham himself draws back from a full-scale attack on the idea of a canon because his spiritual experience is refreshed by returning to the Bible, but he does not believe that this justifies any dogma of normativeness. Barr draws attention to "the accidental nature of the process which led to the formation of the Bible as we know it".[24]

Barr confesses himself not to be convinced by the arguments used but asserts that they have opened up the discussion in a potentially fruitful way. Those who believe in the providence of God may well also believe that there was nothing accidental about the formation of the canon even though it did not happen in a neat and tidy way. After all, the crucifixion is a particularly clear example of the way in which human limitations and even human sin can be overruled to fulfill the purposes of God in history.

One of the strongest reasons for treating the biblical documents as Scripture is found in the concept of their being witnesses to the saving acts of God.[25] But this particular concept is criticized by Barr, who has devoted much of his work to showing the weaknesses of the methodology of the modern "biblical theology" school.[26] He concludes that "in general, then, the possession of proximity to the historical events is an ambiguous quality and it does not of itself validate the status of the existing Bible as theological norm for today."[27]

Barr likewise follows Evans in rejecting the argument that the New Testament derives its authority from the apostles. "The idea that the writings are holy scripture because they are 'apostolic' seems therefore to depend on legends, semantic misunderstandings and erroneous extensions of valid truths".[28] The argument given here is rather brief and seems somewhat facile. It fails to take into account much of the recent work which has been done on the idea of tradition in the New Testament, particularly that of Riesenfeld and Gerhardsson. But it does remind us that we can have no cut and dried proof that all the New Testament documents were written by apostles or by their companions. We have again to admit that the evidence is incomplete and to resort to what many would believe to be a proper assumption, that the God who had gone to such lengths as he did to reveal himself in Jesus Christ for the salvation of mankind would also see to it that a basically reliable record of that revelation was available for all to whom it was addressed.[29]

The problem is that in practice we use the canon selectively. The difficulty is not just that some like Charles Gore go to Paul for preference and others like William Temple to John. It is that for many Christians whole books are practically neglected. K. Aland has drawn attention to this in his important monograph, *The Problem of the New Testament Canon.*[30] He shows that the canon proceeded from the Christian communities rather than being imposed by ecclesiastical authority and that the *regula fidei* had an important role in determining its contents. He asserts that the twenty-seven books of the New Testament canon will not be bettered by any extension though not all the competing documents have survived. Modern demands are always for reduction and in practice the canon is undergoing a reduction and narrowing. He suggests that there are three possibilities open to us. We may accept the situation as it is, or we may try to formulate principles by which we can select from the formal canon to make a new actual canon or we can accept the official canon and see that it is made real by using it all. As a Lutheran he favours the second course of action. But Luther was at his weakest when dealing with the canon and it is unlikely that any new canon could be widely agreed now. It may be that the early church was less naive than is often supposed in its principles of selection and what has been so widely accepted and used for so long should not lightly be overthrown. Barr on the other hand points out that we cannot really change the canon today.

> ". . . formation of scripture and canonization of scripture, are processes which were characteristic of a certain time, a certain stage in the life of the people of God. We are in fact no longer in that stage, it is a matter of history to us, and even historically we are not too well informed of the arguments and categories which were employed."[31]

There are then strong arguments for keeping the canon as it is and seeking to understand it more seriously.

3. THE DEVELOPMENT OF DOCTRINE

It is possible to take the Bible as a norm in the sense that it gives us the raw materials of the Christian faith but to hold a theory of the development of doctrine which renders its authority very much secondary to that of the church in successive ages. Newman's "Essay on the Development of Christian Doctrine" is a classical statement of this position. Hanson points out that he had to abandon the idea that the consubstantiality of the Son had always been taught in the church as a *disciplina arcani.* He demonstrates the attractiveness of the idea that the contemporary church in each age can correct the decisions of the church in ages before. "People whose historical consciences cannot accept the old theory can readily accept this one".[32] He goes on to criticize Newman's approach and shows how the Bible ceases to be the norm of faith. "Indeed, the Bible becomes less and less relevant as the progress of history leaves it further and further in the dim past".[33]

If this approach leads to the development of doctrine which is contrary to that revealed in the Bible or to the making of assertions about supposed historical events without any evidence from the Bible or other contemporary sources, it seems to stand self-condemned. On the other hand it has to be admitted that the doctrines of the incarnation and the trinity cannot be read straight out of the New Testament. It was necessary for the theologians to grapple with the phenomena of the New Testament and then try and formulate some systematic statement of orthodox belief. The great majority of the church's leaders and thinkers have accepted for centuries that the formulations were correct. Yet the formulation of the creeds and their acceptance as subsidiary norms has also recently come under attack. Turner shows the importance of the work of systematization and the making of a coherent whole.[34]

There is nothing absolute about the creeds and there is no *a priori* reason why the contemporary church should not seek to restate the doctrines which they contain in more modern thought-forms. Indeed this is the task of the church in every age in its role as "a witness and a keeper of holy Writ". Perhaps Hanson is over-optimistic when he asserts that the Ecumenical Movement will be the means by which we come to a full understanding of Christianity. "The Holy Spirit has given the Church a norm of faith in the Bible, but only a united church can fully understand that norm."[35] This process of understanding and formulating is of course something quite different from that of adding to the faith of the Bible and of providing for the Bible a framework of interpretation which will not let it stand as it should in judgement over the church. The very fact of the number of questions that are open now is itself witness to the failure of the church at any period in history to provide a scheme of biblical interpretation which will satisfy the church at all subsequent times.

4. PERMANENT AND TEMPORARY FACTORS

While there have always been major philosophical problems in supposing that revealed facts about the nature of God or his action in Christ could be changed, it is much easier to suppose that there are secondary matters where there could be development from age to age. Within the New Testament itself we find for instance the "Apostolic Decree" of Acts 15. This was something formulated and promulgated by the leadership of the church as a result of a top-level conference, but the evidence of the New Testament writings as a whole is that its effect was decidedly limited. It was a ruling about practice rather than doctrine. The Pauline churches came to live under grace rather than law but did not think themselves to be overthrowing the authority of the Old Testament. They were recognizing the temporary nature of the approach to the Law under the old covenant. It is interesting to note that nowhere in the New Testament is there made explicit a division between the moral principles and the legal and ceremonial aspects of the Pentateuch but the whole life-style of the churches indicated that most Christians had taken the point that there was a difference between them. There is therefore no *a priori* reason for supposing that ethical instructions given to individual churches or Christians in the New Testament were supposed to have universal validity in that form. The precise application of the story of the rich young ruler (Mk. 10:17–22) to every Christian would seem to be a recipe for chaos, though every one should face up to its basic moral challenge.[36]

The question of church order is now also treated by most scholars as a secondary question. It is true that Paul tries to impose some measure of conformity upon the Corinthian church (1 Cor. 11:16; 14:33–36), but he never treats this as of fundamental importance. The diversity in church order between the Pauline churches and that at Jerusalem suggests that there is no one given form of order and ministry in the New Testament which is valid for everyone everywhere.[37] To say this does not mean to deny that there are important principles connected with the organization of the church and the ordering of its ministry and sacraments, nor to deny that serious error can occur in these areas and that the best possible pattern should be aimed at. But it does mean that we have passed the day of sterile inter-denominational quarrels, with each side trying to justify its position as the exclusively right one by an appeal to Scripture.

The possibility of development in the field of ethics or church order is made possible by an understanding of the need for cultural transposition between the world and the church of the New Testament and the world and the church of today. The most often quoted example of this concerns Paul's injunctions about headdress in 1 Corinthians 11. Most twentieth century Christians do not find excessive difficulty in understanding that the principle underlying this can be applied to dress today, in whatever way is appropriate to the national or local conditions. Again it seems likely that the New Testament writers by and large accepted the social and political conditions of their day but taught such radical principles of love and of the dignity of man that in the end society would be transformed by this teaching. A particular social order provided the framework in which they practised the Christian life, but they did not have the opportunity of shaping the legislation of professedly Christian states.

There is, as Barr points out, a great danger in "cultural relativism". This would mean "a marked passivity of Christian faith and theology in relation to whatever happens to pass current in the culture of our own time".[38] The New Testament would lose its authority if it could not stand in judgement over the democratic ideals of white Anglo-Saxon Protestants as much as over the tyranny of Herod or of Nero. The principles of human nature, human conduct and human relationships do not change from age to age and the New Testament principles are available for translation into our situation.

Does the principle of translation into twentieth century terms allow for demythologization? The subject has been more fully treated above,[39] and one must agree that there is an urgent need for translating the gospel into present-day terms. This is very different from listing what modern man can and cannot believe, which is often more a statement of what some theologians with a certain philosophical background can and cannot believe. A true demythologization of something like the ascension, showing the real truth which was being expressed in the biblical language and relating that to modern thought and knowledge, does nothing to diminish the authority of the New Testament. To rewrite the whole gospel story to fit our own contemporary prejudices is a different matter altogether. We should rather, in dialogue with the Scriptures, allow them to help shape our presuppositions.[40]

Many of the issues mentioned above find their crystallization in a problem currently facing many sections of the Christian church. Should women be ordained to the presbyterate? While some frankly ignore the biblical evidence as irrelevant to the contemporary church, those who take the New Testament seriously have to grapple with the issues above. What does the New Testament actually say about the ministry of women? Is it a primary or secondary matter? Does the Pauline discussion of the order of creation in relation to the question make it an issue of theological principle rather than of church order? What sort of cultural transposition do we have to make and is it so great that we may almost have to demythologize the biblical doctrine of creation? Has the development of understanding which eventually brought freedom to slaves also now grown ripe for the freeing of women from any restrictions on their ministry? In what sense do we talk about views being "scriptural" or "unscriptural"? Does the matter have to be instanced or commanded in the New Testament or is it simply sufficient that it is not forbidden? Can those who claim that genuine pentecostal phenomena ended with the apostolic age at the same time claim the pattern of the apostolic church to be normative for women's ministry?[41]

V. *Conclusion*

Since the religion and science controversies of the last century intelligent Christians have been learning increasingly to see that God works through all sorts of means for which some explanation other than divine action may also be given. There is no longer any need to posit a "God of the gaps". If this is true both in matters of doctrinal and historical truth and also in ordinary Christian living, there should be no great difficulty in applying the same principle to biblical criticism. If the careful literary and historical study of the Bible suggests that it came into its present form in certain ways which are explicable at the human level, that does not mean that it is not also the word of God. While some solutions of critical problems would be hard to square with any theory of the inspiration and authority of the Bible, the majority are neutral. The discovery of the role of the early church or the role of the evangelist in the compilation of the Gospels makes them no less authoritative than if they had all been simply a verbatim record of what Jesus said and did. A fearless attempt to interpret the New Testament correctly will do more to strengthen than to undermine its authority.[42] For the authority of the Bible comes home most clearly to us when we understand it as fully as we are able to do. This understanding is built up for the church as a whole by the work which scholars and devout Christians have done in trying to grapple with the true meaning of the text and its application in each generation. The New Testament has the authority of a once-for-all revelation which witnesses to a once-for-all redemption, though the church has always found that, in the words of John Robinson (one of the Pilgrim Fathers), "The Lord hath more light and truth yet to break forth out of His holy word." Nonetheless the church has been given a basic norm by which to guide and shape her life and which will act as a judge if she neglects it.

The Bible has been given to us to provide eternal principles and not as a direct solver of current problems. If it is rightly accepted as a norm its principles will be seen to bear on contemporary situations and it is one of the sad facts of the present church scene that there seems to be little understanding of how to apply biblical teaching.[43] All the tools at our disposal must be used to elucidate the original meaning of the text, but there is needed in addition an understanding of the contemporary world, not just from a secular point of view, but with reference to the way in which the Spirit is working. It is very rarely the scholar sitting isolated in his study who discovers anything really fresh in the message of the scriptures. The task of understanding and application needs interplay between evangelist, pastor and layman in the world on the one hand and theologian on the other. The individual Christian should be able to go to the New Testament and find "a command, a promise or a warning, an example to follow or an error to avoid".[44] But he will do this, not by reading the Bible in isolation so that he fails to contextualize what he has read, but by engaging in study of the text and discussion of its meaning with other Christians also. The authority of the New Testament, rightly understood, will never be fully experienced in this life. But if Christians approach it desiring to hear the voice of God speaking to them they will find that the Spirit takes the word in the church and makes it for them something living and active. Only by those with such an attitude can its true authority be found.

NOTES

1. See above, ch. 2.
2. *Interpretation* 25 (1971), pp. 36f. Cited in J. Barr, *The Bible in the Modern World* (London 1973), p. 37.
3. These are set out by J. Barr in "The Authority of the Bible – A Study Outline", *Ecumenical Review* 21:2 (1969), pp. 135–150.
4. See the discussion of the concept of authority by E. Jüngel, G. Krodel, R. Marle and J. D. Zizioulas in *Ecumenical Review* 21:2 (1969), pp. 150–166.
5. *The Bible in the Modern World,* pp. 27–29.
6. For a fuller discussion of the authority of Jesus see H. von Campenhausen, *Ecclesiastical Authority and Spiritual Power in the Church of the First Three Centuries* (E.T. London 1969), pp. 1–11.

7. See above, ch. 16.
8. Cf. C. H. Dodd, *According to the Scriptures* (London 1952); R. T. France, *Jesus and the Old Testament* (London 1971).
9. Cf. Robin Nixon in a forthcoming symposium on morality and law "Fulfilling the Law – Law and Liberty".
10. See above, ch. 10.
11. D. R. Catchpole refers on p. 167f. to two verses whose authenticity seems to be in doubt. As far as Matthew 18:17 is concerned, there need be no difficulty in seeing "Gentile" and "tax-collector" as terms for typical outsiders which could have been used by Jesus here and in 5:46f. It is part of the paradox of grace that heathen and sinners are those who respond to the Gospel. Matthew 23:2f. has always presented more problems, particularly in the first phrase of verse 3. Jesus could have spoken such words to discourage antinomianism and at the same time to lead his disciples to a deeper understanding of the real meaning of the Law. There is similar teaching in 5:17–20 which leads on to the profound dealing with attitudes in 5:21–48. The meaning might be "Do whatever they tell you, but not in the way they do it." The statement of their "not doing" followed by examples of their "doing" indicates some sort of paradox. In verse 23 the practice of justice, mercy and faith (cf. Micah 6:8) is shown to be the true observance of Pharisaic legal teaching (cf. Luke 11:42 where not neglecting legal observance is also referred to). Matthew is a careful writer and should be allowed a measure of consistency even where there is paradox. He must have been as aware as modern writers of the difficulty of the saying (unless we have missed its meaning altogether). That apparent difficulty provides in itself some evidence of authenticity. It prepares the way by contrast for Jesus' last charge "teaching them to observe all that I have commanded you" (Matt. 28:20). For fuller discussion, particularly of the importance of context, see Robert Banks, *Jesus and the Law in the Synoptic Tradition,* (Cambridge 1975), pp. 173ff.
12. See above, ch. XI.
13. As does E. J. Carnell, *The Case for Orthodox Theology* (London 1959), pp. 57f. His attempt to make Romans and Galatians the touchstone of everything in the New Testament needs a more convincing rationale than he provides.
14. See W. Bauer, *Orthodoxy and Heresy in Earliest Christianity* (E.T. London 1972). His thesis is discussed critically by H. E. W. Turner, *The Pattern of Christian Truth, A Study in the Relations between Orthodoxy and Heresy in the Early Church* (London 1954), pp. 39–80. See also A. A. T. Ehrhardt, *The Framework of the New Testament Stories* (Manchester 1964).
15. Cf. E. Käsemann, *New Testament Questions of Today* (E.T. London 1969), pp. 236–251.
16. See F.J. Leenhardt, *Two Biblical Faiths, Protestant and Catholic* (E.T. London 1964).
17. See E. Käsemann, "The Problem of a New Testament Theology", NTS 19 (1972–73), pp. 235–245; R. Morgan, *The Nature of New Testament Theology* (London 1973).
18. Cf. I. H. Marshall, "Palestinian and Hellenistic Christianity: Some Critical Comments", NTS 19 (1972–73), pp. 271–287.
19. *The Bible in the Modern World,* p. 23.
20. "Wherein lies the Authority of the Bible?" in L. Hodgson (*et al.*), *On the Authority of the Bible* (London 1960), pp. 81–96; "The Use of the Bible in Modern Theology", BJRL 52 (1969), pp. 178–199.
21. *The Churchman* 86 (1972), pp. 166–173.
22. C. F. Evans, *Is "Holy Scripture" Christian? and Other Questions* (London 1971), p. 35: "If it was the case that religious models, and especially the Old Testament, were in the end too much for Christianity, so that a time came when it was no longer possible to say, 'These are writings which have belonged from the first to our movement, they are the best we have and they have recommended themselves', and one could only say "This is holy scripture", does it follow that this is of the nature of the case, and that the church has always to think in this way?"
23. D. E. Nineham, "The Use of the Bible . . .", pp. 197f.
24. *The Bible in the Modern World,* p. 43: "The acceptance of books as canonical did not proceed on the basis of theological considerations which we could share today, but on the

basis partly of geography and the rivalries of the major churches in ancient times, partly of historical accident, partly of sheer fantasies or falsehoods, through which books were attributed to 'apostles'."

25. As R. P. C. Hanson puts it: "The Bible is the record of revelation, and this record takes the form of historical witness. It constitutes testimony to an unique activity of God, to an unique course of events which happened to an unique people, and finally to an unique Person. This is what causes the uniqueness of the Bible; what constitutes its uniqueness is not the form or forms of the Biblical literature, which are in fact most of them to be found in many other literatures and cultures as well, but its subject." (*The Bible as a Norm of Faith* (Durham, 1963), p. 7; cf. *Tradition in the Early Church* (London 1962), pp. 213–224).

Similarly Turner states: "The Bible then is the primary norm not only as the earliest, the most complete, the most wide-ranging in time and space record of God speaking, God acting, but also as containing within its pages the words and acts of God which bring salvation. It is the record in word and deed of salvation history" (art. cit., p. 168).

26. *The Semantics of Biblical Language* (Oxford 1961); *Old and New in Interpretation. A Study of the Two Testaments* (London 1966).

27. *The Bible in the Modern World,* p. 81.

28. Ibid., p. 81.

29. The problem of pseudonymity has been discussed above (see ch. 5). It would create considerable difficulties to suppose that a document whose title was deliberately intended to deceive the church about its authorship should be accepted as Holy Scripture. On the other hand, there are literary conventions which are not intended to mislead contemporary readers of documents, and if it could be convincingly shown that such had been used in the title of a "wrongly ascribed" New Testament document, there is no reason to exclude it from the canon on that account.

30. *The Problem of the New Testament Canon* (London 1962). Cf. E. Schweizer, *Neotestamentica* (Zürich/Stuttgart 1963), pp. 208–210.

31. *The Bible in the Modern World,* p. 154.

32. *The Bible as a Norm of Faith,* p. 16.

33. Ibid., p. 16.

34. Art. cit., p. 170: "This the New Testament itself, which is more concerned with spearhead thrust than with lateral roundedness, did not itself undertake. The drawing of the appropriate doctrinal inferences and their thinking together with each other in an appropriate thought-context was a subsequent but indispensable task. To do it justice the church did not hurry over its task, kept firmly in touch with the Bible throughout (biblical commenting went on side by side with philosophical theology) and did not overdefine. It had the advantage over later ages in undertaking the task together and reaching its result through a confluence of different approaches and traditions, though not without dispute or acrimony. Its unity was not seen as incompatible with diversity. It was fortunate too that a set of philosophical coordinates were available which formed a common universe of discourse between the church and its secular contemporaries."

35. *The Bible as a Norm of Faith,* p. 23. For the idea of a continuing revelation to be tested by reference to the Christ of the New Testament, see E. Schweizer, op. cit., pp. 211f.

36. The action of the youthful Origen serves as a warning. For the problem of ethical diversity in the New Testament, see J. L. Houlden, *Ethics and the New Testament* (Harmondsworth 1973).

37. Cf. W. D. Davies, *A Normative Pattern of Church Life in the New Testament – Fact or Fancy?* (London 1950).

38. J. Barr, *The Bible in the Modern World,* pp. 46f.

39. See above, ch. XV.

40. See above, ch. III.

41. For literature on the subject see: K. Stendahl, *The Bible and the Role of Women, A Case Study in Hermeneutics* (Philadelphia 1966); *Why Not? Priesthood and the Ministry of Women,* ed. M. Bruce and G. E. Duffield (Abingdon 1972); *The Ordination of Women to the Priesthood* (Church Information Office, London 1972); *Evangelicals and the Ordination of Women,* ed. C. Craston (Bramcote 1973).

42. G. E. Ladd, *The New Testament and Criticism* (London 1970).
43. See J. D. Smart, *The Strange Silence of the Bible in the Church, A Study in Hermeneutics* (London 1970); B. S. Childs, *Biblical Theology in Crisis* (London 1972). Nineham confesses to not seeing any relevance to the present situation in many passages of the Bible (art. cit., pp. 181f.).
44. The things which users of the Scripture Union notes are encouraged to look for when reading the Bible.

CHAPTER XVIII

EXPOUNDING THE NEW TESTAMENT

John Goldingay

"Exegesis", "exposition", and other words in this field are used in various ways. In this chapter, however, "exegesis" refers to elucidating a verse or passage's historical meaning in itself, "exposition" to perceiving its significance for today.[1] "Interpretation" and "hermeneutics" cover both these major aspects of the task of understanding the Bible.

All four words are sometimes used synonymously, however. In part this reflects the fact that these two major aspects of interpretation have often not been sharply distinguished. The "classic" evangelical treatments of Stibbs[2] or Berkhof[3] simply assume that if you can understand a passage's "meaning", the question of its "significance" will look after itself. Consequently, all that is required of the preacher is "to say again what St. Paul has already said". His message to us will then be self-evident. There is of course a realization that a literal application of a text will sometimes be illegitimate. On the one hand, social and cultural changes make anxiety about women's hats unnecessary today and our job in expounding 1 Corinthians 11 is not to dictate fashion to contemporary ladies but to see what principles underlie Paul's specific injunctions there. On the other hand, the change in theological era effected by Christ's coming complicates the application of the Old Testament to God's New Testament people. With such provisos, however, the application to today of the Bible's eternal message has not seemed difficult.

Earlier chapters of this book have shown how modern study of the Bible has raised major problems for this approach, and "the strange silence of the Bible in the church"[4] witnesses to it. The development of critical methods, even when most positive in its conclusions, has made interpreting the New Testament much more complicated. What if "John (has) written up the story (of Jesus and the Samaritan woman) in the manner he thought appropriate" which is thus "substantially the story of something that actually happened"[5] – but not entirely so? What about tradition- and redaction-criticism which, far from revealing "the historical Jesus", might seem to remove any possibility of knowing what his actual words were, let alone of saying them again? And, while the study of the New Testament's religious background may not seem threatening in the same way, to be told that to try to understand a particular passage "without a copy of the Book of

Enoch at your elbow is to condemn yourself to failure" [6] may be daunting.

Nor can we still assume that when the exegetical problems are solved, the application will look after itself. Modern study has striven to read the Bible in its historical context as a document (or an anthology) from a culture quite different from ours which thus speaks to quite different circumstances. [7] The situation of the church, the customs of society, the very nature of life were unique (as those of every culture are unique – they are not even uniform within the Bible itself). But the Bible's message relates to the particulars of that situation. There is thus a "hermeneutical gap" not only between the event and the account of it in the Bible, but also between the Bible and us, because of the chasm between its situation and ours; a gap which yawns widest when the Bible speaks of the supernatural realities which are the very heart of its concern but which are missing from "modern man's" world-view – hence the pressure to "demythologize" them. [8] Thus elucidating God's message to Timothy does not establish what is his word to us, to whom he might actually have something very different to say. Indeed, "simply to *repeat* the actual words of the New Testament today may well be, in effect, to say something different from what the text itself originally said", [9] and to contribute further to the "death of the Word". Our task is to stand first in the Bible's world, hearing its message in its terms, then in the world of those to whom we have to speak – as we see Jesus doing in the parables [10] – if we are to relate the two.

Paradoxically, however, we can in fact only rightly hear the Bible's message as we do bridge the gap between its world and ours. Appreciating its meaning in its own day, even "objectively", [11] cannot be a cool, "academic" (in the pejorative sense) exercise. We may only be able to do so in the act of working out and preaching the equivalent (which may well not mean the identical) message today. Thus exegesis and exposition are interwoven after all, and sometimes the exegete cannot resist nudging the preacher, [12] while the preacher finds himself having to come back with additional questions about exegesis.

So how does the expositor go about his task? In exposition "as with most other human activities . . . practice precedes theory". [13] Thus the pages that follow attempt to suggest answers to this question in connection with the passages exegeted in Chapter 14 above.

I. *Matthew 8:5–13*

(1) What is the point of this story about the centurion's servant? The subject is *faith* – but this is too broad a definition to be satisfying. Quantitatively, most of the passage is an example of the nature of faith, which casts itself without qualification on Jesus (verses 5–10); but this cannot be *the* point of the whole, because it does not cover verses 11–13. The Lukan parallel does have such a purport; the difference between the two shows how one has to treat each version in its own right as bearing a distinctive message. Often we have been so concerned with harmonizing parallel

passages that we have failed to listen to them in their distinctiveness. It is significant that Tatian's *Diatessaron* is not in the canon! Matthew gives the story an eschatological orientation by introducing the saying about the messianic banquet (verses 11–12). He thus turns a story about the nature of faith into one about the cruciality of faith: "the central importance of faith not only for healing but for salvation, for inclusion in the true people of God for whom his eschatological blessings are reserved".[14] This summary also indicates how the parts relate to the whole: verses 5–10 describe the *nature of faith,* verses 11–13 *the cruciality of faith* both *in this life* (verse 13) and *with regard to the kingdom* (verses 11–12). At least, this is the logical order, and it corresponds to the material's critical history (that is, it reflects the awareness that verses 11–12 are Matthew's addition). In the passage itself the eschatological blessing precedes the physical one. I think this is Matthew's way of making the former his climax after the dramatic tension established by verses 5–10; the final verse is now only a coda.

(2) The exposition of the first section will concentrate on the main point of *the nature of faith.* Although the passage illustrates Jesus' positive attitude to soldiers and a soldier's consideration for his "boy", it is not *about* the ethics of war or about how to be a good employer, any more than John 4 is about how to win people for Christ.[15] The passages may have implications in these areas – but "the crucial problem in the theory and practice of interpretation is to distinguish between possible implications that do belong to the meaning of a text and those that do not belong".[16] One check on this, in the case of the Bible, is to ask whether what is claimed to be implicit is elsewhere explicit. Thus since Jesus is elsewhere set forth as an example of ministry and Paul in his ministry exemplifies many of the features of pastoral care described in John 4, we might infer that the chapter by implication offers a model for ministry even though we cannot ask John whether he intended it that way (and even if, in fact, we could, and the idea proved not even to have been at the back of his mind). We can use the passage thus; though by imposing our questions on a passage we may miss the questions it intended to raise.

What then is faith, according to this first section of Mt. 8:5–13? And also, what does the word suggest to the minds of our congregation? Matthew does not mean "believing things that are not true" or "mental assent"; nor by the attitude of faith does he mean "we expect well of life", refusing to yield to scepticism or despair;[17] nor, however, is this Paul's "saving faith". It is a practical confidence in Jesus' power to heal, based on a conviction of his supreme authority,[18] the praying faith that the believer is called to exercise in his Lord when he is in need,[19] the faith that lays hold of the Lord's power to act.

Jesus has not found such faith *inside* God's people, now he finds it outside. Within the context of Jesus' ministry, this means among Jews as opposed to Gentiles, but to expound the text in such terms would be exactly to repeat its words and thereby to convey a very different meaning. The church would no doubt enjoy a sermon warning the Jews of the possibility of losing their places in the kingdom. But now it is the church itself that is in danger of being of little faith (cf. the challenge of Rom. 11:17–21). Thus it is offered the example of an outsider with the warning "Make sure that Jesus does not have to say of you 'With no-one in the church have I found such faith'". Quite consistently the significance of the Jews as we expound the gospels is that they warn us of what the church may become; we are not the sinner in the parable but the Pharisee.

(3) Similarly, the passage's climax (verses 11–12) goes on to give the church a warning on *the cruciality of faith for salvation:* "Many will sit at table with Paul, Augustine, and Calvin, while the members of the church are missing". And we must beware of identifying the missing members with the obviously nominal or those who do not share our particular orthodoxy (or non-orthodoxy). Part of the point of the passage is that the axe falls on those who least expect it, and the sermon must confront those present with the danger they may be in themselves, not bolster their false security by lamenting the fate of those absent.

But how are we to understand the picture of the eschatological banquet and its alternative of outer darkness, weeping, and gnashing of teeth? Jesus takes up what were customary ideas (cf. Lk. 14:15) which also however appear elsewhere in the Bible (Is. 25; Rev. 3:20; 19:9, 17) in contexts which indicate their symbolic significance. Behm[20] describes the picture of the eschatological banquet as "a meaningful expression for perfect fellowship with God and with Christ in the consummation". This, however, is a colourless abstraction until we have re-expressed it in contemporary symbolism. Think of the best party you've ever been to – when things have gone well, people have enjoyed themselves, made new friends; think of the wedding that makes the reunion of old friends possible; or the gathering together of the scattered family at Christmas, or even the more intimate wedding anniversary meal out for two. Recall the feel of such occasions; and then imagine being left out of the in-crowd, the black sheep of the family, the rejected lover. *That* is how heaven and hell will feel.[21]

Beyond the need for such "desymbolizing" of these verses there arises also the question of demythologizing them. Inside the imagery of the banquet is the "myth" of historical consummation, of final fulfilment and loss. That this "myth should be interpreted not cosmologically, but anthropologically or, better still, existentially"[22] is unlikely, since the first century expression of the faith had open to it a non-eschatological form such as was maintained by the Sadducees, but this was rejected and the eschatological form chosen. Admittedly men today do not think in eschatological terms (except for the "doomwatch" syndrome?), but then they are not often despairing existentialists either;[23] the call to decision is also strange to them. But neither the call to decision nor its eschatological motivation seem to be merely part of the first century expression of the faith. They *are* part of "the stumbling-block of the Gospel".[24]

(4) The closing verse of the pericope asserts the *cruciality of faith* in its other aspect, *in this life.* The verse's meaning is clear – the boy was healed.

But various answers are given to the question of its significance for us.

(a) As the sick experienced healing in Jesus' day, so they may now; the passage encourages expectant prayer for healing. This is the simple, obvious interpretation. It is also the approach that leads to prescribing ladies' headgear. Further, it is often belied by experience. This must make us consider possible alternatives – without letting experience have the final word either way, lest we become confined within the limitations of what we currently experience.

(b) Miraculous healings were a sign that God's Kingdom had come in Jesus, but as such they were confined to his (and his apostles') earthly ministry and do not occur today; the passage encourages faith in Christ as the one who proved himself by these signs. This interpretation matches the church's general (though not universal) experience; but the theological justification for connecting miracle exclusively with the time of Jesus and the apostles is at best an argument from silence, at worst contradicted by such passages as 1 Corinthians 13:8–13 (which implies that spiritual gifts, apparently including healing, have a place in the church until Christ's coming).

(c) Physical healing is part of the total wholeness which Christ brought, whose more important aspects are the non-physical; the passage thus encourages us to seek spiritual wholeness (forgiveness, renewal) in Christ. Again, this fits experience, though it is in danger of being an argument not from silence, but from invisibility – there aren't miracles you can see but there are miracles that you can't see (or are there?[25])! And there is no evidence that physical healing, which certainly *can* symbolize spiritual healing, always does so.[26]

(d) Christ's healing miracles are part of his restoring creation's unspoilt state, which is continued by the efforts of science; the passage encourages us to seek physical healing from Christ through medicine. This approach is even more congenial to the modern mind – too much so for comfort. Can we really imagine that Matthew would acknowledge this as a valid expression of his message for a later age?

We must, in fact, if we are to expound the passage aright, return first to exegesis. General approaches to the problem of interpreting the significance of miracles must give way to looking at particulars. Matthew surely indicates how he understood the incident's significance by his insertion of the eschatological passage, which moved the emphasis from faith's physical consequences onto (not the spiritual in a general sense but) the eschatological. He was certainly challenging the church to manifest an expectant, praying faith in the face of whatever crises threatened (these would include, but not be confined to, illness);[27] but his emphasis is on the fact that the question whether or not the church manifests such faith is of importance beyond the challenge of coping with earthly crises.

The final verse of this passage thus exemplifies a most difficult aspect of exposition: how may we decide between different opinions as to the application of a passage whose historical-critical meaning may be agreed? The answer lies in going back to exegesis: an even more rigorous approach to the question "What was the author saying?" provides guidelines for interpreting the passage now. The story was in applied form when it reached Matthew – it was a "pronouncement story", one less interested in the miracle than in the words which accompanied it;[28] Matthew has further applied it. The Gospel itself thus suggests the area of application of the story within which we may work out more precisely how it applies to us.[29]

(5) The insights of source-, form-, and redaction-criticism thus clarify the expositor's task. But they also add to his problems, for they show that the narrative is by no means a straightforward account of an event and its significance in Jesus' actual ministry. It is a redactor's rewriting of oral tradition's recasting of any actual event: can it still retain its authority for us?

The gospels do not simply describe "history as it actually happened" (that will o' the wisp); they preach the significance of Jesus to the church of their day. But if this was the evangelist's aim, then we believe that the Holy Spirit who is the inspirer of Scripture inspired them to do this well. We have gained a daughter, and not lost a son – for the disciplines of criticism can also take us back behind this preaching, into the meaning of Jesus' teaching and ministry in its original historical context. We are enriched rather than deprived as we can see what the Spirit was saying in several different situations.

(6) The evangelist, then, is the model expositor, in that he adapts and transforms the story so that it may speak to his congregation's situation. But does this mean that we too are free to do what we like with the tradition as we receive it – to adapt and transform it with the creativity that the Spirit inspires in us? Does historical-critical exegesis matter after all – does not Matthew's example (or John's, or other New Testament writers' in their use of the Old Testament) encourage us to ignore his meaning and let the words mean today whatever we feel needs to be said?

The Spirit may indeed in this way cause new light to break out of God's word; "charismatic exegesis"[30] may still be a spiritual gift. Many have had the experience of being blessed by some word from Scripture taken in a sense which they now realize was strictly invalid, though in keeping with the general tenor of the Bible. At least it spoke relevantly to us, and was not the mere dead word from the past which historical-critical exegesis has often turned the Bible into. Nevertheless such exegesis should be the starting-point of exposition, because:

(a) While it is not clear that the Bible's exegetical practice is meant to be normative for us,[31] historical-critical exegesis is an expression of our elemental awareness of history as modern men, which seeks to understand other ages in their own terms before asking what insights they have for us. "Charismatic" exegesis is an anachronism.

(b) Historical-critical exegesis establishes what God was saying at one point, and that the crucial point for the faith. It enables us then to move from the known to the unknown, from the general area of application to the specific, and gives us the former as a check on the latter. While we may be sure that the evangelists were inspired, modern charismatic exegesis cannot be checked!

Exposition is *both* a cerebral *and* a pneumatic exercise. The mind is involved in extrapolating from what we know God was saying then to what he is saying now, though we see the Spirit's activity in this process too. The Spirit will give flashes of insight but is active also as these are examined, tested, and followed up by the mind. Surely we need this combination (1 Cor. 14:15).

II. *1 Peter 3:18–22*

(1) If exposition involves starting from a passage's central idea which is developed in its various parts, then this will seem a passage as difficult to expound as to exegete if there is no real train of thought running through it – as many commentators have concluded. The exegesis, however, has suggested that the unity of the passage lies in what it says "to those facing fierce hostility in the name of Christ",[32] in its attempt to answer the question: "Why should a Christian be prepared to die?" Because:

18a	Jesus set you an example
18b	He is worth suffering for
18c	Death is followed by resurrection
19–20a	He is Lord of the evil powers
20b	Judgement on sinners is only being delayed
20c	Minorities have been saved in the end before
21	Your baptism is the guarantee of your salvation
22	He is Lord of all.

Presumably this will be a sermon with eight points!

This passage exemplifies the occasional nature of the Bible, which was produced in response to specific historical situations. What are we to do with a passage that answers this particular question, in a day when martyrdom is not a threat?

(a) There will be times when its message is awefully relevant, and such times need preparing for. If we have not formulated our attitude to persecution (like that to dying generally) before it happens, the moment itself may be too late. So the passage can be preached as part of educating the people in the whole counsel of God.

(b) In less sharp ways than was the case for Peter's readers, all Christians face hostility. The powers of evil which stood behind their persecution assail us too, finding embodiment in more petty (perhaps only verbal) attacks, which *a fortiori* Peter's argument covers.

(c) We all have to be prepared to die (Mk. 8:34), and that daily (Lk. 9:23). Jesus himself has, perhaps, by anticipation provided the area of application of Peter's message.

We must beware however of the besetting sins, the occupational hazards of the expositor who worships the god "relevance": blunting the edge of Peter's message and losing the pointedness of the specific by generalizing or trivializing or spiritualizing it away. We must somehow feel this bite in our exegesis and communicate it in our exposition.

(2) Jesus "died on behalf of the unjust . . . His death was an effective, once-for-all sacrifice to make atonement for (your?) sins, so that you might be restored to fellowship with God" – so verse 18, which "is steeped in Old Testament sacrificial ideas".[33] And so, often, are our sermons. Peter uses this terminology (as well as ideas from contemporary post-biblical Jewish writings – verses 19–20) because it speaks to his readers, whether Jewish or non-Jewish, who know about cult and sacrifice. But we do not move in that world. And therefore while, to understand the Bible, we must learn to think in that world's terms, we must also learn to speak *of the same realities* in our own world's terms. This is not just for the sake of outsiders (it is not to such, in fact, that the New Testament expounds the technical working of the atonement), not even just for the sake of younger Christians who have not yet got into the Biblical world, but for our own sakes, so that we ourselves may more effectively hear the gospel. It is not enough to *explain* what atonement, sacrifice, substitution are; a metaphor that needs explaining is thereby shown to have lost its force. And in this particular case explaining it does not solve the problem. For the idea of sacrifices to propitiate God is so foreign that people may still find it objectionable when they understand it. They cannot help evaluating it from within the terms of our attitudes – which are also culturally determined, of course, but that is less easy to appreciate! We need to go on further in exegesis to find out what is expressed by the metaphor, and then to find a new metaphor which says as much as the old.

Unpacking this particular metaphor reveals various layers:

(a) At its heart is the experience – perhaps a universal human one, certainly one we share with the biblical world – of estrangement and reconciliation, and the cost involved in this.

(b) This experience suggests a metaphor for understanding relationships between God and man: things come between these parties too.

(c) Sacrificial systems provide a way of effecting reconciliation as the cost is symbolically paid by the offending party and symbolically accepted by the other side.

(d) The Old Testament describes one particular version of this. Note that God himself prescribes the system and thus takes the initiative in reconciliation.

(e) The New Testament takes up aspects of the Old Testament sacrificial system as a metaphor for understanding the cross: Christ was bearing the cost by offering himself.

(f) His achievement breaks the bounds of the metaphor, however, in that he was as much on the side of the offended party as on the offender's: God was in Christ reconciling . . .

Having analysed the biblical metaphor, we need, in re-expressing it, to remove its cultic aspect, which is strange to our world, without losing the atonement's objective side (what it means for God), as well as the subjective side (the need to win man back to God). We might recall how, when we are attacked, instinct tells us to put up our weapons and return the blow – like for like, eye for eye, abuse for abuse. It's as if hostility has a force which must be dissipated, and we have to ensure its deflection away from us back to the other person, so that it can be absorbed there. Alternatively, however, we can let that force strike us, affect us, hurt us, be absorbed by us. Man's rebellion against God (which admittedly does not lie near the surface of his consciousness but is the theological significance of his general self-seeking aggressiveness, his hostility to other men, made in God's image, and his self-destructiveness) is also a hostility which must be absorbed somewhere – it can't just disappear into thin air. The cross is in history the concretizing of God's acceptance of man's hostility, his refusal to return it. God copes with the sin which prevents fellowship between himself and man by absorbing its force in himself and thus dissolving it.[34]

(3) Jesus "went to the fallen angels awaiting judgement in their place of confinement, and proclaimed to them the victory won by his redeeming death . . . These were those spirits who rebelled against God in the days of Noah, while God in his mercy was still withholding the punishment of the flood".[35] Here is a different world of thought which again raises the question of demythologizing.

Demythologizing the "spirits in prison" might mean

(a) Shedding the particular *imagery* of personal, supernatural evil as it is conceptualized here, while still maintaining that "there is about (Evil) . . . the subtlety of a malevolent personality rather than the crudity of a blind, irrational force . . . (A) degree of perverted ingenuity is required to make the world go quite so wrong".[36] The sin that led to the flood did not just have its origin in man.[37]

(b) Shedding not merely this particular imagery but also the *personal nature* of supernatural evil itself, seeing it as powers, forces, laws of an impersonal kind, but still recognizing that there is more to evil than the sinful acts of sinful men.

(c) Shedding any idea of the *supernatural nature* of evil, stressing that Peter is not here arguing the existence of spirits and of angels, authorities and powers (verse 22), but asserting the risen Christ's lordship over these entities which were only too real to people. The demythologized equivalents for us are the driving forces of love, power, knowledge, success and failure, present and future, death and life – all with the peculiar ambiguity of the spirits in that they are sometimes good, sometimes tragic and deadly.[38]

The Creator's restraint of, and now Christ's lordship over these demythologized powers must indeed be preached because they *are* the powers we are aware of. But we should also realise that the powers of evil are greater than we are aware of. Paul does explicitly indicate that there is in the activity of evil another level than the merely human: "We wrestle not against flesh and blood but against principalities . . ." (Eph. 6:12). The conceptualization may need updating, but there is something ontological to re-express.

And what of the way the experience and achievement of Christ is described?

(a) He was made alive in the spirit (verse 18): even if the conceptualization is mythical on the surface, the claim here made of Jesus is that he rose from death in history.

(b) He went to preach to the spirits, went to heaven (verses 19, 22 – *πορευθείς* each time): here is language that presupposes a three-dimensional heaven, but the reality is one that we may seek to re-express, perhaps in terms of *other* dimensions than those of time and space.

(c) He is at God's right hand (verse 22): the three-dimensional heaven may be presupposed here, but more likely writer and readers understood this particular expression as a metaphor drawn from earthly life (cf. Ps. 110); we must not be over prosaic in interpreting the Bible, and treat the writers as too unsophisticated.

(4) The picture in mythical terms of the evil powers that threaten the Christian (verses 19, 22) brackets a linking in historical terms of the days of Noah and of the readers (verses 20–1): a "typical" relationship is ascribed to the latter. Is typology arbitrary?[39] How does it work?[40]

(a) Typology is (here anyway) not a method of exegesis but one of exposition. It does not aspire to be a guide to the original meaning of the flood story but starts from the historical reality (this is not allegory) and uses typology as a means of suggesting its significance for a new day, in the light of Christ's coming.

(b) Near the heart of the answer to the question "What holds the two Testaments together?" is the fact that both deal with the same people, through whom the God of Israel who is also the God and Father of our Lord Jesus Christ is working out his purpose in the world. This link is implicit here, indeed explicit if *ἀντίτυπον* does go with *ὑμᾶς*, though it is assumed rather than argued. But it provides part of the rationale for trying to relate what God did with his people in Old Testament times to what he is doing with them now.

(c) Very probably the significance of baptism as a symbolic undergoing of death/judgement as the gateway to new life/salvation is in the author's mind. This theological significance of baptism is thus similar to that of the flood.

(d) There is no clear evidence to indicate whether or not Peter meant to extend the parallel as far as asserting that Noah was saved by means of water – rather than simply that water was involved on both occasions.[41]

It seems to me to be unreasonable to accuse Peter of being "arbitrary" in his use of typology here. Indeed, I doubt if this really is what is usually meant by typology; he is not suggesting that in Christian baptism you find the real meaning or fulfilment of the flood, but that the former performs an equivalent function to the latter (cf. RSV rather than NEB or JB), that there is a relationship of analogy between them.[42]

(5) Can we ourselves use this expository method, then? Can we suggest other analogies to the flood? And if so, how can we safeguard ourselves

from being arbitrary?

(a) The Old Testament regards the sea as an embodiment of the powers of chaos which assert themselves against God and threaten his people; the flood is an example of the sea at work in this way, though only under God's control. "The Lord sits enthroned over the flood" and thus protects his people (Ps. 29:10–11). This idea might be further applied by taking the flood as a type of danger that threatens the church, perhaps by God's own hand but under his control (an understanding perhaps implicit in the New Testament[43]). On the other hand, to take the wood of the ark as a type of the cross[44] is to move into a wholly new area of parallelism and to take a chance point of contact (the use of wood) as of intrinsic significance, thus making a "form-mistake".[45]

(b) In that the flood story is about God's judgement, it can be used as a way of picturing the final judgement (cf. 2 Peter 3), and it seems reasonable to claim that the writer of Genesis would not have regarded this application of his story as inconsistent with his original intention. On the other hand, to take Noah in his humiliation as a type of Christ[46] seems to go against the way the author presents him, even if it fits in with modern work on such myth as may underlie the narrative.[47]

The fact that the New Testament uses typology does not bind us to do so;[48] but some application of a principle of analogy such as is illustrated here enables us to work on biblical passages, not as a substitute for but on the basis of historical-critical exegesis. But two criteria which set boundaries to the validity of the exercise are that we move within areas of application and development of ideas suggested by the Bible itself,[49] and we apply the passage in the spirit of the original writer.

III. *The Expositor's Method*

There are no rules that guarantee effective fulfilment of the task of interpretation, but it may be helpful to summarize some guidelines in the light of the exercise above – not that these can be neatly separated or put in strict sequence; they rather tend in practice to interact, and insight on a later point will throw corrective light on conclusions reached earlier.

– Base your understanding of the text's significance for us on its original meaning (rather than treating the text as a mere jumping-off ground for your own thoughts).

– Be open to and expectant of finding in the text something fresh, even contradictory of what you thought (rather than letting your theological tradition constrict you to finding only what you knew already).

– Keep listening to what the text says, hearing it through on the questions it raises (rather than cutting it off in mid-sentence because it has answered the questions we are interested in).[50]

– Work persistently at a precise understanding of the specific central point of the passage, so that you can express in a phrase what it is that holds the passage together; and also at how the parts relate to it and to each other (rather than being satisfied with an understanding only of individual words and verses, or with a general impression which misses the author's particular purpose here, or with too narrow a definition which leaves one or two aspects of the passage unembraced).

– Identify the particular circumstances, issues, questions, problems, and mistakes which the writer was dealing with, and consider how far these were peculiar to his situation (rather than assuming that what he says is without context).

– Consider in the light of this understanding what was his specific aim here and what exactly he says to the situation (rather than presuming that his statements and imperatives are necessarily general and universalizable). "In order to find out (a man's) meaning you must . . . know what the question was"[51]

– Note the particular connotations with which he uses theological or other words or concepts, such as faith, salvation, election (rather than reading into such words what they may not mean in this particular context).

– Distinguish symbol, metaphor, and myth from literal presentation, e.g. by parallel usage in the Bible or elsewhere, though realizing that the ancient mind may not have made the distinction which is inevitable for us (rather than being woodenly "literalist").

– Get the feel of such images so that they may have the impact on you that they had on the original readers (rather than being exclusively cerebral in approach to interpretation).

– Elucidate what such language is referring to (rather than assuming either that the medium is the message[52] or that we know the meaning of familiar images such as the good shepherd or being in Christ).

– Establish how concepts present develop within the Bible (e.g. within the Old Testament, between the Testaments, between Jesus, the tradition, Mark, and the other evangelists, between Jesus and Paul) as a means to seeing pointers as to their significance for us.

– In these tasks use the resources available: a synopsis, commentaries – more than one[53] – and if possible reference works such as TDNT, NIDNTT and other wordbooks; listen to such authorities as witnesses whose testimony can help *you* make an informed decision as to where the evidence leads (rather than assuming that scripture's perspicuity means that I can rely on my own uninformed intuition, or that its obscurity means that I must turn scholarly books into paper popes).

– Use tools such as source-, form-, and redaction-criticism as creative hermeneutical aids, with discernment but openness (rather than reverting to a precritical approach on the assumption that they can never be of constructive help or can only be used by experts).

– Identify the particularities of your situation today when set over against those of the Bible: differences in culture, in the church's situation, and so on (rather than failing to locate the exposition's target).

– Ask what angles of the biblical message especially apply here, without failing to preach the whole counsel of God, or to ask whether it is the passage that is irrelevant or rather whether we are[54] (rather than assuming that because all Scripture is equally inspired it is all always equally applicable).

– Know your congregation, know the connotations that words and concepts (e.g. flesh, soul) have for them, know where they are, know their hangups (rather than forgetting that you are trying to communicate with a specific audience).

– Discern how the attitudes, assumptions, and challenges, implicit and explicit in the passage differ from yours and your congregation's and confront them (rather than finding only false comfort in what confirms us in our present position).

– Apply without trivializing, and reinterpret where necessary without losing the principles expressed in the original word (rather than assuming either that this specific expression of God's will necessarily relates directly to a different age, or that it is so time-conditioned that it can be of no help to us now).[55]

– Resymbolize and remythologize so that the significance of the original may be felt anew (rather than only reusing biblical symbols just because they are biblical ones).

– Let the dynamic of the passage's own development, as you understand it, determine the dynamic of your presentation – e.g. the sermon's structure or the Bible study outline (rather than assimilating it to some preconceived sermon pattern or set of Bible study questions).

– Avoid flaunting critical data in the pulpit, but where it is relevant be open with your congregation about how you understand the origin of the Bible (rather than maintaining a double standard whereby the simple believer is left in blissful ignorance of the truth of the Bible's origin[56] – something less defensible now than it was in the days when criticism was carried on without a thought for its implications for the doctrine or the preaching of Scripture).

– Seek to lead your congregation into the same position of being confronted by the text as you have occupied in your preparation.

– Remember that the next time you approach this passage you are a different person and may find new light there[57] (rather than assuming that you have now understood it once and for all). Freshness of approach – not inventiveness, but openness and expectancy – is of key importance in the preacher (or any Bible student).

> So here I am . . .
> Trying to learn to use words, and every attempt
> Is a wholly new start . . .

These words from "East Coker" express T. S. Eliot's hopelessness about ever being able to say adequately what needs to be said. The expositor too will recognise the impossibility of ever speaking adequately of God and his ways with men, but by the same God's grace may be less despairing, and may make the aim expressed here his own.

NOTES

1. For the distinction between meaning and significance, cf. E. D. Hirsch, *Validity in Interpretation* (New Haven/London 1967), pp. 8, 62–63.
2. A. M. Stibbs, *Understanding God's Word* (London 1950); *Expounding God's Word* (London 1960; revised ed. 1976).
3. L. Berkhof, *Principles of Biblical Interpretation* (Grand Rapids 1950).
4. The title of a book by J. D. Smart (London 1970).
5. Above, p. 12f.
6. Above, p. 265.
7. Above, p. 345.
8. Above, pp. 294–300.
9. Above, p. 309.
10. Above, p. 320.
11. Cf. above, p. 252f.
12. E.g. above p. 259.
13. R. Mackenzie, *Concilium* 10:7 (1971), p. 11.
14. Above, p. 263f.
15. Cf. above, p. 14.
16. Hirsch, p. 62. Note that "implications" denotes what is implicit in the inherent meaning of the text itself, and is to be distinguished from the "significance-for-us" of the text's total (explicit and implicit) "meaning-in-itself".
17. So G. A. Buttrick in *The Interpreter's Bible* (New York and Nashville 1951), Vol. VII, p. 341.
18. Above, p. 260.
19. See the treatment of faith in Matthew by H. J. Held, op. cit. on p. 278, n.7 above, pp. 275–299.
20. TDNT II, p. 34.
21. In *The Becomers* (London 1973), pp. 89–106, Keith Miller suggests in some detail how heaven's reality will need to be presented in many different ways as a man's needs and growth as a person develop.
22. Bultmann; cf. above, p. 295.
23. Cf. A. Kee, *The Way of Transcendence* (Harmondsworth 1971), pp. 49–51.
24. Cf. above, pp. 298–300.
25. Cf. J. V. Taylor's doubts as to whether Christians often manifest such renewal in *The Go-Between God* (London 1972), p. 124.
26. The exposition is parallel to Strauss's interpretation of the miracles as Jesus himself appeals to them, as indicating the moral effects of his doctrine (see p. 304, n.37 above)!
27. Cf. again Held, loc. cit.
28. Cf. above, p. 254.
29. On the evangelists' fixing areas of application of material that comes to them, see (with explicit reference to the parables) A. C. Thiselton in SJT 23 (1970), especially pp. 458–461, 466–8.
30. See G. C. Berkouwer, *Holy Scripture* (Grand Rapids 1975), pp. 110ff., and Ellis pp. 000 above.
31. Cf. R.N. Longenecker in Tyn.B 21 (1970), p. 38; also J. Barr, *Old and New in Interpretation* (London 1966), p. 131.
32. Above, p. 265f.
33. Above, p. 267.
34. Of course this analogy does not say all that needs to be said about the atonement (no more than any one biblical metaphor does); but it does re-express in non-cultic terms the idea of reconciliation, substitution, and the price being paid by God himself.
35. Above, p. 277.

36. Colin Morris, *The Hammer of the Lord* (London 1973), p. 54.
37. Cf. B. S. Childs, *Myth and Reality in the Old Testament* (London 1962^{2}), pp. 50–9 on Gen. 6:1–4.
38. Cf. Paul Tillich's sermon on "Principalities and Powers" in *The New Being* (London 1956), pp. 50–9 (reprinted in *The Boundaries of Our Being* (London 1973), pp. 189–97); also R. Bultmann, *Theology of the New Testament* (London 1952), § 21.3, 26.3. There is also a fascinating sermon of Tillich's on "Heal the Sick; Cast out the Demons" in *The Eternal Now* (London 1963), pp. 47–53 (*The Boundaries of Our Being*, pp. 49–55) in which he seems to rejoice in using the "mythological" language!
39. So Beare in his commentary, in loc.
40. Cf. above, 273f.; but note the critique of James Barr, op. cit., chapter 4.
41. Cf. above, p. 272f.
42. I wonder in fact whether *ἀντίτυπον* here does not have its more usual meaning of "copy" (the flood being the "original"), rather than the unusual meaning "fulfilment" (the flood then being the "foreshadowing") as is generally assumed.
43. Cf. G. Bornkamm in Bornkamm, Barth, and Held, op. cit., p. 57.
44. So Justin Martyr, *Dialogue with Trypho*, – 138.
45. Cf. Barr, op. cit., p. 117.
46. Examples in Helen Gardner, *The Business of Criticism* (London 1966), pp. 90ff.
47. Cf. Gardner, pp. 96–7.
48. Cf. n. 31 above.
49. Cf. n. 29 above.
50. Cf. W. W. Johnson, *Interpretation* 20:4 (1966), pp. 423–4.
51. R. G. Collingwood, quoted in the Tillich Festschrift *Religion and Culture*, edited by W. Leibrecht (London 1958), p. 147.
52. Cf. A. C. Thiselton, *The Churchman* 87:2 (1973) p. 96, on the necessity for statements such as "Jesus is Lord" to have ontological as well as existential content.
53. Cf. above, p. 264.
54. Cf. Smart, op. cit., p. 164.
55. Cf. O. M. T. O'Donovan in TSFB 67, pp. 15–23.
56. Cf. Smart, op. cit., pp. 68–76.
57. Cf. Barr, op. cit., p. 197.

Bibliography

Bibliography

Norman Hillyer

Oral tradition has it that the late Professor T. W. Manson once remarked that only one hundred books were needed to study any subject. On that score the titles which follow should prove more than adequate.

The chapters in the present volume already include references to books and articles. But these may be simply to illustrate a detail in the argument or to indicate where profounder thoughts on a particular point can be found. The purpose of this bibliography is more general. The books and articles listed here are those which contributors to *New Testament Interpretation* consider most helpful in carrying the reader further. In many cases a single title is selected as a "best read".

New Testament Interpretation sets out to be a telescope sweeping over the subject of its title. Since these lists were compiled Paternoster Press have begun publishing the equivalent of the microscope in *The New International Dictionary of New Testament Theology,* edited by Colin Brown (3 vols, 1975-78). This work includes bibliographies – sometimes extensive – on individual topics found in the NT.

CHAPTER II

THE HISTORY OF NEW TESTAMENT STUDY

J. BARR, *Old and New in Interpretation* (London: SCM Press 1966). A critical assessment of current trends.

C. K. BARRETT, "Joseph Barber Lightfoot", *Durham University Journal* 64 (1972), pp. 193ff. Inter alia, compares Lightfoot with Baur.

– *Westcott as Commentator* (London: Cambridge University Press 1959).

E. C. BLACKMAN, *Biblical Interpretation* (London: Independent Press 1957). A short history.

– *Marcion and his Influence* (London: SPCK 1948).

C. E. BRAATEN, *History and Hermeneutics = New Directions in Theology*

Today, ii (London: Lutterworth Press 1968). Surveys contemporary trends.

R. Bultmann, "Is Exegesis without Presuppositions Possible?" E.T. in *Existence and Faith,* ed. and tr. S. M. Ogden (London: Hodder and Stoughton 1961), pp. 289ff.

– "New Testament and Mythology", E.T. in *Kerygma and Myth,* ed. and tr. R. H. Fuller (London: SPCK 1953), pp. 1–44.

– "The Problem of Hermeneutics", E.T. in *Essays Philosophical and Theological,* tr. J. C. G. Greig (London: SCM Press 1955), pp. 234ff. Three pioneering and epoch-making essays.

Cambridge History of the Bible, volumes i–iii (London: Cambridge University Press 1963–70). Covers all aspects of Bible study from the beginning until today.

C. W. Dugmore (ed.), *The Interpretation of the Bible* (London: SPCK 1944). A symposium, covering the main phases of history of interpretation.

G. Ebeling, *Word and Faith* (Philadelphia: Fortress Press 1963). One influential line of contemporary hermeneutics.

E. E. Ellis, *Paul and his Recent Interpreters* (Grand Rapids: Eerdmans 1961).

F. W. Farrar, *History of Interpretation* (London: Macmillan, 1886). The classic work; Bampton Lectures for 1886.

E. Fuchs, *Marburger Hermeneutik* (Tübingen: Mohr 1968). Another influential line of contemporary hermeneutics.

R. H. Fuller, *The New Testament in Current Study* (London: SCM Press 1963). A popular survey of current criticism and interpretation.

W. W. Gasque, *A History of the Criticism of the Acts of the Apostles* (Tübingen: J. C. B. Mohr 1975; Grand Rapids: Eerdmans 1975).

R. M. Grant, *A Short History of the Interpretation of the Bible* (London: A. & C. Black 1965). The best short history.

R. P. C. Hanson, *Allegory and Event* (London: SCM Press 1959). Patristic interpretation, especially Origen.

H. Harris, *David Friedrich Strauss and his Theology* (Cambridge University Press 1973).

– *The Tübingen School* (Oxford: Clarendon Press 1975).

W. F. Howard, *The Romance of New Testament Scholarship* (London: Epworth Press 1949). A popular account of some Bible interpreters.

W. G. Kümmel, *The New Testament: The History of the Investigation of its Problems* (London: SCM Press 1972). The most thorough treatment of the subject: German/Lutheran slanted.

G. W. H. Lampe and K. J. Woollcombe, *Essays on Typology* (London: SCM Press 1957). Discussion of the modern resurgence of typology.

S. C. Neill, *The Interpretation of the New Testament, 1861–1961* (Oxford: University Press 1964). A well-informed account, doing full justice to British interpreters.

D. E. Nineham (ed.), *The Church's Use of the Bible Past and Present*

(London: SPCK 1963). A symposium, raising important practical issues.

T. H. L. PARKER, *Calvin's New Testament Commentaries* (London: SCM Press 1971).

J. M. ROBINSON, *A New Quest of the Historical Jesus* (London: SCM Press 1959).

J. M. ROBINSON and J. B. COBB, Jr, *The New Hermeneutic = New Frontiers in Theology, ii* (New York: Harper and Row 1964).

K. SCHOLDER, *Ursprünge und Probleme der Bibelkritik im 17. Jahrhundert* (München: Chr. Kaiser 1966).

A. SCHWEITZER, *The Mysticism of Paul the Apostle* (London: A. & C. Black 1931). Schweitzer's own interpretation of Paul.

– *Paul and his Interpreters* (London: A. & C. Black 1912). Survey of 19th-century works on Paul.

– *The Quest of the Historical Jesus* (London: A. & C. Black 1910). Survey of 19th-century Lives of Jesus.

B. SMALLEY, *The Study of the Bible in the Middle Ages* (Oxford: Blackwell 1952[3]). A standard work.

A. SOUTER, *The Earliest Latin Commentaries on the Epistles of St Paul* (Oxford: Clarendon Press 1927).

J..F. WALVOORD (ed.), *Inspiration and Interpretation* (Grand Rapids: Eerdmans 1957). A symposium by very conservative Americans, critical of most modern trends.

A. S. WOOD, *Captive to the Word* (Exeter: Paternoster Press 1969). Luther's doctrine and interpretation of Scripture.

– *The Principles of Biblical Interpretation* (Grand Rapids: Zondervan 1967). Deals with Irenaeus, Origen, Augustine, Luther, and Calvin.

J. D. WOOD, *The Interpretation of the Bible* (London: Duckworth 1958). A useful history.

Best read: Kümmel, with Neill a close runner-up for the period it covers.

CHAPTER III

PRESUPPOSITIONS IN NEW TESTAMENT CRITICISM

R. BULTMANN, "Is Exegesis without Presuppositions Possible?" E.T. in *Existence and Faith*, ed. and tr. S. M. Ogden (London: Hodder and Stoughton 1961, 1964).

– "The Problem of Hermeneutics" E.T. in *Essays Philosophical and Theological*, tr. J. C. G. Greig (London: SCM Press 1955) pp. 234–261.

Both Bultmann works are summarised in this chapter.
O. CULLMANN, "The Necessity and Function of Higher Criticism", in *The Early Church* (London: SCM Press 1956), pp. 3–16.
H.-G. GADAMER, *Wahrheit und Methode* (Tübingen: Mohr 1973²; E.T. Truth and Method, London: Sheed and Ward 1975). Likely to remain the classic discussion for some time.
E. D. HIRSCH, *Validity in Interpretation* (New Haven: Yale University Press 1967). Includes a summary and critical discussion of Gadamer.
E. KÄSEMANN, "Vom theologischen Recht historisch-kritischer Exegese", ZTK 46 (1967), pp. 259–281.
J. KNOX, *Criticism and Faith* (Nashville: Abingdon Press 1952)
A. NYGREN, *Meaning and Method: Prolegomena to a Scientific Philosophy of Religion and a Scientific Theology* (London: Epworth Press 1972). Wide-ranging and clear.
R. E. PALMER, *Hermeneutics: Interpretation Theory in Schleiermacher, Dilthey, Heidegger, and Gadamer* (Evanston: Northwestern University Press, 1969)
J. M. ROBINSON, "Hermeneutics since Barth", in *The New Hermeneutic,* ed. J. M. Robinson and J. B. Cobb (New York: Harper and Row 1964), pp. 1–77. A survey of the recent discussion.
G. TURNER, "Pre-understanding and New Testament Interpretation", SJT 28 (1975), pp. 227–242.

CHAPTER IV

SEMANTICS AND NEW TESTAMENT INTERPRETATION

J. BARR, "Common Sense and Biblical Language", *Biblica* 49 (1968), pp. 377–387. Discussion of Hill's book, below.
– The Semantics of Biblical Language (Oxford: University Press 1961).
T. BOMAN, *Hebrew Thought Compared with Greek* (Philadelphia: Westminster Press 1961).
K. L. BURRES, *Structural Semantics in the Study of the Pauline Understanding of Revelation* (Ann Arbor: University Microfilms Xerox 71–1810).
D. CRYSTAL, *Linguistics* (Harmondsworth: Penguin Books 1971).
G. FRIEDRICH, "Semasiologie und Lexikologie", TLZ 94 (1969), cols. 801–816.
E. GÜTTGEMANNS, *Offene Fragen an die Formgeschichte des Evangeliums* (Munich: Kaiser 1971²).
– *Studia Linguistica Neotestamentica* (Munich: Kaiser 1971).

D. HILL, *Greek Words and Hebrew Meanings: Studies in the Semantics of Soteriological Terms* (Cambridge University Press 1967).
J. LYONS, *Introduction to Theoretical Linguistics* (Cambridge University Press 1968). Especially chapters 9, 10 on Semantic Principles and Semantic Structure (pp. 400–481).
– *Structural Semantics* (Publications of the Philological Society 20) (Oxford: Blackwell 1963).
E. A. NIDA, "Implications of Contemporary Linguistics for Biblical Scholarship", JBL 91 (1972), pp. 73–89.
– *Towards a Science of Translating* (Leiden: Brill 1964).
R. H. ROBINS, *General Linguistics* (London: Longmans 1964).
F. de SAUSSURE, *A Course in General Linguistics* (London: Peter Owen 1960).
J. F. A. SAWYER, *Semantics in Biblical Research* (London: SCM Press 1972).
K. A. TANGBERG, "Linguistics and Theology", *Bible Translator* 24 (1973), pp. 301–310.
A. C. THISELTON, "The Meaning of *sarx* in 1 Cor. 5:5. A fresh approach in the light of logical and semantic factors", SJT 26 (1973), pp. 204–228
– "The Supposed Power of Words in the Biblical Writings", JTS 25 (1974), pp. 283–99.
– "The Semantics of Biblical Language as an Aspect of Hermeneutics", *Faith and Thought* 103 (1976), pp. 108–20.
S. ULLMANN, *The Principles of Semantics* (Oxford: Blackwell 1957[2]).
– *Semantics: An Introduction to the Science of Meaning* (Oxford: Blackwell 1962).

Best read: Barr, *Semantics.*

CHAPTER V

QUESTIONS OF INTRODUCTION

K. ALAND, *The Authority and Integrity of the New Testament* (London: SPCK 1965). A series of essays on problems arising from a critical study of the text.
D. GUTHRIE, *New Testament Introduction* (London: Tyndale Press 1970[3]). Includes extensive bibliographies on the criticism of NT books.
C. L. MITTON, *The Epistle to the Ephesians* (Oxford: Clarendon Press 1951). A discussion of the problem of the authorship of Ephesians. Concludes it is non-Pauline.

A. Q. MORTON and J. McLEMAN, *Paul, the Man and the Myth. A Study in the Authorship of Greek Prose.* (London: Hodder and Stoughton 1966). An attempt to provide a statistical basis for determining questions of authorship.

J. A. T. ROBINSON, *Redating the New Testament* (London: SCM Press 1976).

CHAPTER VI

THE RELIGIOUS BACKGROUND

H. D. BETZ, "Jesus as Divine Man", in *Jesus and the Historian,* ed. F. T. Trotter (Philadelphia: Westminster Press 1968), pp. 114–133. Compares the concept of "divine men" in Hellenistic thought and the NT.

W. BOUSSET, *Kyrios Christos* (Nashville: Abingdon Press E.T. 1970 from German 5th edn). The standard work on the origins of the title "lord" and its significance in earliest Christianity.

J. H. CHARLESWORTH(ed.), *John and Qumran* (London: G. Chapman 1972).

D. DAUBE, *The New Testament and Rabbinic Judaism* (London: Athlone Press 1956).

W. D. DAVIES, *Christian Origins and Judaism* (London: Darton, Longman and Todd 1962).

– *Paul and Rabbinic Judaism* (London: SPCK 1970[3]). Davies' two books provide probably the most comprehensive and readable accounts of the ways in which Judaism can illuminate the Sitz im Leben of the early church. Much useful information in a readily accessible form.

A. DEISSMANN, *Light from the Ancient East* (London: Hodder and Stoughton 1927[4]). The classic example of how to utilize comparative texts in the exposition of the NT.

J. D. M. DERRETT, *Law in the New Testament* (London: Darton, Longman and Todd 1970).

P. FIEBIG, *Jüdische Wundergeschichten des neutestamentlichen Zeitalters unter besonderer Berücksichtigung ihres Verhältnisses zum Neuen Testament* (Tübingen 1911). A basic text on its subject. Brings together much otherwise inaccessible information.

W. FÖRSTER, *Palestinian Judaism in New Testament Times* (Edinburgh: Oliver and Boyd 1964).

R. H. FULLER, *Interpreting the Miracles* (London: SCM 1961). Deals with the problems of miracle in general, and the particular issues raised by the NT.

M. HENGEL, *The Son of God* (E.T. London: SCM Press 1976). Argues that the main background to NT christology is to be found not in Hellenism but in Judaism, especially Jewish wisdom concepts.

J. M. HULL, *Hellenistic Magic and the Synoptic Tradition* (London: SCM 1974). A comparative study of the relative interest of the evangelists in the magical arts of the Hellenistic age.

B. LINDARS, *New Testament Apologetic* (London: SCM 1961). Examines the ways the early Christians presented their faith to people of diverse religious and cultural backgrounds.

J. G. MACHEN, *The Origin of Paul's Religion* (London: Hodder and Stoughton 1921). A classic exposition, arguing for the dependence of Paul on Jesus himself. Though now dated in its treatment of Hellenistic religion (especially Gnosticism), it still contains much useful material.

B. M. METZGER, *Historical and Literary Studies: Pagan, Jewish, and Christian* (NT Tools and Studies 8) (Leiden: Brill 1968).

J. MURPHY-O'CONNOR (ed.), *Paul and Qumran* (London: G. Chapman 1968).

A. RICHARDSON, *The Miracle Stories of the Gospels* (London: SCM 1941). A simple introduction to the subject of miracle and the gospel miracle stories.

L. SABOURIN, "The Miracles of Jesus", in *Biblical Theology Bulletin* 1 (1971), pp. 59–80; 4 (1974), pp.115–175; 5 (1975), pp. 146–200. A useful series of articles surveying the state of contemporary scholarship on the gospel narratives.

W. SCHMITHALS, *Gnosticism in Corinth* (Nashville: Abingdon Press 1971). A thorough exposition of Paul's Corinthian correspondence, analysing the causes of the discontent in Corinth and the origins of Paul's theology.

H. VAN DER LOOS, *The Miracles of Jesus* (*Nov Test Supp.* 9) (Leiden: Brill 1968[2]). The most comprehensive work there is on its subject, but a massive and tedious volume to read.

E. M. YAMAUCHI, *Pre-Christian Gnosticism* (London: Tyndale Press 1973). A competent introduction to a complex subject.

Best read: Follow up footnotes in the chapter for particular points. No one book, apart from Machen's – now rather old and with nothing on Gnosticism, deals with the subject comprehensively and covers *both* Jewish and Hellenistic background.

CHAPTER VII

HISTORICAL CRITICISM

R. BULTMANN, *Existence and Faith* (London: Hodder and Stoughton 1961).

F. G. DOWNING, *The Church and Jesus* (London: SCM Press 1968)

D. FULLER, *Easter Faith and History* (London: Tyndale Press 1968).
F. HAHN, "Probleme historischer Kritik", ZNW 63 (1972), pp. 1–17.
V. A. HARVEY, *The Historian and the Believer* (London: SCM Press 1967).
E. KRENTZ, *The Historical-Critical Method* (London: SPCK 1975).
G. E. LADD, *The New Testament and Criticism* (Grand Rapids: Eerdmans 1967).
R. R. NIEBUHR, *Resurrection and Historical Reason: A Study of Theological Method* (New York: Scribner 1957).
J. I. PACKER, *"Fundamentalism" and the Word of God* (London: Inter-Varsity Press 1958).
W. PANNENBERG, *History as Hermeneutic* (New York: Harper and Row 1968).
– *Revelation as History* (London: Collier-Macmillan 1969).
N. PERRIN, *Rediscovering the Teaching of Jesus* (London: SCM 1967).
J. M. ROBINSON, *A New Quest of the Historical Jesus* (London: SCM 1959).
A. SCHWEITZER, *The Quest of the Historical Jesus* (London: A. and C. Black 1911^2).
E. TROELTSCH, "Uber historische und dogmatische Methode in der Theologie", *Gesammelte Schriften* (Aalen: Scientia Verlag 1962 = 1922), II, pp. 729–753.
J. WENHAM, *Christ and the Bible* (London: Tyndale Press 1972).
W. WREDE, *The Messianic Secret* (Cambridge: Jas Clarke 1971) (E.T. of German work, first published in 1901).

CHAPTER VIII

SOURCE CRITICISM

W. A. BEARDSLEE, *Literary Criticism of the New Testament* (Philadelphia: Fortress Press 1970).
E. de W. BURTON, *Some Principles of Literary Criticism and their Application to the Synoptic Problem* (Chicago University Press 1904).
B. C. BUTLER, *The Originality of St Matthew* (Cambridge University Press 1951). A recent defence of the Augustinian order of the Synoptic Gospels, i.e. Mt. – Mk – Lk.
J. DUPONT, *The Sources of Acts* (London: Darton, Longman and Todd 1964).
W. R. FARMER, *The Synoptic Problem* (London: Collier-Macmillan, 1964). A readable and forceful history of research into the Synoptic Problem. Good in its criticisms of Marcan priority; less convincing in its arguments for the Griesbach order Mt. – Lk. – Mk. Very useful for further bibliography.

R. T. Fortna, *The Gospel of Signs* (Cambridge University Press 1970).

D. Guthrie, *New Testament Introduction* (London: Tyndale Press 1970[3]). Contains what is probably as good an introduction to the Synoptic Problem as is available in English.

A. M. Honoré, "Statistical Study of the Synoptic Problem", Nov.T 10 (1968), pp. 95–147.

W. G. Kümmel, *New Testament Introduction* (London: SCM Press 1975[2]).

H. Palmer, *The Logic of Gospel Criticism* (London: Macmillan 1968). A philosopher's look at the methods and assumptions of gospel criticism.

E. P. Sanders, *The Tendencies of the Synoptic Tradition* (Cambridge: University Press 1969). Examines how gospel traditions develop and calls into question some common assumptions.

T. Schramm, *Der Markus-Stoff bei Lukas* (Cambridge University Press 1971).

D. M. Smith, Jr, *The Composition and Order of the Fourth Gospel* (New Haven: Yale University Press 1965).

B. H. Streeter, *The Four Gospels: A Study of Origins* (London: Macmillan 1924). For many years the standard book in English on the Synoptic Problem, defending Marcan priority and the "Four Document" hypothesis.

G. W. Styler, "The Priority of Mark", in C. F. D. Moule, *The Birth of the New Testament* (London: A. and C. Black 1966[2]). A recent quite effective defence of Marcan priority in reply to Butler (above).

CHAPTER IX

FORM CRITICISM

J. A. Baird, *Audience Criticism and the Historical Jesus* (Philadelphia: Westminster Press 1969). Computer analysis of the sayings of Jesus in the light of the audiences addressed. A fresh approach which fires broadsides at some widely accepted axioms of radical form criticism.

G. R. Beasley-Murray, *Preaching the Gospel from the Gospels* (London: Lutterworth Press 1965[2]). Suggests how form criticism can be of positive help in interpreting and preaching from the Gospels.

R. Bultmann, *The History of the Synoptic Tradition* (Oxford: Blackwell 1968[2]). This and the following work are the classic examples of German form criticism, although Bultmann is much more radical than Dibelius.

M. Dibelius, *From Tradition to Gospel* (Cambridge: James Clarke 1971; rp of 1934 edn).

W. G. Doty, "The Discipline and Literature of New Testament Form Criticism", ATR 51 (1969), pp. 257–319. Discusses principles and methods in form criticism, and includes an invaluable bibliography of 238 titles.

E. E. ELLIS, "New Directions in Form Criticism", in G. Strecker (ed.), *Jesus Christus in Historie und Theologie* (Tübingen: J.C.B. Mohr 1975), pp. 299–315.

E. V. McKNIGHT, *What is Form Criticism?* (Philadelphia: Fortress Press 1969). The best basic book on the subject, including critiques of Bultmann, Dibelius, and others.

G. N. STANTON, "Form Criticism Revisited", in M. D. Hooker and C. J. A. Hickling (ed.), *What about the New Testament?* (London: SCM Press 1975), pp. 13–27.

V. TAYLOR, *The Formation of the Gospel Tradition* (London: Macmillan 1965[2]). An example of the more cautious British approach to form criticism.

Best read: McKnight.

CHAPTER X

TRADITION HISTORY

R. S. BARBOUR, *Traditio-Historical Criticism of the Gospels* (London: SPCK 1972).

R. BULTMANN, *The History of the Synoptic Tradition* (Oxford: Blackwell 1968[2]).

D. G. A. CALVERT, "An Examination of the Criteria for Distinguishing the Authentic Words of Jesus", NTS 18 (1971–72), pp. 209–219.

F. HAHN, *The Titles of Jesus in Christology* (London: Lutterworth 1969).

M. D. HOOKER, "Christology and Methodology", NTS 17 (1970–71), pp. 480–487.

– "On Using the Wrong Tool", *Theology* 75 (1972), pp. 570–581.

J. JEREMIAS, *New Testament Theology I: The Proclamation of Jesus* (London: SCM Press 1971).

E. KÄSEMANN, "The Problem of the Historical Jesus", in *Essays on New Testament Themes* (London: SCM Press 1964), pp. 15–47.

L. E. KECK, *A Future for the Historical Jesus* (London: SCM Press 1973).

R. P. MARTIN, *Carmen Christi: Philippians 2:5–11 in Recent Interpretation and in the Setting of Early Christian Worship* (Cambridge University Press 1967).

N. PERRIN, *Rediscovering the Teaching of Jesus* (London: SCM Press 1967).

H. SCHÜRMANN, *Traditionsgeschichtliche Untersuchungen zu den*

Synoptischen Evangelien (Düsseldorf: Patmos-Verlag 1968).
D. F. STRAUSS, *The Life of Jesus Critivally Examined* (London: SCM Press 1973; originally pub. 1835–36).

Best read: Barbour.

CHAPTER XI

REDACTION CRITICISM

D. GUTHRIE, *New Testament Introduction* (London: Tyndale Press 1970[3]), pp. 214–219.
J. L. MARTYN, *History and Theology in the Fourth Gospel* (New York: Harper and Row 1968).
N. PERRIN, *What is Redaction Criticism?* (London: SPCK 1970). A valuable introduction, if used with care.
J. ROHDE, *Rediscovering the Teaching of the Evangelists* (London: SCM 1968). An interesting survey of recent work on the Gospels, revealing the diverse nature of the conclusions reached by redaction critics.
R. H. STEIN, "What is *Redaktionsgeschichte?*" JBL 88 (1969), pp. 45–56.

Best read: Perrin.

CHAPTER XII

HOW THE NEW TESTAMENT USES THE OLD

R. BLOCH, "Midrash", *Dictionnaire de la Bible: Supplément,* Vol. 5 (Paris 1957), cols. 1263–81.
F. F. BRUCE, *Biblical Exegesis in the Qumran Texts* (London: Tyndale Press 1960).
P. BORGEN, *Bread from Heaven* (Leiden: Brill 1965).
D. DAUBE, *The New Testament and Rabbinic Judaism* (London: Athlone Press 1956).
J. W. DOEVE, *Jewish Hermeneutics in the Synoptic Gospels and Acts* (Assen 1954).

C. H. DODD, *According to the Scriptures* (London: Nisbet 1952; Collins Fontana 1965).
E. E. ELLIS, *Paul's Use of the Old Testament* (Edinburgh: Oliver and Boyd 1957).
R. T. FRANCE, *Jesus and the Old Testament* (London: Tyndale Press 1971).
L. GOPPELT, *Typos: die typologische Deutung des Alten Testaments im Neuen* (Gütersloh 1939; rep. Darmstadt: Wissenschaftliche Buchgesellschaft 1969; E.T. forthcoming from Eerdmans, Grand Rapids).
R. H. GUNDRY, *The Use of the Old Testament in St Matthew's Gospel* (Leiden: Brill 1967).
A. T. HANSON, *Jesus Christ in the Old Testament* (London: SPCK 1965).
– *Studies in Paul's Technique and Theology* (London: SPCK 1974).
J. R. HARRIS, *Testimonies,* 2 vols. (Cambridge University Press 1916, 1920).
L. HARTMAN, *Prophecy Interpreted* (Lund: C. W. K. Gleerup 1966).
D. M. HAY, *Glory at the Right Hand: Psalm 110 in Early Christianity* (Nashville: Abingdon Press 1973).
T. HOLTZ, *Untersuchungen über die alttestamentlichen Zitate bei Lukas* (Berlin: Akademie-Verlag 1968).
R. N. LONGENECKER, *Biblical Exegesis in the Apostolic Period* (Grand Rapids: Eerdmans 1974).
O. MICHEL, *Paulus und Seine Bibel* (Gütersloh 1929; rep. Darmstadt: Wissenschaftliche Buchgesellschaft 1972).
M. RESE, *Alttestamentliche Motive in der Christologie des Lukas* Gütersloh: Mohn 1969).
H. M. SHIRES, *Finding the Old Testament in the New* (Philadelphia: Westminster Press 1974).
K. STENDAHL, *The School of St Matthew* (Lund: C. W. K. Gleerup 1954; Philadelphia: Fortress Press 1968).
A. SUHL, *Die Funktion der alttestamentliche Zitate und Anspielungen im Markusevangelium* (Gütersloh: Mohn 1965).
G. VERMES, *Scripture and Tradition in Judaism* (Leiden: Brill 1961, 1973[2]).

CHAPTER XIII

APPROACHES TO NT EXEGESIS

J. BARR, *Old and New in Interpretation* (London: SCM Press 1966).
R. E. BROWN, "Hermeneutics" in *The Jerome Bible Commentary* (London: G. Chapman 1968) (section 71).

– *The Sensus Plenior of Sacred Scripture* (Baltimore: St Mary's University, 1955)

W. G. Doty, *Contemporary New Testament Interpretation* (Englewood Cliffs, NJ 1972).

J. Ernst, *Schriftauslegung* (München: F. Schöningh 1972).

K. Frör, *Biblische Hermeneutik* (München: Chr. Kaiser 1961).

T. R. Henn, *The Bible as Literature* (London: Lutterworth 1970).

J. Jeremias, *New Testament Theology I: The Proclamation of Jesus* (London: SCM Press 1971).

– *The Parables of Jesus* (London: SCM Press rev. edn 1963).

– *Rediscovering the Parables* (London: SCM Press 1966).

K. Koch, *The Growth of the Biblical Tradition* (New York: Scribners 1969).

G. E. Ladd, *The New Testament and Criticism* (Grand Rapids: Eerdmans 1967).

E. Linnemann, *Parables of Jesus* (London: SPCK 1966).

A. B. Mickelsen, *Interpreting the Bible* (Grand Rapids: Eerdmans 1963).

B. Rigaux, *The Letters of St Paul* (Chicago: Franciscan Herald Press 1968). A survey of modern discussion.

J. Schreiner, *Einführung in die Methoden der biblischen Exegese* (Tyrolia: Echter 1971).

J. D. Smart, *The Interpretation of Scripture* (London: SCM Press 1961).

K. Stendahl, "Biblical Theology, Contemporary" in *The Interpreter's Dictionary of the Bible* (Nashville: Abingdon Press 1962) (vol. 4, pp. 418–432).

N. Turner, *Grammatical Insights into the New Testament* (Edinburgh: T. and T. Clark 1965). Based on the Greek NT, but with transliterated characters.

R. A. Ward, *Hidden Meaning in the New Testament* (London: Marshall, Morgan and Scott 1969). Helpful exposition of key Greek terms, in English characters.

U. Wilckens, *Was heisst Auslegung der Heiligen Schrift?* (Regensburg: F. Pustet 1966).

A.N. Wilder, *Early Christian Rhetoric* (London: SCM Press 1964). American title: *The Language of the Gospel* (New York: Harper and Row 1964).

H. Zimmermann, *Neutestamentliche Methodenlehre* (Stuttgart: Verlag Katholisches Bibelwerk 1974[4]).

Best read: Doty (or Ladd).

CHAPTER XIV

EXEGESIS IN PRACTICE: TWO EXAMPLES

For essential principles and methods:

O. KAISER and W. G. KÜMMEL, *Exegetical Method: a Student's Handbook* (New York: Seabury 1967), pp. 35–48.

For the "tools" required for NT exegesis:

F. W. DANKER, *Multi-purpose Tools for Bible Study* (St Louis: Concordia 1970^{3}). Includes essays on how to use the major tools of biblical exegesis.

R. T. FRANCE (ed.), *A Bibliographical Guide to New Testament Research* (Cambridge: Tyndale Fellowship, 1974^{2}).

W. G. KÜMMEL, *Introduction to the New Testament* (London: SCM Press 1975^{2}), pp. 23–28: "The Most Important Tools for the Study of the New Testament".

D. M. SCHOLER, *A Basic Bibliographical Guide for New Testament Exegesis* (Grand Rapids: Eerdmans 1973^{2}).

CHAPTER XV

DEMYTHOLOGIZING – THE PROBLEM OF MYTH IN THE NT

I. G. BARBOUR, *Myths, Models and Paradigms* (London: SCM Press 1974). On the diverse functions of language.

H.-W. BARTSCH (ed.), *Kerygma and Myth* (translated and edited by R. H. Fuller; Vol. I, London: SPCK 1953; Vol. II, 1962; both volumes combined, 1972). Contains Bultmann's famous essay "The New Testament and Mythology" together with other contributions to the debate it sparked off.

C. E. BRAATEN and R. A. HARRISVILLE (eds), *Kerygma and History* (Nashville: Abingdon 1962). Includes several essays on myth in the NT.

R. BULTMANN, *Jesus Christ and Mythology* (London: SCM Press 1960). Popular lectures delivered in English in USA.

A. CUNNINGHAM (ed.), *The Theory of Myth: Six Studies* (London 1973). University of Lancaster Colloquium – includes papers on Eliade, Lévi-Strauss and Mary Douglas.

I. HENDERSON, *Myth in the New Testament* (London: SCM Press 1952). A still useful critique of Bultmann.

R. W. HEPBURN, "Demythologizing and the Problem of Validity", in *New*

Essays in Philosophical Theology, ed. A. Flew and A. Macintyre (London: SCM Press 1955).

R. A. JOHNSON, *The Origins of Demythologizing: Philosophy and Historiography in the Theology of Rudolf Bultmann* (Leiden: Brill 1974). The most penetrating analysis of the origin and development of Bultmann's thought.

G. S. KIRK, *Myth: Its Meaning and Function in Ancient and Other Cultures,* (Cambridge University Press 1970). A classical scholar tackles the wider questions of myth, particularly the anthropological theories of C. Lévi-Strauss.

W. G. KÜMMEL, "Mythische Rede und Heilsgeschehen im Neuen Testament", and "Mythos im Neuen Testament", in *Heilsgeschehen und Geschichte* (Marburg: N. G. Elert 1965). Approaches the problem from a "salvation-history" standpoint.

J. MACQUARRIE, *The Scope of Demythologizing* (London: SCM Press 1960). A valuable assessment of the debate to date of writing; perhaps Macquarrie's best work.

G. MIEGGE, *Gospel and Myth in the Thought of Rudolf Bultmann* (London: Lutterworth Press 1960). An Italian Waldensian's contribution.

S. M. OGDEN, *Christ without Myth* (New York: Harper and Row 1961). Perhaps the single most penetrating critique of Bultmann.

W. PANNENBERG, "The Later Dimensions of Myth in Biblical and Christian Tradition", in *Basic Questions in Theology,* vol. 3 (London: SCM Press 1973). A review of approaches to the problem, particularly in biblical scholarship.

J. W. ROGERSON, *Myth in Old Testament Interpretation* (Berlin: de Gruyter 1974). Describes how the concept of myth has been used in OT interpretation since the end of late 18th century, including chapters on Lévi-Strauss and Paul Ricoeur.

G. STÄHLIN, art, *mythos,* in TDNT 4, pp. 762–795.

D. F. STRAUSS, *The Life of Jesus Critically Examined* (London: SCM Press 1973; originally pub. 1835–36).

CHAPTER XVI

THE NEW HERMENEUTIC

P. J. ACHTEMEIER, *An Introduction to the New Hermeneutic* (Philadephia: Westminster Press 1969).

E. BETTI, *Die Hermeneutik als allgemeine Methodik der Geisteswissenschaften* (Tübingen; J. C. B. Mohr 1972[2]).

R. BULTMANN, "Is Exegesis without Presuppositions Possible?" E.T. in *Existence and Faith,* ed. and tr. S. M. Ogden (London: Hodder and Stoughton 1961, 1964) pp. 342–351.

– "The Problem of Hermeneutics", E.T. in *Essays Philosophical and Theological,* tr. J. C. G. Greig (London: SCM Press 1955), pp. 234–262.

G. EBELING, *God and Word* (Philadelphia: Fortress Press 1967).

– *Introduction to a Theological Theory of Language* (London: Collins 1973).

– *Theology and Proclamation* (London: Collins 1963). A debate with Bultmann about Jesus and the kerygma.

– *Word and Faith* (London: SCM Press 1963). Essays on various subjects including hermeneutics.

– *The Word of God and Tradition* (London: Collins 1968).

E. FUCHS, *Gesammelte Aufsätze* (3 vols) esp. vol. 1: *Zum hermeneutischen Problem in der Theologie: die Existentiale Interpretation* (Tübingen: Mohr 1959). Essays on various aspects of the hermeneutical problem.

– "The Hermeneutical Problem", in J. M. Robinson (ed.), *The Future of Our Religious Past: Essays in Honour of Rudolf Bultmann* (London: SCM Press 1971), pp. 276–278.

– *Hermeneutik* (Tübingen: Mohr, 1970[4]). Lectures on general principles, followed by discussion of specific types of biblical language.

– *Marburger Hermeneutik* (Tübingen: Mohr 1968).

– *Studies of the Historical Jesus* (London: SCM Press 1964). Some essays on history and faith, some on hermeneutics and language.

R. W. FUNK (ed.), *History and Hermeneutic* (J Th.Ch. 4)

– *Language, Hermeneutic, and Word of God* (New York: Harper and Row 1966). A survey of modern thinkers, followed by excellent examples of hermeneutic at work.

H.-G. GADAMER, *Wahrheit and Methode* (Tübingen: Mohr 1973[3]). Standard work on philosophical hermeneutics.

M. HEIDEGGER, *An Introduction to Metaphysics* (New Haven: Yale University Press 1961).

– *Unterwegs zur Sprache* (Pfullingen: Neske, 1960[2]).

R. E. PALMER, *Hermeneutics: Interpretation Theory in Schleiermacher, Dilthey, Heidegger, and Gadamer* (Evanston: Northwestern University 1969). Excellent discussion of the philosophical side of the subject.

N. PERRIN, *Jesus and the Language of the Kingdom* (London: SCM Press 1976).

J. M. ROBINSON and J. B. COBB, Jr, *The Later Heidegger* (*New Frontiers in Theology* 1) (New York: Harper and Row 1963).

– *The New Hermeneutic* (*New Frontiers in Theology* 2) (New York: Harper and Row 1964). Includes essays by Fuchs and Ebeling; historical introduction and critical discussion.

J. D. SMART, *The Interpretation of Scripture* (London: SCM Press 1961).

– *The Strange Silence of the Bible in the Church* (London: SCM 1970).

P. STUHLMACHER, "Neues Testament und Hermeneutik – Versuch einer

Bestandaufnahme", ZTK 68 (1971), pp. 121–161.
– "Thesen zur Methodologie gegenwärtiger Exegese", ZNW 63 (1972), pp. 18–26.
– "Zur Methoden- und Sachproblematik einer konfessionellen Auslegung des Neuen Testaments", in *Evangelischer-Katholischer Kommentar zum Neuen Testament: Vorarbeiten* (Zürich: Benziger/Neukirchen: Neukirchener 1972), IV, pp. 22–45.
A. C. THISELTON, "The Parables as Language-Event", SJT 23 (1970), pp. 437–468. Comments on Fuchs' hermeneutic.
– "The Use of Philosophical Categories in NT Hermeneutics", *The Churchman* 87 (1973), pp. 87–100.
– "Understanding God's Word Today", in J. R. W. Stott (ed.), *Christ the Lord* (London: Collins Fontana 1977).
W. WINK, *The Bible in Human Transformation: Towards a New Paradigm for Biblical Study* (Philadelphia: Fortress Press 1973).

Best read: Funk, *Language;* Robinson and Cobb, *New Hermeneutic.*

CHAPTER XVII

THE AUTHORITY OF THE NEW TESTAMENT

K. ALAND, *The Problem of the New Testament Canon* (London: Mowbrays 1962).
J. BARR, *The Bible in the Modern World* (London: SCM Press 1973). A searching analysis of the problem of biblical authority in an age of criticism.
– *Old and New in Interpretation* (London: SCM Press 1966). A study of the relationship between the two Testaments.
W. BAUER, *Orthodoxy and Heresy in Earliest Christianity* (Philadelphia: Fortress Press 1971).
H. von CAMPENHAUSEN, *Ecclesiastical Authority and Spiritual Power in the Church of the First Three Centuries* (London: A. and C. Black 1969).
E. J. CARNELL, *The Case for Orthodox Theology* (London: Marshall, Morgan and Scott 1961). A short conservative exposition.
B. S. CHILDS, *Biblical Theology in Crisis* (Philadelphia: Westminster Press 1970). Problems facing the modern Biblical Theology movement.
A. A. T. EHRHARDT, *The Framework of the New Testament Stories* (Manchester: University Press 1964).
C. F. EVANS, *Is "Holy Scripture" Christian? and Other Questions* (London: SCM Press 1971). A collection of radical essays.

R. P. C. HANSON, *The Bible as a Norm of Faith* (Durham University Press 1963).
– *Tradition in the Early Church* (London: SCM Press 1962).
E. KÄSEMANN, *New Testament Questions of Today* (London: SCM Press 1969). A wide-ranging collection of essays.
– "The Problem of a New Testament Theology", NTS 19 (1972–3), pp. 235–245.
G. E. LADD, *The New Testament and Criticism* (Grand Rapids: Eerdmans 1967). A positive survey of the main types of criticism, from a conservative standpoint.
F. J. LEENHARDT, *Two Biblical Faiths, Protestant and Catholic* (London: Lutterworth Press 1964).
R. MORGAN, *The Nature of New Testament Theology* (London: SCM Press 1973). A translation of material by William Wrede and Adolf Schlatter, with a long introductory essay.
D. E. NINEHAM, "The Use of the Bible in Modern Theology", BJRL 52 (1969–70), pp. 178–199.
J. I. PACKER, "Hermeneutics and Biblical Authority", *The Churchman* 81 (1967), pp. 7–21.
J. W. ROGERSON, "Biblical Studies and Theology: Present Possibilities and Future Hopes", *The Churchman* 87 (1973), pp. 198–206
H. SCHLIER, *The Relevance of the New Testament* (London: Burns, Oates 1967). Essays by a leading German Roman Catholic scholar.
E. SCHWEIZER, *Neotestamentica* (Zurich/Stuttgart: Zwingli Verlag 1963). A collection of essays on NT themes.
J.D. SMART, *The Old Testament in Dialogue with Modern Man* (London: Epworth Press 1965). An attempt to show the relevance of the OT today.
– *The Strange Silence of the Bible in the Church* (London: SCM Press 1970). An examination of the problems of relating the Bible to the twentieth century.
H. E. W. TURNER, "Orthodoxy and the Church Today", *The Churchman* 86 (1972), pp. 166–173.
– *The Pattern of Christian Truth: A Study in the Relations between Orthodoxy and Heresy in the Early Church* (London: Mowbrays 1954).

Best read: Barr, *Bible;* Ladd.

CHAPTER XVIII

EXPOUNDING THE NEW TESTAMENT

D. L. BAKER, "Typology and the Christian Use of the Old Testament", SJT 29 (1976), pp. 137–157.

– *Two Testaments, One Bible* (Leicester: IVP 1976).

J. BARR, *The Bible in the Modern World* (London: SCM Press 1973). A critique of the traditional approach to the Bible's significance, with suggestions as to what it can and should mean today.

– *Old and New in Interpretation* (London: SCM Press 1966). Primarily concerned with the OT. Includes a critique of the idea of typology.

K. BARTH, *Church Dogmatics I: The Doctrine of the Word of God* (Edinburgh: T. and T. Clark 1956) (sections 19:1–2, 21:2). Barth on interpretation.

G. C. BERKOUWER, *Holy Scripture* (Grand Rapids: Eerdmans 1975).

R. W. FUNK, *Language, Hermeneutic and Word of God* (New York: Harper and Row 1956). A sometimes intelligible introduction to the new hermeneutic, with application to epistles and parables.

H.-G. GADAMER, *Truth and Method* (London: Sheed and Ward 1975).

H. GARDNER, *The Business of Criticism* (London: Oxford University Press 1966). Literary critical studies, with implications for biblical interpretation.

J. GOLDINGAY, "The Authority of Scripture in Recent Debate", *Christian Graduate* 28:3 (1975), pp. 65–68.

– "Inspiration, Infallibility, and Criticism", *The Churchman* 90:1 (1976), pp. 6–23.

E. HALLER, "On the Interpretative Task", *Interpretation* 21 (1967), pp. 158–166. Useful insights concerning the task of interpretation.

A. T. HANSON, *Studies in Paul's Technique and Theology* (London: SPCK 1974). Examination, defence, and qualified advocacy of Paul's methods of interpretation. First half rather technical.

E. D. HIRSCH, *Validity in Interpretation* (New Haven/London: Yale University Press 1967). Concerned primarily with literature and poetry, but with one eye on the hermeneutics of Bultmann. Useful critique of Gadamer.

W. W. JOHNSON, "The Ethics of Preaching", *Interpretation* 20 (1966), pp. 412–431. Useful insights into the task of interpretation.

R. N. LONGENECKER, *Biblical Exegesis in the Apostolic Period* (Grand Rapids: Eerdmans 1975).

– "Can we Reproduce the Exegesis of the New Testament?" Tyn.B 21 (1970), pp. 1–38. Examines the NT's methods of exegesis and asks whether we have to follow them ourselves.

T. W. MANSON, "Preaching and Exegesis", in *Neutestamentliche Studien für Rudolf Bultmann* (BZNW 21) (Berlin: Töpelmann 1954). Preaching the Bible as an aid to understanding the Bible.

A. NYGREN, *The Significance of the Bible for the Church* (Philadelphia: Fortress Press 1963). Includes chapters on the OT's use of the NT and on the value of historical-critical study to the interpreter.

O. M. T. O'DONOVAN, "The Possibility of a Biblical Ethic", TSFB 67 (1973), pp. 15–23. Asserts that biblical teaching is in fact universalisable, consistent, and prescriptive.

R. E. PALMER, *Hermeneutics* (Evanston: Northwestern University Press 1969). Concerned with general hermeneutics. Includes valuable surveys of modern approaches.

C. F. SLEEPER, "Ethics as a Context for Biblical Interpretation", *Interpretation* 22 (1968), pp. 443–460. Insights into the task of interpretation, starting with our concern with ethical and social issues.

J. D. SMART, *The Interpretation of Scripture* (London: SCM Press 1961). Thorough general survey from a main-stream American perspective.
– *The Strange Silence of the Bible in the Church* (London: SCM Press 1970). Useful brief introduction to recent hermeneutical debate.

A. M. STIBBS, *Understanding God's Word* (London: IVF 1950; revised, Leicester: IVP 1976).
– *Expounding God's Word* (London: IVF, 1960) Introductions to interpretation and exposition that antedate the modern debate, but are still useful.

A. C. THISELTON, "The Parables as Language-Event", SJT 23 (1970), pp. 437–468. Appreciative critique of the new hermeneutic.
– "The Use of Philosophical Categories in New Testament Hermeneutics", *The Churchman* 87 (1973), pp. 87–100. The usefulness and limitations of the perspectives of existentialism, the new hermeneutic, and linguistic philosophy.
– "Understanding God's Word Today", in J. W. R. Stott (ed.), *Christ the Lord (London: Collins Fontana 1977).*

T. C. VRIEZEN, *An Outline of Old Testament Theology* (Oxford: Blackwell 1970[2]). Includes sections on the tasks of exegesis and exposition (ch. 4).

W. WINK, *The Bible in Human Transformation* (Philadelphia: Fortress Press 1973).

Y. WOODFIN, "The Theology of Preaching", SJT 23 (1970), pp. 408–419.

"Are the Scriptures Losing their Importance?" *Concilium* 10:5 (1969). A Roman Catholic analysis of the reasons.

"From Text to Sermon"; series of articles in *Interpretation* 20–23 (1966–9)

"Theology, Exegesis, and Proclamation", *Concilium* 10:7 (1971) *Roman Catholic studies.*

Best read: The *Interpretation* articles especially Haller.

INDEXES

INDEX OF NEW TESTAMENT PASSAGES DISCUSSED

INDEX OF AUTHORS QUOTED

GENERAL INDEX

INDEX

INDEX